The Social Worlds of Higher Education

The Social Worlds of Higher Education

Handbook for Teaching in a New Century

Edited by:

BERNICE A. PESCOSOLIDO
Indiana University

RONALD AMINZADE
University of Minnesota

PINE FORGE PRESS

Thousand Oaks, California
London • New Delhi

For information, address:

Pine Forge Press
A Sage Publications Company
2455 Teller Road
Thousand Oaks, California 91320
E-mail: sales@pfp.sagepub.com

SAGE Publications Ltd.
6 Bonhill Street
London EC2A 4PU
United Kingdom

SAGE Publications India Pvt. Ltd.
M-32 Market
Greater Kailash I
New Delhi 110 048 India

The social worlds of higher education: Handbook for teaching
in a new century / [edited by] Bernice A. Pescosolido and
Ronald Aminzade.
    p. cm.
  Includes bibliographical references and index.
  ISBN 0-8039-8613-8 (cloth: acid-free paper)
  ISBN 0-8039-9045-6 (pbk.: acid-free paper)
  1. College teaching—Social aspects—United States. 2. College
teachers—United States—Social conditions. 3. Education,
Higher—Social aspects—United States. 4. Educational
change—United States. I. Pescosolido, Bernice A. II. Aminzade,
Ronald, 1949-
  LB2331.S53 1999
  378.1é2—dc21   98-25533

Production Editor: Wendy Westgate
Production Coordinator: Windy Just
Designer/Typesetter: Janelle LeMaster
Indexer: Teri Greenberg
Cover: Ravi Balasuriya

Printed in the United States of America

99 00 01 02 03 04 7 6 5 4 3 2 1

About the Editors

Bernice A. Pescosolido is Chancellor Professor of Sociology at Indiana University and Director of the National Institute of Mental Health-funded Indiana Consortium for Mental Health Services Research. Along with Brian Powell, she directs the Preparing Future Faculty Program for the Department of Sociology and serves on the Executive Committee of the Future Faculty Teaching Fellowship Program. As a member of Indiana University's Faculty Colloquium for Excellence in Teaching, she is a member of the Steering Committee, organized one of its yearly retreats, and has chaired the statewide selection committee for the past five years. At the national level, she is on the editorial board of the journal *Teaching Sociology* and has presented teaching or training workshops for a number of conferences. Specific teaching interests include rethinking graduate education, cross-disciplinary training for those in the medical and social sciences, the use of media in teaching, and ethical issues in teaching and training.

Ronald Aminzade is Professor of Sociology at the University of Minnesota. He also has taught at the University of Wisconsin, the University of Lund, and the University of Amsterdam. He has received a College of Liberal Arts Distinguished Teaching Award, a diversity grant from the Bush Faculty Development Program on Excellence and Diversity in Teaching, and a grant to create a Teaching Resources Center in his department. He served as a "resource teacher" for the Bush Program, mentoring junior faculty in various colleges and departments. His teaching and research interests focus on political sociology, social movements, historical sociology, and East African politics and society. In 1997–1998, he was a fellow at the Center for Advanced Study in the Behavioral Sciences.

About the Contributors

Howard Aldrich is Kenan Professor of Sociology, Director of the Industrial Relations Curriculum, and Adjunct Professor of Business at the University of North Carolina at Chapel Hill.

Thomas A. Angelo is Associate Professor and Director of The Assessment Center at the School for New Learning, DePaul University. Primarily interested in improving learning quality and teaching effectiveness, he is best known for collaborating with K. Patricia Cross to develop classroom assessment and classroom research.

Julie E. Artis is a Ph.D. candidate in sociology at Indiana University. Interested in law, family, and life course, she is completing her dissertation, a study of how motherhood and fatherhood are represented in state child custody laws and how judges, lawyers, and parents define good parenting.

Brian Ault is Instructor of Sociology at the University of Minnesota and Research Associate with the Minnesota Higher Education Services office.

Paul Baker is Distinguished Professor of Educational Administration and Foundations at Illinois State University. He currently studies the mandates of school reform and the processes of school improvement.

Robert B. Barr is Director of Institutional Research and Planning at Palomar College in San Marcos, California. During the past 11 years, he has conducted a number of statewide research studies and served on numerous statewide committees and organization boards.

Robert N. Bellah is Professor of Sociology at the University of California, Berkeley.

Allan Bloom is Professor in the Committee on Social Thought and the College Co-Director of the John M. Olin Center for Inquiry into the Theory and Practice of Democracy at the University of Chicago. He has taught at Yale University, the University of Paris, the University of Toronto, Tel Aviv University, and Cornell University.

Stephen Brookfield is Professor in the School of Education at St. Thomas University in St. Paul, Minnesota. He is author of *Developing Critical Thinkers* (1987) and *Understanding and Facilitating Adult Learning* (1986).

Steven M. Cahn is Professor of Philosophy at the Graduate School of the City University of New York. He is the author of *Saints and Scamps: Ethics in Academia* (Rowman & Littlefield, rev. ed., 1994) and the editor of *Affirmative Action and the University: A Philosophical Inquiry* (Temple University Press, 1993) and *The Affirmative Action Debate* (Routledge, 1995).

Craig Calhoun is Professor in and Chair of the Department of Sociology at New York University.

Daniel F. Chambliss is Sidney Wertimer Professor and Chair of the Department of Sociology at Hamilton College in Clinton, New York. He has published two books, *Champions: The Making of Olympic Swimmers* (1988) and *Beyond Caring: Hospitals, Nurses, and the Social Organization of Ethics* (1996).

Erwin Chemerinsky is Legion Lex Professor of Law and Political Science at the University of Southern California. He concentrates on constitutional law and civil rights issues.

Burton R. Clark is Allan M. Carter Professor of Higher Education Emeritus in the Graduate School of Education and Information Studies at the University of California, Los Angeles.

Patrick Dilger is currently a freelance writer in the Public Affairs Office at Southern Connecticut State University, New Haven, and Director of the University News Bureau at SCSU. He is a former newspaper reporter.

Dean S. Dorn is Professor of Sociology at California State University, Sacramento. He is a former editor of the journal *Teaching Sociology* and currently is the executive officer of the Pacific Sociological Association.

Troy Duster is affiliated with the Department of Sociology at the University of California, Berkeley. His research interests include deviance, law, science, and ethnicity. His publications include *Persistence and Continuity in Human Genetics and Social Stratifications, The Stratification of Culture as the Barrier to Democratic Pluralism,* and *The Prism of Heritability and the Sociology of Knowledge.*

Mark Edmundson is Professor of English at the University of Virginia.

Richard Edwards is Senior Vice Chancellor for Academic Affairs at the University of Nebraska–Lincoln. As an economist, his scholarly work has focused on the tensions between the requirements for efficiency and profitability within the economic system and those of democratic rights within the political system.

Peter Elbow is Professor of English at the University of Massachusetts–Amherst. He directed the writing program at the State University of New York at Stony Brook and taught at the Massachusetts Institute of Technology, Franconia College, Evergreen State College, and Wesleyan University.

Elizabeth Ellsworth is Associate Professor in the Department of Curriculum and Instruction and a member of the Women's Studies Program at the University of Wisconsin–Madison. She teaches graduate courses on the interrelations of media, culture, and curriculum, and she has taught special topic courses on the intersections of gender, race, and class in curriculum and instruction.

Donald L. Finkel is a faculty member at Evergreen State College, where he has been teaching since 1976. He is the coauthor, with William Ray Arney, of *Educating for Freedom: The Paradox of Pedagogy* and recently completed a book titled *Teaching with Your Mouth Shut.*

Jeremy Freese is a Ph.D. candidate in sociology at Indiana University. His areas of interest include sociology of the family and quantitative methods.

Norman Furniss is Professor of Political Science and West European Studies at Indiana University. His research and teaching interests focus on the problems of modernization and political change in advanced industrial states, with particular attention to the European experience.

Jane Gallop is Distinguished Professor of English and Comparative Literature at the University of Wisconsin–Milwaukee. She is the author of numerous books including *Thinking through the Body, The Daughter's Seduction,* and *Around 1981: Academic Feminist Literary Theory.*

Thomas J. Gerschick is Assistant Professor of Sociology at Illinois State University. His research foci include the intersection of disability and gender and pedagogy.

Diane Gillespie is Professor of Liberal Studies at the University of Washington at Bothell, where she teaches interdisciplinary courses in society, ethics, and behavior. Her book, *The Mind's We: Contextualism in Cognitive Psychology,* emphasizes the importance of social interaction and context in cognition and learning.

Gerald Graff is the George M. Pullman Distinguished Service Professor of English and of Education at the University of Chicago, where he has been teaching since 1991. His special interests include American literature, critical theory, and the curriculum.

Harvey J. Graff is Director of the Division of Behavioral and Cultural Sciences and Professor of History at the University of Texas at San Antonio. Author of *The Literacy Myth, The Legacies of Literacy,* and *Conflicting Paths: Growing Up in America,* he currently is writing a book on the city of Dallas, Texas.

Elizabeth Grauerholz is Associate Professor in the Department of Sociology and Anthropology at Purdue University. Her research focuses on how power and gender interact and get played out in various social arenas including the classroom.

Charles S. Green, III has taught at the University of Delaware, at the University of Virginia, and for the past 23 years at the University of Wisconsin–Whitewater. His recent research has focused primarily on teaching and learning in higher education.

Amy Gutmann is Laurance S. Rockefeller University Professor of Politics at the University Center for Human Values at Princeton University. Her major publications include *Democratic Education* (Princeton University Press, 1987), *Liberal Equality* (Cambridge University Press, 1980), *Democracy and Disagreement* (with Dennis Thompson) (Harvard University Press, 1996), and *Color Conscious* (with Anthony Appiah) (Princeton University Press, 1997).

Diane F. Halpern is Chair of the Department of Psychology at California State University, San Bernardino. She is the author of *Thought and Knowledge: An Introduction to Critical Thinking* (Lawrence Erlbaum, 3rd ed., 1996).

Sara C. Hare is a Ph.D. candidate in sociology at Indiana University. She received her master's degree from the Claremont Graduate University in women's studies in religion.

Elizabeth Higginbotham is Professor in the Department of Sociology and Criminal Justice at the University of Delaware. For many years, she was on the faculty of the Center for Research on Women at the University of Memphis, where she was coordinator of curriculum transformation projects.

Carole E. Hill is Professor of Anthropology at Georgia State University. She is a cultural anthropologist who has published extensively in the areas of medical and applied anthropology.

Patrick J. Hill served from 1983 to 1990 as Provost at Evergreen State College, where he now teaches.

bell hooks (deceased) wrote and spoke widely on issues of race, class, and gender. Her books include *Ain't I a Woman, Black Women and Feminism, Killing Rage,* and *Talking Back: Thinking Feminist and Thinking Black.*

Pat Hutchings is Senior Scholar at the Carnegie Foundation for the Advancement of Teaching, where she directs a five-year national project, the Carnegie Teaching Academy, intended to foster a scholarship of teaching that will lead to deeper, more lasting forms of student learning.

Walter R. Jacobs is a Ph.D. candidate in sociology at Indiana University. His doctoral dissertation explores autoethnographic construction of public university classrooms as postmodern spaces.

Arthur Levine is President of Teachers College, Columbia University.

Sølvi Lillejord is Project Coordinator and Assistant Professor in the Department of Applied Education at University of Bergen in Norway. She is working on her Ph.D. at the University of Bergen, doing research on school evaluation, organizational learning, special education, and school management.

Brett McKenzie attended the U.S. Naval Academy and served in the U.S. Navy until the late 1980s, when he left active duty to attend the Harvard Graduate School of Education. For the past 10 years, he has worked at Bryant College, the Naval War College, and Brown University, assisting with the integration of technology and teaching.

Eleanor Miller is Associate Professor of Sociology at the University of Wisconsin–Milwaukee. Her current work is on Azoran immigrants to Lowell, Massachusetts.

G. Stephen Monk is Associate Professor of Mathematics at the University of Washington at Seattle.

Craig E. Nelson is Professor of Biology and of Public and Environmental Affairs at Indiana University, where he has been since 1966. He has received several awards for distinguished teaching from Indiana University as well as nationally competitive awards for distinguished teaching from Vanderbilt and Northwestern universities.

David M. Newman is Associate Professor of Sociology at DePauw University.

Parker J. Palmer is a senior associate of the American Association for Higher Education and senior advisor to the Fetzer Institute, for whom he designed the Teacher Formation Program for K-12 teachers. He is a highly respected teacher who works independently on issues in education, community, spirituality, and social change; he offers workshops, lectures, and retreats in this country and abroad. The author of such widely praised books as *The Company of Strangers, The Active Life,* and *To Know As We Are Known,* he holds a Ph.D. from the University of California at Berkeley. He lives in Madison, Wisconsin.

Richard Paul is widely recognized as a major leader in the national and international critical thinking movements. He has published more than 40 articles and five books on critical thinking in the past five years.

Brian Powell is Professor, Director of Graduate Studies, and Co-Director of the Preparing Future Faculty Program in the Department of Sociology at Indiana University. His research focuses on the consequences of familial structure, educational systems, and gender on life chances.

Gerald T. Powers is Professor in and Director of the Ph.D. Program at the Indiana University School of Social Work. His teaching and research interests have been shaped by four decades of direct practice and consulting experiences in a variety of human service delivery systems.

Linda Ray Pratt is Chair of the Department of English at the University of Nebraska–Lincoln. She is a past president of the American Association of University Professors.

R. Eugene Rice is Scholar-in-Residence and Director of the Forum on Faculty Roles and Rewards at the American Association for Higher Education. Until recently, he was vice president and dean of the faculty at Antioch College, where he continues to hold an appointment as professor of sociology and religion.

Mary Romero is Professor of Justice Studies at Arizona State University. She is the author or *Maid in the U.S.A.* (Routledge) and coeditor of *Challenging Fronteras: Structuring Latina and Latino Lives in the U.S.* (Routledge) and *Women and Work: Race, Ethnicity, and Class* (Sage).

Kent L. Sandstrom is Associate Professor in the Department of Sociology, Anthropology, and Criminology at the University of Northern Iowa. His most recent publications focus on how men with AIDS manage emotions, negotiate sexual relationships, and preserve vital and valued selves.

Marilyn R. Schuster is Professor of French and Comparative Literature at Smith College, where she also served for two years as an academic dean. With Susan Van Dyne, she coordinated the original Smith College Curriculum Transformation Project, and they have participated in the Advisory Committee on the Study of Women since its founding.

Jean Harold Shin is a Ph.D. candidate in sociology at Indiana University. His dissertation research is on perceptions of work alienation in a postindustrial economy, and his teaching background has included courses in social change, social organization, and introductory sociology.

Lawrence C. Soley is Colnik Professor of Communication at Marquette University. He previously taught at the University of Minnesota, University of Georgia, Pennsylvania State University, and City University of New York.

Mary Deane Sorcinelli is Associate Provost for Faculty Development and Director of the Center for Teaching at the University of Massachusetts–Amherst. She also holds an associate adjunct professorship in the Department of Educational Policy, Research, and Administration.

Teresa Sullivan is is Vice President and Graduate Dean at the University of Texas at Austin, where she also is Professor of Sociology and Law. She has been active in the movement to improve the professional development of graduate students who teach.

John Tagg is Associate Professor of English at Palomar College in San Marcos, California, where he has taught since 1982. He has pioneered a number of pedagogical innovations at Palomar including team-taught learning community courses and on-line distance learning.

William G. Tierney is Professor and Director of the Center for Higher Education Policy Analysis at the University of Southern California.

Charles Tilly is Joseph L. Buttenweiser Professor of Social Science at Columbia University.

Susan R. Van Dyne is Associate Professor of English at Smith College, where she also served for four years as an academic dean. She and Marilyn Schuster coordinated the original Smith College Curriculum Transformation Project, and they have participated in the Advisory Committee on the Study of Women since its founding.

James A. Vasquez is Professor in the College of Education at the University of Washington at Seattle.

About The Publisher

Pine Forge Press is an educational publisher, dedicated to publishing innovative books and software throughout the social sciences. On this and any other of our publications, we welcome your comments, ideas, and suggestions. Please call or write to:

Pine Forge Press
A Sage Publications Company
2455 Teller Road
Thousand Oaks, CA 91320
805-499-4224
E-mail: sales@pfp.sagepub.com

Visit our World Wide Web site, your direct link to a multitude of online resources:

www.pineforge.com

Contents

Taking on the Canon and Saving Civilization: Statements from the Culture War

The Power of the Perspective: The Teaching Imagination across the Social Sciences

Section C

The Tenure Debate

The Debate on Affirmative Action

The Debate on Student-Faculty Relations

The Debate on the Ownership of Knowledge

The Forgotten Journey to the Classroom

PART III

Charting the Landscape of Higher Education in the 21st Century

Preface

The challenges of the new century provide the overall theme for this book. Our purpose is to take a broad look at teaching issues at the end of this century, both informing and being informed by social science perspectives. Our job is to help understand the dynamics of social change in higher education and the challenges posed by the newly emerging institutional landscape of the 21st century. One key challenge concerns the "apartheid of instruction" that Wilson (1985) describes as the tendency to view research and teaching as almost entirely different enterprises. Although some institutions of higher education may continue to have the luxury of having three strata of faculty (i.e., those who see themselves exclusively as researchers with little need to pay attention to teaching, those who see themselves exclusively as teachers with little need to pay attention to research, and those who see themselves as critically engaged in both), greater pressure from state governments and trustees combined with the decrease in federal funds for research and higher education in general makes this unlikely. The social changes of the next century will call for a greater integration of the identities and efforts of faculty. In that sense, we see this book as representing the next logical step, the next generation of the concern for teaching and higher education reflected in works such as *Teaching Sociology: The Quest for Excellence* (Campbell, Blalock, and McGee 1985). We have agreed to edit this book in the hope of breaking down the wall between teaching and research and between those in the academic community who identify themselves as teachers and those who identify themselves as researchers.

We engaged in conversations with colleagues, primarily but not exclusively throughout the social sciences, across a range of colleges and universities. This new era requires broad rethinking—laying out the changing contours of higher education and the challenges that confront us; arguing about divergent perspectives on the relationship between higher education and social change; setting out potential principles to organize our work, offering a view on the conceptual tools at our disposal; and (finally) providing a concrete set of materials that translate concepts into tools for use in the classroom, the committee, and the career. For example, too often we hear the belief expressed that it is impossible to evaluate quality teaching with the same rigor and merit-based standards with which we approach research. But there is valid and reliable research from our colleagues in education and across a variety of disciplines that has addressed these issues; student evaluations do, in fact, provide useful data, even if of a limited nature. They measure primarily organization, perceived instructor interest in student learning, and perceived fairness in evaluation. All research faculty need to have at least passing acquaintance with this research. But although it has become fashionable to tout the banner of multidisciplinary work or programs, we rarely take this seriously in the practice of teaching. Likewise, those who devote themselves to teaching sometimes ignore well-known disciplinary contributions and research standards. There is a problem with the attempt to gather and evaluate baseline information about teaching practices, assessment, study habits, and the like by great teachers who are not trained in appropriate research methods.

Our own interest in this effort arose from two realizations over the past few years. The first, enhanced by efforts of Carla Howery and Edward Kain through the materials and workshops of the American Sociological Association's Teaching Services Program, was that many of the strong research departments in sociology, not just the pioneering places such as the University of Washington, have developed serious teacher training programs as part of their graduate curricula. We stood among the many younger faculty in graduate departments who developed these programs virtually in isolation from others engaged in similar initiatives. We struggled on our own to discover and manage the literature on teaching, to become conversant with the larger public debates on the status of teaching, and to create courses and programs that would engage students intellectually as well as pragmatically. We also turned to those in our field who have created and nurtured expertise in undergraduate teaching. Together, we reached a second realization—that what stimulated our conversations about our own departmental and disciplinary efforts was not just a love for teaching and a concern for students but also a fascination with the social aspects of teaching. We saw no necessary bifurcation between teaching and research issues on how amenable they were to social science examination and explication. We often were frustrated by the lack of a sociological perspective on the larger societal debates about higher education and the process of teaching. We hope that this book will go a long way toward sparing others the arduous tasks of discovering basic teaching issues on their own and to convincing them, if not inspiring them, on the relevance and responsibility of sociology and the other social sciences to address the challenges to higher education. This is not simply a matter of distilling the most crucial findings and experiences from our education colleagues. We need to embrace the insights we can gain from taking the perspectives of other disciplines, including the social sciences, to understand the teaching enterprise.

These ideas about teaching, higher education, and society guided our preliminary choices for the organization of the book, topics to be included, and pieces we have solicited and reprinted. Our original notion was to balance "classic" pieces and new contributions. We soon came to realize that addressing the diverse challenges of the 21st century essentially involved planning and writing in a collaborative effort rather than simply gathering pieces tied to one another through introductions to parts of the book and articles. To that end, we brought together a small set of individuals to help shape the book and fill gaps in our understanding of teaching and learning. The members of the Editorial Board represent the team that has produced this effort to date. The members of the Advisory Board form a larger community of contributors, reviewers, and commentators selected because of their prominence in teaching and learning debates, their contributions to these efforts in their own departments, their disciplines, and their willingness to serve in this important position.

We have chosen to make the thrust of the book inclusive without being pristinely multidisciplinary. Much of what is known about teaching, learning, and the process of passing this information on to our professionals-in-training comes from outside sociology, outside the social sciences. Consequently, we considered topics and contributions from a very broad range of authors and include pieces from many different disciplinary affiliations.

We strove for a balance between theory and practice in this book. The book is divided into conceptual tools and methods tools. The former are the focus of the *Handbook,* and the latter are organized into the *Fieldguide* on the included CD-ROM. Printed in its totality, the materials on the file constitute the *Fieldguide;* in parts, they provide selected classroom materials, teaching checklists, topical bibliographies, and practical guides. We have set the *Fieldguide* up to trace the issues and decisions that teachers face as they proceed through the semester or quarter, dealing first with issues of course design (e.g., syllabi construction, textbook evaluation), followed by classroom presentation and interaction issues (e.g., lecture styles, discussion), and ending with evaluation (e.g., assignments, grading, portfolios). It includes many of the classic teaching tools and tips that experienced teachers will recognize (e.g., Peter Frederick's "The Dreaded Discussion: Ten Ways to Start"). Our hope is that we have provided the critical context for the practical tools provided in the *Fieldguide*.

We see the audience for this book as threefold. The first and primary audience is the students and faculty involved in teacher training at the graduate level, primarily but not limited to sociology and the other social science disciplines. This directly answers our call for basic and relevant materials to fill the gap in the training of the future professorate. The second audience is faculty, whether just starting out or tenured, who have not had the benefit of any training in the task that occupies a good part of their daily lives in colleges and universities. Whether they are curious about current debates or looking for some basic checkpoints for what they are doing in the classroom, we hope the book offers a broad set of resources. Again, although we expect sociologists to be most attentive to our effort, we have targeted the social sciences more generally because of our own curiosity about what the perspectives of other social sciences bring to teaching issues. Third, because one of the unique features of this effort is to bring the perspective of the social sciences to bear on current debates, we hope that a small audience will be found in the general community of teachers.

How to Use This Book and the *Fieldguide*

Because we view the larger debates on higher education and what professors do in their classrooms as inextricably intertwined, we address both through the *Handbook* and the *Fieldguide*. However, these materials can be used by faculty and students in three different ways.

First, we realize that many professors enter the classroom initially with little or no training. Their focus is on the practical, day-to-day tasks that face them. They rarely have time to reflect on larger issues. To that end, the *Fieldguide* may be the first set of materials of use. This approach also would fit with teacher training courses that are timed to coincide with the first semester of teaching for graduate students.

Second, even first-time teachers have experience with teaching and learning. Having them consider some of the larger issues upfront might shape the way in which they approach and organize their teaching. Here, the book would set the context for the later use of the *Fieldguide* and would fit with teacher training courses required *before* students take on their first assignments.

Finally, the *Handbook* and the *Fieldguide* could be used together throughout a seminar or across a sequence of courses to make the link among debates, principles, and tools.

Acknowledgments

This book has taken many years; many conversations, meetings, phone calls, and e-mails; and a good deal of faith on the part of authors and Pine Forge Press's Steve Rutter. It originally was conceived in conversations, primarily at the American Sociological Association meetings among faculty at Ph.D. departments who had begun to develop courses, activities, and projects around issues of teaching, presentation, and professional development. Many, of course, had come from the "pioneer" departments in which such efforts had been done, sometimes for many years—at the University of Washington, Fred Campbell and Tad Blalock's teaching seminars; at Yale University, Kai Erikson's sociological craft course; at Northwestern University, Howie Becker's writing course; and at the University of North Carolina, Everett Wilson's teaching course. Others remembered their own early careers or had watched as their junior colleagues struggled to start their teaching careers amid the pressure of research productivity and service commitments. Still others commented on the issue of professional responsibility in training the next generation of the professorate.

For whatever reason, this conversation often was too distant from ongoing conversations in the Undergraduate Education Section of the association, from the larger debates in associations such as the American Association of Higher Education, and from those sociologists who had gone to the public and private sectors. Much of the journey of this book has been to try to bridge these communities, bringing in their concerns and their contributions to understanding what and how we teach and what this means for our undergraduates, our colleagues, and the public as well as for our Ph.D. students.

In our initial conversations with Steve Rutter, he suggested that we bring together a small group of people to start to build bridges within sociology. At his house in California one weekend, the members of the editorial board who were available met and began the arduous process of trying to figure out what was needed to push these conversations further into the mainstream as a regular part of the way in which we think. Dean Dorn, who had just completed his editorship of *Teaching Sociology*, brought an encyclopedic knowledge of people, research, and issues in higher education; Jodi O'Brien's enthusiasm provided a great source of continuing energy; and Chris Wright-Isak came with the unique viewpoint from corporate America (and a Ph.D. in sociology from the University of Chicago). Over the weekend, we discussed ideas, formats, audience, potential contributors, the balance of original and published pieces, and an endless list of other issues. From this, we began the long task of developing an outline, calling contributors, and asking advice from the list of senior scholars who would become our Advisory Board. About seven generations after that first outline, we settled, more or less, on the format of the present volume, with the *Handbook* and the *Fieldguide* as separate volumes, the latter with more of an electronic efficiency and utility.

Perhaps one of the most often discussed issues over most of the development of the project was the boundaries of the project. Was it to be a project by and for sociologists? Some thought this best because it was such a risky endeavor as it was. As we mentioned earlier, we had felt that sociologists were not as involved in the larger national debates on teaching, learning, and higher education as they might be given their expertise in social institutions, social inequality, organizations, socialization, and social interaction. But as we talked to our colleagues in the other social sciences, we found that they too were struggling to develop new courses along these lines and discovering the same separation of communities of expertise. In the end, we realized that what we were trying to do here might be of use to a range of others, and there was little doubt that any number of people on the national scene could provide invaluable contributions to our theme of understanding and rebuilding the social worlds of higher education.

In the end, hundreds of individuals have had some hand in the production of these two volumes—more than 150 contributors, dozens of reviewers, our editorial and advisory board members, our colleagues, directors of teaching centers, librarians, journal and newsletter editors, authors, and college teachers. Carla Howery, director of the Teaching Service Program of the American Sociological Association (ASA), was always there when we needed her wisdom. The students and co-instructor in S606 ("Sociological Issues in College Pedagogy," Spring 1997, in Indiana University's Preparing Future Faculty program) read and commented on each piece. Members of this group—Camilla Salusbury, Carla Shirely, Matt Oware, Sara Hare, Terri Demon, Rob Carini, and Tamara Darnold —were invaluable and provided a good deal of optimism for thinking about the next generation of college teachers. The critical responses of graduate students to required readings for the "Teaching Sociology" seminar at the University of Minnesota helped us to decide which articles to reprint. Judy Howard, Kathleen Blee, and Ted Wagenaar provided thoughtful and detailed reviews of the entire manuscript while William Roy, Neil Smelser, and Marta Fulop provided insightful comments on the editors' essays.

We acknowledge our universities for their continued support of these types of issues and projects. At the University of Minnesota, the Bush Program on Excellence and Diversity in Teaching has provided a great source of inspiration, ideas, and resources. Indiana University, the

Teaching Resources Center, the Dean of Faculties Office, and particularly Eileen Bender and the Faculty Colloquium for Excellence in Teaching, which she directs, have been inspiring. The Center for Advanced Study in the Behavioral Sciences provided financial support that enabled Ron Aminzade to devote his time and energy to this project. To show their appreciation for the support provided for this project by the ASA, the co-editors are donating all royalties to the ASA's Fund for the Improvement of Teaching.

Mary Hannah provided clerical assistance, great fortitude in collecting permissions, and a constant care to getting these materials in, and in shape, for Pine Forge Press. We thank the Research and University Graduate School at Indiana University, as well as Dean George Walker, for support that included some of Mary's time. No doubt, Mary was a cornerstone to the completion of this project. J. Scott Long, chair of the Department of Sociology, and Susan Platter, administrative assistant, also offered encouragement and support.

The staff at Pine Forge Press always were helpful and patient, especially Jean Skeels, Windy Just, and Sherith Pankratz. Finally, Steve Rutter's insights regarding the growing importance of teaching and the need for scholarly materials to improve teaching, training, and learning were ahead of their time.

We owe special thanks to Gary Trudeau, who gave us permission to use his brilliant work throughout the book and to do so without the usual costs. No other person has tapped into the angst of the modern university and commented on it more insightfully than Trudeau. Those of us who are a part of higher education have been able to laugh at ourselves through our sometimes disheartening circumstances, sometimes ridiculous situations, and sometimes moments of great reward through his social commentary. We thank Norman Furniss for his special efforts in contacting Trudeau and without whose efforts this wonderful addition to the book would not have been possible.

Finally, we thank our families for subsidizing this project through endless substitution of household responsibilities, offering their encouragement, and being a source of energy and inspiration.

References

Campbell, Frederick L., Hubert M. Blalock, Jr., and Reece McGee, eds. 1985. *Teaching Sociology: The Quest for Excellence.* Chicago: Nelson-Hall.

Wilson, Everett K. 1985. "Apartheid and the Pathology of Sociology Instruction." Pp. 25-47 in *Teaching Sociology: The Quest for Excellence,* edited by Frederick L. Campbell, Hubert M. Blalock, Jr., and Reece McGee. Chicago: Nelson-Hall.

Teaching for What and for Whom? The Social Worlds and Structural Paradoxes of the University at the End of the 20th Century

Bernice A. Pescosolido
and Ronald Aminzade

In American colleges and universities, issues of teaching and learning have taken an unprecedented place in the center of often heated discussions about higher education. As few as five years ago, when the *Chronicle of Higher Education*'s headlines read "Concern Rises over Faculty Productivity," the issues were likely to target research grants and scholarly productivity. Today, that same headline might be followed by an article on faculty's classroom time and student learning. From both within and outside educational institutions, serious questions have been raised about the aims of learning we hold, the methods we use, the quality of the instruction we provide, and the contributions we make to the larger society. All of these concerns arise while the demands for research and service escalate. Campbell noted in 1985 that the "age of academic exuberance" has been replaced by a "time of contraction," leaving a legacy of poor teaching in its wake. But in the past 10 years, frustration by faculty combined with a growing demand for accountability from taxpayers supporting higher education and parents facing rising tuition costs has placed the quality and quantity of teaching on the public agenda. No one has better captured the different facets of the "crisis" in higher education in a public forum than Gary Trudeau. As his strip on the increasing racial diversity of American universities shows, the challenges often are paradoxical. We find it difficult to embrace some students' requests, to understand the new "corporate" and "managed" stance of administrators, and the public consternation with revered institutions of higher education.

As we stand at the threshold of a new century, we face a set of dramatic challenges to higher education. We have agreed to edit a book on teaching to address these challenges. This book is based on three premises. First, as already noted, the institution of higher education is undergoing radical shifts. Colleges and universities of the next century will look substantially different from their current profiles. Second, these shifts reflect not only changes in theories of learning and teaching but also large changes in society that already have begun to transform higher education and its teaching tasks. We have come to understand that the world is complex and growing ever more so. There are those who have argued that modern society is characterized by rapid social change, change of an unheralded pace. In many of these societal changes lie the source of discontent about higher education and the call for many of the banner issues of the day including cultural diversity, international efforts, and interdisciplinary connections. In brief, what goes on in colleges and universities cannot be divorced from the larger society in which teachers and students operate. Third, the improvement and institutionalization of good teaching will require a broad, concerted, and truly multidisciplinary effort. A multidisciplinary view holds the potential to add insights over and above what those in education have worked hard to demonstrate. Social scientists and others in the university must embrace basic understandings of the process of learning and teaching that those, primarily in schools of education, have theorized and systematically examined. But only by bringing unique disciplinary insights to the study of teaching and learning will we be able to fully comprehend and respond to current dilemmas. We argue that the current wave of critical issues for higher education and their connection to large-scale social changes can be understood only by taking into account the perspectives of those who study these changes on a day-to-day basis. This lies outside the purview of pedagogical theory and research. We, as sociologists and members of the social science community, purport to understand society; we should be struggling to define and describe the contours of the new landscape, new social forms, and their direct and indirect consequences for higher education. In essence, the two intertwined threads that run through this book lie in the attempt to create a new imagery to reclaim both the value of education and the value of social science, particularly sociological knowledge in the teaching enterprise. This book represents one key and crucial way in which to pay more attention to the joint tasks of the creation and dissemination of knowledge, the twin core of what we do as professors.

Logic of the Book

The proposed book is divided into three main parts: (I) Surveying the Social Landscape of Higher Education at the End of the 20th Century: Pressures from the Outside, (II) Mapping Issues in the Social Worlds of Higher Education: Arguments from the Inside, and (III) Charting the Landscape of Higher Education in the 21st Century. The first and third parts each contain fewer essays that link the larger context of higher education to the classroom. We have organized the essays within each of these sections to follow a micro-macro logic—from larger contexts, to institutional structures, to classroom features, to personal issues. The first essay in each part examines the larger changes in society that have led to questions from inside and outside the academy about the "business as usual" in higher education. The next set of essays focuses in detail on how these questions and trends affect the structure, meaning, and goals of higher education. The final set brings these issues squarely into the classroom by examining how they have changed the day-to-day life of the classroom, teachers, and students. The key continuum within parts is temporal; they move from how we have come to this point and where we stand now to charting directions for the future.

The middle part of the book follows four themes (sections) organized around the key social worlds or networks in which professors participate and the key social relations that define obligations and expectations within academia. The purpose of referring to "social worlds" is to emphasize the complexity of the different roles that professors hold and the myriad social relationships in higher education.

A. *The Social World of Professors and Their Students: A First Glimpse.* Every attempt to teach centers on students and requires shared understandings between students and faculty about what we are doing and how we are going to do it. Issues include approaches to teaching, active and cooperative learning, student expectations, community service learning, learning communities, and instructional responsibilities to minority students.

B. *The Collegial World of Professors: The Classic Arguments.* This theme addresses conversations among college professors about what we do both inside and outside the classroom to educate our students. Debates concern how we do or should do our work as teachers, perceive our students, decide on standards and requirements, and evaluate our own performance and that of our students. One of the central debates in higher education revolves around the boundaries of disciplines, the push for inter- or multidisciplinary programs or instruction. These arguments about problem-based restructuring of higher education require a better, sharper understanding of the contrasts and similarities among disciplines. The subsection on the teaching imagination across the social sciences contains a set of select essays in which social science scholars distill the unique insights and approaches of their disciplines to provide background for the debate and discussion among social scientists about the central theme in their teaching.

C. *Professors in a Changing University and a Changing Society.* This section includes discussions about the organizational logics governing higher education, the relevance of what we teach, and the corporatization of higher education. The latter encompasses controversial issues concerning the organization of our academic workplaces including part-time labor, the attack on tenure, and post-tenure review. This section also addresses contentious issues concerning race, gender, and sexuality including affirmative action, sexual harassment, and the ethical responsibilities of faculty. Our responses to these issues not only shape what we do and how we define ourselves but also offer a model to those considering careers in tomorrow's universities.

D. *The Personal Worlds of Professors: Past, Present, and Future.* To discuss teaching and higher education without bringing in issues of "self" provides a safe but unrealistic examination of the key resource of any profession. Faculty must be concerned with the pressures that confront them as individuals and as those charged with training the future professorate. The essays in this section concern teaching excellence and teaching styles; building trust with students; teaching across the boundaries of race, class, and sexuality; and generational differences among faculty. The essays addressing this final issue are organized so as to trace the journey to the classroom, using a life course approach to document different generational perspectives and experiences.

Reference

Campbell, Frederick L. 1985. "Turning toward Teaching." Pp. 3-22 in *Teaching Sociology: The Quest for Excellence,* edited by Frederick L. Campbell, Hubert M. Blalock, Jr., and Reece McGee. Chicago: Nelson-Hall.

PART I

Surveying the Social Landscape of Higher Education at the End of the 20th Century

Pressures from the Outside

The Debate: College Teachers, the New Leisure Class

Gene I. Maeroff

Do you have any idea how many hours a week the average college teacher actually spends in class with students?

A total of 9.8 to 10.5 hours, according to various surveys. That's right—an amount of time slightly greater than the workday of most Americans. And the average is inflated by the schedules of community college teachers who spend 15 to 16 hours a week in the classroom. What makes these astonishing figures especially noteworthy right now is the hand-wringing in one state after another over constraints on the budgets for higher education and the difficulty of holding the line on tuition.

Twenty states made midyear cuts in their budgets for higher education during the 1992-1993 academic year. The University of California system has slashed $900 million from its budget during the past four years. The City University of New York proposes to consolidate academic programs on its various campuses. The "flagship" campus of the University of Maine has embarked on a program to cap enrollments and eliminate 20 administrative positions and 10 academic programs.

Meanwhile, little is mentioned about the work schedules of faculty members. *Productivity* is a dirty word when it comes to higher education.

This is not to say that all of higher education's fiscal pressures could be relieved simply by assigning more class hours to professors. There are grounds and buildings to maintain, new structures to build and equip, research to fund, libraries to stock, students to feed and house, and administrative expenses. Yet, the cost of an education to a

AUTHOR'S NOTE: Adapted from "College Teachers, the New Leisure Class." Reprinted with permission of *The Wall Street Journal,* © 1993, Dow Jones & Company, Inc. All rights reserved.

student and his family surely must have some connection to the productivity of faculty members.

Many faculty members have two or even three days a week when they never enter the classroom. Most faculty members say that they spend about an hour a week preparing for each hour of teaching. Together, instruction and preparation account, on average, for approximately 20 hours a week. It is widely acknowledged, though, that some professors lecture from the same notes for several years with but a soupcon of change.

So, how does a professor use the remainder of his workweek? Figures gathered by the Higher Education Research Institute at UCLA help answer the question. The work schedule is filled out largely by conducting research and then writing about the findings, advising and counseling students, attending committee meetings, and performing administrative tasks.

But there is great unevenness in uses of time from institution to institution and even among faculty members in the same department. Pressures to do research are enormous on younger scholars who are seeking promotion and tenure.

While some members of the faculty are constantly pressed for time, others find abundant opportunities for playing tennis, running errands, taking on consulting assignments that generate extra income, and merely doing nothing special.

By their own admission, almost half the full-time faculty say that they spend no more than four hours a week on research and scholarly writing. As a corollary, 45 percent of the nation's entire professoriate had no professional writings accepted or published during a given two-year period.

Almost 90 percent of faculty members say that they give no more than eight hours a week either to counseling students or to attending meetings, and more than half of the entire faculty give less than four hours a week to either of those tasks.

Certainly, any conscientious professor does a lot of reading and reflecting, but so do professionals in other fields, and no one necessarily pays them for the time involved. The schedule on campus adds up to a pleasant life for most faculty members, who are at least working at jobs they like. And they get summers off.

Few grow rich, but most earn between $40,000 and $70,000 for their nine-month year. Average faculty salaries range from $32,420 for assistant professors at baccalaureate colleges to $66,780 for full professors at doctoral-level universities.

The point here is that the work schedule taken for granted in higher education ought to be examined in recognition of current fiscal exigencies.

A Letter in Response to Article (in *The Wall Street Journal*)

I was absolutely appalled by Mr. Maeroff's article. How dare he! Leisure class indeed! Took me several hours at the beach just to calm down, but I did manage to come up with numerous juicy and wholly appropriate responses. Really felt great. Was going to write it all down and send a letter to the *Journal*. But morning came, have to teach a class at 3:30 today, and figured, nah, why bother? Going to go ahead with the regular game plan and get in a few hours of fishing before class.

—Atul Gupta
Associate Professor of Finance
Bentley College
Waltham, Mass.

1

Introduction to the Changing Landscape of Higher Education

Ronald Aminzade and Bernice A. Pescosolido

Something has changed in higher education. The faculty, looking back over their teaching careers, remember different students, different times, and different climates. Trudeau's cartoon paints an image of change that lays the blame at the feet of students who somehow have been able to "bully" professors into lowering standards.

As Maeroff's *Wall Street Journal* piece declares, a simple but different problem has produced an American higher education in shambles. The trouble lies at the feet of a privileged group of professors with too much time, too high pay, too little motivation, and little to show for it after all. Instead of this overly simplified and egregiously errant picture, we provide a complete and complex set of arguments about the times and conditions that have given rise to such virulent critiques of colleges and universities. Furthermore, we take on these issues as debates about causes and consequences. A basic premise of social science is that understanding comes only through considering phenomena in larger contexts. Some current critiques claim that colleges and universities have thwarted their original, purer goals of education. But institutions of higher education always have pursued many goals beyond teaching, negotiated varied relationships with multiple constituencies, and reflected and responded to larger social, histori-

cal, and political forces. In the 20th century, the institutional landscape of higher education has been transformed dramatically. The essays in this first part document this transformation and discuss the challenges and opportunities it creates for teaching and learning. These essays link the larger context of higher education to the classroom, examining larger changes in society that have led to questions from inside and from outside the academy about "business as usual" in higher education. They focus on how these questions and trends affect the structure, meaning, and goals of higher education, bringing these issues squarely into the classroom by examining how they have changed the day-to-day life of the classroom, teachers, and students. All of the essays in this part highlight issues of power, accountability, and conflict as key dimensions of the larger historical and institutional contexts within which we teach.

Part of this transformation, Craig Calhoun (Chapter 2) argues, is the emergence of a highly differentiated system of colleges and universities, stratified by access to resources, by selectivity of admissions and composition of student bodies, and by rewards and working conditions for faculty. Americans' access to higher education following World War II reinforced a vision of equality of opportunity that conflicts with a reward and prestige hierarchy that differentiates institutions. These differences tend to be ignored by observers who limit their observations to a small number of elite institutions despite the rapid growth of two-year postsecondary schools, a decline in the number of liberal arts colleges, and the expansion of multicampus state university systems. Calhoun's analysis suggests that we reconsider a "one size fits all" approach to higher education and instead acknowledge diversity among institutions, students, and faculties through varying our instructional techniques, educational standards, career tracks, and research and scholarship norms. This is simultaneously an obvious and a controversial suggestion.

Although sympathizing with the desire to tailor teaching and learning to the diverse backgrounds and institutional locations of professors and students, some readers might fear that such an approach will reproduce and reinforce, rather than challenge, existing inequalities among institutions. It is a fear and frustration captured so well by Trudeau's exasperated professor: adjusting our educational standards to take into account differences in student abilities and commitments may lead to lowered standards and expectations and a consequent failure to adequately challenge our students. Burton Clark (Chapter 5, this volume) suggests that many professors already spend an inordinate amount of time on remedial education, a situation that amounts, in his words, to "a dumbing down of the intellectual life of academic staff" (p. 55). Institutional differentiation, he argues, translates into very different everyday experiences for faculty members in teaching loads, burdens of remedial education, disciplinary identification, employment security, and faculty governance. The solution suggested by his analysis entails struggling for increased professionalization and professional control to give all professors the motivation and power to confront the systematic problems of second-

arization, excessive teaching, and a fragmented academic culture. Whether professionalization, rather than unionization, can meet these daunting challenges remains a contentious issue.

However, the story of higher education in America, argues Teresa Sullivan (Chapter 3), cannot be read with one legend as one story. It is a mix of successes, failures, and unmet expectations. Despite expanded access to colleges and universities providing economic benefits, pathbreaking research, and cultural enrichment, the general public remains wary of institutions that no longer guarantee good jobs, continually raise tuition, and inadequately assess learning outcomes. Sullivan suggests the likelihood of even greater differentiation and specialization in the future due to "institutional overload" created by expanded functions and the growing demands of multiple constituencies with conflicting goals. Arthur Levine (Chapter 4) also predicts increased specialization, or a "boutiquing" of higher education, in response to stable or declining resources and growing demands for accountability. He attributes the change to a shift from a growth industry to a mature one. Inadequate and inappropriate institutional responses to these changes, he suggests, have angered the government and are likely to produce increased government regulation and diminished faculty participation in governance.

From larger context to organizational realities, the threat of bureaucratic control by those outside the academy is real, but the often bleak picture painted by analysts of higher education always depends on contemporary development and, in this historical moment, is brightened by recent developments. A buoyant economy, growing faculty agitation for shared governance in response to attacks on tenure, and increased faculty recognition of the need to create new mechanisms of accountability, such as post-tenure review procedures, might forestall moves for increased government regulation. More difficult, perhaps, will be crafting an adequate response to what Clark portrays as poorly prepared students, in need of remediation, whose learning styles contrast with faculty teaching styles.

In our view, meeting this challenge will require not only redesigning our institutions and its structures but also rethinking and re-working the classroom.

Charles Green and Dean Dorn (Chapter 6) explore the implications of the topographical change in higher education described and analyzed by Calhoun, Clark, and Sullivan for what goes on within our classrooms. They argue for less heavy reliance on lecturing, pointing out obstacles to more discussion-oriented teaching as well as opportunities offered by recent teaching reform movements. Some of the challenges they highlight, such as growing conflicts within classrooms, reflect their own institutional locations. Although perhaps more prominent at their institutions, these challenges are common to all colleges and universities where working-class and first-generation college students come to learn. Other challenges, such as generational differences between faculty and students, corporatization, and rapid technological change, impinge on classrooms in a variety of different institutions.

Given the time and energy that overcoming these obstacles will require, the widespread myth of an underworked faculty highlights the need for educators to inform legislators and the general public about what they do. Despite the negative publicity, most faculty still spend the majority of their working time teaching and express a strong commitment to the endeavor. The real problem, as Clark suggests, might lie in the irony that many academics teach too much, making it difficult for them to keep up with scholarship in their disciplines and resulting in academic burnout, especially at two-year colleges.

2

The Changing Character of College: Institutional Transformation in American Higher Education

Craig Calhoun

From medieval centers of faith and learning to finishing schools for the aristocracy and respectable clergy, from normal schools for teacher training to technical institutes in engineering, from intimate liberal arts colleges to sprawling multidimensional universities, institutions of higher education have changed character, constituency, and mandate over the centuries. Such institutions have been pressed into the service of many goals beyond education per se and certainly beyond teaching. They have been called on to save souls; to preserve books, documents, films, and other records of past cultural production; and to advance science, technology, and national economic competitiveness.

Recurrently, there have been waves of doubt both inside and outside higher education about how well these institutions do their jobs. Such a wave recently subjected America's colleges and universities to widespread criticism and scrutiny.[1] Much of this came from the political right (the pendulum swinging, perhaps, to the opposite extreme from the 1960s). Some of it was a result of simple misunderstanding, with institutions of higher education having been startlingly incompetent at explaining themselves to the broader public (perhaps because their leaders and faculty thought themselves above doing so). But some of the criticism also hit home.

Colleges and universities do have problems with accountability, with maintaining appropriate reward structures, and with motivating and reviewing faculty after the tenure stage. Doubts about how well undergraduates are served are eminently reasonable. So too are questions about whether all the research produced is valuable. There are problems with the internal governance systems (and external regulatory regimes) that have produced rapidly rising costs and swelling cadres of administrative staff. A striking feature of the criticisms, the self-analyses and defenses of educators and administrators, however, is that they are cast at a very general level. They do not focus with adequate seriousness on the differences in mission and nature that distinguish America's colleges and universities. Likewise, they are commonly historically naive, operating with reference to an unspecified "golden age" when all classes were small and taught by the best faculty, when all students were attentive and found good jobs on graduation, and when the content of courses was at once intellectually stimulating and universally inoffensive.

Although the golden age is mythical, American higher education has indeed been powerfully transformed in the postwar era. First, the field grew enormously. Second, the balance among different types of institutions was altered during this expansion. Third, the balance also shifted among teaching, scholarship, and research as basic components of academic work. These changes were linked, and each mattered greatly. In this chapter, I address structural transformations in American higher education that form the background to recent complaints about and attempts to improve teaching. These have changed the student population, the organization of colleges and universities, and the work and career patterns of professors. In a later chapter (Chapter 52), I take up some possible directions of further transformation now underway. Throughout, I try to draw attention to some implications of these transformations for teaching, especially with reference to my own discipline, sociology.

A Forgotten Background

Both the sheer number of colleges and universities and the population of students in higher education have grown enormously. The most dramatic phase of this growth (on most indicators) came after World War II. More than half the colleges and universities operating in the United States today did not even exist before the war (Lucas 1996:12). The pattern of growth is, however, long-standing and deeply woven into American expectations for democracy, culture, and (above all) social mobility. Growth was more or less continuous until the 1980s, when a combination of economics, demographics, and politics brought it to an end and even produced some retrenchment.

At the time of the revolution, the United States had only 9 colleges, the largest of which enrolled only a few hundred students. By 1802, 19 more colleges were established. By the eve of the Civil War, there were 250. Religious denominations led the way in founding these colleges, but civic boosterism also played a major role.[2] The predominant orientations of these schools were toward training the clergy and other learned professionals, such as lawyers, and providing a classical education for the sons of the wealthy.

A wider range of practical concerns was expressed in the next phase of expansion, marking a more general and continuing pattern; growth in numbers also has brought a diversity of types of institutions (Oakley 1992; Brubacher and Rudy 1997). One of the biggest changes was the growing presence of women in higher education. A range of new women's colleges were founded, and women were admitted to some of the older schools. Oberlin College led the way, opening as a coeducational college in 1833. After the Civil War, the pace of change quickened in this area (as in other areas).

In 1862, Congress passed the Morrill Act authorizing land grants and funding to a new class of public universities. With gathering momentum, the land grant schools began to dot the country and especially the new states added west of the original colonies. The Morrill Act also provided crucial support for expansion of public institutions designed to educate African Americans. These complemented the growing ranks of private black colleges and institutes.[3] While some of these aimed high in their academic programs, many initially focused on manual skills and practical crafts, reflecting not only prejudices about what blacks should study but also ambivalence about whether technical subjects were appropriate alternatives to classical education.

For most of the history of American education, a mixture of classics and religious education had dominated with minimal challenge. Greek and Latin were considered basic to college education and often were required for graduation (although actual standards may have meant that most students achieved a good deal less than complete mastery). Modern (vernacular) literary and, to some extent, historical classics were widely added to the required curricula. But even secular philosophy was minimally taught, and science was much less so (despite the prominence of the image of Franklin's and Jefferson's scientific enthusiasms in our retrospective views of American history). This was, in many ways, a continuation of the struggle between "ancients and moderns," with antecedents as far back as Greek contests over whether learning was rightly grounded in rhetoric (and oral traditions such as that of the Homeric epics) or in philosophy (and science). The ancients were in the lead for the first 150 years of American higher education.

The bias in favor of gentlemanly classics eroded throughout the second half of the 19th century. The foundings of the Massachusetts Institute of Technology and Cornell in 1865 were pioneering examples of what would become a 19th-century enthusiasm for higher education in applied science and technology. The Civil War is an only partly arbitrary watershed. As often happens, the war showcased the power of technological innovation (although in higher education, economic motives may have mattered more than military ones). Thereafter, more and more place was made in college curricula for scientific education. By this was meant not only knowledge of the natural sciences but also an increasing respect for the scientific method, as codified by Bacon or typified by Newton. Above all, this meant the notion that methods of systematic inquiry could yield knowledge unavailable to the ancients. Religious support for higher education contin-

ued, but with a shift away from the dominance of the early elite Protestant groups. Expansion and upward mobility brought colleges sponsored by Baptists, Methodists, Disciples of Christ, and other "low church" denominations. Immigration expanded the ranks of Catholics and (later) Jews, who in turn founded new religiously affiliated schools. In nearly all cases, the new religiously sponsored schools also included a range of nontraditional—neither classical nor strictly religious—subjects in their curricula.

The teaching of science, and more generally of an orientation to knowledge as a matter of new inquiry rather than as mastery of classics, received a further enormous boost in the 1870s. A pivotal moment in the transformation of American higher education was the introduction of the German model university with its hierarchy of degrees and emphasis on research and specialized knowledge. This had been developing through the 19th century but took cohesive form after 1871, when it was institutionalized as an instrument of national advancement.[4] The model was imported to America almost immediately, with its symbolic focus the founding of Johns Hopkins University in 1876. From Johns Hopkins, the model of the Ph.D. degree spread rapidly, transforming American higher education and eventually becoming the standard qualification for professorships in most fields. Master's and other graduate degrees also proliferated. Soon, it began to be common for professional education in law, medicine, and other fields to come only after a bachelor's degree. With this new model in place, older colleges transformed themselves into universities. On its 150th anniversary in 1896, for example, the College of New Jersey officially changed its name to Princeton University. King's College similarly made itself into Columbia University. Harvard University's president, Charles Eliot, frankly acknowledged the impetus that Johns Hopkins gave to institutional transformation:

I want to testify that the Graduate School of Harvard University, started feebly in 1870 and 1871, did not thrive until the example of Johns Hopkins forced our faculty to put their strength into the development of instruction for graduates. And what was true of Harvard was true of every other university in the land which aspired to create an advanced school of arts and sciences. (quoted in Brubacher and Rudy 1997:182)

New universities also were created following the Johns Hopkins model, perhaps most paradigmatically the University of Chicago but also Stanford University.[5] The numbers of graduate students and the proportion of faculty time spent on graduate students began to climb around the country. Associated with this change was an increasing reconceptualization of the university as a center for research and a growing view that alongside teaching, producing this research should be an expectation for faculty.

This new model of the university set the stage for a further expansion and transformation of the field of higher education in the United States. Even so, higher education remained unusual and mainly an option for elites until the 20th century. Fewer than 3 percent of the nation's population at the close of the 19th century had ever attended college, let alone graduated. By contrast, more than 20 percent of Americans have college degrees today, and 65 percent of young adults at least start college (about two-thirds of these graduate). Between 1840 and 1970, college enrollments rose 417 times, while the population of the country multiplied only 12 times (Carnegie Commission on Higher Education 1972). Most of this growth came in the 20th century and especially in the postwar period. Not only has baccalaureate education spread through the population, post-graduate education also has grown exponentially. Many more Americans get *graduate* degrees today than received bachelor's degrees 100 years ago.[6]

Another important restructuring currently is under way and likely will prove to be a crucial phase in this longer term history. The implications of these transformations for teaching and learning, as well as for the nature of specific institutions and the character of the entire field of higher education, are very great. They also are commonly underestimated or altogether unrecognized. This is so largely because two of the most distinctive features of American higher education have been (a) a greater degree of institutional heterogeneity than any other country in the world and (b) a tendency to mask institutional differentiations and deny their significance.

U.S. higher education both perpetuates and obscures dramatic differences among institutions in financial and other resources. It reproduces and, at least to some extent, conceals a profound prestige and reward hierarchy. Because so many institutions give the same basic degrees—B.A. and B.S., M.A. and Ph.D.—and because these degrees have been offered for such a long time, it often is hard for people to keep in mind that they mean different things at different institutions and at different points in time. It is almost as though people thought that to call attention to these differences was to challenge the very democratic impulse of American education and society more generally.

Growth and Differentiation

After World War II, returning veterans supported by the G.I. Bill flooded American colleges and universities, helping to spark expansion even in relatively hard times. On a smaller scale, the same thing happened after the war in

Korea. Even more dramatically, the veterans of both wars (and their generational cohorts) produced a sustained baby boom. This, combined with economic growth and advancing technology, led to an explosion in demand for higher education in the 1960s. New colleges and universities were founded, and existing ones were expanded. In 1947, there were 2.3 million students in U.S. colleges and universities, up from 1.5 million before the war; by 1994, the number was 14.2 million. The proportion of young adults graduating from high school rose from less than 7 percent at the turn of the century to about 50 percent at the end of World War II, peaked at 77 percent in 1968-1969, and (although it has fallen back) remains at more than 71 percent. The proportion of these high school graduates going on to college rose from 45 percent in 1960 to 65 percent (exclusive of vocational and trade schools) in the mid-1990s. Some 43 percent of high school graduates go on to four-year schools, and another 22 percent go on to two-year colleges. Well over 1 million bachelor's degrees are granted each year. To offer these higher levels of education, the number of faculty grew from 246,000 in 1949-1950 to nearly 1 million today. Graduate education grew more than commensurately. As late as 1920, only 615 Ph.D. degrees were awarded in the United States. Today, more than 43,000 are awarded each year (U.S. Bureau of the Census 1976; National Center for Educational Statistics [NCES] 1996, 1997). Both the educational meaning and job market value of college degrees changed, as did the relationship of higher education to social class and social policy.

This story of growth has profound, but surprisingly often overlooked, implications for teaching. The students of the 1990s are strikingly different from those of earlier periods. They are more diverse, less exclusively upper and middle class, and more commonly immigrants and members of minority groups. Of at least equal importance, however, they are not in any similar aggregate sense an elite. Neither is a college degree training them for membership in an elite. A college degree is increasingly *standard*—at least for the middle class—rather than a mark of distinction. Having one sets one apart from only a little more than half of one's generation. As we know from studies of credentialism, college diplomas are increasingly required for positions that earlier were held by high school graduates or even dropouts (Collins 1979). This in itself does not mean that students gain only the same level of education in college that previous generations gained in high school (a common but false assumption). Today's college students learn a great deal, but (at least for liberal arts majors) much of this learning is not directly and narrowly related to their postgraduation jobs. Rather than establishing specific skills, graduating from college (like graduating from high school earlier) establishes an overall capacity to perform—a matter of discipline and will as much as learning—that employers value.

College education remains important to elite status; indeed (a few billionaire dropouts notwithstanding), it is more so than ever. Nearly all upper class Americans are college educated, but only a minority of colleges and universities train such elites—and a much smaller minority do so than in the past. This pattern already was apparent in research conducted in the 1970s. Coleman and Rainwater (1978) studied the impact of college graduation on lifetime earnings potential (from paid employment, i.e., already putting aside the question of where those with inherited wealth went to gain education commensurate with that wealth). The 15 percent of students who attended the country's most elite private institutions could expect to earn 84 percent more, on average, than those who had not graduated from college. The 45 percent who attended the next tier of still somewhat selective private colleges and leading state university campuses could expect an earnings boost of 52 percent. But—and this was the shocker—those who graduated from the rest of the country's colleges and universities could expect, on average, no net earnings gain compared to those who did not complete college. The differences remained significant even when controlled for father's education, race, and region.

This pattern has changed in two crucial respects (although there is no new study with comparable data to document changes precisely). First, the gap between the average earnings of college graduates and the rest of the population has widened. This is a result of both credentialism and the disappearance of well-paid (especially unionized) manual jobs in favor of often poorly paid service sector work. This means that less prestigious colleges might pay off better than before compared to failure to attend college.[7] Second, however, there has been an increasing inequality in earnings of college graduates that has increased the advantage of elite education compared to nonelite education. This applies independent of choice of major (although, of course, some majors also result in higher earnings [Kominski and Sutterlin 1992]). Rewards flow very disproportionately to those at the top of most lines of work (Frank and Cook 1995). These top positions go disproportionately to graduates of about 10 percent of America's colleges and universities (and, indeed, disproportionately to the most prestigious within that 10 percent). Thus, the shift away from educating elites—either those of inherited position or those who aspired to become elites through entering learned professions—has happened in most of the higher education sector but not in its most prestigious institutions.

This shift (where it has occurred) is of basic significance. It changes how well students are prepared for college, what students (and their families) want out of it, and what they in fact get out of it. I do not want to imply a "night and day" contrast; college students had career aspirations 100 years ago as well. After graduation, many students of earlier generations also entered occupations in which they could make relatively little use of what they studied.

One implication is simply that students of a much wider range of abilities and preparation go on to college. This is not simply a question of their level of knowledge in specific subject matters but rather of their capacities for following lectures, reading textbooks, analyzing problems, writing expository essays, and so on. A significant part of the decline that teachers report in their students' skills actually is better described as an expansion in the proportion of students going to college. One of the reasons for misperception is that teachers often tacitly compare their current students and contemporary institutions not to others they have experienced as teachers but rather to their own college and graduate school years. Because most teachers attended schools more prestigious, selective, and academically rigorous than the ones in which they teach, it is easy for them to confuse differences in types of institutions with changes over time. This effect is enhanced by the fact that teachers' impressions of their own college years do not involve systematic data or even widespread observations (such as those they make of students today) but rather are recollections of their own peer and reference groups.

Second, sheer growth in numbers of students and in the proportion of students in each age cohort to go on to college had an impact on the differentiation of educational institutions and settings for instruction. Although the full impacts of this were not felt at once, an increasing proportion of postsecondary education began to be carried out in two-year schools, whether or not oriented to eventual transfer into bachelor's degree programs.[8] By 1972, public four-year institutions (including universities) taught 48 percent of U.S. students in higher education, private four-year schools taught 22 percent, and public two-year schools taught 28.7 percent.[9] In the 1990s, the proportion taught in public four-year institutions has fallen to 40 percent, that in private four-year schools has slipped slightly to 20 percent, and that in two-year public institutions has risen to 37 percent (NCES 1997). The growing prominence of two-year schools was not the only result. Universities gained in proportionate enrollment compared to liberal arts colleges, and with the dramatic expansion of multicampus state university systems, the internal character and social role of universities changed even while the name held constant. The University of North Carolina, for example, originally was a single campus at Chapel Hill. That campus did not reach the 10,000-student mark until the 1960s, then quickly doubled again. In the same postwar period, the university was expanded to a 16-campus system for which the Chapel Hill campus is a flagship but is neither the largest nor the most typical campus. "Commuter" or "comprehensive" campuses became the fastest growing parts of many state university systems (and in some ways represented a step between community colleges and flagship research campuses).

Consider the disparity that is introduced between the students at the most elite and least elite institutions. Differences in grades, test scores, and other indicators vary dramatically. So do differences in parental socioeconomic status (SES) and "cultural capital." The gap continues to widen. With regard to SES, for example, between 1972 and 1992 there was an approximately equal gain in postsecondary enrollment for both high- and low-SES students, but this was recorded almost entirely in differ-

TABLE 2.1 Percentages of All Students in Achievement Test Quintiles Attending Two-Year Versus Four-Year Institutions within Two Years of High School Graduation

	Test Quintile	1972	1992
Four-year institutions	1 (low)	10	12
	2	22	27
	3	40	50
	4 (high)	70	77
Two-year institutions	1 (low)	13	27
	2	17	30
	3	17	25
	4 (high)	11	12

SOURCE: National Center for Educational Statistics (1997).

ent types of institutions (NCES 1997). Enrollment of low-SES students increased at two-year institutions only, while enrollment of high-SES students increased at four-year institutions. This was a period when the number of public two-year or community colleges quadrupled to account for more than 40 percent of all institutions in American higher education (Oakley 1992:78). Within two years, 65 percent of high-SES 1972 high school graduates attended four-year colleges, whereas for 1992 graduates that figure had risen to 70 percent. Low-SES students continued to attend four-year colleges at the rate of just under 19 percent. By contrast, low-SES enrollment in two-year schools rose from 11 to 22 percent, but high-SES enrollment at two-year schools edged up only from 15 percent to a little less than 17 percent. The contrast in achievement test scores is equally striking (NCES 1997). Table 2.1 shows the widening gap between the two types of schools. (Note that these data lump together all four-year schools from the most selective to the majority with nearly open admissions policies.[10]

Table 2.1 reveals that the population of students entering two-year schools has become increasingly skewed toward the lower end of achievement score results, while that at four-year schools has become increasingly skewed toward the high end. This is not necessarily a problem. This disparity might suggest an appropriate division of educational labor. Either way, there are important implications for teaching. The same textbooks, techniques and styles of instruction, and assignments are unlikely to be appropriate for both sets of institutions. Whether the same standards of educational attainment exist is a distinct question; indeed, whether the standards *should* be the same is open to debate. Is it reasonable to expect students at schools where the majority of students enter in the bottom 40 percent of national achievement test takers to achieve at the same level as those at schools where the majority come from the top 20 percent of such test takers? If not, then what does this mean for the notion that community college credits should be accepted for transfer to four-year schools? What does it mean for the production and use of textbooks? The market for textbooks lies disproportionately at the lower end of the higher education prestige hierarchy but also includes some higher end schools, especially relatively large ones. Publishers have an interest in stopping authors from introducing content that will be deemed too complex, or at too high a reading level, for students in two-year schools. Introductory sociology, in particular, is taught very disproportionately at two-year institutions. This contributes to the tendency for textbooks to present sociology at relatively low levels as well as in highly standardized form and content. This happens more with sociology than with subjects more disproportionately taught in four-year schools, such as physics and history, and the resulting textbooks help to shape the image of the field.

Among four-year schools and universities, there also are great disparities, many the result of recent structural changes in American higher education. Perhaps the most basic transformation has been the increasing numerical domi-

nance of public institutions.[11] This is not just a matter of number but also a matter of size. "Almost 90 percent of the institutions enrolling more than 10,000 students are public, whereas 87 percent of those enrolling 1,000 or fewer are private" (Oakley 1992:79). Although public institutions dominate numerically, they are underrepresented among the most elite institutions by almost any ranking. This means that students who can pay for education at private schools can receive an extra benefit in the struggle over class positions. Private schools are more likely to offer small classes, personal attention, and a variety of support services. They also are much more likely to provide their students with the experience of residence in a college community. Although some state universities are able to offer this, the majority of students enrolled in public higher education attend commuter schools, many with only a fraction of the extracurricular activities and institutional support available in residential schools (NCES 1996).

The character of private colleges also has been changing. Most basically, there has been a decline in the number of traditional, freestanding liberal arts colleges. These are perhaps the most distinctively American institutions of higher education. Their key feature is that they focus overwhelmingly—usually entirely—on students seeking bachelor's degrees. Harvard, Yale, Princeton, and many others of the country's oldest and most famous schools were founded as liberal arts colleges, but as I noted earlier, they transformed themselves into universities, mainly in the late 19th century. The same thing happened at many of the older state universities such as Rutgers University and the University of North Carolina.[12] This means centrally that they added graduate and professional programs. They continued to teach liberal arts curricula but within the context of much larger institutions. This usually meant that faculty had divided responsibilities, teaching both graduate and undergraduate students. Undergraduate liberal arts programs were commonly administered in a "College of Arts and Sciences."

Although the rhetoric of most such universities (both public and private) still stresses that these undergraduate colleges are "the heart of the university," in fact over the years funding and attention have flowed disproportionately to other parts of the university. The biggest gains have not come in graduate schools of arts and sciences with their attendant research programs, some recent critics notwithstanding.[13] They have come in professional schools; these have been impressively successful in attracting both students and especially financial resources.[14]

Recent years have seen a substantial decline in the number of liberal arts colleges. How steep depends on the definition one uses. Between 1970 and 1987, there was a decline from about 715 to 570 in the number of private, independent four-year schools (Carnegie Commission on Higher Education 1987). Most of this was due to reclassification, as many grew large and came to be incorporated into universities. Quite a few others simply closed their doors. While community colleges and large universities grew in the 1960s and 1970s and gained substantial new resources, most liberal arts colleges did not. This left many vulnerable when the economic and demographic environment grew less favorable in the 1980s. Those colleges that remained small and autonomous were divided by the Carnegie Commission on Higher Education into two groups. The first, about 140 of the total, consisted basically of those that offered primarily liberal arts bachelor's degrees and were more or less highly selective in admissions. Prestigious examples included Amherst, Carleton, Reed, and Williams universities. These schools also often were relatively well endowed financially, and in any case were able to attract students willing to pay high tuition because of the educational experiences the schools offered (both curricular and extracurricular) and their success in placing students in graduate and professional schools.

The second group of liberal arts colleges offered a similar mix of degrees in earlier years but were generally not very selective in admissions and had much less in the way of financial resources. A key result was that they came into direct competition with what the Carnegie Commission calls "comprehensive universities and colleges," particularly the less selective branch campuses of public university systems but also a number of relatively small private universities. Competition over tuition costs was debilitating to many small colleges, as students and their families chose less expensive public institutions or attended private ones only when they could get financial assistance. More transformative, however, was competition over courses of study. The less selective small colleges moved away from their traditional emphasis on the liberal arts, adding more and more courses and majors in business and other directly job-related fields. "Their survival threatened in a rapidly shifting marketplace, the bulk, it seems, of the institutions we are accustomed to think[ing] of as liberal arts colleges have in fact transformed themselves into 'something else'—for want of a better term—into 'small, professional college[s]' " (Breneman 1990, quoted in Oakley 1992:77-78). Breneman (1990) estimates, in fact, that no fewer than 317 of what had been liberal arts colleges stopped granting even 40 percent of their degrees in liberal arts subjects. This reduced the total number of "real" liberal arts colleges from 540 to 212.[15]

This was one dramatic institutional manifestation of the general rise in popularity of professional, career-oriented baccalaureate programs. This combined with the growth of community colleges to mean that the majority of students in American higher education, and the majority of those taking sociology classes, no longer was comprised of liberal arts students.

Teaching, Research, and Career Tracks

A common weakness in discussions about teaching is that participants often assume teaching to be a single skill, with the same techniques—and even content—appropriate to students of different levels and in different types of institutions. No doubt, there are considerable continuities, but there also are important disjunctures.

One could start with a catalog of basic questions about differences in preparation:

- Do students know how to grasp arguments in or take notes on lectures?
- Are students ready to read primary source materials or only textbook presentations?
- Are students at ease with basic graphical and tabular presentations of statistical material, or is the ability to understand this material one of the things they need to learn in a sociology class?
- Do students have basic computer skills to enable them readily to incorporate specialized software or computer-based research efforts into their classes?
- Do students know (or have reason to know) much about other disciplines or interdisciplinary fields, thus making it important for their teachers to situate sociology among these?
- Have students studied any significant amount of (or specific content in) world history or comparative cultures? Put an-

other way, how much and what type of knowledge should instructors take for granted? (This is a question not just about "level" of school but also about whether or not sociology is taught after a common core of general education classes.)

- What proportion of students live on or have easy access to a campus environment, with its learning resources (and common cultural referents)?

To this, one could add differences in racial, ethnic, and class mixes. Schools also vary greatly in the patterns of aspirations that motivate their students.

A somewhat related question is whether there is any reason for undergraduate classes to mirror and attempt to cover the basic fields of scholarship and research into which a discipline is divided. The primary rationale for doing so lies in the notion that one is mastering the field for the purpose of continued intellectual activity in that field. The major, in this sense, developed in the context of the modern research university and as a counterpart to its organization of graduate education and scholarly publication. But changes in the nature of undergraduate education suggest that this might not be very relevant.

Sociology is a good example. Relatively few students within liberal arts programs major in sociology. The most important teaching sociologists do in such programs often will be for nonmajors (although these nonmajors might take more than one course, and there might be no reason for those they take to start with a conventional introductory survey). It might be appropriate to design courses that introduce sociological thinking and modes of inquiry in relation to various topics without attempting to cover literatures or subfields. In non-liberal arts schools, sociology might be taught more often to majors, but these majors seek preparation for specific types of jobs (few, if any, of which carry the title "sociologist"). In some settings, sociology is closely tied into criminal justice or law enforcement majors; in others, it might be tied into labor or industrial relations. Sociologists teaching in more professional majors have special obligations to be able to impart specific job-related skills, of course, but also to bring a sociological perspective to bear on the applied field. Again, this suggests teaching that is not precisely a mirror of the research enterprise.[16] Knowledge of sociology as a discipline might matter little to students in such settings, but contributions of sociological knowledge to certain types of job performance might matter a great deal. In such cases, the teaching sociologist takes on an obligation continually to renew his or her knowledge of how professionals in the given field actually work and not only how sociology works as a research enterprise.

The more general question of whether there is in fact a mutually supportive relationship between teaching and research is, of course, a vexed one. Virtually no one is absolutely against research, of course, yet virtually no one maintains that high school teachers should be evaluated on their performance as researchers. It is clear that their jobs require teaching skills and effort and are enhanced by keeping up with new developments in the fields they teach, but high school teachers are neither given facilities and time nor given incentives for original research. This is generally true even for those who teach high school students more talented and better prepared than those at many colleges (either because of the overall character of the high school in question or because the teachers are assigned honors classes). The question appropriately arises: Why should we have different expectations of college teachers? Unfortunately, the question is not readily answerable in that form.

To get a more precise understanding of the issue, we should abandon the notion that college teaching is one task. We could then ask the question: For which college teachers should we consider research requirements appropriate? This would be largely a matter of taking seriously differences among institutions of higher education but also could vary among levels and programs within individual institutions. In fact, many institutions already have tacitly recognized this (although few will announce it publicly). Large universities, for example, apparently do not believe that being a researcher in linguistics, literature, or education is necessary for success as a teacher of foreign languages. This is demonstrated by the extent to which such teaching is done by adjunct or non-tenure-track faculty or by foreign graduate students who are native speakers but not necessarily researchers in fields related to their teaching.[17] Similarly, to the extent that universities employ adjunct and temporary faculty to do a large part of their teaching, they would appear tacitly to acknowledge that they do not see research as an important complement to teaching, at least at introductory levels. Of course, in both cases the universities could be making mistakes, responding inappropriately to economic pressures. But the point remains valid, I think, that the positive link between teaching and research does not reasonably apply equally across types of institutions, levels of instruction, and levels of student preparation.

The issue extends beyond the teaching-research link. It is desirable that all teachers at all levels of instruction from elementary grades to postgraduate keep up with scholarship in their fields of instruction. It is desirable, in other words, that they engage in both scholarship and teaching, whether or not they engage in "original" research (or "the production of new knowledge"). But this is a desideratum that applies unequally. We expect different levels of mastery and continual expansion of knowledge on the parts of seventh-grade social studies teachers and college sociology instructors. We do, I think, also expect different levels of scholarship from those who specialize in teaching introductory sociology and those who also teach a range of upper division undergraduate classes. Not least, we expect—or should expect—a considerably different level of scholarship to be demonstrated by those who teach graduate classes and supervise master's and doctoral work.[18] Whatever our empirical expectations, however, an ideological commitment to the notion that college teaching is a single occupation weakens our ability appropriately to differentiate norms for teachers called on to do different types of work.

Good teaching is valuable at all levels and in different types of institutions, but it must mean somewhat different things and imply different types of work. The extent to which an instructor should focus time and energy on the mastery of teaching techniques, for example, might vary. A variety of special techniques might be appropriate at the introductory level that are not appropriate at the graduate level. At the graduate level, substantive mastery of the latest research in a field might count for more relative to teaching technique than it does at the introductory level. A similar differentiation might apply to different levels even of introductory teaching where different student populations have been enrolled. At present, we muddle the issue by seeking to place some requirements for research on and offer some rewards for research to all types of college teachers. A simple bit of evidence is the way in which many (I suspect most) institutions decide whether to pay for a teacher to attend a scholarly meeting. The teacher gets financial support only if he or she is presenting a paper, not if the teacher proposes to listen to papers, learn from them, and incorporate the new knowledge into his or her teaching. This is, remarkably, true of entirely undergraduate institutions as well as research universities. It not only seems to be a questionable allocation of institutional resources and a curious signal, it makes scholarly meetings less effective by encouraging more speaking, less listening, and less selectivity for presentations of the best research.[19]

The point is not that faculty at community colleges or four-year schools focused on applied skills rather than on liberal arts might not in fact be good researchers; this does indeed happen, just as some professors at research universities do no research. It also has been the case that high school teachers publish noteworthy scholarly works. More impressive is the relatively strong research performance of teachers at the more selective arts colleges. Good research is valuable to the discipline wherever it is produced. It might not be equally valuable, however, to all the different types of institutions that employ sociologists. Research is much more supportive of the specific mission of some schools than others, and it is more likely to make an instructor helpful to some populations of students than others.[20]

Despite this, however, research accomplishments are the most readily marketable of academic credentials. Graduate education is organized accordingly, and the pattern continues through the production of articles and books and the winning of research grants by professors. Those who see publications as the primary ticket to career mobility are not wrong, although this does not mean that the system that makes them right is in all regards a good one.

Lewis (1996) argues that published research is the most effective "capital" in academic job markets for understandable reasons. First, it is relatively easy to measure, directly in volume and by means of reputation in quality. Second, whether or not it contributes much to teaching, it can contribute a good deal to institutional reputation. This is significant because schools inevitably are in the business of marketing degrees. That is, students (and their families) choose and pay for colleges on the basis of expected labor market returns, not just for the pleasure of learning. The research productivity of faculty is relatively strongly correlated with the value of degrees. This might be partly because the same institutions with the resources to support strong faculty research (and, in effect, to buy strong faculty) are able to be highly selective in their admissions policies. This not only means that the more able students they enroll go on to predictably greater career success simply for that reason but also means that each student gains from having more able classmates. A large part of education actually comes from fellow students, not from teachers, and what teachers can offer is shaped by overall preparation of those in their classes. If the students in selective schools also are from higher class backgrounds, then so much the better for their value as members of the social networks through which graduates seek jobs and make business connections.

This suggests why institutions "buy" researchers, even when they assign them to work largely as teachers.[21] Lewis's (1996) explanation works better, however, for relatively elite liberal arts colleges and research universities. Other schools, from community colleges to comprehensive universities, depend less on and gain less from competition in the market for research-based reputations. This is partly because other sources of distinction remain salient (e.g., percentage of faculty with Ph.D. degrees, which is basically invariant among more elite schools). It also is because modest productivity can achieve local distinction, and applied research linked to local concerns might be of greater value than national reputation. The prestige of research might matter more when a nonselective school seeks to change its niche

(e.g., to shift from two-year to four-year or from four-year to graduate) than it does in competing for students within its established niche. Even where research adds relatively little to an institution's competitive position, it might be a priority for some instructors. This might be because they harbor other ambitions. Even where these professors do not have immediate intentions of seeking to change employers, many are shaped by the ambitions they harbored while in graduate school. They seek to make the professorships they hold live up to those that they observed or to which they aspired while students. The long drought in academic employment centered on the 1980s (longer in some fields than others) made this issue more acute. Many scholars whose graduate school performances would (a decade or two earlier) have landed them in research universities or selective liberal arts colleges found themselves in branch campuses of state universities, nonselective colleges, or community colleges.

Research is important not only to the careers of individual scholars but also to the prestige of graduate departments. These are evaluated not only on the research of their own current members but also on the research and placements of the students they train. As a result, they have an incentive to overvalue placement in universities and to undervalue primarily teaching institutions. In addition, grant income has become important to the budgets of a whole class of universities. The presence of Ph.D. programs along with substantial funded research was used to distinguish an elite of *research universities* from the rest of the institutions called *universities*. These institutions continued to attract a disproportionate share of the best prepared students and offered the greatest return to student (and family) investment in educational credentials (compared to other universities, not independent liberal arts colleges, which have their own internal hierarchy). To a considerable extent, however, this dominant group of universities began to reward their faculty more for research and publications and less for teaching.[22]

The differentiation of academic institutions has produced differentiated labor markets for teachers and researchers. Lewis (1996) generalizes that "teaching, what most faculty are hired to do and what most do most of the time, does not figure prominently in the academic labor market" (p. 27). Aside from the emphasis on research at the more selective and better funded schools, the biggest reason probably is difficulty rendering teaching skills demonstrable, transferable, and sufficiently distinctive. Let me take up each point briefly.

Recognition as a good teacher is largely local. Although teaching awards and formal evaluations help teachers demonstrate their skills more broadly, there is very little common understanding of how to evaluate these compared to the pecking order among journal and book publishers. Teaching, moreover, is something done for and addressed to students, whereas research is done for and addressed to colleagues. This means that publishing good research directly generates recognition (even if we sometimes complain that it does not do so accurately enough); citation indexes are a measure of this direct generation of recognition. By contrast, most recognition of teaching achievements is indirect. This means that capacity to identify good teachers at a distance is limited. Most jobs (almost by definition) are located at a distance. An important (if slightly ironic) approach to this problem comes in attempts to demonstrate teaching skills by publishing articles about teaching. These not only disseminate useful knowledge to other teachers but also advertise an author's commitment to and possibly innovation in teaching.[23]

Second, teaching skills might not be readily transferable across populations of students and types of schools or programs. What makes for success in a small liberal arts college might not work well in a large, minimally selective school and might bore or frustrate students in a highly selective school.[24] There are instructors gifted as seminar leaders who handle larger classes poorly, and (perhaps less often) there are superb lecturers who do less well at maintaining a high intellectual level in the "give and take" of small classes. If this is so, or even if it is simply perceived to be so, it inhibits the potential for upward mobility of instructors through movement to different levels of types of institutions. Excellent research will be more effective at moving someone from a branch campus of a state university to a flagship campus than excellent teaching will be at moving someone from a nonselective liberal arts college to a highly selective one.

Third, and perhaps most troubling, teaching has become increasingly commoditized. That is, it is bought on the basis of volume rather than quality. Differentiations among teachers matter relatively little once some basic threshold of performance is passed. There are many faces to this; increasing reliance on adjunct, temporary, and term contract faculty is perhaps the most extreme. The current pattern reflects the conjuncture of several factors.

Colleges and universities face fiscal constraints, leading them to economize by making instruction more of a volume production process; larger class size and cheaper teachers seem to spell efficiency. At some institutions, this means a change in the full-time equivalent load and pay for teachers generally. At others, it means an increasing differentiation between classes of faculty. Some faculty are rewarded and/or assigned the time and resources to do work that enhances the institution's reputation;

others, especially non-tenure-track faculty, teach more and are paid less. Enrollment growth in recent decades has come disproportionately in fields outside the traditional liberal arts. This means that teaching in many traditional liberal arts fields has been reduced primarily to introductory-level courses. Community colleges are the extreme examples of this, but versions exist at all levels of institutions. For example, even Ivy League schools rely on non-tenure-track faculty to teach foreign language courses or expository writing. At a wide range of schools, temporary faculty are used to teach large enrollment "service" courses in many fields. At many nonselective institutions, which compete with each other for students in job-related tracks and compete partly on price grounds, low-cost and low-level liberal arts courses became especially attractive. Costlier investments have to be limited to the fields that attract the students. More than 40 percent of college and university faculty today work on a temporary basis, double the percentage of the early 1970s (Brubacher and Rudy 1997:402; NCES 1997).

In addition to temporary and adjunct faculty, graduate students play a substantial role in the teaching of sociology—mainly, of course, in the larger, Ph.D.-granting institutions. The role of graduate students in teaching is a common target for critics of American universities. Most, however, speak in ignorance. It is true that using graduate students saves money compared to hiring more faculty. It is possible that in the absence of graduate students, faculty would teach more undergraduates, but it is unlikely that additional assignments to current faculty could come close to making up for the loss of instructors. Most basically, however, the critics assume that graduate students are poorly qualified to be teachers or perform poorly in the classroom. Both assumptions are false. Gradu-

ate students who teach today typically have master's degrees, their equivalents, or still higher level educations. What critics fail to recall is that before the 1960s, most college and university faculty in the United States also lacked doctorates. The spread of the doctorate as a standard faculty credential has taken place only in the past 40 years (albeit starting from roots in the late 19th century, as discussed earlier). Today's graduate student teachers are highly educated and in most cases have been chosen for admission to Ph.D. programs based on highly selective criteria. Moreover, graduate students generally get good teaching evaluations.[25] Graduate students are more likely than faculty to have received formal instruction in how to teach, largely because such instruction has proliferated only in recent years. At many universities, it is mandatory for graduate students before they are given responsibility for a class, but it is not mandatory for faculty.

Despite all of this, most faculty in all but the most research-oriented schools spend most of their time teaching. The National Survey of Postsecondary Faculty showed that teaching takes up more than 70 percent of the working time of instructors in two-year schools, 65 percent of working hours of those in liberal arts colleges, and only 45 percent of the working hours of those in research universities (NCES 1996). Most spend much more time on teaching than extrinsic rewards would dictate, suggesting that they find it intrinsically rewarding or at least identify with the task. Not least of all, surveys suggest that most faculty think of themselves primarily as teachers and that not only do few shirk teaching in favor of research, the vast majority make little effort to produce research.

There is, however, an evident oversupply of potential faculty. Whatever the economic wisdom of the career choices individuals have made, this has been exacerbated by faculties that have promoted the production of many more Ph.D. holders than the labor market could easily bear. To a lesser extent, the same pursuit of prestige and rewards associated with research helped drive the expansion of graduate programs. Colleges sought to turn themselves into universities; campuses founded with only undergraduate degree programs first demanded the right to offer master's degrees and then Ph.D. degrees. When the job market turned down in the 1970s, many long-standing graduate programs were very slow to cut their student intake (even while worrying about student quality). Faculty had become accustomed to teaching graduate rather than undergraduate courses, to having students to supervise, and to having teaching and research assistants. Institutions often depended on graduate students for inexpensive teaching. In addition, the creation of new Ph.D. programs continued at a rapid rate. This has been driven by ambitions of faculty, institutions, and localities with relatively little attention to the labor market. Tending to faculty egos in this way not only deflated the market value of a Ph.D. with the award of increasing numbers of new doctorates but also led to a muddying of the distinctions among the mandates and niches of different types of academic institutions. Although the University of North Carolina system continued to designate only two of its campuses as research universities, for example, in the 1980s and 1990s it authorized a number of other branch campuses to award doctorates. This was done in the face of advice that isolated departmental Ph.D. degrees would be weaker than those embedded in full-fledged, multidisciplinary graduate schools. More to the point, it happened even in fields such as history, in which the job market already was revealing a tremendous excess of new Ph.D. holders over jobs. Nationally, sociology has gained the distinction of being the social science

in which the largest proportion of degrees are granted outside the most prestigious programs (D'Antonio 1992).

This might reflect a different pattern of quality control compared to other disciplines, but it also reflects a minimally acknowledged substantive differentiation of the discipline of sociology. At the major Ph.D.-granting universities, research is paramount and ever more specialized. Students commonly develop a strong command of only a single subfield of the discipline. Elsewhere, knowledge of multiple subfields and an orientation to sociology in general may be stronger. Indeed, some graduate departments, clear about the likely teaching positions in which many of their graduates will find work, explicitly encourage students to gain enough knowledge to teach in several different branches of the discipline.

There also are differences in the subfields emphasized. Some branches of sociology that are prestigious and powerful in the research universities are not even taught in many undergraduate schools; demography is one example. At the same time, some other fields of sociology are much less likely to be taught in the most prestigious departments but are prominent in less prestigious schools; criminology is perhaps the prime example. There is a robust market for sociologists prepared to teach in criminal justice programs or able to offer relevant courses. Yet, in the dozen most prestigious Ph.D.-granting departments of sociology, there are only 3 faculty members who list criminology as a specialty in the American Sociological Association (ASA) *Guide to Graduate Departments*[26] Including people who list deviance and social control as areas only raises the number to 5 out of some 300 faculty members.

The point can be extended. It is not simply that some specialties are high prestige and others are low prestige, it is that the development of an active job market for graduates of programs with an applied emphasis actually is correlated with low prestige for the relevant field of study. That which comes to be taught as an applied specialty at the undergraduate level is not taught much in the most prestigious graduate programs. Applied emphases apparently have some of this effect even when not linked so heavily to faculty in top graduate departments. Thus, there is a sharp disjuncture between the concerns of the elite graduate programs and those in which the majority of sociologists actually teach. This is not just a disjuncture between graduate and undergraduate programs in which criminology, medical sociology, and (to a lesser extent) sociology of education are prominent fields of study. These train the faculty for the relatively large number of positions available in those fields as well as for nonacademic jobs. Likewise, there is a great deal of research in each of these three areas; funding might actually be more readily available for work in these fields than in many specialties associated with higher prestige institutions—comparative historical sociology, collective behavior and social movements, and stratification.[27] But the research in criminology, medical sociology, and education seems to have less impact on the field of sociology as a whole and to remain more compartmentalized within each subfield. This is not, of course, because the topics lack intrinsic interest; each has been the subject of widely recognized sociological classics, and each also is one of the areas of greatest public concern in the contemporary United States.[28]

What we need to grasp is that disciplines seem surprisingly different when viewed from the vantage point of different types of institutions. Here, as in many regards, it is relevant to note that the highly publicized battle over teaching versus research actually obscures the issue. The major distinction in what is taught lies, as Oakley (1992) summarizes,

not between the universities with a substantial commitment to graduate education and the four- and two-year undergraduate colleges, but between the universities and top tier of four-year colleges, on the one hand, and the less highly selective four- and two-year colleges, on the other. (p. 116)

We can be more precise.[29] Those universities that are highly selective and the highly selective liberal arts colleges teach a different sociology, by and large, from the rest of the institutions of higher education. The difference is not only a greater preponderance of introductory over specialized courses, it is a difference in what types of specialized sociological knowledge are taught.[30] The reason lies largely in the preparation and aspirations of the students who attend the different institutions.

Conclusion

I have suggested that perhaps the single most salient feature of American higher education is the enormous differentiation among institutions. Different in form, function, size, mandate, prestige, selectivity, and resources, colleges and universities nonetheless project a surprisingly common and confused public image. This has contributed to a lack of clarity among funders, students, and critics of various perspectives. But despite the confusions, American higher education also is enormously vital and impressively successful in meeting the needs of a very wide range of students and of other constituencies such as purchasers of research. The diversity of institutions is a crucial basis for this vitality.

I have argued that poorly recognized transformations in institutional patterns and student enrollments have dramatically altered teaching and academic employment in the postwar era. Changes in who is enrolled in higher education and in the types of institutions that enroll them account for many differences in the overall field of higher education that are poorly perceived as declines. But these changes also demand that those who would improve teaching and learning take seriously the differences among the environments in which these occur and the student populations with which different teachers work. A populist tendency to mask the structural and cultural differences behind the words *college, university,* and *professor* makes this hard to accomplish.

Notes

1. See, among many, Bloom (1987), D'Souza (1991), Kimball (1990), Smith (1990), and Sykes (1990). These (and other) major book-length critiques launched a wave of investigations and attacks from foundations and local interest groups. It is worth noting that the peak phase of the attacks, like that of the "culture wars" and rebellion against a changing literary canon with which both were associated, seems to have passed.

2. One of the major transformations in late 19th- and 20th-century American higher education has been its overwhelming secularization. See Marsden (1994).

3. Schools also were created to educate Native Americans, although their history is quite different. The most famous private effort to create a college for Indians resulted in the creation of Dartmouth College, one of America's oldest and most prestigious schools, which quickly shifted its mission. Others were founded by the federal government, many as boarding schools designed to educate talented Indian youths for lives away from their tribes and reservations or for leadership in transform-

ing the lives of their people in accord with the orientations of the dominant powers.

4. The University of Berlin had been founded in 1810 and became a showplace for Prussian leadership and reform of state institutions. After the unification of Germany, Prussian models became still more influential. Berlin was not uniquely responsible for the "German model" imported to America, however. Indeed, under Münchausen, Hanover's Halle University initiated partly similar trends even earlier, including pioneering in the recruitment of "star" professors based on their publications. See McClelland (1980).

5. Clark University was founded as an all-graduate university, although this model did not take root. Clark soon opened its doors to undergraduates. The leadership of distinguished psychologist G. Stanley Hall and the demand for possessors of the new higher degrees were not enough to provide the institution with an adequate income, mission, or identity (Veysey 1965). This foreshadows a continuing ambivalence about graduate education in American research universities—an eagerness to embrace the conception of knowledge that places research and specialized graduate education at its core and a desire to "sell" institutions to funders and the public on the basis of their role in undergraduate education. This is no doubt due in large part to the ambivalence of the (ultimately funding) public itself about science, specialized research, and the balance of different roles in the mission of the university. Oddly, although Chicago was perhaps the most important direct follower of the Johns Hopkins model, its reputation today is at least equally shaped by its later adoption of the "great books" teaching format that flourished as a reaction against the emphasis of "new inquiry" in the research universities.

6. More than 400,000 Americans receive master's degrees each year (U.S. Bureau of the

Census 1997). To get an idea of the continuing speed of this change, consider that as recently as 1985, only 289,000 Americans received master's degrees.

7. Research is needed on this point. It seems likely that if tendencies toward polarization of the labor market continue, then the extent to which degrees from nonselective colleges will qualify graduates for "middle-class" jobs will decline.

8. A prominent early model for community colleges stressed their role as "junior" counterparts to four-year institutions and universities and promoted the idea that typical students could be conceptualized as "freshmen" and "sophomores" destined, if successful, to transfer into baccalaureate programs. As Brint and Karabel (1990) show, this ideal was not fully realized—partly, they argue, because local business groups seized on the community colleges as tax-supported providers of training closely tied to corporate skill requirements rather than to broader educational agendas. An implication of this was that community colleges often extended the vocational tracks of secondary schools more than opening up new paths to bachelor's degrees and (with them) to social mobility. Whatever the ultimate degree objective or attainment of students, community colleges came between the 1960s and 1990s to play a proportionately larger and larger role in the teaching of introductory sociology. Predictably, they exerted a significant influence on the preparation and development of introductory sociology textbooks. In the 1990s, community colleges have once again been targeted for extensive development (boosted by proposed tax credits).

9. Private two-year schools taught between 1.2 and 2.1 percent of students throughout the postwar period.

10. The National Center for Educational Statistics does not differentiate among four-year colleges and universities in this regard, but only about 200 are selective, and they probably account for most of the high-SES students.

11. This has been a striking change among two-year and community colleges as well. We now tend to take public funding of these for granted, almost as definitional. In fact, private two-year schools once were fairly widespread but declined in the postwar era, while the rest of higher education grew. In the 1970s and 1980s, the number of private two-year colleges decreased by 50 percent, while the number of public two-year institutions quadrupled (Ottinger 1989; NCES 1997).

12. Thus, the recent trend of establishing public, elite liberal arts colleges is something of a return to an earlier pattern under changed circumstances. The University of North Carolina at Asheville aspires to something of the instructional mission of Chapel Hill in an earlier day, although this now means a different niche in the overall ecology of higher education. The College of New Jersey has adopted not only the original name of the school that became Princeton but something of the institutional design that characterized Rutgers in an earlier day.

13. The mistaken notion that research-oriented graduate schools rather than professional schools have been the primary beneficiary of a shift in focus away from undergraduates is prominent, for example, in Sykes (1990).

14. It is common for academics committed to the liberal arts to complain that this is an altogether new phenomenon, conceived by upstart quasi-intellectual professions and unfairly relegating teachers of the liberal arts to a lower status. In fact, the issue already was old when Kant intervened into the "conflict of the faculties" at the end of the 18th century. As academic guilds gave way to universities in the late Middle Ages, "they came customarily to be divided into 'faculties,' with the faculty of arts being

regarded as preparatory to the 'superior' professional faculties of medicine, law, and theology" (Oakley 1992:18). Indeed, for a long time, the terms *doctor* and *professor* were used only for those who taught (and were formally *masters*) in the superior faculties, not in the arts (Rashdall 1936). Thus, the 19th- and 20th-century American pattern in which liberal arts bachelor's degrees became a common foundation for graduate professional degrees was, to some extent, a reconstruction of an earlier pattern.

15. Breneman's (1990) figure of 540 small colleges (before deducting those no longer classifiable as liberal arts schools) is slightly lower than that of the Carnegie Commission because of differences in classification. A common criticism is that some such colleges teach material that should be taught in high school. A somewhat oblique support for this comes in Arum's (1998) finding that states that spend more on high school vocational programs spend less on college-level ones and vice-versa.

16. Likewise, it is important to avoid fetishization of the new. One example comes in college textbooks. Bringing out ever more frequent editions (largely to defeat the used book market), publishers are at pains to demonstrate that each is truly an advance over those that came before. Many make a point, for example, of the proportion of citations that reference works published since the previous textbooks. One effect of this, however, is to shift the contents of such textbooks away from presentations of enduring sociological knowledge and toward more emphasis on current events (and semipopular or ad hoc sociological interpretations of them). This fetishism of the new oddly accompanies a conservatism about some organizing devices such as the long outdated and never quite coherent notion that theory comes in three schools—functionalism, conflict, and symbolic interaction—or the organization of tables of contents.

17. Whereas being a researcher in literature might be only distantly related to teaching language, research in linguistics and language acquisition might be important. Schools do well to develop career tracks for language teachers and incentives to acquire and exercise those skills.

18. In the fight over teaching versus research, scholarship sometimes is all but forgotten. As funded research projects and ostensibly original publications became the primary indexes of academic achievement, the value traditionally placed on *having*—as distinct from *producing*—knowledge was eroded. Command of a broad field—or of multiple or interdisciplinary fields—and depth of specialized knowledge both lost proportionate rewards. Even teaching was easier to measure, at least with student appreciation or sheer numbers of students "processed" as indicators. A key impact of the declining prestige and reward accorded scholarship was to undermine the unity and intellectual coherence of intellectual fields including sociology. There was not much payoff for investment in learning about sociology in general (Calhoun 1992). To the extent that such knowledge was pursued, it often was by the writers of introductory sociology textbooks and instructors specializing in introductory sociology, and both activities became somewhat declassé. This happened, in significant part, precisely because of the emphasis on creating new knowledge rather than on transmitting, reproducing, and interpreting existing knowledge.

19. The American Sociological Association, in particular, operates a policy motivated by antielitism. This not only ensures a very wide access to chances to present scholarly work but also selects members for committees based on criteria of representation. In some cases, these

criteria run directly counter to recognition of distinct missions of different types of schools (as in mandates that committees to judge scholarly achievement always include faculty from non-research-oriented schools).

20. Here I speak only of research to advance sociological knowledge as such, not research on the teaching of sociology. The latter is a welcome, relatively new development and, of course, may appropriately be distributed differently.

21. There are, of course, other reasons including the extent to which researchers bring in outside money. This clearly is valued by administrators, although many do not examine it carefully enough. Some large grants are "profitable" for institutions receiving them, but many are not. They call for matching funds and other commitments of institutional resources. This is an especially problematic issue away from the most active research institutions. Externally funded research might appear to be more valuable where it is rarer, but it also might cost much more to administer because of lack of economy of scale and differences in the nature of the research itself and the preexisting institutional facilities. A further issue is the increasing shift to proprietorial research as universities and their faculties try to join forces with private industry. Who benefits and how are questions needing much more careful research. For one helpful account buttressed unusually by comparative data, see Slaughter and Leslie (1997).

22. Often denied by top administrators, this reward structure is evidenced both in the fact that leading researchers commanded higher salaries than leading teachers (even disregarding differential opportunities for supplemental pay) and in the criteria for promotion and tenure. The administrators, in what has become one of their major public rituals, not only deny the reality of differential rewards but also declare that teaching and research clearly and unequivocally reinforce each other. It is likely true that many of the same qualities (e.g., intellectual vitality) go into the makeup of both good teachers and good researchers, but the administrators disingenuously ignore the impact of the incentive structure under which faculty work and the fact that with both days and careers relatively short, faculty have to make judgments about where to invest their time and energy.

23. An emphasis on innovation might be more important to getting articles on teaching published than to actual teaching. Many of the most useful skills and approaches, after all, already are known if inadequately disseminated or practiced.

24. Let me make clear that this does not mean that work on teaching skills and performance does not matter as much in more selective schools. On the contrary, skills matter everywhere—but sometimes different skills. Also, the common pattern of learning how to teach by conscious or unconscious imitation of one's own good teachers probably works better for those who teach in schools similar to those they attended.

25. Teaching evaluations at the two universities where I have been a professor and an administrator suggest that some graduate students are among the most successful and highly praised teachers, whereas the mean for graduate students falls only slightly below that for faculty.

26. I examined the data listed in the 1997 ASA guide for every faculty member listed as holding a regular full-time appointment in sociology for any department that was listed in the top 10 in *either* the National Research Council or *U.S. News & World Report* rankings. There are about 300 faculty members in

the 12 departments; they list a median of three fields each.

27. In each of these fields, there are several times as many faculty members in the top graduate departments as there are in criminology, medical sociology, and sociology of education. Here are the tallies from this quick review (obviously hardly a detailed and systematic study, but the variance is substantial) compared to 1996 membership in the ASA section most closely identified with the subfield in question:

	Faculty in Top Departments	Section Membership
Criminology	3	625
Medical Sociology	9	948
Education	12	550
Collective Behavior and Social Movements	23	555
Stratification	33	n/a
Comparative/Historical	45	540

Interestingly, there is no ASA section on stratification.

28. The cynic might actually assert that prestige in sociological work is inversely related to relevance to applied careers or public discourse. Without cynicism, one can see that greater esteem flows to studies that address problems pointed up by other sociologists' work than to those that directly tackle public issues or apply sociological inquiry to practical problems.

29. Oakley (1992) is at pains to distinguish selective from nonselective liberal arts colleges but tends to lump universities together as research institutions, at least in this part of his analysis.

30. The more selective schools also tend to sponsor different interdisciplinary fields from the less selective schools—cultural studies, social studies of science, and gender and sexuality, for example, rather than criminal justice, family development, and recreation and leisure stud-ies. Likewise, the "culture wars" have been disproportionately a dispute in the more selective schools. Behind some of the differences lie not only market niches but also the contrast between settings in which faculty determine curricula and appointments to a greater extent and those in which administrators act with more complete authority.

References

Arum, Richard. 1998. "Invested Dollars or Diverted Dreams: The Effect of Resources on Vocational Student Educational Outcomes." *Sociology of Education* 71 (2).

Bloom, Allan. 1987. *The Closing of the American Mind: How Higher Education Has Failed Democracy and Impoverished the Souls of Today's Students.* New York: Simon & Schuster.

Breneman, David W. 1990. "Are We Losing Our Liberal Arts Colleges?" *College Board Review,* Summer, pp. 16-29.

Brint, Steven and Jerome Karabel. 1990. *The Diverted Dream: Community Colleges and the Promise of Educational Opportunity in America, 1900-1985.* New York: Oxford University Press.

Brubacher, John S. and Willis Rudy. 1997. *Higher Education in Transition: A History of American Colleges and Universities.* New Brunswick, NJ: Transaction Publishers.

Calhoun, Craig. 1992. "Sociology, Other Disciplines, and the Project of a General Understanding of Social Life." Pp. 137-95 in *Sociology and Its Publics,* edited by T. Halliday and M. Janowitz. Chicago: University of Chicago Press.

Carnegie Commission on Higher Education. 1972. *A Statistical Portrait of Higher Education.* Berkeley, CA: Carnegie Foundation for the Advancement of Teaching.

———. 1987. *A Classification of Institutions of Higher Education*. Princeton, NJ: Carnegie Foundation for the Advancement of Teaching.

Coleman, R. P. and L. Rainwater. 1978. *Social Standing in American: New Dimensions of Class*. New York: Basic Books.

Collins, Randall. 1979. *The Credential Society*. New York: Academic Press.

D'Antonio, William V. 1992. "Recruiting Sociologists in a Time of Changing Opportunities." Pp. 99-136 in *Sociology and Its Publics*, edited by Terence C. Halliday and Morris Janowitz. Chicago: University of Chicago Press.

D'Souza, Dinesh. 1991. *Illiberal Education: The Politics of Race and Sex on Campus*. New York: Vintage.

Frank, Robert H. and Philip J. Cook. 1995. *The Winner-Take-All Society*. New York: Free Press.

Kimball, Roger. 1990. *Tenured Radicals: How Politics Has Corrupted Higher Education*. New York: HarperCollins.

Kominsky, Robert and Rebecca Sutterlin. 1992. *What's It Worth? Educational Background and Economic Status: Spring 1990*. U.S. Bureau of the Census, Current Population Reports, Household Economic Studies. Washington, DC: Government Printing Office.

Lewis, Lionel S. 1996. *Marginal Worth: Teaching and the Academic Labor Market*. New Brunswick, NJ: Transaction Publishers.

Lucas, Christopher J. 1996. *Crisis in the Academy: Rethinking Higher Education in America*. New York: St. Martin's.

Marsden, George. 1994. *The Soul of the American University: From Protestant Establishment to Established Nonbelief*. New York: Oxford University Press.

McClelland, Charles M. 1980. *State, Society, and University in Germany: 1700-1914*. Cambridge, UK: Cambridge University Press.

National Center for Educational Statistics. 1996. *Digest of Educational Statistics*. Washington, DC: U.S. Department of Education.

———. 1997. *The Condition of Education*. Washington, DC: U.S. Department of Education.

Oakley, Francis. 1992. *Community of Learning: The American College and the Liberal Arts Tradition*. New York: Oxford University Press.

Ottinger, Cecily A., ed. 1989. *Higher Education Today: Facts in Brief*. Washington, DC: U.S. Department of Education.

Rashdall, Hastings. 1936. *The Universities of Europe in the Middle Ages*. 3 vols. Oxford, UK: Oxford University Press.

Slaughter, Sheila and Larry L. Leslie. 1997. *Academic Capitalism: Politics, Policies, and the Entrepreneurial University*. Baltimore, MD: Johns Hopkins University Press.

Smith, Page. 1990. *Killing the Spirit: Higher Education in America*. New York: Viking.

Sykes, Charles T. 1990. *ProfScam: Professors and the Demise of Higher Education*. New York: St. Martin's.

U.S. Bureau of the Census. 1976. *Historical Statistics of the United States*. 2 vols. Washington, DC: Government Printing Office.

———. 1997. *Statistical Abstract of the United States, 1996*. Washington, DC: Government Printing Office.

Veysey, Lawrence R. 1965. *The Emergence of the American University*. Chicago: University of Chicago Press.

3

Higher Education and Its Social Contracts

Teresa Sullivan

Amerian higher education is generally recognized as one of the wonders of the modern world. In its rich diversity, its general accessibility, and its multiple roles, American higher education is touted internationally and closely woven into the texture of community life domestically. Despite its record of success, however, higher education receives sustained criticism for rising tuition, declining access, aloofness from the larger community, and mismanagement. This chapter looks to "institutional overload," an institutional analog to role overload for individuals, as a source of the frustration felt both within and outside academe. First, I review the successes of American higher education. Second, I review the criticisms of higher education. Then, I show how institutional overload helps us to understand the paradox of success and criticism.

Higher Education:
The Success Story

American college degrees are widely admired and, to an increasing extent, are being copied in other nations. After only a century, the American Ph.D. has become the standard credential of research capability, largely displacing or transforming many of the European degree programs on which it originally was modeled.

Master's degrees, although sometimes overlooked by commentators, appear to confer additional value in the marketplace and are the threshold credential for many professional and semiprofessional occupations (Conrad, Haworth, and Millar 1993). About 305,000 master's degrees are conferred each year. The bachelor's degree, once a mark of the privileged classes, by 1995 was held by nearly a quarter of the adults over 25 years of age. More than 1.1 million bachelor's degrees are awarded each year, and more than 60 percent of high school graduates every spring annually enroll in colleges the following fall (U.S. Bureau of the Census 1996:191).

Providing such degrees and offering courses is generally seen as the main function of higher education, and in 1994 more than 14.2 million people were enrolled in American colleges and universities (U.S. Bureau of the Census 1996:181). These students constitute an economic presence that sometimes is overlooked. Although most of the states calculate the financial value only of their export *products,* higher education ranks as a leading export *service* of the United States. One example of its success has been its attractiveness abroad. In 1994, when the United States admitted 894,000 immigrants, there were 493,000 foreign students enrolled in American colleges

(U.S. Bureau of the Census 1996). In other words, for every 2 immigrants admitted, we also admitted 1 international student to pursue a degree. In many cases, the immigrants who were legally admitted had previously earned degrees as students.

A second example of the economic value of the student body is its function as a stable tourist industry. Unlike the regular tourist industry, which brings visitors to spend money in a locality for a few days or weeks at the most, a college brings visitors who stay for nine months at a time. Anyone familiar with a "college town" will recognize the contribution of a college to the local economy, whatever additional ambivalence burdens town-gown relations. Within some states, higher education takes on the trappings of a major industry, where the colleges are playing host to large numbers of college students.[1] Across the United States, the ratio of college enrollees to the population ages 18 to 24 years is about 0.57, but for Massachusetts (with its 118 institutions of higher education) the ratio rises to 0.78. Part of that increase might come from high proportions of Massachusetts citizens who go on to higher education, but some of it also might come from the immigration of citizens of other states to attend school.

American higher education offers a place for nearly every student, from community colleges with open-door admissions to the most selective universities, where fewer than 15 percent of applicants are admitted. Combinations of full-time and part-time course work, distance learning and correspondence courses, courses offered through television and the Internet, and an amazing diversity of degree plans and areas of study have proliferated throughout the country. Public and private institutions compete with one another, spurring innovation. This proliferation of institutional forms and course formats has given the United States the most acces-sible higher education on the globe for any time period in history.

Besides its role in educating individuals, however, higher education by now fulfills a number of other functions within the country. Indeed, the students in residence on the campus might be a relatively small subset of the people who are affected by a college or university in the course of a given day. Through its research and public service, the college or university has the potential to reach many more people than merely those who are registered as degree students.

Since World War II, the research university has been charged with researching and solving a variety of problems facing the country, from the technical aspects of semiconductor manu-facturing to the design of space stations, from the development of vaccines against AIDS to the improvement of student achievement in the K-12 school systems. Although there are a few freestanding research institutions, for the most part, the alliance of research with education has remained stable.[2] Because American industry often has neglected research and development in favor of more short-range objectives, the research role of higher education has been seen as good for business. Indeed, the value of higher education to the general economic health of the nation and the community has been enthusiastically promoted.

Sociologists have been quick to recognize how American firms have reduced their workforces by outsourcing business services and by using independent contractors to replace permanent employees (Hodson and Sullivan 1995). They have been much less likely to understand how their own campuses serve a similar function. Businesses outsource their research needs to the local campus, and they have come to count on reasonably priced (if not free) consulting services, relatively low-cost research solutions conducted by eager (albeit low-paid) student workers, and continuing development of basic research that might be practical in the future. It is hard to see why a corporation would fund its own research office if it is located near a university. Even if the university charges a high overhead rate, the costs probably still are much lower than they would be if the company expanded its payroll to provide permanent employment for researchers and their staff and to provide equipment and libraries to support their research.

Colleges and universities also provide service beyond their teaching and research efforts. Many communities rely on universities for art and music, entertainment, and enrichment. University museums, sponsored children's groups, dramatic productions, and concerts add much to the cultural life of many cities. Aside from the Olympics, colleges serve as the major venue for amateur athletics in most team sports and dual sports as well as many of the individual sports. College student bodies provide volunteers for charitable and educational enterprises in the community, and college faculties often sit on the boards of local social service agencies, school, hospitals, and museums as part of their public service function. Churches, synagogues, legislatures, public libraries, clinics, and preschools benefit from the involvement of university faculty and students. Many college campuses function almost as parks, with the public welcome to stroll the quadrangles and attend many public events. Even private schools have become public spaces. The term *campus* has passed into the American lexicon to indicate not just the grounds of a college but also a general green space surrounding and enhancing a built environment.

Although little effort has been made to quantify the value of these public services, universities add to the quality of life of their immediate communities. As universities provide more material on-line and through the elec-

tronic media, their public service boundaries also widen to include even more possible recipients. Through audiences, patients, clients, and spectators, higher education affects many more than the 14 million people who are enrolled as students.

Higher Education: The Critique

More recently, however, observers have claimed that higher education has broken its social contract with the country (Commission on National Investment in Higher Education 1996). Few accuse the universities of abandoning their research role or of reducing their economic impact on the community. There is no widespread outcry that university concerts have declined in sound or technique or that college football no longer is exciting. University teaching hospitals still are generally acclaimed for offering the highest quality medical care, and millions of school-age children still are loaded onto yellow buses to visit the universities' museums of natural history. University World Wide Web sites and libraries still are widely consulted, and journalists still call professors for expertise on foreign affairs and social problems.[3]

The students themselves, however, often express disappointment that social problems are not more easily resolved on campus. They often are restive that racism, sexism, and homophobia—not to mention crime and illness—cannot be banned from the campus. The restless impatience with campus imperfection can be distinguished in principle from the critique developed in what follows, in part because one is more likely to be internal and the other more likely to be external.

The terms of the social contract that matter for the critics seem to hinge on a posited trade-off between generous access to higher education in return for a substantial level of financial support. The critique centers almost totally on the suspicion that the fulfillment of other functions has diluted the central mission—to educate the students.[4] Whatever good things colleges might do for their communities and the local economies, the most important outcome remains what colleges can do for the individual student. At bedrock, the social contract involves a tacit recognition that in a wage economy, where most parents cannot bequeath jobs or even substantial capital to their children, education is the key to both social stability and social mobility. The contract is deemed broken when education "does not work," either because initial access to education has deteriorated or because the educational outcomes are not as desirable as expected. Parents enter into the contract on behalf of other citizens either as taxpayers or tuition payers (or both), but the general public also is viewed as a partner in the contract.

Jobs as Outcomes

One outcome that parents expect is a degree that will command a wage in the marketplace. Education is the principal stepping-stone to the world of work. As access to higher education widened in the decades following World War II, the "hidden curriculum" of the college campus socialized young adults into the norms of the world of work including being punctual, showing independence, working hard, valuing technology, and accepting both bureaucracy and hierarchy. Completion of a degree is certification both of mastery of some knowledge matter (although knowledge that might grow obsolete) and the character traits required to complete a challenging goal. College is the finishing touch on most young people's educations. Its generalized value is expected to pay off in the labor market, even if students have

not majored in one of the more vocational specialties.

Not every country places such a functional burden on higher education. In many European countries, strong apprenticeship programs are viable alternatives to education as a threshold to work. Although it is true that many American colleges are adopting aggressive internship programs, genuine apprenticeship programs in the United States are generally limited to some of the trade unions, and the unionized fraction of the labor force has steadily declined. Universal or near universal military service plays a similar role in some countries and once played a greater role in the United States in preparing young people for the labor force. Although the content of combat military specialties may have few applications in the civilian job market, the "hidden curriculum" of discipline, responsibility, and comprehension of a bureaucracy is valued by many employers. Trade schools, although plentiful, seem to appear increasingly in newsprint accompanied by stories of fraud in student loan programs, and many of them provide obsolete skills with limited placement opportunities. Even traditional on-the-job training often is outsourced to the local community college instead of being provided by the employer.

Thus, the alternatives to college for preparing students for the workforce have diminished rapidly, a surprising deinstitutionalization in a modern economy. An unsurprising result is that a college degree no longer is a guarantee of a "college" job. One possible conclusion is that there is an oversupply of college graduates based on the increased number of college graduates who are in "high school" jobs (Hecker 1992, 1995; but see Tyler, Murnane, and Levy 1995). Structural changes in the wage economy, especially the rapid deployment of electronic technology and the frenzy of downsizing, have affected the levels of stability even in the "college" jobs. Young graduates have faced layoffs and uncertainty even in the big "blue chip" firms that were reputed for their job security. Parents who see their college graduate offspring suffering in the job market are understandably worried, and many of them will blame the college.

Sociologists immediately will see the possibility of a Mills (1959) insight—that the individual troubles of many graduates might be masking a social problem, in this case the chic of "lean and mean" within management circles having created many thousands of insecure part-time, temporary, contingent, and marginal jobs. The entrepreneurship of the worker and the glamour of the individual corporation sound better in the pages of the leading business magazines than in the accounts of adult children struggling to feed a family and pay off the credit card bills. If parents hit on a different structural explanation—that the faculty could not or would not teach their children in college—then they will blame higher education for adverse employment outcomes and claim that higher education has broken the social contract.

Skills as Outcomes

The sociologist who says that the labor market has changed certainly is correct. But perhaps the parent who says that the college has failed to teach (or that the student has failed to learn) also might be correct. One recent study found that between 1971 and 1987, there was a long-term rise in the share of university-educated workers taking jobs in which the average educational level is much lower (i.e., high school), but that after 1987 the percentage of university-educated workers in "high school" jobs began to decline among younger workers while rising among older, male, university-educated workers. This study found that the workers who experienced downward occupational mobility had, on average, a lower level of

functional literacy than did other college graduates (Pryor and Schaffer 1997). Graduates with better functional literacy were experiencing rising real wages and were in reasonably high demand.

Can it be possible that the graduates of the finest higher education system in the world can lack functional literacy on graduation? It is possible, and the graduation of poorly prepared students does not occur merely in the lower reaches of higher education. Labor force competition has made the "Gentleman's C" unmarketable (except perhaps in the social classes already endowed with capital), and competition among colleges for freshman students has made grade inflation more palatable. If college grade point averages cannot be trusted, then new measures will be demanded. Colleges are being pressed to develop more assessments of outcomes. College exit examinations, capstone examinations in the major, and new rounds of standardized tests already are being tried in some locations.

Colleges, in turn, complain about the ill-prepared students graduating from high schools. A weak K-12 system inevitably will affect higher education. Within the stratification of institutions, some schools will suffer the ill effects much later than will others. More selective schools might keep the underprepared at a distance, for example, but will then encounter the third prong of the critique—inadequate access.

Access

The issue of access to higher education can be phrased in terms of class, race, and gender. Each characteristic was used for years to keep groups of students from attending college or to sharply limit their attendance to a relatively small group of specialized institutions. Interest in diversity has now led virtually every institution to seek additional students from among the traditionally underrepresented populations. Formerly all-women's schools court male high school seniors, and formerly all-men's schools seek to recruit women students (and athletes). Previously all-white institutions seek minority students, and historically black or Hispanic institutions seek white students. If ever there was near universality of access, it would seem to be today.

The flaw in this analysis lies in the continuing social stratification of the larger society and of the institutions within the higher education system. Families with access to capital and high incomes have been able to provide educational advantages for their children that the threadbare K-12 public systems often cannot provide. These advantages often translate into higher grades, a wider range of extracurricular activities, and higher test scores. These characteristics, viewed as meritorious by college admissions committees, help ensure admissions of the relatively well off to the relatively well regarded among the many institutions of higher learning.

Many of these relatively well-off students can afford the tuition at the more selective schools. Others, however, even in so-called "need-blind" admissions strategies, will be able to pay the tuition principally by mortgaging their futures through student loans. Some students, even with the help of the need-blind financial aid, decide that they cannot swing the debt or that they will attend less expensive schools. Others will know so little about the college process—and find their high school counselors so overworked—that the possibility of financial aid will not be fully explored.

Thus, in the final analysis, the argument about access usually is bracketed with dollar signs. What students can afford, what parents can afford, and what colleges can offer in aid all become enormously important variables in the full access equation. With parents already worried about their own roles in downsizing workplaces, and with concerns about the placement prospects even of college graduates, it is not surprising that some families refuse the risks and send their children to less impressive schools or to no schools at all.

The Broken Contract from the Other Side

But why is the tuition so high and rising, often above the level of general inflation? Observers have pointed the finger of blame at many potential culprits. Other functions of the university are immediately suspect. The tuition dollars are really subsidizing the research, they claim, or undergraduates are really subsidizing graduate students. Other possible culprits include the cost of the football team, the cost of student services, and the increased staff required to handle new regulatory requirements. Business owners pay marked-down prices for contract research, and students make up the difference. The endowment is unwisely invested, or unionized clerical workers or faculty demand too much money.

Above all, the time allocation of the faculty is blamed for the increase. Because the faculty do research, it is argued, they are not available to teach as many hours, and inferior substitutes are provided to the students, who nevertheless have to pay higher prices to support both the regular and "shadow" faculty.[5] Student service bills increase because the faculty no longer will serve as academic advisers, career advisers, library acquisitions officers, admissions committees, recruiters, and alumni association liaisons. Expensive specialists are hired in the place of the faculty.

There are many other possible culprits for the financial crises that plague many colleges. The cost of technology, for example, rarely has been adequately planned in any budget, and yet students need access to adequate computing power and to current software. With replacement costs of equipment coming due in cycles as short as three years, most colleges are scrambling to find recurring money to stay in place with technology. Similarly, library acquisitions budgets have been under extreme strain from the extraordinary inflation of printed materials. Hardly able to cope with those costs, libraries now face large and growing costs for electronic resources.

A new spirit of consumerism has arisen among students and their parents with comparison shopping, discounts, and the other paraphernalia of a retail enterprise. For private schools, consumerism takes the form of "sticker shock." For public schools, it takes the form of increased regulation by legislatures that are providing ever smaller proportions of the operational budget. Additional competitors to colleges have arisen in the form of proprietary schools, some under corporate auspices, that offer degrees and course credit. Because these parents and students also are constituents, legislators are sympathetic to their pleas to keep college tuition in the public institutions affordable.

Observers within the academy, on the other hand, point to the withdrawal of government support and the increasingly focused nature of corporate support as signs that the social contract has been broken from the other side. Higher education has provided generally wide access, but the social support that was the tacit reciprocation has eroded. Colleges have sought to fill the gap by increasing user fees (tuition). Tuition increases are a dangerous tactic because the increased revenue must be balanced against possible losses from students who leave. And at all times, the complex system of higher education pits one institution against another, en-

couraging ruinous discounts in the recruiting of a freshman class. Far from being a typical not-for-profit institution, the university is in fact in a highly competitive market for students, faculty, research grants, and contracts. The prestige that results from success in this competition helps ease the difficulty of the competition in the next round.

Besides raising tuition, many schools are following their own versions of downsizing and contingent labor. Although the institution of tenure remains fairly strong, the new systems of accountability such as posttenure review and exit examinations for students suggest that university constituencies are not satisfied with the performance of all faculty. Tenure (and academic freedom) is suspect as the last refuge of scoundrels among the faculty. Administrators try to balance the demands for accountability with the means to pay the bills. Although not many administrators accept the allocation of faculty time as the scapegoat for college financial woes, there is substantial demand for further job control of the faculty. Parents without job security, and students who are afraid they never will achieve job security, are not necessarily sympathetic with the professoriate's argument for tenure as a bulwark of academic freedom.

Higher education lags other industries in other organizational respects. Just as downsizing has come more slowly to academe than to the corporation, higher education remains somewhat unusual among American industries in retaining many different, fairly local, competing "firms." In most American industries, smaller firms have been squeezed out in favor of larger, more efficient, oligopolistic firms or franchise operations have replaced many small, independent enterprises. This tendency to oligopoly is quite general in manufacturing and is coming to prevail in some of the service industries. "Mom and pop" grocery stores and restaurants have been replaced by 7-Eleven convenience stores and McDonald's fast food restaurants. Local dress stores and dime stores stand empty a few blocks from the new mega Wal-Mart and K-mart stores. Many small software companies have been eclipsed by the rise of giant Microsoft. Another decade might bring us the development of mega-universities or large universities that franchise smaller schools to offer trademarked courses or degree programs.

Most schools grapple with the issue of the extent to which a corporate model is appropriate for them. Some aspects of the corporate model might lie ahead for faculty, including the greater prevalence of the "free agent" faculty member, whose loyalty to any one institution is tenuous and to whom no institution bears loyalty. Administrators are likely to find themselves more concerned with cost containment than with curriculum. For the institutions themselves, the development of franchised courses and libraries, the attachment of weaker institutions to stronger ones in larger organizational forms, and the development of a limited monopoly power might lie in the future. None of these alone will be adequate to contain tuition or to maintain the widest access.

Institutional Overload

Sociologists have long talked about role overload as a key concept in microsociology. Most introductory textbooks explain the concept and its application in understanding role conflict. Coser (1974) introduced the idea of the "greedy institution," the institution that takes up more and more of a worker's time. Indeed, both role overload and the greedy institution might come to mind in describing the position of contemporary faculty, who often handle their many responsibilities by working even longer hours.

But this overload at the micro level might reflect an overload at the institutional level. Human societies often tie great expectations and multiple functions to certain dominant institutions. Dominant institutions, almost by definition, deal with recurring critical issues posed by the intellectual, economic, and social forces of the society. In many societies, the family has been the dominant institution, and it labors under a sort of corporate role overload. The family is expected to simultaneously play many roles, some of which are in conflict with each other. Other institutions similarly have been expected to serve many constituencies in many ways. In Europe in the Middle Ages, the Church and the monarchy were overloaded with both expectations and functions. Both institutions lost power as their functions gradually devolved on more specialized institutions.

Perhaps the American university is experiencing an overload of functions and expectations. It is not too far-fetched to view higher education as a dominant institution. Universities and colleges train the next generation in multiple fields; they solve problems and invent technology; they provide great literature, art, music, and theater; they entertain and inform; and they are hailed as the generators of economic growth and the producers of new workers. They are sought for expertise in all fields and on all topics for knowledge of languages and mathematics as well as the literature and history of all ages and places. They are expected to help young people "find themselves" and provide role models for deprived population groups. Colleges and universities are expected to preserve the self-esteem and enhance the mental health of students but also to provide candid rankings for employers. In the pursuit of these multiple goals, they often are chaotic, noisy, swirling maelstroms of ideas and passionate convictions.

American universities are dominant institutions because they confront the recurring problem of America's belief in equality and the realization of individual potential with its need for a sorting mechanism to generate and allocate some economic mobility. In the face of unlimited demand for economic mobility, universities rank-order students, fields, and each other. An institution that struck a social contract positing equality of access faces the devil's bargain of offering unequal results at the end of four years.

Over the long run, specialization of various types usually resolves the role conflict of the individual or institutional overload in dominant institutions. It seems likely that further differentiation and specialization will be proposed as solutions for the issues that face American higher education. These developments are likely to be viewed as insufficient and unsatisfactory, and they eventually will erode the dominance of higher education. The current dilemmas of the social contract are phrased in terms of dollars and access, but the ultimate issues are more abstract and would persist even if current funding were increased by an order of magnitude.

With all of its flaws and structural dilemmas, however, the university is attractive precisely because its social contract, even if adequately realized, crystallizes for us a part of the central American ideology. Ideals, like the perfect institution, also are unattainable but no less appealing for their ineffability.

Notes

1. Private colleges are principal attractors of the nonresident student because they have a single tuition; state universities are more likely to limit the number of nonresidents numerically and/or by imposing higher tuition on them.

2. Even some institutions established to be research entities, such as the RAND Corporation (Research ANd Development), have now developed small degree programs.

3. To be fair, there does seem to be disappointment that progress on some research problems is so slow. There still is no cure for all cancers, fusion remains only a distant dream for cheap energy, and America continues to struggle with issues of racism despite decades of research. On the other hand, critics recognize that these are difficult research problems that will not be easily solved. Professors' inability to resolve educational problems is not so easily tolerated.

4. As one "op-ed" columnist put it, "With each passing year, education and American universities have less and less to do with each other. Football is just part of the problem" (Murchison 1997).

5. Graduate teaching assistants often are seen as the link in this chain of blame; faculty teach graduate students, who teach undergraduate students, even though the undergraduates pay prices high enough to "earn" faculty instructors. One problem with this line of analysis is the assumption that teaching assistants are inferior teachers. Research at my institution has shown that graduate student instructors earn teaching evaluations that are essentially the same as those of assistant professors.

References

Commission on National Investment in Higher Education. 1996. *Breaking the Social Contract: The Fiscal Crisis in Higher Education.* Santa Monica, CA: RAND.

Conrad, Clifton F., Jennifer G. Haworth, and Susan B. Millar. 1993. *A Silent Success: Mas-*

ter's *Education in the United States*. Baltimore, MD: Johns Hopkins University Press.

Coser, Lewis A. 1974. *Greedy Institutions: Patterns of Undivided Commitment*. New York: Free Press.

Hecker, Daniel E. 1992. "Reconciling Conflicting Data on Jobs for College Graduates." *Monthly Labor Review,* July, pp. 3-12.

———. 1995. "College Graduates in 'High School': A Commentary." *Monthly Labor Review,* December, p. 28.

Hodson, Randy and Teresa A. Sullivan. 1995. *The Social Organization of Work*. 2d ed. Belmont, CA: Wadsworth.

Mills, C. Wright. 1959. *The Sociological Imagination*. New York: Oxford University Press.

Murchison, William. 1997. "Universities, Education Drift Apart." *Dallas Morning News* (December 3).

Pryor, Frederic L. and David Schaffer. 1997. "Wages and the University Educated: A Paradox Resolved." *Monthly Labor Review,* July, pp. 3-15.

Tyler, John, Richard J. Murnane, and Frank Levy. 1995. "Are More College Graduates Really Taking 'High School' Jobs?" *Monthly Labor Review,* December, pp. 18-27.

U.S. Bureau of the Census. 1996. *Statistical Abstract of the United States, 1996-1997.* Washington, DC: Government Printing Office.

4

How the Academic Profession Is Changing

Arthur Levine

In the years ahead, the academic profession can be expected to change dramatically. Five forces are propelling the change: (1) the changing attitudes and demands of higher education's patrons; (2) the changing characteristics of college students; (3) the changing conditions of employment in higher education; (4) the rise of new technologies; and (5) the growth of private sector competitors. Most of the impetus for change is coming from sources outside the academy, over which higher education has little control.

The Changing Attitudes and Demands of Higher Education's Patrons

In the late 1980s and 1990s, government support for higher education decreased, both financially and politically. Two rationales have generally been offered to explain the reductions. The first is that these are hard times for the government, so it has less money to give away. The assumption is that when the govern-

ment is flusher, higher education will receive additional support. The second explanation is that government priorities have changed. Higher education has given way in importance to prisons, health care, and highways. Even in the area of education, preference is now given to schools over colleges and children over adults. The assumption is that the change is temporary, and higher education's priority will rise again in the future—what goes around comes around.

I would suggest a third reason, one that is likely to be far more permanent. American higher education has become a mature industry. More than 60 percent of all high school graduates are now going on to some form of postsecondary education. increasingly, this is viewed in state capitols as a sufficient number or even as an overexpansion of higher education. There is no government enthusiasm for increasing the college attendance rate to 70 or 80 percent.

This represents a dramatic change in the condition of American higher education. Throughout this century, colleges and universities have been a growth industry. Except during the world wars and for two years of the depression, enrollment has risen every year. In the decades following World War II, the first and most persistent demand that government made

AUTHOR'S NOTE: "How the Academic Profession Is Changing," reprinted by permission of *Daedalus,* Journal of the American Academy of Arts and Sciences, from the issue entitled, "The American Academic Profession," Fall 1997, Vol. 126, No. 4.

of higher education was to increase its capacity to provide a college education for more and more people. Rising government support was the norm; obstacles to increasing enrollments were swept away. Government's principal role was to expand higher education and increase opportunities for access. More and more faculty were hired, public institutions of higher education multiplied, and government aid was targeted at private schools to promote expansion. Few questions were asked. This is generally the lot of growth industries in America.

The government, however, treats mature industries very differently. It seeks to regularize or control them. It asks hard questions about their cost, efficiency, productivity, and effectiveness. It attempts to limit their size and funding. It diminishes their autonomy and demands greater accountability. This is precisely what is happening to higher education today. The government, in scrutinizing the cost of the enterprise, is asking questions of colleges and universities that have never been asked before. The price of higher education is being attacked loudly and continually, funding formulas are being reexamined, and financial aid is shifting from grants to loans.

Questions of productivity and efficiency are being raised, particularly in regard to the professorate. How much should faculty teach? What is the appropriate balance between teaching and research? How much should it cost to educate a student? Can campuses and faculties be replaced by new technologies? Should there continue to be lifetime employment or tenure for faculty?

What programs should colleges offer? How much course and program redundancy is necessary? What should the balance be between graduate and undergraduate education? Should faculties continue to make these decisions, as they have historically?

Questions of effectiveness are being asked, too. Why are graduation rates not higher? Why should it take students more than four years to graduate from college? Why do colleges offer remedial education?

The government is shifting the terms of the relationship between higher education and the public. The focus is moving from teaching (what faculty do in their classrooms) to learning (what students get out of their classes). The emphasis is moving from courses and credits (process) to what students achieve as a result of a college education (outcomes). In short, the state is demanding greater accountability from higher education, and that burden is resting increasingly on the shoulders of the faculty. Several states, Florida for one, have already imposed tests on higher education to measure student achievement.

The effects of these changes on higher education are profound. As a growth industry, colleges and universities could generally rely on additional resources annually. Growth and progress were treated as synonyms. New activities were a matter of addition: the new was simply added to the old.

Today, with resources either stable or declining, this is no longer possible. Change is expected to occur by substitution. If something new is added, something old must be eliminated. If growth is to occur, it can occur only in selective areas. Colleges and universities are being forced to choose limited targets for investment. If colleges are unwilling to do this themselves, the government is increasingly willing to help them make the choices. The government is becoming more involved and is quite prepared to make decisions that were once regarded as the prerogative of the faculty.

The net result is likely to be a "boutiqueing" of higher education. That is, most colleges and universities in the country are fundamentally alike in terms of the curriculum and academic programs they offer. For the most part, institutions vary largely in terms of the number of professional programs they provide and the relative size of their upper division and graduate programs; in this sense, most institutions are comprehensive. This is increasingly the case even among colleges that were once exclusively devoted to liberal arts. Today, institutions of higher education are being forced to make selections, eliminate overlapping or redundant offerings, and make themselves more specialized. They are moving away from being something akin to full-service department stores toward being more sharply focused boutiques. The common wisdom today is that higher education must do more with less; the reality is that institutions will have to do less with less, putting existing programs and faculty positions in jeopardy, as is the case with downsizing in business today.

These changes are likely to be permanent. They will not go away when the government has more money or higher education's relative priority in the public agenda rises. And higher education's response to these new conditions has only served to further anger and frustrate the government. Instead of making cuts, as the government intended when resources were reduced, higher education's first response was to raise more money. Tuition prices were increased well above inflation. More admissions officers were hired to attract more students. More development staff [were] hired to raise more money. More student-affairs professionals were hired to reduce attrition. And more finance staff [were] hired to control spending. Higher education soon found that these steps only increased costs and did not produce more revenue—though they did set off a firestorm of criticism, especially regarding the price of tuition.

The second response was to cut costs around the edges, making across-the-board budget cuts, imposing hiring freezes, and deferring maintenance. The stated goal was to preserve institutional quality, staff morale, and student access. The reality was that preserving quality turned out to be a synonym for maintaining every program and every faculty member on campus, making it also a synonym for preserving morale. Only the commitment to access was allowed to wither. It has been preserved rhetorically and abandoned financially on many campuses. At bottom, this strategy sacrificed quality to avoid rocking the boat. Strong and weak programs were cut equally, and staff reductions followed. Random attrition patterns, rather than institutional priorities, determined the changes to be made. All in all, it was akin to a ship hitting an iceberg and the captain announcing as the boat sinks that his highest priority is to save the crew. The next priority is to avoid any inconvenience as the ship goes down by continuing all activities—the midnight buffet, the bingo game, and the shuffleboard tournament. The third priority is to repair the ship. And the fourth and final priority, should time permit, is to save the passengers. Besides penalizing students and sacrificing academic quality, this approach does not save enough money, making campus decision-making and decision-makers look very bad publicly, particularly the faculty, who are viewed as being self-concerned and intransigent.

This caused institutions of higher education to attempt a third response, that is, choosing priorities distinguishing between the areas central to an institutional mission and more marginal activities that could be reduced or eliminated. To accomplish this, the usual mechanism has been to create a strategic planning committee comprised of at least eighty-seven members, which, after two years of weekly meetings, manages to select one program for cuts that has not had a student in three years. This gross intrusion into the fabric of the institution leads to a faculty vote of no confidence in the president, who then resigns. A new president is selected, who says the problem can be overcome by raising more money, and the cycle begins again.

This is, of course, a parody of decision-making in higher education. However, it is true that the government believes more and more that colleges and universities are dragging their feet and are selfish and unconcerned about the public good. The government is more critical of higher education today than it ever was of the schools.

This is likely to affect the professorate in a variety of ways. In the years ahead, the faculty role in governance is likely to diminish. Boards of trustees will become more active in the management of educational institutions. Government regulation of higher education will increase and encompass such matters as faculty work loads and tenure. Higher education is entirely unready for this change. Not long ago, I visited a research university in a state in which the legislature was considering a bill that would tie faculty salaries entirely to the amount of time spent in the classroom. When I asked the faculty at this university what they thought about this, their answer was "intellectual McCarthyism." This represents a major communication failure. The faculty completely misread the message of disapproval and censure that the legislature was sending them. This kind of response is likely to lead to further criticism of the academy in general and of professors in particular. More sensational books like *ProfScam* can be anticipated, along with legislative inquiries. Demands for accountability from institutions and their faculties are also likely to increase and, if not heeded, to become mandates.

The Changing Characteristics of Students

Perhaps the greatest change in higher education in recent years has to do with who the students are. During the 1980s and early 1990s, the lion's share of growth in college enrollment came from students often described as nontraditional. Half of new students were twenty-five years of age or older, 74 percent of the increase was female, and 56 percent were part-time students. By 1993, 38 percent of all college students were over twenty-five years of age, 61 percent were working, 56 percent were female, and 42 percent were attending part-time. Less than a fifth of all undergraduates fit the traditional stereotype of the American college student—eighteen to twenty-two years of age, attending full-time, and living on campus.[1]

What this means is that higher education is not as central to the lives of many of today's undergraduates as it was to previous generations. It is becoming just one of many activities in which they engage everyday. For many, college is not even the most important of these activities—work and family often overshadow it.

As a consequence, older, part-time, and working students, especially those with children, said in a national study I conducted of undergraduate attitudes and experiences between 1992 and 1997 that they wanted a different type of relationship with their colleges than undergraduates have historically had. They preferred relationships like those they already enjoyed with their bank, their gas company, and their supermarket.

Think about what we want from our bank. We want an ATM on every corner. We want to know that when we get to the ATM, there will be no line. We want a parking spot right in front of the ATM. We want money available the moment our checks arrive at the bank—or perhaps the day before. And we want no mistakes unless they are in our favor. There are also things we do not want our bank to provide—softball leagues, psychological counseling, or religious services. We can arrange those things without [the bank's] assistance or additional cost.

Students are asking for roughly the same kind of service from their colleges. They want their colleges nearby and open during the hours most useful to them—preferably, around the clock. They want easy, accessible parking (in the classroom would not be at all bad), no lines, and a polite, helpful, and efficient staff. They want high-quality education at a low cost. For the most part, they are willing to comparison shop, placing a premium on time and money. They do not want to pay for activities and programs they do not use or can get elsewhere. Increasingly, students are bringing to higher education exactly the same consumer expectations they have for every other commercial enterprise with which they deal. Their focus is on convenience, quality, service, and cost. They believe that since they are paying for their education, faculty should give them the education they want, and they make larger demands on faculty than students in the past ever have [made]. They are also the target audience for alternatives to traditional higher education. They are likely to find distance education appealing, offering the convenience of instruction at home or in the office. They are prime candidates for stripped-down versions of college, located in the suburbs and business districts of our cities, that offer low-cost instruction made possible by heavy faculty teaching loads, with primarily a part-time faculty, limited numbers of majors, and few electives. Proprietary institutions of this type are springing up around the country.

Traditional undergraduates are also changing in ways that will affect the faculty who teach them. They are not as well prepared to enter college as their predecessors. As a result, there is a growing need for remediation. According to a national survey of student affairs officers that I conducted in 1997, within the last decade nearly three-fourths (73 percent) of all colleges and universities experienced an increase in the proportion of students requiring remedial or developmental education at two-year (81 percent) and four-year (64 percent) colleges. Today, nearly one-third (32 percent) of all undergraduates report having taken a basic skills or remedial course in reading, writing, or math. In 1995, more than three-fourths of all colleges and universities offered remedial reading, writing, or math courses. Between 1990 and 1995, 39 percent of institutions reported that enrollments in these areas had increased, while only 14 percent reported a decrease.[2]

According to a survey by the Higher Education Research Institute, only one-quarter (25 percent) of faculty believe their students are "well-prepared academically," while less than four in ten (39 percent) gave them even a "satisfactory" or "very satisfactory" rating in terms of their quality.[3] The result is that faculty are being forced to teach more and more basic skills courses, dumb down the level of their classes, and reduce the number of advanced courses they offer, therefore enjoying their teaching and their students less than in the past. The 1997 student affairs survey showed that 45 percent of faculty feel less comfortable with students today than in the past. This feeling is more pronounced at four-year schools (53 percent) than at two-year colleges (37 percent).

There is another hurdle even more daunting than remediation—the widening gap between the ways in which students prefer to learn and the ways in which faculty prefer to teach. According to research by Charles Schroeder of the University of Missouri–Columbia, more than half of today's students perform best in a learning situation characterized by "direct, concrete experience, moderate-to-high degrees of structure, and a linear approach to learning. They value the practical and the immediate, and the focus of their perception is primarily on the physical world." On the other hand, three-quarters (75 percent) of faculty "prefer the global to the particular; are stimulated by the realm of concepts, ideas, and abstractions; and assume that students, like themselves, need a high degree of autonomy in their work." In short, students are more likely to prefer concrete or practical subjects and active methods of learning, while faculty are predisposed to abstract and theoretical subject matter and passive methods of learning. The result, says Schroeder, is frustration on both sides and a tendency for faculty to interpret as deficiencies what may simply be natural differences in learning patterns.[4] This mismatch may cause faculty to think every year that students are less and less well prepared and for students to think their classes are incomprehensible. This is certainly the case with faculty. The 1997 student affairs survey revealed that at 74 percent of colleges and universities, faculty complaints about students were on the rise; there is little difference between two-year (72 percent) and four-year (77 percent) colleges. In the years ahead, there will be enormous pressure on faculty to change the ways [in which] they teach to match the ways in which students learn. In the final analysis, student tuition dollars are likely to be more powerful than faculty preferences.

There are other reasons that the classroom experience is becoming less appealing to faculty. Forty-four percent of institutions report rises in student disruptions of class over the past five years. Plagiarism or cheating has increased on more than a fifth of college campuses (21 percent) and three-quarters of deans of students say undergraduates are less likely to believe plagiarism is wrong. A majority also would describe their campuses as politically correct (57 percent) and report that students feel un-

comfortable expressing unpopular opinions (54 percent). And on top of this, 40 percent of all colleges and universities are experiencing increased threats of litigation by students.[5] The campus is becoming less and less of a community for faculty and their students. Because a majority of undergraduates are now working and increasing proportions are attending college part-time, faculty are spending less time with their students and thus do not know their students as well. The degree to which this is occurring varies considerably across different types of colleges, as Burton Clark's essay in this issue of *Daedalus* [reprinted in Chapter 5 of this volume] indicates.

Finally, current undergraduates are costing their institutions more than their predecessors did. Student aid is growing dramatically on many campuses, as the fastest-growing populations in the country have the lowest incomes and can least afford to attend college. The cost of student services is also rising substantially. For instance, students are coming to college more damaged psychologically than in the past, owing to family, sexual, drug, eating, and other disorders. More than three out of five colleges and universities (61 percent) report expanded use of psychological counseling services.[6] The resources to support these activities are coming out of revenues that in the past would have been used to fund academic programs and faculty positions. For the past decade, administrative budget lines have been growing much more quickly than faculty lines.

The Changing Conditions of Faculty Employment[7]

College and university professors are being criticized today for low productivity—not working enough, with too little consequence. This criticism is coming in part from the states.

Many state legislators and policy makers believe that faculty members at public colleges and universities care little about undergraduate education, especially education at the freshman and sophomore levels. Faculty members are viewed as being more concerned with graduate education and their research, publication, and other professional activities.[8]

The criticism is also coming from blue ribbon commissions within higher education:

Our best guess is that professors in 1990 spend less time in the classroom than their counterparts before the Second World War. There is a general feeling that faculty spend less time advising, teach fewer courses outside their specialties, and are less committed to a commonly defined curriculum.[9]

Several distinguished academics have also joined the fray.

When I began to teach, a "full load" was six courses a year; it is commonly five now, and there is [a] movement underway to reduce it to four. Seven courses a year would seem to me to be a reasonable number, a number that . . . would allow all the research activity a professor felt compelled to do.[10]

And a raft of sensational books have been published, seemingly on a daily basis, on the shortcomings of higher education. One of the earliest described college professors this way. (1) They are overpaid, grotesquely underworked, and the architects of academe's vast empire of waste. (2) They have abandoned their teaching responsibilities and their students. To the average undergraduate, the professorate is unapproachable, uncommunicative, and unavailable. (3) In pursuit of their own interest and research, academic politicking, and cushier grants, they have left the nation's students in the care of an ill-trained, ill-paid, and bitter academic underclass. (4) They have distorted university curricula to accommodate their own narrow and selfish interests rather than the interests of their own students. (5) They have

created a culture in which bad teaching goes unnoticed and unsanctioned and good teaching is penalized. (6) They insist that their obligations to research justify their flight from the college classroom, despite the fact that fewer than one in ten makes any significant contribution to [his or her] field.[11]

What is ironic is that the mounting criticism of faculty and their work loads does not comport with the facts. The realities are these. Faculty members are working longer, not shorter hours. The first study of faculty work load, conducted in 1919, found that professors worked 46.8 hours a week.[12] Research in the 1970s showed roughly the same length for a faculty week (44 hours). However, by 1992 that number had risen to 53 hours. Faculty at research universities worked the longest week (56 hours) and those at two-year colleges worked the shortest (47 hours).[13]

Moreover, faculty hours in the classroom have not systematically declined in recent years. What has occurred is far more complex. In 1975, 1984, and 1989, the Carnegie Foundation studied the median number of hours faculty spent in the classroom each week.[14] They examined five different types of institutions—research universities, doctoral-granting universities, comprehensive colleges and universities, liberal arts colleges, and two-year colleges. Over the decade and a half of the study, median classroom hours, which the foundation reported in ranges, changed in a variety of ways. The minimum number of hours in the classroom declined across all institutional types. However, the maximum number of hours remained constant at research universities and actually increased at doctoral universities and community colleges. In contrast, declines in maximum hours occurred at liberal arts and community colleges. In short, faculty are teaching undergraduates both less and more, depending upon where they teach and how they fit into the median range. Plummeting faculty work loads are merely a figment in the minds of higher education's most productive critics. The reality—particularly if one includes graduate teaching hours, which have risen since the 1970s—is very different.

It is also true that faculty are spending a smaller proportion of their time teaching, but they are nonetheless spending more hours teaching. In the original 1919 study, faculty spent 63 percent of their time on teaching, 8 percent on research, and 29 percent on other activities. A 1988 study found that faculty now spend 56 percent of their time on teaching, 16 percent on research, 13 percent on administration, 4 percent on community service, 5 percent on professional development, and 7 percent on other activities.[15] However, faculty at two-year colleges were spending an even higher percentage of their time on teaching (71 percent), while those at four-year colleges [were spending] less time (52 percent).[16] Yet even for faculty at four-year institutions, this translates into a greater number of teaching hours than the 1919 faculty.

On top of this, teaching still remains the key interest of most faculty. In surveys in 1969, 1975, and 1989, the Carnegie Foundation asked faculty whether their interests were primarily in teaching or research. Roughly the same question was asked by the Higher Education Research Institute in 1996. Over nearly thirty years, the proportion of faculty responding affirmatively to teaching remained an astounding seven out of ten.[17]

The picture that emerges of the professorate is very different from the popular image. Despite claims to the contrary, academic life has changed relatively little in recent years. However, disenchantment with higher education on the part of the government and the public over issues such as cost and lack of responsiveness seems sufficient to render the facts irrelevant. Accordingly, substantial changes can be expected in the years ahead. There are currently approximately 584,000 college and university faculty. "Seven in ten hold an earned doctorate, half are age 40 to 54 years, and more than six in ten have the security of a tenured position."[18]

The Rise of New Technologies

The wild card that has the greatest capacity to change faculty life in this situation is new technologies. Several years ago, I had a conversation with the editor of one of the nation's major metropolitan daily newspapers. He said his newspaper would be out of the newspaper business within the next two decades. Instead, he said, the news would be delivered electronically. Subscribers would be able to design the newspaper they receive. For instance, they might want to begin the day with sports. The headlines and front-page news on their daily paper would accordingly focus on athletics. They might have young children and therefore ask that political news be excised, and so forth. This has enormous import for curriculum design; it means the age of textbooks is coming to an end. Faculty will be expected to custom design their own course readings, and these readings will be geared to the demographics of the class being taught. They can and should be updated with each subsequent class. The days of teaching from old yellow lecture notes is approaching an abrupt conclusion.

In the same vein, I recently read an article in an airline magazine that described the travel agency of the future. Through virtual reality, a traveler considering different vacation venues would be able to experience various possibilities. The traveler would be able [to] hear, feel, and see different locales. [The traveler] could walk the beaches, climb the mountains, enter the historic landmarks, and inspect the restaurants, hotels, and shops. The same could be done with historic locales. One could visit fifth-century Rome, eighteenth-century America, or fifteenth-century Paris. Imagine smelling the smells of fifteenth-century Paris—they must have been putrid. Imagine walking the cobblestones, entering the great and not-so-great buildings, and seeing the people on the street. This would have revolutionary consequences for pedagogy. How will a standard lecture on fifteenth-century Paris compare with the experience of actually being there? As technology advances, we can anticipate profound changes in the nature of instruction. The only real question is the degree to which this will be something that replaces the faculty or whether it will supplement the faculty. In either case, it will mean a very different role for the professorate.

Already, technology is available with the capacity to fundamentally change the nature of college instruction. Today, it is possible for Stephen Graubard to give a lecture at the House of the Academy in Cambridge, for me to attend that lecture in New York, and for a third person to watch and listen to it in Tokyo, for example. All of us would, for all intents and purposes, be in the same classroom. I could, for instance, electronically nudge the student in Tokyo and say I missed Professor Graubard's last comment. My question would be translated into Japanese, and the update would be translated back into English. Professor Graubard could ask my Japanese colleague and me to prepare a joint project for the following class session. The point is this: if we can do all of these things electronically, why does higher education any longer need the physical plant called a campus? In the years since World War II, the goal for American higher education has been to overcome geographic barriers to attending college by putting a campus within reach of most

Americans. Geography is a barrier that electronic education minimizes and perhaps has the capacity to eliminate. If that is the case, why would a state like California need nine research universities? Why does New York need sixty-four state colleges? Why should any university be forced to employ a lesser scholar or teacher? Faculty will work across campus and state boundaries, as they already have begun to do. Reducing the barrier of geography will profoundly change the nature of the college and university faculty, perhaps in number, but certainly in expectations, roles, and activities.

The Growth of Private Sector Competitors

Higher education is a business with revenues in the hundreds of billions of dollars and a reputation for low productivity. This is causing the private sector to look increasingly at postsecondary education with a gleam in its keen eyes. As the chair of a major university's board of trustees confided recently, if higher education were a publicly traded stock, it would be overripe for a hostile takeover.

In this regard, two recent activities are worth noting. The first is the development of a new breed of higher education institution characterized by the University of Phoenix, now the largest private college in America, enrolling fifty thousand students. Traded on the NASDAQ exchange, this profit-making college is regionally accredited, offering degrees from associate through master's and soon the doctorate. The faculty, which boast traditional academic credentials, are all part-timers, having other forms of primary employment in the fields in which they teach. The equivalent of a full-time faculty member would teach a dozen courses a year. Class syllabi are uniform, prepared every three years by professionals and practitioners in the subject area. In other words, faculty teach the courses; they do not prepare or design them. Students attend classes at convenient hours as a cohort, taking precisely the same courses in sequence. There are no electives. In recent years, the University of Phoenix has added an on-line version of [its] courses, used by three thousand students. They offer programs from coast to coast, put an emphasis on assessment of student learning and faculty teaching, and have plans to expand enrollment to two hundred thousand students over the next decade.

The University of Phoenix is the largest example of proprietary higher education, but it is not unique, and its example is being watched not only by other entrepreneurs but also by Wall Street and venture capital firms. We will see more institutions like it in the future. What they will mean for faculty is a vastly different role, one that does not include participation in governance, and minimal activity in curriculum planning. The emphasis will be on increasing teaching productivity and eliminating scholarly expectations. Total salary costs will be lower, and all or most faculty will be part-time.

Other, more traditional corporations are also eyeing the higher education market. There is an underlying belief that colleges and universities are making precisely the same mistake that the railroads made. The railroads believed they were in the railroad business; they focused on making bigger and better railroads. The problem is that they were actually in the transportation industry and, as a result, were derailed by the airlines. Similarly, it can be said that higher education is making the mistake of thinking it is in the campus business, when in reality it is in the very lucrative education business. High-technology and entertainment companies are viewing non-campus-based education as an opportunity. The head of one of the major state

university systems in the United States recently said his biggest fear is that, before long, the private sector will go to the state capitol demanding the opportunity to bid on the state university contract. At the moment, several major companies, such as Disney, IBM, and Bell Atlantic, are exploring technology and learning as an investment opportunity, with greater capital and speed than higher education. Partnerships between the private sector and campuses in this area are mushrooming. Industry is the driving force and senior partner in most of these relationships. With the right company offering education and degrees—that is, a company with an admired name, a record of cutting-edge accomplishments, and a consumer orientation—the public may well find the alternative very attractive. The implications for faculty of this new education alternative are difficult to contemplate, but one can be assured that the change will be profound.

Conclusion

In 1819, Washington Irving wrote "Rip Van Winkle," a story about a man who fell asleep for twenty years. He awakened unaware of the length of his slumber and proceeded to walk around the village in which he lived. He found that "the very village was altered; it was larger and more populous. There were rows of houses which he had never seen before, and those which had been his familiar haunts had disappeared. Strange names were over the doors— strange faces at the windows—everything was strange." The same was true of the village populace: "The very character of the people seemed changed. There was a busy, bustling, disputatious tone to it, instead of the accustomed phlegm and drowsy tranquillity." Rip Van Winkle concluded, "Everything changed and I'm changed, and I can't tell what's my name or who I am."

Washington Irving's story was an allegory. It was more than a tale of a man who overslept; it was an account of the relentlessness of change in America, of an era of overwhelming demographic, economic, global, and technological changes called the Industrial Revolution. Rip Van Winkle was intended to be Everyman trying to orient himself to an unfamiliar world, which seemed to be changing radically overnight.

Today's faculty may be living through a comparable period. As one *Newsweek* observer put it, "It wasn't until recently that I began to get some inkling of what poor Rip must have been feeling the day he finally opened his eyes and rejoined that world." This just might be an equally eye-opening period for all of us who live and work in the world of academe.

Notes

1. *The Digest of Educational Statistics* (Washington, D.C.: Department of Education, 1995), 167, 179, 189; *Digest of Educational Statistics* (Washington, D.C.: Department of Education, 1996), 179, 189, 324; *Condition of Education* (Washington, D.C.: Department of Education, 1995), 142, 379; Youth Indicators, *Indicator* 67 (1996).

2. National Center for Educational Statistics, "Remedial Education at Higher Education Institutions, Fall 1995-October 1996," NCES-97-584.

3. Eric L. Dey, Alexander W. Astin, and William S. Korn, "The American Freshman: Twenty-Five Year Trends, 1966-1990," Higher Education Research Institute, Graduate School of Education, University of California, Los Angeles, September 1991, 37-38.

4. Charles C. Schroeder, "New Students—New Learning Styles," *Change* 25(4) (Sept./Oct. 1993): 21-26.

5. Arthur Levine, student affairs survey, 1997.

6. Ibid.

7. The material on criticism of the professorate and the research on a changing work load come from an unpublished manuscript by Arthur Levine and Jana Nidiffer, "Faculty Productivity: A Background Paper," 1994.

8. Daniel T. Layzell (Legislative Budget Office, State of Arizona), "Tight Budgets Demand Studies of Faculty Productivity," *Chronicle of Higher Education* 19 February 1992, B2-B3.

9. Pew Foundation Higher Education Roundtable, "The Lattice and the Ratchet," *Policy Perspectives* 2(4) (1990).

10. Page Smith, *Killing the Spirit: Higher Education in America* (New York: Viking, 1990), 192-193.

11. Charles Sykes, *ProfScam: Professors and the Demise of Higher Education* (New York: St. Martin's Press, 1990), 5.

12. Leonard Koos, *The Adjustment of Teaching Load in a University* (Washington, D.C.: U.S. Government Printing Office, 1919).

13. *Digest of Educational Statistics*, 1996, Table 223.

14. Unfortunately, [these] data [are] now eight years old. More recent studies have used categories of institutional types or other divisions of faculty activities, so they are not comparable to the earlier Carnegie [Foundation] studies. The most recent Carnegie Foundation study conducted in 1992-1993 is not yet available either.

15. Koos, *The Adjustment of Teaching Load in a University*.

16. S. M. Russell, F. S. Fairweather, and R. N. Hendrickson, *Profiles of Faculty in Higher*

Education Institutions, 1988 (Washington, D.C.: National Center for Education Statistics, August 1992), 51-52.

17. Carnegie Foundation for the Advancement of Teaching, *The Condition of the Professorate: Attitudes and Trends* (Princeton, N.J.: Carnegie Foundation for the Advancement of Teaching, 1989), 63.

18. Eugene J. Haas, "The American Academic Profession," in Philip G. Altbach, ed., *The International Academic Profession: Portraits of Fourteen Countries* (Princeton, N.J.: Carnegie Foundation [for the Advancement of Teaching], 1996), 342.

5

Small Worlds, Different Worlds: The Uniqueness and Troubles of American Academic Professions

Burton R. Clark

Different worlds, small worlds. Institutional differentiation interacts with disciplinary differentiation in a bewildering fashion that steadily widens and deepens the matrix of differences that separate American academics from each other.

Systematic Problems

When we pursue the different worlds of American professors by emphasizing disciplinary and institutional conditions, deep-rooted problems that are otherwise relegated to the background or only dimly perceived come to the fore. Five systemic concerns may be briefly stated as problems of secondarization, excessive teaching, attenuated professional control, fragmented academic culture, and diminished intrinsic reward and motivation.

Secondarization and Remediation

The long evolution from elite to mass to universal access in American postsecondary

AUTHOR'S NOTE: "Small Worlds, Different Worlds: The Uniqueness and Troubles of American Academic Professions," reprinted by permission of *Daedalus*, Journal of the American Academy of Arts and Sciences, from the issue entitled, "The American Academic Profession," Fall 1997, Vol. 126, No. 4.

education has not been without its costs. One major undesirable effect is a change in the conditions of the academic life that occurs when academics confront poorly educated students who come out of a defective secondary school system and flow into higher education by means of open access. Academic work then revolves considerably around remedial education. Faced with entering students whose academic achievement is, for example, at the level of ninth-grade English, faculty first have to help the student progress to the twelfth-grade or traditional college entry level, thereby engaging in the work of the high school. Mathematics instructors may find themselves facing students whose achievements measure at the sixth-grade level and hence need to complete some elementary schoolwork as well as their secondary education. Well known by those who teach in nonselective four-year colleges and especially in community colleges, this situation may seem surprising, even shocking, to others. But like the night and the day, it follows from the structure and orientation of American secondary and postsecondary education. If secondary schools graduate students whose achievement is below the twelfth-grade level, as they commonly do, and if some colleges admit all or virtually all who approach their doors, then college faculties will engage in K-12 work. Remedial education is spread throughout American higher education, from leading universities to community colleges, but it is relatively light when selectivity is high and quite heavy when selection is low or even nonexistent.

The problem of teaching poorly prepared students is compounded in the two-year college by its concentration on the first two years of the four-year undergraduate curriculum and on short-term vocational and semiprofessional programs. This curricular context calls for repetitive teaching of introductory courses. Since community colleges experience much student attrition during and after the first year of study, due to a variety of personal, occupational, and academic reasons, teaching is concentrated in first-year courses. In each department, it is usually the general introductory course or two that must be taught over and over again, with little or no surcease. Upper division courses, let alone graduate courses, are rarely available. While some course diversity can be found at the second-year level, the departmental task is to cover the introductory materials semester by semester, year in and year out. The teaching task is then closer to secondary school teaching than what is found in selective universities. The task of remedial education adds to the downward thrust, requiring sub-college work on a plane below the regular first-year instruction.

Inherent and widespread in current American education, this teaching context receives relatively little attention in academic and public discussions. It is virtually an institutional secret that academic life is so often reduced to the teaching of secondary school subjects. With due respect to the difficulties of the work and the often deep devotion of involved staff to the welfare of underprepared students and immigrant populations, this widely found situation amounts to a dumbing down of the intellectual life of academic staff. Subject content is limited to codified introductory material. Educational euphemisms allow us to blink at this undesired effect of American-style comprehensive secondary schooling and universal higher education, but they do not allow us to escape it. The situation marginalizes faculty. Eroding "the essential intellectual core of faculty work," it de-professionalizes them.[1]

Excessive Teaching

The complaint that professors do too much research and too little teaching has been prevalent for almost a hundred years. When William James wrote about "the Ph.D. octopus" shortly after the turn of the century, he pointed to the increasing preoccupation of professors in the emerging universities with specialized research, graduate students, and doctoral programs. Since then, the protest of too much research has been a perennial battle cry of the American reformer seeking more emphasis on undergraduate programs and on their general or liberal education components in particular. The 1980s and early 1990s have seen a strong resurgence of this point of view inside and outside the academy. Careful critics beamed their messages at research universities, would-be universities, and even four-year private and public colleges that have opened their faculty reward systems to the research imperative. They understand that professors teach when they supervise students in the preparation of master's and doctoral theses. They are sometimes aware that in the best private liberal arts colleges, professors involve their undergraduate students in research as an effective way to teach and to learn.[2] But the critical comment overall has turned into a generalized charge that "professors" should do less research and more teaching, meaning undergraduate teaching. In the popular press, and even in the academic press, careful targeting is forgone. In the extreme, a minimization of teaching by professors is portrayed as part of a "scam."

But across the dispersed American professorate, the reality is the reverse: more academics teach too much than teach too little. Fifteen hours of classroom teaching each week is far too much for the maintenance of a scholarly life; even twelve hours is excessive. But as noted earlier, most institutional sectors present such loads, specifying assignments that are two to three times greater than [those] of professors in research-based institutions. Twelve and fifteen hours a week in the classroom at the college level tends to push professors out of their disciplines. A sense of being a scholar is reduced as the "physicist" becomes entirely a "teacher of physics" [and] the "political scientist" a "teacher of political science"—and then mainly as teachers of introductory courses only. Interest flags in what is going on in the revision of advanced topics; command of the literature weakens. Excessive teaching loads apparently are now becoming a source of academic burnout, importing into higher education the teacher burnout long noted as a problem in the K-12 system. A 1989 Carnegie Foundation faculty survey found that the share of the full-time faculty "intending to retire early" was 25 percent in research universities, 26 percent in liberal arts colleges, and a huge 49 percent in two-year colleges.[3] A setting characterized by heavy introductory teaching propels academics toward early retirement twice as much—one-half of the total staff!—as settings where professors have light teaching loads, involvement in research, and a more scholarly life as traditionally defined.

Weakened Professional Control

As indicated earlier, command structures are not unheard of in American colleges and universities. Professors in research universities

and leading private four-year colleges certainly encounter trustee and administrator influence. Their professional position is also increasingly challenged by the professionalization of administrative occupations clustered around central management; in the words of Gary Rhoades, "Faculty are increasingly 'managed' professionals in organizations increasingly run by 'managerial professionals'."[4] But academics in these favored sites generally have strong countervailing power of a professional kind that is rooted in their personal and collective expertise. Department by department, professional school by professional school, they exercise much internal control. They expect to dominate in choosing who to add to the faculty and what courses should be taught. They expect to be consulted in many matters rather than to receive orders from those in nominally superior positions. But in public and private comprehensive colleges and especially in community colleges, the foundations of authority change. Subject expertise becomes more diffuse, occasionally amounting only to sufficient knowledge in the discipline to teach the introductory course to poorly prepared students, while at the same time the role of trustees and administrators is strengthened, sometimes approaching the top-down supervision found in local school districts. Such managerialism is particularly evident in public sector institutions, especially when they are exposed to state assertions of accountability.

Adding greatly to the vulnerability of academic professionals to political and administrative dictate is the marginal position of part-time faculty. In all institutional sectors, part-timers have long been with us: witness the traditional use and abuse of faculty spouses in part-time work in foreign language departments of research universities. But the use of part-timers grew greatly during the last two decades as a form of mobile and inexpensive labor. It unfortunately turns out that floating student "clienteles" require dispensable academic staff, hence the deteriorating situation for staff in community colleges where a majority of faculty now serve part-time. The part-timers themselves have only marginal influence, and their large numbers weaken the influence of full-time faculty vis-à-vis trustees and administrative staff. A relatively powerless proletariat exists in American academic life, centered in employment that is part-time and poorly paid.

Experiments are underway in the two-year colleges, we should note, to create new forms of academic professionalism that are centered on "the disciplines of instruction" rather than on disciplinary affiliation.[5] This approach emphasizes the importance of translating knowledge into more understandable forms by such means as course revision and media preparation. Certain attitudes about teaching, as well as forms of teaching, become the possible basis for professional identity. But while community college instruction has become a career in its own right, it remains highly unlikely that a strong sense of professionalism can be constructed when disciplinary foundations are weak, part-time work is the main form of employment, and top-down bureaucratic control remains widespread.

Fragmented Academic Culture

All-encompassing academic values are increasingly hard to find in American academic life. The claims frequently made by reformers that academics must somehow find their way back to agreement on core values and assume an overarching common framework become less realistic with each passing year. Different contexts, especially institutional ones, promote different values. Even common terms assume different meanings. "Academic freedom" in one context means mainly the right to do as one pleases in pursuing new ideas; in another, not to have an administrator dictate the teaching syllabus one uses; in another, the right to teach evolution in a college where the local board of trustees is dominated by creationists; in yet another, the right to join an extremist political group. Promotion criteria vary from an all-out emphasis on research productivity to weight put solely on undergraduate instruction, from complicated mixtures of teaching and research and several forms of "service" to heavy weighting of years on the job and seniority rights. As mentioned earlier, professional schools must value their connection to outside professions as well as to other parts of their universities, thereby balancing themselves between two sets of values in a way not required in the letters and science departments. The grounds for advancement then become particularly contentious. All such differences in outlook among academics widen as differentiation of academic work continues.

Diminished Intrinsic Reward and Motivation

Under all the strengths and weaknesses of American academic life, we find the persistent problem of the professional calling. When academic work becomes just a job and a routine career, then such material rewards as salary are placed front and center. Academics stay at their work or leave for other pursuits according to how much they are paid. They come to work "on time" because they must (it is nailed down in the union contract); they leave on time because satisfaction is found after work is concluded. But when academic work is still a calling, it "constitutes a practical ideal of activity and character that makes a person's work morally inseparable from his or her life. It subsumes the self into a community of disciplined practice and sound judgment whose activity has meaning and value in itself, not just in the output or profit that results from it."[6] A calling transmutes narrow self-interest into other-regarding and ideal-regarding interests: one is linked to peers and to a version of a larger common good. The calling has moral content; it contributes to civic virtue.

Professionalization projects seek to provide vehicles by which multitudes of workers are transported to a calling, where they find intrinsic motivation as well as the glories of high status and the trappings of power. The academic profession is lucky in that it has abundant sources of intrinsic motivation in the fascinations of research and the enchantments of teaching. Many academic contexts offer a workaday existence rich in content and consequence. As a confederative gathering, the academic profession's continuing promise lies considerably in the provision of a variety of contexts that generate "absorbing errands."[7] In that promise lies the best hope in the long term for the recruitment and retention of talent.

But when such contexts fade away or become severely weakened, the errands run down and talented people search for other fascinations and enchantments. The systemic problems I have identified—secondarization, excessive teaching, weakened professional control, fragmented academic culture—point to structural and cultural conditions that run down the academic calling.

Notes

1. Earl Seidman, *In the Words of the Faculty: Perspectives on Improving Teaching and Educational Quality in Community Colleges* (San Francisco, Calif.: Jossey-Bass, 1985), 275.

2. See Robert A. McCaughey, *Scholars and Teachers: The Faculties of Select Liberal Arts Colleges and Their Place in American Higher Learning* (New York: Barnard College, Columbia University, 1994).

3. Carnegie Foundation for the Advancement of Teaching, "Early Faculty Retirees: Who, Why, and with What Impact?" *Change* (July/August 1990): 31-34. On burnout in community colleges, see Cohen and Brawer, *The American Community College*, 90-93.

4. Gary Rhoades, "Reorganizing the Faculty Work Force for Flexibility," *Journal of Higher Education* 67 (6) (November/December 1996): 656.

5. Cohen and Brawer, *The American Community College*, 96-100.

6. Robert N. Bellah, Richard Madsen, William M. Sullivan, Ann Swidler, and Steven M. Tipton, *Habits of the Heart: Individualism and Commitment in American Life* (Berkeley and Los Angeles, Calif.: University of California Press, 1985), 66.

7. A metaphor attributed to Henry James. Exact reference unknown.

6

The Changing Classroom: The Meaning of Shifts in Higher Education for Teaching and Learning

Charles S. Green, III and Dean S. Dorn

Previous chapters discussed a number of macro-level trends in higher education. In this chapter, we discuss how these trends affect teaching and learning at the micro level, that is, in the classroom.[1] The issues addressed are teaching as if learning mattered; unprepared, overly burdened students (Generation X?); what to teach (is there a canon?); conflicted classrooms; can we do more with less?; and technology (boon, boondoggle, or speed up?).

Teaching as if Learning Mattered

Teaching as a Tradition-Bound Endeavor

The favored methods of undergraduate instruction are the lecture and the discussion. To be sure, there are differences in emphasis among institutions; large state-supported universities tend to rely more on the former, whereas small private colleges rely more on the latter (Boyer 1987:146-54). Nevertheless, both have remained enshrined in the pantheon of teaching virtues for well over 100 years (Levine 1978:171-73). This persistence of tradition is remarkable, considering how little evidence there is to support the effectiveness of lecture and discussion and that academics typically think of themselves as the avant-garde, open and accepting to new ideas. We shall not tarry at trying to explain the persistence of tradition. Instead, we elaborate a bit on the ineffectiveness of our traditions and take note of recent movements seeking to improve teaching.

Lecturing

One wag has argued that the lecture is a mechanism by which the notes of a professor are transferred to the notes of a student without passing through the head of either. That might be something of a cheap shot. On the one hand, professors probably think a lot, at least when their notes originally are written; on the other hand, students think about—or at least memorize—notes to prepare for examinations. But

EDITORS' NOTE: For some innovative uses and guidelines for using technology, see Innovative Routes to Learning section, Using Technology subsection in the *Fieldguide,* and for some ideas about the shift from teaching to learning, see Creative Ways of Engaging Students subsection in the *Fieldguide.*

two processes are at work that make the wag's argument too often true.

First, in delivering lectures orally, professors fail to take into account that student attention spans are barely more than 20 minutes, so gaps in lecture notes occur and misunderstandings emerge as contexts of points are missed. It must be emphasized that it is sloppy reasoning for professors to argue that students' incomprehension is due to their brains being addled by television. For one thing, professors complained about student inattentiveness well before television existed (H. Horowitz 1987; Moffatt 1989, 1991). Moreover, anyone who has attended more than a few academic conferences has seen professors nod off, doodle, and in other ways visibly show inattentiveness to one another's lectures.

The second process is related to the first. Professors lecture and students take notes at a far slower pace than either can silently read the same material. In a 50-minute period, a professor can deliver about 2,500 to 5,000 words. In that same period of time, even the slowest student can read those words twice from written text, and adept readers can read them up to *10 times*. Comprehension is far better when material is read and *read several times*. In short, if we are serious about comprehension, then we should stop lecturing so much.

Finally, heavy reliance on lecturing implies a mind-set in which learning is assumed to involve professors pouring knowledge from their fonts of wisdom into students' empty skulls. The evidence is now overwhelming that this orientation to teaching is counterproductive; it induces students to take an alienated and superficial approach to studying and results in, at most, only short-term memorization of content (Kember and Gow 1994; Rau and Baker 1989; Rau and Heyl 1990; Kuh, Pace, and Vesper 1997).

Discussion

If lecturing at students is a poor way in which to teach, then one might wonder whether discussion must be an effective way in which to ensure not only comprehension but also higher order cognitive skills such as analysis, synthesis, and evaluation. We think that discussion can be highly effective, to the extent that it tailors teaching to the unique repertoire of interests and learning abilities that each student brings to the classroom (cf. Chickering and Gamson 1987:4; Frederick in the *Fieldguide*). But discussion is extremely demanding of professors; not only must they have mastered the content of their disciplines, they must be able to improvise almost instantaneously in the classroom how best to convey that content (e.g., through questioning, prompting, challenging) to each student (Nunn 1996) and how best to manage the group dynamics (Fassinger 1995:19; Billson 1986; Rau and Heyl 1990). What little "hard" evidence there is about discussion suggests that very few professors are both willing and able to do this well (Ellner and Barnes 1983; Nunn 1996). Moreover, discussion is labor intensive and therefore very expensive. That also has deterred its wider use.

Reform Movements

For more than 25 years, there has been an attempt to change the culture of academic sociology so as to increase the importance accorded to teaching within the American Sociological Association (ASA) in particular and within the profession in general (Little and Bowker 1997; Mauksch and Howery 1986; Rau and Baker 1989; Baker and Rau 1990). This reform has stressed increasing the attention given to teaching in the ASA's and regional and state associations' annual meetings and governance structures. This reform also has stressed creating and disseminating methods of classroom instruction that deemphasize traditional lecturing and discussion in favor of methods whose effectiveness has been established through careful research. The latter include a variety of "benign disruptions" (Goldsmid and Wilson 1980:84-97, 297-98) designed to foster critical thinking, collaborative learning exercises and projects, learning communities, role-playing, case examples, the one-minute paper, simulation games, frequent and immediate feedback on work, and opportunities for students to revise and improve work before it receives a final grade (see *Fieldguide* for many examples of these methods). In addition, there have been efforts to excite students about science in general and sociology in particular by blurring the lines between teaching and research. As Goldsmid and Wilson (1980) put it nearly 20 years ago, "We conclude that it is a serious error, if not a mortal sin, to see teaching and research as contending, incompatible roles. If they are in fact so defined, they need not be—must not be, if we are to teach competently" (p. 34).

Despite the cogency of this argument, what has been done since to blur these lines has served mainly to show how difficult the task is (for two good case studies, see Schmid 1992 and Pestello et al. 1996). In fact, whether research and teaching are locked in a zero-sum relationship or whether they can be synergistic depends on the relative importance given to teaching and research, the level and quality of the students being taught, and the type of research being done (Baker and Zey Ferrell 1984; Baker 1986). Thus, it should come as no surprise that a recent meta-analysis of 58 studies concluded that "the common belief that research and teaching are inextricably entwined is an enduring myth. At best, research and teaching are very loosely coupled" (Hattie and March 1996:529).

One final aspect of this reform movement deserves notice—the attempt in sociology as well as in other disciplines to define scholarship more broadly so as to include under that rubric course syllabi and instructional materials as well as published research (Rice 1986; Boyer 1990).

A second reform effort, the so-called assessment movement, has emerged that transcends the discipline of sociology. It is much misunderstood, even in the academic world (Sharkey 1996). For example, we have encountered fevered conspiracy theories in the newsletter of an ASA section and on the Internet attributing the emergence of assessment to profit-hungry capitalists, legislators captive of the latter, and governing boards beholden to both—all allegedly seeking to deskill and disempower the professorate.

Assessment is not the product of a recent conspiracy. Rather, it has a long and complicated history that we will not attempt to review here; suffice it to say that the history is an honorable one (Adelman 1986; Sharkey 1992). Assessment simply means quality control and improvement, goals to which we think all academics should be committed. Indeed, our professional autonomy is contingent on our achieving these goals. That is, there is a tacit compact by which society gives professors autonomy in deciding what is taught and how it is taught, in return for which we provide quality education (Pescosolido 1991; Sullivan, this volume). Thus, assessment should be seen *not* as illegitimate external interference but rather as a professional obligation to earn public confidence, thereby enabling us to *keep* that autonomy (Katz 1994; Power 1997; Ewell 1991, 1994).

Specifically, assessment requires (1) finding out what students knew and could do on entering college and what they know and can do on graduating; (2) finding out what happens between entry and exit, that is, which students fail to learn as much as we expect of them and why; (3) finding out what institutions, professors, and students themselves can do to maximize the learning of all students (Astin 1997; Hutchings 1992; Eckert et al. 1997). Thus, assessment requires program evaluation and systematic organizational change, activities in which sociologists should be at the forefront (Hutchings 1992; Sharkey 1992).

Unprepared, Overly Burdened Students: "Generation X"?

Unprepared Students

It is important to place the issue of students' unpreparedness in both historical and sociological perspective. First, professorial complaints about students' laziness, lack of prior preparation, stupidity, and the like can be traced at least as far back as colonial times; thus, it is hardly a new issue (H. Horowitz 1987; Furniss in this volume). Second, it hardly seems to matter how well prepared students are because professors from institutions that differ vastly in admissions standards uniformly complain about their students. For example, we have heard community college faculty express envy at the types of students we (at comprehensive state universities) have; our colleagues' wish lists include students as good as those at the University of California, Berkeley, and the University of Wisconsin–Madison; we have heard faculty from the latter institutions waxing enviously over Harvard University, University of Chicago, and Stanford University students; and we have met faculty from the latter institutions who reminisce nostalgically over how good their *former* students were. In short, it might

appear that this is a nonissue. But it merits some further examination because it is a far more complex issue than most faculty gripe sessions reveal. The notion of "preparedness" is itself complex. By "prepared," do we mean how knowledgeable students are when they enter college, or do we mean the amount of effort and seriousness that they devote to their studies?

If by preparedness we mean the latter, then it is not so clear that there has been much change. Historians and sociologists of higher education have noted the existence of a "collegiate" subculture that emerged in the mid-19th century. This subculture emphasizes getting a "well-rounded education," which means that "sociability" (i.e., partying), making "good connections," and socioemotional maturation are valued at least as much as is cognitive growth. This subculture was elaborately legitimated, and it resisted control by faculty and administration. For example, one of the authors (Green) recalls learning the following song lyrics his freshman year (1955) at the University of Virginia: "From Rugby Road to Vinegar Hill, we're gonna get drunk tonight. The faculty's afraid of us, they know we're in the right." (More systematic documentation of this resistance can be found in Jencks and Riesman 1968:35-50; Litt 1969:89-102; H. Horowitz 1987; Kett 1977; Moffatt 1989.) This subculture was pervasive at even elite universities until admissions standards began, after World War II, to be based more consistently on merit rather than on class, race, religion, and gender. Moreover, the impact of more meritorious admissions standards on classroom performance has been enormous. According to one series of studies, public school graduates admitted to Harvard and other elite universities since the 1960s earn higher grades and are far more likely to be elected to Phi Beta Kappa than are private school graduates. These results cannot be accounted for by differences in aptitude, as measured by SATs (Zweigenhaft 1991, 1992, 1993). Thus, although the sharp increase in grades over the past 25 years or so has been attributed to "grade inflation" (Levine 1994; Pedersen 1997), it appears that the grade increase is better attributed to the increasingly closer match between students' abilities and academic ambitions and institutions' demands and expectations (Pascarella and Terenzini 1991:388-90, 624-29; Clark 1987:4-23; see also Freese, Artis, and Powell in this volume). In short, less able students and those able students who prefer being "collegiate" over being "grade grubbers" and/or intellectuals are less likely than was the case in the past to be admitted to, *and failed from,* more demanding institutions. Now they wind up at Rutgers University instead of Harvard, or at a comprehensive state university instead of a second-tier university or liberal arts college, or at a community college instead of a comprehensive state university. We faculty who are at less demanding institutions complain but largely tolerate the less able students and the "collegiates" because they provide us with our jobs (cf. Moffatt 1991). Administrators and even a few faculty at more demanding institutions can enjoy the luxury of wondering whether their students should not, perhaps, have a bit more fun (see Gose 1996 on the issue of introducing more fun at the University of Chicago).

If by preparedness we mean what students bring to college with them, then it is clearly true that things have changed for the worse. Most institutions were built relatively recently to accommodate the perceived needs of a growing and technologically more sophisticated economy (Litt 1969; Jencks and Riesman 1968; Key 1996; Clark 1987). Thus, colleges and universities, especially state-supported ones, have over the past 100 years been admitting larger and larger numbers of students, the majority of whom are *first-generation students who come*

to us initially unprepared in numerous ways as compared to those whose parents have college degrees.

- There is a lack of family support, both financial and in terms of values, for entering and completing college (Brooks-Terry 1988; Billson and Brooks-Terry 1987; Ross 1990; Cabrera, Nora, and Castañeda 1993).
- There is a lack of knowledge of higher education environments—their traditions, rules, vocabularies, and so on (York-Anderson and Bowman 1991).
- Students are vocationally oriented as opposed to interested in education for its own sake (Billson and Brooks-Terry 1982).
- First-generation students "do not join, do not socialize, and do not study hard" (Billson and Brooks-Terry 1982:70; see also Cabrera et al. 1993), nor do they seek advice or help from faculty or staff (Tinto 1985, 1988).
- First-generation students are somewhat more likely to work and spend nearly *twice as many hours working* as do their second-generation peers (Billson and Brooks-Terry 1982; see also Stern and Nakata 1991).
- Conflicting demands of home, job, and college result in very high attrition rates (Brooks-Terry 1988).

Overly Burdened Students

As we have just noted, the college performance of first-generation college students is especially problematic. However, the financial burdens they face recently have become even more serious, and the burden on middle-class second- and third-generation students has increased sharply as well (Passell 1997; Geraghty

1997; "The Widening Gap" 1996). There are at least three sources of these burdens: (1) shifts in federal assistance from grants to loans (Vanden Brook 1996; College Board 1996); (2) declining state support for universities and students as resources being redirected to prison construction, K-12 education (in some states), welfare, and health (Hossler et al. 1997; Arenson 1996; Butterfield 1995; Geraghty 1997; Levine 1997); and (3) increasing real costs of college education due in large part to the growth of administrative and nonteaching staff costs. Other costs, including faculty salaries, have barely kept up with inflation (Leslie and Rhoades 1995; Gumport and Pusser 1995). Recent statistics show that increasing percentages of middle-class students are working, working longer, and assuming great amounts of debt (Stern and Nakata 1991; Vanden Brook 1996; Hartle 1994; "Anxiety over Tuition" 1997).

Generation X?

Media "hype" implies that the current generation of students is vastly different from previous generations. We agree. But we wish to point out that some of those differences are trivial and do not create any classroom problems that well-trained instructors cannot handle. Other differences, however, have impacts in the classroom that are more difficult to deal with.

"Generation X" (Gen. X) is different from the generation of this chapter's authors. The historical events we experienced in our formative years (e.g., World War II, the "bomb" and the Iron Curtain, Korea, Vietnam, the Kennedy and King assassinations, McCarthyism) are not Gen. X'ers; they cite the Gulf War, the O. J. Simpson trial, the *Challenger* explosion, the end of the cold war, and the death of rock stars such

as Kurt Cobain. The world they enter is different from ours in other respects as well. For example, those of us born in the 1930s were part of a tiny cohort and so did not face much competition in the market. Moreover, our competitors were other Americans and, among the latter, we of the Depression-era cohort of faculty (most of us are white males) benefited from gender and race discrimination. Gen. X'ers were born into a cohort among whose members must be counted not only Americans but also all of their age peers in the global economy.

When Gen. X'ers are compared to faculty born in more recent generations (i.e., "boomers"), there still is a significant generation gap. Although boomers did not face *international* competition in their young years to the same extent that Gen. X'ers now do, they faced and still face far more competition within the United States because their cohort is so large. Like the Depression-era birth cohort, but unlike Gen. X'ers, boomers vividly remember formative events in their youth such as Sputnik, the war in Vietnam, the civil rights and women's movements, assassinations, and Watergate. (For a recent compendium of research on Gen. X, see Craig and Bennett 1997.) Yet, there always has been a generation gap (and often a social class gap as well) between students and professors. We have coped with these differences before and so can continue to do so (Bohmer and Briggs 1991; Cohen 1995; N. Davis 1992; Eells 1987; Gimenez 1989; Reed 1994).

Other differences concern us more. As we noted earlier, financial aid is down, yet students are expected to pay a much higher proportion of their costs than was expected of us. This translates into pressures on professors—to demand less in terms of homework, papers, and the like. It also translates into pressures imposed on students to finish college as soon as possible. This pressure can come from two sources: (1) students and their families who want to minimize their costs and (2) financially strapped institutions. The outcome of these pressures is that students have become less willing to tolerate failures (which may require repeating courses), less willing to take risks (e.g., take a "hard" course), and less willing to experiment (e.g., take a course for the sheer pleasure of it).

Another difference that concerns us is that Gen. X students are more likely than earlier generations of students to be from lower and working-class backgrounds.[2] This means that they are far more likely to have experienced the stresses of poverty, increasing the possibility of abusive, dysfunctional family life while growing up (Hotaling, Straus, and Lincoln 1989; Marsh 1990). As noted earlier, they also are more likely to be overly burdened by increasing family and work obligations while in college. The crises fostered by these stresses manifest themselves in the classroom in myriad ways—the student who breaks down during a lecture or discussion on family violence; the student who misses many classes because no one else is available to care for his ill mother; the student who publicly and heatedly challenges the professor, arguing that "a good whipping" not only does not hurt kids but is in fact good for them; the student whose only responses to an intellectual challenge consist of profanity and threats of violence.

Another troubling issue is the increasing number of Gen. X students who enter college without college-level skills in reading, English, and mathematics. The ability to read is key to success in college, but research documents a continuing decline in reading ability ("College Students Can't Read?" 1992). Two of the largest systems of higher education, City University of New York and the California State University system, have dealt with this issue by offering more remedial courses (Knowlton 1995; Moloney 1996; Richardson 1995). States with

increasing populations of non-native English speakers, such as California, Texas, and Florida, are struggling with this issue. In the next century, a tidal wave of new students, many from immigrant backgrounds, will hit higher education institutions in these states. The problem is compounded by a decline in standards in K-12 so that substantial percentages of native English speakers arrive at college and cannot be placed in college-level English courses (Stewart 1995).

After entrance, many of these students enroll in courses such as introductory sociology, social problems, and lower division statistics without first acquiring college-level prerequisite skills in English, reading, and mathematics. Professors who are experts in their content areas have little formal training in teaching students to become competent in these skills. In the meantime, college textbooks and reading material have become more complex (e.g., postmodern theory, quantitative research methods). This is frustrating to faculty who are not prepared to deal with the situation and to students who often blame the school system (Stewart 1995). One result is low retention rates for first-year college students.

What to Teach: Is There a Canon?

It certainly would make teachers' lives easier if there were a canon, but there is not. For more than a decade, the humanities have been arguing over *the* canon, with meetings of the Modern Language Association in particular being a virtual battleground. Political scientists have been battling over area studies, and anthropology has been threatened from within and without by the emergence of "cultural studies." In sociology, one can find pale imitations of and musings about a canon, and these can be somewhat helpful in identifying important works to add to one's own "must read" list and to assign students. For example, in May 1996, *Contemporary Sociology* published retrospective reviews of the 10 most influential books (but not necessarily sociology books or the most meritorious books) of the past 25 years. The July-August 1996 issue of *Footnotes* contained some additional suggestions but surprisingly few radical challenges to the list. The July 1996 issue of *C.S.* contained a short statement by each of 42 sociologists identifying his or her favorite books. So, there might be a modicum of consensus about the "best books." The consensus ends there.[3]

A sizable minority (possibly even a majority) of sociologists agree that the discipline is in trouble, but the diagnoses are wildly disparate (see, e.g., recent works such as I. Horowitz's [1993] *The Decomposition of Sociology,* Lemert's [1995] *Sociology after the Crisis,* Levine's [1995] *Visions of the Sociological Tradition,* and Wolfe's [1996] *Marginalized in the Middle*).

With respect to theory construction, the micro/macro distinction we once learned was so important is under attack and, it is argued, should be replaced by the concept of "fractals" (Goldstone 1990). One can choose from among the classic divisions in sociological theory (e.g., conflict, functionalism, exchange, symbolic interaction) or from any of the newer emphases such as social constructionism, feminism, networks, rational choice, structuration, and queer theory. With respect to research methods, there is similar disarray. Old-fashioned positivism still has its adherents (J. Davis 1990; Lieberson 1985; Huber 1995, 1997), but there are a variety of qualitative postmodernist approaches from which to choose (e.g., Denzin 1996, 1997; Denzin and Lincoln 1994).

We choose to see this disarray and dissensus as something of a good thing. Possibly, we are less troubled than our younger peers because we cannot remember when our discipline was

ever unified. Indeed, Hargens (1990) documents that sociologists' discouragement about their discipline extends at least as far back as the mid-1960s *and* has been exaggerated by the press as well as by disaffected elders in the discipline. We instead see some good in chaos because it is symptomatic of a lively discipline, one reexamining and reconstituting itself and thereby revitalizing itself. Moreover, this chaos can be used to enliven teaching by showing students that knowledge is not a fixed, unalterable product but rather a process of creation, criticism, revision, and even revolution.

Thus, disarray and dissensus can be viewed as merely pessimistic labels for phenomena that could justifiably be relabeled as *a cornucopia of goodies from which one may choose without fear of severe sanction.* In fact, feminist pedagogy, with its emphasis on replacing the "lone wolf" expert at the head of the class with collaborative and dialogic learning, is ideally suited for a chaotic sociology in particular and the other social sciences as well (cf. Maher and Thompson 1994; Baxter Magolda 1992).

Conflicted Classrooms

Over the past few years, there have been sessions of state, regional, and national annual meetings devoted to topics such as rage, hostility, hate, and conflict in the classroom. Discussions on these topics also may be found on the Internet. Although we doubt that such problems pervade all classrooms, it is clear that enough professors encounter and have trouble dealing with them to make it worth our while to discuss them here (see also Gershick in this volume). We have not seen any systematic research on the extensiveness, let alone the causes, of conflicted classrooms. So, the discussion that follows is best described as "informed guesswork." We think that the rise of conflicted classrooms can be traced to six classes of factors. We discuss each in turn.

First, there is a vast gulf in political views between the public and academics. For example, 18 percent of adults identify themselves as left or liberal, whereas 40 percent of professors in general and 78 percent of sociology professors identify themselves as left or liberal (Hamilton and Hargens 1993). This widening gulf, or "backlash," may well be what is showing up in our classrooms. But we think that this is only a necessary condition for classroom conflict, not a sufficient one.

Second, as noted earlier in this chapter, increasing proportions of our students are the first in their families to attend college. That is, they might come from encapsulated lower and working-class cultures. They are highly likely to be socially conservative, especially with respect to sexual behavior and to both political and religious deviance. Violation of their standards is far more likely to evoke strong and violent punishments than is the case for more cosmopolitan, often middle-class, students (Collins 1975:61-79, 1988:187-226; Bourdieu 1984; Fischer 1982). Thus, the intensity of response that some professors have experienced when dealing with controversial topics might be attributable to the first-generation and/or working-class background of their students.

Third, first-generation students are, for obvious economic reasons, more likely to attend colleges that neither require residence nor even provide residence halls (e.g., community colleges). Furthermore, even when they do attend residential colleges, they are more likely than second-generation students to commute and to stay uninvolved (Billson and Brooks-Terry 1982). Therefore, these students seldom experience the "other curriculum" outside the classroom that can (although we professors seldom acknowledge it) reinforce classroom learning about tolerance and empathy—day-to-day conversations and involvement in common activities with people from diverse backgrounds (Kuh 1995; Moffatt 1989; Pascarella and Terenzini 1991; Pascarella et al. 1996; Astin 1993). To put it another way, commuter students' experience of other students might be desegregated but not fully integrated. Moreover, it is not only commuting that can prevent an integrated experience. Multiculturalism carried too far (e.g., separate residence halls, seating areas in dining halls, separate cultural and recreational areas) also can hinder the attainment of cross-cultural understanding, tolerance, and empathy (Kuh 1995; Pascarella et al. 1996).

Fourth, new and especially interdisciplinary curricula may be introducing students to issues of class, race, and gender far sooner than was the case even a generation ago. In addition, we have become much more concerned with integrating materials on race, gender, and class throughout every course.[4] Ironically, by becoming better educators, we may have made the classroom a more difficult place in which to teach.

Fifth, conflict in the classroom may be related to the race, ethnicity, or gender of the professor, to the interaction between professors' and students' ascribed characteristics, or to both. Yet, the evidence is mixed. For example, with respect to gender, some observational studies have shown gender differences in faculty behavior, whereas others have not; surveys of students reveal few perceived gender differences in behavior among professors (cf. the literature reviews in Auster and MacRone 1994 and Fassinger 1995). There are numerous studies of interaction effects (Constantinople, Cornelius, and Gray 1988; Crawford and MacLeod 1990; Statham, Richardson, and Cook 1991; Feldman 1992), but most of these suggest that gender per se is *not* a systematic, patterned source of protracted conflict. On the other hand, a longitudinal study of a professor's pregnancy while teaching a feminist course showed that "the meanings students attached to their professor depended chiefly on how the situation [class size and pregnancy] constrained both their interaction with her and their perception of her gender performance" (Baker and Copp 1997:40). Thus, a professor's credibility and authority might depend on students' gendered expectations of the professor; controversial course content can intensify that relationship (cf. Maher and Thompson 1994; Smith, Morrison, and Wolf 1994; M. Moore 1997; V. Moore 1996). With respect to race and ethnicity, although we have heard numerous anecdotes about problems faced by minority professors, there is a paucity of rigorous research published on the issue. We suspect that the authority and credibility of minority faculty might depend on factors similar to those experienced by women.

Sixth, increasing numbers of students are arriving at college classrooms without an appreciation for or an understanding of the importance of respect and civility that have long been hallmarks of college instruction. Troublesome behavior in the classroom is not a relentlessly cheerful topic. Even though most extremely disruptive behaviors do not occur daily, one or two per semester are enough to be discouraging (Weimer 1988). Whether there are more troublesome students in our classes in 1997 than in 1961 is difficult to know, but we do know that many faculty members have had students in their classes who have behaved so inappropriately that they were disruptive (Appleby 1990; Ludewig 1994; Sorcinelli and Brell 1990).

Faculty reports of irritating behavior that is disruptive to the teaching-learning process include a lengthy list of student offenses—cheating on examinations, missing class and asking "Did I miss anything important?," placing their heads on their desks or falling asleep during class/lecture, being excessively tardy and absent on examination days, failing to read the assigned textbook or material, not bringing required materials to class, and missing lecture and expecting the professor to provide a personal encore (Ludewig 1994). Other "disrespectful" behaviors seem to be increasing as well—leaving class early without prior notification, eating in the classroom, reading newspapers in class, doing homework for other classes during lecture, talking on the cell phone during class, complaining about course requirements, requesting extensions for due dates, making statements that seem to have nothing to do with the topic, cursing, wearing hats in the classroom, and making racist, sexist, and homophobic remarks about other students (Midwest Sociological Society 1996). The offenses have become so commonplace that faculty are adding a "classroom behavior" section to their course outlines, and we know of some sociology departments that have adopted a "Classroom Code of Conduct" (see *Fieldguide* for a University of San Diego example). Thus, the social order of the classroom is increasingly a negotiated one, where the authority of professors no longer is taken for granted.

Although the classroom may have become a more difficult place to teach, we do not think that the situation is hopeless. For one thing, the very diversity of the classroom presents opportunities waiting to be exploited by imaginative teachers. For example, carefully moderated discussions and debates on controversial topics can bring together people who might not otherwise have the opportunity to do so (Cohen 1995; Aminoff 1995). Two especially important guidelines are as follows:

1. Institute courtesy rules (no one else talks when someone has the floor, no interrupting, etc.) (Emerick 1994).

2. The composition of debate, project, and discussion groups should be diverse with respect to students' knowledge and experience (Thompson 1993; see also Billson 1986; Yamane 1996).

Furthermore, classroom diversity itself can be the focus of both theoretical and methodological questions (cf. Arnold 1995; Moreman 1997). Examples include the following:

1. What is meant by diversity? (gender, race, ethnicity, age, class, or all of these?)

2. How diverse *is* the classroom?

3. What are the consequences of diversity? (Are there differences among class members over the acceptability of abortion, and are these traceable to gender, race, religion, or social class?)

4. What are the causes of classroom diversity? (Is California more diverse than Wisconsin? Is California State University, Sacramento, more or less diverse than Occidental College in Los Angeles? Is the University of Wisconsin–Whitewater more or less diverse than nearby Beloit College?)

Finally, we wish to emphasize that although we think our sociological imaginations can contribute greatly to both understanding and coping with classroom conflict, there are individual circumstances where we will fail. Almost no one can cope with students who are psychotic, are irredeemably bigoted, or threaten physical harm to professors and other students. Such students must be dropped from class—if necessary, even removed forcibly by campus police. Otherwise, the education of the rest of the class will suffer.

Can We Do More with Less?

Roughly 80 years ago, Veblen (1918) published *The Higher Learning in America: A Memorandum on the Conduct of Universities by Businessmen.* Despite its oversimplifications (cf. Riesman 1953), the book was a perceptive and witty critique of the infusion of business values into academic life. Veblen's (1918) critique was directed at the corruption that results when colleges and universities become dependent on contributions by the wealthy to grow and prosper. At the turn of the century, his analysis was most applicable to new and ambitious private institutions such as the University of Chicago (see also Honan 1995 on contemporary New York University). Today, his analysis can be extended to public colleges and universities as well because, as we noted earlier, state funds account for a decreasing share of public higher education's revenues (Levine 1997). In fact, institutions such as the University of Michigan and the University of Wisconsin system (Fox 1996) now publicly refer to themselves as "state assisted." What type of corruption does a Veblen-esque analysis of today's academic life reveal? Generally, corruption results from the failure by business and academia alike to recognize that their very different goals (profit vs. talent development and knowledge creation) can be realized only through different means (i.e., governance structures) (Etzioni 1975; Collins 1975).

One specific corrupting influence is the emphasis on efficiency (i.e., on lower costs). This emphasis has both direct and indirect impacts on the classroom. One direct impact is on class size. Because faculty have failed to define educational quality in terms of measurable learning outcomes, by default education has become defined by "time in place," that is, as the number of semester hours or quarter hours of credit a student completes with a passing grade.[5] Implicit in this definition is the assumption that education does not change students and that they merely absorb information via lectures while "in place." (Veblen might not have appreciated the irony of faculty complicity in their own corruption.) Faculty *productivity,* then, is readily defined as the number of student credit hours attributable to that professor, and *efficiency* is the number of student credit hours per dollar of professor cost. It is obvious from the standpoint of this type of business mentality that it is much more efficient to teach larger classes than smaller ones.

Because faculty seldom have deigned to describe and defend what they do outside the classroom, it *should* come as no surprise to faculty (although this has not been the case) that there are demands for teaching more classes (i.e., to increase their workloads) (Wilson 1997). Moreover, it is obvious that faculty efficiency can be further improved if students do not have to either repeat courses or flunk out, hence the current emphasis on *retention,* with its not-so-implicit message to faculty to "dumb down" course content and/or to inflate grades. Retention often is defended publicly not only for reducing the costs to the institution but also for reducing the costs to students and their parents (Geraghty 1996). Thus, the customers must be kept happy, even though to do so would be the ultimate corruption of academic values. In contrast to the way in which businesses treat customers, we do not admit students who in our opinion will not benefit from our service, and we make students "buy" things they might not want (e.g., general education courses). (For a more detailed critique of the student as customer metaphor, see Mwachofi et al. 1995; see also Nicklin 1995.)

Another corrupting influence is the emphasis on managerial flexibility. Such flexibility typically is defended in terms of business values and business metaphors. For example, it is argued that because educational institutions are like businesses, they face financial crises such as reduced or shifting demands for their products. It follows, then, that universities should respond to crises the same way in which businesses do; faculty tenure needs to be relaxed, if not done away with altogether, and increasing reliance must be placed on full- or part-time academic staff (Rhoades 1996; Magrath 1997; Leik 1997; Lauderdale 1997; Wood 1997; Chait 1997).

It never occurs to educational administrators infected by or beholden to this business mentality that insecurity breeds lower effectiveness; insecure faculty are more likely than tenured faculty to dumb down their courses or inflate grades to preserve their jobs. Moreover, insecure faculty have no loyalty to institutions per se or even to one another (Leatherman and Magner 1996; Altbach 1995). In short, the vaunted cost-consciousness of the business mentality fails to take into account the inappropriateness of its policies when applied to education (Cameron and Tschirhart 1992; Kerlin and Dunlap 1993).

A final corrupting influence is the short-term, "quick fix" mentality of businesspeople and their sympathizers in academe. This influence manifests itself in the faith in technology, the subject of the next section.

Technology: Boon, Boondoggle, or Speed Up?

Our answer to the question posed in the section title is "yes—all three." Seriously, we think that in evaluating the impact of technology, we must distinguish among different types of technology (e.g., the Internet, multimedia CD-ROMS), and we must anticipate that each type will affect different people in different ways. We first discuss the Internet and then "distance learning."

The Internet promises all types of wonderful things for our students. We can, for example, envision the day when classes in sociology across the world share viewpoints, personal experiences, and findings from their studies and projects. The Internet already has facilitated communication among students and between students and faculty. Thus, new forms of groups are emerging across the world, uniting us as never before. Yet, sociologists know that as people are united within boundaries of groups, these very boundaries also separate them from other people (Cerula, Ruane, and Chayko 1992). In short, the Internet is likely to have paradoxical consequences.

There is no question that interactive satellite technology will bring courses to people who otherwise would not have been able to take them. What troubles us is that so many administrators treat this type of distance learning as a panacea for escalating costs, trying to use technology to wrest sharp increases in productivity from faculty (cf. Fox 1996; Blumenstyk 1994). As we noted in the previous section, the notion of increased productivity is predicated on a definition of education that assumes that education merely involves students absorbing information from an expert source. Thus, the greater the number of students, the greater the efficiency or productivity. But what if education really involves—or really *should* involve—the development of higher order cognitive skills such as critical thinking? Virtually everything we know about how to cultivate critical thinking skills suggests that it is a labor-intensive process of interaction and communication (Brooks 1997; Paul 1993; Himmelfarb 1996; Ashworth 1996; see also Rudenstine 1997, who argues instead that the new technology *intrinsically* helps develop higher order skills). Thus, administrators are deluding themselves—and the public—with exaggerated claims about the potential of multimedia education in general

and distance learning in particular (Yonke 1997). Moreover, we would be remiss in not noting that faculty, by legitimating and preserving the tradition of the lecture, have contributed to the notion that education can be had "on the cheap." Finally, we wish to point out a deliciously ironic potential inherent in distance learning. It seems to us that if carried to its ultimate and logical extreme, distance learning would involve just a few professors in each discipline working with a production team to produce videotapes for worldwide broadcasting (Hamilton and Miller 1997). That means almost no more professors, no more university campuses, *and no more administrators.*

Conclusion

In this chapter, we have raised a number of the important classroom issues instructors are likely to face in the 21st century—new pedagogies that focus on learning outcomes, the implications of the changing composition of the student body, disagreement over what to teach, conflicted classrooms, financial exigencies, and new technologies. There is one still lively issue we did not address: are student evaluations of teaching merely Nielsen rating-like gimmicks that force professors to compromise standards and become mere entertainers? We think that this issue deserves to be buried. Thousands of studies and several meta-analyses of those studies have now been published, and the results are conclusive; carefully crafted and administered instruments not only are highly reliable but also *validly measure the impact of teachers on student learning* (Cohen 1981; Feldman 1989; Abrami, d'Apollonia, and Cohen 1990).[6] Part II of this volume provides more detailed discussions of this and other issues we raised in this chapter. The *Fieldguide* provides practical ways in which to cope with those issues.

Notes

1. The issues we discuss in this chapter were not chosen by guesswork alone. Both authors have been deeply engaged in the American Sociological Association's (ASA) teaching movement for many years. That engagement has included conducting workshops on teaching, conducting numerous evaluation visits to sociology departments, providing refereeing and editing services for the journal *Teaching Sociology,* and serving as officers in the ASA's Section on Undergraduate Education and in its Committee on Teaching. Both authors have been active in state and regional associations and try to keep abreast of what is happening in higher education at all levels—micro (classroom), meso (institutional), and macro (societal and even world system). Finally, Dorn (1996) recently interviewed a nonrandom but diverse sample of 36 sociologists, asking them (among other things) about issues that concern them now and about what they see as key issues for the future. Thus, although we are unable to rank which issues are of gravest concern to which types of instructors, we do believe that we have at least identified issues of great concern to significant numbers of instructors.

2. In 1996, 26.8 percent of the fathers and 24.1 percent of the mothers of new freshmen admitted to four-year, moderately selective public institutions had completed college degrees (Higher Education Research Institute 1997). The college completion percentages were twice those in the 1950s and early 1960s, before the explosion of enrollments in public four-year institutions (Jencks and Riesman 1968).

3. Connell (1997) argues that a sociological classical canon (e.g., Marx, Durkheim, Weber) was created in the 1930s in the United States in response to the rupturing of a prior European worldview founded on the premises of progress and imperialism. Collins (1997) argues that Connell's (1997) analysis of the reasons for the emergence of this canon is flawed but agrees that the sociological study of canons is worthwhile.

4. This is most noticeable with respect to sociology textbooks. Over the past decade, *Teaching Sociology* has published several reviews criticizing textbook authors for failing to integrate material on race, gender, or class—or on all three—into all chapters of textbooks.

5. See Nordvall and Braxton (1996) for a definition of educational quality that is based on outcomes.

6. Student evaluations are not valid measures of the appropriateness of course content; of the difficulty of assignments, tests, and examinations; or of the adequacy of reading assignments. These judgments are best left to peer review.

References

Abrami, P. C., S. d'Apollonia, and P. Cohen. 1990. "The Validity of Student Ratings of Instruction: What We Know and What We Do Not." *Journal of Educational Psychology* 82:219-31.

Adelman, C., ed. 1986. *Assessment in Higher Education: Issues and Contexts.* Washington, DC: U.S. Department of Education, Office of Research and Improvement.

Altbach, P. G. 1995. "The Pros and Cons of Hiring 'Taxicab' Professors." *Chronicle of Higher Education,* January 6, p. A133.

Aminoff, S. 1995. "The Family History Exercise: Developing Positive Awareness in Culturally Diverse College Classrooms." *Teaching Sociology* 25:155-58.

"Anxiety over Tuition: A Controversy in Context." *Chronicle of Higher Education,* May 30, pp. A10-AI9.

Appleby, D. C. 1990. "Faculty and Student Perception of Irritating Behaviors in the College Classroom. *Journal of Staff, Program, and Organization Development* 10:41-46.

Arenson, K. 1996. "Cuts in Tuition Assistance Put College beyond Reach of Poorest Students." *The New York Times,* January 27, p. AI9.

Arnold, F. W. 1995. "Developing and Teaching a Cultural Pluralism Course in One of America's 'Uneasy Salad Bowls': Immigration and Ethnicity in Los Angeles." *Teaching Sociology* 23:94-110.

Ashworth, K. H. 1996. "Point of View: Virtual Universities Could Produce Only Virtual Learning." *Chronicle of Higher Education,* September 6, p. A88.

Astin, A. 1993. *What Matters in College: Four Critical Years Revisited.* San Francisco: Jossey-Bass.

————. 1997. "Point of View: Our Obsession with Being 'Smart' Is Distorting Intellectual Life." *Chronicle of Higher Education,* September 26, p. A60.

Auster, C. J. and M. MacRone. 1994. "The Classroom as a Negotiated Social Setting: An Empirical Study of the Effects of Faculty Members' Behavior on Students' Participation." *Teaching Sociology* 22:289-300.

Baker, P. J. 1986. "The Helter-Skelter Relationship between Teaching and Research: A Cluster of Problems and Some Small Wins." *Teaching Sociology* 14:50-66.

Baker, P. and M. Copp. 1997. "Gender Matters Most: Interaction of Gendered Expectations, Feminist Course Content, and Pregnancy in Student Course Evaluations." *Teaching Sociology* 25:29-43.

Baker, P. J. and W. C. Rau. 1990. "The Cultural Contradictions of Teaching Sociology." Pp. 169-87 in *Sociology in America,* edited by H. J. Gans. Newbury Park, CA: Sage.

Baker, P. J. and M. Zey-Ferrell. 1984. "Local and Cosmopolitan Orientations of Faculty: Implications for Teaching." *Teaching Sociology* 12:82-106.

Baxter Magolda, M. B. 1992. *Knowing and Reasoning in College: Gender-Related Patterns in Students' Intellectual Development.* San Francisco: Jossey-Bass.

Billson, J. M. 1986. "The College Classroom as a Small Group: Some Implications for Teaching and Learning." *Teaching Sociology* 14:143-51.

Billson, J. M. and M. Brooks-Terry. 1982. "In Search of the Silken Purse: Factors in Attrition among First-Generation Students." *College and University* 58:57-75.

————. 1987. "A Student Retention Model for Higher Education." *College and University* 62:290-305.

Blumenstyk, G. 1994. "Networks to the Rescue? States Hope Technology Can Keep down Tuition and Expenses and Let Them Reach More Students." *Chronicle of Higher Education,* December 14, pp. A21-A25.

Bohmer, S. and J. L. Briggs. 1991. "Teaching Privileged Students about Gender, Race, and Class Oppression." *Teaching Sociology* 19:154-63.

Bourdieu, P. 1984. *Distinction: A Social Critique of the Judgement of Taste.* Richard Nice, trans. Cambridge, MA: Harvard University Press.

Boyer, E. L. 1987. *College: The Undergraduate Experience in America.* New York: Harper & Row.

————. 1990. *Scholarship Reconsidered: Priorities for the Professorship.* Princeton, NJ: Carnegie Foundation for the Advancement of Teaching.

Brooks, J. M. 1997. "Beyond Teaching and Learning Paradigms: Trekking into the Virtual University." *Teaching Sociology* 27:1-14.

Brooks-Terry, M. 1988. "Tracing the Disadvantages of First-Generation College Students: An Application of Sussman's Option Sequence Model." Pp. 121-34 in *Family and Support Systems across the Lifespan,* edited by S. K. Steinmetz. New York: Plenum.

Butterfield, F. 1995. "Prison-Building Binge in California Casts Shadow on Higher Education." *The New York Times,* April 12, p. A32.

Cabrera, A. F., A. Nora, and M. B. Castañeda. 1993. "College Persistence: Structural Equations Modeling Test of an Integrated Model of Student Retention." *Journal of Higher Education* 64:123-39.

Cameron, K. S. and M. Tschirhart. 1992. "Postindustrial Environments and Organizational Effectiveness in Colleges and Universities." *Journal of Higher Education* 63:87-108.

Cerula, K. A., J. M. Ruane, and M. Chayko. 1992. "Technological Ties that Bind: Media-Generated Primary Groups." *Communication Research* 19:109-29.

Chait, R. 1997. "Thawing the Cold War over Tenure: Why Academe Needs More Employment Options." *Chronicle of Higher Education,* February 7, pp. B4-B5.

Chickering, A. W. and Z. F. Gamson. 1987. "Seven Principles for Good Practice in Undergraduate Education." *American Association for Higher Education Bulletin* (March).

Clark, B. R. 1987. *The Academic Life: Small Worlds, Different Worlds.* Princeton, NJ: Carnegie Foundation for the Advancement of Teaching.

Cohen, L. 1995. "Facilitating the Critique of Racism and Classism: An Experiential Model for Euro-American Middle-Class Students." *Teaching Sociology* 23:87-93.

Cohen, P. A. 1981. "Student Ratings of Instruction and Student Achievement: A Meta-analysis of Multisection Validity Studies." *Review of Educational Research* 51:281-309.

College Board. 1996. *Trends in Student Aid.* New York: College Board.

"College Students Can't Read?" 1992. *The Teaching Professor* 6:1.

Collins, R. 1975. *Conflict Sociology: Toward an Explanatory Science.* New York. Academic Press.

———. 1988. *Theoretical Sociology.* San Diego: Harcourt Brace Jovanovich.

———. 1997. "A Sociological Guilt Trip: Comment on Connell." *American Journal of Sociology* 102:1558-64.

Connell, R. W. 1997. "Why Is Classical Theory Classical?" *American Journal of Sociology* 102:1511-57.

Constantinople, A. P., R. R. Cornelius, and J. Gray. 1988. "The Chilly Climate: Fact or Artifact?" *Journal of Higher Education* 59:527-50.

Craig, S. C. and S. E. Bennett, eds. 1997. *After the Boom: The Politics of Generation X.* Lanham, MD: Rowman & Littlefield.

Crawford, M. and M. MacLeod. 1990. "Gender in the Classroom: An Assessment of the 'Chilly Climate' for Women." *Sex Roles* 23:101-22.

Davis, J. A. 1990. "Comment on 'The Essential Wisdom of Sociology.' " *Teaching Sociology* 18:531-32.

Davis, N. J. 1992. "Teaching about Inequality: Student Resistance, Paradigms, and Rage." *Teaching Sociology* 20:232-38.

Denzin, N. K. 1996. *Interpretive Ethnography.* Thousand Oaks, CA: Sage.

———. 1997. "Whose Sociology Is It? Comment on Huber." *American Journal of Sociology* 102:1416-23.

Denzin, N. K. and Y. S. Lincoln, eds. 1994. *Handbook of Qualitative Research.* Thousand Oaks, CA: Sage.

Dorn, D. S. 1996. *Voices from the Classroom: Interviews with Thirty-Six Sociologists about*

Teaching. Washington, DC: ASA Teaching Resources Center.

Eckert, C. M., D. J. Bower, K. S. Stiff, A. J. Hinkle, and A. P. Davis. 1997. "Students' Knowledge and Faculty Members' Expectations: The Case for Classroom Assessment." *Teaching Sociology* 25:150-59.

Eells, L. Workman. 1987. "So Inequality Is Fair? Demonstrating Structured Inequality in the Classroom." *Teaching Sociology* 15:73-75.

Ellner, C. L. and C. P. Barnes, eds. 1983. *Studies of College Teaching.* Lexington, MA: D. C. Heath.

Emerick, R. E. 1994. "A Conversation on Classroom Etiquette in Introductory Sociology Courses." *Teaching Sociology* 22:341-44.

Etzioni, A. 1975. *A Comparative Analysis of Complex Organizations.* Revised and enlarged ed. New York: Free Press.

Ewell, P. 1991. "Assessment and Public Accountability: Back to the Future." *Change,* November-December, pp. 12-17.

———. 1994. "A Matter of Integrity: Accountability and the Future of Self-Regulation." *Change,* November-December, pp. 24-29.

Fassinger, P. A. 1995. "Understanding Classroom Interaction: Students' and Professors' Contributions to Students' Silence." *Journal of Higher Education* 66:82-96.

Feldman, K. A. 1989. "The Association between Student Ratings of Specific Instructional Dimensions and Student Achievement: Refining and Extending the Synthesis of Data from Multisection Validity Studies." *Research in Higher Education* 30:583-645.

———. 1992. "College Students' Views of Male and Female College Teachers: Part I—Evidence from the Social Laboratory and Experiments." *Research in Higher Education* 33:317-75.

Fischer, C. S. 1982. *To Dwell among Friends: Personal Networks in Town and City.* Chicago: University of Chicago Press.

Fox, P. 1996. "A Plan for Now and the Future: UW System Unveils a Budget that Advocates New Technology, Other Initiatives to Prepare for a New Millennium." *Wisconsin Ideas,* October, pp. 1, 8.

Geraghty, M. 1996. "More Students Quitting College before Sophomore Year, Data Show." *Chronicle of Higher Education,* July 19, pp. A35-A36.

———. 1997. "Finances Are Becoming More Crucial in Students' College Choice, Survey Finds." *Chronicle of Higher Education,* January 17, p. A41.

Gimenez, M. E. 1989. "Silence in the Classroom: Some Thoughts about Teaching in the 1980s." *Teaching Sociology* 17:184-91.

Goldsmid, C. A. and E. K. Wilson. 1980. *Passing on Sociology: The Teaching of a Discipline.* Belmont, CA: Wadsworth.

Goldstone, J. A. 1990. "Sociology and History: Producing Comparative History." Pp. 275-92 in *Sociology in America,* edited by H. J. Gans. Newbury Park, CA: Sage.

Gose, B. 1996. " 'U. of Chicago Social Life' May No Longer Be an Oxymoron." *Chronicle of Higher Education,* November 15, p. A49.

Gumport, P. and B. Pusser. 1995. "A Case of Bureaucratic Accretion: Context and Consequences." *Journal of Higher Education* 66:493-520.

Hamilton, K. and S. Miller. 1997. "Internet U: No Ivy, No Walls, No Keg Parties." *Newsweek,* March 10, p. 12.

Hamilton, R. and L. Hargens. 1993. "The Politics of the Professors." *Social Forces* 71:603-27.

Hargens, L. L. 1990. "Sociologists' Assessments of the State of Sociology, 1969-1984." *American Sociologist* 20:200-8.

Hartle, T. W. 1994. "Point of View: How People Pay for College: A Dramatic Shift." *Chron-*

icle of Higher Education, November 9, p. A52.

Hattie, J. and H. W. Marsh. 1996. "The Relationship between Research and Teaching: A Meta-analysis." *Review of Educational Research* 66:507-42.

Higher Education Research Institute. 1997. *The American Freshman: Norms for Fall 1996.* Los Angeles: University of California, Los Angeles, and American Council on Education.

Himmelfarb, G. 1996. "Point of View. A Neo-Luddite Reflects on the Internet." *Chronicle of Higher Education*, November 1, p. A56.

Honan, W. H. 1995. "A Decade and a Billion Dollars Put New York University at Top." *The New York Times,* March 20, pp. A1, A12.

Horowitz, H. L. 1987. *Campus Life: Undergraduate Cultures from the End of the Eighteenth Century to the Present.* New York: Knopf.

Horowitz, I. L. 1993. *The Decomposition of Sociology.* New York: Oxford University Press.

Hossler, D., J. P. Lund, J. Rarnin, S. Westfall, and S. Irish. 1997. "State Funding for Higher Education: The Sisyphean Task." *Journal of Higher Education* 68:160-90.

Hotaling, G. T., M. A. Straus, and A. J. Lincoln. 1989. "Intrafamily Violence and Crime and Violence Outside the Family." Pp. 315-75 in *Family Violence*, edited by U. Ohlin and M. Toury. Chicago: University of Chicago Press.

Huber, J. 1995. "Institutional Perspectives on Sociology." *American Journal of Sociology* 101:194-216.

———. 1997. "Of Facts and Fables: Reply to Denzin." *American Journal of Sociology* 102:1423-29.

Hutchings, P. 1992. "Behind Outcomes: Contexts and Questions for Assessment in Sociology." Pp. 6-25 in *Assessing Undergraduate*

Learning in Sociology, edited by S. Sharkey and W. Johnson. Washington, DC: ASA Teaching Resources Center.

Jencks, C. and D. Riesman. 1968. *The Academic Revolution.* Garden City, NY: Doubleday.

Katz, S. N. 1994. "Point of View: Defining Education Quality and Accountability." *Chronicle of Higher Education,* November 16, p. A56.

Kember, D. and L. Gow, 1994. "Orientations to Teaching and Their Effect on the Quality of Student Learning." *Journal of Higher Education* 65:58-74.

Kerlin, S. P. and D. M. Dunlap. 1993. "For Richer, for Poorer: Faculty Morale in Periods of Austerity and Retrenchment." *Journal of Higher Education* 64:348-77.

Kett, Joseph F. 1977. *Rites of Passage: Adolescence in America, 1790 to the Present.* New York: Basic Books.

Key, S. 1996. "Economics or Education: The Establishment of American Land Grant Universities." *Journal of Higher Education* 67:196-220.

Knowlton, S. 1995. "Question about Remedial Education in a Time of Budget Cuts." *The New York Times,* June 7, pp. B8, B11.

Kuh, G. D. 1995. "The Other Curriculum: Out-of-Class Experiences Associated with Student Learning and Personal Development." *Journal of Higher Education* 66:123-55.

Kuh, G. D., C. R. Pace, and N. Vesper. 1997. "The Development of Process Indicators to Estimate Student Gains Associated with Good Practices in Undergraduate Education." *Research in Higher Education* 38:435-54.

Lauderdale, P. 1997. "University Workers, Tenure under Fire." *Pacific Sociologist* (May 3-4).

Leatherman, C. and D. K. Magner. 1996. "Faculty and Graduate Student Strife over Job Issues Flares on Many Campuses." *Chronicle of Higher Education,* November 29, pp. A12-A14.

Leik, R. K. 1997. "There's Far More than Tenure on the Butcher Block: The Crisis at the University of Minnesota." *Pacific Sociologist* (May 3-4).

Lemert, C. 1995. *Sociology after the Crisis.* Boulder, CO: Westview.

Leslie, L. L. and G. Rhoades. 1995. "Rising Administrative Costs: Seeking Explanations." *Journal of Higher Education* 66:187-212.

Levine, A. 1978. *Handbook on Undergraduate Curriculum.* San Francisco: Jossey-Bass.

———. 1994. "To Deflate Grade Inflation, Simplify the System." *Chronicle of Higher Education,* January 19, p. A133.

———. 1997. "Point of View: Higher Education's New Status as a Mature Industry." *Chronicle of Higher Education,* January 31, p. A48.

Levine, Donald. 1995. *Visions of the Sociological Tradition.* Chicago: University of Chicago Press.

Lieberson, S. 1985. *Making It Count: The Improvement of Social Research and Theory.* Berkeley: University of California Press.

Litt, Edgar. 1969. *The Public Vocational University: Captive Knowledge and Public Power.* New York. Holt, Rinehart & Winston.

Little, J. K. and L. H. Bowker. 1997. "The Legacy of Hans Mauksch: Institutionalizing the Teaching Movement in the American Sociological Association." Unpublished manuscript, Humboldt State University.

Ludewig, L. M. 1994. "Ten Worst Student Behaviors." *The Teaching Professor,* May, p. 2.

Magrath, C. P. 1997. "Point of View: Eliminating Tenure without Destroying Academic Freedom." *Chronicle of Higher Education,* February 28, p. A60.

Maher, F. A. and M. K. Thompson. 1994. *The Feminist Classroom: An Inside Look at How Professors and Students Are Transforming Higher Education for a Diverse Society.* New York: Basic Books.

Marsh, H. W. 1990. "Two-Parent, Step-Parent and Single-Parent Families: Changes in Achievement, Attitudes, and Behaviors during the Last Two Years of High School." *Journal of Educational Psychology* 82:327-40.

Mauksch, H. O. and C. B. Howery. 1986. "Social Change for Teaching: The Case of One Disciplinary Association." *Teaching Sociology* 14:73-82.

Midwest Sociological Society. 1996. Panel on "Student/Faculty Conflict over Classroom Content and Style: What Is Happening?" presented at the meeting of the Midwest Sociological Society, Chicago.

Moffatt, M. 1989. *Coming of Age in New Jersey: College and American Culture.* New Brunswick, NJ: Rutgers University Press.

———. 1991. "College Life: Undergraduate Culture and Higher Education." *Journal of Higher Education* 62:44-61.

Moloney, W. J. 1996. "Reading at 8th-Grade Level in College: Concern over Need for Remedial Reading Programs." *The Washington Post,* December 8, p. 7.

Moore, M. 1997. "Student Resistance to Course Content: Reactions to the Gender of the Messenger." *Teaching Sociology* 25:128-33.

Moore, V. A. 1996. "Inappropriate Challenges to Professorial Authority." *Teaching Sociology* 24:202-6.

Moreman, R. D. 1997. "A Multi-cultural Framework: Transforming Curriculum, Transforming Students." *Teaching Sociology* 25:107-19.

Mwachofi, N., P. Gilbert, M. Strom, and H. Cohen. 1995. "Reflections on the 'Student-as-Customer' Metaphor." *Teaching Forum* 16:1-3. (Undergraduate Teaching Improvement Council, University of Wisconsin System)

Nicklin, J. L. 1995. "The Hum of Corporate Buzzwords." *Chronicle of Higher Education,* January 27, pp. A33-A34.

Nordvall, R. C. and J. M. Braxton. 1996. "An Alternative Definition of Quality of Undergraduate Education." *Journal of Higher Education* 67:483-97.

Nunn, C. E. 1996. "Discussion in the College Classroom: Triangulating Observational and Survey Results." *Journal of Higher Education* 67:243-66.

Pascarella, E. T., M. Edison, A. Nora, L. S. Hagedom, and P. T. Terenzini. 1996. "Influences on Students' Openness to Diversity in the First Year of College." *Journal of Higher Education* 67:174-95.

Pascarella, E. T. and P. T. Terenzini. 1991. *How College Affects Students: Findings and Insights from Twenty Years of Research.* San Francisco: Jossey-Bass.

Passell, P. 1997. "Rise in Merit-Based Aid Alters College Market Landscape." *The New York Times,* April 9, p. A18.

Paul, R. W. 1993. *Critical Thinking.* Revised, 3d ed. Santa Rosa, CA: Foundation for Critical Thinking.

Pedersen, D. 1997. "When an A Is Average: Duke Takes on Grade Inflation." *Newsweek,* March 3, p. 64.

Pescosolido, B. 1991. "The Sociology of the Professions and the Profession of Sociology: Professional Responsibility, Teaching, and Graduate Training." *Teaching Sociology* 19:351-61.

Pestello, F. G., D. E. Miller, S. L. Saxton, and P. G. Donnelly. 1996. "Community and the Practice of Sociology." *Teaching Sociology* 24:148-56.

Power, B. Miller. 1997. "Point of View: The Danger Inherent in Abusing Academic Freedom." *Chronicle of Higher Education,* June 20, p. A52.

Rau, W. and P. J. Baker. 1989. "The Organized Contradictions of Academe: Barriers Facing the Next Academic Revolution." *Teaching Sociology* 17:161-75.

Rau, W. and B. Heyl. 1990. "Humanizing the College Classroom: Collaborative Learning and Social Organization among Students." *Teaching Sociology* 18:141-55.

Reed, M. S. 1994. "Digging up Family Plots: Analysis of Axes of Variation in Genograms." *Teaching Sociology* 22:255-59.

Rhoades, G. 1996. "Reorganizing the Faculty Workforce for Flexibility: Part-Time Professional Labor." *Journal of Higher Education* 67:626-59.

Rice, R. 1986. "The Academic Profession in Transition: Toward a New Social Fiction." *Teaching Sociology* 14:12-23.

Richardson, L. 1995. "Students Who Want Extra Help: One-Year Limit on Remedial Work at CUNY Dismays Many." *The New York Times,* July 1, p. A21.

Riesman, D. 1953. *Thorstein Veblen: A Critical Interpretation.* New York: Scribner.

Ross, K. 1990. "Eight Myths about Minorities in Higher Education." *College Board Review* 155:12-19, 45.

Rudenstine, N. L. 1997. "Point of View: The Internet and Education—A Close Fit." *Chronicle of Higher Education,* February 21, p. A48.

Schmid, T. J. 1992. "Classroom-Based Ethnography: A Research Pedagogy." *Teaching Sociology* 20:28-35.

Sharkey, S. R. 1992. "Assessment as a Conversation about Teaching." Pp. 26-55 in *Assessing Undergraduate Learning in Sociology,* edited by S. R. Sharkey and W. S. Johnson. Washington, DC: ASA Teaching Resources Center.

———. 1996. "Who's 'Sitting Beside' Whom? Language and Politics in Assessing Students' Learning." *Teaching Sociology* 24:122-26.

Smith, D. G., D. E. Morrison, and L. E. Wolf. 1994. "College as a Gendered Experience: An Empirical Analysis Using Multiple Lenses." *Journal of Higher Education* 65:696-725.

Sorcinelli, M. D. and C. D. Brell. 1990. "Dealing with Troublesome Behavior in the Classroom." Unpublished manuscript, Center for Teaching, University of Massachusetts at Amherst.

Statham, A., L. Richardson, and J. A. Cook. 1991. *Gender and University Teaching: A Negotiated Difference.* Albany: State University of New York Press.

Stern, D. and Y. Nakata. 1991. "Paid Employment among U.S. College Students." *Journal of Higher Education* 62:25-43.

Stewart, J. W. 1995. "Remedial Cal State Students Blame School System." *The Los Angeles Times,* January 8, p. B1.

Thompson, M. E. 1993. "Building Groups on Students' Knowledge and Experience." *Teaching Sociology* 21:95-99.

Tinto, V. 1985. "Dropping Out and Other Forms of Withdrawal from College." Pp. 28-43 in *Increasing Student Retention,* edited by L. Noel, R. Levitz, D. Saluri, and Associates. San Francisco: Jossey-Bass.

———. 1988. "Stages of Student Departure: Reflections on the Longitudinal Character of Students Leaving." *Journal of Higher Education* 59:438-55.

Vanden Brook, T. 1996. "Increase in Student Borrowing Troubles College Administrators." *Milwaukee Journal Sentinel,* October 2, p. B2.

Veblen, T. 1918. *The Higher Learning in America: A Memorandum on the Conduct of Universities by Businessmen.* New York: Viking.

Weimer, M. 1988. "Ideas for Managing Your Classroom Better." *The Teaching Professor,* February, pp. 3-4.

"The Widening Gap in Higher Education: A Special Report." 1996. *Chronicle of Higher Education,* June 14, pp. A10-A17.

Wilson, R. 1997. "Faculty Leaders in N.Y. and California Unite on Productivity Issues." *Chronicle of Higher Education,* February 28, p. A12.

Wolfe, A. 1996. *Marginalized in the Middle.* Chicago: University of Chicago Press.

Wood, J. 1997. "Tenure under Attack: Recent Problems and Solutions." *Pacific Sociologist* (May 6).

Yamane, D. 1996. "Collaboration and Its Discontents: Steps toward Overcoming Barriers to Successful Group Projects." *Teaching Sociology* 24:378-83.

Yonke, Eric. 1997. "Technology and the Humanities: Can Multimedia Education Transform Liberal Learning?" *Teaching Forum,* April, pp. 6-8. (Undergraduate Teaching Improvement Council, University of Wisconsin System)

York-Anderson, D. C. and S. L. Bowman. 1991. "Assessing the College Knowledge of First-Generation and Second-Generation College Students." *Journal of College Student Development* 32:112-16.

Zweigenhaft, R. L. 1991. "The Accumulation of Cultural and Social Capital: The Differing College Careers of Prep School and Public School Graduates." Unpublished manuscript, Gilford College, Greensboro, NC.

———. 1992. "The Application of Social and Cultural Capital: A Study of the 25th Reunion Entries of Prep School and Public School Graduates of Yale College." *Higher Education* 23:311-20.

———. 1993. "Prep School and Public School Graduates of Harvard: A Longitudinal Study of the Accumulation of Social and Cultural Capital." *Journal of Higher Education* 64:211-25.

PART II

Mapping Issues in the Social Worlds of Higher Education

Arguments from the Inside

The critiques of higher education have not come simply from the outside. The very nature of academic work leads to critical analyses, and the very structure of colleges and universities leads to different constituencies and issues of concern. The students, the faculty, and the administration all constitute, to some degree, different communities with unique cultures. Furthermore, within these communities, there are clear distinctions in viewpoints and behaviors. Understanding the points of both agreement and disagreement within these communities is of great importance. Of even greater significance is how individuals in these communities view the nature and meaning of the relationships forged within and between their memberships.

We have chosen to call these the "social worlds" of higher education to be consistent with our topographical metaphor and to highlight the network ties inherent in the day-to-day life of higher education. Social worlds emphasize the complexity of the different roles that professors hold—as teachers, colleagues, citizens, and unique individuals—and the myriad social relationships in which they are involved in higher education. This second part of our book, then, follows four themes organized around the social worlds in which professors participate and the key social relations that define obligations and expectations within academia. We begin this part, as we did the first part, with a controversial statement that strikes at the heart of the debate. We begin Part II and each of the sections on the social worlds with a Trudeau cartoon that, characteristically, captures a key tension in the debates about what we teach, how we teach, and what type of relationship we establish with our colleagues and our students.

Here, at the start of Part II, Trudeau's cartoons repeatedly remind us of the various ways in which a consumerist mentality on the part of students can undermine higher education. Such a mentality, according to Mark Edmundson, is what most students bring to the classroom. In his unflattering portrait, the current generation of students are passive, cautious, and unenthusiastic consumers who are unwilling to take risks or be criticized and who expect to be entertained and diverted rather than challenged and educated. The culture of the university, he believes, reinforces this consumerist ethos, as is evident in its physical layout, college brochures, relaxed grades and requirements, and celebrity graduation speakers.

Edmundson's views undoubtedly are shaped by his institutional location at an elite private research university, where he admittedly comes into contact with few low-income or first-generation students. Nevertheless, consumerist attitudes and values are widespread, and they present a serious challenge to a faculty committed to teaching critical thinking.

Edmundson's celebration of genius may be one path to critical thinking, but the danger is that it lends itself to an individualized and elitist solution rather than to a collective one. The solution, in our view, is not simply for professors to champion the appreciation of genius but also to reorganize higher education along the lines suggested by advocates of learning communities. By creating new forms of community and developing strong programs of community service learning, we can hallenge both the competitive individualism and the consumerism that impede the teaching and learning of critical thinking.

The Debate: On the Uses of a Liberal Education— As Lite Entertainment for Bored College Students

Mark Edmundson

It's a lack of capacity for enthusiasm that defines what I've come to think of as the reigning generational style. Whether the students are sorority fraternity types, grunge aficionados, piercer/tattooers, black or white, rich or middle class (alas, I teach almost no students from truly poor backgrounds), they are, nearly across the board, very, very, self-contained. On good days, they display a light, appealing glow; on bad days, shuffling disgruntlement. But there's little fire, little passion to be found.

How did my students reach this peculiar state in which all passion seems to be spent? I think that many of them have imbibed their sense of self from consumer culture in general and from the tube in particular. They're the progeny of 100 cable channels and omnipresent Blockbuster outlets. TV, Marshall McLuhan famously said, is a cool medium. Those who play best on it are low-key and nonassertive; they blend in. Enthusiasm quickly looks absurd. The form of character that's most appealing on TV is calmly self-interested though never greedy, ttuned to the conventions, and ironic. Judicious timing is preferred to sudden self-assertion. The TV medium is inhospitable to inspiration, mprovisation, failures, and slipups. All must run perfectly.

Naturally, a cool youth culture is a marketing bonanza for producers of the right products, who do all they can to enlarge that culture and keep it grinding. The Internet, TV, and magazines now teem with what I call persona ads, ads for Nikes and Reeboks and Jeeps and Blazers that don't so much endorse the capacities of the product per se as show you what sort of person you will be once you've acquired it. The Jeep ad that features hip, outdoorsy kids whipping a Frisbee from mountaintop to mountaintop isn't so much about what Jeeps can do as it is about the kind of people who own them. Buy a Jeep and be one with them. The ad is of little consequence in itself, but expand its message exponentially and you have the central thrust of current consumer culture—buy in order to be.

Most of my students seem desperate to blend in, to look right, not to make spectacles of themselves. (Two students having an argument under the portico turned out to be acting in a role-playing game.) The specter of the uncool creates a subtle tyranny. It's apparently an easy standard to subscribe to, this Letterman-like, Tarantino-like cool, but once committed to it, you discover that matters are rather different. You're inhibited, except on ordained occasions, from showing emotion, stifled from trying to achieve anything original. You're made to feel that even the slightest departure from the reigning code will get you genially ostracized. This is a culture tensely committed to a laid-back norm.

One of the lessons that consumer hype tries to insinuate is that we must never rebel against the new, never even question it. If it's new—a new need, a new product, a new show, a new style, a new generation—it must be good. So maybe, even at the risk of winning the withered, brown laurels of crankdom, it pays to resist newness worship and cast a colder eye.

Praise for my students? I have some of that too. What my students are, at their best, is decent. They are potent believers in equality. They help out at the soup kitchen and volunteer to tutor poor kids to get stripes on their resumes, sure. But they also want other people to have a fair shot. And in their commitment to fairness, they are discerning; there you see them at their intellectual best. If I were on trial and innocent, I'd want them on the jury.

What they will not generally do, though, is indict the current system. They won't talk about how the exigencies of capitalism lead to a reserve army of the unemployed and nearly inevitable misery. That would be getting too loud, too brash. For the pervading view is the cool consumer perspective, where passion and strong admiration are forbidden. "To stand in awe of nothing, Numicus, is perhaps the one and only thing that can make a man happy and keep him so," says Horace in the *Epistles,* and I fear that his lines ought to hang as a motto over the university in this era of high consumer capitalism.

Doonesbury

BY GARRY TRUDEAU

The Social World of Professors and Their Students: A First Glimpse

The central relationship in higher education is the one between teacher and student. As is shown by Trudeau's rendering of a typical classroom activity, handing back papers, these perspectives often are not in sync and make little sense to either party. Part of the debates in the past 20 years have centered on who our students are, what they are like, what they want, and what we believe they should get from higher education. These debates, while centering on students, most often involve differing opinions about our students. In this section, we asked our authors to take on some debates about students and our approach to them. Every attempt to teach centers on students and requires shared understandings between students and faculty about what we are doing and how we are going to do it. Students and faculty occupy different social worlds and often are separated from their students by generational, racial, ethnic, class, and gender differences. Given these barriers to communication, which are compounded by the exercise of power and authority, dialogues based on trust and mutual understanding appear difficult. Yet, successful teachers have managed to overcome these barriers. They connect with their students in invigorating and energizing teaching and learning experiences. The authors in this section suggest that such experiences are more likely when we move beyond the dyadic teacher-student relationship and exercise our professorial authority in creative and cooperative ways that tap into students' motivations, experiences, learning styles, and desires. A number of authors suggest that empowering experiences can be generated by the creation of participatory learning communities that acknowledge the civic responsibilities entailed by democratic values. Democracy presupposes communication rooted in mutual respect, an appreciation of cultural differences, and a willingness to question our own cherished beliefs and to entertain opposing views.

A cardinal rule of good teaching is to know your audience. This is not easy. It requires that we understand what our students bring with them into the classroom. This can be accomplished by incorporating active and experiential learning activities into our teaching methods. The essays in this section discuss students' prior knowledge and experience, student responsibilities to the larger community, ways in which professors can exercise their authority within classrooms to maximize student learning, and the importance of attending to learning styles to fulfill our responsibilities to minority students.

One of the book's basic premises is that knowledge from social sciences can assist us in improving learning by students and satisfaction of faculty. Diane F. Halpern (Chapter 7) provides one such contribution from cognitive psychology, on the need to understand learning processes better. Her account emphasizes the failure of traditional pedagogies to enable students to apply the principles they learn in the classroom to the real world. Halpern suggests that professors need to use diverse teaching methods for different types of learning and be more attentive to the prior knowledge and experiences, and to the implicit and explicit beliefs, that students bring to the classroom. In a similar way, Paul Baker (Chapter 8), a sociologist, argues that new forms of community are necessary to advance student and faculty learning and to grapple with problems of low teacher morale and limited faculty involvement with students. The solution, he argues, must be communal rather than individual or technical. It requires the creation of supportive communities that extend beyond the classroom into departmental structures and university-community partnerships. Baker lays out a set of principles on which such learning communities can be built and suggests a variety of skills and dispositions that facilitate their creation. The creation of learning communities entails a major reorganization of our institutions and a ethinking of curricula, pedagogy, and the current structure of time and space within academia. Given the scope of necessary changes, some critics might dismiss Baker's vision as "utopian." However, Thomas A. Angelo (Chapter 9), named recently as one of higher education's younger leaders, provides persuasive evidence that the forces that can produce meaningful learning communities already are present in higher education. The seeds of change, he argues, already exist in the form of numerous concrete "levers" that will foster the transformation.

Donald L. Finkel and G. Stephen Monk (Chapter 10) suggest that the problem extends beyond the consumerist culture of students to the individualistic culture of the faculty. Their diagnosis identifies an "Atlas complex" that leads teachers to dominate their classrooms, remain cut off from what students know and do not know, and bear a heavy burden of responsibility. Their solution, student-student interaction and collaborative group learning, does not entail faculty abdication of authority but rather entails sharing responsibilities and exercising authority in different ways. As many of us know from experience, successful learning groups require extensive preparation to guide discussion and give structure to interaction in a manner that effectively differentiates and redistributes teaching functions.

A pedagogy of active and experiential learning designed to foster critical thinking provides an alternative way in which to confront the passivity and consumerism of our students. The goal is to foster what Richard Paul (Chapter 11) labels the "intellectual virtues" of humility, courage, empathy, integrity, perseverance, faith in reason, and a sense of justice (fair-mindedness). Paul argues that attainment of this goal will require the transformation of our teaching, as well as our curricula, away from superficially absorbed content and shallow coverage and in the direction of depth, fundamental ideas, synthesis, and the empathetic appreciation of alternative viewpoints.

The creation of learning communities promises to solve yet another pressing problem facing higher education, the alarmingly high attrition rates of minority students. James A. Vasquez and Nancy Wainstein (Chapter 12) argue that greater attention to learning styles not only will improve the overall quality of education but also will meet the needs of minority students, who are ill served by culturally inappropriate pedagogies. They suggest a number of instructional strategies involving greater attentiveness to student motivations, values, and learning styles; high expectations; cultural sensitivity; and cooperative and active learning.

Although most readers are likely to sympathize with their call for faculty to acknowledge responsibilities to minority students, some might question their assumptions of cultural difference and point to the diversity that exists among minority populations.

7

The War of the Worlds: Why Psychology Helps Bridge the Gap between Students' and Professors' Conceptual Understanding

Diane F. Halpern

If you like horror stories, this one should terrify you. In a random telephone survey of more than 2,000 adults, conducted by the Public Opinion Laboratory at Northern Illinois University, 21 percent of the respondents said they believed that the sun revolved around the earth; an additional 7 percent said they did not know which revolved around which.

I have no doubt that virtually all of these adults were taught in school that the earth revolves around the sun; they may even have written it on a test. But, in fact, they never altered their incorrect mental models of planetary motion because their everyday observations didn't support what their teachers told them. People see the sun "moving" across the sky as morning turns into night, and the earth seems stationary while that is happening.

Students can learn the right answers, even recite them in class, and yet never incorporate

them into their working models of the world. The objectively correct answer that the professor accepts and the student's personal understanding of the world can exist simultaneously, each unaffected by the other. Outside of class, the student continues to use the personal model because it has always worked well in that context. Unless professors address specific errors in their students' naive models of the world, the students are not likely to replace their own models with the correct one promoted by professors.

Students' personal notions of how the world works influence what they learn in every academic discipline. In a now classic study conducted in the late 1970s, two University of Minnesota psychologists, Mark Snyder and Seymour Uranowitz, presented short stories about a woman named Betty to two groups of undergraduates. The stories were identical, except that one group read an additional sentence in which [group members] were told that "Betty is now a lesbian."

One week later, the students returned for a test on the story they had read. The group that had read that Betty was a lesbian was much

AUTHOR'S NOTE: This is a reprint of an article originally published as Halpern, Diane F., "The War of the Worlds: When Students' Conceptual Understanding Clashes With Their Professors," *Chronicle of Higher Education,* March 14, 1997, pp. 84-85. Used with permission.

more likely than the other group to recall reading that "Betty never dated men." In fact, both groups had read that she dated men occasionally. Students' beliefs about the world—in this example, about lesbians—influenced what they recalled from a simple story.

Perhaps one more example will convince you. Have you ever waited with a group of people for an elevator? Invariably, someone will keep pushing the call button. If you ask the button-pushers why they continue pushing, they will explain their belief that the elevator will come more quickly if it "knows" they are impatient. This sort of naive belief is highly resistant to change because it is repeatedly confirmed in real life. In fact, after an interval of button-pushing, the elevator arrives, just as the button-pusher predicted.

Cognitive psychology provides models of human learning and knowing—that is, how people acquire, organize, retrieve, and use information—that can help us teach students to put aside their naive models of the world. To educate our students successfully, we must incorporate into our teaching an understanding of the way in which learners organize knowledge and represent it internally and the way in which these representations resist change when learners encounter new information.

But despite all that cognitive psychologists now know about what happens when people learn, urban planner Donald Schön's observation in *The Reflective Practitioner* remains true: most teachers "have gained relatively little from cognitive psychology." It seems that even cognitive psychologists apply to their teaching very little of what they know about their academic discipline. The gap between empirically validated theory and practice is wide. One of my favorite examples of this is the deadly dull three-hour lecture I once sat through on the shortness of people's attention spans.

Let me suggest some basic principles of human cognition that should serve as a guide for college-level instruction:

- What and how much students learn in any situation depends heavily on their prior knowledge and experience. We must not think of our students as blank slates, but as slates that may need to be edited, updated, and revised to reflect new, correct information.

- To change students' incorrect or incomplete mental models, we need to understand their implicit and explicit beliefs and design our instruction so that we expose the errors explicitly and make the benefits of the new models obvious. Otherwise, students may be able to produce a correct answer on a test, but their underlying understanding of the phenomenon involved may not change.

- Learning and remembering involve multiple, interdependent processes. No single set of learning principles will help all students learn in every situation, particularly because what Students learn and recall partly depends on what they already "know." So educators must be prepared to use different pedagogical methods if they see that their students are having trouble absorbing and retaining information. Some types of learning—such as mastering the plot of a popular movie—occur without our conscious awareness; the learning seems effortless and automatic. Other types—such as memorizing the names of the facial nerves or understanding how to multiply in matrix algebra—require a great deal of concerted effort and may call for a variety of teaching methods.

- Experience often "teaches" us things that are, in fact, wrong, but our daily lives do not always provide immediate feedback that demonstrates the errors. To promote critical thinking about the judgments we make, educators need to provide systematic and corrective feedback. For example, research indicates that most jurors believe that they can tell from a person's demeanor whether she or he is telling the truth. Yet Paul Ekman, a psychologist at the University of California, San Francisco, who studies lying, has found that people generally can't tell when someone is being truthful or not. We may not find out that someone has lied to us, though, and without evidence that our judgments about someone's honesty have been wrong in the past, we are overconfident about our ability to detect deceit. A technique that Ekman has used successfully to dispel students' assumptions about this ability is to have convincing liars "testify" to law students during a class—and later on in the session admit their deceit.

- Because students frequently fail to apply what we have taught them in class to the real world, we must focus part of our teaching on "transferability." For instance, virtually all students who have taken courses in social sciences or statistics can tell you that a correlation between two variables doesn't necessarily mean that a change in one variable causes a change in the other. Most students who have had course work on this topic can compute a correlation coefficient for a set of data and provide examples of positively and negatively correlated variables. But when, for example, they read a newspaper report of a study that found that children who eat breakfast are better readers by the end of first grade, many of these same students don't recognize that eating breakfast did not necessarily cause the first graders to be better readers. Making frequent use of real-life examples in class helps students recognize the principles we are teaching when they encounter them operating outside of school.

Applying these principles of cognitive psychology in our classrooms can begin at the start of each semester. The teacher can start by having students give their own explanations of the subject to be studied—for example, state how they believe selected topics in psychology are linked, describe what would happen if a certain chemical were heated, or explain how they would determine the value of a variable. Students often are surprised to discover that they already have beliefs about such topics.

Then the teacher can present the facts, stressing the ways in which reality is similar to or different from the students' initial understanding of it. Using a few real-world examples that require the students to apply underlying principles will help ensure the replacement of [the] old understanding with correct information. Later in the semester, the teacher can again ask the students for their own explanations of important principles and how their understanding differs from their original conceptions. Having students reflect on their prior knowledge, [their] subsequent learning, and their current understanding increases the likelihood that they will internalize what they are taught in class.

The most important reason for making sure that our students can apply to the real world what we are trying to teach them in class is that the world is changing at an accelerating rate. As specific situations change, the importance of the underlying principles—and students' ability to recognize and apply them to new settings—becomes even more critical.

Demand is increasing for a new type of employee, sometimes called "knowledge workers" or "symbol analysts." They need to be able to carry out multistep operations, manipulate abstract symbols and ideas, acquire new information efficiently, and remain flexible enough to recognize new paradigms. If we fail to address the fact that too many students leave our classrooms unable to transfer principles and understanding to new domains of knowledge, we will create a workforce for tomorrow that is superbly prepared only for yesterday's problems.

8

Creating Learning Communities: The Unfinished Agenda

Paul Baker

Professors in the social sciences live a double life as members of a discipline dedicated to study of human affairs and as participants of various groups found in the academy. However, theories and research on human groups, for example, often have failed to inform our practice as teachers in the classroom, colleagues in the department, and contributors to the shared governance of our colleges and universities. In Wilson's (1985) words, "We belong to the knowledge professions, college and university teachers, yet our work proceeds in dark ignorance" (p. 25). The gap between theory and practice is further complicated by the continuous turmoil surrounding institutions of higher education at the end of the 20th century. How can academics gain a better understanding of their organizational workplace and translate that understanding into new commitments to build viable workgroups of mindful engagement for students and faculty alike? One response to this question calls for a sociological lens to examine the sociologist's place of work. I focus on the need for new forms of community inside and beyond the academy. Furthermore, I argue that the challenging agenda of building

learning communities is an essential step in the larger goal of advancing student and faculty learning. Before proposals for community building are presented, I want to call attention to the current state of affairs in higher education.

The Lonely Work of Teaching

Anyone who takes a serious and honest look at education in America at any level, kindergarten through graduate school, will encounter endless reports and documented cases of a serious crisis. Although the rhetorical claims of "good teaching" often accompany awards to "outstanding teachers," the same colleges and universities often are hiring a reserve army of temporary instructors who receive poverty wages for their work. The morale of teachers seems to be at a new low. Teachers often feel overextended and underappreciated. The work often seems mindless and mechanical. On too many occasions, it is boring and dispiriting to both teachers and students. The heart of the crisis in American education is the lonely work of teachers who often feel disconnected from administrators, colleagues, and many of their students.

The crisis of isolated teachers is not new. Waller (1932) conducted the pioneering re-

EDITORS' NOTE: For ideas on learning groups, see Creative Ways of Engaging Students subsection in the *Fieldguide* (particularly Weast; Wright; McKinney and Graham-Buxton; Lerner).

search in this field in the 1920s (*Sociology of Teaching*). In the 1950s and 1960s, Sputnik and the civil rights movement inspired a wave of school reforms, but subsequent study of these initiatives led to sobering conclusions about the difficulties of meaningful change in educational organizations. Two books in particular documented the problem: Sarason's (1971) *The Culture of Schools and the Problem of Change* and Lortie's (1975) *School-Teacher*. The central problem of both books is the isolated, fragmented, and privatized world of teaching. These classic studies offer significant insights to students of higher education (Baker 1986).

In the second half of the 20th century, public schools are not alone in facing the challenges of educational change. The Vietnam War and the student protest movement generated considerable interest in reforming colleges and universities. Sociologists such as Riesman, Gusfield, and Gamson (1971) documented the problems of disconnected youths and the prospects for new structures of shared community and engaged learning. It was an era of new reforms with residential colleges and interdisciplinary curricula. But the reforms faded by the 1970s, and recent observers such as Boyer (1990), Moffatt (1989), and Astin (1993) have written about serious problems of a fragmented community in our colleges and universities. In a national study, Massy, Wilker, and Colbeck (1994) observe, "For a myriad of reasons, faculty are unwilling or unable to communicate with one another" (p. 11). In most departments and on most campuses, they encountered "hollowed" collegiality. Relationships among faculty are superficial and "collegiality remains thwarted with regard to faculty engagement with issues of curricular structure, pedagogical alternatives, and student assessment" (p. 19).

My own inquiries at Illinois State University have documented the problem of lonely teachers on more than one occasion (Baker and Zey-Ferrell 1984; Zey-Ferrel and Baker 1984). Let me cite one case. I interviewed a random sample of 120 professors regarding their work as teachers and researchers and the networks of support that they relied on to sustain their work. Distinct patterns emerged from these interviews. First, research work involved very elaborate and strong networks of collaboration inside the university and throughout the nation (indeed, the world). Professors who engage in research are continually consulting and collaborating with fellow researchers wherever they can be found. But teaching is different. Teaching generates very few occasions of active collaboration either inside the university or beyond.

My interviews suggested that there are two ideal types of lonely teachers. First, there are "splendid isolationists" who affirm the American values of rugged individualism. These self-confident teachers see no need to consult with anyone about issues of teaching, learning, or assessing student work. In one of my interviews, I asked a professor whether he ever consulted with his colleagues about teaching. He seemed puzzled. "No," he said, "I am the best teacher in the department. Who would I talk to?" The second type of lonely teacher is strikingly different. These are "demoralized loners" who consult with no one because they carry bitter disappointments about their students and colleagues. They feel very lonely and are sure that no one at the university cares about them. When they were asked about networks of support that sustained their teaching, they mentioned no one inside the academic world. On occasion, they expressed appreciation for a spouse or a close friend.

I also know the moments of loneliness as a teacher. Several years ago, I worked hard to revise a course, making it more rigorous, intellectually exciting, relevant, and worthwhile. I came to class the first day full of enthusiasm, and my students responded with a chorus of complaints. I was making them work too hard. My writing assignments were wrong. This was not an English course. I felt rejected by the very people I wanted to know. I came back to my office with a sense of defeat and disgust. I sat at my desk dejected. That day, I had picked up a Gideon's Bible that was on my desk. I began to skim through it aimlessly. I came to the second chapter of proverbs: "Wisdom utters her voice in the streets. . . . How long ye simple ones? You fools of knowledge. . . . I will laugh at your calamity; I will mock when your fear cometh. . . . Your destruction will come as a whirlwind." I felt better. Divine powers would deal with those know-nothing students.

How is it that we who teach often seem disconnected from the students we have come to serve? And why do we remain silent with our colleagues on issues of teaching? These questions are grounded in a keen awareness of the idealism we brought with us as teachers. We often sense a gap between the ideals we brought to our teaching careers and the subsequent experiences of isolation and marginality. What is to be done on behalf of teaching and learning? How do we move from loneliness and despair to community and hope? There are no quick answers to these questions—no magic wands, no silver bullets, no quickstep solutions.

There are no fail-safe formulas for overcoming the problems of faculty isolation. One of the ironies of this situation is that many faculty members do not believe their isolation is a problem to worry about. Nevertheless, I argue that conditions of hollowed collegiality and limited involvement with students are serious challenges to the academy. Teachers can respond to these challenges, in part, by turning to the work of social scientists who have identified the critical tasks of developing productive groups in which participants are guided by common goals, a strong sense of interdependence, sustained commitment to attainable

results, and continuous renewal. I want to examine some of this literature by presenting a heuristic framework for the revitalization of teaching and learning. I define this practical model as a learning community.

The Idea of a Learning Community

The idea of a learning community requires a fundamental shift of mind about relationships among teachers, students, and administrators. It rejects the long-standing assumptions of individualism that have dominated educational debate for many decades. For example, the problems of public schools often are attributed to one source—teachers. The problems are individual and technical. Teachers do not know much (they have weak intellects), and they do not know how to teach what little they know (they have limited skills). The solution follows: fix the teachers. Get rid of the bad ones (through screening tests and technical evaluations), and raise the standards for those who stay and are recruited in coming years.

In universities, the problems of education also are individualistic and rather simpleminded. Now, the culprit is not the teachers but rather the students (who were poorly educated in the schools by inept teachers). The professors are fine; they have impressive credentials to prove their intelligence and expert capacities. The problems are ill-prepared students and bureaucratically inclined administrators.

On occasion for brief periods of time, colleges and universities have looked on teachers as the problem. In the 1970s, foundations became interested in the problems of retrenchment facing college teachers. Millions of dollars were spent on "teaching-learning centers." Illinois State University had such a center supported by the Kellogg Foundation. I was assigned to the center for two years as a "teaching fellow." We fellows had office hours at the center to consult with teachers who were invited to come by to discuss their teaching problems. But few teachers stopped in for advice. The fellows often discussed their limited clientele. Why did teachers not stop by to get "fixed"? One of my colleagues explained our situation: "The teaching-learning center is the venereal disease (VD) clinic for teachers. Who wants to admit they have VD if they can hide it?" In short, Illinois State University had individualized the problems of teaching and learning and had privatized the solution.

In schools, colleges, and universities, the problems of teaching and learning often are reduced to individuals (either teachers or students) who have various deficits in knowledge, skills, and motivation. The solutions that are recommended often are technical (e.g., greater training, more computer technology, additional requirements for the information explosion, new tests to screen out the incompetent or to certify achievement). The blame is found in individuals who must be fixed or punished. We live in an age of individualism, and we clamor for technical solutions to our educational problems.

The fundamental problems of education are not individual or technical but rather communal. Because the basic problems are communal, we must shift our focus to broader and more complex issues that involve the formation of productive groups and the creation of supportive communities. In short, sociologists and others are challenged to address the tasks of building learning communities. What do I mean by the term *learning community?* Let me respond briefly by examining both terms (*learning* and *community*) and then connecting them as a joint term (*learning community*).

Learning

I begin with a basic assumption borrowed from numerous scholars at the turn of the century such as Lev Vygotsky, George Herbert Mead, and John Dewey. Learning and human development always are embedded in a social and cultural context. I appreciate Rogoff's (1990) metaphor that children (as well as adults) are best understood as "apprentices in thinking." They are "active in their efforts to learn from observing and participating with peers and more skilled members of their society, developing skills to handle culturally defined problems with available tools, and building from these givens to construct new solutions within the context of sociocultural activity" (p. 7). We are born as utterly dependent creatures, and much that we need as functioning adults can be acquired only through the mechanisms of social and cultural transmission. The only way in which we can learn is from fellow humans.

Furthermore, the need to learn never stops throughout our lifetimes. We are necessarily lifelong learners, and the experiences of learning are continuous and relational. The developmental psychologist, Alan Fogel, argues that all thinking and learning can be seen as embodied cognitions in social settings:

The human mind and sense of self must . . . be understood as evolving out of the historical process of personal relationship formation between the self and other individuals. Upon close examination, one finds that the workings of the mind and ways in which we perceive and understand ourselves is remarkably like the form of our personal relationships. (Fogel 1993:4)

I have just stated taken-for-granted truths of the sociological tradition. Teaching and learning are communal activities. Yet, the full implications of these ideas rarely are taken into account by those who design formal learning settings in places such as schools, colleges, and universities.

Community

This term is terribly elusive. It is like other important key words—art, democracy, morality, creativity, and the like. We keep probing the meaning of the term without being definitive. In recent years, there has been a renewed interest in community (Bellah et al. 1985; Etzioni 1993). My own thoughts borrow heavily from Selznick (1992), who insists that community does not presume territory or locality and that it can vary in size from an international group of scientists to a research team in a laboratory. It is a group that can have a great deal of variation on various aspects of community. Community is not an "all or nothing" proposition. According to Selznick, "The emergence of community depends on the opportunity, and the impulse toward, comprehensive interaction, commitment, and responsibility" (p. 359). In terms of this chapter, I focus on the relatively small groups of personal interaction that allow people to sort out the good, the bad, and the ugly. Naroll (1983) calls these groups "moralnets." I accept his premise that the vitality and well-being of a society, its institutions, and its members depend on a rich array of strong communal groups.

Learning Community

There are many people who write about learning communities (Christensen, Garvin, and Sweet 1991; Gabelnick et al. 1990). The term has many meanings. I use the term to mean a relatively small group that may include students, teachers, administrators, and others who have a clear sense of membership, common goals, and the opportunity for extensive face-to-face interaction. The definition includes groups such as classrooms, laboratories, committees, advisory groups, interdisciplinary teaching teams, participatory action research teams, schools, residential colleges, and aca-demic departments. These groups are not necessarily learning communities, but all have the potential (with varying degrees of development) to become learning communities.

There are two fundamental features of a learning community.

All members of the group are learners. In a learning community, everyone is given opportunities and is expected to be a fully engaged learner. Stratified positions are not used to separate some members as "learned" (experts) and others as "ignorant" (novices). Although group members have different levels of authority, knowledge, and skill, all are defined as learners—students, staff, teachers, administrators, parents, and community members. All members are appreciated as participants in the community; part of the meaning of participation is the willingness to learn and the opportunity to teach others.

The group is organized to learn as a whole system. Group learning is as important as individual learning. The group learns as a whole team by having members share common assumptions, goals, information, and decisions. Hidden agendas are anathema. Members work together in collaborative tasks such as finding problems, collecting and analyzing data, solving problems, taking risks, setting priorities, making action plans, and celebrating the contributions and achievements of everyone.

Whereas the preceding definition of a learning community and its two basic features provides a framework for examining various workgroups, a few exemplary cases can illustrate the types of organizational learning I see as appropriate models for all teachers, kindergarten through graduate school. First, one of the best examples of a learning community is Dewey's laboratory school at the University of

Chicago in its formative years (1896-1904), when theories of learning were constantly tested in the real world of practice (Mayhew and Edwards 1936). Everyone worked hard, but they also shared in the excitement of creating a new learning environment for students and teachers alike.

A second special learning community is the Highlander School founded by Myles Horton in the 1930s (Horton 1990). For many decades, Highlander was the training center for labor organizers and civil rights leaders such as Rosa Parks and Martin Luther King, Jr. The training emphasized dialogue among fellow participants as well as among those who opposed their aims. Horton borrowed many ideas from Dewey. He once wrote Dewey a letter of appreciation but explained that he was not a disciple. Dewey wrote back, "I'm so delighted to find that you don't claim to be a disciple. My enemies are bad enough, but my disciples are worse" (p. 45). There is little room for dogmatic allegiance in learning communities.

Communal Principles of Learning Communities

There is no comprehensive theory of learning communities. In this section, I identify six salient themes that provide some of the scaffolding for building a learning community. I mention these themes as an exploratory exercise in constructing a set of working concepts to guide the work of theory and practice.

Communication and the Power of Dialogue

In recent years, several students of highly effective groups have discovered the power of dialogue in communication among participants (Senge 1990; Isaacs 1994). Buber (1965) has developed a theory of dialogical relationships. His most widely recognized distinction is "I-Thou" and "I-It" relationships. "I-Thou is a relationship of openness, directness, mutuality, and presence," whereas "I-It, in contrast, is the typical subject-object relationship in which one knows and uses other persons or things without allowing them to exist . . . in their distinctive uniqueness" (Buber 1965, as quoted in Friedman et al. 1996:xiv). We necessarily have many I-It relationships in our daily lives. These relationships may be polite and civil, but under certain circumstances an I-Thou relationship may occur when I meet the other as a fully acknowledged person and the other responds in like fashion. This is a moment of dialogue that allows movement toward discovery, new understanding, insight, and sensitivity to participants. According to Burbules (1993), "Dialogue represents a continuous, developmental communicative interchange through which we stand to gain a fuller apprehension of the world, ourselves, and one another" (p. 8). In many respects, the next five themes are derived from the more encompassing ideas of the communicative act as dialogue (see also Habermas 1984).

Mutuality

A key aspect of dialogue is mutuality. In relationships of mutuality, there is genuine commitment to know the other person by "experiencing the other side." Such mutuality requires a willingness to explore issues that are important to other people, active listening, and the capacity to grasp the concreteness of others' experiences. According to Wilson (1985), teachers often ignore the lessons of mutuality. "Probably the greatest gulf between instructor and students derives from the instructor's ignorance of the extra-academic matters that preoccupy the student: sports, sex, family, religion, the shock of deviant behavior, relations with roommates, work demands, and the like" (p. 31). He goes on to suggest, for example, that sociology courses are ideal settings to explore the texture of student life. The multiple social realities in any sociology classroom can be seen as a gateway to studying broader social patterns of class, religion, gender, politics, and community.

Mindful Engagement

Mindful engagement is another aspect of learning communities. By this term, I mean the vital sense of presence in which participants relate to one another with honesty, energy, and an alertness to the situation (Langer 1989). In the field of theater, actors are aware of this issue; they use the phrase "to be in the moment." The opposite of "being in the moment" is the actor who is going through the lines without a sense of critical choices and creative energy intended by the playwright. Lev Vygotsky writes about mindful engagement in which the teacher creates social situations that are capable of "rousing the mind to life" (Tharp and Gallimore 1988).

Mindful engagement is the penetrating moment when participants are willing and able to stretch toward new opportunities to learn. Robert Park shares such an occasion from his college years. After a miserable freshman year at the University of Minnesota, he transferred to the University of Michigan. "It was Calvin Thomas, who was then teaching German at Michigan, who first taught me how poor a student I was. He returned my first class paper with the remark inserted that if my work was six times as good at the end of the semester as it was then that he could not pass me. Then I settled down to work" (quoted in Baker 1973:253). Thanks to Thomas, Park began his journey to become one of the most celebrated teachers in the history of sociology. His students praised him for the mindful engagement they encountered in his seminars.

Double-Loop Learning

The concept of double-loop learning originated with Bateson (1979), but Argyris (1993) has made extensive use of the term in his writing on learning organizations. Much learning in organizations is single loop. It is learning that asks, "What am I supposed to do?" In single-loop learning, the question is, "What does the boss want, and what do I do to please the boss?" But in double-loop learning, a new level of dialogue is encouraged. Double-loop learning asks, "Why should I (or anyone else) do this in the first place?" Double-loop inquiry raises a whole range of new questions about purpose, governing values, and larger issues of context. All questions are encouraged in open dialogue.

Many times, organizational norms inhibit the critical questions of double-loop learning from surfacing. One sits through a long meeting filled with tension and all types of hidden agendas, knowing full well that the real issues never will be discussed. Later in the parking lot, some of the same people will examine the same issues with a sense of energy, engagement, and uninhibited freedom. Argyris has suggested that sometimes members of groups in formal settings may have average IQs of about 120, but in their deliberations around the table, the IQs decline to about 65. How does one explain the discrepancy? In part, it is because people are not free to engage in double-loop learning.

Zone of Proximal Development

The concept of zone of proximal development (ZPD) was developed by Vygotsky in the early part of the 20th century (1978). According to Vygotsky (1978), children (and people at all age levels) have two levels of development: actual and potential. These two levels define the boundaries on the ZPD. As teachers interact with students, or as leaders interact with followers, there always are opportunities to enable learning to occur inside the ZPD. Good teachers and leaders learn to work inside the ZPD through continuous interaction that tests the capacity to move the zone toward new potential for learning.

My intuitive discovery of the ZPD occurred in my efforts to teach critical thinking to undergraduates. In my Social Problems class, I wanted students to read and think at the same time. For years, I was frustrated because I was teaching beyond the students' ZPD. I had to back up. We began with newspapers and commonsense conversations about social problems that made sense to students. Throughout the semester, we progressively moved to more complex thinking tasks with more sophisticated social science literature (Baker, Anderson, and Dorn 1993). But I had to start where the students were, not where I believed they should be. I taught by creating tension between their actual development and the next levels of advancement inside the ZPD. This is not teaching down to students; rather, it is teaching them realistically to new levels of achievement. The experience is not easy for either the teacher or the students; in many instances, it is a case of benign disruption (Baker and Jones 1976).

The Dialectic between Structure and Freedom

In learning communities, freedom and structure always need each other. Structure without freedom is stifling tyranny, but Freeman (1986) reminds us that we can suffer from the "tyranny of structurelessness." In recent years, organizational analysts have seen the simultaneous need for both structure and freedom. Weick (1978) writes about the need for tight and loose coupling, and Quinn (1988) writes about the dialectical connection between flexibility and control. In learning communities, participants honor the freedom of individ-

ual members while they simultaneously insist on the members honoring the necessary structures of the group. A. Bartlett Giamatti, former president of Yale University, identifies this dialectical tension in his description of the university as "a free and ordered space." In this world of freedom and order, a paradox is affirmed. "Independence is achieved through consenting to interdependence" (Giamatti 1988:82).

In learning communities, structure is crucial as a shared framework for dialogue. It provides the rules and roles that make sense to us as individuals and as a group. At the same time, these rules must allow considerable space for meaningful creativity on the part of members of the group. This freedom is necessary for the creativity, energy, enthusiasm, commitment, and capacity to solve complex problems. Nyden and his colleagues (1997) describe this balance in their Policy Research Action Group (PRAG). "PRAG has consciously walked the thin line between enough *structure* to get things done efficiently and enough *flexibility* so that it can be responsive to changing needs and to new ideas that emerge in the research and action process" (p. 23).

Academic Settings for Building Learning Communities

My discussion of learning communities has emphasized the interpersonal relationships in relatively small groups. Can the principles of shared learning found in these small settings be applied to larger and more complex systems such as colleges and universities? This is an important question, but even a cursory response exceeds the limits of this chapter. Rather than examine the critical issues of organizational learning in the university, I turn attention to three settings in which academics can play vital roles in fostering new opportunities for collaborative learning: the classroom, the department, and action research partnerships with community organizations.

The Classroom

College teaching has well-established conventions that are in sharp contrast to the communal principles of a learning community. For example, the habit of placing the professor in front of the room for a 50-minute lecture still is common practice. The only questions typically asked are, for example, "How do you spell Gemeinschaft?" or "What was the third point?" The custom of lecturing has attracted critics for many years. To quote Wilson's aphorism, "Telling is not teaching, and listening is not learning." Academic freedom is another convention of higher education, and teachers are not bound to classroom habits that maximize social isolation and diminish opportunities for active learning. The classroom is a "free and ordered space" for teachers who are willing to take risks of dialogical relationships with their students. Classrooms can be different, and teachers are in a position to practice their craft as builders of learning communities. Teachers who are inclined to explore various strategies of collaborative learning can turn to a substantial body of literature. Mention is made here of a few leading sources.

The intellectual pioneers of collaborative classrooms were Kurt Lewin and John Dewey. Their ideas were synthesized and tested by Herbert Thelen at the Human Dynamics Laboratory at the University of Chicago. Thelen (1954) applied these findings and insights to a wide range of classroom settings. His classic book, *Dynamics of Groups at Work,* still is worth careful study, but in recent years other educators have taken up the challenge of transforming the classroom (Joyce and Weil 1986). At Harvard University, several teachers who are committed to discussion teaching have written a series of thoughtful essays on the classroom as a learning community (Christensen et al. 1991). In various articles and an important book, Bruffee (1993) provides a wealth of practical wisdom and philosophical reflection on the promises of collaborative learning. The study of classrooms is vast; these references are the small tip of a huge iceberg.

The preceding references are taken from several disciplines. Attention is now given to the work of two sociologists. William Rau and Barbara Sherman Heyl have spent several years developing collaborative learning groups (CLGs) in their sociology classes (Rau and Heyl 1990; Heyl and Rau 1994). On the first day of class, they organize the students into small groups that typically range in size from four to six students. Students are expected to assume various work roles in their groups (e.g., discussion leader, report writer). Roles are rotated each week, and specific tasks are given each time the class meets. The major work of the groups is to discuss critically specific reading assignments. Students must complete the readings before coming to class and must be prepared to respond to a series of probing questions provided by the teacher. Initially, students work on these questions alone; then, they join their groups for deeper study and reflection. Deliberations of each group are recorded by the report writer. This is not a blow-off bull session. Members of the CLG are expected to create a report that is richer than individual responses to the same questions. It is to be richer in the sense that group reports have "more ideas or angles on the problem, more details, and more examples than any one person's individual worksheet" (Heyl and Rau 1994:1). Rau and Heyl assess both individual achievements and the collective achievements of the CLG.

According to Rau and Heyl, many benefits are derived from CLGs. Their research provides evidence that students learn more substantive content, have greater satisfaction with the course, and enjoy getting to know other students. Heyl and Rau (1994) also report a dramatic instance in which the CLG broke down the racial isolation of two polar groups in his Formal Organization class. The research findings and experiences of Heyl and Rau have been repeated many times by teachers who create collaborative learning environments. Collaborative learning can advance academic achievement and foster greater sociability in the classroom.

The Department

The department is the primary governing unit of the faculty. It is the place where critical decisions are made about teaching, learning, curriculum, recruitment of colleagues, and career advancement. It is a place of central importance, yet it rarely is defined as a learning community. One student of higher education, Alexander Astin, has argued that despite the relatively small size of departments, they actually are characterized by individualism, competition, and specialization. The challenge is to move beyond an aggregation of individual faculty members to a viable work group of common interests, shared responsibilities, and inclusive opportunities for students and staff. Any movement toward community building must incorporate a serious examination of the department's instructional agenda.

Robert Barr and John Tagg have made a persuasive case for the need for a new paradigm for undergraduate education. They define this paradigm as a shift from teaching to learning (Barr and Tagg 1995 [reprinted in Chapter 54 of this volume]). Their new paradigm is an ideal topic for debate in any department committed to the renewal of its educational mission. I am in strong agreement with their central thesis: departments must take responsibility for learn-

ing at the collective level as a department as well as at the individual level as faculty members. The department is not an aggregation of teachers; rather, it is a collective unit with collective accountability for student learning. It never is sufficient to define faculty work in terms of teaching. More important, open inquiry must be pursued on what students should learn and have actually learned.

Barr and Tagg (1995) have written a powerful polemic on the urgent need to enhance learning opportunities for students. Their polemic polarizes teaching versus learning. I prefer to see teaching and learning as one integral process that includes planning, actual practices, and evaluation of various outcomes. All aspects of the teaching-learning process should be open to departmental scrutiny—the goals of the curriculum articulated in various courses, the means of instruction practiced by faculty, and the assessment of learning outcomes demonstrated by meaningful gains in knowledge and skills. The process allows for continuous study and renewal. These ideas are not new (Goldsmid and Wilson 1980), but they remain crucial to the working agenda of academic departments committed to the principles of a learning community.

A critical question faces those who want to enhance learning opportunities for undergraduate students: how can department leaders mobilize broad, inclusive faculty commitments to the public work of teaching and learning? The task cannot be done by one or two faculty members who are identified as having a special interest in teaching. A complex work agenda awaits any department committed to disciplined inquiry and rigorous application of ideas that advance teaching and learning. At one level, all faculty might consider themselves to be generalists about a wide range of topics related to teaching and learning, but collaborative departments should go beyond the work of generalists. Various topics require concentrated study as theory and practice. Let me suggest a few topics to illustrate specialized inquiry by members of the department:

- Issues of assessment of student learning
- Small group processes that enhance learning
- Critical thinking and other topics of higher order reasoning
- Field-based learning opportunities for majors
- Effective use of new computer technologies
- Essential knowledge and analytical skills of all majors

These topics and others of interest to the faculty provide a working agenda for individuals and small task groups. A department with a graduate program would generate other topics of interest. Because the teaching and learning process, in all its complexity, is a common responsibility, everyone should find a topic or project that is both intellectually engaging and of genuine benefit to the department. Hopefully, specialization within the department does not lead to fragmentation but instead leads to integration. This is an ideal in all successful organizations.

University-Community Partnerships

The first generation of academic sociologists and their students often ventured into the larger community to participate in the social reforms of their day. They had strong ties to the social settlements, churches, and other agencies committed to improving social conditions for immigrants and the urban poor. By the 1920s and 1930s, this progressive agenda was passed on to the emerging profession of social work. Aca-

demic sociology turned to the systematic development of empirical methodologies and European social thought as more appropriate avenues for intellectual recognition. But each generation of academic sociologists has had a small group of social activists who kept the flame burning for a more direct and relevant role for sociology in the world of human affairs. Interest in social action research has been gaining momentum in the past quarter-century. In the 1990s, the commitment to community service and participatory action research has expanded on many fronts (Whyte 1991; Park 1993). These developments provide new opportunities to build learning communities that connect the university to the larger community.

Community building requires two parties to acknowledge gaps that separate them, even though they might share common interests and recognize the value of working together. Such gaps currently exist between academic sociologists and community leaders. Sociologists produce research about community problems, but community leaders frequently are unable to use the research in their attempt to solve local problems. New arrangements are needed to connect academic sociologists and community leaders in a partnership that is of mutual benefit to both parties. Nyden and his colleagues (1997) provide a framework for developing university-community collaborative research. This framework is grounded in years of dialogue between researchers and community activists. Their deliberations led to a new forum for planning and action—the Policy Action Research Group. PRAG is a network of collaborative arrangements among 4 universities and 15 community organizations in the Chicago metropolitan area. It is an exemplary case study of building learning communities that extend beyond the walls of the university.

In 1988, the John D. and Catherine T. MacArthur Foundation recognized the need to reassess its work with various community development programs in Chicago's neighborhoods. After much discussion with community leaders, city officials, and faculty with a special interest in urban affairs, the foundation sponsored a three-day conference, the writing of several position papers, and two think tanks to help design a new model for collaborative action research. PRAG solicited research ideas from community organizations, and 12 projects were funded. Each project had undergraduate or graduate interns, community organization staff, and university professors mentoring the interns. The projects ranged from writing a manual on toxic waste in neighborhoods to creating a blues/jazz historic cultural district. The participatory research action projects were highly successful, and leaders in community organizations and university faculty began to explore other possibilities for collaboration. "PRAG enabled professors and students to find research projects that allowed them to use their knowledge and skills at the same time [as] they were developing policy projects that would have a real impact on families and communities" (Nyden et al. 1997:22). In the past six years, PRAG has supported more than 130 projects. PRAG is one university-community collaborative network in one metropolitan area. Similar networks exist in Minneapolis, in Philadelphia, and statewide in Ohio. These networks and numerous university-community partnerships provide concrete evidence of building learning communities through participatory action research.

The Unfinished Agenda of Academia

The title of this chapter includes the subtitle "the unfinished agenda." This phrase has two meanings. First, each generation of teachers must reexamine their teaching agendas as pio-

neers who face a new challenge. Barzun (1991) writes of this aspect of the unfinished agenda: "The perpetual task of the educational reformer is to say: Look! Whatever your good intention was fifty years ago, it has now hardened into a deadly, oppressive, meaningless routine. Since you are not likely to capture the freshness of the former effort, let me urge a new effort" (p. 54). Teachers of sociology and other social sciences who research individual-group-organization linkages have the unfinished agenda of further developing the theoretical understanding and empirical research essential to improving the teaching-learning environments in which we work. As teachers, we have the opportunity to redesign the learning tasks in our classrooms and beyond. In short, there is an unfinished agenda of theory, research, and practice for those who are interested in building learning communities.

Creating learning communities is an unfinished agenda in another way: community building always is unfinished work. Let me quote Buber (1992) on this issue:

The empirical community is a dynamic fact. It does not take away [a person's] solitude but fills it, makes it positive. It thereby deepens the consciousness of responsibility for the individual. The community does not have its meaning in itself. (p. 86)

It is the abode where ultimate concerns can be known, where the deepest joys in life can be celebrated.

If one knows this, then one also knows that community in our time must ever again miscarry. The monstrous and dreadful phenomenon of individualism so prevails that one cannot simply bring about healing [and] rescue in one single blow. But the disappointments belong to the way. There is no other way than that of this miscarrying. (p. 86)

As professors who practice our craft in academic settings, we have the opportunity to belong to many learning communities. One of the joys of teaching is the joy of participating in learning communities. Numerous authors cited in this chapter write about the deep enjoyment they experience in their work as co-learners in collaborative settings. I accent joy. As William James reminds us, "To miss the joy is to miss all." There is no joy greater than building learning communities.

References

Argyris, Chris. 1993. *Knowledge for Action: A Guide to Overcoming Barriers to Organizational Change.* San Francisco: Jossey-Bass.

Astin, Alexander. 1993. "Higher Education and the Concept of Community." David Dodds Henry lecture (No. 15). Urbana-Champaign: University of Illinois.

Baker, Paul. 1973. "The Life Histories of W. I. Thomas and Robert Park." *American Journal of Sociology* 79:243-60.

———. 1986. "The Helter-Skelter Relationship of Teaching and Research." *Teaching Sociology* 14:50-66.

Baker, Paul, Louise Anderson, and Dean Dorn. 1993. *Social Problems: A Critical Thinking Approach.* 2d ed. Belmont, CA: Wadsworth.

Baker, Paul and Janet Jones. 1976. "Benign Disruption in the Classroom." *Teaching Sociology* 7:27-44.

Baker, Paul and Mary Zey-Ferrell. 1984. "Local and Cosmopolitan Orientations of Faculty: Implications for Teaching." *Teaching Sociology* 12:82-106.

Barr, Robert and John Tagg. 1995. "From Teaching to Learning: A New Paradigm for Undergraduate Education." *Change,* November-December, pp. 13-25.

Barzun, Jacques. 1991. *Begin Here: The Forgotten Conditions of Teaching and Learning.* Morris Philipson, ed. Chicago: University of Chicago Press.

Bateson, Gregory. 1979. *Mind and Nature.* New York: Bantam Books.

Bellah, Robert, Richard Madsen, William Sullivan, Ann Swidler, and Steven Tipton. 1985. *Habits of the Heart: Individualism and Commitment of American Life.* New York: Harper & Row.

Boyer, Ernest. 1990. *Campus Life: In Search of Community.* Princeton, NJ: Carnegie Foundation for the Advancement of Teaching.

Bruffee, Kenneth. 1993. *Collaborative Learning: Higher Education, Interdependence, and the Authority of Knowledge.* Baltimore, MD: Johns Hopkins University Press.

Buber, Martin. 1965. *Between Man and Man.* Ronald Gregor Smith, trans. New York: Macmillan.

———. 1992. *On Intersubjectivity and Cultural Creativity.* S. N. Eisenstadt, ed. Chicago: University of Chicago Press.

Burbules, Nicholas. 1993. *Dialogue in Teaching: Theory and Practice.* New York: Teachers College Press.

Christensen, Roland, David A. Garvin, and Ann Sweet, eds. 1991. *Education for Judgement: The Artistry of Discussion Leadership.* Boston: Harvard Business School Press.

Etzioni, Amitai. 1993. *The Spirit of Community.* New York: Crown.

Freeman, Jo. 1986. "The Tyranny of Structurelessness." Pp. 5-16 in *Untying the Knot: Feminism, Anarchism and Organization.* Montreal: Bevy of Anarchist/Feminists.

Friedman, Maurice, Pat Boni, Lawrence Baron, Seymour Cain, Virginia Shabatay, and John Stewart, eds. 1996. *Martin Buber and the Human Sciences.* Albany: State University of New York Press.

Fogel, Alan. 1993. *Developing through Relationships: Origins of Communication, Self, and Culture.* Chicago: University of Chicago Press.

Gabelnick, Faith, Jean MacGregor, Roberta S. Matthews, and Barbara Leigh Smith. 1990. "Learning Communities: Creating Connections among Students, Faculty, and Disciplines." In *New Directions for Teaching and Learning,* edited by Robert E. Young. San Francisco: Jossey-Bass.

Giamatti, A. Bartlett. 1988. *A Free and Ordered Space.* New York: Norton.

Goldsmid, Charles A., and Everett K. Wilson. 1980. *Passing on Sociology: The Teaching of a Discipline.* Belmont, CA: Wadsworth.

Habermas, Jürgen. 1984. *The Theory of Communicative Action.* Boston: Beacon.

Heyl, Barbara and William Rau. 1994. "Collaborative Learning Strategies: Implications for Creating Learning Communities in the Classroom." Paper presented at meeting of the Illinois Sociological Association, Peoria, IL, October.

Horton, Myles, with Judith Kohl and Herbert Kohl. 1990. *The Long Haul: An Autobiography.* New York: Doubleday.

Isaacs, William. 1994. "Dialogue." Pp. 357-64 in *The Fifth Discipline Fieldbook,* edited by Peter Senge, Art Kleiner, Charlotte Roberts, Richard Ross, and Bryan Smith. New York: Doubleday.

Joyce, Bruce and Marsha Weil. 1986. *Models of Teaching.* 3d ed. Englewood Cliffs, NJ: Prentice Hall.

Langer, Ellen J. 1989. *Mindfulness.* Reading, MA: Addison-Wesley.

Lortie, Dan C. 1975. *School-Teacher: A Sociological Study.* Chicago: University of Chicago Press.

Massy, William, Andrea K. Wilker, and Carol Colbeck. 1994. "Overcoming Hollowed Collegiality." *Change,* July-August, pp. 11-20.

Mayhew, Katherine and Anna C. Edwards. 1936. *The Dewey School.* New York: Appleton-Century.

Moffatt, Michael. 1989. *Coming of Age in New Jersey: College and American Culture.* New Brunswick, NJ: Rutgers University Press.

Naroll, Raoul. 1983. *The Moral Order.* Beverly Hills, CA: Sage.

Nyden, Philip, Anne Figert, Mark Shibley, and Darryl Burrows. 1997. *Building Community: Social Science in Action.* Thousand Oaks, CA: Pine Forge.

Park, Peter. 1993. "What Is Participatory Research? A Theoretical and Methodological Perspective." In *Voices of Change: Participatory Research in the United States and Canada,* edited by Peter Park et al. Westport, CT: Bergin & Garvey.

Quinn, Robert E. 1988. *Beyond Rational Management: Mastering the Paradoxes and Competing Demands of High Performance.* San Francisco: Jossey-Bass.

Rau, William and Barbara Heyl. 1990. "Humanizing the College Classroom: Collaborative Learning and Social Organization among Students." *Teaching Sociology* 18:141-55.

Riesman, David, Joseph Gusfield, and Zelda Gamson. 1971. *Academic Values and Mass Education.* New York: Doubleday.

Rogoff, Barbara. 1990. *Apprenticeship in Thinking: Cognitive Development in Social Context.* New York: Oxford University Press.

Sarason, Seymour. 1971. *The Culture of Schools and the Problem of Change.* Boston: Allyn & Bacon.

Selznick, Philip. 1992. *The Moral Commonwealth: Social Theory and the Promise of Community.* Berkeley: University of California Press.

Senge, Peter M. 1990. *The Fifth Discipline: The Art and Practice of the Learning Organization.* New York: Doubleday.

Tharp, Roland G. and Ronald Gallimore. 1988. *Rousing Minds to Life: Teaching, Learning, and Schooling in a Social Context.* New York: Cambridge University Press.

Thelen, Herbert A. 1954. *Dynamics of Groups at Work.* Chicago: University of Chicago Press.

Vygotsky, L. S. 1978. *Mind in Society.* Cambridge, MA: Harvard University Press.

Waller, Willard. 1932. *Sociology of Teaching.* New York: John Wiley.

Weick, Karl. 1978. "Educational Systems as Loosely Coupled Systems." *Administrative Science Quarterly* 23:541-52.

Whyte, William Forte, ed. 1991. *Participatory Action Research.* Newbury Park, CA: Sage.

Wilson, Everett K. 1985. "Apartheid and the Pathology of Sociology Instruction." Pp. 25-47 in *Teaching Sociology: The Quest for Excellence,* edited by Frederick Campbell, Hubert Blalock, and Reece McGee. Chicago: Nelson-Hall.

Zey-Ferrell, Mary Baker, and Paul J. Baker. 1984. "Faculty Work in a Regional Public University: An Empirical Assessment of Goal Consensus and Congruency of Actions and Intentions." *Research in Higher Education* 20:399-426.

9

The Campus as Learning Community: Seven Promising Shifts and Seven Powerful Levers

Thomas A. Angelo

Throughout its history, American higher education has adapted and reinvented itself repeatedly in response to social, economic, and political changes. And it will again. Today, much as happened at the end of the nineteenth century and again after World War II, new ways of envisioning and organizing academic life are emerging, signs of another historic renewal of academic culture. This time around, however, the changes center less on building new institutional structures, redefining the curriculum, or expanding access and more on the very heart of higher education—on improving teaching and learning.

In what was likely the most widely read higher education article of 1995, Robert Barr and John Tagg characterize these changes as a shift from our current teaching-centered model of undergraduate education to a new learning-centered paradigm. As Barr and Tagg see it, the

AUTHOR'S NOTE: This is a reprint of an article originally published as Angelo, Thomas A., "The Campus as Learning Community: Seven Promising Shifts and Seven Powerful Levers," *American Association for Higher Education,* 49 (9): May 1997, pp. 3-6. Used with permission.

EDITORS' NOTE: For ideas on learning groups, see Creative Ways of Engaging Students subsection in the *Fieldguide* (particularly Weast; Wright; McKinney and Graham-Buxton; Lerner).

primary purpose of colleges and universities in this new paradigm will be to "produce learning" rather than to provide instruction, with traditional teaching only one of several possible means of bringing about the learning we want.

Although the word *paradigm* always makes me a bit queasy (Thomas Kuhn reportedly tried to withdraw the term from use late in his life), I think Barr and Tagg are right on target. One outcome of the paradigm shift will be the transformation of our colleges and universities, from the "teaching factories" or "educational shopping malls" they too often resemble into authentic "learning communities."

Collaboration, Connection, Community

The phrase may have a congenial ring to it, but what exactly *is* a learning community? Several definitions exist, but most center around a vision of faculty and students—and sometimes administrators, staff, and the larger community—working collaboratively toward shared academic goals in environments in which competition is deemphasized. In a learning community, faculty and students alike have both opportunity and responsibility to learn from and help teach each other. Faculty become less transmitters of information and more designers of learning environments and experiences, expert guides, coaches, and practicing master learners.

While there are many variations on the theme, learning communities typically feature purposive groupings of students, shared scheduling, significant use of cooperative and/or collaborative learning approaches, and an emphasis on connecting learning across course and disciplinary boundaries. For example, anywhere from 20 to 100 students may be enrolled as a cohort in a cluster of conceptually linked courses from diverse disciplines organized around a theme such as "Body and Mind," "The Environment and Community Health," or "Schools and Families." Faculty explicitly design and teach these linked courses to foster coherence and connections. Students typically also attend a weekly group meeting facilitated by a peer adviser. Through course work and meetings, students learn academic content *and* the learning and group process skills needed for the shift from an individualistic to a cooperative academic culture.

But imagine extending this model beyond two or three courses, to transform an entire department, program, school, or campus into a learning community. Now imagine not just students but also faculty working together as members of learning communities, collaborating on and connecting their teaching, scholarship, and service in meaningful ways. For some faculty, such campus-wide learning communities would represent the fulfillment of long-held aspirations. Many hunger for the community of scholars they expected to find in academic life. The recent explosion of newsletters, books, conferences, listservs, and Web sites focused on teaching and learning is an indication of the depth of that longing.

Of course, a faculty's personal and professional fulfillment isn't reason enough to invest in learning communities. We must first ask how

effective such communities are at producing student learning. The results to date are promising. Research done by Vincent Tinto and others demonstrates that learning communities can produce significant gains in student involvement, learning, satisfaction, social connectedness, persistence, and retention. These benefits accrue to "remedial" and "nonremedial" students in community colleges and research universities alike.

I'm convinced that developing a more cooperative academic culture is vital for our very survival. Just as employers consistently tell us that our graduates need well-developed teamwork skills to thrive in the workplace, faculty need to develop similar skills in order to prepare our students well. Within the academy's walls, real and virtual, we'll need better collaboration than we can currently muster to survive coming political and financial shocks. In the biggest of big pictures, if we're to cope with our planet's increasingly complex problems, we must educate highly effective team workers capable of making connections across all kinds of boundaries. And we must do all this much more efficiently at lower cost—or sacrifice hard-won gains in equity and access.

Fundamental Shifts

The challenge, then, is to improve both instructional productivity and learning quality to create productive learning communities. Realizing this vision will require several fundamental shifts in our standard operating procedures, moving us toward the "campus-wide learning community" ideal I've described. The good news is that many promising shifts are already under way and that powerful "levers" are available to hasten the transformation.

Space limitations preclude detailed discussion here, but let me offer a short list of seven positive shifts and seven proven levers we can employ to construct a more productive learning-focused campus.

Shift 1: From a Culture of Largely Unexamined Assumptions to a Culture of Inquiry and Evidence

---

Much of our standard practice depends on implicit and often highly questionable assumptions. For example, our system of courses and credits assumes that all students learn all subjects at the same rate. Typical general education survey courses assume a "vaccination" model of learning, that a dose of Freshman Composition cures writing ills for the next three years. And some diversity efforts assume that simply throwing very different students together in the same environment will lead to greater tolerance and appreciation of diversity.

Lever 1: Assessment. The assessment "movement" prods us to examine our assumptions by turning them into empirical, "assessable" questions. Could more students learn calculus well if we gave them more time? Do students who succeed in freshman writing courses write demonstrably better in subsequent courses? Does simple coexistence with diversity lead to more open attitudes? After more than a decade of effort, a wide range of assessment tools exists to help us find out what's broke, what isn't, and just how well our well-intentioned innovations are working.

Shift 2: From a Culture of Implicitly Held Individual Hopes, Preferences, and Beliefs to a Culture of Explicit, Broadly Shared Goals, Criteria, and Standards

---

The notion of community implies shared goals and values that inform our decisions and actions. To get anywhere together, we first have to agree on the destination. To create meaningful learning communities, we'll need to develop shared goals for student learning outcomes, shared criteria for assessment and evaluation, and shared standards for measuring student and faculty success.

Lever 2: Goal-, criteria-, and standards-setting methods. Several methods for building broad agreement on goals, criteria, and standards have been developed in the corporate world and in K-12 education. Some of the most promising are TQM/CQI approaches such as "open-space technology" and "future search" and a method used in writing across the curriculum known as "primary trait analysis." Whatever the methods, the aim is to create common ground by developing trust, a shared language, and shared values.

Shift 3: From a Teaching Culture that Ignores What Is Known about Human Learning to One that Applies Relevant Knowledge to Improve Practice

---

For far too long, most college faculty were uninformed about applicable research on learning and teaching, and far too many were dismissive of its potential value. Imagine if other applied professions, such as medicine or engineering, took the same dim view of research! Today, by contrast, many current and future faculty are interested in understanding and applying the research base.

Lever 3: The research and practice literature on teaching and learning. After more than fifty years of research in psychology, cognitive science, and education, there are some general, well-supported principles of teaching and learning to inform our professional practice. Recent books by Wilbert McKeachie, Pascarella and Terenzini, and Gardiner, among many others, offer useful research syntheses and practical related suggestions.

Shift 4: From a Narrow, Exclusive Definition of Scholarship to a Broader, Inclusive Vision

In his widely read 1990 book, *Scholarship Reconsidered,* the late Ernest Boyer made a persuasive argument for broadening our vision of scholarly work from the traditional scholarship of discovery—research and publication—to include the scholarships of integration, application, and teaching. Several factors, including the end of the cold war and consequent decline in research funding, have spurred interest in changing the model.

Lever 4: The faculty evaluation system. Like everyone else, faculty tend to do what they are evaluated on and rewarded for. Therefore, the faculty evaluation system used for retention, tenure, promotion, and merit decisions is a powerful lever for redirecting time and effort. Inspired by Boyer's challenge, campuses throughout the country are working to develop ways to assess and value a broader range of scholarship. The American Association for Higher Education's Peer Review of Teaching project and its Forum on Faculty Roles and Rewards are two efforts to move this agenda "from ideas to prototypes." Among the most promising approaches for documenting and displaying scholarship currently being field-tested and refined are teaching portfolios and course portfolios.

Shift 5: From an Academic Culture that Tends to Ignore Costs to One that Attempts to Realistically Account for Direct, Deferred, and Opportunity Costs

The "cost disease" threatens the health of higher education generally and the very existence of many particular institutions. Yet, for the most part, we lack accurate information on the real costs and benefits of our programs and activities on which to base decisions. There's no general agreement, for example, on what the appropriate "unit" would be in a cost-per-unit accounting of learning. Without better accounting, in the broadest sense, we can't really determine our productivity, much less improve it.

Lever 5: New accounting models and methods. Innovations in accounting, such as activity-based accounting and full-costing, are beginning to be adapted and applied to academic units, informing our assessment and decision making. Inside the academy, leaders such as Alan Guskin, Robert Zemsky, William Massy, and Stephen Ehrmann are developing and disseminating new models, indicators, and measures of teaching and learning "productivity."

Shift 6: From a Culture that Emphasizes and Privileges Individual Struggle for Private Advantage to One that Encourages Collaboration for the Common Good and Individual Advancement

While it's critical to change the evaluation and reward systems for individual faculty and the testing and grading systems for individual students to encourage and reinforce community, it's also necessary to teach all involved how to work together effectively. Research has demonstrated that nearly all students learn more and better through well-structured, well-run group work than on their own and that it particularly benefits the less privileged and less prepared. Consequently, I see the decision to employ—or not to employ—cooperative methods as an ethical choice, not simply an instructional one. And since research also indicates that group process is the major determinant of group effectiveness, we need to train both faculty and students in group process skills.

Lever 6: Cooperative and collaborative education methods. A rapidly growing body of research on and practical expertise in these approaches can guide and inform our efforts. The National Center for Teaching, Learning, and Assessment is one excellent source for recent materials. Books and articles by David and Roger Johnson, Karl Smith, and Kenneth Bruffee are also key resources.

Shift 7: From a Model of Higher Education as Primarily a Quantitative, Additive Process to One that Is Fundamentally Qualitative and Transformative

---

To many, higher education equals course taking and credit collecting, as if the simple adding up of experiences necessarily [leads] to any significant learning. But just as no pile of bricks, however numerous, necessarily makes a building; no list of courses, however long, necessarily equals an education. All too often, however, students are awarded degrees primarily for persisting, and employers complain that our graduates lack basic skills and knowledge.

Lever 7: Competency-based, mastery learning. One way around this debasing academic "bean counting" is to decouple course taking and grades from degree granting. It would require that we define the competencies (what learners must demonstrably know and be able to do) that we most value, the core criteria for evaluating those competencies, and the standards for how well students must perform and then develop adequate means to assess them. In a productive, competency-based learning commu-

nity, students could potentially demonstrate their mastery of some or most aspects of the curriculum without taking courses, but they could never become "certified" simply by taking courses.

Conclusion

The natural and necessary connection between competency-based learning and assessment brings us full circle, a transit that underlines the necessary connectedness of all these shifts. Progress toward a more productive, more authentic form of academic community will require movement on many fronts at once—many shifts propelled by many levers.

Selected Resources for Making the Shifts

1. *To a culture of inquiry and evidence*
   Banta, T. W., et al. (1995). *Assessment in Practice: Putting Principles to Work on College Campuses.* San Francisco: Jossey-Bass.
   Gardiner, L. F., C. Anderson, and B. L. Cambridge, eds. (1997). *Learning through Assessment: A Resource Guide for Higher Education.* Washington, DC: AAHE.

2. *To a culture of explicit, broadly shared goals, criteria, and standards*
   Brigham, S. E. (November/December 1996). "Large-Scale Events: New Ways of Working across the Organization." *Change* 28 (6): 28-37.
   Stark, J. S., K. M. Shaw, and M. A. Lowther. (1989). *Student Goals for College and Courses: A Missing Link in Assessing and Improving Academic Achievement.* ASHE-ERIC Higher Education Report, No. 6. Washington, DC: School of Edu-

cation and Human Development, George Washington University.

Walvoord, B. E., and V. Anderson. (November/December 1995). "An Assessment Riddle." *Assessment Update* 7 (6): 8-9, 11.

3. *To a teaching culture that applies relevant knowledge to improve practice*

Gardiner, L. F. (1994). *Redesigning Higher Education: Producing Dramatic Gains in Student Learning.* ASHE-ERIC Higher Education Report, No. 7. Washington, DC: School of Education and Human Development, George Washington University.

McKeachie, W. J., et al. (1994). *Teaching Tips: Strategies, Research, and Theory for College and University Teachers.* 9th ed. Lexington, MA: D. C. Heath.

Menges, R. J., and M. D. Svinicki, eds. (1991). *College Teaching: From Theory to Practice.* New Directions for Teaching and Learning, No. 45. San Francisco: Jossey-Bass.

Pascarella, E. T., and R. T. Terenzini. (1991). *How College Affects Students: Findings and Insights from Twenty Years of Research.* San Francisco: Jossey-Bass.

4. *To a broader, more inclusive vision of scholarship*

Cross, K. P., and M. H. Steadman. (1996). *Classroom Research: Implementing the Scholarship of Teaching.* San Francisco: Jossey-Bass.

Hutchings, P., ed. (1995). *From Idea to Prototype: The Peer Review of Teaching—A Project Workbook.* Washington, DC: AAHE.

Rice, R. E. (1996). *Making a Place for the New American Scholar.* New Pathways

Working Paper series, Inquiry No. 1. Washington, DC: AAHE.

5. *To an academic culture that attempts to realistically account for costs*

Ehrmann, S. C. "The Flashlight Project: Spotting an Elephant in the Dark." Available on the AAHE Web site: www.aahe.org/elephant.

Guskin, A. E. (July/August and September/October 1994). "Reducing Student Costs and Enhancing Student Learning," Parts 1 ("Restructuring the Administration") and 2 ("Restructuring the Role of Faculty"). *Change* 26 (4): 2229 and 26 (5): 16-25.

Plater, W. M. (May/June 1995). "Future Work: Faculty Time in the 21st Century." *Change* 27 (3): 22-33.

Zemsky, R., and W. E. Massy. (November/December 1995). "Toward an Understanding of Our Current Predicaments: Expanding Perimeters, Melting Cores, and Sticky Functions." *Change* 27 (6): 40-49.

6. *To a culture that encourages collaboration for the common good—and individual advancement*

Bruffee, K. A. (1993). *Collaborative Learning: Higher Education, Interdependence, and the Authority of Knowledge.* Baltimore, MD: Johns Hopkins University Press.

Gabelnick, F., J. MacGregor, R. Matthews, and B. L. Smith, eds. (1990). *Learning Communities: Creating Connections among Students, Faculty, and Disciplines.* New Directions for Teaching and Learning, No. 41. San Francisco: Jossey-Bass.

Goodsell, A., M. Maher, and V. Tinto. (1992). *Collaborative Learning: A Sourcebook for Higher Education.* University Park, PA: National Center for Teaching, Learning, and Assessment.

Johnson, D. W., R. T. Johnson, and K. A. Smith. (1991). *Learning: Cooperation in the College Classroom.* Edina, MN: Interaction.

7. *To a model of higher education that is qualitative and transformative*

Barr, R. B., and J. Tagg. (November/December 1995). "From Teaching to Learning: A New Paradigm for Undergraduate Education." *Change* 27 (6): 12-25.

Campbell, W. E., and K. A. Smith, eds. (1997). *New Paradigms for College Teaching.* Edina, MN: Interaction.

Education Commission of the States. (1995). *Making Quality Count in Undergraduate Education.* Denver, CO: Education Commission of the States.

10

Dissolution of the Atlas Complex

Donald L. Finkel and G. Stephen Monk

The Atlas Complex

Professor A is just concluding the culminating lecture on one of his favorite topics in his field. In earlier lectures, he painstakingly laid the groundwork, explaining each element and placing each detail of the theory in its proper relationship to the others. Today, he carefully ties the various components together to exhibit one of the most beautiful and powerful theories that he knows of. Each time that he lectures on this theory, he more clearly understands its depth and subtlety, and his lectures improve accordingly. Students find the theory difficult, and so he has learned to inject humor, personal views, and dramatic emphasis to get it across. Today, Professor A's pacing and timing work perfectly. He ends just in time to allow for his usual five minutes of questions. He asks, "Are there any questions?" A few students look up from their notebooks, but nothing else happens. He fills the silence by raising some questions that naturally arise from the theory. Then, he answers the questions. The students dutifully record the answers. One student asks a polite question about a specific fact in the lecture, and Professor

AUTHOR'S NOTE: This is a reprint of an article originally published as Finkel, Donald L. and G. Stephen Monk, "Teachers and Learning Groups: Dissolution of the Atlas Complex," in *Learning in Groups: New Directions for Teaching and Learning #14*, edited by C. Bouton and R. Y. Garth (Jossey-Bass), 1983, pp. 83-97. Used with permission.

A uses the occasion to expound still more on the theory. Another student asks the inevitable question about how much of the material will be on the exam. When the bell rings, Professor A is stirred by mixed emotions. He is pleased with how well he pulled the lecture together—it is easily the best version that he has given—but he is bothered by how little the students seem to have been moved by it. He has enough experience to know what the absence of real questions means. The students probably admire both his performance and the theory. But they do not feel the power of the theory, and they do not grasp how economically it answers so many deep questions. What must he do to get the excitement of his subject across to students?

Professor B is conducting a seminar in her own field of research. The topic for discussion is one of the seminal works in the field. Some students ask her to clarify certain passages, and she is able to do so clearly and completely. Then, she asks a question that she believes to be central to the issues that underlie the work, and one of the brighter students responds in a very thorough and lengthy manner. But inevitably, the student does not understand the full depth of the issue, and Professor B has a strong impulse to correct and clarify the student's answer. However, as an experienced seminar leader, she stifles this impulse and asks the students if they have any response to the first student's answer.

Another student says that he disagrees with the first student and proceeds to give his own long and complete answer. Now, Professor B has two shallow and slightly incorrect answers to clear up. After doing so, she asks another question. She fixes her eye on one of the quieter students, and the student responds very tentatively, so that Professor B must encourage him and help to fill in the details missing from his answer. These separate, truncated dialogues between Professor B and each of her students continue until, out of something approaching desperation, she presses one student on what he means by one of his too neat, almost glib answers. As the student retreats into silence, a feeling of defeat overcomes Professor B. The work that they are discussing always stimulates her thinking with the freshness of its perspectives and insights. At each reading, it raises new questions in her mind. How can it fail to motivate a discussion as involving as those she had with fellow students in graduate school? The cause of the dry, ritualistic seminar before her must be herself, she reasons. She has not asked the right questions.

Both these teachers are the central figures in their classrooms. Like most of their colleagues, they assume full responsibility for all that goes on. They supply motivation, insight, clear explanations, even intellectual curiosity. In exchange, their students supply almost nothing but a faint imitation of the academic performance that they witness. Both teachers so thoroughly dominate the proceedings that they are cut off from what the students know or are confused about. For their part, the students form a group of isolated individuals who have no more in common than their one-to-one relationship with the same individual. While Professors A and B exercise their authority through control of the subject matter and the social encounter in the classroom, they lack the power to make things happen for their students. They

are both caught in the middle of their classes by a host of mysterious forces—hidden assumptions, hidden expectations, and the results of their own isolating experience. We call this state the "Atlas complex."

In this chapter, we first examine the phenomenon of the Atlas complex. In the next section, we describe a third teacher, Professor C, who is very present in his class but who is not caught in the middle. This example allows us to broaden our perspective on the social organization of the typical college course and on the particular hold that it has on the teacher. Finally, we show the many ways in which this social system can be modified to free teachers from the middle without violating their sense of themselves as teachers. Such modifications should broaden and enrich their view of what they can accomplish as teachers. The result should be a more fulfilling teaching experience and a greater sense of what is possible—in short, a dissolution of the Atlas complex.

The Two-Person Model

Most teachers and students conceive of the heart of education as a two-person relationship. The ideal relationship is that of tutor and tutee alone in a room. Classes are seen only as an economic or pragmatic necessity in which one person—the teacher—either simultaneously engages in ten or three hundred two-person relationships with separate individuals or addresses a single undifferentiated entity—the audience. Teachers who view their classes as an elaboration of the two-person model are cut off from the potential energy and inspiration that lie in student-to-student interaction or in the mutual support that a group of individuals working toward a common goal can provide. Consequently, it becomes the responsibility of teachers to provide motivation, enlightenment, and a sense of purpose. Like Atlas, such teachers support the entire enterprise.

The sense of fixedness that stems from the two-person model of teaching has both a cognitive and a social component. The cognitive component stems from the teacher's expertise in subject matter, while the social component results from the teacher's occupying the role of group leader in the classroom. Teachers invest a large quantity of their time, energy, and hard work in becoming experts in their disciplines. They have a comprehensive understanding of their subjects and detailed knowledge of their subjects' intricacies and skills. How can they withhold these things? And if students do not get the point the first time, what can teachers do but give again or give more? By the very terms of the encounter, students lack something that the teacher has in abundance; thus, every activity in which the teacher does not give this "something" must play a secondary role. Teachers assume that their principal task is one of improving the ways in which they express their expertise. Clear and precise explanation can always be articulated and sharpened; penetrating questions can always be made more penetrating.

The social component of the sense of fixedness derives from the teacher's role of group leader. The literature on the social psychology of small groups (Slater, 1966) demonstrates that most groups in their early stages can be described precisely by the two-person model; that is, each member acts as if he or she were in an exclusive dyadic relationship with the leader. It is a long and arduous process for group members to break their dependence on the leader and to form mutual bonds with one another. But teachers are more than just leaders. Their expertise in the subject matter exacerbates the problem that all leaders face if they want to distribute responsibility to the individual members of the group. The teacher is the very em-

bodiment of the group's goal—the subject matter. There is no doubt that teachers have all the answers. Why should students look to anyone else?

These forces hold teachers in place with their Atlas-like burden of responsibility. They prevent teachers from sharing some of their responsibilities with the group's members. But some teachers do try to make such a change. They allow individual students to take turns at leading the class, they form study groups of various kinds, they try to restrict their role in discussion to that of facilitator or resource person. And, when they encounter the intensity of the forces, they find themselves pushed back into the center by a cognitive force, by a social force, or by both.

The most striking consequence of allowing students to interact directly and collectively with subject matter without the teacher's mediation is that the teacher comes face to face with students' own partially formed and inadequate conceptions of the subject. As experts with carefully articulated and elaborate views of their subjects, and as representatives of their disciplines, teachers are bound to feel a strong personal discomfort in the presence of the kinds of imprecise, loosely connected, unintegrated comprehension that students have of their subjects. Thus, the very act of opening up and listening to students forces the teacher-expert back into the middle because imprecise explanations cannot go unrefined, because all the connections have to be made, and because final conclusions have to be drawn. In short, the teacher returns to the center in order to mediate between the students and the material.

For their part, students are likely to resist the teacher's attempt to step out of the middle because they perceive this switch in roles as an attempt to abandon responsible leadership. Students who feel abandoned resent their teacher, and consequently they do not develop the enthusiasm necessary for learning. This in turn leads the teacher, who tries to innovate and share responsibility for learning, to become cynical about students. The primary reason for this sequence of reactions is that when [the teacher switches] from the role of expert to the role of helper, [his or her] expertise gets lost. If students have no way to draw on the teacher's knowledge of the subject, it is natural that they learn less. The attempt to break the two-person model and to cause students to draw on the resources of the group can easily lead to a lowering of the intellectual goals of the class in the eyes of both teacher and students. And since this is usually judged to be unsatisfactory, the teacher returns to the role of expert, and the students settle back into their seats to take in the teacher's illuminating words.

We have described the way in which the cognitive and social aspects of the two-person model keep teachers in the middle of their classes, carrying all the burden and responsibility of the course on their own shoulders. We have also described how the forces that typically operate on teachers, both from within and without, tend to move them back to the center when they try to leave it. People approach teaching with a set of conventional beliefs about the teacher's role that are strongly reinforced by being in the middle. Years of experience then fuse these beliefs into a whole, so that they cannot be differentiated, questioned, or tested. Instead, they form a complex—a monolithic and undifferentiated state of mind that gives teachers so much responsibility for everything that goes on in the class that they cannot move—a state of mind that we call the Atlas complex.

But a teacher who takes responsibility for all that goes on in the class gives students no room to experiment with ideas, to deepen their understanding of concepts, or to integrate concepts into a coherent system. Most teachers

agree that these processes, together with many others, are necessary if students are to understand a subject matter. Any teacher will say that the best way of learning a subject is to teach it—to try to explain it to others. Scientists agree that intellectual exchange, discourse, and debate are important elements in their own professional development. Almost anyone who has learned something well has experienced the particular potency that a collaborative group can have through its ability to promote and make manifest such intellectual processes as assimilating experience or data to conceptual frameworks, wrestling with inadequacies in current conceptions, drawing new distinctions, and integrating separate ideas. The evidence that collective work is a key ingredient to intellectual growth surrounds us. Yet, to judge by the typical college course, most teachers do not believe that it is either appropriate or possible to foster these important processes in the classroom.

Professor C

Before we examine how the Atlas complex can be dissolved, we will describe a class that does not have a teacher in the middle and that still benefits from the teacher's expertise. This should show that change is possible—that the forces holding the teacher in the middle are not irresistible. It should also illustrate the point of view that we wish to advance in the next section.

Professor C walks into his class of forty students and hands out a photocopied "worksheet" to every student. The students continue to chatter as they glance at the worksheet, start to form groups of five (as the worksheet instructs them to do), and seat themselves around the tables in the room. Gradually, the noise level falls as students read through the worksheet. Then, it rises again as they begin to engage in discussion with one another over the questions on the sheet. After a few minutes, Professor C joins one group, where he quietly watches and listens but does not talk. A few minutes later, he moves to another group. After listening to the discussion there, he suggests to group members that they are not getting anywhere because they misunderstand the example given in the first question. He tells them to draw out in pictures what the example describes, and as they do so, he makes clarifying comments. He listens as discussion resumes, then moves to yet another group. Meanwhile, many students are not only talking but also making notes as they do. Some groups are engaged in heated discussion; others are quieter, as individuals pause to think or to listen to a member who reads a passage aloud from reading that accompanies the worksheet. In one way or another, however, all the groups are working with the sequence of questions and instructions contained in the worksheet.

Professor C may seem to be a teacher with no real function; indeed, he may even seem irresponsible. But keeping a class of forty students actively involved with course material with a minimum of direct support from the teacher requires an artfully written set of instructions and questions. Professor C puts all his expert knowledge, his most provocative questions, and his insights about how students comprehend the material into the worksheets. Breaking his own finished knowledge of his discipline down into its component processes [and] then provoking students to discover these processes takes at least as much intellectual work as a finely crafted series of lectures would require. But having done this work and set the students to interacting with one another and with the worksheet, he becomes free to perform a number of helping teaching functions as well as to expound, probe, or press on the basis of his expertise. He can also take time just to listen to students. He is free to choose. (For a more

complete description of the worksheet approach and its uses, see Finkel and Monk, 1978, 1979.)

Professor C revises his worksheets after watching his class interact with them (this is where listening becomes important), just as Professor A revises his lectures every time that he gives them. The difference is that Professor C bases his revision on direct observation, while Professor A must rely on his own perception of how he has done, supplemented by a few polite questions and test results. Like Professor B, Professor C always feels that livelier and deeper conversation would result if he only could ask better questions. The difference is that Professor C has had the opportunity to be an outside observer of students' conversation without the concerns of a discussion leader; thus, Professor C can gain a clearer view of what actually happens than even most seminar leaders can.

We offer the example of Professor C not as a model for Professor A, Professor B, or any other teacher to imitate. Answers to teaching problems are never that easy. The example of Professor C shows that a teacher can be in his class without being caught in the middle. We use this example to illustrate a principle that lies behind a variety of possible course restructurings and that helps to relieve the teacher of the Atlas complex.

From Roles to Functions

Professor C serves as an expert in his class primarily through his worksheet. Since students focus on it and not on him, he is free to give clear explanations, to press for clearer answers, and to encourage hesitant students. The power of this approach stems from a fundamental differentiation of the teaching functions that make up the role of teacher. When these functions are differentiated and then distributed throughout a course, many of the constricting features that come from the role of teacher disappear and with them [disappear] the peculiar symptoms of the Atlas complex.

Brown (1965, p. 153) observes that "roles are norms that apply to categories of persons." In this case, the category is *teacher,* and anyone who fills that role is expected to follow a certain set of norms in his behavior. Moreover, roles do not exist in isolation; they are defined in interlocking sets, within the context of a given institution. In defining the role of college teacher, we necessarily define norms for college student as well. Social life flows smoothly because of these sets of roles. People enter the social arena knowing in advance what to expect; they have to be confident that the range of unpredictable behavior is strongly limited. Teachers who want to teach in a strikingly different way, for pedagogical reasons, usually find themselves crossing the limits of their role, violating some of the rules that define it. Students will be the first to force them back into doing what teachers are supposed to do, that is, into the conventional role of teacher. Thus, the very predictability that we need from roles can become so rigid by force of habit that the roles of teacher and student become overly restrictive and actually exclude the usual needs of cognitive life in the classroom.

Suppose now that teachers focus not on how they are supposed to behave but on the job that they are supposed to accomplish. Most teachers understand this job to involve such things as getting the students to understand a given theory, having students examine certain phenomena from a new perspective, or teaching students how to perform new skills. Each goal leads to certain mental processes that must be carried out. These processes include organizing and synthesizing a variety of specific facts, ideas, and events into a general scheme, engaging the particulars of a context or experience while maintaining a perspective on its general qualities, and compressing and crystallizing connections made within the discipline or between a discipline and the area that it describes. Each process requires a different form of work from students and a different form of assistance from the teacher. A teacher operates in quite different ways depending on whether students are to organize and synthesize, to engage, or to compress and crystallize. Even within each mental process, the teacher has to make choices to act. We call particular ways of operating in a classroom *teaching functions.*

For instance, to get students to organize and synthesize specific facts and events into a general scheme, the teacher can perform such teaching functions as asking students to give their current interpretations of the specific facts and events, laying out projects that allow students to devise their own schemes, responding to students' work, and presenting the teacher's own organizing scheme.

In designing his worksheet, Professor C performed such teaching functions as interpreting student misconceptions, setting goals and tasks, and analyzing his subject matter. In his classroom, Professor C performs such teaching functions as listening to students, redirecting them, clearing up misunderstandings, and supporting students. Notice that analysis of classroom roles ties behavior to persons (teacher, students), while analysis of teaching functions ties behavior to tasks that must be accomplished. Some teaching functions can be performed just as well by students as by the teacher. Other teaching functions can best be performed by groups of students or even by combinations of student groups. As we show in the next section, a conscious decision about which teaching functions are to be performed by whom and where can be made as part of the design of the organization of the course.

The perspective of teaching functions makes the strong negative effects of thinking in terms of teaching roles quite clear. First, any role is inevitably confining. Many teachers acknowledge that a particular teaching function should be performed but that it is not. They say, "Such things are not done" or "Students won't stand for it." This is only a way of saying that their particular role does not permit it. And, because the role does not permit it, most teachers are not inclined consciously to articulate what teaching functions they deem most important for their students' learning.

Second, the language of roles itself creates dilemmas about the ways in which people are to behave. Teachers ask, "Is my role of teacher one of expert or helper?" as if they must choose between two roles.

The conflict disappears if the teacher performs functions that require expertise at one time and place and functions that require helping at others. To say that students must be *independent* (bold, skeptical, imaginative) and *dependent* (relying on the accumulated knowledge of past generations) sounds like a contradiction, because it is couched in the language of roles. The adjectives prescribe contradictory norms for a category of persons. But if we say instead that some of the activities in which a student must engage require independence and that others require dependence, then the contradiction disappears. There is a time and a place for both independence and dependence when each characterizes a mode of engaging in a specific activity. But as role descriptors, they contradict each other.

Third, roles tend to generate their own work to be done, so that the teacher's activities are determined not by tasks but by roles and expectations. Thus, Professor A becomes a performer caught up in such functions as polishing, timing, and motivating, while Professor B becomes a stage manager of discussions who looks for the perfect sequence of questions so that the actors can play their parts.

Fourth, every role includes several distinct functions. When these functions are performed simply as part of the role, they tend to blur and merge; they are performed simultaneously, but none is performed particularly well. In trying to get feedback after he has spent forty-five minutes driving his points home, Professor A is fooling himself. Likewise, in trying to manage a discussion among students while maintaining high standards of rigor, Professor B performs neither function. A lecturer who gives illuminating examples to stimulate students' thought processes and then immediately gives her own perspective to explain these examples can think of herself as engaging students in a particular context and inviting them to form their own view of it, which she will then enrich. But for students to perform such an activity in fact requires behavior from the lecturer that the students would not tolerate. Thus, Professor B's students do not really go through the process, and she really performs just one function, exposition.

Distributing Teaching Functions in a Course

While most teachers acknowledge that their role is confining and wish to perform a wider array of teaching functions, they find that good intentions, even when backed by strong resolve, do not go far to promote change. To effect genuine change, a teacher must first differentiate teaching functions, then distribute them in the course so that the responsibility for learning is shared with students. Only then can the Atlas complex be dissolved. To do this, the various parts of the course must be clearly distinguished so that the functions appropriate to them can be distributed.

When we think of making structural changes in a formal organization, such as a corporation, the candidates for transformation are immediately apparent. For instance, we can alter channels of communication, change the authority relations between officers, or merge or divide departments. Like a corporation, a course is a social system. However, when it is viewed simply as a teacher and some students, it seems to lack the structural components that a corporation has, and thus it seems to lack candidates for transformation.

To distribute teaching functions, the teacher needs to distinguish three components in his course: specific activities that serve general teaching functions, people responsible for performing these activities, and the "places" in the course where these activities are performed. For instance, a teacher who wants to perform the teaching function of giving his own perspective on the subject can choose among such activities as these: giving a lecture, having students study a few key examples that exemplify the significance of his own perspective, and asking a highly convergent sequence of questions that point to that perspective. Further, there are many choices as to who performs each particular activity. The typical choice is between the teacher and individual students. However, there are additional candidates for this responsibility. Small groups of students working together can take over some teaching functions. In some instances, the entire classroom group can do so. Finally, there is an enormous array of "places" in any course where various teaching functions can be located. The obvious places include class sessions, tests, homework assignments, office hours, lectures, and quiz sections. These can be refined to include such places as Friday's class, critiqued but ungraded homework, files of past tests, required office conferences, and makeup tests.

Once teachers have differentiated the teaching functions to be performed and consciously distinguished the components of their

courses that can be operated on, then they can make local decisions about the specific activities used to realize these functions, about who performs each function, and about where in the course the activity should be carried out. With this strategy for change, teachers can preserve existing activities that already serve important teaching functions and test new activities that may be able to take the place of activities that have not worked out well.

Faced with the complexities of the course as a social system, teachers may well wonder how to get started in such a program for change—particularly since, by our analysis, teachers themselves play such a dominant role in the system. Student learning groups, in which small numbers of students work together in a class without constant assistance from the teacher, can restrict the problem of systematic change to a problem of manageable size. Professor C divided his class into small groups that worked together for two hours, guided by the instructions and questions on the worksheet. Professor C performed many of the expert teaching functions by writing the worksheet, so that he became free in the class to perform many helping functions. Working in groups, the students perform such functions as asking and answering questions, giving support and reinforcement, and providing fresh perspectives on the subject. Each small group of students serves other important functions as well, such as providing carrying energy and bringing out low participators. But the concept of learning groups is extremely elastic. Learning groups can be permanent or temporary. They can work for five minutes, two hours, or even longer at one time. They can be highly structured by the teacher or not. They can be required to devise group products, which are assigned group grades. Or, they can serve primarily as support groups for individuals.

Teachers who decide to use learning groups as part of a class, no matter on how small a scale, have taken a giant step out of the middle of their class because in carrying out their decision, they distribute teaching functions, which forces them to deal with all the key issues involved in such a move. What concrete activities will be carried out in the groups? Who will have the responsibility for these activities? At what time and place in the course will learning groups be used?

Teachers who feel that a commitment to learning groups is too radical a step can take smaller steps in the same direction to divest themselves of some of their Atlas-like burden. For instance, Professor A could begin by distributing his beautifully polished lectures in advance and instruct students to read them as preparation for class. This puts him in a position to use the class time as an opportunity to serve a new teaching function. Since he is concerned with eliciting intelligent and informed questions from his students and with having a chance to respond to them, he can use the class period for just this purpose. He can have students bring prepared questions to class, where they can form the basis for a discussion, or he can simply respond to them publicly. He can take yet another step and use small temporary groups of students to drive the intellectual processes necessary for the assimilation and organization of ideas derived from his lecture. To do this, he can distribute a short list of conceptual questions along with his lecture, which each group of students can be responsible for answering. Student work of this nature would enable him to perform yet another teaching function: critiquing without grading the students' response to his lectures. This teaching function would not only be beneficial to the students, it would [also] help Professor A to revise his lectures because it would give him a sharper view of his students' conception of the subject matter.

In much the same way, Professor B could write her telling and penetrating questions out for students to work on as they do their reading. To reduce her dominant role in the seminar, she can choose a small number of teaching functions to perform during class, to the exclusion of all others. If she still feels that her expertise is not being drawn upon sufficiently, she can designate a segment of the seminar (the last fifteen minutes of each class or the last class of each week) in which she answers student questions or comments on student answers. However, she must do this in such a way that students see clearly that the expected behavior for this segment of the seminar is different from the behavior expected in the rest of the seminar.

In the preceding paragraphs, we have made a number of recommendations about how a course can be changed by distribution of teaching functions. However, it is important to remember that, as a social system, a course is not just a variety of distinct structural components; these components are strongly linked. If a change in one part of the system is to have lasting effect, the teacher must consider how this change interacts with other parts of the system. Change that is not integrated into the system [either will] be isolated and nullified or will distort the entire system. For instance, if learning groups are introduced, then their relation to the evaluation structure of the course must be made very clear. Exams signal to students more clearly than anything else what the teacher really cares about, and students direct their behavior accordingly. Thus, if group work is to be taken seriously, the results of group work must be tested by exams. That is, there should be a clear payoff to students for putting their energies into the new activity. Similarly, if the teacher deems collaborative work among students to be important and the teacher works hard to foster it in class, it makes no sense to grade exams on a curve since students see such grading as a clear message that they are competing with one another.

However far one goes in distributing teaching functions, it is extremely important to set up clear boundaries around the various places in the course to which distinct teaching functions have been assigned. Places can be marked off by such means as a designated day of the week or time [of] the day, a different classroom format, a different medium, a different physical location, or a different mode of evaluation. As long as teachers are absolutely explicit about the nature of the different tasks to be performed in the places marked off by such boundaries, they can ensure the predictability of behavior that people require when they drop stereotypical roles. A lecture carefully organized to give a highly polished overview of the subject indicates one set of behaviors for teacher and students, while a class period in which students work in groups on their first tentative explorations of the subject calls for another. A separate class period in which a panel of students presses the teacher with what they see to be the most important questions on the subject leads to yet another kind of behavior. As long as such class periods are clearly marked off, the diversity of expected behavior can create no confusion. There is a time and a place for students to be receptive and passive, curious and imaginative, challenging and doubting. Similarly, the teacher can assume an authoritative voice for a lecture, become a listener and helper in a worksheet class, and answer questions thoughtfully and carefully before a panel of students. As one boundary after another is crossed in a course, teachers and students can alter their behavior quite radically. All flows smoothly—just as long as the boundaries are absolutely clear.

Dissolution of the Atlas Complex

The perception that each course is in fact a miniature social system is perhaps the key to teachers' dissolution of the Atlas complex. The Atlas complex is a state of mind that keeps teachers fixed in the center of their classroom, supporting the entire burden of responsibility for the course on their own shoulders. This state of mind is hardened by the expectations that surround teachers and by the impact of the experience that results from them. A direct assault on the complex is doomed to fail.

The solution that we propose here is indirect. By focusing teachers' attention on a course as a social system, not on themselves as filling a role, we suggest that teachers can take specific concrete actions that enable them to share responsibilities in the classroom. To do this, teachers must distinguish the various components of a course—the structural parts that comprise the social system—and distribute teaching functions into them.

There is a continuum along which the teacher can make such changes, ranging from small moves that share responsibility with students as individuals, to use of learning groups [that] allows small subgroups of students temporarily to assume a number of different teaching functions, to delegation of major responsibilities to the entire group. We have found that the middle course of action—learning groups— is the most effective way to begin, for it opens up a great number of local possibilities for change while allowing the teacher to keep the fundamental structure of the curriculum and teaching intact.

Most teachers start with a small change, which enables them to experience their teaching in a different way and enriches their view of their course as a social system containing diverse teaching functions. This step leads to alterations in their own and their students' expectations of themselves, which deepen and expand their sense of further possible steps for change in the course. Each further step alters both their experience of teaching and their sense of what is possible. Only in this way is it possible to dissolve the Atlas complex.

References

Brown, R. 1965. *Social Psychology.* New York: Free Press.

Finkel, D. L., and Monk, G. S. 1978. *Contexts for Learning: A Teacher's Guide to the Design of Intellectual Experience.* Olympia, Wash.: Evergreen State College.

————. 1979. "The Design of Intellectual Experience." *Journal of Experiential Education, 38,* 31-38.

Slater, P. 1966. *Microcosm: Structural, Psychological, and Religious Evolution in Groups.* New York: Wiley.

11

Critical Thinking, Moral Integrity, and Citizenship: Teaching for the Intellectual Virtues

Richard Paul

Educators and theorists tend to approach the affective and moral dimensions of education as they approach all other dimensions of learning, as compartmentalized domains, and as a collection of learnings more or less separate from other learnings. As a result, they view moral development as more or less independent of cognitive development. "And why not!" one might imagine the reply. "Clearly there are highly educated, very intelligent people who habitually do evil and very simple, poorly educated people who consistently do good. If moral development were so intimately connected to cognitive development, how could this be so?"

In this [chapter], I provide the outlines of an answer to that objection by suggesting an intimate connection [among] critical thinking, moral integrity, and citizenship. Specifically, I distinguish a weak and a strong sense of each and hold that the strong sense ought to guide not only our understanding of the nature of the educated person but also our redesigning the curriculum.

There is little to recommend schooling that does not foster what I call intellectual virtues. These virtues include intellectual empathy, intellectual perseverance, intellectual confidence in reason, and an intellectual sense of justice (fair-mindedness). Without these characteristics, intellectual development is circumscribed and distorted, a caricature of what it could and should be. These same characteristics are essential to moral judgment. The "good-hearted" person who lacks intellectual virtues will act morally only when morally grasping a situation or problem does not presuppose intellectual insight. Many, if not most, moral problems and situations in the modern world are open to multiple interpretations and, hence, do presuppose these intellectual virtues.

We are now coming to see how far we are from curricula and teaching strategies that genuinely foster basic intellectual and moral development. Curricula are so highly compartmentalized and teaching [is] so committed to "speed learning" (covering large chunks of content quickly) that it has little room for fostering what I call the intellectual virtues. Indeed, the present structure of curricula and teaching not

AUTHOR'S NOTE: This is a reprint of an article originally published as Paul, Richard, "Critical Thinking, Moral Integrity, and Citizenship: Teaching for the Intellectual Virtues," in *Critical Thinking: How to Prepare Students for a Rapidly Changing World*, edited by Jane Willsen and A. J. A. Binker (Foundation for Critical Thinking), 1993, pp. 255-68. Used with permission.

only strongly discourages their development but also strongly encourages their opposites. Consequently, even the "best" students enter and leave college as largely miseducated persons, with no real sense of what they do and do not understand, with little sense of the state of their prejudices or insights, with little command of their intellectual faculties—in short, with no intellectual virtues, properly so-called.

Superficially absorbed content, the inevitable byproduct of extensive but shallow coverage, inevitably leads to intellectual arrogance. Such learning discourages intellectual perseverance and confidence in reason. It prevents the recognition of intellectual bad faith. It provides no foundation for intellectual empathy, nor for an intellectual sense of fair play. By taking in and giving back masses of detail, students come to believe that they *know* a lot about each subject—whether they understand or not. By practicing applying rules and formulas to familiar tasks, they come to feel that getting the answer should always be easy—if you don't know how to do something, don't try to figure it out, ask. By hearing and reading only one perspective, they come to think that perspective has a monopoly on truth—any other view must be completely wrong. By accepting (without understanding) that their government's past actions were all justified, they assume their government never would or could do wrong—if it doesn't seem right, I must not understand.

The pedagogical implications of my position include these: cutting back on coverage to focus on depth of understanding, on foundational ideas, on intellectual synthesis, and on intellectual experiences that develop and deepen the most basic intellectual skills, abilities, concepts, and virtues.

To accomplish this reorientation of curriculum and teaching, we need new criteria of what constitutes success and failure in school. We need to begin this reorientation as early as possible. Integrating teaching for critical thinking, moral integrity, and citizenship is an essential part of this reorientation.

The term "critical thinking" can be used in either a weak or a strong sense, depending upon whether we think of critical thinking narrowly, as a list or collection of discrete intellectual skills, or, more broadly, as a mode of mental integration, as a synthesized complex of dispositions, values, and skills necessary to becoming a fair-minded, rational person. Teaching critical thinking in a strong sense is a powerful, and I believe necessary, means to moral integrity and responsible citizenship.

Intellectual skills in and of themselves can be used either for good or ill, to enlighten or to propagandize, to gain narrow, self-serving ends, or to further the general and public good. The micro-skills themselves, for example, do not define fair-mindedness and could be used as easily by those who are highly prejudiced as those who are not. Those students not exposed to the challenge of strong sense critical thinking assignments (for example, assignments in which they must empathically reconstruct viewpoints that differ strikingly from their own) will not, as a matter of abstract morality or general good-heartedness, be fair to points of view they oppose, nor will they automatically develop a rationally defensible notion of what the public good is on the many issues they must decide as citizens.

Critical thinking, in its most defensible sense, is not simply a matter of cognitive skills. Moral integrity and responsible citizenship are, in turn, not simply a matter of good-heartedness or good intentions. Many good-hearted people cannot see through and critique propaganda and mass manipulation, and most good-hearted people fall prey at times to the powerful tendency to engage in self-deception, especially when their own egocentric interests and desires are at stake. One can be good-hearted and intellectually egocentric at the same time.

The problems of education for fair-minded independence of thought, for genuine moral integrity, and for responsible citizenship are not three separate issues but one complex task. If we succeed with one dimension of the problem, we succeed with all. If we fail with one, we fail with all. Now we are failing with all because we do not clearly understand the interrelated nature of the problem [or] how to address it.

The Intellectual and Moral Virtues of the Critical Person

Our basic ways of knowing are inseparable from our basic ways of being. How we think reflects who we are. Intellectual and moral virtues or disabilities are intimately interconnected. To cultivate the kind of intellectual independence implied in the concept of strong sense critical thinking, we must recognize the need to foster intellectual (epistemological) humility, courage, integrity, perseverance, empathy, and fair-mindedness. A brief gloss on each will suggest how to translate these concepts into concrete examples.

Intellectual humility: Having a consciousness of the limits of one's knowledge including a sensitivity to circumstances in which one's native egocentrism is likely to function self-deceptively; sensitivity to bias, prejudice, and limitations of one's viewpoint. Intellectual humility depends on recognizing that one should not claim more than one actually knows. It does not imply spinelessness or submissiveness. It implies the lack of intellectual pretentiousness, boastfulness, or conceit, combined with insight

into the logical foundations, or lack of such foundations, of one's beliefs.

Intellectual humility arises from insight into the nature of knowing. It is reminiscent of the ancient Greek insight that Socrates was the wisest of the Greeks because only he knew how little he really understood. Socrates developed this insight as a result of extensive, in-depth questioning of the knowledge claims of others. He had to think his way to this insight.

If this insight and this humility is part of our goal, then most textbooks and curricula require extensive modification, for typically they discourage rather than encourage it. The extent and nature of "coverage" for most grade levels and subjects implies that bits and pieces of knowledge are easily attained, without any significant consideration of the basis for the knowledge claimed in the text or by the teacher. The speed with which content is covered contradicts the notion that students must think in an extended way about content before giving assent to what is claimed. Most teaching and most texts are, in this sense, epistemologically unrealistic and hence foster intellectual arrogance in students, particularly in those with retentive memories who can repeat back what they have heard or read. *Pretending* to know is encouraged. Much standardized testing validates this pretense.

Most teachers got through their college classes mainly by "learning the standard textbook answers" and were neither given an opportunity nor encouraged to determine whether what the text or the professor said was "justified by their own thinking." To move toward intellectual humility, most teachers need to question most of what they learned, but such questioning would require intellectual courage, perseverance, and confidence in their own capacity to reason and understand subject matter through their own thought. Most teachers have not done the kind of analytic thinking necessary for gaining such perspective.

I would generalize as follows: just as the development of intellectual humility is an essential goal of critical thinking instruction, so is the development of intellectual courage, integrity, empathy, perseverance, fair-mindedness, and confidence in reason. Furthermore, each intellectual (and moral) virtue in turn is richly developed only in conjunction with the others. Before we approach this point directly, however, a brief characterization of what I have in mind by each of these traits is in order:

Intellectual courage: Having a consciousness of the need to face and fairly address ideas, beliefs, or viewpoints toward which we have strong negative emotions and to which we have not given a serious hearing. This courage is connected with the recognition that ideas considered dangerous or absurd are sometimes rationally justified (in whole or in part) and that conclusions and beliefs inculcated in us are sometimes false or misleading. To determine for ourselves which is which, we must not passively and uncritically "accept" what we have "learned." Intellectual courage comes into play here because inevitably we will come to see some truth in some ideas considered dangerous and absurd and distortion or falsity in some ideas strongly held in our social group. We need courage to he true to our own thinking in such circumstances. The penalties for nonconformity can be severe.

Intellectual empathy: Having a consciousness of the need to imaginatively put oneself in the place of others in order to genuinely understand them, which requires the consciousness of our egocentric tendency to identify truth with our immediate perceptions or long-standing thought or belief. This trait correlates with the ability to reconstruct accurately the viewpoints and reasoning of others and to reason from premises, assumptions, and ideas other than our own. This trait also correlates with the willingness to remember occasions when we were wrong in the past despite an intense conviction that we were right and with the ability to imagine our being similarly deceived in a case at hand.

Intellectual good faith (integrity): Recognition of the need to be true to one's own thinking; to be consistent in the intellectual standards one applies; to hold one's self to the same rigorous standards of evidence and proof to which one holds one's antagonists; to practice what one advocates for others; and to honestly admit discrepancies and inconsistencies in one's own thought and action.

Intellectual perseverance: Willingness and consciousness of the need to pursue intellectual insights and truths in spite of difficulties, obstacles, and frustrations; firm adherence to rational principles despite the irrational opposition of others; a sense of the need to struggle with confusion and unsettled questions over an extended period of time to achieve deeper understanding or insight.

Faith in reason: Confidence that, in the long run, one's own higher interests and those of humankind at large will be best served by giving the freest play to reason, by encouraging people to come to their own conclusions by developing their own rational faculties; faith that, with proper encouragement and cultivation, people can learn to think for themselves, form rational viewpoints, draw reasonable conclusions, think coherently and logically, persuade each other by reason, and become reasonable persons, despite the deep-seated obstacles in the native character of the human mind and in society as we know it.

Fair-mindedness: Willingness and consciousness of the need to treat all viewpoints alike, without reference to one's own feelings or vested interests or the feelings or vested interests of one's friends, community, or nation; implies adherence to intellectual standards without reference to one's own advantage or the advantage of one's group.

The Interdependence of the Intellectual Virtues

Let us now consider the interdependence of these virtues, how hard it is to deeply develop any one of them without also developing the others. Consider intellectual humility. To become aware of the limits of our knowledge, we need the *courage* to face our own prejudices and ignorance.

To discover our own prejudices, in turn, we must often *empathize* with and reason within points of view toward which we are hostile. To do this, we must typically *persevere* over a period of time, for learning to empathically enter a point of view against which we are biased takes time and significant effort. That effort will not seem justified unless we have the *faith in reason* to believe we will not be "tainted" or "taken in" by whatever is false or misleading in the opposing viewpoint. Furthermore, merely believing we can survive serious consideration of an "alien" point of view is not enough to motivate most of us to consider them seriously. We must also be motivated by an *intellectual sense of justice.* We must recognize an intellectual *responsibility* to be fair to views we oppose. We must feel *obliged* to hear them in their strongest form to ensure that we do not condemn them out of our own ignorance or bias. At this point, we come full circle back to where we began: the need for *intellectual humility.*

Or let us begin at another point. Consider intellectual good faith or integrity. Intellectual integrity is clearly difficult to develop. We are often motivated—generally without admitting to or being aware of this motivation—to set up inconsistent intellectual standards. Our egocentric or sociocentric side readily believes positive information about those we like and negative information about those we dislike. We tend to believe what justifies our vested interest or validates our strongest desires. Hence, we all have some innate tendencies to use double standards, which is, of course, paradigmatic of intellectual bad faith. Such thought often helps us get ahead in the world, maximize our power or advantage, and get more of what we want.

Nevertheless, we cannot easily operate *explicitly* or overtly with a double standard. We must, therefore, avoid looking at the evidence too closely. We cannot scrutinize our own inferences and interpretations too carefully. Hence, a certain amount of *intellectual arrogance* is quite useful. I may assume, for example, that I know just what you're going to say (before you say it), precisely what you are really after (before the evidence demonstrates it), and what actually is going on (before I have studied the situation carefully). My intellectual arrogance makes it easier for me to avoid noticing the unjustifiable discrepancy in the standards I apply to you and those I apply to myself. Of course, if I don't have to empathize with you, that too makes it easier to avoid seeing my duplicity. I am also better off if I don't feel a keen need to be fair to your point of view. A little background fear of what I might discover if I seriously considered the consistency of my own judgments also helps. In this case, my lack of intellectual integrity is supported by my lack of intellectual humility, empathy, and fair-mindedness.

Going in the other direction, it will be difficult to maintain a double standard between us if I feel a distinct responsibility to be fair to your point of view, understand this responsibility to entail that I must view things from your perspective in an empathic fashion, and conduct this inner inquiry with some humility regarding the possibility of my being wrong and your being right. The more I dislike you personally or feel wronged in the past by you or by others who share your way of thinking, the more pronounced in my character must be the trait of intellectual integrity in order to provide the countervailing impetus to think my way to a fair conclusion.

Defense Mechanisms and the Intellectual Virtues

A major obstacle to developing intellectual virtues is the presence in the human egocentric mind of what Freud has called "defense mechanisms." Each represents a way to falsify, distort, misconceive, twist, or deny reality. Their presence represents, therefore, the relative weakness or absence of the intellectual virtues. Since they operate in everyone to some degree, no one embodies the intellectual virtues purely or perfectly. In other words, we each have a side of us unwilling to face unpleasant truth, willing to distort, falsify, twist, and misrepresent. We also know from a monumental mass of psychological research that this side can be powerful, can dominate our minds strikingly. We marvel at, and are often dumbfounded by, others whom we consider clear-cut instances of these modes of thinking. What is truly "marvelous," it seems to me, is how little we take ourselves to be victims of these falsifying thoughts and how little we try to break them down. The vicious circle seems to be this: because we, by and large, lack the intellectual virtues, we do not have insight into them, but because we lack insight into them, we do not see ourselves as

lacking them. They weren't explicitly taught to us, so we don't have to explicitly teach them to our children.

Insights, Analyzed Experiences, and Activated Ignorance

Schooling has generally ignored the need for insight or intellectual virtues. This deficiency is intimately connected with another one, the failure of the schools to show students they should not only test what they "learn" in school by their own experience but also test what they experience by what they "learn" in school. This may seem a hopeless circle, but if we can see the distinction between a critically analyzed experience and an unanalyzed one, we can see the link between the former and insight, and the latter and prejudice, and will be well on our way to seeing how to fill these needs.

We subject little of our experience to critical analysis. We seldom take our experiences apart to judge their epistemological worth. We rarely sort the "lived" integrated experience into its component parts, raw data, [or] our interpretation of the data, [and we rarely] ask ourselves how the interests, goals, and desires we brought to those data shaped and structured that interpretation. Similarly, we rarely seriously consider the possibility that our interpretation (and hence our experience) might be selective, biased, or misleading.

This is not to say that our unanalyzed experiences lack meaning or significance. Quite the contrary, in some sense we assess all experience. Our egocentric side never ceases to catalogue experiences in accord with its common and idiosyncratic fears, desires, prejudices, stereotypes, caricatures, hopes, dreams, and assorted irrational drives. We shouldn't assume a priori that our rational side dominates the shaping of our experience. Our unanalyzed experiences are some combination of these dual contributors to thought, action, and being. Only through critical analysis can we hope to isolate the irrational dimensions of our experience. The ability to do so grows as we analyze more and more of our experience.

Of course, more important than the sheer number of analyzed experiences is their quality and significance. This quality and significance depends on how much our analyses embody the intellectual virtues. At the same time, the degree of our virtue depends upon the number and quality of experiences we have successfully critically analyzed. What links the virtues, as perfections of the mind, and the experiences, as analyzed products of the mind, is insight. Every critically analyzed experience to some extent produces one or more intellectual virtues. To become more rational, it is not enough to have experiences [or] even for those experiences to have meanings. Many experiences are more or less charged with irrational meanings. These important meanings produce stereotypes, prejudices, narrow-mindedness, delusions, and illusions of various kinds.

The process of developing intellectual virtues and insights is part and parcel of our developing an interest in taking apart our experiences to separate their rational from their irrational dimensions. These meta-experiences become important benchmarks and guides for future thought. They make possible modes of thinking and maneuvers in thinking closed to the irrational mind.

Some Thoughts on How to Teach for the Intellectual Virtues

To teach for the intellectual virtues, one must recognize the significant differences between the higher order critical thinking of a fair-minded critical thinker and that of a self-serving critical thinker. Though both share a certain command of the micro-skills of critical thinking, they are not equally good at tasks which presuppose the intellectual virtues. The self-serving (weak sense) critical thinker would lack the insights that underlie and support these virtues.

I can reason well in domains in which I am prejudiced—hence, eventually, reason my way out of prejudices—only if I develop mental benchmarks for such reasoning. Of course, one insight I need is that when I am prejudiced it will seem to me that I am not and, similarly, that those who are not prejudiced as I am will seem to me to be prejudiced. (To a prejudiced person, an unprejudiced person seems prejudiced.) I will come to this insight only insofar as I have analyzed experiences in which I was intensely convinced I was correct on an issue, judgment, or point of view, only to find, after a series of challenges, reconsiderations, and new reasonings, that my previous conviction was in fact prejudiced. I must take this experience apart in my mind [and] clearly understand its elements and how they fit together (how I became prejudiced; how I inwardly experienced that prejudice; how intensely that prejudice seemed true and insightful; how I progressively broke that prejudice down through serious consideration of opposing lines of reasoning; [and] how I slowly came to new assumptions, new information, and ultimately new conceptualizations).

Only when one gains analyzed experiences of working and reasoning one's way out of prejudice can one gain the higher order abilities of a fair-minded critical thinker. What one gains is somewhat "procedural" or sequential in that there is a *process* one must go through, but one also sees that the process cannot be followed out formulaically or algorithmically; it depends on principles. The somewhat abstract articulation of the intellectual virtues above will take on concrete meaning in the light of these *analyzed experiences*. Their true meaning to us will be given in and by these experiences. We will often return to them to recapture and rekindle the insights upon which the intellectual virtues depend.

Generally, to develop intellectual virtues, we must create a collection of analyzed experiences that represent to us intuitive models, not only of the pitfalls of our own previous thinking and experiencing but also processes for reasoning our way out of or around them. These model experiences must be charged with meaning for us. We cannot be indifferent to them. We must sustain them in our minds by our sense of their importance as they sustain and guide us in our thinking.

What does this imply for teaching? It implies a somewhat different content or material focus. Our own minds and experiences must become the subject of our study and learning. Indeed, only to the extent that the content of our own experiences becomes an essential part of study will the usual subject matter truly be reamed. By the same token, the experiences of others must become part of what we study. But experiences of any kind should always be critically analyzed, and students must do their own analyses and clearly recognize what they are doing.

This entails that students become explicitly aware of the logic of experience. All experiences have three elements, each of which may require some special scrutiny in the analytic process: (1) something to be experienced (some actual situation or other); (2) an experiencing subject (with a point of view [and] framework of beliefs, attitudes, desires, and values); and (3) some interpretation or conceptualization of the situation. To take any experience apart, then, students must be sensitive to three distinctive sets of questions:

- What are the raw facts, [and] what is the most neutral description of the situation? If one describes the experience this way and another disagrees, on what description can they agree?
- What interests, attitudes, desires, or concerns do I bring to the situation? Am I always aware of them? Why or why not?
- How am I conceptualizing or interpreting the situation in light of my point of view? How else might it be interpreted?

Students must also explore the interrelationships of these parts. How did my point of view, values, desires, etc., affect what I noticed about the situation? How did they prevent me from noticing other things? How would I have interpreted the situation had I noticed those other things? How did my point of view, desires, etc., affect my interpretation? How *should* I interpret the situation?

If students have many assignments that require them to analyze their experiences and the experiences of others along these lines, with ample opportunity to argue among themselves about which interpretations make the most sense and why, then they will begin to amass a catalogue of critically analyzed experiences. If the experiences illuminate the pitfalls of thought, the analysis and the models of thinking they suggest will be the foundation for their intellectual traits and character. They will develop intellectual virtues because they had thought their way to them and internalized them as concrete understandings and insights, not because they took them up as slogans. Their basic values and *their* thinking *processes* will be in a symbiotic relationship to each other. Their intellectual and affective lives will become more integrated. Their standards for thinking will he implicit in their own thinking rather than in texts, teachers, or the authority of a peer group.

Conclusion

We do not now teach for the intellectual virtues. If we did, not only would we have a basis for integrating the curriculum, we would also have a basis for integrating the cognitive and affective lives of students. Such integration is the basis for strong sense critical thinking, for moral development, and for citizenship. The moral, social, and political issues we face in everyday life are increasingly intellectually complex. Their settlement relies on circumstances and events that are interpreted in a variety of (often conflicting) ways. For example, should our government publish misinformation to mislead another government or group which it considers terrorist? Is it ethical to tolerate a "racist" regime such as South Africa, or are we morally obligated to attempt to overthrow it? Is it ethical to support anti-Communist groups that use, or have used, torture, rape, or murder as tools in their struggle? When, if ever, should the CIA attempt to overthrow a government it perceives as undemocratic? How can one distinguish "terrorists" from "freedom fighters"?

Or, consider issues that are more "domestic" or "personal." Should deliberate polluters be considered "criminals"? How should we balance off "dollar losses" against "safety gains"? That is, how much money should we be willing to spend to save human lives? What is deliberate deception in advertising and business practices? Should one protect incompetent individuals within one's profession from exposure? How should one reconcile or balance one's personal vested interest against the public good? What moral or civic responsibility exists to devote time and energy to public good as against one's private interests and amusements?

These are just a few of the many complex moral, political, and social issues that virtually all citizens must face. The response of the citizenry to such issues defines the moral character of society. These issues challenge our intellectual honesty, courage, integrity, empathy, and fair-mindedness. Given their complexity, they require perseverance and confidence in reason. People easily become cynical, [become] intellectually lazy, or retreat into simplistic models of learning and the world they learned in school and see and hear on TV. On the other hand, it is doubtful that the fundamental conflicts and antagonisms in the world can be solved or resolved by sheer power or abstract goodwill. Good-heartedness and power are insufficient for creating a just world. Some modest development of the intellectual virtues seems essential for future human survival and well-being. Whether the energy, the resources, and the insights necessary for this development can be significantly mustered remains open. This is certain: we will never succeed in cultivating traits whose roots we do not understand and whose development we do not foster.

12

Instructional Responsibilities of College Faculty to Minority Students

James A. Vasquez and Nancy Wainstein

The Problem

The shockingly poor performance in public education of minority students[1] from Black, Hispanic, and Native American ethnic groups throughout the years has become a given, even a starting point, for almost any discussion on education for these students. While there is no need to establish basic evidence for a phenomenon so well known, we will present some of the data that demonstrate the attrition of these students, beginning from the high school years through graduate and/or professional schools.

Astin (1982) reports that minority students are "increasingly under-represented at each higher level of degree attainment" (p. 17). He identifies five points at which minority students drop out of the educational system: completion of high school, entry to college, completion of college, entry to graduate or professional school, and completion of graduate or professional school. The loss of minorities at those

AUTHORS' NOTE: This is a reprint of an article originally published as Vasquez, James A. and Nancy Wainstein, "Instructional Responsibilities of College Faculty to Minority Students," *Journal of Negro Education,* 1(4): Fall 1990, pp. 599-610. Used with permission.

EDITORS' NOTE: For a detailed discussion and some teaching ideas, see the Opening Up New Roads: Diversity Issues section in the *Fieldguide.*

five transition points, Astin reports, "accounts for their substantial under-representation in high-level positions" (p. 14).

The figures clearly show that minority students trail White students significantly at each of the transition points identified above. For example, the rate of minority students (Blacks, Chicanos, Puerto Ricans, and/or Native Americans) dropping out of high school is 65 to 165 percent higher than that [of] White students. Among those going on to college (two- and four-year), 11 to 31 percent fewer minority students complete college than [do] Whites. Finally, minority students drop out of graduate or professional schools at rates 10 to 27 percent higher than [those of] Whites (Astin, 1982). Table 12.1 dramatically illustrates the long-term declining effect on 1,000 (hypothetical) students from each group entering high school.

For each population, then, there is a pyramid effect, with a smaller group continuing up the educational structure at each of the graduation/admission points. The issue we must stress, however, is that at virtually every point the pyramid becomes significantly narrower for minority populations.

Astin (1982) further reports that "most observers agree that in recent years the quality of public schooling at both the elementary and secondary levels has deteriorated and that the weaknesses of the public education system are

TABLE 12.1 The Differential Effect of Dropout Rates by Ethnicity Group per 1,000 (Hypothetical) Cases Entering High School

Group	Graduate from High School	Enter College	Graduate in 4 Years	Graduate (4 Years +)	Enter Graduate/ Professional School	Graduate
White	830	373	127	209	30.0	17.0
Black	720	288	70	147	12.0	6.6
Chicano	550	220	29	88	3.6	1.7
Puerto Rican	550	247	32	104	4.0	2.0
Native American	550	170	27	66	2.6	1.4

SOURCE: Astin, A. W. (1982). *Final report of the Commission on the Higher Education of Minorities* (p. 15). San Francisco: Jossey-Bass.

borne most heavily by minority students" (p. 26). Grossman (1984), in his wide-ranging survey of Hispanic professionals, found that they believed, with few exceptions, that schools provide Hispanics with culturally inappropriate education. Other factors associated in the literature with low achievement for minority students include social isolation and economics (Lunneborg & Lunneborg, 1986b, p. 71) and self-concept and the extent of interaction with faculty and peers (Pascarella et al., 1987).

One can hardly question the potential influence of these problem areas on academic performance. While the truth seems to be that "there is less known about why minority students perform as they do in college than is known about White students" (Lunneborg & Lunneborg, 1986a, p. 81), it is strange that virtually nothing is said in the literature—written for the most part, one must assume, by college faculty members—about the need for the faculty to assume greater responsibility for the tragic history of these minority students in higher education.

The Inadequacy of Deficit/Disadvantage Theories

Historically, the most popular explanation for the poor academic records of minority students as a group has been the assumption of deficien-

cies, whether linguistic, sociocultural (Bernstein, 1961), economic, or biological (Jensen, 1969). Yet, minority students may have social and cultural value systems that are significantly different from (although not inferior to) those of majority (mainstream) students and of their teachers. Thus, the use of a cultural deficit/disadvantage explanation for their poor academic performance must be severely questioned.

Moore (1976) challenges the cultural disadvantage hypothesis on the grounds that it does not consider (1) the possible negative effects of the school environment, (2) the effect of teacher behaviors and attitudes toward minority students on student performance, [and] (3) the questionable validity of test scores used to determine levels of academic achievement. Further, it is unable to explain how some teachers can consistently instruct high-risk, disadvantaged, and minority students effectively while others consistently fail to do so. Other reasons noted in current research for rejecting the deficit interpretation of minority student academic performance are its essential orientation to student weaknesses rather than strengths ([Howard] & Scott, 1981; Munroe et al., 1981; Lunneborg & Lunneborg, 1986b), its tendency to ignore context in interpreting performance (Laosa, 1981), and its insensitivity to the struggle minority students endure because they are caught between mainstream American and minority cultures (Greco & McDavis, 1978). According to Sedlacek (1983), these inadequacies in the theory, which turn initial "differences" into "deficits," make deficit interpretations the forerunners of institutional racism.

Much of the recent literature suggests that minority students do not fail academically because of inherent deficiencies but because their differences are not acknowledged or accommodated by educational institutions or the faculty within them. Thus, whereas cultural differences of minority students should be viewed as strengths that contribute positively to the classroom, they are too often seen as deficiencies that must be "corrected" or, at best, disregarded.

The Faculty as Classroom Instructors

Almost nothing in the current literature directly addresses the issue of how college faculty members should adapt their instruction to the cultural distinctiveness of minority students. Until this literature appears, there is little likelihood that faculty will be able to cultivate these strengths in or out of the classroom. This is not to say that educators and researchers have not written about allegedly successful programs for minority students in higher education—they have—but while institutional responsibilities have been described, the need for college-wide support services, remedial classes, and other elements in these programs has been stressed. There remains a peculiar absence of recommendations for instructors about how they might change their own classroom behavior.

For example, the book, *Higher Education and the Disadvantaged Student* (Astin et al., 1972), covers 359 pages, yet less than one and one-half pages are devoted to the subject of teaching. The *Final Report of the Commission*

on the Higher Education of Minorities (Astin, 1982) contains ten chapters (249 pages), and none indicates by its title that the book discusses the type of teacher needed for minority students in higher education. In the chapter entitled "Factors Affecting Minority Educational Progress," no discussion is presented of the type of teaching that might be most effective for minority students at the college level. That report, the product of a contract awarded by the Ford Foundation to the Higher Education Research Institute, was guided by the Commission on the Higher Education of Minorities. One of the four major tasks of the commission was "to identify factors in the social and educational environment that facilitate or hinder the educational development of minority students" (Astin, 1982). However, while the report closes with 66 recommendations in 14 categories, five of which address graduate and professional education, not one of the five presents teaching strategies or techniques for instructors with minority students in their classrooms. To cite a final example, Gandara's (1986) article, "Chicanos in Higher Education: The Politics of Self-Interest," closes with six recommendations for improving the educational attainment of Chicanos in higher education, particularly in California, but not a line is found regarding the need for college instructors to make any changes in their traditional manner of teaching.

Clearly, the role of the instructor in the college classroom is a very key one. Little, if any, solid evidence exists to deny that the instructor's role at this level is or should be less critical than it is at lower levels of education. Roueche and Snow (1977), for example, reporting results of a national survey on existing practices in two- and four-year colleges to solve the learning problems of "nontraditional" students, state simply that the teacher is the key. They cite the instructor's role in deciding the content that will be taught. They claim that content is critical because it must reflect the interests and values of these students. When it does, students "will want to learn the material. In fact, they will probably go beyond that which is required" (p. 116). The report further magnifies the instructor's role by stressing the importance of instructional delivery. Decisions regarding which instructional delivery system will be used, according to Roueche and Snow, are entirely in the hands of the instructor. Thus, the instructor's functions, as evaluator of student performance and as virtually the sole provider of reinforcement to students, are other behaviors that point to the cruciality of the instructor's role in the college classroom.

It is not difficult to understand why some minority students look for that quality called "leadership" in an instructor (Britto, 1983). The term implies much more than simply imparting information. Indeed, the most naturally gifted teachers require some kind of unique preparation before they would be expected to meet the varied needs of minority students. As Fantini and Weinstein (1972) note, "Even the best teachers may not be capable of teaching the disadvantaged without special training" (p. 31). In light of this, it is truly incongruous that, while all other levels of schooling from the first grade on require teachers to have completed some form of specialized and supervised training, at many universities one needs, with few exceptions, absolutely no formal preparation or experience to be an instructor.

We will now discuss nine perspectives found in the literature regarding what is required of college instructors who teach minority students if the true potential of these students—as comprehended by and within their own cultures—is to be achieved. Some of these perspectives take the form of attitudes and concepts to which instructors must attend, [and]

others are more specifically defined as instructional strategies for use in the classroom. We will attempt to present them in an order moving from the general to the more specific.

Basing Instruction on Student Values

Various educators suggest that it is the instructor's responsibility to know the values of minority students and to build on those values. A basic rationale for this seems to be that values underlie students' reinforcement systems. Thus, if students are to feel motivated or rewarded for their performance in the classroom, the instructor must be able to offer inducements and/or rewards that have some tie-in with the students' values. Moore (1976) states that "motivation strategies are necessary" and that it is "more productive to determine what stimulates a student than to argue that the student cannot be stimulated" (p. 18). Grossman (1984) reports a number of recommendations made by his respondents (mostly Hispanic professional educators) on how instructional techniques should be modified for Hispanic students. Numerous culture-related traits appear in these recommendations including family pride, preference for personal forms of rewards and for close personal relationships, cultural expectations of punctuality, global perceptions of reality, preference for cooperative activities, and the need to know about contributions the student's culture has made to society. Grossman concludes by recommending that counselors, educators, psychologists, and others who work with Hispanic students "should take these individual differences into consideration when selecting appropriate instructional, classroom management, counseling, and assessment techniques" (pp. 6, 7, 19, 210).

Matching Teaching and Learning Styles

Gentry and Ellison (1981) suggest that "there are benefits to be derived from matching teaching styles with learning styles" (p. 8). Benefits specifically mentioned by these educators are improved mental health, self-understanding, and learning. They state that students at all levels find greater motivation and perform at higher levels academically when instructional methods complement student learning characteristics. Other researchers have reported similar findings. Barwell (1981), for example, states in reference to Native American students that "arrangement" (in the context of discussions on harmony with nature) as mainstream individuals know the concept is difficult for Native American students to understand. Further, dichotomies such as cause-effect and comparison-contrast are somewhat foreign to these students because they appear "untruthful and complicated to the Indian's sense of order" (pp. 6, 7). Barwell recommends description and, particularly, narration as activities that are more natural for Native American students because their culture has been passed orally from generation to generation.

Barwell (1981) further suggests that, in teaching Native American students, "Above all, the course should be taught holistically" (p. 1). Holistic teaching is suggested by researchers in their elaboration of what is known as field-dependent (sometimes referred to as field-sensitive or field-attentive) learning style (Ramirez & Castaneda, 1974). Basically, this approach to learning (and to teaching) is deductive and proceeds from the general to the particular. Students characterized by this style of learning are said to be most responsive to an overview or "big picture" at the beginning of a lesson. This procedure presumably orients them to the entire field of information to be covered early in the learning process and enables them to proceed to more specific details in a lesson.

Many Mexican American students have also been found to be characterized by the field-dependent learning style. Working with Mexican American students at the lower levels of schooling, Ramirez and Castaneda (1974) have written extensively in this vein, citing the responsiveness of these students to a holistic instructional approach. Grossman (1984) also reports that this survey found both mainstream and Hispanic professionals in agreement that "Hispanic students may do better on tasks which require global perception rather than analysis of detail" and that "educators should adapt their instructional techniques to this cultural difference" (p. 59). Field-dependent students are widely thought by researchers to be particularly responsive to the use of affect by their instructors. Additional support for a field-dependent approach to instruction in the case of minority students is found in Fantini and Weinstein's (1972) recommendation that "these students must be approached with an understanding of their affective as well as their cognitive needs" (Astin et al., 1972, p. 31).

Maintaining High Expectations

Not a few educators affirm the importance of teacher expectations in the college classroom. Britto (1983), for example, stresses the role of the instructor in building "hope" in minority students and states that "when [minority] students know there is hope, they are remarkably generous in their response to subject matter and their instructor" (p. 8). Britto urges the use of the ideas of self-respect and pride to challenge the abilities of students and states that instructors should "dare students to succeed" (p. 8).

To build hope and high expectations in students, it seems, instructors must first have those same expectations of them. In their report on "disadvantaged" students in higher education, Astin et al. (1972) cite Gordon and Wilkerson (1966), who affirm the "critical importance" of the teacher's expectations in influencing student performance (p. 32). They also note that Rosenhan (1966) "presents evidence which suggests that students whose teachers believe they will perform well actually do, regardless of ability" (p. 32). More recently, Lunneborg and Lunneborg (1986a), in seeking to explain factors affecting the low academic performance of minority students in college, state that "an expectation may have been built up among faculty that Blacks in general would perform poorly" (p. 83). They cite data and comparable findings from a study by Edmunds (1984).

Acceptance of Students' Nonparticipation

A specific minority student behavior that might be attributed directly to culture and that has often defied explanation is the lack of interaction and active participation in the classroom by some minority students. This may, of course, be due to inability among language-minority students to comprehend the language of the classroom. Even when such students are progressing well in English, some researchers cite a "silent period," that stage in language learning just preceding the breakthrough to linguistic competence and activity which, in and of itself, appears to be an indication of language growth (Krashen, 1981). Language differences aside, however, other cultural factors may also produce a quiet, inactive type of minority student in the classroom. Barwell (1981), for example, states that Native American students possess a certain "cultural respect for age and authority, which makes their classroom manner appear

shy or inattentive" (p. 1). He elaborates by saying that "the lack of student-to-teacher and student-to-student interaction [is] directly related to the Indian's way of dealing with authority and of being respectful" (p. 6).

Closely related to this explanation of lack of classroom participation is the reputed unwillingness of some minority students, especially those of Asian background, to "challenge" instructors or to ask questions that might be interpreted as questioning an instructor's knowledge or competence. Viewed in this manner, nonparticipation is not a weakness or deficiency but actually a show of respect for the knowledge and skills that faculty members possess. Therefore, it would seem most advisable for college instructors to bear in mind possible cultural explanations for minority students' nonparticipation in classroom discussions and activities.

The Instructor as Problem Solver

The role of the instructor as problem solver is an important one for those with minority students in the classroom. According to Britto (1983), instructors cannot afford to be oriented to subject matter alone; some of their attention must be directed to the specific and more personal needs of individual students. He urges instructors to "break from routine and see how [their] minority students are doing" (p. 7). Moore (1976) stresses a similar concept in his report, stating that "the teacher must accept some responsibility for helping the student determine his goals and help him reach them" (p. 18). Perhaps there is some affiliation between the role of the instructor as problem solver and the tendency of some minority students to view instructors in the role of "leaders," as described above. Apparently, some minority students tend to view their instructors in a more complete, holistic way than do mainstream students (Vasquez, 1988), expecting instructors not only to be providers of information but also to relate to students in ways that involve the two parties in more comprehensive and informal relationships.

The Instructor as Motivator

Instructors must see and accept their responsibility for motivating minority students at the college level. Clearly implicating the instructor's role as motivator, Moore (1976) states that ways "must be learned to make (college-level) students receptive to learning activity" (p. 18). Stressing the importance of the instructor in this activity, Moore continues,

The effects of teacher behavior on motivation cannot be minimized. . . . The statements they make, their availability, the interest they take in their students, the advice they give, the enthusiasm they display—all are facets of their ability to simulate. (p. 19)

Still, from listening to college faculty conversations, one gets the impression that minority students must "grow up"—that they should be largely self-motivated at the college level, as if mainstream students no longer receive culturally appropriate reinforcements and rewards at the college level. In short, if minorities want to "make it in a White man's university," they have to "do it the White man's way." A growing body of literature indicates that culturally appropriate instructional and motivational strategies are effective at the college level and that college instructors should be responsible for knowing about and implementing them.

Encouraging Achievement through Cooperation

Clearly, instructors must recognize that some minority students tend to excel when engaged in cooperative activities as opposed to competitive or individualistic activities. Barwell (1981) reports this finding in relation to Native American students:

This cultural difference has a direct influence on how we should organize classroom activities. Pitting one student's essay against another may prove disastrous. On the other hand, small groups and pairs in writing and criticism tend to work well. (p. 7)

Griffin (see Sedlacek & Webster, 1978) indicates that Blacks also tend to emphasize cooperative activities, while Grossman (1984) reports "high agreement" (82 percent) among Hispanic professionals that Hispanic students were more cooperative and group oriented than Anglo students. This characteristic is especially pertinent for college teachers of minority students for two reasons. First, the typical college classroom tends to be somewhat competitive, if for no other reason than because grades are based so frequently on a curve. Thus, every student in every activity that is graded (consciously or unconsciously) by the instructor is, at all times, in an academic battle with every other student. One can hardly imagine a more effective way to induce a competitive atmosphere in the classroom. Second, college instructors seem to place undue value on work that is done alone by the student. Perhaps there is some justification for this in that grades must be assigned individually at the end of the quarter, but the practice favors some students (those who prefer to work alone) at the expense of others, including many minority students who often indicate that they already feel quite alone and isolated in the university context (Madrazo-Peterson & Rodriguez, 1978).

Oral versus Written Traditions

An additional interesting and helpful insight is provided by Britto (1983) in discussing the differences he found in teaching college composition to minority students. While Britto broadens the application of his findings to minorities in general (and there is some support for this—e.g., Kleinfeld, 1973), it is with specific reference to Black students that he discusses the need for college instructors to understand that minority students participate in a culture that is basically oral in orientation while the mainstream culture is basically oriented to the printed word. Britto cites Smitherman (1977) as follows:

The crucial difference in American culture lies in the contrasting modes in which black and white Americans have shaped their language. . . . a written mode for whites, having come from a European, print-oriented culture; a spoken mode for blacks, having come from an African, orally oriented background. (p. 6)

As Britto (1983) further urges, "This avenue of understanding and study should be pursued by the instructor of college composition who wishes to instruct minorities" (p. 6). The current resurgence of interest in Black Vernacular English as a spoken mode of communication (apparently not accompanied by written form) attests to Britto's and Smitherman's (1977) findings that a strong oral tradition exists among speakers of that dialect. Barwell (1981) provides similar findings relative to Native Americans and suggests that oral tradition among Native Americans exerts a significant influence on learning among students of that ethnic group as well.

Clearly, some ethnic minority students differ from mainstream students in meaningful ways along the lines of oral versus written preferences for transmitting information. Thus, the traditional emphasis, that such a heavy proportion of college learning takes place only when an open book is placed in front of the student, may serve these students inadequately.

Learning by Doing

Just as research has shown that Blacks emphasize learning through oral tradition, other researchers suggest that Hispanics emphasize learning by doing as opposed to learning by hearing. Grossman (1984) suggests that "educators should deemphasize the lecture approach and utilize the direct experience approach with students who learn better this way" (p. 59). Kleinfeld (1973) also reports that some minority students (at lower levels) tend to learn through the "trial and error" method (i.e., observing a parent perform a task to be learned and then attempting it themselves, often with little or no verbal interaction between the two). To some, this suggests a culturally based difference between "teaching" and "training"—the former consisting basically of imparting information verbally and through books and the latter of a kind of on-the-job experience. Training, in this sense, may seem objectionable, as opportunities for schooling of this kind are limited by college facilities, time available from instructors, and so forth. However, a move toward stressing activities that allow learning through direct experience would be a move toward more culturally appropriate instruction for minority college students and, thus, [is] certainly advisable.

Conclusion

Our review of the research literature indicates that deficit/deficiency explanations of minority groups' poor academic performance and attrition at the higher education levels are untenable. A cultural difference perspective not only fits reality better but also suggests practical means for identifying solutions to these most disturbing phenomena. Although most researchers acknowledge that college faculty should be specially trained to respond to minority students (as are teachers at the lower levels of the educational system), our review of the literature found only bits and pieces of the larger program needed to make serious inroads to the solution. The literature that suggests practical strategies for instructing minority students in the college classroom are virtually nonexistent.

Many minority students fail in school not because they are culturally different but because faculty members are unprepared to recognize their cultural distinctiveness as strengths. We have attempted to identify some of these differences and to suggest ways for instructors to build positively upon them. Unless college faculty members are willing to take significantly more responsibility for the failure of minority students in our colleges and universities by adapting their own instructional and counseling services to minorities' cultural preferences and traits, the future of a large and growing percentage of our college population looks rather bleak. Given proper recognition in the college context, however, the cognitive and affective strengths of minority students can bring a renewed sense of humanism and purpose to an educational system sorely in need of such traits.

Note

1. Reference to minority students in this chapter will be primarily to those from Black, Hispanic, and/or Native American ethnic backgrounds. The term *Hispanic* generally will be used to refer to students who are Spanish-surnamed and thus trace their cultural heritage to a country that is Spanish-speaking. In cases where studies or surveys were conducted with a specific Hispanic group such as Puerto Ricans or Chicanos (Mexican Americans), we will identify the specific group by name.

References

Astin, A. W. (1982). *Final report of the Commission on the Higher Education of Minorities*. San Francisco: Jossey-Bass.

Astin, H. S., Astin, A. W., Bisconti, A. S., & Frankel, H. H. (1972). *Higher education and the disadvantaged student*. Washington, D.C.: Human Service Press.

Barwell, J. (1981, March). *Strategies for teaching composition to Native Americans*. A paper presented at the annual meeting of the Conference on College Composition and Communication, Dallas, Texas. (ERIC Document No. ED 199 761)

Bernstein, B. (1961). Social class and linguistic development: A theory of social learning. In A. H. Halsey, J. Floyd, & C. A. Anderson (Eds.), *Education, economy and society* (pp. 288-314). Glencoe, IL: Free Press.

Britto, N. (1983, February). *Teaching writing to minority students*. A paper presented at the annual meeting of the Midwest Regional Conference on English in the Two-Year College, Overland Park, Kansas. (ERIC Document No. ED 233 343)

Edmunds, G. J. (1984). Needs assessment strategy for Black students: An examination of stressors and program implications. *Journal of Non-White Concerns, 12*, 48-56.

Gandara, P. (1986). The politics of self-interest. *American Journal of Education, 95*(1), 256-272.

Gentry, R. & Ellison, V. G. (1981, February). *Instructional strategies that challenge Black college students in the area of exceptional child education.* A paper presented at the Council for Exceptional Children Conference on the Exceptional Black Child, New Orleans, Louisiana. (EMC Document No. ED 204 906)

Gordon, E. & Wilkerson, D. (1966). *Compensatory education for the disadvantaged: Programs and practices, preschool through college.* New York: College Entrance Examination Board.

Greco, M. E. & McDavis, R. J. (1978). Cuban-American college students: Needs, cultural attitudes, and vocational development program suggestions. *Journal of College Student Personnel, 79,* 254-258.

Grossman, H. (1984). *Educating Hispanic students.* Springfield, IL: Charles C Thomas.

Howard, A. & Scott, R. (1981). The study of minority groups in complex societies. In R. H. Munroe, R. L. Munroe, & B. B. Whiting (Eds.), *Handbook of cross-cultural human development* (pp. 113-152). New York: Garland Press.

Jensen, A. R. (1969). How much can we boost IQ and scholastic achievement? *Harvard Educational Review, 39*(1), 1-123.

Kleinfeld, J. (1973). Intellectual strengths in culturally different groups: An Eskimo illustration. *Review of Educational Research, 43*(3), 341-359.

Krashen, S. D. (1981). Bilingual education and second language acquisition theory. In California State Department of Education, *Schooling and language minority students: A theoretical framework* (pp. 51-79). Los Angeles: Evaluation, Dissemination and Assessment Center, California State University.

Laosa, L. M. (1981). Maternal behavior: Sociocultural diversity in modes of family interaction. In R. W. Henderson (Ed.), *Parent-*

child interactions: Theory, research and prospects (pp. 125-167). New York: Academic Press.

Lunneborg, C. E. & Lunneborg, P. W. (1986a, April). Beyond prediction: The challenge of minority achievement in higher education. *Journal of Multi-Cultural Counseling and Development, 14,* 77-84.

———. (1986b). Student-centered versus university-centered solutions to problems of minority students. *Journal of College Student Personnel, 26,* 224-228.

Madrazo-Peterson, R. & Rodriguez, M. (1978, May). Minority students' perceptions of a university environment. *Journal of College Student Personnel, 19*(3), 259-263.

Moore, W., Jr. (1976). *Community college response to the high risk student: A critical reappraisal.* Washington, D.C.: American Association of Community and Junior Colleges.

Pascarella, E., Smart, J. C., Ethington, C. A., & Nettles, M. T. (1987). The influence of college on self-concept: A consideration of race and gender differences. *American Educational Research Journal, 24*(1), 49-77.

Ramirez, M. & Castaneda, A. (Eds.). (1974). *Cultural democracy, bicognitive development, and education.* New York: Academic Press.

Rosenhan, D. L. (1966, September). Effects of social class on responsiveness to approval and disapproval. *Journal of Personality and Social Psychology,* pp. 253-259.

Roueche, J. E. & Snow, J. J. (1977). *Overcoming learning problems.* San Francisco: Jossey-Bass.

Sedlacek, W. E. (1983). Teaching minority students. In J. H. Cones, III, J. F. Noonan, & D. Janna (Eds.), *Teaching minority students* (pp. 39-50). San Francisco: Jossey-Bass.

Sedlacek, W. E. & Webster, D. W. (1978). Admission and retention of minority students in large universities. *Journal of College Student Personnel, 19,* 242-248.

Smitherman, G. (1977). *Talkin' and testifyin'.* Boston: Houghton Mifflin.

Vasquez, J. A. (1988, Spring). Contexts of learning for minority students. *The Educational Forum, 52*(3), 243-253.

Doonesbury

BY GARRY TRUDEAU

The Collegial World of Professors: The Classic Arguments

How the bridge between students and faculty is forged depends, to a great extent, on the conversations—collegial and critical, formal and informal—that we have among ourselves. The essays in this section engage the theme of conversations among college professors about what we do both inside and outside the classroom to educate our students. Issues concern how we do or should do our work as teachers and how we perceive our students, decide on standards and requirements, and evaluate our own performance and that of our students. Recent debates over grade inflation, student evaluations, multiculturalism, and interdisciplinary studies have focused attention on a number of issues that have preoccupied college faculties. Clearly, the faculty are not homogeneous in their response, as Trudeau so succinctly reminds us. The issues include how to assess the product of our labors, the proper content of what we teach, and the disciplinary knowledges and norms that inform how and why we teach. These three themes are highlighted in the essays in this section.

Specifically, the first five essays concern how we evaluate our courses, ourselves, and our students. They identify a number of myths—about undergraduate decline, the trade-off between content and critical thinking, graduate student failure, grade inflation, and teaching evaluation and assessment. These myths circulate within faculties, in corridors, in elevators, and in rest rooms as well as in departmental meetings, justifying current practices, limiting our accountability to students and colleagues, and devaluing teaching. Rejection of these myths leads to a concern with the question raised in the next set of essays in this section: how can we accurately assess how well we are accomplishing the tasks we set for ourselves and our students?

Norman Furniss (Chapter 13) challenges myths about the qualities and qualifications of undergraduates. His documentation makes clear that many complaints of faculty are perennial and not unique to the end of this century. This analysis suggests a far deeper issue than realized because it characterizes writings of frustrated faculty through time. He believes that these misconceptions, which reflect a loss of self-confidence, detract from more important issues of curricula quality and coherence.

Craig E. Nelson (Chapter 14), following up on his pathbreaking work on critical thinking in science, proposes that we focus evaluation not on students' mastery of course content but rather on incremental changes in their views of knowledge. These changes, which accompany learning to think critically, include an ability to perceive uncertainty as real, opinion as insufficient, and analysis as always deeply embedded in values. Our task as teachers, he suggests, should be to support students who are willing to confront the challenges of critical thinking. We can provide explicit criteria, encourage questions about the big picture, and make material accessible. We also must provide opportunities for small group discussions, rehearsals, and uninhibited expression, and we must show students that we care about their learning and are willing to model the behaviors we hope to encourage.

Jeremy Freese, Julie E. Artis, and Brian Powell (Chapter 15) attack a pervasive fiction within academia—the myth of grade inflation. Available evidence simply does not support the contention that professors are increasingly pandering to students by giving higher grades to undeserving students. The narrow media focus on a small number of elite schools that educate a small minority of college students has distorted our picture of reality. This myth, note the authors, allows poorer teachers self-servingly to dismiss the validity of student evaluations and to resist student-centered learning and faculty accountability.

For many of us, evaluating student performance is the most difficult and most painful part of the job. It is a source of conflict with students, often a result of poorly conveyed expectations and nagging questions about how to ensure fairness by delicately balancing the accommodation of individuals' problems with universalistic standards that treat all students equally. The task is complicated because we need to decide not only how to assess students fairly but also what to evaluate.

Debates about assessment extend beyond the classroom. They encompass course evaluation as well as department- and college-wide assessment. Although the latter often is regarded as the province of administrators, concerned faculty with a commitment to meaningful faculty governance must broaden their vision of assessment to include this bigger picture. The essays by Mary Deane Sorcinelli (Chapter 16) and Pat Hutchings (Chapter 17) provide valuable concrete suggestions for using student ratings, colleague evaluations, and self-evaluations of teaching. Teaching assessments, notes Sorcinelli, serve different purposes, including personnel decisions and teaching improvement, and thus require different types of information. This crucial distinction between the summative and formative purposes of evaluation often is disregarded, thereby undermining our efforts to improve teaching. High-quality evaluations, she argues, must be based on multiple sources, encompass activities within and outside the classroom, and assess student learning as well as teaching activities. Hutchings contends that we need to look behind outcomes and assess the social processes and contexts that produce learning. This type of analysis requires answers to a wide range of questions about student experiences and outlooks both inside and outside the classroom. Answers to these questions will help us to better understand the attitudes, values, and dispositions that facilitate learning and the institutional arrangements that improve teaching and learning.

The second group of essays in this section, by Patrick J. Hill (Chapter 18), Gerald Graff (Chapter 19), Robert N. Bellah (Chapter 20), and Troy Duster (Chapter 21), looks at contentious issues within the academy that have generated more heat than light; produced their own distinctive myths; and exposed extensive class, racial, and ideological divisions. Hill grounds the debate over multiculturalism in democratic political theory. He outlines four principal frameworks used to interpret diversity—relativism, universalism, hierarchism, and pluralism—and argues that pluralism is most consistent with democratic values and most likely to promote sustained respectful conversations about difference. Noting that higher education is not currently organized to value diversity as a resource for learning, he contends that implementation of a democratic pluralist vision would require a changed curriculum, serious minority recruitment, and the creation of intercultural and interdisciplinary learning communities.

Graff's review of the debate over multiculturalism suggests that media accounts have highlighted the negative aspects of conflict instead of treating conflict as a sign of vitality and a potential opportunity for teaching and learning. Exposing students to respectful disagreement over controversial issues via collaborative teaching, he says, serves our educational mission better than does fear of controversy, noncommunication, self-contained courses, and a disconnected curriculum. Bellah is less sanguine; he is wary of the adequacy of Graff's solution. He worries about higher education's ability to defend itself from outside attacks given the erosion of common ground among faculty because of heightened class and ideological divisions. Bellah views current conflicts as based on intractable differences that are deeply rooted in incompatible paradigms of moral enquiry. His solution is to avoid inconclusive debates that threaten to produce cynicism and nihilism among students and to instead search for some common ground among the professoriate that can provide the basis for academic community and define the purposes of the university.

Duster brings students and their aspirations and experiences into the debate. He situates current student self-segmentation in historical context, provides evidence of a shared desire among students for more cross-racial interaction, and notes racial differences about whether this should involve individual personal friendships or official programs. His solution is to embrace a cultural pluralism that recognizes differences as valuable resources and redefines competence as the ability to participate effectively in a multicultural world.

One of the central debates in higher education revolves around the boundaries of disciplines, the push for inter- or multidisciplinary programs or instruction. These arguments about problem-based restructuring of higher education require a better and sharper understanding of the contrasts and similarities among disciplines. In the third group of essays in this section, on the teaching imagination across the social sciences, social science scholars distill the unique insights and approaches of their disciplines to provide background for the debate and discussion among social scientists about the central theme in their teaching. These essays highlight the distinctive pedagogical contributions of disciplines using sociology, history, and anthropology as three of many possible illustrations. The authors raise a number of issues concerning what we teach and how we teach it. Charles Tilly's (Chapter 22) contribution, on the uses and limitations of standard stories, suggests that sociology teachers should focus their attention on encouraging undergraduates to criticize, compare, and improve the standard stories that they routinely use to make sense of the social world. In graduate professional training, we can teach the methodological skills needed to construct nonstory alternatives that capture incremental, indirect, unintended, collective, and environmentally mediated effects via equations, tables, and diagrams. But for nonspecialists, Tilly argues, our goal should be to improve students' ability to criticize and revise popular standard stories and replace them with contextualized and superior stories. This ability can be fostered by experiential and active learning activities (e.g., case studies, simulation games, life histories) that encourage students to question, revise, and compare standard stories.

Carole E. Hill (Chapter 23) explores the history, main concepts, and likely future challenges of teaching anthropology. By encouraging students to think comparatively and reflexively, she contends, anthropology enables students to question assumptions about human diversity, critically reflect on their own cultures, and relate to other cultures in a less ethnocentric fashion than that with which they began. In her view, the holistic character of the discipline, its global perspective, and its ability to foster empathy and mutual respect mean that anthropology can play a major collaborative role in creating the interdisciplinary and international curriculum needed for multicultural and civic education.

Harvey J. Graff (Chapter 24) argues that historians, by teaching students to discipline historical imagination with historical context, can make a distinctive contribution to higher education. Using visual materials and case studies, we can encourage students to imagine alternative possible pasts consistent with our knowledge of particular times and places and to use theory and comparison to contextualize and discipline their historical imaginations. History can thereby provide students with a critical perspective on knowledge construction and a better understanding of the foundations of contemporary societies and the relationship between past and future.

In sum, our trespass across the disciplines suggests that the multidisciplinary future of higher education lies in understanding the points of natural overlap coupled with a clear view of the unique perspectives that social science disciplines bring to human behavior. More than ever, to bring to fruition an embrace of multidisciplinary frameworks requires a greater, deeper understanding of these similarities and contrasting angles. Finally, as some college and universities move explicitly to interdisciplinary topic-oriented courses, it requires that professors themselves understand and are able to clearly explain why disciplines that often seem to ask the same questions focus on different angles, try different methods of inquiry, and together offer a fuller, more complete look at the complexities of human behavior such as how people learn, what it means to be educated, and how to teach.

13

Barbarians Inside the Gate?
Why Undergraduates Always Seem Worse
and Civilization as We Know It at the Brink

Norman Furniss

This chapter examines the widespread, but (I argue) greatly exaggerated, feeling that college students today are disturbingly different both from their professors and from previous generations of students. This idea that our students are outsiders—"barbarians"—takes three separable but overlapping forms. First, it is claimed that students are like recent immigrants from another country with fundamentally distinct morals and values. Second, students are barbarians in the sense of being aliens, ignorant of and indifferent to the academic enterprise. Third, it is claimed that students are in danger of becoming barbarians thanks to the ministrations of a clever and unscrupulous faculty. Following Locke's idea that the mind is a *tabula rasa,* it is proposed that students can and do absorb any number of wild and dangerous doctrines and that they emerge eager to propagate them.

I consider each of these potentially overlapping contentions in turn. By any straightforward rendering, I find that there is much less to them than might appear at first glance. They are not new to today's commentators, an observa-

tion that in itself helps put the claims in perspective. And with certain exceptions, the empirical support for these claims either is weak or reflects more complex factors. This is not to say that all is right with our teaching or our students or that all would be fine if only critics would cease their carping. Although not in themselves supported, the claims help focus attention on why we are *teaching* and why we are teaching at colleges and universities.

Before considering these claims in some detail, it is important to acknowledge explicitly the extreme heterogeneity of higher education in the United States. There is nothing equivalent to a "system," however loose, that one can attribute, for example, to most European countries. There is hardly a proposition about higher education in America for which one cannot muster some support or marshall a few counterexamples. In this connection, I have avoided direct references to community colleges (or their functional equivalents) because I do not know enough about them. This omission is not (as yet) of great relevance to teachers at four-year colleges. But we need to remember that the public two-year college sector is huge, comprising more than 900 colleges and enrolling more than half of the nation's first-time college fresh-

---

EDITORS' NOTE: For more discussion of these issues, see Eble's "The Mythology of Teaching" in the *Fieldguide.*

men (Brint and Karabel 1989). The arguments of this chapter do not necessarily apply to the challenges of teaching at these colleges, although my hunch is that they do.

Claim 1: Barbarians as Outsiders

This is the most direct application of the original meaning. Students, actual or potential, are diverse in many ways, most obviously racially and ethnically. This claim is institutionalized at most universities in offices such as Indiana University's Office of Diversity Programs and Instructional Support. Its summer brochure on *Teaching with Student Diversity in Mind* (Office of Diversity Programs and Instructional Support 1996) typically begins by noting that "the changing profile of the college student brings people with different aptitudes and experiences into the classroom. The dimensions of student diversity include age, learning style, skill level, cultural background, physical ability, gender, race, ethnicity, and sexual orientation."

The brochure then makes several suggestions to foster successful teaching such as learning students' names, trying to find ways in which to encourage discussion, and asking students who are not doing well in class to see you about what might be done. These ideas might not be earth-shattering, but they are hardly a frontal assault on "standards."[1] In short, discussions about diversity can lead usefully to renewed concern for effective teaching. The actual extent of this diversity, however, can be easily exaggerated. After reading strictures on teaching with student diversity in mind and then confronting the sea of white, Anglo-German faces in my classes, I was led to wonder whether my experience is qualitatively different. A look at the composition of student bodies as reported in "Changing Demographics of

College Enrollment" (1996) in the *Chronicle of Higher Education* suggests that it is not.[2] I have taken from the report the major public university or universities (e.g., both the University of Washington and Washington State University in the state of Washington) in each of the 50 states. My list of 60 institutions no doubt has some omissions, but the general pattern is clear. Of the 60 schools, only 8 had enrollments of Native Americans, blacks, and Hispanics that, when combined, exceeded 15 percent of the student population. These schools were the University of Arizona (12.2 percent Hispanic); the University of California, Berkeley (18.7 percent combined); the University of California, Los Angeles (18.9 percent combined); Rutgers University (7.8 percent black, 7.1 percent Hispanic, 0.2 percent Native American); the University of New Mexico (22.9 percent Hispanic); City University of New York (a multiculturalist's dream—22.5 percent black, 18.1 percent Hispanic); the University of Texas at Austin (12.4 percent Hispanic, 3.8 percent black, 0.3 percent Native American—in general, the University of Texas system has a significant Hispanic enrollment); and the University of South Carolina, Columbia (14.9 percent black, 1 percent Hispanic, 0.2 percent Native American).

Besides suggesting that the influx of barbarians (outsiders) into our major state institutions of higher education is hardly a deluge, four points can be drawn on the basis of this record. First, there is a large Hispanic enrollment throughout the Southwest and in California. Second, enrollment for blacks is low. This low enrollment is even more disturbing if we examine state schools established in major urban areas with "diversity" as a major mission. At Indiana University–Purdue University at Indianapolis, for example, 7.6 percent of the students are black; the proportion at the University of Illinois–Chicago Circle is just over 10 percent. Third, we should mention specifically the exception of California colleges and universities that indeed achieved a relatively striking measure of diversity. As we know, this diversity is now in danger of eroding.

The final point is one of continuity. Except for California, schools that traditionally have had diverse student bodies continue to have them, whereas elsewhere diversity is high relative only to its near absence in the past. The best example of the former is the university system of the City of New York, established to provide inexpensive education to its large immigrant population. As Hacker (1996) notes, it remains the most ethnically diverse system in the country. In Hacker's spring 1996 class, for example, there were students born in Argentina, Bangladesh, Chile, Colombia, the Dominican Republic, Ecuador, Egypt, El Salvador, Greece, Guyana, Haiti, Honduras, Ireland, India, Iran, Jamaica, Kenya, Pakistan, Paraguay, Romania, Russia, South Africa, Spain, and Trinidad. Here, we see one of the historic glories of the American higher educational system. The contribution not merely to social mobility but also to intellectual development has received numerous testimonials, one of the more recent being from Colin Powell:

I also owe an unpayable debt to the New York City public education system (CCNY). I typified students that CCNY was created to serve, the sons and daughters of the inner city, the poor, the immigrant. Many of my college classmates had the brainpower to attend Harvard, Yale, or Princeton. What they lacked was money and influential connections. Yet, they have gone on to compete with and surpass alumni of the most prestigious private campuses in this country.
I have made clear that I was no great shakes as a scholar. . . . Yet, even this C average student emerged from CCNY prepared to write, think, and communicate effectively. . . . If the Statue of Liberty opened the gateway to this country, public education opened the door to attainment. (Powell 1995:36-37)

These sentiments reflect the aspirations of "outsiders" to become "insiders" as well as the belief that public higher education could and should help in the attainment of this goal.

It remains to situate the challenge of student diversity in a broader perspective. Whatever the practice, the American ideal has been resolutely democratic-meritocratic. Woodrow Wilson put the matter well. While president of Princeton University, he declared (1915, pp. 91, 95) that the modern world

needs at the top not a few but many men with the power to organize and guide. The college is meant to stimulate in a considerable number of men what would be stimulated in only a few if we were to depend entirely upon nature and circumstance. . . . It is for the training of men who are to rise above the ranks. (Wilson 1915:91, 95)

The goal, then, is to draw into the college people from various ranks of life. This goal, of course, is not unique to America. It is similar to that which informed the Chinese examination system at least before the Ching Dynasty (Ping-Ti Ho 1963), and it paralleled the contemporary "meritocratic" reforms in the French university system (Tuilier 1994). It does stand in sharp contrast to the ascriptive values in which the English (not Scottish) universities were grounded and that Wilson laments motivated many Princeton undergraduates before his time.

When one turns from aspirations to practice, however, it probably is not surprising to find that the decisions on who actually has gained admission to particular colleges have been greatly influenced by social pressures and by political preferences and prejudices. Karabel (1984) describes how Harvard, Yale, and Princeton universities confronted what they saw as the "Jewish problem" between the two world wars. The "problem" basically was that by their own criteria, "too many" Jews were being admitted. The solutions, most of which were undertaken first at Harvard, ranged from the transparent—alumni preference (still in effect; see Powell's 1995 reference to "connections") requiring pictures of candidates—to the more subtle such as discovering the virtues of *geographical diversity* (also still in effect). A well-rounded student body, it was argued, must have its quota of (white Protestant) men from Montana and Wyoming. These machinations were justified on the grounds that Jews lacked the requisite character and family background. The remarks of the dean of admissions at Yale were atypical only in being voiced publicly: "The Jew graduates into the world as naked of all attributes of refinement and honor as when born into it" (quoted in Karabel 1984:17).

The results, from the standpoint of the Ivy League universities, were gratifying. The percentage of Jews in the student body fell and then remained level. Blacks, of course, fared worse. Here, the record of Princeton stands out. Oberdorfer (1995) relates the story. Blacks were entirely absent from Wilson's university, with Wilson himself commenting that it was "altogether inadvisable for a colored man to enter Princeton" (quoted on p. 143). The situation reached a point at which Norman Thomas (class of 1905) wrote the *Princeton Alumni Weekly* in 1940 to complain that "Princeton maintains a racial intolerance almost worthy of Hitler" (quoted in Oberdorfer 1995:143). This intolerance remained until 1948, when the New Jersey legislature passed an anti-discrimination law. Princeton had opposed the law as "coercive," but in 1949 the university's president informed the trustees that the law did indeed apply to their university. Subsequently, Princeton admitted a grand total of roughly *two* blacks per year in the 1950s.

In regard to the composition of the student body, then, we can identify a long-standing tension in university admissions policies. On the one hand, the rhetoric surrounding higher education promotes the values of democracy and merit; Wilson, for example, was fond of remarking that if the Angel Gabriel were to apply for admission at Princeton, he would have to pass the entrance examination to get in (e.g., Wilson [1907] 1974a:58, [1908] 1974b:56). On the other hand, the experience has been that the composition of the student body has been considered far too important to be left to the vagaries of either "the market" or "merit." The Angel Gabriel might not have gained admission to Princeton if he failed the entrance examination. But when "too many" Jews were passing, Princeton abolished the examination altogether.

It is now possible, in my view, to place the fuss about "affirmative action" in its proper context. In the sense of attempting to structure orderly admission on the basis of politically or socially derived criteria, affirmative action is not new. What is different is the effort for blacks and Hispanics to match rhetoric with action. The goal, in Wilson's words, is to admit people who, for reasons of "nature and circumstance," might well not have been at the college or university. Not surprisingly, this effort is controversial, and at the time of this writing it faces a number of legal and political challenges, some of which appear likely to succeed, at least in part. For the purposes of this chapter, it is enough to observe that its elimination would have a devastating impact on what student diversity actually exists. The prime case where diversity is a reality rather than an aspiration again is California. We already see the impact of the successful "civil rights referendum" on professional school enrollment. As for undergraduates, Hacker (1996) reports that in 1994, 27.1 percent of the entering freshmen at the University of California, Los Angeles, were Hispanics or blacks. The percentage would have been 6.2 had students been "admitted on academic criteria alone" (p. 21). The relative diversity at some of our major public universities might be short-lived.

In sum, the notion of our students as barbarians (outsiders) finds a certain amount of support. To be sure, the presence of racial and ethnic minorities at our institutions of higher learning tends to be modest. But these modest numbers are more than they were, they are higher than they would be absent purposeful action, and they represent (embarrassingly) a better profile among students than among their instructors. Furthermore, the turning of outsiders into insiders, rising "above the ranks" in Wilson's words, is one of the traditional goals and glories of American universities. That pursuing this goal is now seen as engendering some sort of crisis requiring new methods of instruction, a renewed dedication to "standards," passing "civil rights" referenda, and a host of related (albeit seemingly contradictory) measures tells us more about the nature of higher education than it does about the composition of the student body.

Claim 2: Barbarians as Aliens

I use the word *alien* in the dictionary sense of "different in nature" and "repugnant in nature." Another way in which to view the claim is in reference to the "unchurched." Just as many are said to be not so much opposed to religion as completely and complacently ignorant of its tenets, rituals, and promises, so today's college-age women and men are declared to be unaware of and uninterested in disciplines of the mind or in what constitutes an educated person. There is, of course, one major difference: the unchurched rarely attend religious services; these intellectual barbarians fill our classrooms. This is the claim heard most frequently from faculty in hallways and before the formal start of faculty meetings. It fills our press

with stories of declining SAT scores, the collapse of "standards," and the ignorance of students concerning basic political, historical, geographical, and other "facts." (The standards motif was institutionalized by William Bennett when he was secretary of education in the 1980s; how badly we do in comparison to other countries in a major subtheme. "Ignorance" was popularized by Bloom 1988. Other references follow.) Nor, as we have seen, can the claim be explained away as a necessary or an unfortunate function of the changing profile of the college student. The educational difficulties and outlooks of undergraduates can hardly be attributed to racial diversity. What, then, is the problem?

As with the discussion of barbarians as outsiders, this question must be placed within a broader context. We cannot usefully assess what, if anything, is the matter with our students until we identify the purpose of college education against which abilities and attainments can be measured. Back when university presidents and other officials used to ponder these things, there was a general consensus on the value of a "liberal" education. This was given classic expression by Newman ([1852] 1959) in *The Idea of a University*. Newman took "for granted that the true and adequate end of intellectual training and of a university is not learning or acquirement, but rather is thought or reason exercised upon knowledge" (p. 160). Wilson (1915) echoes this sentiment in stating that college should be "a place of mental discipline" offering "a general intellectual training" designed to "release and quicken the faculties of the mind" (pp. 90, 95). Wilson put his point more directly in an address to students at the Hotchkiss School ([1908] 1974c): "Have you ever fallen in love with the spirit of knowledge? Have you ever desired to be made free of the citizenship of the world of thought and of ideas? If you have not, you have never dreamed the dream of the true college man" (p. 502).

Have not all of us at some point, if only for a moment, fallen under the spell of the "spirit of knowledge"? If not, then why would one embark on the teaching profession? This is all the more reason to remember that generations of students have gone to colleges and universities for multiple purposes. More pressing for many is the economic imperative. When I was growing up, the mantra was that "to get a good job, you need a good education," which meant that to earn good money, you needed a college degree. The relative monetary value of this degree might now be at a historic high; census data show that the income gap between a household headed by a high school graduate and one headed by a college graduate is more than $22,000 ("Pell Grants" 1996:A10). As important as money are issues of status, captured wonderfully by Sinclair Lewis in his presentation of this exchange between George Babbitt and his son:

"Well what do you think, Dad? Wouldn't it be a good idea if I could go off to China or some peppy place and study engineering or something by mail?"
"No, and I'll tell you why, son. I've found out it's a mighty nice thing to be able to say you're a B.A. Some client that doesn't know who you are . . . gets to shooting off his mouth about economics or literature or foreign trade conditions, and you just ease in something like, 'When I was in college—course I got my B.A. in sociology and all that junk'—oh, it puts an awful crimp in their style! . . . It's been worth it, to be able to associate with the finest gentlemen in Zenith, at the clubs and so on, and I wouldn't want you to drop out of the gentleman class." (Lewis [1922] 1955:73)

Small wonder, then, that many students view their college experiences with a set of expectations different from that of their instructors. More surprising might be the discovery of what seems to be a long history of widespread cheating and raucous classroom behavior. I note a few examples. Yale undergraduates in the 19th century, of course, employed "ponies" to translate and simplify their studies (Cross, 1943:52ff). They also resorted to "skinning" (i.e., misrepresentation of who was reciting, the copying of examination papers) as well as outright thievery of examination questions (Anonymous 1871:620-58). Nor, we find, are paper services a new educational bane. The same observer reports more than 100 years ago the presence of persons "who make a business of supplying their classmates with the lesser literary wares at prices varying from fifty cents to five dollars a page." He concludes that "it is probably safe to say that of all the compositions read or handed in, less than half are what they purport to be; that is, written for the occasions on which they were offered and by the individuals who offer them" (p. 647). Classroom deportment was no better. Why? One answer seems to be that, like today, many students either could not or would not absorb the course material. Craig (1962) reports an encounter with a Princeton undergraduate around 1910 who, when asked why he kept disrupting the class, replied that "he couldn't help laughing because the teacher used repeatedly the funniest word he had ever heard. Asked what the word was, he replied, 'Spinoza'" (pp. 34-35). Like today, teachers and educational reformers viewed these activities with dismay and scorn. It becomes quite understandable that Wilson ([1908] 1974c) could conclude that colleges "are getting to resemble a very superior kind of country club" (p. 503), a sentiment seconded 90 years later by Edmundson (1997), who laments that our colleges are fast becoming "northern outposts of Club Med" (p. 49). Also not surprising is Wilson's occasional assignment of blame for this situation to the stupidity of students. Speaking of college men who "haven't any minds," Wilson

([1908] 1974c) was reminded of a man whose head was mentioned. " 'That's not a head; that's just a knot the Almighty put there to keep him from raveling out' (much laughter)" (p. 495). But somehow one doubts that "much laughter" actually greeted this anecdote, which parallels much commentary on students today, with SAT scores replacing references to the Almighty.

More instructive are efforts to fix the blame to particular events because the reasons then need to be offered. Hirsch's (1987) widely cited *Cultural Literacy*[3] traces the beginning of our decline to 1918. It was then that the National Education Association report on "Cardinal Principles of Secondary Education" fatally shifted attention "from subject matter to social adjustment" (p. 118). To this shift can be traced all our ills. "The romantic formalism of the Sixties and Seventies was an extreme yet logical extension of the romantic formalism that has been the dominant theory taught in our schools of education over the past fifty years" (p. 125). This effort and others that would be tedious to name are not, to be sure, examples of rigorous inferential reasoning.[4] What they do highlight is the point I attempted to make earlier in this chapter: there *never was* a "golden age" of American college education when all the students were above average, respectful, and eager to learn. Spinoza makes Hirsch's list of the "5,000 essential names, places, and concepts" that "every American needs to know" but does not know because "we cannot assume that young people know things that were known in the past by almost every literate person in the culture" (p. 8). As already noted, the past does not include late 19th-century Princeton, where Spinoza was a mystery. And I have no doubt that for most college students, he resides in similar obscurity today.

The major difference in reviewing discussions about college students over time is not found in complaints about their qualifications and qualities that are omnipresent. Rather, it is that in the past 20 years or so, there has been a progressive loss of *constructive outrage*—the idea that the current situation is unacceptable and that it can be improved in part through purposeful action. This is what Mannheim ([1936] 1967) refers to as "utopian orientations" that, "when they pass over into conduct, tend to shatter, either partly or wholly, the existing order" (p. 192). Wilson did not just complain about students; he instituted the preceptoral system in a (partially successful) attempt to approach his educational goals.[5]

All too often, what we find today is a loss of self-confidence that we as teachers and college administrators have educational goals apart from satisfying "the market" or (much the same thing) satisfying the "needs" of the state as defined by various public officials. With this loss of self-confidence comes a relinquishment of reformist zeal. Signs include a retreat from teaching undergraduates, a fixation on student *retention* as opposed to student education, and an abandonment of the vision of a curriculum that would foster "thought or reason exercised upon knowledge" in favor of a desperate search to design courses that might appeal to the vagaries of student taste.

In sum, undergraduates do arrive at colleges badly trained and badly motivated. Whether this situation is new or significantly worse than in the past is open to question and is, in any event, rather beside the point. As college teachers, we are better off focusing on those things we can change rather on those things we cannot change. Our main task is to persevere in efforts to make college a place of "mental discipline." Although it is beyond the direct scope of this chapter, I have noted a couple of past experiences that suggest that such efforts can in part succeed. The key might not be whether our students are "better" or "worse" but rather whether our curriculum and educational requirements are more or less coherently focused.

Claim 3: Barbarians as Dupes

This is the most common complaint about the student-teacher relationship from outside the university. To understand this claim, it is useful to refer back to the assumption discussed in the introduction to this chapter that psychologically each individual is a blank state who acquires knowledge and values through experience. The implications for teaching were developed by the French linguistic philosopher Ferdinand de Sassure, for whom "communication [is] the passage of a message from a sender to a receiver who is silent, who exists only as a receptacle" (Readings 1996:155).

From this perspective, teaching becomes a powerful, perhaps necessary, and certainly potentially dangerous enterprise.[6] "Free" inquiry in higher education, although no doubt useful in many ways, has the potential of being critical of the established order, and students have no natural defenses against such criticisms. Even more, the nature of structured "rational" discussion itself can be subversive. Mannheim (1971) makes this point in an insightful essay on "Conservative Thought" in which he finds that once one is compelled to *argue* that the old ways are best because they are the old ways, the game is pretty much up. The old ways persist when they are accepted implicitly without discussion or justification. (For an account of the English class system in this connection, see Ishiguro 1989.)

Higher education, then, can be seen as occupying the troubled boundary between two sets of contending forces. On the one side is a constellation of various "needs"—of political and corporate leaders for an educated workforce, of political and social leaders for a responsible citizenry, of individuals to "get ahead." On the other side are fears that the process will get out of control, that people will emerge not as loyal but rather as discontented workers and citizens. This tension never is resolved definitively. (And it appears to be universal. For the current debate in China, see Miller 1996.) At first glance, it might appear that in the United States the balance would favor needs; aspirations for control might seem to confront a serious impediment in the First Amendment to the Constitution. This obstacle has not, in practice, proved difficult to surmount. The rationale for ignoring it has been offered by William F. Buckley. Buckley (1951) argues that although everyone does have First Amendment rights, these rights can and should be modified by the terms of university employment.

Assuming the overseers of the university in question to have embraced democracy, individualism, and religion, the attitudes of the faculty ought to conform to the university's. Consequently, while reading and studying Marx or Hitler, Laski or the Webbs, Huxley or Dewey, I should expect the teacher whose competence, intelligence, and profundity I take for granted to "deflate" the arguments advanced. (p. 181)

The reason that this alignment is important, he emphasizes, is that teachers such as Charles Lindblom, whose "philosophy is collectivist in the extreme" (p. 91), exert "tremendous influence" (p. 93) over the apparently innocent Yale student body. Once again, the mind of the college student is a tabula rasa.

The easy solution to this problem of the potential corruption of America's youths is to purge the faculty. Babbitt commends this course with zeal:

The worst menace to sound government is not the avowed Socialists but a lot of cowards who work under cover. . . . Irresponsible teachers and professors constitute the worst of the whole gang. . . . These profs are the snakes to be scotched. . . . When it comes to these blab-mouth, fault-finding, pessimistic, cynical university teachers, let me tell you that in the coming year it's just as much our duty to bring influence to have these cusses fired as it is to sell all the real estate and gather in all the good shekels we can. (quoted in Lewis [1922] 1955:154-155)

Now, when these hoary matters of academic freedom and associated professional perks such as tenure are raised, the reception often approaches boredom. Is it not just the "looney left" that really gets in trouble? Or, granted their historical relevance, are these dangers not past? Did not real threats to academic freedom vanish with Senator McCarthy? Neither of these reactions is accurate. To begin with, as we discussed earlier, the inherently subversive activity of dealing with ideas always brings the possibility of trouble no matter what one's political persuasion. An excellent case in point involves William Graham Sumner, who taught political economy at Yale in the latter part of the 19th century and who was a founder of the sociology department. As a self-proclaimed "social Darwinist," Sumner opposed (among other things) private charity to the poor on the grounds that it would encourage the destitute to have more children, who then would further burden the public by their fecklessness. Conversely, he found that "millionaires are a product of natural selection. . . . They get high wages and live in luxury, but the bargain is a good one for society" (Sumner 1914:90).

One would not suppose that these opinions would disturb the powers that be, and indeed there is not evidence that they did. But Sumner also had strong views on free trade. On this matter a faithful follower of John Stuart Mill, whose *Principles of Political Economy* he assigned to his classes, Sumner "damned protectionism as class legislation for the benefit of the

few" (Cross 1943:71). For this heresy against the corporate wisdom of the day, and notwithstanding his favorable view of millionaires, Cross (1943) reports that "many captains of industry denounced him in turn as a man who seemed to regard it as his mission to '*poison the minds*' of a whole generation of Yale students" (p. 73, emphasis added). As Cross tells the rest of the story, these captains of industry were not content with verbal dissent and moved quickly to have Sumner fired. The Yale administration, in a familiar pattern, temporized. It was suggested that Sumner might provide some "balance" by also giving arguments in favor of protectionism, a gambit he dismissed on the grounds that concerning arguments for protection "there were none" to give. Sumner stayed, and Yale was forced to provide the balance by hiring a pro-protection Presbyterian divine from the University of Pennsylvania whose lectures, according to Cross, "appeased the hostile critics of Sumner." The lesson for this essay is that the perceived capacity to "poison the minds" of the students runs the political spectrum. Once again, students are assumed to have minds peculiarly susceptible to such poisoning.

The idea that these pressures are a thing of the past is more easily set aside. After a period of relatively benign neglect from the mid-1970s to the late 1980s, trustees and other college and university overseers have returned to their traditionally more active role. This appears to be the case at both private and public universities. One of the most prominent individuals involved is former Treasury Secretary William E. Simon, whose initiatives on behalf of his educational goals as president of the John M. Olin Foundation deserve separate treatment. Confining ourselves to Lafayette College, Simon (1996) declares that "the activist professors who control many of our universities are openly contemptuous of America and its way of life and are determined to use the classroom to overthrow it" (p. 50). Babbitt is alive and well. Finding no "principled leadership" from the Lafayette administration to deal with this threat, Simon applauds the decision of "many alumni" to withdraw financial support from the college at which he himself is a trustee. Turning to public universities, oversight positions, many of which had been filled in the British phrase by the "great and the good," are experiencing a leavening of people with more directed agendas. Healy (1996) describes the situation at James Madison University, where a new trustee has declared his intention to "go course by course in the James Madison manual to see what I don't like and what I think doesn't have a place on our curriculum" (p. 26). The aim is to eliminate not just poisonous professors but also poisonous courses.

This review allows us to situate the university more precisely in terms of American values and practice. In principle, the "marketplace of ideas" is accorded prime standing. Former Yale President Whitney Griswold (1950-1963) was an eloquent champion of this principle, even (as one might be amazed to hear today) at financial cost to the university. In words extensively cited at the time of his death, he proclaimed, "Ideas won't go to jail. In the long run of history, the censor and the inquisitor have always lost" (*New York Times* quote cited in Overbrook Press 1964:22). In practice, although agreeing that Griswold might be correct, there are a number of people more concerned with the medium and the short run. And the presumed ease by which the opinions of students can be formed or changed ("poisoned"), combined with the purported project of "activist" professors to use the classroom to "overthrow" the American way of life, offers a constantly tempting rationale for "balancing" free speech with other political and social concerns.

This rationale has been worth extracting analytically because it is becoming increasingly overlaid with more utilitarian considerations. If a student's mind is indeed a tabula rasa, then it might be not only shielded from poisonous doctrine but also filled with economically useful knowledge. It might have been enough in Babbitt's day for faculty to "whoop it up for rational prosperity" (Lewis [1922] 1955:155). Now, they are to *teach* it. The state of West Virginia exemplifies this trend. Its legislature recently passed a law with "the overriding goal [of ensuring] that West Virginians are prepared to enter the workforce. The colleges have been put on notice that they will be judged on the basis of their graduates' employability" (Schmidt 1996:A28). As the Democratic governor explained, "If we don't focus on getting people the skills they need to get a job, we have missed the point" (quoted in Schmidt 1996: A28).

This point is becoming pervasive in American higher education. As we have seen, it runs counter to the principles that led to the founding of most colleges and that subsequently animated generations of university reformers. College was not an employment agency, nor was it established to teach "skills." It is ironic that now, at a time when America never has been wealthier, institutions that concentrate on "mental discipline" with the goal of "releasing the quickening the faculties of the mind" are considered luxuries we no longer can afford. The recent turmoil at the University of Minnesota over proposed changes in the meaning of tenure pertain directly to these themes. In one draft of the regents' proposal, professors were instructed to be "industrious and cooperative." *Industrious* clearly meant fostering industry relevant to the state of Minnesota; this was the motivation behind the talk about eliminating programs. In general, it is disturbing, albeit not surprising, that the flashpoint for so much faculty debate focuses on tenure and not on the mission of the college.

Conclusion: Putting Barbarians in Perspective

This review of the contentions that college students are barbarians in various ways leads to findings unlikely to reinforce those who insist that we are faced with a qualitatively different type of student. Yes, the student body is somewhat more "diverse." But the extent of the diversity easily can be overestimated, as can the logically necessary assumption of the relative homogeneity of whites (else an increase in non-white enrollment could *decrease* diversity). Yes, the preparatory training of many students leaves much to be desired. But we always must remember that no educational golden age ever existed and that, *nevertheless,* significant educational reforms were implemented and gains in teaching and learning were made. Yes, there is the temptation to see students as bits of (recalcitrant) clay that instructors can mold for good or (much more frequently, it is feared) for evil. But this view always has been present. Its social and political implications often have been successfully resisted, although I do see the pressures to concentrate on "graduates' employability" as particularly dangerous because they are somewhat more subtle than the straight Babbitt line.

This is not to say that the conclusion that nothing is fundamentally different or wrong with higher education is warranted. Indeed, in many ways, this concern with the nature of the student body, as opposed to what skills we want to impart and why, is emblematic of the loss of self-confidence. The reasons why we see so much lamentation over the decline of "standards," over failures to "reward teaching," and over the pressures from trustees and university administrators to be more "efficient" have little to do with students. They involve the questioning of the role of the university itself as a relatively autonomous institution with its own professionally derived criteria of judgment.

Fundamental debates on this role are essential. I close by mentioning the *physical form* colleges have assumed. It is instructive to see how often the constitutive myth of college origins revolves around the establishment of a library. The library physically locates the college. Students and faculty congregate around it. In a 1924 address, Chauncey Brewster Tinker of Yale summarized this outlook. He declared, "There are three distinguishing marks of a university: a group of students, a corps of instructors, and a collection of books. And of these, the most important is the collection of books" (quoted in Schiff 1996:88). My argument is that, as in the past, essential decisions fall on us as teachers. What do we consider the distinguishing marks of a college? Do they warrant claims that the college be differentiated from the society and the political structure within which it is embedded? Do we have an educational mission that increases the likelihood that our students will graduate prepared—in Powell's words, "to write, think, and communicate effectively"? These, not the supposedly barbaric nature of our students, are our major challenges.

Notes

1. On a more concrete level, although Traub's (1994) *City on a Hill: Testing the American Dream at City College* seems to have raised the ire of many in the educational profession (see, e.g., Donahue 1996), it represents a serious effort to teach a serious subject. Traub's difficulties might relate more to the changing place of reading than to the changing nature of the student body.

2. The following runs counter to most interpretations including the one offered by the authors compiling the data. If one adds "Asians" and "foreigners" to Native Americans, African Americans, and Hispanics, then the remaining "white" category obviously shrinks. This larger "diversity" grouping is not "wrong." But in my view, it obscures our concern with "teaching with student diversity in mind." Asian students have at least as high SAT scores as do their white counterparts. They are a classic case of outsiders who already are insiders. As for foreign students, the overwhelming majority are from Europe or Asia. They might have language difficulties, but these are not the focus of this chapter. Finally, to lump "whites" into one presumably homogeneous group hides great historic internal diversities. One of the unique features of American higher education, as compared to European higher education, has been the extent to which students have been drawn from rural areas and small towns. These (white) students were strikingly different from their urban counterparts, as shown in the case of students from farms who established fraternities (e.g., the agricultural fraternity Alpha Gamma Rho) to facilitate their transition to college life. Today, as rural-urban differences fade, colleges are experiencing a new influx of *older* (mostly white) students. It is as dangerous to understate past diversity as it is to overstate its present dimensions. It also should be noted that, as a result of legal challenges and referenda in Texas and California, the data reported in the 1996 *Chronicle* report ("Changing Demographics" 1996) could well be the high water mark for racial and ethnic diversity.

3. The idea that the essence of "cultural literacy" involves knowledge of various "facts" would, of course, have been greeted with scorn by Newman, Wilson, and others seriously concerned about what constitutes an educated person. Hirsch's fixation on "the facts," which recalls the educational philosophy of Mr. Gradgrind developed so memorably by Charles Dickens in *Hard Times,* points to what is wrong in much of the debate surrounding higher education today.

4. This National Education Association report does seem, for many, to mark a turning point toward mediocrity. A recent example is Sykes (1995), whose title, *Dumbing Down Our Kids: Why American Children Feel Good about Themselves But Can't Read, Write, or Add,* conveys this message. The underlying assumption has to be that education was better before World War I. Evidence in support of this proposition would be hard to find.

5. One finds a host of similar stories of administrators who put their college or university "on the map" through utopian action. At Indiana University, for example, the key figure is former President Herman Wells, who with typical modesty assessed many of his accomplishments at the consequence of "being lucky" (Wells 1980).

6. For these reasons, many English commentators at the time of the Industrial Revolution were dubious of the value of universal education. As one 18th-century author concluded, "It is not easy to conceive or invent anything more destructive to the interests and very foundation principles of a nation entirely dependent on its trade and manufactures than the giving of an education to children of the lowest class of her people that will make them condemn those drudgeries for which they were born" (quoted in Furniss 1920:148).

References

Anonymous. 1871. *Four Years at Yale.* New Haven, CT: Charles C. Chatfield.

Bloom, Alan. 1988. *The Closing of the American Mind.* New York: Simon & Schuster.

Brint, Steven and Jerome Karabel. 1989. *The Diverted Dream: Community Colleges and the Promise of Educational Opportunity in America.* New York: Oxford University Press.

Buckley, William F., Jr. 1951. *God and Man at Yale.* Chicago: Henry Regnery.

"Changing Demographics of College Enrollment." 1996. *Chronicle of Higher Education,* May 24, pp. 32-42.

Craig, Hardin. 1962. *Woodrow Wilson at Princeton.* Norman: University of Oklahoma Press.

Cross, Wilbur. 1943. *Connecticut Yankee.* New Haven, CT: Yale University Press.

Donahue, Patricia. 1996. "Talking to Students." *College Composition and Communication* 47:112-23.

Edmundson, Mark. 1997. "On the Uses of a Liberal Education: As Lite Entertainment for Bored College Students." *Harpers,* July, pp. 39-49.

Furniss, Edgar S. 1920. *The Position of the Laborer in a System of Nationalism: A Study in the Labor Theories of the Later English Mercantilists.* New York: Kelley and Millman.

Hacker, Andrew. 1996. "Goodbye to Affirmative Action?" *New York Review,* December, pp. 21-29.

Healy, Patrick. 1996. "The Republican Contract with Public Colleges." *Chronicle of Higher Education,* April 22, pp. A26-A28.

Hirsch, E. D. 1987. *Cultural Literacy: What Every American Needs to Know.* New York: Vintage Books.

Ishiguro, Kazuo. 1989. *The Remains of the Day.* New York: Knopf.

Jones, Rufus. 1933. *Haverford College: A History and an Interpretation.* New York: Macmillan.

Karabel, Jerome. 1984. "Status-Group Struggle, Organizational Interests, and the Limits of Institutional Autonomy: The Transformation of Harvard, Yale, and Princeton, 1918-1940." *Theory and Society* 13:1-40.

Lewis, Sinclair. [1922] 1955. *Babbitt.* New York: Signet Books.

Mannheim, Karl. 1971. "Conservative Thought." In *From Karl Mannheim,* edited by Kurt Wolff. Oxford, UK: Oxford University Press.

Mannheim, Karl. [1936] 1967. *Ideology and Utopia.* New York: Harvest Books.

Miller, H. Lyman. 1996. *Science and Dissent in Post-Mao China: The Politics of Knowledge.* Seattle: University of Washington Press.

Newman, John Henry Cardinal. [1852] 1959. *The Idea of a University.* New York: Doubleday.

Oberdorfer, Don. 1995. *Princeton University: The First 250 Years.* Princeton, NJ: Princeton University Press.

Office of Diversity Programs and Instructional Support. 1996. *Teaching with Student Diversity in Mind.* Bloomington: Indiana University.

Overbook Press. 1964. *Alfred Whitney Griswold, 1906-1963: In Memorium.* Stamford, CT: Overbook Press.

"Pell Grants." 1997. *Chronicle of Higher Education,* June 22, p. A26.

Ping-ti Ho. 1963. "Family vs. Merit in the Ming and Ching Dynasties." In *The Chinese Civil Service: Career Open to Talent?* edited by Johanna Menzel. Lexington, MA: D. C. Heath.

Powell, Colin. 1995. *My American Journey.* New York: Ballantine Books.

Readings, Bill. 1996. *The University in Ruins.* Cambridge, MA: Harvard University Press.

Schiff, Judith Ann. 1996. "Scholar, Collector, Teacher—Tinker." *Yale Alumni Magazine* 59 (7): 88.

Schmidt, Peter. 1996. "West Virginia Starts Sweeping Overhaul of Public Higher Education." *Chronicle of Higher Education,* July 26, pp. A26-A28.

Simon, William E. 1996. "PC Has a Price." *Academic Questions,* Spring, pp. 50-53.

Sumner, William Graham. 1914. "The Concentration of Wealth." In *The Challenge of Facts and Other Essays,* edited by Albert Galloway Keller. New Haven, CT: Yale University Press.

Sykes, Charles. 1995. *Dumbing Down Our Kids: Why American Children Feel Good about Themselves but Can't Read, Write, or Add.* New York: St. Martin's.

Traub, James. 1994. *City on a Hill: Testing the American Dream at City College.* Reading, MA: Addison-Wesley.

Tuilier, A. 1994. *Histoire de l'Universite de Paris et de la Sorbonne.* Vol. 2. Paris: Nouvelle librairie de France.

Wells, Herman B. 1980. *Being Lucky: Reminiscences and Reflections.* Bloomington: Indiana University Press.

Wilson, Woodrow. 1915. "What Is College for?" In *College and the Future,* edited by Richard Rice. New York: Scribner.

———. [1907] 1974a. "An Address to the Indiana State Teachers' Association." In *The Papers of Woodrow Wilson,* vol. 17, edited by Arthur Link. Princeton, NJ: Princeton University Press.

———. [1908] 1974b. "An Address to a Yale Phi Beta Kappa Dinner." In *The Papers of Woodrow Wilson,* vol. 18, edited by Arthur Link. Princeton, NJ: Princeton University Press.

———. [1908] 1974c. "The Meaning of a College Education: An Address at the Hotchkiss School." In *The Papers of Woodrow Wilson,* vol. 18, edited by Arthur Link. Princeton, NJ: Princeton University Press.

14

On the Persistence of Unicorns: The Trade-Off between Content and Critical Thinking Revisited

Craig E. Nelson

Ten years ago, in "Skewered on the Unicorn's Horn: The Illusion of a Tragic Trade-Off between Content and Critical Thinking in the Teaching of Science," I addressed the nature of critical thinking, how to teach it, and the benefits and costs of doing so (Nelson 1989). I argued that, although many faculty feared that they would have to teach less content if they were to teach critical thinking, the trade-off was actually illusory—as imaginary as the unicorn's horn. Here, I have been asked to revisit this analysis and to explicitly extend it to a wider array of disciplines.

The unicorn still thrives in much of academia. When I introduce faculty to various approaches to fostering critical thinking in their classes, many still initially fear that teaching critical thinking will mean that they have to teach less content. There is, of course, a sense in which these faculty are right. If one measures teaching by what the teacher presents or "covers," then time spent on anything except lecturing on content is, by definition, a reduction in coverage. However, if one asks how to maxi-

mize student learning, then covering as much as possible clearly is a seriously flawed approach.

The effects of replacing a substantial portion of traditional coverage with required, guided student-student interaction have been well documented. For example, McKeachie (1994), in the classic introduction to college pedagogy (now in its ninth edition), summarizes the relevant studies as showing that discussion usually is better than lecture for retention of information after the end of a course, transfer of knowledge to new situations, problem solving, thinking, attitude change, and motivation for further study.

Three examples here will suffice to illustrate the magnitude of the effects often achieved with guided student-student interaction. Adding required peer checking outside of class and structured small group work in class reduced the D and F rate for African Americans taking calculus at the University of California, Berkeley from 60 percent to 4 percent with no reduction in the expectations (Fullilove and Treisman 1990; Treisman 1992). An experienced math professor taught calculus with no F's for the first time in his career after switching some of the homework to reflection in English and using structured small groups during class (Angelo and Cross 1993). Most spectacularly,

---

EDITORS' NOTE: For more discussion and ideas, see Weiss's "But How Do We Get Them to Think?" and Weast's "Alternative Teaching Strategies: The Case for Critical Thinking" in the *Fieldguide*.

in a meta-analysis of studies of several alternative approaches to teaching some key concepts in introductory physics, Hake (1998) found that such approaches always were superior to traditional physics teaching. These approaches usually doubled or even tripled the increase in student understanding produced by traditional physics teaching.

One of the lower levels of critical thinking is right answer, quantitative problem solving in which the entire class is expected to arrive at the same answer, usually by fairly straightforward application of algorithms presented in the class. The preceding examples illustrate that, even at this level, massive improvement in learning to think critically can be achieved dependably by partly or wholly replacing traditional, coverage-focused lecturing with carefully structured, active approaches. Pedagogy matters, and much is already known about how to make it more effective.

However, I feel a deep affinity with those faculty who still are worried about unicorns. Like most faculty, I came from a background where pedagogy was almost a dirty word and where suggestions that college teaching could be taught were ridiculed by full professors of international renown. Any formal knowledge of pedagogy was thus "taboo" (Nelson 1997).

Serendipity intervened. A colleague cited Perry's (1970) *Forms of Intellectual and Ethical Development in the College Years* as essential reading for anyone interested in teaching undergraduates. The central lesson in Perry's scheme is that learning to think critically requires an incremental series of major reorganizations in our students' views of knowledge and knowing. This insight stimulated developments in my teaching that greatly enhanced the students' enthusiasm and fostered more powerful critical thinking and a deeper understanding both of the content and of the nature and limits of science.

Perry's scheme still is central in my considerations of teaching and learning as well as of what critical thinking is and of how to facilitate it. Success at many of the central tasks of liberal, disciplinary, and professional education can only be achieved by implicitly or explicitly fostering the students' progress. In summarizing the scheme and the teaching moves that relate to it, I draw mainly on Perry (1970, 1981), Belenky et al. (1986) and my own earlier expositions of some of these ideas (Nelson 1986, 1989, 1994, 1996, 1997).

A Teacher's Overview of Perry's Scheme and of Its Implications for Fostering Critical Thinking

Perry (1970, 1981) found that students typically enter college with a simple view of knowledge that essentially precludes them from understanding complex issues. Some students progress through a series of transitions to more effective modes of thinking, but a substantial majority graduate unable to deal effectively with uncertainty and complexity. Four modes and the three transitions among them are especially important for understanding college teaching. The formal names for the modes are Perry's. Those in quotes are my attempts at mnemonic tags.

Mode 1: Dualism or "Sergeant Friday"

Truth as Simple and Eternal

In this approach, the intellectual world is seen dualistically as almost exclusively right or wrong, both factually and morally. Students assume that valid questions have certain answers. Right versus wrong spelling and arithmetic ground this perspective. Grades should be equally unambiguous. Like Sergeant Joe Friday, the television detective, students here want "just the facts, ma'am" and expect to memorize them (just) long enough to pass the exam. Thus, they feel that teachers should serve as gigantic, flourescent yellow highlighters who emphasize the parts of the text that must be memorized. Alternatively, teachers should teach *the* unambiguous way (*the* equation) to find *the* right answer. Students here so resist uncertainty that they might question a teacher's competence if shown two ways in which to work a problem.

Furthermore, teachers are not to add to the text; there is plenty there already. We certainly should not disagree with the text; if we were that smart, then *we* would have written it. If the text is not "right," then why are we using it? And, worse, how could anyone decide what parts of the text to believe?

We will have dualists in most classes. Some students approach all classes this way, and many approach some classes this way. Much teaching in freshman courses focuses on two tasks that dualists can do well: memorizing information and solving right answer problems. Such teaching works in the narrow sense of letting the students pass the exams. However, dualistic students might be unable to decide what facts are "relevant" and what algorithms are "appropriate." Thus, paradoxically, focusing teaching on facts and right answer problems might make even these aspects harder for most students to learn.

Transition 1: Perceiving Uncertainty as Real

No one thinks critically about things that seem to them to be unquestionably true. An understanding of both the extent of uncertainty and of its sources is essential. When students understand just the sources, they often assume that uncertainty is just a theoretical possibility and that the material actually is eternal truth.

Alternatively, when uncertainty is rampant in a course but its sources are not understood, students might assume that the uncertainty is the teacher's fault—that if the teacher were competent, then the truth would be clear.

Even when both the extent and sources of uncertainty are clear, students may try to preserve dualism as the general state. When I began teaching the content of ecology in the ways I suggest here, but without any structured student-student discussion, students repeatedly said essentially, "Nelson is a pretty good teacher, but it is a shame that ecology is so uncertain. They should let him teach some real science sometime." This was their way of limiting the range of knowledge that was uncertain.

Students appropriately are reluctant to accept the idea that knowledge is uncertain until they understand how conclusions that presently seem so convincing might be flawed. How can we help students understand the extent and sources of uncertainty in what we teach?

One very powerful tool is the history of knowledge. It is helpful to include examples from mathematics and physics because students often regard these fields as touchstones for certainty.

Kline's (1980) *Mathematics: The Loss of Certainty* summarizes the "calamities" that befell the view that logic alone could establish the structure of reality. If logic provided truth about reality (rather than about imaginary universes that ours only approximates), then space would be Euclidian rather than a function of the distribution of matter, and two quarts of alcohol added to two of water would yield exactly one gallon rather than distinctly less (they dissolve in each other).

Data also fail to yield certainty. What did physicists 100 years ago "know" to be absolutely true beyond all possibility of doubt ever that we now know to be wrong? Important answers include the following: space was thought to be perfectly Euclidian (rather than bent hither and yon by matter), motion was thought to be Newtonian (rather than relativistic), and matter was thought to be indestructible (rather than interconvertible with energy).

The general point is that whether or not scientists ultimately can find certain truth, they often have wrongly thought that they had it. Put differently, the failure of Euclidian geometry shows that even complete agreement among all relevant authorities on good empirical and theoretical grounds for a millennium or so is not adequate to guarantee truth.

Fundamentally, the complexity of reality often allows multiple interpretations of a data set, including some not yet envisioned. This precludes "proof" by even apparently perfect agreement between prediction and data. Hence, the insistence by statisticians that we reject nulls (as we cannot not prove theories). Worse, the same factors that preclude certain proof also preclude certain "falsification." Instead of the hypothesis falsified being wrong, an auxiliary assumption made in testing it might be wrong (e.g., Kitcher 1982). Physicists falsified continental drift by showing that no known physical force could move continents. The "flaw" was not anticipating the discovery of sea floor spreading. But no proof or falsification in any field can ever be guaranteed against the discovery of new forces or against the relevance of additional factors. Hence, the tentativeness or uncertainty of all empirically based knowing.

Even though historical examples often are very powerful, it is important to also focus on more recent shifts, bringing these to bear on the course at hand. Otherwise, the students will fail to understand the tentativeness of current views and might even conclude that, although past ideas have fallen consistently short of truth, present views really are certain. In most disciplines, the normal flow of knowledge, and especially the gradual demise of the unquestioned dominance of "modernist" ideas and the emergence of "postmodern" alternatives, provides a plenitude of examples. Anderson (1990) provides a quick, teachable, multidisciplinary introduction to these alternatives.

Mode 2: Multiplicity or "Baskin Robbins"

Personal Truth

When students first encounter unavoidable uncertainty, they have no way in which to select better options. Instead, they divide reality into two realms. In one, authority still provides correct answers. In the other, absent consensus among authorities, each person's position is fully valid and no one can say that one position is better or worse than another. Lacking any better standard in this second realm, students pick an opinion because it feels intuitively okay, much as one might pick a flavor for an ice cream cone. Such choices are based on feelings or intuition, not on reasoned analysis. Perry termed this mode "multiplicity." Students here often actively distrust authority, reason, abstraction, and especially science (Belenky et al. 1986).

Most graduates from four-year programs have multiplicity as the most sophisticated mode they use spontaneously in thinking about real problems (e.g., Belenky et al. 1986; King and Kitchner 1994). In this sense, liberal, disciplinary, and professional education all fail even for most of the students we graduate.

Transition 2: Perceiving Opinion as Insufficient

Comparisons and Criteria

The transition from dualism to multiplicity required that students recognize the inevitability of important uncertainty on many questions.

The transition from multiplicity to greater sophistication requires the recognition that despite this uncertainty, justified choices can be made. Often, one or more ideas or other human productions (be they poems, economic or scientific analyses, management or nursing plans, or whatever) can be shown tentatively to be superior to most other comparable productions. Alternatively, although there may be a fair range of acceptable productions, many others are demonstrably terrible. Thus, the choices among theories and other human productions must be justified on comparative rather than absolute grounds. And asking "To which theories is this one preferable?" leads naturally to "On what criteria or grounds is it preferable?"

As an example, the big bang theory for the origin of the universe is widely taught, even though it predicts that matter will have been initially spread so evenly that galaxies would never form. Put differently, the big bang theory has been known to be wrong for decades (as galaxies clearly do exist). This illustrates uncertainty. The big bang is taught not because it is "right" or "true," nor is it chosen on feelings or intuition. Rather, it is widely taught because it is "better." The alternative models assume either an unchanging universe or a "steady state" of endless unchanging equilibrium. These are the comparisons. The big bang is better because it accounts for the cosmic background radiation, the changes in the average composition of stars through time, and certain other features of the universe that are left unexplained by the alternative models. Explanation of these additional data sets is one of the criteria on which the big bang model is better than the alternatives.

The basic task here is to explicitly delineate, and to help the students learn to use, the forms of argumentation and the criteria used by our disciplines in deciding which ideas to accept tentatively. Several difficulties interfere with this goal.

First, unfortunately, we often focus our teaching on one (currently) "best" theory (or other production), leaving the comparisons implicit. Thus, we hide the very perspective that the students need to think critically about the material.

Second, many of the transitions we use between modes of representation (e.g., words, drawings, illustrations, equations, graphs) have become second nature to faculty but are not evident from the students' perspective and serve only to make the argument more confusing (Arons 1979).

Third, several aspects of the justification for a choice may have been learned tacitly by faculty (Polanyi 1966) and thus not be easily explained. It took me considerable effort to articulate the forms and criteria for the fields I teach. In sum, we often recognize and present good arguments and good examples without articulating well what makes them good.

Finally, although comparison is the core of much of argumentation in many disciplines, criteria and other aspects of argumentation differ appreciably among fields (e.g., Bruffee 1984, 1994; Hare-Mustin and Marecek 1988). In much of natural and social science, match to external reality is central. Describing real empirical patterns accurately and providing testable causal explanations that account for the patterns are core criteria in any comparison. In some of the humanities, by contrast, match to internal environment is essential, and all of the "facts" can literally be fictional. In other areas, the feasibility and acceptability of the policies or other social actions that emerge from an idea are crucial considerations.

The overall point is not that particular criteria must be used across disciplines. Rather, students cannot learn to think critically until they can use criteria appropriate to our disciplines to select among alternatives. We aid them when we make the comparisons and criteria explicit.

Comparisons are especially effective in most disciplines when they are clearly unbiased (or, if you prefer, minimally biased). I formalize this for students in the areas where I teach by focusing on comparisons that are demonstrably "fair." Fair comparisons are based on new discoveries that could have supported each of the alternatives being compared. Radioactive dating provides a fair test, in this sense, of earlier ideas that the earth is either quite young (based on Biblical interpretation) or hundreds of millions of years old (based on analyses of erosional and depositional rates). It is fair because neither of the earlier theories is based on radioactivity and because it could have supported either or neither of the alternatives. A young earth is rejected in science not because it has a religious source but rather because it fails a long series of fair empirical tests.

A nagging question underlies much student anxiety during this transition: "how can knowledge simultaneously be both uncertain and useful?" I like to take this one level further and ask how knowledge can be wrong and still be useful. If wrong ideas can be useful, then uncertain ones surely can as well.

Consider the brilliance of the flat earth model. The earth is in fact very flat—precisely as flat as the surface of a small pond on a still day. Although the pond is wonderfully flat, it domes imperceptibly up in the middle to exactly match the earth's curvature. Moreover, the flat earth model is by far the most widely used quantitative model of the shape of the earth in practical human applications such as architecture and engineering. (We assume that in a square room, opposite vertical walls will be parallel rather than vertically divergent; this assumes that the earth is flat.) Thus, the flat earth model has precisely the same present scientific validity as do Newton's laws of motion. Both capture important pieces of reality. Both are of immense, quantitatively precise, practical importance. And both are quite wrong and wrong in exactly the same sense. Each is a quantitatively quite good local first approximation that fails spectacularly on larger scales. Our current explanatory models in most, if not all, fields are useful in about these same senses, and many (perhaps all) either are now known to be wrong or will likely turn out to be wrong in about the same sense.

Mode 3: Contextual Relativism or "Teachers' Games"

Understanding Decisions Within Disciplines

After they complete this second transition, students can understand that one can use the criteria and forms of argumentation of a field to tell better from worse and make sense of the chaos of uncertainty in a way that is satisfying to the teacher, if not to oneself. However, many students treat such intellectual activity as either teachers' games or disciplinary games. Often, there is a strong element of sophistry here, albeit not the "any opinion is equally good" of multiplicity. Rather, students now often still think privately that any framework or game is equally good (it is this sense that I emphasize by using the term *games*) and may cynically consider the justified answers teachers require to be "bullshit." Indeed, Perry (1970) found that students who were unwilling to give answers that they did not fully believe often had the toughest time in college. Thus, it helps to emphasize for students that, in most cases, we do not want their own raw opinions. Rather, we want the best answers that they can provide within the rules of our fields.

The students' sophistry and cynicism here show that, despite our delight in their understanding of our disciplines, these students still are not capable of mature critical thinking. They cannot effectively compare alternative paradigms, choose appropriate applications in complex situations, or understand the interrelations, say, of science and public policy. If we do not ask them to treat such issues, we might not realize that even many of our best students fall short of what we expect from a liberal, disciplinary, or professional education.

Why Disciplinary Discourse Is Not Enough

Developing Intellectual Empathy

The necessity for further development can be seen if we examine the development of empathy (Belenky et al. 1986). When we treat issues as dualists, we rely on an authority to provide the answers. We see no validity in asking why authority chose those answers. Authority chose them because they are the truth. Because we do not understand why our group believes as it does, we have no base for understanding why other groups believe differently; they are simply wrong. Indeed, we frequently regard other views as not just factually wrong but also morally wrong—as evil (Perry 1970). Thus, we have no base for either intellectual empathy or tolerance.

In areas we treat with multiplicity, we believe that authority cannot provide dependable answers. If we must pick an answer, then we do so unreflectively (again, like choosing ice cream). Thus, we have no articulated understanding of our choice and, hence, still no grounds for intellectual empathy. But we want others to tolerate our choices and thus expect to tolerate theirs. This leads us to try for unlimited tolerance in areas where we see that there are no clear answers.

In the intellectual "games" of contextual relativism, we understand that people living in different contexts often legitimately believe differently. We might even take as one of our central tasks the attempt to understand how intelligent, even brilliant, people (past and present) ever came to believe things that are so different from those we currently believe (Russell 1945). Thus, we are rapidly developing the capacity for intellectual empathy.

But we still have essentially unlimited tolerance for different frameworks. Great tolerance might seem to be a virtue, but students here often carry it to extremes. Given an introduction to modern German history, they can see that in many ways Hitler was brilliant and effective. But they are reluctant to say that, despite our agreement with parts of Hitler's framework, key parts of what he did were wrong or crazy (Belenky et al. 1986). To make such judgments, one has to assert one's own values as preferable in key ways to some of the alternatives. One has to begin to take stands again, as one once did in dualism, but now based on an articulation of one's own values and analyses and not just as an echo of authority's positions.

I have sketched the rationale underlying this conclusion for the development of intellectual empathy. The same conclusion follows from several alternative considerations. For example, the development of multicultularity follows a sequence of modes or stages very like those of Perry's scheme. Indeed, Bennett (1986) suggests an almost one-to-one correspondence with Perry's modes. Bennett's analysis makes clear that progress beyond the multicultural equivalent of teachers' games is crucial.

The overall point is that contextual relativism fails to provide frameworks for choosing among approaches in nonarbitrary ways and for deciding when and how to combine disciplines (or cultures) in solving real-world problems.

Such frameworks are made necessary by the complexity of these problems; their causes and potential solutions transcend individual disciplines. The teacher's third basic task is to delineate the values inherent in the practice and application of our fields, the limits of our fields, and the consequences that follow from applying them.

Transition 3: Joining Values and Analysis

How can we best foster this third transition, the one that allows deep professional competence and sophisticated ethical judgment? The teacher's basic task is to delineate the values inherent in the practice and application of our fields, the limits of our fields, and the consequences that follow from applying them. Many disciplines strive hard for objectivity. We often misleadingly downplay, especially in science, the role of values in the decisions made both within the field and in its applications (e.g., Graham 1981; Harding 1986, 1993). Morrill (1980) discusses several general approaches for relating values to other content, especially in the social sciences. I have found several approaches to be helpful here.

Hypothesis testing. The role of values at the core of much of natural and social science is well illustrated by our procedures for deciding when evidence is adequate to accept or apply a hypothesis. We use our evaluations of consequences to justify our initial stance toward a hypothesis (accept until shown to be probably false or reject until adequately supported). Why do we usually take an initially skeptical view of hypotheses proposing new effects? When should we take a different stance? Would your stance differ for new food additives versus ethnic spices? For AIDS drugs if you were a patient or the one in charge of regulation? Similar

evaluations let us then decide how much contrary evidence should lead us to reject our initial stance. Consider the 5 percent level for rejecting null hypotheses. Try asking, "Why 5 percent rather than 10 percent or 1 percent?" and "When should another level be used?" Note that 5 percent rarely is appropriate for applying science or for reaching conclusions that have real-world implications. "How sure should we be that a new drug is safe?" provides an example. Such value judgments are central to hypothesis evaluation and application across much of the natural and social sciences (e.g., see Nelson 1986 for the creation *or* evolution and nuclear power controversies; see Hare-Mustin and Marecek 1988 for gender differences; or see any statistics book).

Paradigm choice and paradigm mixing. The central role of values also is evident in decisions as to which paradigm or field we should apply to particular questions. This can be illustrated by considering cases in which different approaches are now used. For example, what are the advantages and disadvantages of addressing schizophrenia as a genetic defect, as a biochemical disequilibrium, or as a response to social stress?

The limits of each of our disciplines usually can be shown by even a brief consideration of how a major real-world problem should be addressed. Biology can demonstrate some consequences of pollution but provides only little pieces of possible solutions. Paul (1982, 1988) suggests that we teach students to expect that each field provides a biased view and that solutions typically require a dialectical interplay of the strengths and weaknesses of various fields. Basseches (1984) emphasizes the importance of the dialectical approaches in achieving advanced levels of critical thinking.

Comparing one's own values to those of one's major. Alverno College (1987; see also Earley,

Mentowski, and Schafer 1980) has developed materials for teaching values at each Perry level in a wide range of disciplines. These materials suggest that each major should teach values analysis in a series of steps graded across several courses. These culminate, in part, in asking seniors to delineate the value commitments inherent in their majors, to compare and contrast those commitments with their own, and to discuss how they see the differences playing out in their careers. With slight rewording, this becomes a very helpful exercise for helping individual faculty reflect on their own commitments and values.

The teacher as the lesson. In verbal presentations of his findings, Perry often emphasized that students at this level have just one question of you as a faculty member: "Are you alright?" The student can see that this new approach to knowing requires both that the student leave behind many of his or her earlier views of why things should be and that the student accept considerable responsibility for himself or herself and his or her world. The student wants to know whether you are happy enough and moral enough. Who the teacher is becomes an essential part of the learning experience in a new and deeper way.

Put differently, students need to see us as faculty modeling the taking of stands securely grounded in our values in the face of uncertainty and complexity. The place where this is most effective is that which affects the students most directly. One way in which to do this is to articulate for ourselves and for the students the answers to questions such as "How are my personal values reflected in the choices I make as to what content to teach and what not to teach?" and "How are they reflected in the choices I make as to what pedagogical approaches to use and what not to use?"

A Bit of Reflection

By now, we have blithely crossed several layers of the taboos that surround teaching. We must not just explore the pedagogical literature, both generally and in our own disciplines, for ways in which teaching can be done better. We also must ask whether the ways in which our disciplines traditionally have been taught, or the ways in which our graduate professors taught, are the most effective ways for our particular students, thus challenging our disciplinary culture. And, in most fields, there is a further taboo against seeing that teaching always is at least implicitly teaching about values both in the content choices and in the choices of pedagogies. But teaching necessarily becomes explicitly about values when we choose to openly model and require "adult" thinking.

Mode 4: Commitment

I have struggled to find a mnemonic for the approach Perry termed "Commitment," emphasizing with a capital C the qualitative distinction from decisions or "commitments" made at the less sophisticated stages. I sometimes just use "adult" thinking here, but not in a descriptive sense, as many adults do not use this approach. Rather, I use it in a hopeful and normative or prescriptive way, asserting that this is the way in which adults usually should think. Belenky et al. (1986) call it simply "constructed knowing."

To operate as sophisticated adults, we must combine "games" and adjudicate among various combinations thereof in different contexts. Thinking becomes more complex and more responsible in several senses (Belenky et al. 1986). We come to see knowledge as constructed rather than discovered. We see decisions as contextual, as based inevitably on approximations, as involving trade-offs among conflicting values, and as requiring that we take stands and actively seek to make the world a better place. We understand that to do significant good, one must risk doing harm, and that to do great good, one must do significant harm (Levinson et al. 1978).

A doctor who is unwilling to risk harming us is useless. Powerful drugs have significant, occasionally lethal side effects. Doctors must accept that some of their patients will be harmed or die from the side effects of drugs and other treatments appropriately administered and from the consequences of appropriately withholding drugs and other treatments. And that is without any mistakes. A parallel argument can be made for teaching: if we do not teach for sophistication, then we harm all of the students, and if we do, then we might occasionally cause more stress than we intended. More generally, trade-offs and risks are the rule, not the exception, in important real-world decisions.

The small minority of students who do use this mode know that problems can be approached from diverse frameworks. They can indeed delineate the advantages and disadvantages of various frameworks, address contexts and trade-offs, and articulate why they advocate or use a particular approach. Most gratifyingly, they take responsibility for the validity of their beliefs and for personally making a difference in the world (Belenky et al. 1986). Education has worked.

When we, as faculty, fail to get students to this level of critical thinking, we leave them poorly prepared to deal with personal and professional decisions. Moreover, this type of thinking is required for any useful approach to the major issues of our times including diversity, social problems, environmental issues, technological change (e.g., in the applications of medicine and genetic engineering), and changing economic and geopolitical systems. These issues all require minds that can grapple successfully with uncertainty, complexity, and conflicting perspectives and still take stands that are based on evidence, analysis, and compassion and are deeply centered in values. This ability must be a major goal of liberal, disciplinary, and professional education. Fostering the sequential transitions is a major route to the goal.

Mosaicism

I have sketched only Perry's main line of development. Students may retreat to earlier modes if the challenges of sophistication become overwhelming. More important, students in intermediate stages (where most are) usually take a mosaic approach. Some areas encompass truth, others include naked opinion, and (for sufficiently sophisticated students) yet others include issues resolvable by disciplinary criteria or trade-offs among disciplines.

Estimates of a student's dominant mode are less helpful for teachers than is insight on how the student is approaching the current topic. Furthermore, Perry emphasizes the importance of learning to apply in new areas the modes one has mastered in others. Explicit comparisons of different topics with those from areas in which the students are more sophisticated sometimes facilitate rapid changes in thinking (Perry 1970). Such comparisons complement the teaching moves that facilitate particular transitions.

The Other Half: Matching Challenge with Support

The most fundamental lesson for teachers from Perry's study is that critical thinking is acquired incrementally. The second key point is that learning critical thinking is existentially as well as intellectually challenging. In asking students to learn to think more critically, we ask them to set aside modes that have served them well and still tie them to family, friends, and prior teachers. (Similarly, when we ask faculty to teach in new ways, we ask them to set aside or modify pedagogical modes that have served them well and still tie them to colleagues and mentors. They, too, need support to help them alter their pedagogy.) Perry's (1970) fine treatment of the existential factors that students face is deeply enriched by that in Belenky et al. (1986). The interplay of intellectual and existential factors dictates a balance of challenge and support in facilitating critical thinking (Knefelkamp 1980). Support has several elements.

Explicitness. The central intellectual challenge is mastering critical thinking and applying it to course topics. Both support and intensified challenge are provided by making uncertainty, criteria, and values explicit and central. I treat these aspects extensively early in the course and then use them to frame subsequent lectures and discussions. Almost daily, I emphasize alternative theories and criteria for evaluation. This requires about 10 minutes per 75-minute "lecture" period. We also usually devote a discussion period and an exam question to the question, "What view of the nature of science is presented in this course?"

Larger perspectives. Critical thinking is facilitated by frameworks that encourage students to ask, "How am I thinking about this?" (McKeachie 1994). Explicitly teaching critical thinking requires students to ask, "What criteria are appropriate here?" and "What values is the author applying here?" I also have students read and discuss Perry (1970). They can then ask, "Am I approaching this as a question of truth, of opinion, of disciplinary criteria, or

what?" A third framework is provided by noting the interplay between positivism (or objectivism) and constructivism that dominates much current intellectual dialogue. Lakoff (1987) and Anderson (1990) both discuss this interplay across broad swaths of the intellectual landscape and draw out its central role in understanding differing views on the nature of knowledge and knowing in a variety of intellectual disciplines. Novick's (1988) analysis, although focused on history, is quite valuable in considering other areas as well.

Accessibility. Lectures and readings that require thinking near the limits of the students' current frameworks may tax their abilities to summarize and anticipate exam questions. If so, then they can study extensively without accomplishing much. Making the material more accessible helps. I distribute lecture outlines that state difficult points and list questions on both lectures and readings. Questions central to main themes are starred. Exams are drawn from these lists and include a disproportionate number of starred questions. Because students might not recognize inadequate answers to the new types of questions, I assign selected questions as homework. The students then discuss them in small groups. Allowing retakes of at least the early exams further encourages mastery of critical thinking (Nelson 1996).

Structured small group discussions. As I noted in the introduction, extensive discussion as an integral part of each course greatly facilitates the mastery of critical thinking processes. Critical thinking must be practiced. It is not a spectator sport. Discussions provide a guided opportunity. Moreover, new ways of thinking might seem less alien when mutually explored. Small group discussions also increase content learning, application skills, and enthusiasm (McKeachie 1986); build rapport; and facilitate out-of-class group study and the deeper understanding it produces.

As a major part of much of my teaching, I have adapted Hill's (1969) approach. The students prepare a worksheet over an assigned reading. They summarize the author's argument, evaluate its support, determine an appropriate burden and level of proof, and then decide whether the argument is adequate. Small groups (five to seven) use the worksheets to structure their discussions. Grades cover preparation and participation (emphasizing roles that foster participation and understanding). This approach produces nearly 100 percent careful preparation for participation discussion and much improved understanding of the ideas at hand. I also use several other discussion approaches including some in nearly every "lecture" period (Nelson 1994).

Rehearsals. Knefelkamp (1980) emphasizes the importance of multiple rehearsals in teaching critical thinking. Multiple opportunities for rehearsing important ideas are provided in the pedagogical approaches I normally use. These opportunities include lecture comprehension, writing and participating in mini-discussions built into the lecture period, individually answering study questions, group review of study questions, discussion preparation, discussion, faculty-led review sessions, the exams, and the option of restudying and doing an exam retake.

Fostering voice. Fostering the students' own voice encourages intellectual change (Belenky et al. 1986). In fostering the recognition of uncertainty, we sometimes must accept opinions as valuable without evaluation. I initially found this troubling because unjustified opinion seemed contradictory to critical thinking. Later, I realized that students had implicitly taught me its importance. They invariably expressed their feelings prior to seriously discussing a reading and asked for an unevaluated "parting thoughts" section on the worksheets. My interpretation is that most of my students use multiplicity as the base where they like to start and end.

I now look for other opportunities to ask for opinions, reactions, or experiences. For example, early in a course, I often ask, "What have you heard to be the problems with evolution?" Questions asking for public perceptions of a field or topic can be used in nearly any course. Similarly, to foster analysis and the integration of values with analyses, we can provide opportunities for students to start their analyses in the modes they normally use. Discussion and study groups provide such opportunities and facilitate out-of-class conversations.

Connected teaching. This concept from Belenky et al. (1986) has two main aspects. First, it is important to show that you care about the students' learning. I do not let covering material take precedence over asking whether my explanations or the students' discussions need to be clarified or elaborated. This requires pacing the lectures so that the students can listen actively instead of acting as dictation machines (lecture outlines help) and stopping occasionally so that the students can decide whether they have questions. Caring also is manifest in knowing the students' names. This is difficult for me. I take the students' pictures and find that I can learn the students' names for classes up to a bit over 100.

The second key aspect of connected teaching is revealing the teacher as an individual striving, like the students, to interpret a complex and uncertain world. Although lectures require much prior thinking, it might seem to the students as if professors spontaneously think the way in which we lecture and, consequently, as if "real" thinking is beyond the students' reach (Belenky et al. 1986). This impact can be softened by exploring new ideas as they emerge during class and by noting how our own personal understanding has changed. Share the changes, the mistakes, and new information (and other factors) that led to changes, the alternatives you have individually explored and rejected, and the changes you are now considering. Sharing the triumphs and the false starts involved in creating new ideas is central. I recently have come to see as central here the explicit explanations of why I am teaching certain content and of whom I expect to benefit by using my pedagogical array.

Student Reactions and the Unicorn Dehorned

How is all of this received by the students? How does it affect the apparently tragic trade-off between teaching critical thinking and teaching content?

Students are more enthusiastic. Students have become more enthusiastic as my goals became clearer and my teaching moves became more effective. Several distinguished teaching awards, two of them student initiated, document their enthusiasm.

Students work harder. The experience of teaching also has changed remarkably. Most of my students seem to hunger and thirst after stronger thinking skills, and many spontaneously see that questions such as "How am I thinking about this?" and "What criteria will help?" apply quite widely.

I formerly took the mastery of the most sophisticated students as evidence that I taught well and that the other students just needed to apply themselves. Perry's study and the many follow-up studies (Moore 1997) show that mediocre performance often reflects not lack of

hard work but rather lack of complex understanding. Many students need to study differently rather than more. Perry's scheme helps us define "differently" for them and for ourselves. It now seems that few of my students fail to work hard enough. The increased support allows many more of them to be successful.

However, some students do find learning to study differently and doing the more advanced critical thinking tasks almost impossibly difficult. In freshman courses, the proportion seems similar to the 15 percent that Arons (1985) found in teaching critical thinking in physics. Recognizing that some students are not yet ready for the tasks I set intensifies the usual dilemmas of grading. I usually design the assessments so that diligent students using early modes can get C's (illustrating yet again the extent to which value judgments must be made in teaching).

Students learn more regular content. The steps that facilitate critical thinking also facilitate content acquisition. These steps affect the way in which lectures are framed more than the details of the material presented. The opportunities for rehearsing critical thinking also serve for rehearsing other content. Students' enthusiasm for discussion and for critical thinking carries over to other content. A higher proportion of the class now masters difficult content. Furthermore, much of the content will be retained as examples of critical thinking processes. The trade-offs between the teaching of processes and the teaching of content that once seemed so evident are, as I noted in the introduction, as imaginary in practice as unicorn horns.

Teaching critical thinking now seems a necessary part of effective college teaching, partly because critical thinking is necessary for effectively understanding and using content and partly because the teaching moves that facilitate critical thinking and the enthusiasm they generate also facilitate the learning of normal content.

Will these approaches work in your classes? I have used them successfully in introductory biology courses, in both science and great books-focused freshman honors courses, in intensive freshman seminars (dealing in part with modernism and postmodernism across the curriculum), and in an upper division course for nonmajors as well as in the upper level majors course I usually teach. These approaches work for the entire array of courses I teach.

More pertinent, perhaps, I have introduced this approach to thousands of faculty in workshops ranging from three hours to three days and more. The responses are almost uniformly enthusiastic. Faculty from many disciplines have spontaneously reported later that it led to major improvements in their classes.

Robustness

Perry's (1970, 1981) framework was of immense help to me in developing this approach. Do the teaching goals and moves depend on Perry's scheme for their validity? No. Many of them parallel goals and moves suggested from diverse bases such as direct analyses of critical thinking tasks in science (e.g., Arons 1985; Hake 1998) and more generally (Paul 1990), from reviews of critical thinking (Kurfiss 1989), educational psychology (McKeachie 1986, 1994), student development generally (Knefelkamp, Widick, and Parker 1978; Cornfeld and Knefelkamp 1978; Kegan 1994), and feminist pegagogy (even in science) (Barton 1998; Barton and Osborne 1998; Harding 1986, 1993; Rosser 1986, 1998; Whatley 1986). The diverse theoretical approaches that Hare-Mustin and Marecek (1988) and Anderson (1990) link

as "postmodern" have implications for teaching that both parallel and enrich those I find in Perry. Parallels and enrichment both also are evident in Belenky et al.'s (1987) synthesis of Perry with feminism and in the many other joinings of Perry's scheme to complementary frameworks (Moore 1997). Perry's scheme remains fundamental among this diversity, however, because it focuses most directly on the development of critical thinking, an objective that is universally acknowledged as a central goal of higher education.

College faculty are in a strange position intellectually. We are very eager to show the rest of the society the advantages of studying what is known about how to do their jobs more effectively. However, most of us have had almost no training in the literature on the theory and practice of college pedagogy, and most of us have made at best only token efforts to remedy this deficit. Indeed, many of us treat pedagogical knowledge as a taboo (Nelson 1997). Not only do we not know the literature, we even assert that there is nothing to be known. Fortunately, this taboo approach is beginning to lose it dominance, as reflected in the very existence of this volume.

Indeed, I believe that the burden of proof is shifting. Those who continue to use only straight lecture to cover the content, with or without traditional labs and large group discussions, may soon be professionally or morally obliged to show that they are at least as effective as they would be if they adopted the approaches that typically are distinctly more effective.

References

Alverno College, Valuing in Decision Making Competence Division, compilers. 1987. *Valuing Education Materials.* Rev. ed. Milwaukee, WI: Alverno College.

Anderson, W. T. 1990. *Reality Isn't What It Used to Be: Theatrical Politics, Ready-to-Wear Religion, Global Myths, Primitive Chic, and Other Wonders of the Postmodern World.* New York: Harper & Row.

Angelo, T. A., & Cross, K. P. 1993. *Classroom Assessment Techniques.* 2nd ed. San Francisco: Jossey-Bass.

Arons, A. B. 1979. "Some Thoughts on Reasoning Capacities Implicitly Expected of College Students." In *Cognitive Process Instruction: Research on Teaching Thinking Skills,* edited by J. Lochhead and J. Clement. Philadelphia: Franklin Institute Press.

———. 1985. "Critical Thinking and the Baccalaureate Curriculum." *Liberal Education* 71:141-57.

Barton, A. C. 1998. *Feminist Science Education.* New York: Teachers College Press.

Barton, A. C. and M. D. Osborne, eds. 1998. Theme Issue: "Pedagogies in Science Education." *Journal of Research in Science Education* 35 (4).

Basseches, M. 1984. *Dialectical Thinking and Adult Development.* Norwood, NJ: Ablex.

Belenky, M. F., B. M. Clinchy, N. R. Goldberger, and J. R. Tarule. 1986. *Women's Ways of Knowing.* New York: Basic Books.

Bennett, M. J. 1986. "Towards Ethnorelativism: A Developmental Model of Intercultural Sensitivity." Pp. 27-69 in *Cross-Cultural Orientation,* edited by Michael Paige. Lanham, MD: University Press of America.

Bruffee, K. 1984. "Collaborative Learning and the 'Conversation of Mankind'." *College English* 46:635-52.

Bruffee, K. 1994. *Collaborative Learning: Higher Education, Interdependence, and the Authority of Knowledge.* Baltimore, MD: Johns Hopkins University Press.

Cornfeld, J. L. and L. L. Knefelkamp. 1978. "The Developmental Issues of Graduate Students: A Model of Assessment." *Chrysalis* 2 (1): 30-41. (University of Maryland, Division of Student Affairs)

Earley, M., M. Mentowski, and J. Schafer. 1980. *Valuing at Alverno.* Milwaukee, WI: Alverno College.

Fullilove, R. E. and P. U. Treisman. 1990. "Mathematics Achievement among African American Undergraduates of the University of California, Berkeley: An Evaluation of the Mathematics Workshop Program." *Journal of Negro Education* 59:463-78.

Graham, L. R. 1981. *Between Science and Values.* New York: Columbia University Press.

Hake, R. 1998. "Interactive-Engagement vs. Traditional Methods: A Six-Thousand-Student Survey of Mechanics Test Data for Introductory Physics Courses." *American Journal of Physics* 66:64. (Available on World Wide Web at http://carini.physics.indiana.edu/SDI)

Harding, S. 1986. *The Science Question in Feminism.* Ithaca, NY: Cornell University Press.

———. 1993. *The "Racial" Economy of Science.* Bloomington: Indiana University Press.

Hare-Mustin, R. T. and J. Marecek. 1988. "The Meaning of Difference: Gender Theory, Postmodernism and Psychology." *American Psychologist* 43:455-64.

Hill, W. F. 1969. *Learning thru Discussion.* Rev. ed. London: Sage.

Kegan, Robert. 1994. *In over Our Heads: The Mental Demands of Modern Life.* Cambridge, MA: Harvard University Press.

King, P. M. and K. S. Kitchner. 1994. *Developing Reflexive Judgement: Understanding and Promoting Intellectual Growth and Critical Thinking in Adolescents and Adults.* San Francisco: Jossey-Bass.

Kitcher, P. 1982. "Believing Where We Cannot Prove." In *Abusing Science: The Case against Creationism,* edited by P. Kitcher. Cambridge, MA: MIT Press.

Kline, M. 1980. *Mathematics: The Loss of Certainty.* Oxford, UK: Oxford University Press.

Knefelkamp, L. L. 1980. "Faculty and Student Development in the 80's: Renewing the Community of Scholars." *Current Issues in Higher Education* 5:13-14.

Knefelkamp, L., C. Widick, and C. A. Parker. 1978. *New Directions for Student Services: Applying New Developmental Findings.* San Francisco: Jossey-Bass.

Kurfiss, J. 1989. *Critical Thinking: Theory, Research, Practice, and Possibilities.* Washington, DC: Association for the Study of Higher Education and ERIC Clearinghouse.

Lakoff, G. 1987. *Women, Fire, and Dangerous Things.* Chicago: University of Chicago Press.

Levinson, D. J., C. N. Darrow, E. B. Klein, M. H. Levinson, and B. McKee. 1978. *Seasons of a Man's Life.* New York: Random House.

McKeachie, W. J. 1986. "Teaching Thinking." *National Center For Research to Improve Postsecondary Teaching and Learning (NCRIPTAL)* 2 (1): 1.

———. 1994. *Teaching Tips: A Guidebook for the Beginning College Teacher.* 9th ed. Lexington, MA: D. C. Heath.

Moore, B. 1997. *Perry Network: Cumulative Bibliography for the Perry Scheme of Intellectual and Ethical Development.* Olympia, WA: Center for the Study of Intellectual Development.

Morrill, R. L. 1980. *Teaching Values in College.* San Francisco: Jossey-Bass.

Nelson, C. E. 1986. "Creation Evolution or Both? A Multiple Model Approach. Pp. 128-59 in *Science and Creation,* edited by R. W. Hanson. New York: Macmillian.

———. 1989. "Skewered on the Unicorn's Horn: The Illusion of a Tragic Trade-Off between Content and Critical Thinking in the Teaching of Science." Pp. 17-27 in *Enhanc-*

ing Critical Thinking in the Sciences, edited by L. W. Crowe. Washington, DC: Society of College Science Teachers. (National Science Teachers Association)

———. 1994. "Collaborative Learning and Critical Thinking." Pp. 45-58 in *Collaborative Learning And College Teaching,* New Directions for Teaching and Learning, No. 59, edited by K. Bosworth and S. Hamilton. San Francisco: Jossey-Bass.

———. 1996. "Student Diversity Requires Different Approaches to College Teaching, Even in Math and Science." *American Behavioral Scientist* 40:165-75.

———. 1997. "Tools for Tampering with Teaching's Taboos." Pp. 51-77 in *New Paradigms for College Teaching,* edited by William E. Campbell and Karl A. Smith. Edina, MN: Interaction Book.

Novick, P. 1988. *That Noble Dream: The "Objectivity Question" and the American Historical Profession.* New York: Cambridge University Press.

Paul, R. 1982. "Teaching Critical Thinking in the Strong Sense: A Focus on Self-Deception, World Views, and a Dialectical Mode of Analysis." *Informal Logic,* May.

———. 1988. "Critical Thinking and the Critical Person. In *Thinking: Progress in Research and Teaching,* edited by D. N. Perkins, J. C. Bishop, and J. Lochhead. Hillsdale, NJ: Lawrence Erlbaum.

———. 1990. *Critical Thinking: What Every Person Needs to Survive in a Rapidly Changing World.* Rohnert Park, CA: Sonoma State University, Center for Critical Thinking and Moral Critique.

Perry, W. G., Jr. 1970. *Forms of Intellectual and Ethical Development in the College Years: A Scheme.* New York: Holt, Rinehart & Winston.

———. 1981. "Cognitive and Ethical Growth: The Making of Meaning." Pp. 76-116 in *The*

Modern American College, edited by A. W. Chickering. San Francisco: Jossey-Bass.

Polanyi, M. 1966. *The Tacit Dimension.* Garden City, NY: Doubleday.

Rosser, S. V. 1986. *Teaching Science and Health from a Feminist Perspective.* New York: Pergamon.

———. 1998. *Re-engineering Female Friendly Science.* New York: Teachers College Press.

Russell, Bertrand. 1945. *A History of Western Philosophy.* New York: Simon & Schuster.

Treisman, U. 1992. "Studying Students Studying Calculus: A Look at the Lives of Minority Mathematics Students in College." *College Mathematics Journal* 23:362-72.

Whatley, M. 1986. "Taking Feminism to the Science Classroom: Where Do We Go from Here? In *Feminist Approaches to Science,* edited by R. Bleier. New York: Pergamon.

15

Now I Know My ABC's:
Demythologizing Grade Inflation

Jeremy Freese, Julie E. Artis, and Brian Powell

When traditional grading standards are relaxed, students learn that success can be accomplished without work, thereby undermining the purpose of education and denying themselves the education they purport to seek. . . . But the consequences of grade inflation are even more severe. Tacitly condoning grade inflation sends the message that it is all right to manipulate a system for personal gain or nonacademic interests. Education was supposed to be above such corruption by valuing ethics and responsibility, challenge and diversity, and above all else, justice and knowledge. . . . This is not the legacy Aristotle or Thucydides had in mind.

—Suzanne E. Fry,
San Diego Union-Tribune
(August 6, 1995)

In a culture where artificial measures of class performance have come to matter more than learning itself, no one should be surprised that college professors are rolling out A students at the rate rabbits roll out bunnies. . . . The problem isn't that college students are too smart, it's that our culture is too dumb. Old notions of firm standards by which to measure

accomplishment and failure—standards the implicit assumption of which was that few achieve and many fail—have been abandoned in favor of the "I'm okay, you're okay" syndrome, the essence of which is that high grades, measureless popularity, and "self-esteem" are part of the American birthright, to be bestowed by entitlement rather than earned by achievement.

—Jonathan Yardley,
The Washington Post
(June 16, 1997)

Recently, there has been a flurry of stories in the media decrying "grade inflation" as the newest crisis in higher education. As exemplified by the opening quotes, the prevailing belief is that professors are much more generous in dispensing A's now than they were in the past and that these rising grades reflect an academy that has forgotten its ideals and adopted a "consumer-driven" ethos where student satisfaction is sought not by providing a rewarding education but by providing the most vacuous of educational rewards—the easy A. Where professors once stood accused of being aloof and indifferent to students' needs, professors now are accused of pandering to students by giving them the grades they want but do not deserve. Some have attributed grade inflation to the increasing number of professors who are children of the liberal 1960s and 1970s and who now lack the hard edge needed to provide students with a "bell-shaped" grade distribution. More insidiously, some have tied grade inflation to the increasing importance of student evaluations and recommendations in determining faculty promotions and pay raises. In this scenario, faculty seek to ingratiate themselves with students and "buy" good evaluations with high grades.

Whatever the cause, individual universities have responded to these reports by taking a variety of measures to show that they are fighting grade inflation. Stanford University has revived the F. Following Dartmouth University's lead, Duke University has proposed coupling its grades with an "achievement index" that takes into account the overall distribution of grades in the students' classes. Among the recommendations to fight grade inflation at Indiana University are grade indexing, greater scrutiny of professors' grades in tenure and promotion decisions, required discussions of the "rigor of department's grading patterns" at annual budget conferences between the dean and departmental chairs, and even contests sponsored by the university teaching center offering a free lunch for the instructor who offered the best tip for keeping grades down.[1]

Whether conducted in the media, faculty meetings, or the classroom, debates about grade inflation usually focus either on who is to blame for the problem or how best to solve it. Less attention is devoted to discerning how widespread grade inflation is or even to verifying that grade inflation *is* widespread. In his classic *An Invitation to Sociology,* Berger (1963) describes the "debunking motif" of the discipline, where sociologists often are lonely skeptics who

demand evidence for what everyone else takes for granted. As teachers, we feel a professional obligation to participate in the ongoing discussion about grade inflation; however, as sociologists, we feel that the first step in this discussion should be determining what the facts about grade inflation are. Here, we cannot rely on watercooler assessments of how things are or recollections of how they used to be but instead must consider the extant data on average grades.

We believe that an inspection of these data shows that most of the claims about grade inflation in higher education are considerably overstated. There is evidence of grade inflation in high schools, among undergraduates at "elite" universities, and among undergraduates generally back in the Vietnam War era. For most colleges and universities, however, evidence that grades have risen in the past 20 years is scant. Moreover, any increases in average grades can likely be accounted for by the demographic and institutional changes in higher education over the past two decades. Indeed, we argue here that the entire debate about grade inflation has been confused by the propagation of a series of myths that contradict the available evidence. By debunking these myths, we seek to introject facts into an issue that has been marred by posturing and nostalgia and to contribute toward a more reasoned dialogue on grading practices in the academy.

Myth 1: Grade Inflation Is an Increasingly Significant Problem at Most Colleges and Universities

To examine the question of whether undergraduate grades are increasingly inflated, we must first clarify what is meant by *grade inflation.* Grade inflation is a separate issue from whether the requirements of undergraduate classes have become easier or whether the expectations of professors have changed. Instead, the question is simply whether the grades given by universities are higher now than they were in the past. If class requirements or professors' expectations have slackened without a concurrent change in the distribution of grades, then one would think this is a matter better addressed by recommending that professors assign more extensive or difficult work rather than by revamping universities' grading policies.

When our home university, Indiana University, first began alerting faculty to the supposed problem of grade inflation, the senior author (Powell) dutifully checked whether or not he was part of the problem by examining his grade distributions from the first sociology class he had ever taught (in 1980) through the first class he had taught at Indiana (in 1985) and all classes since. He found that his grades had remained essentially the same over this period. His reaction to this was ambivalent. He was pleased that he had been consistent over time, as this meant that the grade inflation that was supposedly rampant within the university could not be his fault. At the same time, he also had thought that he had become a better teacher since the first time he taught and that students were getting more out of his classes, and so he would have thought that students should be getting higher grades in his class now than when he first started teaching. One of our colleagues has remarked that his goal is to have everyone receive an A (although this never has come close to being realized) because for everyone to earn an A would imply that he had imparted mastery of the material to all students.

Satisfied that he was not to blame for grade inflation, the senior author became suspicious when he discussed the problem with his colleagues in the sociology department because all of those who had looked back at their grades

also reported little change. Obviously, if grade inflation was indeed rampant at Indiana, then someone had to be responsible for it. We checked the department's records and found that our colleagues had been telling the truth; the average grade given within our department have remained consistently between a 2.7 and 2.9 over the past two decades.

Perhaps instructors within the sociology department were impervious to the pressures that had led to grade inflation elsewhere in the university. Yet, we found that average grades throughout the university have been remarkably consistent over the past two decades. In the fall semester of the 1973-1974 academic year, undergraduates earned an average grade of 2.86. In the fall semester of the 1996-1997 year, the average grade was 2.90—hardly a difference worth considering as a crisis of standards or pedagogical integrity.[2]

Media reports of grade inflation have focused on elite schools, for example, Harvard, Stanford, and Duke universities. These reports are not inaccurate; there is clear evidence of an increase in the average grades at these schools, although, as we discuss later, possible explanations of this change extend far beyond the frequent lament that professors are lowering their grading standards. The evidence of grade inflation at public universities and "non-elite" private colleges, however, is much more suspect. The best evidence to confirm or disconfirm claims about grade inflation at the national level would seem to come from the large surveys by the National Center of Education Statistics that include college transcripts as part of their data. Using these data, Adelman (1995) finds that over the past two decades, the mean grade point average (GPA) for all college students who earned bachelor's degrees actually *declined* from 2.98 to 2.89. In short, when the nation's undergraduates are considered as a whole, there is not only no such thing as grade inflation but quite possibly a slight grade deflation. The absence of rising grades is not a feature of just one department or one university but rather of undergraduate life in general. The most prominent exception is at the nation's most elite schools, which have received the majority of attention from the media on this issue but still house only a small minority of America's college students.

Even in schools where there is evidence that grades have increased, however slightly, we have no reason to believe that this increase is attributable to the actions of individual professors grading too generously, despite the claims of a professor writing for *The Washington Post* who wrote, "The younger members of the [faculty] have never even known what a C was all about—let alone what a Gentleman's C was" (Twitchell 1997:C23). As sociologists, we try to teach students how to distinguish between individualistic and social structural explanations of behavior. And yet, discussions of grade inflation often deteriorate into individualistic attributions of certain professors giving higher grades. Indeed, an apparent assumption of grade inflation is that nothing has changed structurally within certain universities or within higher education that can explain increasing average grades. On closer inspection, we suggest that claims about grade inflation and its origins must take into account a number of demographic and institutional factors.

Changing Gender, Racial, and Age Composition of Students

Over the past several decades, virtually every college and university has experienced increases in the number of female, Asian American, and "nontraditional" students. Evidence shows that female students work harder, have a greater commitment to academic performance, and do better in college than their male counterparts. Indeed, because the sharpest rise in coeducation occurred in the late 1960s and early 1970s, the undisputed grade changes in this era may have been largely due to the rise of coeducation.[3] Similarly, for a variety of reasons, Asian Americans earn higher average standardized test scores (especially in mathematics and the sciences) and high school GPAs on matriculating in college and tend to do better than members of other racial/ethnic groups while in college. At Indiana University, the number of Asian Americans has increased sixfold over the past 20 years. Among nontraditional students, a large number are returning women, who, as a group, have been highly successful in the classroom. Any one of these compositional changes could explain fluctuations in a school's overall average grades; all should be taken into account in any examination of why some schools' grades might be changing.

Improving Student Credentials

For elite institutions at least, today's incoming freshmen have better credentials (e.g., standardized test scores, high school grades) now than they did just 20 or 30 years ago. Competition for admission to elite universities is extremely keen, more so than in the past. Although we do not argue that incoming freshmen at all colleges and universities have better credentials than they did 20 years ago, those schools with the greatest increases in grades are precisely those with the most dramatic rises in the quality of their incoming students.

Changes in the Classroom

Since the 1970s, most colleges and universities have made extensive changes in curricula. Schools now require fewer courses, especially in the sciences, mathematics, and foreign languages. Schools have given more latitude to students in course selection and have encouraged independent studies, tutorials, and internships. A byproduct of these changes may have been slight increases in grades. Students historically have performed better in their elective courses than in required ones, especially science and mathematics. Indeed, some have argued that humanities and social science departments are primarily responsible for grade inflation because the average grades in these departments generally are higher than those in natural sciences and mathematics. This argument, however, ignores the fact that these disciplinary differences occurred *before* the alleged rise in grades. Rather, the minor increments in grades might be a function of changes in the distribution of courses, and not of the shifts in grading strategies of professors.

The Rise in Professional Schools

As students and parents increasingly seem to equate a college education with occupational training, more schools have expanded their professional programs. More students at Indiana University, for example, are graduating with professional degrees in business, public administration, education, nursing, health sciences, and recreation, while fewer students are earning degrees in the liberal arts. This shift offers yet another explanation for the minor increases in overall grades. Grades typically are higher in professional schools than in liberal arts programs. In 1995-1996, the average course grade at Indiana's College of Arts and Sciences was 2.81, as compared to 2.90 in the business school, 3.21 in the optometry school, 3.36 in the education school, and 3.43 in social work. Differences in grades among these schools have not varied appreciably over time, but the changing distribution of students within these schools has, accounting for an overall slight increment in grades.

Withdrawal Inflation

Although there is equivocal evidence of grade inflation, there is persuasive evidence of withdrawal inflation. More students are exercising their option to withdraw from a course. If more students withdraw, then grades may fluctuate even if professors maintain the same grading standards. As an illustration, 4.8 percent of all students registered in classes at Indiana University in 1978-1979 withdrew, compared to 7.4% in 1995-1996. Although we cannot know with certainty all students' reasons for withdrawing, our experiences in the classroom suggest that students who withdraw often are faring poorly. If we assume that the average grade of students who withdraw is a D, then the 2.6% increase in withdrawals that occurred at Indiana should translate into an approximately .05 increase (on a 4-point scale) in the average grade, which is actually greater than the observed increase in grades in that period (.04). Thus, although universities and colleges may wish to reexamine policies regarding withdrawals, we should not confuse problems resulting from such policies with those resulting from changing faculty grading standards.

Myth 2: A Grade of C Did, and Should, Indicate "Average" Performance

Perhaps one reason for the unquestioning adherence to the myth of grade inflation is a corollary myth: that C was and should be average. In the debate over grade inflation, some critics decry that the average grade of college students is not a C but rather between a B and a B–. These critics remain nostalgic for the bell curve in which C or the "Gentleman's C," the allegedly normative standard for "average" students from several decades ago, is the modal grade. They dismiss the B/B– average as yet another example of the Lake Wobegon syndrome, in which "all the children are above average."

The Gentleman's C was and is more myth than fact. It is mathematically impossible in most grading systems employed in modern colleges and universities. At Indiana University, for example, a student must maintain a C (2.0) average to avoid being placed on probation; students who consistently earn less than a 2.0 average cannot remain on campus. By definition, then, the only way for the mean grade of college graduates, and college students in good standing, to be a C would be if there is no variation in grades whatsoever—a violation of statistical assumptions of normal distributions and of virtually every professor's experience with students. If there is a normal distribution in grades, then the tail ends of this distribution for college graduates, and other successful college students, must be C (2.0) and A (4.0), not F (0.0) and A, and the median should be approximately a 3.0, not a 2.0. Because the 2.0 minimum requirement has been long-standing at Indiana and at most other universities and colleges, it should not be surprising that B (or B–) is regarded as average and has been for a long time and that this is why grade distributions have remained fairly constant for so long.

Before unreflectively equating C with "average," we must ask "average compared to whom?" To students in the course? To students in the university? To students in all universities and colleges? To all adults, regardless of whether they attend colleges or universities? Another way in which to demonstrate the social construction of the meaning of "average" and why it does not necessarily translate into a C is to examine grades among graduate students. If we really believe that C indicates "average," then should we be alarmed that the GPA of graduate students typically is between 3.5 and

3.7 (e.g., 3.56 in 1973-1974 and 3.66 in 1995-1996 at Indiana University)? Of course not. Most professors understand that graduate students must maintain a 3.0 average (and, in some cases, a 3.3 average) to continue their studies. Consequently, any grade lower than a B, in effect, is equivalent to a subpar performance. It is, therefore, no surprise that B+ or A– is considered "average" and that the GPA of graduate students is approximately halfway between the highest possible (A) and lowest acceptable (B) grade.

Myth 3: One Can Buy Good Teaching Evaluations with Good Grades

---

In seeking to explain the allegedly significant and alarming rise in student grades, some have offered yet another myth: that grade inflation is the result of universities and colleges' overly solicitous focus on student needs and demands. In the eyes of proponents of this myth, grades have increased primarily because postsecondary institutions and their professors are pandering to students. Advocates of this position attribute the rise in student influence and, in turn, the rise in grades to two factors: student activism in the 1960s and 1970s and the advancement of a business-centered and profit-driven university system that bases its policies and decisions on consumer (i.e., student) demands.

Student Activism

Certainly, increasing student activism affected many fundamental changes in the curriculum, the role of students, and the expectations of professors. Activism called into question the infallibility of professors, on the one hand, and the relative lack of power and knowledge of students, on the other, and it encouraged students to take a more active role in their education. Students also insisted that they should have the right to evaluate the very people who evaluated them—professors. Thus, although there were student evaluations of professors prior to the 1960s and 1970s, they were used far more frequently thereafter.

Business-Centered University/ College Policies

Given the large number of baby boomers in academia, it is not surprising that many view the rise of student activism of the 1960s and 1970s with almost nostalgic fondness but see as insidious the rise of a more profit-motivated (tuition-driven) university philosophy. As operating costs have increased, universities have become more attuned to their client base—students—and to demands of legislators for state schools to become more accountable to the public. Such accountability has led to a renewed emphasis on teaching, "relevance," and "student needs" as well as, correspondingly, a greater reliance on student input (i.e., student evaluations). In turn, student evaluations have become increasingly influential in tenure and promotion decisions and even in annual pay raises, especially at schools that have explicitly allocated some proportion of annual pay increments to reward teaching excellence.

This reliance on student evaluations has not been uniformly praised. Critics question whether students can fairly and knowledgeably evaluate teaching and contend that giving students indirect sway over faculty promotions and raises inevitably compromises faculty grading by, in effect, pressuring professors to confer higher grades to students than they deserve. Such reasoning implies that students can be bought with higher grades and that faculty can be bought with high student evaluations.

Such reasoning has not been borne out by experiences in our department (sociology) at Indiana University. Examining the grading practices of professors in our department since 1990, we found that the professors who have won departmental or university teaching awards gave slightly *lower* grades than did their colleagues who have not won such awards. Moreover, our graduate student instructors who have received the highest student evaluations were, on average, no more lenient than those who have received the poorest evaluations. Furthermore, looking at evaluations across courses, we find that student reports of the grades they are receiving in a class correlate poorly with their overall evaluations of the instructor,[4] whereas overall evaluations correlate strongly with students' assessments of instructors' clarity, enthusiasm, fairness, and impartiality.[5]

Our findings are consistent with the bulk of literature on this topic, which indicates that students' evaluations are at most weakly correlated with students' grades (Doyle 1983; d'Apollonia and Abrami 1997; Felder 1992; Lowman 1990; Marsh 1987; Marsh and Roche 1997; McKeachie 1990).[6] Contradicting this general pattern of findings is the recent and highly publicized study by Greenwald and Gillmore (1997) that finds student evaluations to be positively correlated with grading leniency; however, Marsh and Roche (1997), d'Apollonia and Abrami (1997), and McKeachie (1990) all raise cogent criticisms to this study's methodology. It is perhaps telling that far more press has been given to Greenwald and Gillmore's (1997) claims about the connection between evaluations and grading leniency than to the preponderance of evidence that has failed to find such a connection. Moreover, student evaluations correspond surprisingly closely with professors' evaluations of one another's teaching (Aleamoni 1978; Felder 1992; Lowman 1990; Marsh 1987). Consequently, although it might be convenient for some to ignore the overall literature and argue that high evaluations are a response to high and undeserved grades, such reasoning is at best ill informed and at worst self-serving.

Conclusion

Part of teaching sociology is showing how many claims about social phenomena that are widely circulated in the media cannot stand up to close, empirical examination. In this chapter, we have shown that the much-hyped crisis of grade inflation within undergraduate education does not reflect actual trends in grading over the past 20 years, which in reality have remained mostly stable. Moreover, even in those institutions where there is clear evidence of grade inflation, the most common explanation of grade inflation is unlikely. Rather than attributing grade inflation to the increasing softness of individual professors or of even a whole generation of new professors, we described a variety of compositional and institutional changes in universities that may lead to increases in average grades.

Whereas we have questioned the myths surrounding grade inflation in this chapter, sociologists typically are not content simply to debunk myths; they also seek to explain the persistence of the myths. If we are correct that widespread cries about grade inflation are misguided, then the inevitable next question is why so many in the media, the academy, and the general public have been quick to embrace the idea that grades are inappropriately rising, especially given the ready availability of alternative explanations and the relative lack of hard evidence. Perhaps most obviously, grade inflation is consonant with the belief that America has undergone wholesale deterioration of values and cultural standards. In *The Way We*

Never Were, Coontz (1992) suggests that contemporary debates about the family are hopelessly clouded by public nostalgia for the days when every family was a wholesome "traditional family," a nostalgia that Coontz argues is based more on selective memory and wishful thinking. Discussions of higher education might be similarly clouded by a self-enhancing tendency of past college graduates to believe that today's college students are being graded much easier than they were graded.

At the same time, although the popularity of the grade inflation myth might stem partially from a memory-distorting nostalgia, it should be pointed out that the widespread belief in grade inflation also serves the interests of some parties. The idea of grade inflation provides a shield for those in the academy who resist student-centered learning and forgo opportunities to make their course content as accessible as possible to students. Grade inflation allows these professors to claim that they are refusing to pamper today's spoiled students. To hear some tell it, the professors who give the lowest grades and who receive the worst evaluations are actually the best teachers because they refuse to "buy" their students' evaluations by handing out high grades to all. In this way, the myth of grade inflation can make the bad teacher accountable to no one because it demeans the credibility of student evaluations, one of the few systematic means of monitoring college teaching. It is thus perhaps perverse that some universities are experimenting with the idea of offering rewards to professors who do the most to "combat" grade inflation. Such systems might reward some instructors who make high demands for excellence but also would reward those instructors whose students perform poorly according to classroom standards because they are not learning anything.

In addition, claims of grade inflation also provide fodder for those who have made a cottage industry out of attacking the academy. Over the past two decades, various villains have been held up as representing the ills of higher education—the deadbeat professor, the professor too focused on research to have any time for students, the foreign professor who cannot communicate with students, and the hopelessly incompetent graduate student instructor. To this list, one can add the professor popular with students because he or she gives A's to nearly everyone in class. In all of these cases, one might be able to locate isolated examples, but charges that these ills are rampant within the academy are consistently refuted by the available evidence.

A recurring theme of critiques of higher education is that universities have acquired political, research, or administrative agendas that are at cross-purposes with their supposed goal of educating students in "the basics" needed for successful careers. This theme is evident in the argument that rewarding high student evaluations gives professors strong incentive to loosen their standards and that this degradation of standards has caused an unjustified increase in average grades. By showing that extant claims of grade inflation are overstated, we provided evidence that grading practices do not seem to have been affected by the increased emphasis on student evaluations. Consequently, the alleged conflict between students evaluating teachers and teachers being able to demand excellence from their students should itself be considered more a matter of myth than truth.

Notes

1. The only entry the center received was by one of the authors of this chapter (Powell), whose entry was titled "There is no such thing as a free lunch . . . or grade inflation." The center decided not to award a winner.

2. These figures are based on semester grade point averages of students. Using an alternative measure, average grades of courses, we find the same pattern. Of course, there has been some fluctuation in average grades between 1973 and 1996, with an initial decrease between 1973 and 1984 and an upswing since then, but these changes have been trivial.

3. This, of course, is not to deny the influence of the Vietnam War on rising grades in the late 1960s and early 1970s. One frequently used explanation for rising grades in the Vietnam War era is that professors graded students more generously to help them meet the criteria necessary for keeping their draft deferments (or that students worked harder to keep their deferments).

4. For example, in our analysis of courses taught by graduate student instructors this year, we found a slightly *negative* correlation (−.09) between average grades and student evaluations of the instructor.

5. In discussing the link between course evaluations and grades, we compare the average evaluations for a class to that class's average grade. This comparison is appropriate for examining the claim that higher average evaluations are obtained by those instructors with more generous average grades. Within individual classes, students who are performing better in the course tend to evaluate the instructor more positively. This might be for a variety of reasons; for example, students who enjoy a class more than do their peers might put more effort into their studies. Yet, if higher grades per se caused higher student evaluations, then we would expect average class grades to be correlated with average class evaluations, which research has shown is not the case.

6. Research *has* shown that student evaluations are correlated with class size, course level, academic discipline, and (perhaps most tellingly) students' sense of fairness in the evalu-

ation process (Lowman 1990; McKeachie 1990).

Acknowledgment

We gratefully acknowledge Robert Fulk and Kathryn Henderson for their helpful suggestions and input.

References

Adelman, Cliff. 1995. "A's Aren't That Easy." *The New York Times,* May 17.

Aleamoni, L. M. 1978. "Development and Factorial Validation of the Arizona Course/Instructor Evaluation Questionnaire." *Educational and Psychological Measurement* 38: 1063-67.

Berger, Peter L. 1963. *Invitation to Sociology: A Humanistic Perspective.* Garden City, NY: Doubleday.

Coontz, Stephanie. 1992. *The Way We Never Were: American Families and the Nostalgia Trap.* New York: Basic Books.

d'Apollonia, Sylvia and Philip C. Abrami. 1997. "Navigating Student Ratings of Instruction." *American Psychologist* 52:1198-208.

Doyle, Kenneth O., Jr. 1983. *Evaluating Teaching.* New York: Free Press.

Felder, Richard M. 1992. "What Do They Know, Anyway?" *Chemical Engineering Education* 26:134-35.

Greenwald, Anthony G. and Gerald Gillmore. 1997. "Grading Leniency Is a Removable Contaminant of Student Ratings." *American Psychologist* 52:1209-17.

Lowman, Joseph. 1990. *Mastering the Techniques of Teaching.* San Francisco: Jossey-Bass.

Marsh, Herbert W. 1987. *Students' Evaluations of University Teaching: Research Findings, Methodological Issues and Directions for Future Research.* New York: Pergamon.

Marsh, Herbert W. and Lawrence A. Roche. 1997. "Making Students' Evaluations of Teaching Effectiveness Effective: The Critical Issues of Validity, Bias, and Utility." *American Psychologist* 52:1187-97.

McKeachie, Wilbert J. 1990. *Teaching Tips: A Guidebook for the Beginning College Teacher.* Boston: Houghton Mifflin.

Twitchell, James B. 1997. "Stop Me before I Give Your Kid Another 'A'." *The Washington Post,* June 4, p. C23.

16

The Evaluation of Teaching: The 40-Year Debate about Student, Colleague, and Self-Evaluations

Mary Deane Sorcinelli

In the past 40 years, there have been more than 2,000 books, articles, monographs, opinions, and stories written about the evaluation of teaching. Most of this work has dealt with the technical aspects of evaluation, especially the reliability and validity of student ratings. In fact, the literature on student ratings turns out to be the largest single body of research in the field of higher education studies (Marchese 1997). Other studies have focused on linkages between the processes of teaching development and evaluation (e.g., the development and use of teaching portfolios), and some have discussed the dynamics of evaluation in particular disciplines such as sociology and psychology or from particular perspectives such as gender or career stage (Theall 1997).

Most recently, the debate has sharpened as legislatures, parents, and students demand that teaching evaluation processes contribute more directly not only to the individual development of faculty but also to student learning outcomes and to institutional accountability. They argue

that evaluation needs to move beyond examining an individual faculty member's teaching to whether such assessment brings about deeper, longer lasting forms of learning for students and contributes to the collective curricular and instructional goals of the department, college, and institution (Braskamp and Ory 1994).

This chapter, which attempts to tame the voluminous literature on teaching evaluation, is divided into three sections. In the first, I consider some important considerations in evaluating teaching effectiveness. Next, I offer basic suggestions for collecting information. Last, I discuss how faculty and departments can use this evidence to evaluate and improve teaching.

The Concept of Teaching Evaluation

Simply thinking about procedures for evaluation raises challenging questions. Why evaluate? What aspects are included? What dimensions can be evaluated? Who should provide information? What methods can gather it? How can a faculty member or department use this information to make decisions?

EDITORS' NOTE: See Sorcinelli's guides and forms for evaluation in the *Fieldguide* ("Self-Evaluation of Teaching" and "Faculty Evaluation by Colleagues").

Why Evaluate?

There are two key reasons for evaluating teaching: to aid in administrative decisions (e.g., tenure, promotion in rank, salary increases) and to diagnose areas for improvement. For personnel decisions, faculty need *summative* information that measures overall teaching effectiveness and student learning. For improving teaching, faculty want *formative* information that can help identify strengths and problems. Despite some commonalties between these purposes, distinguishing their differences is critical. It influences sources and types of information collected, criteria focused on, how information is analyzed and reported, and to whom findings go.

Who and What Methods Should Provide Information?

The quality of evaluation, be it for teaching improvement or personnel decisions, is higher if multiple sources of information are used. This proposal for a more holistic assessment of teaching and learning need not be daunting. Students, colleagues, and instructors themselves can adequately assess the teaching responsibilities of most faculty.

On nearly all campuses, information from students is collected primarily through ratings, although letters, interviews, and measures of learning sometimes are used. Peer evaluation of teaching has not been developed to anywhere near a comparable level of practice and use. When colleagues are involved, their likely role is to review the materials or results of teaching (e.g., syllabi, assignments, examinations, grades) or to evaluate an individual's contribution to the unit's teaching mission. They less frequently observe in classrooms, especially for personnel decision making. Increasingly, instructors have been encouraged to assess their own teaching through an annual report or teaching portfolio for personnel decisions and similar self-appraisal or consultation for teaching improvement. To these principal sources and methods may be added the contributions of other individuals who have had the opportunity to observe some aspect of teaching or materials that reflect on the quality of teaching.

What Aspects Are Included?

At all education levels, teaching is being viewed more broadly and connected more directly to student learning. Good teaching is more than good in-class teaching behaviors. It encompasses aspects such as classroom instruction; advising, supervising, and mentoring students; developing learning activities (e.g., course revisions, textbooks, software); and developing as a teacher. This broader view of teaching and learning attempts to demonstrate that the professor has the responsibility to create a learning environment that includes, but is not limited to, the classroom. (Braskamp and Ory 1994; Menges 1990).

What Dimensions Can Be Evaluated?

Researchers have recognized the extreme complexity of teaching and its evaluation (Centra 1993; Braskamp and Ory 1994). Still, research going back to the beginning of this century, using different methods and viewpoints (e.g., faculty, students, administrators, alumni), has arrived at quite consistent agreement on general characteristics of effective teaching. Most studies point to instructor enthusiasm, organization and clarity, stimulation of interest, positive interactions with students, and knowledgability. These dimensions not only emphasize what teachers *do* but also are related to the *outcome* of effective teaching—student learning (Centra 1993; Feldman 1988; Braskamp and Ory 1994).

Collecting Information on Teaching

The next three subsections are organized around sources—students, colleagues, and self—for collecting information on teaching. They focus on the foremost method for collecting information from each source—student ratings, colleague evaluation of course materials, instructional contributions and classroom visits, and self-evaluation through annual reports and teaching portfolios. Considered are areas in which each source can make judgments, methods for collecting information, research on the quality of such information, and suggestions for personnel decisions or teaching improvement. For a comprehensive review and examples of other sources and information on which faculty may draw (e.g., student interviews, letters, measures of learning), there are several campus evaluation handbooks that are especially helpful (Centra et al. 1987; Davis 1988; Ory 1990; Sorcinelli 1986).

Student Evaluation of Teaching

Students provide an important perspective on teaching; they are the recipients of instruction. Students are in a good position to report on the extent to which a teacher prepares for class sessions, communicates clearly, stimulates interest, and demonstrates enthusiasm and an interest in students. Generally, students are not competent to judge the knowledge of the instructor or the scholarly content and currency of the course.

National studies of how college teaching is evaluated have found that systematic student ratings are the foremost method for tapping student judgment, in part because they are easiest to administer and score as well as least costly and time-consuming (Centra 1993; Braskamp and Ory 1994). In terms of reliability, validity, and usefulness, data provided by students are the most investigated aspect of faculty evaluation with the greatest weight of consistent, positive supporting evidence. Unfortunately, because it often is emphasized as the sole measure of teaching and is not carefully collected and reported, it remains the most suspect aspect of faculty evaluation (Theall 1997).

Research on Student Ratings

As noted earlier, literature that examines student evaluations is extensive. Two areas that encompass several issues and have been studied extensively are the reliability and validity of student ratings. Research on the reliability of student ratings typically has asked either (1) whether different students evaluating the same class and instructor agree on the teacher's effectiveness or (2) whether student ratings are stable over time. Studies on validity have asked (1) the extent to which students' evaluations correlate with other measures thought to reflect effective teaching and (2) whether there are biasing factors in student ratings. The answers to all of these questions boil down to this: research is largely supportive of student ratings, but they do have their limitations. The good news is that student evaluations correlate with other measures of teaching effectiveness (e.g., trained observers, faculty, alumni) and are remarkably stable over time. The cautionary news is that although overall ratings of an instructor are relatively unaffected by a wide variety of factors thought to be potential biases, there are a few background variables such as class size, discipline, prior student interest in the subject (e.g., required/elective, major/nonmajor), and expected grade that merit attention in personnel decisions. In addition, one study has suggested that the psychometric properties of student evaluations are less an issue than is the way in which data are collected and interpreted by departments and institutions (Theall and Franklin 1990).

As this book goes to press, in fact, renewed debates on student evaluations have begun in terms of their correlation with grades or their invalidity or unreliability—issues that have been studied extensively (Williams and Ceci 1997). Student ratings are both valid and reliable, but like any data, they can be misinterpreted and misused. The real problem with student ratings, researchers and practitioners in the field argue, is their frequent misuse by administrators and faculty on promotion and tenure committees. More effort needs to be directed toward research on the proper use and interpretation of student ratings (Arreola 1995; Theal and Franklin 1990).

Suggestions for Use

Given these findings, there are a number of matters that should be taken into account when using student ratings for personnel decisions or teaching improvement (Sorcinelli 1986).

Use multiple sources. For whatever purpose results may be used, student ratings represent only one source of information about teaching (see teaching evaluation as a triangle: student ratings, peer ratings, self-reports).

Obtain a sufficient number of raters. At least 8 to 10 raters, preferably 15 or more, is the recommended number. The proportion of a class that rates an instructor is important. If a fifth or more of class members are absent or choose not to respond, then the results might not be representative.

Use multiple sets of ratings. Ratings from only one course or one term might not represent a teacher's performance (for course improvement, ratings from a single course can be helpful). For personnel decisions, use five or more sets of evaluations taught over more than one semester.

Take into account course characteristics. Small classes (less than 15 students) often receive slightly more favorable ratings. Courses required by the university that are not a part of a student's major or minor tend to receive somewhat lower ratings. Ratings also may differ because of the nature of the course (e.g., humanities vs. social or natural sciences). For each characteristic, the differences are slight, but together they might be significant.

Rely more on summary items (e.g., how effective the course was overall) than on other items for personnel decisions. Overall ratings of the teacher or course tend to correlate higher with student learning than do specific diagnostic items. Therefore, decisions initially should focus on the overall evaluation items.

For teaching improvement, use diagnostic items and written comments. Summary items provide limited feedback; diagnostic items and students' written comments in response to open-ended questions can help point to teachers' strengths and weaknesses. Although studies have shown that some teachers can improve after receiving rating results, change is more likely if a knowledgeable colleague or teaching improvement consultant can help interpret scores, provide encouragement, and suggest teaching improvement strategies. Collecting feedback at mid-semester rather than at the end, soliciting comments through e-mail, and making use of "one-minute papers" are other ways in which to gather input from students (Centra 1993).

Use comparative data, but with caution. Student ratings tend to be favorable; comparative data (preferably local norms) provide a context within which faculty and administrators can interpret individual reports. It is important not to overinterpret; differences of less than 10 percentage points on any item or factor generally are not critical (e.g., 4.74 vs. 4.79 on a 5-point scale).

Employ standard procedures for administering forms in each class. When results will be used in personnel decisions, it is critical. Someone other than the teacher (e.g., student, staff member) should distribute, collect, and return questionnaires to a central office. The teacher should not be present during the process. Ratings should be administered in the final week or two of the class, preferably not after or during a final examination. Evaluation results should not be returned to instructors until after they have reported grades for the course.

Do not overuse forms. "Evaluation fatigue" may occur if ratings are too long or are required in every course in every term. For personnel decisions, a short form (4 to 6 summary items) should suffice. For improvement, a medium form (16 to 20 items) or a long form (30 to 36 items) is appropriate. A random or representative selection of courses is recommended, particularly for tenured professors.

Colleague Evaluation of Teaching

Surveys of how college teaching is evaluated demonstrate a dramatic increase in the use of faculty colleagues as raters of teaching effec-tiveness, for both teaching improvement and personnel decisions (Centra 1993). Colleagues, including department chairs, are in an excellent position to assess instructors' content knowledge as reflected by course materials (e.g., syllabi, readings, assignments, tests), student achievement (e.g., examinations, papers, presentations), and contributions to the department's teaching mission (e.g., teaching assistant, honors, theses, curriculum work). Colleagues are in a less advantageous position to judge teaching through classroom visits. The disadvantages of colleague evaluation (particularly class visits) are that it might affect collegiality, overburden faculty members in terms of time and effort, suffer from problems of sampling and rater unreliability, and duplicate information available from students.

Evaluation of Course Materials

Colleagues who have expertise in the discipline of a faculty member can evaluate course materials (e.g., syllabi, reading lists, textbooks, handouts, assignments, graded examinations) within a teaching dossier or portfolio. Although such examination still is not practiced systematically, it offers several advantages. It properly uses faculty expertise, is relatively nonthreatening, and can be done in a reasonable period of time. In addition, peers do not need to visit classrooms to gain insight into teaching effectiveness. It also is appealing because it can be used for both personnel decisions and teaching improvement. At many campuses, review of course materials appears to be limited to promotion and tenure dossiers but could be used to foster teaching improvement. Sharing of materials between junior and senior faculty might help clarify standards and stimulate the exchange of ideas.

Despite the potential for peer review of course syllabi, student assignments, or other documentary evidence of effective teaching, little research has been published on their reliability or validity (Centra 1993). Root (1987) did study colleague evaluations of teaching, research, and service dossier materials for tenure and promotion and found the reliabilities of the evaluations of the six-member committee to be very high (above .90) for each of the three areas, with the strongest agreement being in the area of research. The Root study supported the use of colleague evaluations of course materials, concluding that evaluation is most effective when the committee reviews materials according to a list of specific criteria. The following types of questions tend to be useful (adapted from French-Lazovik 1981):

- What is the overall quality of the course materials?
- What types of intellectual tasks were set by the instructor, and how thoughtfully engaged were the students?
- Do the course materials reflect current scholarship in the field? Do they reflect an adequate breadth and depth of coverage? Are they too advanced for a majority of enrollees?
- As demonstrated by course materials, to what extent is this instructor providing an optimum environment for student learning?
- Given the level of the course, do testing and grading practices seem appropriate?

A number of institutions do have forms that suggest areas for colleague examination and review. They include sample questions for colleague evaluation of course materials such as the course description, reading lists and textbooks, assignments and homework, and examinations and quizzes. Other forms include assessment of out-of-class contributions to teaching such as curriculum development,

undergraduate and dissertation advising, teaching assistant supervision, and participation in teaching development (Centra et al. 1987; Davis 1988; Ory 1990; Sorcinelli 1986).

Evaluation of Classroom Teaching

Colleagues who have expertise in the discipline and training in what to observe can provide evaluative information through classroom visits. In particular, a colleague's observation of aspects of teaching such as breadth and depth of material covered, the relation of such material to the syllabus and goals of the course, and incorporation of recent developments in the discipline could offer a more informed appraisal of the instructor's mastery of content than could students' perceptions. Of all ways in which to collect information about teaching for personnel decisions, however, classroom observation by colleagues is by far the most infrequently used method.

Literature on colleague evaluation of classroom teaching is inconclusive. Some researchers report that the value of observing teaching for promotion and tenure is dubious (Cohen and McKeachie 1980; Scriven 1987), whereas others (French-Lazovik 1981) conclude that carefully gathered and judiciously interpreted observations are capable of solid judgment on merit increases, promotion, and tenure. There is consensus that peer observation has enjoyed considerably more success as a strategy for improvement, and a system must be carefully crafted if used for personnel decisions.

If a department or campus decides to develop a system of evaluation by colleagues for promotion, tenure, or salary decisions, then it will need to decide on several procedural issues. Will the program be voluntary or mandatory, which faculty members will participate, how will observers be selected, how often will colleagues visit, will observers receive training and use a standardized form or process, and how will such observations be reported?

If the purpose of visitation is teaching improvement, then greater flexibility of sources and methods is possible. The simplest procedure is for faculty to ask colleagues to observe and review their teaching. Even more helpful are observations by experienced colleagues from similar academic disciplines or teaching improvement consultants often available through campus teaching centers. For departments interested in developing colleague visitation programs, there are several detailed guides on using colleagues as coaches, team teachers, and instructional consultants (Keig and Waggoner 1994; Paulsen and Feldman 1995; Sorcinelli 1984).

Suggestions for Use

The following overall guidelines for colleague evaluations are based on research and examples of successful practice (Centra 1993).

Use committees of colleagues to evaluate teaching for tenure and promotion decisions. Evaluations should be based on a dossier or portfolio of instructional materials, student evaluations of a range of courses, and (if possible) class observation. As few as three colleagues can provide sufficient reliability, and brief training sessions for the team will increase reliability of the judgments.

Do not give classroom observations undue weight in summative evaluations. Colleagues have only limited time to spend visiting classes and often have different views about teaching. Class visits can be used to supplement other types of information about teaching performance.

Encourage faculty to work together to improve instruction. Several successful models for collaboration include mentoring programs that link junior and senior faculty (Sorcinelli 1995); the Lilly Teaching Fellows Program, which provides teaching consultation, mentoring, and teaching seminars for pretenure faculty (Sorcinelli and Austin 1992); the Partners in Learning Program, which allows faculty to work in pairs to understand how students learn (Katz and Henry 1988); and the national American Association for Higher Education Teaching Initiative, which offers exemplars for peer collaboration and review (Hutchings 1996). Incentives for involvement can include a reduced teaching load, monetary rewards, or acknowledgment of such efforts in tenure and promotion decisions.

Self-Evaluation of Teaching

Self-evaluation of teaching can range from personal reflection to formal assessment intended for promotion, tenure, or salary committees. As a source of information used to evaluate teaching in colleges and universities, self-evaluation has gained popularity in recent years. In particular, a great deal of thought and writing has been devoted to the concept of the teaching portfolio as a means for encouraging both self-assessment and peer review of teaching (Anderson 1993; Centra 1993; Edgerton, Hutchings, and Quinlan 1991; Seldin 1991, 1993).

Self-Evaluations

Self-evaluations need to be distinguished from descriptive self-reports of teaching such as annual reports and teaching portfolios. Research clearly indicates that self-evaluations of teaching should not be emphasized in personnel decisions. Feldman (1989) reviewed studies that compared self-evaluation of teaching to evaluations given by current students, colleagues, and administrators and did not find much agreement between teachers' views of themselves and others' views of them. Centra (1993) suggests, however, that self-ratings for instructional improvement can be very useful. (For examples of the use of self-administered rating forms, as well as audio and videotape analysis and faculty development contracts for self-improvement of instruction, see Centra et al. 1987; Davis 1988, 1993; Ory 1990; Sorcinelli 1986.)

Self-Reviews

Self-reviews such as annual reports to describe annual professional activities or personal statements for tenure and promotion can provide a useful framework for assessing teaching effectiveness. Many campuses use a standard self-report form for annual reviews (Centra 1993). Such forms seek information on teaching, student advising, research, and service or outreach. Some reports not only ask what individuals did but also ask how well they think they did it and what their plans are for the future.

Whereas self-ratings of overall teaching effectiveness lack credibility for academic personnel reviews, personal statements or narratives that provide evidence of teaching competence give colleagues a context for interpreting and understanding a candidate's teaching activities and accomplishments. In such statements, candidates may outline a philosophy of teaching; discuss their contributions to the teaching, advising, and curricular needs of the department and university; explain teaching preferences and strengths; detail teaching accomplishments and future goals; describe efforts to develop teaching competence; and interpret student ratings and colleague judgments (Sorcinelli 1986).

Teaching Portfolios

Self-reports completed by faculty traditionally have been limited to the reports of activities as described heretofore. However, Paulsen and Feldman (1995) note that recently they have been expanding into a showcase for reflective practice, namely the teaching portfolio. Briefly, a teaching portfolio is a means for documenting teaching. Seldin (1991) suggests that a portfolio allows faculty to "display their teaching accomplishments for examination by others. And in the process, portfolios contribute both to solid personnel decisions and to the professional development of individual faculty members" (p. 3).

Teaching portfolios usually contain some combination of two basic ingredients: artifacts of teaching and explanatory and reflective statements by faculty. Most often, faculty start off with a faculty description of teaching responsibilities and a reflective statement about their philosophies of teaching and perhaps their histories as teachers. They go on to give more specific artifacts—firsthand evidence such as syllabi, tests, examples of student work with comments or responses, and videotapes of classes or conferences as well as secondhand evidence such as student evaluations and reports from colleagues who have observed their teaching or materials. Several publications outline a range of possible items for inclusion (Anderson 1993; Edgerton et al. 1991; Seldin 1991, 1993). But the key notion of the teaching portfolio is not that of merely compiling items; rather, it is the artifacts plus the reflective comments on them that make the portfolio meaningful.

No research has been conducted to investigate whether or not teaching portfolios improve instruction or correlate with other measures of good teaching such as student ratings. And studies of faculty perceptions of the value of portfolios are mixed. At one large state university, faculty participants reported that portfolios were accurate portrayals of their teaching effectiveness (Seldin and Annis 1993). At another university, however, faculty found that the process did not provide enough time or direction and was focused on "administrative uses" rather than on faculty development (Robinson 1993). A study at a community college by Centra (1993) found that if portfolios were used for personnel decisions, several colleagues independently reviewing the materials according to specific criteria increased the credibility of the review process. Instructors also desired an opportunity to discuss the results of the review with the review committee or with one of its members.

It seems obvious that faculty can benefit from the process of documenting and reflecting on their own teaching. When thoughtful guidelines and procedures are in place, numerous accounts from both participating faculty members and faculty developers do report that developing teaching portfolios improves instruction (Paulsen and Feldman 1995). In fact, although institutions have adopted and promoted the teaching portfolio to enhance the status of teaching or personnel decision making, its greatest potential might be in the area of faculty development, both for individual faculty members and for the colleagues with whom they talk about their teaching.

Lessons Learned

What, then, have we learned from 40 years of researching and debating the merits of evaluating teaching? First, it is critical to determine from the outset how evaluative information will be used. Personnel decisions require information that measures overall teaching effectiveness, the information needs to be drawn from multiple sources and methods, and its collection needs to be uniform. Teaching improvement requires information that can help identify strengths and problems. The information might come from multiple perspectives, but its collection can be relatively informal. Such information is developmental and confidential; it should not be released for personnel decisions.

Second, evaluation of teaching is complex, and no one source tells the entire story; each has particular strengths and limitations. Students, colleagues, and instructor self-evaluation provide a basis for informed judgment. For personnel decisions, the most defensible student information is from summary items on student rating forms. Specific items on student rating forms are best suited for improvement because they provide detailed and diagnostic information. Student written comments, interviews, and letters are more useful for teaching improvement, although they may assist in personnel decisions to confirm or add meaning to student ratings.

For personnel decisions, colleagues can evaluate course materials and instructional contributions to the department. Classroom visits can improve teaching. For their successful use in tenure and promotion, there needs to be careful planning and training as well as support of all faculty in the unit.

The type of self-evaluation used also depends on purpose. Personal statements and self-reports for annual reviews can be valuable in personnel decision making, especially if they tie together other evaluative materials and judgments on teaching. Teaching portfolios are particularly useful for developing and improving teaching. They can be helpful in personnel decision making if structural support systems that encourage their development and evaluation are in place.

Finally, any teaching evaluation efforts will work best within a larger institutional culture that supports a comprehensive view of both individual and collective teaching efforts. Such cultures are defined by supportive academic leaders (from department chairs to senior administrators), faculty ownership, a sense of collegiality and community around teaching, a campus-wide center for teaching or faculty development program, and recognition of teaching development and excellence within the institution's formal reward structures (Sorcinelli and Aitken 1995). If one were looking for a way in which to fulfill the important responsibility of developing and assessing teaching, then here might be the place to begin.

References

Anderson, E., ed. 1993. *Campus Use of the Teaching Portfolio*. Washington, DC: American Association for Higher Education.

Arreola, R. A. 1995. *Developing a Comprehensive Faculty Evaluation System*. Bolton, MA: Anker.

Braskamp, L. A. and J. C. Ory. 1994. *Assessing Faculty Work*. San Francisco: Jossey-Bass.

Centra, J. A. 1993. *Reflective Faculty Evaluation*. San Francisco: Jossey-Bass.

Centra, J. A., R. C. Froh, P. J. Gray, and L. M. Lambert. 1987. *A Guide to Evaluating Teaching for Promotion and Tenure*. Acton, MA: Copley.

Cohen, P. A. and W. J. McKeachie. 1980. "The Role of Colleagues in the Evaluation of College Teaching." *Improving College and University Teaching* 28:147-54.

Davis, B. G. 1988. *Sourcebook for Evaluating Teaching*. Berkeley: University of California, Office of Educational Development.

———. 1993. *Tools for Teaching*. San Francisco: Jossey-Bass.

Edgerton, R., P. Hutchings, and K. Quinlan. 1991. *The Teaching Portfolio: Capturing the Scholarship of Teaching*. Washington, DC: American Association for Higher Education.

Feldman, K. 1988. "Effective College Teaching from the Students' and Faculty's View: Matched or Mismatched Priorities?" *Research in Higher Education* 28:291-344.

———. 1989. "Instructional Effectiveness of College Teachers as Judged by Teachers Themselves, Current and Former Students, Colleagues, Administrators, and External (Neutral) Observers." *Research in Higher Education* 30:137-94.

French-Lazovik, G. 1981. "Peer Review: Documentary Evidence in the Evaluation of Teaching." Pp. 73-89 in *Handbook of Teacher Evaluation*, edited by J. Millman. Beverly Hills, CA: Sage.

Hutchings, P. 1996. *Making Teaching Community Property*. Washington, DC: American Association for Higher Education.

Katz, J. and M. Henry. 1988. *Turning Professors into Teachers: A New Approach to Faculty Development and Student Learning*. Phoenix, AZ: Oryx.

Keig, L. and M. D. Waggoner. 1994. *Collaborative Peer Review*. ASHE-ERIC Higher Education, Report No. 2. Washington, DC: George Washington University.

Marchese, T. 1997. "Student Evaluations of Teaching." *Change*, September-October, p. 4.

Menges, R. J. 1990. "Using Evaluation Information to Improve Instruction." Pp. 104-21 in *How Administrators Can Improve Teaching*, edited by P. Seldin. San Francisco: Jossey-Bass.

Ory, J. C., ed. 1990. *Teaching and Its Evaluation: A Handbook of Resources*. Urbana-Champaign: University of Illinois, Office of Instructional Resources.

Paulsen, M. B. and K. A. Feldman. 1995. *Taking Teaching Seriously*. ASHE-ERIC Higher

Education, Report No. 2. Washington, DC: George Washington University.

Robinson, J. 1993. "Faculty Orientations toward Teaching and the Use of Teaching Portfolios for Evaluating and Improving University-Level Instruction." Paper presented at the annual meeting of the American Educational Research Association, Atlanta, GA, April.

Root, L. S. 1987. "Faculty Evaluation: Reliability of Peer Assessment of Research, Teaching, and Service." *Research in Higher Education* 26:71-84.

Scriven, M. 1987. "Validity in Personnel Evaluation." *Journal of Personnel Evaluation in Education* 1:9-23.

Seldin, P. 1991. *The Teaching Portfolio: A Practical Guide to Improved Performance and Promotion/Tenure Decisions.* Bolton, MA: Anker.

———. 1993. *Successful Use of Teaching Portfolios.* Bolton, MA: Anker.

Seldin, P. and L. Annis. 1993. "The Teaching Portfolio." *Journal of Staff, Program, and Organizational Development* 8:197-201.

Sorcinelli, M. D. 1984. "An Approach to Colleague Evaluation of Classroom Instruction." *Journal of Instructional Development* 7:11-17.

———. 1986. *Evaluation of Teaching Handbook.* Bloomington: Indiana University, Dean of the Faculties Office.

———. 1995. "How Mentoring Programs Can Improve Teaching." Pp. 125-36 in *Improving College Teaching,* edited by P. Seldin. Bolton, MA: Anker.

Sorcinelli, M. D. and N. D. Aitken. 1995. "Improving Teaching: Academic Leaders and Faculty Developers as Partners." Pp. 311-24 in *Teaching Improvement Practices,* edited by A. L. Wright. Bolton, MA: Anker.

Sorcinelli, M. D. and A. Austin, eds. 1992. *Developing New and Junior Faculty.* New Directions for Teaching and Learning, No. 50. San Francisco: Jossey-Bass.

Theall, M. 1997. "Evaluation of Faculty Performance: The State of the Art and the State of the Practice." Paper presented at the annual meeting of Professional and Organizational Development in Higher Education, Haines City, FL, October.

Theall, M. and J. Franklin, eds. 1990. *Student Rating of Instruction: Issues for Improving Practice.* New Directions for Teaching and Learning, No. 43. San Francisco: Jossey-Bass.

Williams, W. M. and S. J. Ceci. 1997. "How'm I Doing: Problems with Student Ratings of Instructors and Courses." *Change,* September-October, pp. 12-23.

17

Behind Outcomes:
Contexts and Questions
for Assessment

Pat Hutchings

Thus far, much of the activity undertaken in the name of assessment has been shaped primarily by questions about *outcomes*. There are reasons for this focus; attention to outcomes counters long reliance on resources and reputation as tests of quality, and outcomes as benchmarks for what graduates know and can do are the natural concern of both policymakers (whose mandates often drive assessment) and educators. Nevertheless, the promise of assessment—mandated or otherwise—is improved student learning, and improvement requires attention not only to final results but to *how* results occur. Assessment "behind outcomes" means looking more carefully at the processes and conditions that lead to the learning we care about; it means not only measuring "results" but examining broader social processes involved in realizing the outcomes a campus or program might define.

AUTHOR'S NOTE: Adapted and excerpted from Pat Hutchings (1989), "Behind Outcomes: Contexts and Questions for Assessment," Washington, DC: American Association for Higher Education, Assessment Forum). © 1989 AAHE. Reprinted with permission.

EDITORS' NOTE: See Hutchings' materials in the *Fieldguide* on portfolios ("A List of What Teaching Portfolios Are and What They Are Not" and "The Teaching Portfolio: Possible Models").

Such a focus is well matched to the increasing involvement of faculty in assessment, especially at the department level. Indeed, it has become clear that the department or program is a particularly appropriate and powerful context for assessment "behind outcomes." Many of the questions we can productively ask about our impact on students (particularly in larger institutions) can be answered more sharply and suggestively at the departmental or program level than at the level of the entire campus, where information becomes too general, even rarified, to be very helpful. The department is also the setting in which a more integrated view of learning makes natural sense, where the line between what students know, what they can do, and what they believe is most intriguingly blurred, and where "good assessment" (integrated, performance-based, rich in feedback) is closest to what good teaching has always been about.

Assessment has, on some campuses, already begun moving in these directions. In hopes of moving it further, this [chapter] suggests and explicates nine areas of inquiry for assessment that gets behind outcomes, with appropriate methods for addressing them and with resources for further work.

1. What do we know about students who enter our institution?

2. How are course-taking patterns related to outcomes?

3. How do students experience the institution?

4. What is the student's contribution to learning?

5. What do students learn over time in a program of study?

6. How do out-of-class experiences contribute to learning?

7. What are students able to do with what they know?

8. What patterns characterize students' movement through the institution?

9. What judgments can students make about their learning?

The need for a more comprehensive view of the tasks of assessment has become increasingly evident. It is needed, first, because the current focus on outcomes often misses the mark when it comes to improvement. The significance of outcomes—and their implications for improvement—depends on context: being able to lay final effects up against information about where students started and what happened to them along the way, about the match between student expectations and institutional intentions. Information about outcomes alone does little to suggest which educational processes are responsible for those outcomes and [does] little, therefore, [to suggest] how to make improvements.

Secondly, assessment focused solely on outcomes may miss what many campus practitioners are finding most valuable about assessment: new, richer conversations about educational purposes and processes. A faculty member in a large research university reports that it was only in the context of assessment (in her case, state mandated) that "department members actually sat down and talked with each other about what they do with students in their classes." At its best, assessment raises and illuminates practical, day-by-day questions about teaching and learning. What do we expect our students to know and be able to do? What do we do in our classes to promote the kinds of learning we seek? What texts do we, collectively, teach, and how do we choose them? What expectations and goals do students bring to our classes? What motivates them? Which students would benefit from which classroom teaching strategies? Does the students' experience in my class relate to what happens in yours? How can we help students make connections between classroom learning and experiences outside the classroom?

These questions lead to a third perspective: not only is a focus on outcomes too narrow, but assessment needs a broader conception of learning. For decades, teachers and researchers alike have been aware that intellectual development is significantly affected by aspects of personal development; the cognitive and affective domains, far from being neatly separable, influence each other and develop (or don't) in connected ways. Given this circumstance, assessment aimed only at final outcomes of an intellectual character necessarily falls short. It leaves too many important areas for growth, too many sources of potential learning, unexamined. The first and unique purpose of a college is indeed intellectual development, but to understand that development one needs a broader view of the whole student and of the college experience.

This [chapter], then, argues for an expanded view of assessment—one that continues the emphasis on outcomes but strives to get behind them, to understand how they come about. Getting behind outcomes implies two departures from early assessment practice: greater attention to matters along the way, in order to know more about which students learn what under what conditions; and a broader focus, directed not only at academic achievement but [also] at aspects of student growth and development that faculty care about.

A metaphor may be suggestive. Assessment, as it's envisioned in this [chapter], looks less like a graduation *snapshot* than it does like a *movie:* "scenes" from the student's college experience, behavior and achievement over time, seen in multiple settings and contexts, from various points of view, sorted out and interpreted by thoughtful, involved audiences—including students themselves.

New Questions for Fuller Answers

Turning assessment from a snapshot to a movie means looking more closely at a wide range of student learning and development, over time, in various settings; it means increased attention to campus climate, in class and out. But which of the many dimensions of this broad scene should assessment focus on? Which questions are most fruitful? Which methods will help answer those questions, and which are most do-able? What will lead most directly to improvements for students?

What follows are nine areas for pushing ahead with assessment "behind outcomes."

What Do We Know about the Students Who Enter Our Institution?

Information about entering students—individually and as a group—is essential to mak-ing sense of outcomes down the line. Without it, there's little context for interpreting or judging the amount and quality of learning that subsequently occurs—be it in a general education program or a major field of study—and little prospect for improvement. Just as important, however, and more immediately, knowing students at entry can lead to better course design, more accurate placement, more effective advising and support services—and, as a result, better conditions for teaching and learning.

What kinds of information are at issue here? Nothing very fancy: demographic data, records from high school and other previous preparation, statements written for admission, ACT/SAT scores, results from placement exams, and so on. In fact, much of this information is already routinely gathered; it's here and there, in various offices, managed by people who may or may not see its relevance to improving learning. In many institutions, then, a first step is to find out where that information is located and how to bring the important pieces together to begin constructing a bigger, more suggestive picture for faculty, advisors, and students themselves.

Knowing what information is and is not already collected may also suggest further points of inquiry. What is known about the student's goals and expectations? What perceptions does she have of herself as a learner? What are her assumptions about college? What does she think she'll be *doing* as a college student? How about after college? Is she anxious? Does she have a place to study? Does she hold a job off campus? Answers to questions like these point toward ways to help individual students; in the aggregate, they may suggest ways to make freshman-year programs and services more responsive to realities.

The value of focusing assessment on such questions is highlighted by a project undertaken at Rhode Island College, where, several years ago, entering students received a "Personal Learning Plan" to help them chart their course through college. A detailed questionnaire, completed prior to registration, asked students about goals and expectations (What grades do you hope to attain? How many hours a week will you study?), lifestyle and support systems (Do you live at home/in an apartment/on campus? Does your mother/father/spouse . . . support your educational aspirations?), and other learning-related issues. Results from the questionnaire, along with more routine information from the admissions office, placement exams, and personal interviews, were translated into a detailed, individual advising document. (ACT-COMP results were included in an early version but dropped because they provided too little feedback helpful to students.) The Personal Learning Plan advised students about course load, time management, areas of academic strength and weakness, needs for assistance, course selection, and student activities.

How Do Student Course-Taking Patterns Relate to Outcomes?

Getting outcomes means understanding how students moved toward them; it implies looking at what courses they took (and didn't), in what combinations, at what points, how well they did in them, and to what effect. How do students travel through the twists and turns of curricular options? Do part-time and transfer students follow different routes? What patterns can be discerned? What gaps and problem points? Are students graduating without ever taking a history course? Is there, by virtue of courses chosen, a more common general education core than distribution requirements suggest? Do we like the way it looks? Are there relationships between course-taking patterns and retention? Levels of achievement? Outcomes?

These questions are now being asked at a national level. The U.S. Department of Education's Office of Educational Research and Improvement has been undertaking a large-scale transcript analysis project (PETS, the Postsecondary Education Transcript Sample). It also funded a project that involves a sample of 1,500 students from five institutions to develop methods of transcript analysis and assessment that can describe the effects of different course work patterns on the general learned abilities of college students. A monograph from the Association of American Colleges, *Structure and Coherence,* wades into similar waters. Based on transcripts from thirty-five diverse institutions, its author, Robert Zemsky, analyzes student choices across the curriculum and offers preliminary statistical conclusions about the state of the undergraduate curriculum nationally; he presents a method for describing the shape of the "real" curriculum on individual campuses.

The Association of American Colleges (AAC) has also, more recently, overseen work directly related to course-taking in the major, including sociology. As part of a project on "Study in Depth," AAC assembled task forces of faculty representing twelve different disciplinary associations. These ambitious, large-scale projects explore important new ground about the impacts of course-taking patterns, but more modest, local approaches may be useful, too. On many campuses, the major is a locus of current assessment effort. Departments might do well, as part of a larger set of methods, to look at student course-taking patterns. One scenario might be an afternoon department meeting where fifty transcripts get passed around the table and discussed by faculty. Do successful sociology majors take more math than those who encounter difficulties or change majors? Is success related to where they encounter statistical methods? Fieldwork? Are upper level courses founded on false assumptions about courses taken during the freshman and sophomore years?

A next step might be more focused evaluation of student work in light of courses taken. Faculty might work together to rate student papers from a senior seminar, then lay the results against information about which students took what routes into that seminar. Such an exercise would raise interesting—and difficult—questions about departmental course sequencing; it also focuses faculty attention on learning beyond their own classroom, on the "what does it all add up to" question that lies behind powerful assessment.

The point, then, of focusing assessment on student course-taking patterns is not just to find the glitch and fix it but to look more systematically at how students move through the curriculum. We learn something about the effectiveness of a program by assessing student outcomes; we learn how a program *works* by relating those outcomes to patterns of study that led to them.

How Do Students Experience and Understand Their Program of Study?

Knowing who our students are and what courses they take goes some distance toward a clearer picture of how we can improve what we do for them. But we want to understand, as well, what it *means,* from a student point of view, to be a student at this institution, enrolled in this major, these classes, with these fellow students, these faculty. What works and what doesn't? What, in the student's opinion, promotes learning? What hinders it?

Many departments (and entire campuses as well) are now using assessment as an occasion to explore the student experience. Some construct their own surveys; many adopt an available commercial instrument (ACT and ETS both offer one) and add local questions. Some survey not only current students but [also] alumni. A particularly useful instrument is C. Robert Pace's College Student Experiences Questionnaire (CSEQ), which asks students about their experiences with courses, co-curricular activities, faculty, and each other. The CSEQ now comes with norms and is available in a community college form. It is particularly helpful in looking at "the other side" of assessment—that is, not just institutional contribution to learning but [also] *student* effort (a subject taken up below).

Methods that move beyond "customer satisfaction" to get at student understandings of their *learning* are particularly helpful. One might, for instance, ask students how one course builds on another. What connections can they see and articulate? Can they (and do they) apply what they learn in class to a family or work situation? Do they think their instructors pay attention to "real-world" applications? How do they see themselves changing as a result of their studies?

Surveys are an economical way to gather some of this information, in standard ways, over time. An alternative, more probing method for understanding student experience is the interview. They're labor intensive and don't yield neat, summary data, but interviews, a method to which sociologists bring special expertise, have several virtues.

For one, a carefully designed and conducted interview can provide rich contextual data about who learns what under which conditions (this, again, the "behind outcomes" objective). It was in part to ask questions about which students learn what under [which] conditions that the University of Maryland at College Park undertook a massive longitudinal study, employing one-to-one interviews, during the 1980s. [The researchers] looked, for instance, at the educational experience of resident vs. commuter students; at the impact of employment on student satisfaction and retention; and at the academic experience of black students, transfer students, and students who drop out. The interviews that fed into reports in these areas not only produced rich data; they were, participants report, a powerful staff development experience.

Moreover, interviews are good for *students*—an occasion for reflection and a way for students to get signals about institutional and departmental values and expectations. (The late Joseph Katz once commented that the single best thing an institution could do for students was to have a faculty member sit with them for an hour and discuss their learning.)

The argument here is not that every department should do interviews. It is, once again, that clearer, deeper understandings of the students' educational experience are a prerequisite to improving outcomes.

What Is the Students' Contribution to Learning?

What (and how well) students learn is a function of teaching, curricula, and broader campus culture; but it's also significantly a function of *student* effort.

To assess learning outcomes without taking into account the students' responsibility for and contribution to those outcomes is to ignore key questions. What expectations, goals, and motivation do students bring to their work? How do they spend their time? How many hours a week

do they study, and how do they allocate those hours? How much do they use the library, and for what purpose? Do they seek out help when they're falling behind? How often do they talk with other students about classwork or books they've read? Do they try to apply what they learn outside the classroom?

Questions about student effort clearly cross over into those from the previous category—the student experience. And many of the same methods are appropriate. The [CSEQ] asks questions relevant to effort, motivation, and use of time. Surveys and interviews are pertinent, as are more indirect methods such as recording student attendance at cultural events, monitoring library use, and the like.

Trickier than concerns about how to gather such data are those of using them. Faced with a finding that full-time students study six hours a week (a Massachusetts state college learned this when it asked students how they spend their time), what do faculty do? Cut back on homework? Lower expectations? "No" and "maybe" are probably the answers here, but the larger point is that knowing more about what students bring to their studies has implications for how we teach, organize curricula, [and] conduct orientation and, most of all, for how we talk with students about our expectations and their involvement. For many of today's first-generation college students, the "givens" of academe are not given at all. Knowing that students study only a few hours a week, we need to tell them, as clearly and explicitly as possible, that "a careful reading of this chapter will take you four hours," that "writing this paper means writing three drafts and turning it in on time." Being more explicit about expectations and "criteria" is, in fact, a central motif in the most successful assessment programs. More important, it's key to student *learning* itself.

Student effort and motivation is a complex subject, but it's a promising focus for assessment, one that sidesteps a variety of political threats (Will the information be used to evaluate faculty?) and methodological problems (Is Instrument X or Y valid for our program?) while putting an issue squarely on the table. At the least, data on student effort can do what assessment does best: start and inform an essential conversation.

How Does Learning Progress, over Time, in a Given Program of Study?

In assessment's earlier days, a lot of attention went to the value-added model of assessment. There's a right idea behind that model—that college effectiveness is not a matter simply of outcomes but [also is a matter] of student growth, of documented learning over time, [of] distance covered. Unfortunately, value-added came, in many cases, to mean two snapshots taken with a standardized instrument: before and after, pre- and posttest, with little attention to the experiences in between or to explanation. But, as colleges are coming to see, to improve academic growth over time, one needs fuller, more continuous information.

Both as a metaphor for how to think about assessment and as a method, a suggestive notion here is the portfolio: an assembly and analysis of student work done over time—an archive, if you will, through which questions about learning can be framed and explored. Unlike standardized tests, with their machine-reported scores, portfolios put explicit emphasis on human judgment and meaning making.

The most familiar version of portfolio assessment focuses on writing: samples of student writing over time, be it from a variety of disciplines (to get a reading on cross-cutting outcomes) or from within the major. But the concept of a portfolio becomes more suggestive when thought of not simply as a folder of student papers but as an archive of work of various kinds and in various formats, assembled from class (and perhaps out-of-class) activities, publicly documenting academic growth. One might, for instance, compile from assignments done in various contexts a portfolio of student "work samples" within the major: exams from a methods class, memoranda prepared at an internship site, videotapes of presentations, [or] a longer research paper done in a capstone course.

Alverno College employs portfolios, and for similar purposes. Its assessment center maintains an archive of each student's work that includes a videotape of speeches, beginning with one at entry and concluding with an upper level, extemporaneous speech on a concept in her major field, samples of writing at various stages and from various courses; the student's *self*-assessment and extensive written feedback from external assessors (mostly professionals from the community) of several assessment center simulations; and other samplings of work, all grist for final narrative transcripts written by departmental faculty for each of their majors.

Portfolios aren't quickly or cheaply done, nor do they yield neat, bottom-line data. They do offer several benefits. First, their very unwieldiness makes them less subject to misuse than [do] apparently simpler, single-score methods. Second, the act of compiling the portfolio is almost always educational for students; it's hard to imagine a more powerful assignment than asking students to go back over their work of several years, to sort and cull and finally select items (the best and worst) for a portfolio, and to analyze that assembly for patterns, strengths and weaknesses, [and] implied next steps. Third, portfolio methods lend themselves to "co-assessment," to discussion among interested parties, including the student herself, about the quality of the work and its implications. One can imagine, for instance, a conference between a student—let us say a second-semester junior majoring in psychology—her departmental advisor, a faculty member from her support area in philosophy, and the director of student services with whom she's been working on a peer-advising project. The portfolio—and the student's analysis of the work included in it—is the prompt for a conference, whose real point then becomes in-depth feedback and a talking through of next steps, future areas of study, and options following graduation.

How Do Students' Out-of-Class Experiences Contribute to (or Impede) Their Learning?

In 1984, a National Institute of Education commission on the "conditions of excellence" called for (and entitled its report) "Involvement in Learning." At issue, among other things, were the ways students spend out-of-class time and the extent to which they enter into campus intellectual life; recommendations included strengthening out-of-class activities "that have academic functions or academic overtones: debate teams, language clubs, publications, performance groups, political clubs, and international exchange groups" (p. 35). Today, more and more campuses are calling for assessment of out-of-class experiences and dimensions of student growth that transcend course-based conceptions of learning.

These are, of course, areas [in which] some disciplines are particularly interested. In addition, educators in "student affairs" have traditionally studied broader impacts of college on individual development, for example, in the area of student values, personal orientation, and maturation. Today's assessment movement presents the occasion to bring this work to bear more systematically on the improvement of student learning.

The good news is that these are outcomes that many faculty care deeply about and purposefully pursue. Within the disciplines, one can find attention to such "softer" outcomes. In sociology, for instance, one finds many faculty concerned not only with student knowledge of frameworks and facts but [also] with a disposition (that is, something beyond an ability) to step back and be critical, an orientation toward social change, and the capacity to link individual experience with the larger sociohistorical context. Faculty in literature often look not only for ability to analyze a text but [also for] a deeper, more personal engagement with literature. At the institutional level, many college catalogs posit values that students are to develop—or state as objectives various perspectives, awarenesses, attitudes, sensibilities, or dispositions, the sources for which would be both in and out of class. There are important kinds of learning, for which a variety of assessment methods are available, ranging from standardized batteries and focused interviews to observation studies and student self-report.

A second focus might be the co-curriculum, in whole or [in] part, college sponsored (clubs, sports, public events) or informal (that which students create for themselves). The questions here are familiar. To what extent are students involved with out-of-class campus life? How does such involvement relate to in-class performance or later success? What abilities and values does the co-curriculum seem to advance? In whom? Are those values congruent with the college's goals and curricular intents? In the name of assessment, various colleges have examined Greek systems, student TV viewing, and off-campus work; several are looking at student-faculty interaction out of class and activity participation rates over time; [and] one university did an ethnographic study of freshman dorm life (with dismaying findings).

A third point here is less a new topic than a perspective and a reminder that in applying the techniques and answering the questions of other sections of this [chapter], the learning/growth, cognitive/affective, in-class/out-of-class nexus be kept in mind. So, for example, should departmental faculty elect to interview graduating students about experiences in the major, their questions might include attention to the values [the students perceive they] were taught (and learned) in departmental classrooms. Portfolio assessment can illuminate not only growth of knowledge and abilities but [also] more personal, affective areas of development such as creativity, persistence, and initiative.

What's at issue here again is assessment that looks at the whole student and the full college experience. Learning doesn't occur in a vacuum, and to improve it we need to look beyond the department, beyond the classroom, beyond narrow conceptions of learning.

What Are Students Able to Do with What They Know?

The outcomes many educators and policymakers care most about have to do with what students can do with what they know, with how well they can put the pieces together and apply knowledge in new situations.

This is a concern many "outcome measures" miss. Standardized tests in particular tend to look at learning in terms of discrete pieces of knowledge (as "items") and tend, consequently, to be weak predictors of performance in the work world. But beyond needs for predictive measures of outcome, the larger need here is for assessment that (a) coincides with a view of learning that encompasses both knowing and doing, (b) connects with and enables such learning during the college years, and (c) is in itself educative. That need can be met by "performance-based" assessment.

Performance assessment is less a single method than a way of thinking about learning; it has to do with developing in students abilities to comprehend, connect, and apply. In a community college automotive technology program, for example, quite specific knowledge components and diagnostic/repair abilities are the objective; instructors bring these together over the semesters in a sequence of practical exercises designed for feedback to students. At two years' end, there may indeed be a summative, culminating project for students to accomplish, one final test of "knowledge in action," but it has been preceded and set up by a consistent pattern of instruction along the way. In effect, the connections between teaching and assessment become seamless: teaching entails assessment, the assessment teaches.

So too in other "applied" fields. In social work, for instance, there's a tradition of performance-based assessment (and learning). Students are expected to develop a set of skills which they can demonstrate and apply in real settings.

Indeed, where the objective is to assure end-of-program professional competence and readiness for practice, performance-based assessment becomes the method of choice. Here college faculties are learning from corporate and governmental counterparts (who've been at these questions since the 1940s) about the "assessment center" method. The assessment center is less a place than a process that attempts to identify the components of professional effectiveness, then observe their development in candidates through a series of carefully structured, juried exercises. The Teacher Assessment Project at Stanford in the late 1980s offered a much-watched example. Researchers there designed assessment center methods for teacher certification. Candidates participating in the several-day experience engaged in a number of "real world" simulations—critiquing curricula, designing lesson plans, teaching in various class situations—with their performances observed and judged by expert teachers. Parallel efforts exist in medical education, nursing, business, architecture, and a variety of other professional and pre-professional fields.

Parenthetically, research demonstrates the superiority of the assessment center over other methods in predicting future performance in a wide range of work settings. Not surprisingly, too, the candidates who do better in assessment center exercises are those who aren't seeing them for the first time, whose prior learning has attended to the knowing-doing nexus. Indeed, many educators who push end-of-study performance assessment hope that its tie to licensing and certification (which makes it matter to students and therefore to their teachers) will in time nudge underlying patterns of instruction toward greater attention to application and doing.

Examples of performance assessment are most evident within the professions, such as nursing, engineering, [and] teacher education, where standards of practice are comparatively more visible and agreed upon. Of course, there is also a sense in which departments preparing students for disciplinary graduate school are also routinely conducting performance assessment: asking students to "do" sociology or chemistry in ways that they will have to do it in graduate school as well—through the writing of research papers, conducting of laboratories, or whatever.

What is particularly intriguing, however, is to think of what "performance" and its assessment mean outside of the framework of training for the professions or graduate school. What does "performance" mean in the liberal arts and general education? How can faculty observe students "doing sociology" or "doing chemistry" as part of their broad development in the liberal arts? How can faculty observe the traces of their teaching in the way students approach issues in their own lives and in their communities?

Done over time, then, performance assessment becomes a powerful adjunct to the teaching and learning process. It provides a faculty with rich information about how well students are able to integrate and apply knowledge and [with] a look at "softer" but important learning in areas such as creativity, persistence, empathy, and personal values. Most important (once more), the assessment center and related experiences look behind outcomes to learning processes that are inherently involving and educational for students.

What Broad Patterns Characterize Our Students' Movement through the Institution?

A fact brought to light by assessment is that many campuses have no systematic way to track student movement through the institution. How many graduate? In what length of time? Who leaves, and where do they go? What patterns characterize the persistence of women or returning students? Information about how students, as groups and individuals, progress (or don't) is, once again, essential to getting behind outcomes.

Concerns about retention naturally fuel an interest in these matters, and some campuses have established a "longitudinal database" or "integrated student information system" for purposes of tracking (and maximizing) enrollment. Understanding and improving student *learning*, however, means developing a somewhat different system, one that addresses not only broad-scale administrative or management questions but [also] *educational* questions about student attainment.

Toward such a system, a first step may be to think carefully about what questions it should address and therefore what kinds of information to collect. Academic and student development faculty in particular, but also administrators, librarians, and computing specialists, need to work together to formulate questions and concerns the database should address. This wider participation not only produces better guidelines for data collection but [also] reinforces stakeholding and the likelihood that data will be brought to bear in solving problems.

What Judgments Are Students Able to Make about Their Own Learning?

Research shows that students who are self-conscious about themselves as learners learn more. Teachers know this from experience; students who understand their own process as writers can repeat their successes, [and] those who can figure out that they study better with a group are steps ahead. What this implies is that assessment should be not only *of* (and for) students but [also] *by* them.

Work at Alverno College is suggestive; there, a focus on the student's ability to self-assess begins at entry. With a curriculum organized around eight outcomes (communications, analysis, problem solving, aesthetic response, etc.), Alverno faculty naturally want to know as much as possible about each student's beginning-level effectiveness in those areas; but because of a commitment to independent learning, they also want to know about and encourage *student* reflectiveness about their own knowledge and abilities.

Thus, to assess the ability to "speak on one's feet," Alverno asks entering students to prepare and deliver (and have videotaped) a short speech on the question, "Should applicants be screened or should college be open to anyone who wants to try?" Following a workshop which introduces the concept and strategies of self-assessment, the student sits down with a trained assessor to watch and critique the videotape of her performance. The focus is on the student's understanding of her own work and the charting of a course for improvement—courses to be taken, opportunities to practice, and so forth. This process is repeated many times over four years until the ability to self-assess becomes a refined habit.

The larger point here is the important one: mechanisms can be found (self-assessment is but one) to involve students in assessment, to provide useful feedback, to help students themselves get behind outcomes, [and] to understand and take charge of their own learning. The goal here is simple and by now familiar: that in the name of *assessing* learning, learning occurs.

Themes and Implications

The nine questions above often overlap. Running through them are six larger points that sociology faculty involved in assessment would do well to keep in mind.

Outcomes are not enough. That is, we need to lay what we learn about outcomes up against what we know about the goals and programs of the college including the character of its curriculum, teaching, and out-of-class life. Further, we need to know who our students are, about their goals and level of effort, and about how they experience the institution. The point is to get "behind outcomes" to the conditions of learning—to get information that will help improve those conditions.

Getting behind outcomes implies a broader focus for assessment, one that looks beyond narrowly conceived cognitive outcomes to the attitudes, values, and dispositions that necessarily undergird learning. Indeed, distinctions between the cognitive and [the] affective, the in-class and the out-of-class, are blurred in many of the outcomes we care most about: tolerance, creativity, abilities to solve problems and work with others. We need assessment predicated on a view of learning that is integrated and multidimensional.

Using assessment to get behind outcomes means that more people, using a wider variety of methods, will look at a broader range of concerns; it means a more complex array of information that will never lend itself to neat, bottom-line scores and reports. A next challenge in assessment is to find ways to communicate and *use* complex qualitative information both inside and outside the institution. "Meaning-making" and dissemination strategies may be more important than how information is gathered.

Choices about what to assess and how to do so should be governed first and foremost by what's good for students. The best methods involve students in creating or improving conditions of learning and are in and of themselves educative. A corollary here is that such assessment will be done primarily by those who regularly work with students—academic and student development faculty—and not by third-party experts.

A broader conception of the tasks of assessment means a broader involvement by people from across the institution. Assessment for improvement is not a one-office, data-gathering operation but a total institutional responsibility, an ultimate interdisciplinary challenge. Assessment issues are cross-cutting: in class and out, student effort and faculty teaching, student preparation and institutional expectation. To get the big picture in view, we need teams of people representing diverse perspectives and expertise—faculty from various academic disciplines, student development faculty and staff, admissions staff, advisors, administrators, students, and alumni. The goal of assessment is a mind-set: that quality improvement is everybody's business.

Sociologists and other social scientists come to the assessment movement with specific skills related to qualitative and quantitative research, very well suited to working to improve the validity and reliability of the tools they use to discover what their students have actually learned. They also enjoy a "structural" view of their work setting which helps them identify and make better use of the institutional resources and networks they need to improve teaching and learning in the individual classroom, department, or institution. They have effective conceptual tools, therefore, to define and implement the kinds of assessment most likely to improve the quality and character of student learning.

Taking on the Canon and Saving Civilization

Statements from the Culture War

18

Multiculturalism: The Crucial Philosophical and Organizational Issues

Patrick J. Hill

In higher education today and in American society at large, we are wrestling with an incredible explosion of diversity. There are those who deem higher education complicitous with society's leadership in depreciating or ignoring the diversity of human experience; their attempt, consequently, is to provide institutional and curricular status of a nonmarginal sort for enterprises like women's studies, ethnic studies, and Latin American studies. Then there are those who judge the early responses to diversity to have been more or less appropriate under the circumstances; who worry about incoherence, fragmentation, and "particularism" in the curriculum; and who want to clarify what students should be led to regard as central and what as marginal. In one way or another, all these parties are concerned with the comparative value of the diverse visions and with how we are to conceive their relationship.

This [chapter] attempts to clarify the crucial philosophical and organizational issues that

AUTHOR'S NOTE: *Change,* July-August, 1991, pp. 39-47. Reprinted with permission of the Helen Dwight Reid Educational Foundation. Published by Heldref Publications, 1319 Eighteenth St., N. W., Washington, D.C. 20036-1802. Copyright © 1991.

EDITORS' NOTE: See the Opening Up New Roads: Diversity Issues section in the *Fieldguide.*

underlie the current struggles in higher education about multiculturalism. The [chapter] is in two parts. The first examines the explosion of diversity and evaluates four major frameworks that have been employed in the West to comprehend or order diversity. The second part reflects on the ramifications of these frameworks for current and possible approaches to the conduct of higher education.

Four Frameworks

"The hallmark of modern consciousness," Clifford Geertz observes insightfully, "is its enormous multiplicity." Diversity of opinion, of course, is hardly new; it was, for example, radical diversity of opinion more than 300 years ago that shaped the philosophical projects of Montaigne and Descartes. The novelty in the contemporary engagement with diversity is a function of other novelties.

Awareness on the part of most Western thinkers of the collapse of the Enlightenment goal of objective reason, in the light of which it was hoped to sort and hierarchize the great diversity of opinion. Gadamer's rehabilitation of the concept of prejudice as an inevitable feature of all human thinking may by itself symbolize how far we have moved from the ideal of a disembodied objective mind.

The related awareness, partly philosophical and partly political, of the socioeconomic and political dimensions to the development and sustaining of knowledge-claims. Whereas the claims of scientists were falsely cloaked in the mantle of pure objectivity, the knowledge-claims of other groups (e.g., women, minorities, persons of color, Third World persons) were and are suppressed, invalidated, and marginalized.

The growing incapacity of groups hitherto exercising monopolizing control over judgments of truth and worth to sustain such power. The wealth of Japan and the Arab nations, for example, and the voting power of women and the elderly in the United States have forced accommodations by the established order to a newly emerging one.

The realization on the part of many of the intrinsic beauty and worth of the diverse voices—a realization that came to many people in the United States through the black revolution of the '60s. This shift in consciousness was crisply expressed by Octavio Paz:

The ideal of a single civilization for everyone, implicit in the cult of progress and technique, impoverishes and mutilates us. Every view of the world that becomes extinct, every culture that disappears, diminishes a possibility of life.

Diversity, again, is not new, and intellectuals have not needed the stimulations of today to construct its analysis. In Western thought, four major frameworks have been employed in the analysis of diversity:

(1) *Relativism,* which in one way or another regards all knowledge-claims as self-contained within particular cultures or language communities and which recognizes no higher or commensurable ground upon which objective adjudication might take place

(2) *Perennialism* or *universalism,* which sees commonalities or constancies in the great variety of human thought and which frequently (as in the influential work of Frithjof Schuon) regards those constancies as the essential and more important aspect of diverse historical phenomena

(3) *Hierarchism,* which attempts to sort or rank the multiplicity by a variety of means, among them establishing criteria or methods of inquiry that divide knowledge from opinion or interpreting world history and human development in such a way that certain opinions and behavior are progressive, developed, and/or mature while others more or less approximate those ideals

(4) *Pluralism,* which in its democratic version is central to the analysis of this chapter and which I will therefore spend a longer moment here to expand upon

In the philosophical and political traditions of American pluralism, diversity has played a prominent role. Nowhere was diversity more prominent than in the epistemology and social philosophy of John Dewey. Though aware of the idealized dimension of his thinking, Dewey grounded both science (as a way of knowing) and democracy (as a way of life) in a respect for diverse opinion:

It is of the nature of science not so much to tolerate as to welcome diversity of opinion, while it insists that inquiry brings the evidence of observed facts to bear to effect a consensus of conclusions—and even then to hold the conclusions subject to what is ascertained and made public in further new inquiries. I would not claim that any existing democracy has ever made complete and adequate use of scientific method in deciding upon its policies. But freedom of inquiry, toleration of diverse views, freedom of communication, the distribution of what is found out to every individual as the ultimate intellectual consumers, are involved in the democratic as in the scientific method.

In linking science and democracy, Dewey welcomed not just the diversity of opinion of highly trained scientists; he [also] welcomed as an intellectual and political resource the diversity of every human being:

Every autocratic and authoritarian scheme of social action rests upon a belief that the needed intelligence is confined to a superior few, who because of inherent natural gifts are endowed with the ability and the right to control the conduct of others. . . . While what we call intelligence may be distributed in unequal amounts, it is the democratic faith that it is sufficiently general so that each individual has something to contribute.

For Dewey, the inclusion of diverse perspectives becomes an ethical imperative:

The keynote of democracy as a way of life may be expressed, it seems to me, as the necessity for the participation of every mature being in the formation of the values that regulate the living of men [sic] together . . . . All those who are affected by social institutions must have a share in producing and managing them.

Finally, appreciation of diversity is linked by Dewey to visions of human nature and community. The resources of diversity will flourish in those social and political forms that allow the pooling of the experience and insights of diversely constituted individuals. Not that the pooled insight is inherently preferable to the workings of intelligence in an individual or within a single-language community—Dewey is

forever appreciative of the value of small communities—but that the pooling is an escalation of the power of human intelligence:

The foundation of democracy is faith in the capacities of human nature; faith in human intelligence and in the power of pooled and cooperative experience. . . . What is the faith of democracy in the role of consultation, of conference, of persuasion, of discussion, in formation of public opinion, which in the long run is self-corrective, except faith in the capacity of the intelligence of the common man [sic] to respond with common sense to the free play of acts and ideas which are secured by effective guarantees of free inquiry, free assembly, and free communication.

In pooled, cooperative experience, Dewey is saying, the powers of human intelligence are increased and human nature or capacity is completed.

This view, or at least the narrowly epistemological dimension of it, is affirmed in other traditions. In Gadamer, the essential and unavoidable partiality of the human knower must be corrected or supplemented in dialogue. In *The Genealogy of Morals,* Nietzsche states the epistemological value of cooperative inquiry quite succinctly:

The more affects we allow to speak about one thing, the more eyes, different eyes we can use to observe one thing, the more complete will our concept of this thing, our objectivity, be.

Interpreting Diversity

What is at issue among these four competing philosophic frameworks? How might we go about choosing among them?

The philosophical issue in most general terms is the appropriate interpretation of diversity: how to give it its proper due. In an older style of doing philosophy—what Rorty terms the metaphysical as opposed to the "ironist" view—we would now seek to determine which one of these frameworks is true to the nature of things, in this case to the phenomenon of diversity. In a post-metaphysical mode of doing philosophy, we recognize that each of these frameworks is an interpretation, a value-laden interpretation of the variety of human experience. No neutral ground exists upon which we might stand to evaluate either the values or the frameworks objectively.

The choice among the frameworks is to be made (assuming, as I judge to be the case here, that each has dealt honestly and intelligently with the full range of available data) not in terms of conformity to the nature of things but in terms of each framework's appropriateness for sustaining the values of the culture or language community. The question of the adequacy of each of the interpretations of diversity, then, will be answered differently in different cultures. All answers will be value-laden answers that cannot be justified without reference to these values.

In the United States and much of the Western world, we are at least nominally committed to a democratic social order. The evaluation that follows of the four frameworks is thus done within the context of that cultural commitment. The judgments reached are not abstract ones about the correspondence of particular frameworks to the nature of things but judgments about their appropriateness to sustaining the vision of "pooled and cooperative experience" articulated above. Crucial to each of those judgments will be the extent to which diversity is "welcomed" and incorporated democratically into pooled experience as well as the extent to which each framework can suggest a relationship of self and diverse other that might motivate the kind of conversation capable of sustaining a public sphere.

With these considerations and a frank commitment to democratic values in mind, I make the following observations about the frameworks for explaining diversity.

(1) *Relativism.* This is the framework that accords enduring centrality to diversity, both to the fact of diversity and to its defense, if not its nurturance. The endless attempts of philosophers to discredit the logical foundations of relativism are convincing to themselves but ineffective in undermining the attractiveness and strength of its straightforward recognition of diverse, frequently nonintersecting (or impermeable) modes of thinking. While those who describe themselves as relativists will endlessly be dogged with logical objections, the opposite position—what Geertz calls "anti-relativism"—can mask a great lack of appreciation for the profound, intractable diversity of our time.

From the standpoint of democratic values, the problem with relativism is less its logical incoherence than its comparative incapacity to motivate interest or conversation—an incapacity which may stem more from the individualism of our culture than from the framework itself. If we all live in separate and/or incommensurate reality-worlds, the motivation to inquire into the world of the diverse other can be readily relegated to the anthropologist or world traveler. For democracy to work, its citizens must sense if not a commitment to a shared future, then at least an occasional need for each other.

(2) *Perennialism or universalism.* These philosophies do not ignore diversity, as is frequently charged. They could not uncover perennial themes in diverse cultures or epochs without first immersing themselves in the diversity. Perennialists would claim that they do accord diversity its proper due; indeed, their system is not incapable of explaining anything.

The problem with perennialism from the standpoint of democratic values is less its capacity to explain diversity than the comparative noncentrality it accords it. If the dialogical other is inevitably going to be viewed as an instantiation of a previously known pattern— or, more generously, if the dialogue is at best going to force a modification of a previously known pattern in the light of which I and the other will then be seen as instantiations—it is understandable that the other may feel his/her uniqueness depreciated and forced to fit a mold. Genuine appreciation of diversity must be found to some extent upon an expectation of novelty.

(3) *Hierarchism.* Philosophies or theologies or social systems that hierarchize or sort differences according to some historical or developmental scheme are obviously taking diversity— especially inequality—seriously. It is not ignored. It is ranked and explained (or explained away, critics would say).

While inequality is a fact of life and some sort of ranking may for the near term be unavoidable, what is disturbing to a theorist of democracy is the way in which whole epochs and entire peoples—e.g., Native Americans, women, the physically challenged, and the so-called underdeveloped nations—have been and continue to be marginalized and their experiences depreciated in such rankings. Democratic social theory cannot in the end be satisfied with an egalitarian epistemology—because some insights and truths are more appropriate than others to particular situations and because we wish to encourage the development of continually diverse perspectives. Still more opprobrious to democratic social theory as an interpretation of human diversity and inequality is a system of ranking joined to a hierarchical structure of association; in any such system, the epistemologically marginalized remain politically vulnerable and effectively voiceless. Whatever inequality currently exists is worsened and perpetuated by structures that de facto operate (in Dewey's words) "as if the needed intelligence" to participate meaningfully "were confined to a superior few."

(4) *Democratic pluralism.* Within the context of a commitment to democratic values, the diversity of the world's peoples is to be welcomed, respected, celebrated, and fostered. Within that context, diversity is not a problem or a defect, it is a resource. The major problem within all pluralistic contexts (including relativism) is less that of taking diversity seriously than that of grounding any sort of commonality. It is the problem of encouraging citizens to sustain conversations of respect with diverse others for the sake of their making public policy together, of forging over and over again a sense of a shared future.

Conversations of respect and the making of public policy in a democracy cannot be based on mere tolerance—on the "live and let live" or "to each his own" attitudes of individualistic relativism—at least not in the Jeffersonian and Deweyan, as opposed to the Federalist, vision of democracy. Democracy needs something at once more binding or relating of diverse viewpoints and something that grounds the respect in a public sphere, in a world or situation that is at least temporarily shared. It is impossible to respect the diverse other if one does not believe that the views of the diverse other are grounded in a reality—the democratic version of reality— that binds or implicates everyone as much as do our own views.

Conversations of respect between diverse communities are characterized by intellectual reciprocity. They are ones in which the participants expect to learn from each other, expect to learn nonincidental things, expect to change at least intellectually as a result of the encounter. Such conversations are not animated by, nor do they result in mere tolerance of, the preexisting diversity, for political or ethical reasons. In such conversations, one participant does not treat the other as an illustration of, a variation of, or a dollop upon a truth or insight already fully possessed. There is no will to incorporate the other in any sense into one's belief system. In such conversations, one participant does not presume that the relationship is one of teacher to student (in any traditional sense of that relationship), of parent to child, of developed to underdeveloped. The participants are co-learners.

* * *

My paradigms of such conversations of respect are drawn from my experience in interdisciplinary academic communities. Not all interdisciplinary conversations, to be sure, are respectful. Social scientists often view English professors as providing a service, the service of illustrative examples of their truths, or as high-class entertainment. Humanists often assume that scientists are value-blind dupes of the military-industrial complex. Other interdisciplinary conversations, somewhat less disrespectful, are so complementary as to involve little or no diversity of substance.

In genuinely respectful conversations, each disciplinary participant is aware at the outset of the incapacity of his/her own discipline (and, ideally, of himself/herself) to answer the question that is being asked. Each participant is aware of his/her partiality and of the need for the other. One criterion of the genuineness of the subsequent conversations is the transformation of each participant's understanding or definition of the question—perhaps even a transformation of self-understanding.

This definition of a conversation of respect may strike many as too demanding, uncritical, or relativistic. It seems to suggest that the respect easily acknowledged as appropriate to

conversations between Christians and Buddhists or between Palestinians and Jews is also appropriate to conversations between biologists and philosophers, between those in higher education and those currently excluded. Or, worse yet, between systems of beliefs on the one hand modernized to accommodate contemporary science and philosophy and, on the other, fundamentalists, traditionalists, pantheists, and all sorts of local and tribal and idiosyncratic cognitive systems.

I have three responses to these concerns. First, we foreclose the ethnographic task that Geertz and others have urged upon us as appropriate to the contemporary explosion of diversity if we presume that we will not discover something about the life of the mind and something valuable for all of us in a dialogue with the radically diverse other. Second, I do not regard these boundary-crossing conversations as the only conversations worth having or the only activity worth engaging in; they just deserve far more of our energy at this time than we have been allotting to them. Third, in view of the collapse of Enlightenment values, of the crisis of the planetary environment, and the many critiques of universalism, the reluctance of modern thought to engage in conversations with communities that retain pre-industrial values ought to be considerably less than it was a quarter of a century ago. The deep distrust of modernity for everything that originated prior to the 16th century has less and less to recommend it.

One last observation about the four frameworks of interpretation: although particular versions of the four have done so, none of them (as presented in general terms here) attends adequately to the politics of knowledge, to the postmodern awareness of the interplay between power and truth. Democracy's celebration of the diversity of knowers is a healthy corrective to the alternatives of hierarchism, but democracy's framework attends no more sufficiently than the others to the de facto inequality among these alternatives and to the impact of that inequality upon the pursuit of truth. A fuller analysis of the nature of thinking in democratic contexts, which I have attempted elsewhere, would attend to (a) the habits of mind appropriate to participation in a democracy and (b) the creation of conditions under which the power of pooled intelligence might be fully realized.

Having looked at the fact of diversity—at the principal interpretations of it—and attempted to evaluate those interpretations in the context of a democratic pluralism, I turn now to three more topics: (1) the philosophical underpinnings of the current organization of higher education including the implications of that organization for liberal education, (2) how higher education would be differently organized with the philosophical underpinnings of democratic pluralism, and (3) possible objections to my analysis.

Organizational Philosophy

Let me begin with this introductory observation. Higher education, judged by the standards of democratic pluralism, does not take seriously even the diversity within its walls, much less the diversity outside its walls. The diversity of disciplinary or ideological perspectives is muted by what the recent national study of the major conducted by the Association of American Colleges called "the ethos of self-containment." Even in institutions that take interdisciplinarity seriously, the diversity most frequently worked with is not the challenging diversity of unshared assumptions or excluded peoples but the congenial diversity of presumed complementarity. Wedded as most of higher education is to the notion that the point of teaching is to transmit what we already know,

few (too few, unfortunately) agree with Gerald Graff in seeing a positive pedagogical function for exposing our students to unresolved conflict.

At first blush, and from the point of view of the student, the organization of the university appears relativistic. It appears that each major, surely each division, constitutes a separate reality-world or, to borrow a recent phrase of Isaiah Berlin's, a "windowless box." The organization of the university seems intended to facilitate each student's discovering a reality-world in which he/she will feel comfortable. The departments, especially across divisional lines, are at best tolerant of each other, displaying in practice and in their requirements for their majors no great need of each other. Given these assumptions, they pay appropriately little attention to other departments or to general education, both because the major is believed to be self-contained and because there is little to no agreement on what might be significantly common across fields of inquiry. Indeed, the disciplines are often viewed, consistent with their historical origins, as correctives to each other.

From the point of view of the self-contained major, the liberally educated person is defined by the habits of mind appropriate to the particular department. From the point of view of the undeclared student, liberal education is de facto defined in a myriad of ways, and the message of the university as a whole seems to be: define it whichever way you like.

The university, of course, is only speciously relativistic. Hierarchy pervades the institution. Although messages of what is or is not important frequently escape a student's perusal of the catalogue or passage through the pork-barreled distribution requirements, the truth is that the university oozes with uncoded messages about centrality and marginality. While these messages vary from institution to institution, we are all familiar with the value judgments inherent in distinctions like the hard and soft sciences, graduate and undergraduate, required and optional. Discerning observers see the value judgments in the size of departments and buildings, in grading patterns, in the willingness or unwillingness to waive prerequisites, in the frequency of tenure-track appointments, and in the denial of departmental status and budgets to areas like women's studies.

Liberal education in the hierarchical university is spoken of in much the same individualistic terms that an outright relativist might employ: "Do what you're good at." But there is no mistaking the fact that, in the hierarchical university, all the disciplines are not equally valuable. By and large, it is believed by students and professors alike that the better and more serious students will be found in the prestigious departments. It is not a value-free observation to report that so-and-so majored in biochemistry at Johns Hopkins.

What about universalist or perennialist assumptions in the current organization of the university? These assumptions, of course, pervade the separate disciplines themselves (otherwise there would be no point to Geertz's critique). But the assumptions are not apparent in the organization of the university. General education, wherein one would expect the commonality of human experience or disciplinary paradigms to be addressed, is a poor stepchild in most colleges and universities. The university is organized to encourage research and teaching within unshared paradigms. If there are constancies in human cultures and disciplines, the traditional university is certainly not set up to encourage the boundary-crossings that might uncover them.

Democratic Pluralism?

What about democratic pluralism and the conversations of respect upon which it thrives? To what extent is the traditional university grounded on those assumptions?

In my judgment, most universities are not grounded at all on these assumptions. I will make this point by sketching a few features of what a college/university so grounded might look like.

A college that looked upon diversity as a vital resource for learning and wished, therefore, to encourage conversations of respect under conditions in which unshared or disparate power would not inhibit those conversations would devote itself to three tasks. Two of the tasks are now being done in a token fashion; the third is not being done at all.

Such a college would make it the highest priority to recruit women, minorities, persons of color, and persons from other cultures to their faculties and student bodies as soon as possible. As a temporary measure, a measure of significant inadequacy, such colleges would undertake a massive retraining of their faculties (mis)educated in one discipline and one culture.

The second step is a prerequisite of significant multicultural education. Having hired some women and persons of color from North America and around the world, it would thus be easy to claim, as many colleges now do, that they are giving diversity its due because they have a study-abroad program, because 10 percent of the faculty are tenured women, because they have a Nigerian in the history department, or because they require one course in non-Western culture. These colleges are still in the grips of the windowless boxes of relativism. In such colleges, it is still quite possible for the vast majority of students and faculty to happily go their independent ways with no experience of a conversation of respect—a transforming conversation of respect—with another culture.

Were a college or university truly committed to democratic pluralism, it would proceed to create conditions under which the representatives of different cultures need to have conversations of respect with each other in order to do their everyday teaching and research. As colleges are set up now, there is, except in the highly sequenced departments, virtually no interdependence of the various departments and frequently little of the members of the same department. A democratically pluralistic college would make war upon the ethos of self-containment, upon all boundaries that inhibit or make unnecessary conversations of respect between diverse peoples. General education would be radically reconceived to immerse students in such conversations, in full interaction with their majors. Team-taught programs and interdisciplinary/intercultural majors would become the central (though not the exclusive) mode of study.

The point requires even further elaboration. We would not have changed much if all we achieve is a sprinkling of multicultural courses in the departments: "Multicultural Cities" in the sociology department, five courses on the Far East in a 120-course history department, or a cross-listed elective for biology majors on the "History of Chinese Medicine." We need to reconceive and restructure the curriculum so that the inquiry cannot be conducted without the contributions or even the presence of the currently marginalized. We would no longer find separate courses on health taught mostly by white males in separate departments of biology, sociology, and philosophy, but instead [would find] a team-taught program of 32 credits on "The Human Body in Interdisciplinary and Intercultural Perspective," or "Health and Sickness in Interdisciplinary and Intercultural Perspective," or "Self, Nature, and World in Interdisciplinary and Intercultural Perspective."

Marginalization will be perpetuated, in other words, if new voices and perspectives are added while the priorities and core of the orga-

nization remain unchanged. Marginalization ends and conversations of respect begin when the curriculum is reconceived to be unimplementable without the central participation of the currently excluded and marginalized.

This point was made in a different language by a team that visited Brown in 1990. It contrasted the idea of diversity—of mere diversity—with what I have been calling conversations of respect in democratic pluralism:

> By contrast to the idea of [mere] diversity, which gives primary regard to the mere presence of multiple ethnic and racial groups within the community, pluralism asks of the members of all groups to explore, understand, and try to appreciate one another's cultural experiences and heritage. It asks a leap of imagination as well as a growth of knowledge. It asks for a most difficult outcome: cultural self-transcendence.

Meaningful multiculturalism, in other words, transforms the curriculum. While the presence of persons of other cultures and subcultures is a virtual prerequisite to that transformation, their "mere presence" is primarily a political achievement (which different groups will assess differently), not an intellectual or educational achievement. Real educational progress will be made when multiculturalism becomes interculturalism.

What might such an exploration in intercultural education look and feel like to the student in a democratically pluralistic university? I have framed an answer in terms of the habits of mind I have seen developed by the most responsive students in experiments approximating what I am advocating.

Such persons have immersed themselves in a sustained learning community, a community that is intercultural and interdisciplinary. They have studied something of great human significance and have experienced how their understanding deepens with the additions of each relevant perspective of another discipline, culture, or subculture. They have mastered or at least internalized a feeling for more than one discipline, more than one culture. They know the value and indeed the necessity of seeking many and diverse perspectives, most particularly the inevitable *partiality* of those perspectives. They have mastered the skills of access to those perspectives. They have mastered the skills in understanding and integrating these diverse perspectives. They are comfortable with ambiguity and conflict. Tolerance, empathic understanding, awareness of one's own partiality, openness to growth through dialogue in pluralistic communities—all of these things have become part of their instinctive responses to each novel situation they encounter. (They might even characterize those who proceed otherwise as uncritical thinkers.)

There is one last point I wish to make about the organization of democratically pluralistic colleges. I return to the aforementioned report at Brown to preface the point:

The ideal of pluralism toward which we would have the university strive is one that can only be realized when a spirit of civility and mutual respect abounds, when all groups feel equally well-placed and secure within the community because all participate in that spirit.

I am less concerned at the moment with the "spirit of civility and mutual respect" than I am with its consequence: "When all groups feel *equally well-placed and secure within the community.*" How would an institution make this happen for currently excluded or marginalized peoples?

In a previous age, we might have been content to say that such security would be provided by allowing all voices to have access to or be represented at the decision-making table. We are now too aware of the interplay of power and knowledge and of the partiality of

our own listening to be satisfied with such an answer. Colleges serious about "equal placement and security" would have to be concerned with neutralizing the impact of unshared power in teaching and research as well as in personnel decisions.

I see no holding back from concluding that this suggests an end to the currently inhibiting system of rank, tenure, and promotion. I am not saying flatly that the whole system must be abandoned (though I have heard worse ideas), but if it is not, then ways must be found (as they were found in the Federated Learning Communities and its spinoffs) to conduct the conversations of respect fully within the curriculum but entirely without consequences one way or another for promotion and tenure decisions.

Six Objections

Many reasonable objections might be raised to restructuring the university along the lines I have suggested. Less in the hope of responding definitively to them than in the hope of enhancing the plausibility of a democratically pluralistic vision of the university, I will respond briefly to the objections I have most frequently encountered.

(1) Granted, we are living in a radically diverse world, runs the first objection. It is impossible, however, without undermining the coherence of the academic enterprise, to take all of that diversity seriously.

In reply: I am not suggesting that every institution has to mirror all the diversity in the world. The full diversity should be mirrored by the entire system of higher education or (less so) by institutions in a region or state. What is important for a single institution is that a challenging, relevant diversity pervade the curriculum and that its students are thereby exposed to the liberal education experiences described above.

(2) A second objection, inspired by the developmental view of human diversity: It is all well and good to acknowledge the explosion of diversity in our awareness. But all these diverse viewpoints are not equally worthwhile. It is romantic and unreasonable to believe that Native American society, pre-industrial Latin America, or the Gaelic-speaking people of the west of Ireland have as much to contribute to the understanding and shaping of the modern world as do Americans and Europeans and the Japanese.

In reply: I do not expect Native Americans to leapfrog in the near future over the Japanese and Americans in the production of smart bombs or compact discs. But by and large, I will expect, until proven otherwise in sustained conversations of respect, that the marginalized cultures of the world have much to contribute to medicine, to agricultural science, to our understanding of the relationship of humanity and the environment, to child rearing, to therapy, and to dozens of other important things. The advanced industrial nations of the world have cornered the market on neither wisdom nor science.

(3) A related hierarchical objection: Can any education be serious that does not focus centrally on Western civilization? Even ignoring the fact that it is our heritage (and ought therefore to be the focus of our education), it is the most

powerful and influential force on the planet.

In reply: I am not suggesting that we not study Western civilization or that it be marginalized or caricatured as the sole root of the world's many problems. I am suggesting, rather, (a) that both in its origins (as Martin Bernal has urged) and in its current form it be studied in interaction with other cultures and with its own subcultures (which are also our heritage) and (b) that this study take the form of a dialogue with members of those other (sub)cultures in situations of "equal placement and security." Political science majors, for example, ought regularly to encounter professors from Latin America and Africa in dialogue with North American professors on issues of democracy and sociopolitical organization. Biology majors likewise should participate in curricular-based dialogues with Chinese professors who question the assumptions of Western medicine. While students could scarcely come away from such experiences without some awareness of the partiality of Western approaches, they would also likely leave with as much or more appreciation of the strengths of our approaches than is fostered by the current noncomparative, sprawling, unfocused, and unconnected curriculum.

(4) A universalist might object: There is no great need to study Buddhist psychology because the essence of it is available in Jung; and [there is] no great need to read Vine Deloria because his tribalism is not significantly different from the decentralist tradition in America or Russia.

In reply: If these intellectual phenomena are as similar as the objection supposes, that conclusion should emerge in a sustained conversation of respect with Buddhists and Native Americans. We are all too familiar with the distortions and depreciations that occur when a dominant culture or an isolated individual attempts to interpret another by incorporating it into what is already familiar. Additionally, the objection presupposes, contrary to the assumptions of democratic pluralism, that the alleged similarities of these intellectual phenomena are more significant than their diversity.

(5) A more general (and politically more difficult) version of the previous objection: One or another invasion of diversity has characterized the whole of at least Western history. Geertz and the multiculturalists are exaggerating the significance of contemporary diversity. Diversity is already receiving its appropriate due.

In reply: In a democratic society, the issue under discussion is not only the philosophical issue of according diversity its proper due but [also] the politico-philosophical issue of how that judgment is made. Were the predominantly white and male establishment of higher education to decide what changes need to be made to accord contemporary diversity its due, the response would reflect the partiality of [its members'] experience and aspirations. Were that decision to emerge from a democratic process in which the currently marginalized and excluded had participated from positions of "equal placement and security," the judgment would understandably be of a different sort. Ultimately, we come face-to-face with the depth or shallowness of what Dewey (in a text cited earlier) called "the democratic faith."

(6) The last, and most frequently heard, objection: Changes of the sort being discussed would inevitably lead to a watering down, if not a complete collapse, of standards.

In reply: There is little doubt that standards would change, just as the standards of the individual disciplines evolve in many interdisciplinary inquiries or as the skills one values in tennis change from singles to doubles. Whether the new standards are as challenging as the old depends less on the intrinsic nature of these different intellectual enterprises than on the integrity and respectfulness of the conversations.

Conclusion

It is easy to read contemporary experience in the light of simpler times, of a more familiar order, and to regard the explosion of diversity as productive of fragmentation, incoherence, and conflict. From the standpoint of democratic pluralism, wherein diversity is a resource, the explosion is challenging and unsettling but highly welcome. I thus prefer the metaphor of inchoateness to the backward-looking metaphor of fragmentation. We are not staring wistfully at the fragmented ruins of a temple once whole but poring over the recently discovered jottings for a novel whose form or plot has yet to emerge.

If higher education were to take as its role the creation of new structures of dialogue and invention and cooperative discovery (i.e., structures appropriate to an inchoate world), there may indeed emerge a new world order. I speak not of an order in which technologically powerful Americans try to bring the diversity of the world to heel but of a new world order that empowers hitherto excluded peoples of our [nation] and other nations to contribute their experience on an equal footing to our collective understanding of ourselves, society, and the world.

19

Conflict in America

Gerald Graff

If we believe what we have been reading lately, American higher education is in a disastrous state. As pictured in a stream of best-sellers, commission reports, polemical articles, and editorials, the academic humanities in particular look like a once-respectable old neighborhood gone bad. The stately old buildings have been defaced with spray paint, hideous accumulations of trash litter the ground, and omnipresent thought police control the turf, speaking in barbarous, unintelligible tongues while enforcing an intolerant code of political correctness on the terrorized inhabitants.

Having lived in this neighborhood for the last thirty years as a teacher of literature, a department chair, a lecturer at numerous universities, and a curriculum consultant at some, I find it hard to square these lurid accounts with my experience. There is something truly astonishing about the degree of exaggeration, patent falsehood, and plain hysteria attained by the more prominent of these accounts. Much of the hysteria comes from simple fear of change, but much of it comes from the mysterious na-

ture of certain precincts of the academic world to both other academics and the public. When a country is little known, fabulous and monstrous tales readily circulate about it, and any abuse can be passed off as typical.

It is true that staggering changes have occurred in the climate of academic life over the course of my professional life. I started graduate school in 1959, so my career spans the abyss between today's feverish struggles over books and the days when the literary canon—the body of literature thought to be worth teaching—seemed so uncontroversial that you rarely heard the word "canon." It is also true that social and cultural change has brought difficult new problems in the areas of admissions, hiring, and campus life. In my view, however, these are the problems of success, a consequence of the vast superiority of today's university in intellectual reach and cultural diversity to the relatively restricted campus culture of a generation ago. That today's university is rocked by unprecedented conflicts is a measure of its vitality, not its decline. As I see it, the challenge is to turn these very conflicts to positive account by transforming a scene of hatred and anger into one of educationally productive debate.

Though I am sympathetic to feminism, multiculturalism, and other new theories and practices that have divided the academy, I do not argue that these movements have the final word about culture—only that the questions

AUTHOR'S NOTE: This is a reprint of a chapter originally published as "Conflict in America," in *Beyond the Culture Wars: How Teaching the Conflicts Can Revitalize American Education*," by Gerald Graff, copyright © 1992. Reprinted by permission of W. W. Norton & Company, Inc.

EDITORS' NOTE: See the Opening Up New Roads: Diversity Issues section in the *Fieldguide*.

they are raising deserve to be taken seriously. Yet one would never guess from the overheated and ill-informed accounts given by today's popular critics that the issues in the battle over education are ones on which reasonable people might legitimately disagree. Arguments that at the very least are worthy of debate—like the argument that political factors such as race, class, gender, and nationality have influenced art and criticism far more than education has traditionally acknowledged—have been reduced by their opponents to their crudest and most strident form and thus dismissed without a hearing. A complex set of issues that cry out for serious debate has been fumed into a clear-cut choice—as one prominent conservative puts it—"between culture and barbarism."

No doubt it pleases such critics to think of themselves as last-ditch defenders of civilization against the invasion of barbarian relativists and terrorists. But if the goal is constructive educational reform, then such apocalyptic posturing is a dead end. One does not have to be a tenured radical to see that what has taken over the educational world today is not barbarism and unreason but simply conflict. The first step in dealing productively with today's conflicts is to recognize their legitimacy.

We need to rethink the premise that the eruption of fundamental conflict in education has to mean educational and cultural paralysis. My argument is that conflict has to mean paralysis only as long as we fail to take positive advantage of it.

Acknowledging the legitimacy of social conflict, however, is not an easy thing even for Americans of goodwill. We may not hesitate to embrace cultural diversity, but when diversity leads to clashes of interests, as it naturally will, we find ourselves at a loss. Such conflict seems vaguely un-American, a legacy of the less abundant societies of the Old World. President Bush echoed an old American tradition when he recently declared that class conflict is "for European democracies. . . . It isn't for the United States of America. We are not going to be divided by class."

In fact, there is little reason to think we Americans are any less divided by class than other nations, but we are certainly better at concealing it from ourselves. A combination of affluence and geography has enabled more fortunate Americans to avoid noticing unpleasant social conflicts by the simple device of moving away from them. In times past, there was the frontier settled mostly by conquerable Indian tribes, to which Americans could flee when urban conflict became too intense. More recently, the flight has been out to suburbs and malls, on freeways which let us drive past our social problems, or into high-rises from which those problems need be viewed only from a distance.

In our mass-produced fantasies, we are virtually obsessed with conflict, but of a stylized, unreal, or commercially trivialized kind. Our popular films and television programs often deal with the sorts of conflicts that can be resolved by a fistfight, a car chase, or a shootout at the OK Corral. Our TV commercials stage endless disputations between partisans of old and new improved brands of soap, toothpaste, or deodorant, including the great debate over whether we should drink a particular beer because it is less filling or because it tastes great. Other commercials present modern life as a conflict-free utopia in which races freely intermingle and the world's ethnic groups join hands on a hillside to hymn their desire to buy the world a Coke. Our national obsession with athletic contests (one I fully share) is at least partly explained by the fact that conflict in sports, unlike in real life, is safe and satisfying, with clear-cut winners and losers.

Lately, however, conflicts over race, gender, and ethnicity have become so frequent and conspicuous that we seem to be getting more accustomed to dealing with them. This is seen in the public fascination with social conflict films like *Do the Right Thing, Thelma and Louise,* and *Dances with Wolves* and with events like the Clarence Thomas-Anita Hill sexual harassment hearings. Yet the same conflicts that we have begun to accept in society still stick in our craw when they appear in education. The race, class, and gender conflicts that national newsmagazines treat as understandable and legitimate in films and public hearings have been depicted by these same magazines as a catastrophe for education.

Clearly, we still long to think of education as a conflict-free ivory tower, and the university *tries* to live up to this vision. While it welcomes diversity and innovation, it neutralizes the conflicts which result from them. This it does by keeping warring parties in noncommunicating courses and departments and by basing the curriculum on a principle of live and let live: I won't try to prevent you from teaching and studying what you want if you don't try to prevent me from teaching and studying what I want.

The effects of this amiable rule of laissez-faire have by no means been all bad, and it would be a serious mistake to try to abolish it entirely. It has enabled the American curriculum to relieve the increasingly conflicting pressures placed on it by painlessly expanding its frontiers, adding new subjects, courses, and programs without asking those in control of the already established ones to change their ways. It is only by such peaceful coexistence that the university could have achieved the improbable feat of becoming modern society's chief patron of cultural innovation without ceasing to stand for staunchly traditional values.

The modern university has from the beginning rested on a deeply contradictory mission. The university is expected to preserve, transmit, and honor our traditions, yet at the same time it is supposed to produce new knowledge, which means questioning received ideas and perpetually revising traditional ways of thinking. The smooth functioning of the modern university has depended on a silent agreement to minimize this conflict between old and new, and times of relative affluence have afforded the room to pursue both missions without fatal collisions. This explains how it is possible for both the left and the right to believe with some reason that the opposing party is in charge.

Today, however, we see the end of the growth economy that for so long enabled the university to cushion its conflicts by indefinitely expanding the departmental and curricular playing field. Meanwhile, the contradictions that have accumulated as the academy has diversified have become so deep, antagonistic, and openly political that it has become impossible to prevent them from becoming visible to outsiders. In no other American institution do we find such a mind-boggling juxtaposition of clashing ideologies: corporate managers side by side with Third World Marxists, free market economists with free-form sculptors, mandarin classical scholars with postmodern performance artists, [and] football coaches with deconstructive feminists. Peaceful coexistence is increasingly strained, and it is harder to hold the conflicts at bay by the silent agreement not to wash dirty linen in public.

The result is today's educational crisis. It is a sign of the university's vitality that the crisis is happening so openly there. The academic curriculum has become a prominent arena of cultural conflict because it is a microcosm, as it should be, of the clash of cultures and values in America as a whole. As the democratization of culture has brought heretofore excluded groups into the educational citadel, with them have come the social conflicts that their exclusion once kept safely distant. A generation ago, decisions about what was worth teaching and what counted as "culture" were still circumscribed by a relatively homogeneous class with a relatively common background. Today new constituencies—women, blacks, gays, and immigrant groups from Asia and Latin America in particular—demand a say in how culture will be defined. And even more offensive to those who are used to having their way without controversy, these upstarts are now often in a position to put their ideas into practice. A less "canonical" faculty and student body implies a less canonical curriculum, dramatizing the fact that culture itself is a debate, not a monologue.

Never comfortable with conflict to begin with, we are naturally prone to interpret these challenges as symptoms of disintegration. Many of the well-publicized horror stories about intolerant political correctness on campus—when they have not been shown to be simply bogus—seem to me a symptom not of left-wing McCarthyism, as has been charged, but of fear in the face of controversy. In some cases, at least, I believe that what teachers have perceived as "harassment" is simply the novel experience of being in a minority and having to argue for one's beliefs instead of taking them for granted. Some overzealous proponents of cultural diversity have indeed behaved obnoxiously in attempting to sensitize their student and faculty colleagues whether they wish to be sensitized or not. But it is not necessarily a symptom of intolerance if a feminist student challenges a teacher's interpretation of Henry James for acceding to a stereotype about women or if a black student asks why a slave diary has not been assigned in a course on the Civil War.

I suspect that the teachers who have reacted to such criticisms by canceling their courses and offering themselves to the media as helpless victims of political correctness would have done better to stay and argue the issues with their students. Good teachers, after all, *want* their students to talk back. They know that student docility is a far more pervasive problem than student intransigence. Good students, for their part, appreciate teachers who take strong positions on controversial questions—though they do not appreciate brainwashing.

If the public furor over political correctness has shed more heat than light, it has at least proved that the gap between American culture and the ivory tower has closed. There is an old joke that academic disputes are especially poisonous because so little is at stake in them. But the stakes are no longer so trivial. Today's academic disputes over which texts should be taught in the humanities, over the competing claims of Western and non-Western culture, and over the pros and cons of affirmative action and codes regulating hate speech mirror broader social conflicts over race, ethnicity, and privilege. Even the quarrels sparked by esoteric literary theories about the pertinence of gender questions to the study of Shakespeare echo debates over sex roles in the larger society provoked by feminists, gay activists, and the entry of women into the professional workforce. At a moment when many in our society are questioning traditional assumptions about romantic love, heterosexuality, the nuclear family, abortion, aging, free speech, and the American flag, we should not be too outraged that decisions about which books to assign no longer go without saying.

But if outrage is not a helpful response to the conflicts occasioned by new interests, ideas, and constituencies, neither is the liberal complacency that has been content to say, "Sure, we can handle that innovation; we'll just add a new course on it." The current educational crisis has exposed the limitations of the live-and-let-live philosophy of curriculum, enabling conservatives to take the lead in the education debate and attract many disillusioned liberals to their side. The conservatives speak powerfully because they recognize the incoherence of a curriculum that is content to go on endlessly multiplying courses and subjects like boutiques at a mall. Unfortunately, the conservatives' only prescription for curing this incoherence is to superimpose a higher order on the curriculum, an order that they like to call the "common culture" but that is really only *their* idea of order, one contender among several competing ones.

The history of modern American education has pitted the liberal pluralist solution (everyone do his or her own thing) against the conservative solution (everyone do the conservatives' thing). What is happening today, I believe, is that both the liberal pluralist and the conservative solutions have outlived their usefulness. Everyone doing his or her own thing has made a mess of the curriculum, but cleaning up the mess by reverting to a narrowly defined traditional curriculum can only make a far worse mess. Since such a traditional curriculum would mean cutting away the vast areas of the world of knowledge and culture that do not fit the conservative vision of reality, it could be institutionalized only by forcing it down the throats of dissenting teachers and students. But then the same holds for the extreme radical vision.

Antagonistic as they are in most respects, the liberal pluralist and the conservative solutions are actually two sides of the same coin; neither is able to imagine any positive role for cultural conflict. Liberal pluralists are content to let cultural and intellectual diversity proliferate without addressing the conflicts and contradictions that result, whereas conservatives would exclude or shut down those conflicts. Neither strategy works in a world in which cultural and philosophical conflicts, increasingly, can no longer be evaded or shut down. A combination of changing demographic patterns in the wider culture, making student bodies and faculties more diverse, and unsettling new ideas in the academic disciplines, challenging traditional disciplinary axioms, has created conflicts that cannot be successfully coped with by the traditional educational philosophies and curricular structures, much less by shaking our fists, shouting about relativism and lost standards, and calling for a return to the eternal verities. A solution, however, is latent in the problem itself, if only we can stop listening to those who tell us that controversy is a symptom of barbarism and that education was better in the past because it was calmer.

Where the university *has* failed—and here is the point on which many on the right, left, and center should be able to agree—is in making a focused curriculum out of its lively state of contention. Too much of the current debate is simply irrelevant to the educational problem as it is experienced by the struggling student. The most neglected fact about the culture war is that its issues are clearer and more meaningful to the contending parties than they are to that student. It is not the conflicts dividing the university that should worry us but the fact that students are not playing a more active role in them.

It won't matter much whose list of books wins the canon debate if students remain disaffected from the life of books and intellectual discussion, as too many have been since long before any canon revisionists arrived on the academic scene. It is easy to forget that for most American students, the problem has usually been how to deal with books in general, regardless of which faction is drawing up the reading list. Here educators are wasting a major opportunity, for the conflicts that are now adding to the confusions of students have the potential to help them make better sense of their education and their lives. There is really no other choice. These conflicts are not going to go away, and students need to learn to deal with them in the culturally diverse world in which they already live and will live after graduation.

The best solution to today's conflicts over culture is to teach the conflicts themselves, making them part of our object of study and using them as a new kind of organizing principle to give the curriculum the clarity and focus that almost all sides now agree it lacks. In a sense, this solution constitutes a compromise, for it is one that conflicting parties can agree on. But it is really a way of avoiding the evasive compromise represented by the pluralist cafeteria counter curriculum, which leaves it up to students to connect what their teachers do not.

In an important sense, academic institutions are *already* teaching the conflicts every time a student goes from one course or department to another, but they are doing it badly. Students typically experience a great clash of values, philosophies, and pedagogical methods among their various professors, but they are denied a view of the interactions and interrelations that give each subject meaning. They are exposed to the *results* of their professors' conflicts but not to the process of discussion and debate they need to see in order to become something more than passive spectators to their education. Students are expected to join an intellectual community that they see only in disconnected glimpses. This is what has passed for "traditional" education, but a curriculum that screens students from the controversies between texts and ideas serves the traditional goals of education as poorly as it serves those of reformers.

Nobody wants to turn the curriculum into a shouting match, of course. But the curriculum is already a shouting match, and one that will only become more angry and polarized if ways are not found to exploit rather than avoid its philosophical differences. When teachers in rival camps do not engage one another in their classrooms, all sides get comfortable preaching to the already converted. We get clashing forms of political correctness that become ever more entrenched the less they are forced to speak to one another. In a vicious circle, opposing viewpoints are so rarely debated that on the rare occasions when they are, the discussion is naturally hostile and confused, and this result then seems to prove that reasoned debate is not possible. Here, as I see it, is the essence of the problems of "Balkanization," separatism, and particularism that have come so to worry us: not the lack of agreement but of the respectful disagreement that supposedly is the strength of democracies and educational institutions.

That is why, however admirable the intention, adding courses in non-Western culture to existing general education requirements (as is now being done or contemplated at many schools and colleges) will only once more postpone the debate that has always been avoided in the past. It is not that non-Western courses are inherently separatist, as so many charge, but that *the established curriculum is separatist,* with each subject and course being an island with little regular connection to other subjects and courses. It is important to bring heretofore excluded cultures into the curriculum, but unless they are put in dialogue with traditional courses, students will continue to struggle with a disconnected curriculum, and suspicion and resentment will continue to increase. For the same reasons, the new field of "cultural studies" should be an open debate about culture and not the euphemism for various kinds of leftist studies that it has become. At the least, cultural studies and women's studies courses should be in dialogue with traditional ones.

In addition to being educationally defective, a disconnected curriculum in which one hand never knows what the other is doing is also very expensive. The cafeteria counter curriculum evolved, after all, during a period of affluence when universities had the luxury to hire specialists in almost everything and encourage them to go their separate ways. Such an ill-coordinated mode of organization would put a commercial firm out of business in a few months, and it may now put many universities out of business if they do not find ways to make teaching more collaborative. For reasons of both economy and pedagogy, we need to rethink what I call the course fetish and the myth of the great teacher, which rest on the notion that by some law of nature, teaching must be a solo performance.

I grant that making harsh disagreements productive for education is not easy. How will departments and colleges agree on what to disagree about? Who will determine the agenda of debate and decide which voices are included and excluded, and how will the inequalities between students and teachers, the tenured and the untenured, the eminent and the obscure, be overcome? Some will see the introduction of non-Western texts into traditional introductory courses not as a debatable issue but as a capitulation to political pressure. Others will rightly be offended by proposals to debate questions like "Did the Holocaust really happen?" or "Is homosexuality a disease?" where no reputable scholar considers the question open or where it is framed in a way that puts one group on the defensive.

Numerous teachers, departments, and colleges have managed to overcome these obstacles. They have recognized that students need to see the connections [among] the different interpretations, ideas, and values in the curriculum if they are to enter actively into academic discussions. The point was made best by an instructor who had joined with several colleagues to teach an introductory literature course: "Our students were able to argue with us because they saw us arguing with each other."

These teachers and institutions pick up at the very point at which today's disputes have become deadlocked. They assume that there is something unreal about the either/or choice we have been offered between teaching Western or non-Western culture, that in a culturally diverse society, a wide range of cultures and values should be and will be taught. But they also see that teaching different cultures and values implies teaching them in relation to one another so that the differences and points of intersection become comprehensible. I find it much easier to clarify the traditional idea that great literature is universal when I teach feminist critiques of that idea. Opposing texts and theories need one another to become intelligible to students. As one of my students put it after our class had read Joseph Conrad's *Heart of Darkness* alongside the very different treatment of Africa by the Nigerian novelist Chinua Achebe, *Things Fall Apart,* she thought she better understood the Europeanness of Conrad because she now had something to compare it with.

Teaching the conflicts has nothing to do with relativism or denying the existence of truth. The best way to make relativists of students is to expose them to an endless series of different positions which are not debated before their eyes. Acknowledging that culture is a debate rather than a monologue does not prevent us from energetically fighting for the truth of our own convictions. On the contrary, when truth is disputed, we can seek it only by entering the debate—as Socrates knew when he taught the conflicts two millennia ago.

20

Class Wars and Culture Wars in the University Today: Why We Can't Defend Ourselves

Robert N. Bellah

It has become obvious for quite some time that the American university is under siege. Ours is not the only institution to be so beset, but after decades of public favor, we are not used to taking a defensive posture. Further, it is not at all obvious that the academic profession is in any position to defend itself because of the growing divisions among us, divisions which are intensifying, both materially and intellectually, all the time. Contention in the university is normal, even desirable, but we have come close to losing the common ground that can be the only basis for self-defense.

Let me turn to some objective facts which have begun to have serious consequences for us in the university. The disintegration of the postwar institutional order, spurred on by Thatcherism, Reaganism, and then by the end of the cold war, has been going on for quite some time, but those who celebrate that disintegration as well as those who are alarmed by it appear only recently to have begun to describe it accurately. One way of putting it is to say that all the primary relationships in our society, those between employers and employees, between lawyers and clients, between doctors and patients, between universities and students, are being stripped of any moral understanding other than that of market exchange. Business has no obligation to its employees, to the communities in which it operates, or to the larger society. The same forces that are uprooting decades-long practices in industry are to be found at work in medicine, education, and even the church and the family. To put it in Pierre Bourdieu's terms, we could say that the economic field is encroaching even more than ever on the autonomy of the other fields.

For a thoroughly chilling description of the new America, where market forces are to determine every aspect of our lives, read Newt Gingrich's *To Renew America,* published in the summer of 1995, when he still had thoughts of running for president. Instead of medicine, we have the health care industry; instead of the university, we have the education industry. These are not metaphors but the direct imposition of the logic of the economic field on the

AUTHOR'S NOTE: This is a reprint of an article originally published as Bellah, Robert N., "Class Wars and Culture Wars in the University Today: Why We Can't Defend Ourselves," *Academe,* July-August, 1997, pp. 22-26. Used with permission.

EDITORS' NOTE: See the Opening Up New Roads: Diversity Issues section in the *Fieldguide.*

other fields. Gingrich argues that doctors, for example, should be seen not as authorities but as employees, and we should see ourselves not as patients but as customers, shopping for the best medical buy to be had. Similarly, professors have no right to tenure since they too are merely employees, put there to supply customers with educational services, and again, at the lowest possible cost.

In a recent article entitled "Anger in the Academic Workplace," Judith Sturnick well describes the feelings that arise when those called to university teaching find things changing rapidly beneath their feet:

The academic workplace as we knew it, and to which we committed our professional lives, is slipping away from us. The process of change has left us in the grip of grief, and anger is a particularly strong phase of that mourning. Restructuring, which was merely a threat four years ago, is now a reality. . . . Although our much-vaunted autonomy may have been as much fiction as fact, we no longer believe we have control over our own destiny. Public support for higher education is a tattered garment. Downsizing has left us with fewer people and more work to be done. The quality of our lives has been affected at every level. . . . The destruction of the mythos of community has cut a wide swath across our collective psyches. (*The Academic Workplace,* Fall-Winter 1996, p. 5)

The university has never been a particularly egalitarian institution, but the inequalities we are experiencing today mirror what is going on in the larger society. Robert Reich has described the emerging three-class typology of our current socioeconomic life as an overclass living in the safety of elite suburbs, an underclass quarantined in surroundings that are unspeakably bleak and often violent, and a new anxious class trapped in the frenzy of effort it takes to preserve their standing.

The most striking feature of this new class system in the university is the appearance of a genuine underclass. We have sensed for quite some time that such a thing existed, but the evidence now is overwhelming. In the November-December 1995 issue of *Academe,* Cary Nelson describes the plight of very large numbers of graduate students today. He begins by asking a riddle: "In three letters, what is the name of a lengthy and expensive cultural enhancement program for term employees in the academy—employees, in other words, who have been hired for a fixed term and no longer? . . . The answer is the Ph.D." The crushing fact is that many, perhaps most, of these Ph.D.'s who staff our courses in any large university (Nelson says graduate students teach over two-thirds of the courses, about 500 classes a year, in his English department at the University of Illinois) will never get a tenure-track job. Heavily exploited before receiving the degree, afterward they may spend some years as itinerant part-timers and eventually—after eight, ten, or fifteen years—they will have to find a different line of employment, at what cost to their own self-esteem and the viability of their families we can only imagine. This growing body of temporary or term employees is our academic underclass.

The overclass, of course, are the academic stars, the winners in the academic division of our winner-take-all society. These are professors whose salaries are not 225 times that of the average worker, as are the salaries of CEOs, but are nonetheless several times those of beginning assistant professors and an even larger multiple of the stipends of graduate student teaching assistants. When they are holders of chairs, they may have released time from teaching and lavish funds that pay, among other things, for travel and for research assistants, something of which I have some firsthand knowledge. I need not mention the even more extravagant salaries and perquisites that go to administrators in some of our public and private universities.

The academic anxious class are those tenured or tenure-track professors who, as Judith Sturnick puts it, are already dreaming of retirement at the age of forty, whose idealistic commitment to the profession no longer makes sense, [and] who are overburdened with increased teaching loads and unprepared students. Like other members of the anxious class, their salaries have barely kept up with inflation, and even tenure isn't very comforting if their unit, or even their institution, seems threatened with economic inviability. At a place like Berkeley, it is mainly the assistant professors who make up the anxious class, but at more vulnerable institutions, it may include most of the faculty.

This growing tripartite class division within the university creates major strains on whatever sense of common interest remains, making solidarity in defense of academic autonomy increasingly difficult. The bitterness of the Yale teaching assistants strike is an indication of how destructive academic class struggle can be. I must say frankly that I support the teaching assistants—unionization is the only way for them to protect themselves from extreme exploitation—but unionization does not sit well with my sense of what the university ought to be. As a corollary, I would like to find some way to hold down high-end salaries of both administrators and academic stars, but in view of antitrust legislation and the mood of the times, this might, ironically, be harder to do than [to] recognize unions for teaching assistants.

If there are sharp material divisions within the university, there are also sharp intellectual ones. I will not comment on the fact that many of our colleagues do not think of themselves as intellectuals at all but only as specialists within disciplines or sub-disciplines, and their sense of collective solidarity does not extend beyond those limits. I will turn instead to another kind of disjunction now widespread in the university, not the contrast between fields of specialization but the contrast between competing academic ideologies. Let me draw on Gerald Graff's book, *Beyond the Culture Wars* (New York: Norton, 1992):

An undergraduate tells of an art history course in which the instructor observed one day, "As we now know, the idea that knowledge can be objective is a positivist myth that has been exploded by postmodern thought." It so happens the student is concurrently enrolled in a political science course in which the instructor speaks confidently about the objectivity of his discipline as if it had not been exploded at all. "What do you do?" the student is asked. "What else can I do?" he says. "I trash objectivity in art history, and I presuppose it in political science."

To some of us these days, the moral of [such] stories would be that students have become cynical relativists who care less about convictions than about grades and careers. In fact, if anything is surprising, it is that more students do not behave in this cynical fashion, for the established curriculum encourages it. The disjunction of the curriculum is a far more powerful source of relativism than any doctrine preached by the faculty.

Graff proposes to overcome these breaks in intellectual discourse by having, say, positivists and postmodernists teach together so that the disjunctions can be faced and the students may better understand them, which is a step in the right direction but may not be enough. The most helpful book I know for thinking about fundamental intellectual conflicts in the contemporary university is Alasdair MacIntyre's *Three Rival Versions of Moral Enquiry*. MacIntyre reminds us that the reigning paradigm in the present university is of relatively recent origin, arising together with the research university in the late nineteenth century. This is the paradigm of what MacIntyre calls encyclopedia, though what he means is the paradigm of science as the only valid form of knowing. He reminds us that this paradigm came to power through ousting another paradigm, what he calls tradition, one rooted in Christian theology and the Greek and Latin classics. This older paradigm has never been completely banished, although theology has been pretty successfully confined to divinity schools that are clearly marginal to the conception of the research university.

The third competing paradigm is relatively recent as a major force in the university, although it goes back at least as far as Nietzsche. This is what MacIntyre calls genealogy but is pretty much what we mean today by postmodernism. As the reference to Nietzsche indicates, the third paradigm represents a profound doubt about the whole Enlightenment scientific enterprise, a question about whether its claim to truth is only a form of will to power. The recent rise of postmodernism in the university is undoubtedly related to doubts about the whole modern project brought on by a series of crises in the twentieth century to which there is no end in sight.

While the remaining defenders of premodern tradition also have their doubts about science as the only basis of truth, they cannot join hands with the postmodernists, whose assumptions they reject. The postmodernists return the compliment by asserting that tradition, too, has no objective authority but is, like modernity, based only on a will to power. These are oversimplifications, yet I think they get at deep, apparently intractable differences in the university that no amount of conversation of the sort Graff advocates is likely to resolve. MacIntyre sums up our situation as follows:

Hence debate between fundamentally opposed standpoints does occur, but it is inevitably inconclusive. Each warring position characteristically appears irrefutable to its own adherents; indeed, in its own terms and by its own standards of argument, it is in practice irrefutable. But each warring position equally seems to its opponent to be insufficiently warranted by rational argument. It is ironic that the wholly secular humanistic disciplines of the late twentieth century should thus reproduce that very same condition which led their nineteenth-century secularizing predecessors to dismiss the claim of theology to be worthy of the status of an academic discipline.

The outcome can be summarized as follows. We have together produced a type of university in which teaching and enquiry in the humanities (and often enough also in the social sciences) are marked by four characteristics. There is first a remarkably high level of skill in handling narrow questions of limited detail. . . . Secondly, in a way which sometimes provides a direction for and a background to these exercises of professionalized skill, there is the promulgation of a number of large and mutually incompatible doctrines, often conveyed by indirection and implication, the doctrines which define the major contending standpoints in each discipline. Thirdly, insofar as the warfare between these doctrines becomes part of public debate and discussion, the shared standards of argument are such that all debate is inconclusive. And yet, fourthly and finally, we still behave for the most part as if the university did still constitute a single, tolerably unified intellectual community, a form of behavior which testifies to the enduring effects of the encyclopedists' conception of the unity of enquiry. (pp. 7-8)

MacIntyre feels [that] the kind of debate Graff calls for will only be discouraging, interminable, and insoluble, given fundamentally different starting points, and that the solution might better be to divide our universities into three categories: traditional, scientific, and postmodern. At least then students would get some coherent sense of the world and not be tempted by cynicism and nihilism.

The direction in which I would go is less radical than that of MacIntyre but more demanding than that of Graff. One reason I hesitate to go all the way with MacIntyre is that the three categories he has so acutely analyzed are within many of us as well as between us. Although part of me is deeply rooted in the world of tradition, not only religiously but [also] philosophically (in Germany, I understand, I am sometimes referred to as a left-wing Aristotelian, an odd designation for [Germans] since they presume Aristotelians will be right-wing), I would be lacking in self-knowledge if I did not recognize how profoundly I have been formed by the Enlightenment and even by its positivist offspring, nor would I be honest if I denied that I have learned from the postmortem critiques of modernity. Rather than opt for a situation which would force me to choose between parts of myself, I would attempt to find some common ground in defense of which a broadly based collectivity of academic intellectuals might stand. Perhaps MacIntyre's emphasis on moral inquiry can provide an avenue for the exploration of this possibility.

An effort in this direction by Robert Heilbroner and William Milberg in their recent book, *The Crisis of Vision in Modern Economic Thought,* might be exemplary for more disciplines than economics. They distinguish between analysis and vision: "By analysis," they write, "we mean the process of deducing consequences from initial conditions, of attending scrupulously to chains of reasoning, and of guarding against the always present temptation to substitute demagoguery for intellectual exchange" (p. 4). By vision, they point to what for most economists remains "precognitive," that is, notions of the "rightness or wrongness, the inevitability or malleability, of the arrangements of power and prestige that we discover in all human societies." These elements, which they call "political and moral," actually form the basic concepts, such as "class, property, and even power itself" that provide the place where analysis begins (p. 14).

For Heilbroner and Milberg, "vision" is that kind of moral and political seeing which provides the "primitive concepts" of the social sciences, that is, the concepts that are themselves not scientifically derivable (though they certainly have historical, moral, and political derivations) but which provide the foundations of analysis. It is precisely this aspect of vision that drops below the consciousness of positivist science, which nonetheless cannot do without primitive concepts any more than the rest of us. Contemporary economists who ignore the question of vision and attempt to confine themselves to analysis end up deriving their primitive concepts from common sense or from an abstract deductive schema called "rational actor theory," which in the Anglo-Saxon world is only another version of common sense. Heilbroner and Milberg argue that vision must be a conscious part of the social scientific enterprise, as was the case, for example, with John Maynard Keynes, even, though it is more like art than science; a new vision is a new way of seeing, just as Manet, in Bourdieu's example, allowed us to see the world in a new way. Nonetheless, the moral and political bases of such visions are available to, and require, criticism and reformulation.

The research university has never in fact pursued pure science cut off from the surrounding world. From the beginning, it has been mobilized by business and government for purposes quite beyond the university itself. War, which looms so large in the twentieth century, has always mobilized the university, never more than in World War II, but also in its long aftermath of the cold war. I might remind you that the University of California made the atomic bombs for the United States military for forty-five years and still is in charge of monitoring the weapons to see that they maintain their effectiveness and of designing potential new ones, a function many of us in the faculty have long opposed but which we have never managed to eliminate. With the end of the cold war, mobilization for economic competitiveness has become very much the order of the day, with a wide variety of effects in both public and private universities.

What I would suggest is that, rather than imagine that the university can escape such mobilization and return to an ivory tower that never existed, we might ask whether the purposes to which the university is put are the right ones, the ones we as intellectuals would autonomously choose. Are we a good university contributing to a good society when we concentrate on war or economic competitiveness but think much less about the environment or poverty or the new world disorder? More fundamentally, can we construct a vision of the social world which is not dominated by the contemporary economic or political fields but has at least a degree of moral autonomy? In a common effort to think about the political and moral bases of our inquiry, we could call on the insights of traditional, scientific, and postmodern intellectuals, not in order to attain an unreachable, and even an undesirable, consensus but to regain the initiative in defining our own enterprise, which is, after all, neither to become functionaries for the prevailing economic and political powers nor to secede into the guarded, gated communities that elite research universities are tempted to become. A good place to begin would be to consider how we can resist the destructive consequences of growing class polarization in the larger society and in our own institution.

21

An Emerging Reformulation of "Competence" in an Increasingly Multicultural World

Troy Duster

A Fierce and Angry Debate and a Poverty of Vision

The current national debate about multiculturalism, group identity, and expansion of the curriculum tends to be fierce and binary. It is saturated with a surprising level of mean-spiritedness and apocalyptic forebodings that are, on the surface, hard to explain. For example, in the *Wall Street Journal* in July 1991, Irving Kristol wrote an essay entitled "The Tragedy of Multiculturalism" in which he stated that "multiculturalism is a desperate strategy for coping with the educational deficiencies, and associated social pathologies, of young blacks." A host of commentators have summarily dismissed courses designed to include more of the contributions of ethnic, cultural, and racial groups as nothing more than "feel good

AUTHOR'S NOTE: This is a reprint of an article originally published as Duster, Troy, "An Emerging Reformulation of 'Competence' in an Increasingly Multicultural World," in *Beyond a Dream Deferred*, edited by Becky W. Thompson and Sengeeta Tyagi (University of Minnesota Press), 1993, pp. 231-255. Used with permission.

EDITORS' NOTE: See the Opening Up New Roads: Diversity Issues section in the *Fieldguide*.

courses" or a "victim's revolt" (Aufderheide 1992; D'Souza 1991).

A full cadre of critics with the peculiar self-appointed name of the National Association of Scholars made their positions public long before any could have had an opportunity to review the serious intellectual content of dozens of new and renovated courses being developed at Berkeley to satisfy a new single-course requirement.[1] Responding primarily to the most recent push to change the New York State curriculum for a fuller multicultural content, Arthur Schlesinger, Jr., has published a short book that he entitled, with uncharacteristic hyperbole, *The Disuniting of America: Reflections on a Multicultural Society* (1992).

So far, we are given only two choices in this debate: either assimilation and the shedding of ethnic, religious, and cultural differences or ethnic, racial, tribal war. The latter image—Bosnia and Lebanon—is conjured as the only alternative to assimilation. Weiner (1992) appropriately identifies this binary set of alternatives as a setup, a reduction to the absurd.[2] If we are limited to these two choices, and if only a fool or a villain would choose war, the implicit injunction is that all reasonable people would choose assimilation.

To his credit, Schlesinger (1992) does mention, however briefly, an alternative to this binary and otherwise debased debate. In 1915, Horace Kallen wrote an essay for *Nation* entitled "Democracy versus the Melting Pot" in which he provided a sharp contrast to a "shedding of differences" and assimilationist vision of America. Kallen argued that we should not aspire to a melting away of differences [and] that the persistence of ethnic groups and their distinctive traditions was a potential source of enrichment.

Kallen (1915) was responsible for the metaphor of the symphony: different instruments and different parts that blend into a harmonic whole. This conception that Kallen came to call "cultural pluralism" represents neither assimilation nor enclaved warfare. There is a new outlook developing in America. It is not the assimilationist version of shedding differences, nor is it Kallen's holding onto differences in a symphonic blend of harmony. It is sometimes cacophonous—and conflictual—and it is certainly quite different from mere shedding and acquisition. It is both a holding onto and something new. While the whole nation struggles with the new immigration, nowhere is the issue more self-consciously addressed than in education. It is very much a part of our current college campus scene, very much at the root of the debate over multiculturalism, and often very much obscured by the passionate adversaries in this debate, who have reduced the matter to good guys and bad guys battling an evil citadel or defending a sacred one.

Sociohistorical Context of Current Student Self-Segmentation

In the past decade, the increasing social and ethnic heterogeneity of the nation's college campuses has captured the attention of media pundits, higher education administrators, and many faculty members. Unfortunately, the troublesome aspects of this development have dominated most of the public debate. One major issue that has absorbed the media is that many students' social lives are segmented in ways that reaffirm their ethnic, racial, and cultural identities. This segmentation, now routinely referred to as "Balkanization," causes surprise, chagrin, and even some derision. It is characterized as an unseemly reversion to "tribalism" that gets in the way of the search for common ground.

There is something both old and new here. Although typically treated as a new and alarming development, segmentation is quite an old phenomenon and has been replayed throughout the history of higher education in America. Social historians who study U.S. colleges and universities know that the Hillel and Newman foundations played important roles for Jewish and Catholic students, respectively, for much of this century. With the assistance of such organizations, parties, dances, study groups, and sometimes residences were routinely "self-segregated," often in response to active discrimination against Jews and Catholics elsewhere on campus.

Today's critics are suffering from a selective cultural amnesia when they portray African-American theme houses and Chinese student associations as newly created enclaves that destroy the search for common ground. Even into the 1980s, the most prestigious fraternities at Yale, Michigan, Harvard, and Berkeley had never admitted a Jew, much less an African-American or an Asian. The all-Jewish fraternity was common as late as the 1960s, and when a Chinese-American, Sherman Wu, pledged a fraternity at Northwestern in 1956, it was such a sensation that it made national news and generated a folk song. Over the years, some mild hand-wringing occurred about discrimination, but no national campaign was launched against the "self-segregation" of the all-white, all-Anglo fraternities.

Yet, despite this long tradition, I believe something new is occurring on campuses that may help explain the hysterical response that we have been hearing. The new development is a demographic shift that the long-dominant white majority sees as a threat to its cultural hegemony. At the Berkeley campus of the University of California, the undergraduate student body has been rapidly and dramatically transformed. In 1960, more than 90 percent of the students were white. In 1980, the figure was about 66 percent. Today, it is about 45 percent. The first-year class in the fall of 1992 signaled an even more striking change for those who still think of Berkeley in 1960s terms. For the first time in history, whites did not make up the largest proportion of the incoming class; instead, it was Asian-Americans, who accounted for about 35 percent. Only 30 percent of the class were Americans of European ancestry. Nearly 20 percent of the class were Chicanos/Latinos, and nearly 8 percent [were] African-Americans. If this pattern holds, well over 60 percent of the Berkeley students will be "of color" by the end of the 1990s.

Although it will not be quite as dramatic in some other regions of the country, this coloring of the campus landscape reflects a vital and constantly unfolding development in American social life. Although they are symbolized by the dramatic Berkeley figures, the ramifications go far beyond the percentages of different ethnic and racial groups on college campuses. The ramifications of demographic change certainly tug at the curriculum and challenge the borders of faculty turf and expertise. But the fundamental issues tapped by this change go to the heart of American identity and culture. Bubbling just beneath the surface of all the national attention devoted to "political correctness" and "quotas"

is a complicated question that, stated most simply, is this: What does it mean to be an American? A related question is [this:] How does one become an American? It is a complex issue.

The controversy over diversity at Berkeley, much like the battle over the social studies curriculum in New York State, is a struggle over who gets to define the idea of America. Are we essentially a nation with a common—or at least a dominant—culture to which immigrants and "minorities" must adapt? Or is this a land in which ethnicity and difference are an accepted part of the whole, a land in which we affirm the richness of our differences and simultaneously try to forge agreement about basic values to guide public and social policy?

Critics of the current visible wave of segmentation argue that "Balkanization" threatens the ties that bind civil society. But civil society in a nation of immigrants is forever in flux, and the basic issue always has been which group has the power to define what the values and structures of their common society will be. We should learn something from our history. Being an American is different from being French or Japanese or almost any other nationality because, except for Native Americans, there actually is no such thing as an American without a hyphen. We are a nation of immigrants. Generations of immigrants have struggled to balance both sides of the hyphen, to carry on some aspects of the culture of the old country while adopting the norms and customs of the new. Today, many of their descendants continue to find comfort in an identification with the old country—however tenuous it may be—that provides a sense of belonging to a recognizable collectivity. A sense of belonging, of being one with others like oneself, helps to overcome the isolation of modern life while paradoxically also allowing a sense of uniqueness.

This is the same phenomenon we see being reenacted on campuses all over the country today, the difference being that the actors are no longer all white. At a place like Berkeley, there is no longer a single racial or ethnic group with an overwhelming numerical and political majority. Pluralism is the reality; no one group is a dominant force. This is completely new. We are grappling with a phenomenon that is both puzzling and alarming, fraught with tensions and hostilities yet simultaneously brimming with potential and crackling with new energy. Consequently, we swing between hope and concern, between optimism and pessimism, about the prospects for a common social life among peoples from different racial and cultural groups. Are members of particular groups isolated or interacting, segregating or integrating, fighting or harmonizing? Who is getting ahead or falling behind?

It may well be that we have too narrowly conceived the options as either/or. It may be that as a nation we have cast the problem incompletely and thus incorrectly.

External Sameness, Internal Differences

By talking directly to students for nearly two years, we were able to make a nuanced reading of how students interpret what is going on on campus, as opposed to the partial images reported in the media. We tried to come up with a systematic way to characterize the problems of group perception and came up with an analogy to how participants experience a social movement. It is axiomatic that no social movement is as incoherent as it appears from within [or] as coherent as it appears from without. If you are on the left (at least in recent decades), you see such internal variation as Trotskyism, Stalinism, different versions of progressive labor, democratic socialism, and so on. But if you are on the right, you tend to see only "the left";

it all looks pink over there. And of course, the opposite is also true; if you are on the right, you can identify single-issue anti-abortionists, fiscal conservatives, and all kinds of other right-wingers, but from the left, all you see is this thing called "the right." It is the same thing when you are studying ethnicity. Asian-Americans, for example, are likely to be aware of strong and important internal differences among them: generational differences (whether a Japanese is Nisei or Sansei), whether a person is foreign born or native, and, of course, which Asian nationality. But if you are white, all you are likely to see are "Asians." Likewise, blacks distinguish between streetwise kids from East Oakland and the offspring of a black suburban professional, but to many Asians, whites, and Latinos, they are all just "blacks."

Converging Desire for Diversity, Diverging Conceptions

A remarkable 70 percent of all undergraduate students at Berkeley agree with this statement: "I'd like to meet more students from ethnic and cultural backgrounds that are different from my own."[3] Negotiating the terrain of interethnic relations in a situation where none is the majority is a new experience for most of the people on campus. While Berkeley's undergraduate students generally say they want interracial experiences and contacts—on or off the campus—members of different ethnic and racial groups tend to chart this terrain in different ways. In general, the desire for diversity is not being sufficiently acknowledged, much less constructively addressed, in any of the current debates about affirmative action, quotas, and self-segregation. This shared interest in diversity should be an important starting point.

Despite the variation and diversity within and across groups, there are clear distinctions in how different groups of students construct, experience, and understand their time at Berkeley and in their expressions of interest in greater interethnic, intercultural contact. More than 72 percent of African-American respondents to the Freshman Survey were "interested" or "extremely interested" in programs to promote racial understanding. In sharp contrast, only about 43 percent of white respondents expressed such an interest, and nearly 30 percent said that they were not very interested or probably would be too busy for such activities.[4] In fact, survey data show whites to be the least interested of all groups in programs meant to promote racial understanding.

Yet when we compared the Freshman Survey findings to data from our group interviews, an interesting difference in responses by ethnic and racial groups surfaced. In the group interviews, white students, with much greater frequency than African-Americans, routinely and consistently expressed interest in having more contact and friendships with African-American students, whom they experienced as being cliquish and somewhat closed to interracial contact. The white students' willingness to be friendly, indeed "to be friends" at the personal level, is prima facie evidence of goodwill and lack of racism. In contrast, African-American students most often among the ethnic groups indicated a preference for same-group friendships and for same-group social activities and organizations. They were most likely to report these experiences as more comfortable and resonant with shared values and experiences. To generalize from the combined findings of the survey of undergraduates, the Diversity Project, and the 1990 Freshman Survey, while whites tended to express a willingness and desire to be friends with African-Americans, they were less likely to want interracial contact in the context of special programs, courses, or activities that structure interethnic contacts. At the other end,

African-Americans were far more likely to want special programs and activities and [were] less interested in developing cross-racial friendships and social activities. These three data sets suggest that while both African-American and white students want more interracial experiences and contacts, they want them on different terms. African-Americans want more classes, programs, and other institutional commitments and responses. Whites want more individual personal contacts developed on their own.

These data suggest again the polymorphous character of interethnic relations on campus. The task is to provide all students with a range of safe environments and options where they can explore and develop terms that they find comfortable. In the absence of such opportunities, the tendencies remain for each group to see the others from a distance in terms of images, stereotypes, stories, and myths that are not informed by direct contact and experience.

Diversity: Sometimes Zero-Sum, Sometimes Mutual Enhancement

The overwhelming sense of our group discussions with students was that the students were ambivalent and contradictory when it comes to increasing ethnic and racial diversity. This ambivalence was not only within groups but also often [within] the same person. White students were the most likely to give voice to the zero-sum aspect of the new diversity. When whites thought in terms of their group interest (racial or ethnic or color interests) in being admitted to college, for example, they were most likely to feel squeezed out of what they considered their slice of the pie—squeezed, on the one hand, by "undeserving" affirmative action admits and, on the other hand, by "overly competitive" Asian-Americans. At the same time, some white students could also see that ethnic and racial diversity in their midst enhanced their own education and ability to live in an increasingly diverse society.

Asian-American students were the most conflicted of all the groups of students about a policy to diversify the student body.[5] Chicano/Latino Americans, African-Americans, and Native Americans voiced the strongest support for an explicit polity of student diversification via affirmative action, yet their knowledge of how and why such a policy operates was no greater than that of whites and Asians. Thus, while it can be said that students could be divided into two camps, for and against a policy of diversification, it would ultimately be inaccurate because it fails to capture the deep and gnawing reservations among the supporters and some strong sympathy even among the detractors. Therefore, implications must be drawn with sensitivity to the complexity of the situation.

Students from every group were divided about affirmative action admissions policies, and even some students who expressed strongly positive or negative views were, upon closer examination, at variance. If there is a single pattern that emerged from the study, it is that the students are deeply conflicted, disturbed, divided, and confused about affirmative action as a policy, yet they support the idea of diversity. How this value conflict unfolds in the day-to-day relations between and among students provides some of the richest material about diversity on campus.

A theme heard frequently among white and Asian-American students is that affirmative action undercuts the university's traditional color-blind, equal opportunity approach to recruitment by rewarding students of color for having too much "fun" and "goofing off" in high school. This subverts the university's meritocratic principles, it is claimed, and the policy is characterized as unfairly admitting "unqualified, "undeserving" students who thereby "steal" the spots to which qualified students are "entitled." Using the moral language of Protestantism, these students make distinctions between "deserving" and "undeserving" students based on the amount of effort exerted in high school.

Given this operating assumption among many of the white and Asian students that we interviewed, it is not surprising that black, Chicano/Latino, and Native American students routinely expressed the feeling of "not belonging" at Berkeley. One African-American undergraduate said, "I feel like I have 'affirmative action' stamped on my forehead." Another noted, "We're guilty until proven innocent." And yet another said, "There's no way to convince whites we belong here. We do backflips and they still wouldn't accept us." When these students do well in class, they report, their classmates and teachers frequently express surprise or portray them as being somehow different from other students of color, an exception to the rule. "What is your SAT score?" is a question many freshmen resent when they feel that behind the question is the assumption that they have [low scores].

It is precisely this reification of the academic index that makes some of the black and Chicano/Latino students chafe at what they take to be the assumption on the part of whites that while the white and Asian-Americans "belong" on campus, blacks and Chicano/Latinos are there only because of affirmative action. It is in this sense that the general controversy over affirmative action colors much of the substance of the ethnic and racial relations within and between groups and penetrates social and academic life in diffuse and indirect ways. Reference to the legitimacy of the academic index wavered under certain conditions. White students, for example, shifted their ground and questioned the index when the idea of "Asian over-representation" surfaced.[6] At that point, "well-roundedness" emerged as a competing criterion to the academic index.

What white students overlook is that far more whites have entered the gates of the ten most elite American institutions of higher education through "alumni preference" than the combined number of all the blacks and Chicanos who have entered through affirmative action. Data for the entering freshman class at Harvard in 1988 show that alumni preference accounted for more admissions than all the African-American, Mexican-American, Native American, and Puerto Rican registrants combined.[7] At Berkeley in 1989, 24 percent of the white students were admitted based upon criteria other than or in addition to the academic index.[8]

Many students, but especially those from European and Asian backgrounds, expressed their dismay, frustration, and reservations about a race-based affirmative action policy that did not take class or socioeconomic status into account. We heard the leitmotiv of resentment, the refrain of "lack of fairness," when a middle-class black or Chicano/Latino student was admitted, while either a white or an Asian student with a better academic index score or a poor white or Asian was not. There is a tension between the feeling that middle-class Chicano/Latinos and blacks are given unfair preference at Berkeley and the reality that, on the whole, white and Asian students come from families with significantly greater economic resources than do African-American and Latino students.[9] Since there are more poor white people in the United States than there are middle-class people of color, a class-based affirmative action policy would necessarily bring in more whites. Unless such a policy explicitly "bumped" wealthier whites, it would reduce the number and proportion of people of color. Thus the historical advantage of whites, codified in law and practice for more than a century, is revisited by such a policy.

What it means to be an educated American in this context is just emerging, and only recently has it been possible to see some of the likely contours of this identity. The meaning of being a citizen in a diverse society cannot be based on mindless homogenization, assimilation, or "melted down" integration. It will revolve instead around new meanings of diversity, perhaps close to Kallen's version of pluralism. In a pluralist society, ethnic and racial groups can maintain distinctive cultures, organizations, and identities while they participate in the larger community. Individual members of ethnic and racial groups may choose to live in delimited communities, marry within their own group, and sometimes even work at similar occupations. While this sustains and promotes their ethnic identity and culture, they also relate to others. This interaction between [and among] groups is often less intimate and occurs in the realm of politics, economics, and education.

Competence in the context of pluralism will mean being able to participate effectively in a multicultural world. It will mean being "multicultural" as well as multilingual. It will mean knowing how to operate as a competent actor in more than one cultural world, knowing what is appropriate and what is inappropriate, what is acceptable and unacceptable in behavior and speech in cultures other than one's own. Competence in a pluralist world will mean being able to function effectively in contexts one has until now only read about or seen on television. It will mean knowing how to be "different" and feeling comfortable about it, being able to be the "insider" in one situation and the "outsider" in another.

Defined this way, pluralism in America can be achieved only if everyone does some changing. Every group will need to learn new ways of navigating in territories in which they do not have the power to define what is normal. No one will be immune from this process. For some groups of color, this will mean learning how to be "the majority." For whites in California, it may sometimes mean learning how to be "a minority." Addressing these issues will be an important aspect of a university education in the coming decade.

When they give voice to their idealism, this is what Berkeley's undergraduates say they want. Despite the reservoir of goodwill with which they arrive on campus in that first semester, they most often come up against the second stage of diversity, the zero-summing, the socially formed sense of enclaves that are difficult to penetrate. They would, of course, prefer to get to what we have called the "third experience" and just bypass the second, but it may well be that a period of self-segregation or Balkanization may strengthen identity and community as a prerequisite to being able to bring that strength to bear on the larger communal experience.

In this third experience of diversity, the public sphere is enriched precisely because members come from heterogeneous backgrounds, ways of thinking, [and] ways of formulating and solving problems. A special value is placed upon a contribution to the whole, or to the common collective experience, because contributing members bring something to that experience that is unique. In order to have a third stage of diversity, and in order to get to the stage in which people will come together across their differing ethnic/cultural/racial experiences and create a greater whole, each group must be able to draw upon the integrity of its own cultural experience. Each must have a sense of distinct cultural identity and carry the distinctiveness of culture, experience, space,

place, perspective, and orientation in order to make its particular contribution to the larger collective enterprise.

Notes

Selected segments of this [chapter] appear in the following publications: "Understanding Self-Segregation on the Campus," *Chronicle of Higher Education,* September 25, 1991; " 'They're Taking over' and Other Myths," *Mother Jones,* September 1991; and the *Diversity Project,* Berkeley: Institute for the Study of Social Change, University of California, 1992. (The segments that appear here were written by the author, who was principal author of the report.)

1. The American cultures requirement at Berkeley, passed by the Academic Senate, requires that each student admitted (beginning in the fall of 1991) must take one course that compares three of five ethnic/racial/cultural groups. More than twenty-five such courses have been and are being developed. At the time when the criticism was being leveled, most of these courses were still on the drawing board, and there could have been no chance for the critics to have reviewed syllabi, course outlines, reading lists, or general intellectual content.

2. "The acrimony generated by the current debates over multiculturalism has created extreme positions in academe. At one extreme is the view that we should teach only the history and values of Western civilization; at the other is the notion that we should focus chiefly on the origins and histories of particular ethnic groups. Those who refuse to subscribe to either position seem strangely paralyzed and silent. It is imperative that we find intellectual models

that support cultural diversity without erecting battle lines that discourage understanding and tolerance and that breed racism" (Weiner 1992: B1, B2).

3. This finding is from *Promoting Student Success at Berkeley: Guidelines for the Future,* the report on a study conducted by the Commission on Responses to a Changing Student Body released by the chancellor in 1991.

4. These data are from the Office of Student Research, *1990 Freshman Survey: Berkeley's Ten Supplemental Questions by Ethnicity and Gender,* February 1991. See also Table 5 of the *Diversity Project* final report, 1991.

5. The more affluent and assimilated Asian-Americans had strong concerns about the *practice* of affirmative action that focused on issues of "academic standards," meritocratic criteria, and inherent problems with "race-based" policies. Other Asian-Americans argued on behalf of affirmative action as an important wedge for undoing some of the historical effects of discrimination.

6. As Deborah Woo (1990) has pointed out, the very collapse of the category permits a conception of "over-representation" in the university that masks internal differentiations [among] Japanese-American enrollment (which declined significantly between 1980 and 1989), Korean-American enrollment (which has tripled), and Chinese-American enrollment (which has remained the same).

7. Jerome Karable and David Karen, "Go to Harvard, Give Your Kid a Break," *New York Times,* December 8, 1990.

8. Interview with Pamela Burnett, associate director, Office of Undergraduate Admissions, October 17, 1991.

9. The median family income for white students is nearly double that for blacks.

References
[and Suggested Reading]

Aufderheide, P., ed. *Beyond PC: Toward a Politics of Understanding.* St. Paul, Minn.: Graywolf, 1992.

Crèvecoeur, J. Hector St. John de. *Letters from an American Farmer.* 1782. Reprint. New York: Fox, Duffield and Co., 1904.

D'Souza, D. *Illiberal Education: The Politics of Race and Sex on Campus.* New York: Free Press, 1991.

Glazer, N., and D. P. Moynihan. *Beyond the Melting Pot: The Negroes, Puerto Ricans, Jews, Italians, and Irish of New York City.* Cambridge, Mass.: MIT Press, 1970.

Hall, S. "Ethnicity: Identity and Difference." *Radical America* 23, no. 4 (1991).

Kallen, H. M. "Democracy versus the Melting Pot." *Nation* 100 (February 18-25. 1915): 190-94, 217-20.

Karabel, J. "Status-Group Struggle, Organizational Interest, and the Limits of Institutional Autonomy: The Transformation of Harvard, Yale, and Princeton, 1918-1940. *Theory and Society* 13, no. 1 (January 1984): 1-40.

Kristol, I. "The Tragedy of Multi-culturalism." *Wall Street Journal,* July 31, 1991.

Light, I., and E. Bonacich. *Immigrant Entrepreneurs: Koreans in Los Angeles, 1965-1982.* Berkeley: University of California Press, 1988.

Oren, D. A. *Joining the Club: A History of Jews at Yale.* New Haven, Conn.: Yale University Press, 1985.

Portes, A., and R. G. Rumbaut. *Immigrant America: A Portrait.* Berkeley: University of California Press, 1990.

Schechner, R. "An Intercultural Primer." *American Theater,* October 1991: 28-31, 135-36.

Schlesinger, A., Jr. *The Disuniting of America: Reflections on a Multi-cultural Society.* New York: Norton, 1992.

Synnott, M. G. *The Half-Opened Door: Discrimination and Admissions at Harvard, Yale, and Princeton, 1900-1970.* Westport, Conn.: Greenwood, 1979.

Wechsler, H. S. *The Qualified Student: A History of Selective College Admissions in America.* New York: Wiley, 1977.

Weiner, A. B. "Anthropology's Lessons for Cultural Diversity." *Chronicle of Higher Education,* July 22, 1992: B1, B2.

Woo, D. "The Over-representation of Asian-Americans: Red Herrings and Yellow Perils." *Sage Race Relations Abstracts* 15, no. 2 (May 1990).

Zangwill, I. *The Melting-Pot: Drama in Four Acts.* New York: Macmillan, 1920.

The Power of the Perspective

The Teaching Imagination across the Social Sciences

22

The Trouble with Stories

Charles Tilly

Born in England but soon transplanted to Ontario, Stephen Leacock left Canada to do a Ph.D. with Thorstein Veblen at the University of Chicago. After four years, Leacock returned definitively to Canada, but this time to Montreal; he eventually chaired McGill Uni-

AUTHOR'S NOTE: Ronald Aminzade, Mustafa Emirbayer, Roberto Franzosi, Herbert Gans, Jan Hoem, John Krinsky, Charles Lemert, John Markoff, Ann Mische, Victor Nee, Bernice Pescosolido, Francesca Polletta, Marilynn Rosenthal, Harrison White, and Viviana Zelizer provided helpful comments on earlier drafts. I also have benefited from an electronic discussion of these issues initiated by Polletta and then joined energetically by Jeff Broadbent, Marco Giugni, Jack Goldstone, Jeff Goodwin, Michael Hanagan, Roger Karapin, Howard Lune, and Heather Williams. It is only fair to record that (1) Mische, Polletta, and some of the electronic debaters vigorously dispute my claims that what I call *standard stories* are relatively invariant in structure and dominant in everyday social analyses and that (2) I have done no formal collection and analysis of stories to back up my arguments. I base my assertions about the form and prevalence of standard stories not only on everyday observation, some experience in life history interviewing, and long exposure to written accounts (fictional and otherwise) of social life but also on impressions gained from cataloging and coding perhaps 150,000 reports concerning different types of popular contention that my collaborators and I have abstracted from periodicals, administrative correspondence, chronicles, and related sources. Fortunately, the dispute is open to empirical adjudication; it should encourage readers to bring their own observations and evidence to bear on the actual structure of everyday storytelling. However such an empirical inquiry comes out, its results will clarify the origins, structures, and effects of social stories and thereby help specify effective ways in which to teach, learn, investigate, and explain social processes.

versity's Department of Economics and Political Science. In that vein, his *Elements of Political Science* (Leacock 1921) merited translation into 17 languages. As Leacock grew older and wiser, however, he turned increasingly from economics and political science to humor such as his droll classic *Literary Lapses*. He titled that book's final story "A, B, and C. The Human Element in Mathematics." It concerns stories. Leacock ([1910] 1957) wrote,

The student of arithmetic who has mastered the first four rules of his art, and successfully striven with money sums and fractions, finds himself confronted by an unbroken expanse of questions known as problems. These are short stories of adventure and industry with the end omitted, and though betraying a strong family resemblance, are not without a certain element of romance.

The characters in the plot of a problem are three people called A, B, and C. The form of the question is generally of this sort:

"A, B, and C do a certain piece of work. A can do as much work in one hour as B in two or C in four. Find how long they work at it." (p. 141)

A, B, and C rowed on rivers, pumped water from cisterns, dug ditches, and otherwise competed strenuously, always to the disadvantage of C. Leacock ([1910] 1957) reveals what he learned from survivor D: C died of exhaustion after yet another grueling contest with A and B. A then lost interest in competition as B languished in his grief until he "abjured mathematics and devoted himself to writing the history of the Swiss Family Robinson in words of one syllable" (p. 146).

Under Leacock's pen, the abstract relations of algebra give way to human interest stories. His readers can chuckle because they instantly recognize the conceit. Alas, the same does not hold for sociology's readers. The trouble with reading, writing, and learning sociology is straightforward but formidable; people ordinarily cast their accounts of social life as stories—stories, as we shall see, with distinctive causal structures. Such stories do crucial work in patching social life together. But sociology's strongest insights do not take the form of stories and often undermine the stories people tell.

By *stories,* I do not mean rhetoric, the artful use of language to convince readers that the writer tells the truth. Nor do I mean the straightforward chronologies of events that appear in sources such as personnel records, marriage registers, and machine inspection logs. Although reading notes, court proceedings, political tracts, and advertisements sometimes incorporate stories in the narrow sense I am pursuing here, I am not including all of them under the heading "stories." I mean the sequential, explanatory recounting of connected, self-propelled people and events that we sometimes call tales, fables, or narratives. Let us call these sequential, explanatory accounts of self-motivated human action *standard stories.*

Standard Stories

To construct a standard story, start with a limited number of interacting characters, individual or collective. Your characters may be persons, but they also may be organizations such as churches and states or even abstract categories such as social classes and regions. Treat your characters as independent, conscious, and self-

motivated. Make all their significant actions occur as consequences of their own deliberations or impulses. Limit the time and space within which your characters interact. With the possible exception of externally generated accidents—you can call them "chance" or "acts of God"—make sure that everything that happens results directly from your characters' actions.

Now, supply your characters with specific motives, capacities, and resources. Furnish the time and place within which they are interacting with objects that you and they can construe as barriers, openings, threats, opportunities, and tools—as facilities and constraints bearing on their actions. Set your characters in motion. From their starting point, make sure that all their actions follow your rules of plausibility and produce effects on others that likewise follow your rules of plausibility. Trace the accumulated effects of their actions to some interesting outcome. Better yet, work your way backward from some interesting outcome, following all the same rules. Congratulations, you have just constructed a standard story.

In writing your standard story, you have crafted a text that resembles a play, a television sitcom episode, a fable, a news item, or a novel. But you also have produced something like the following:

- The account that a jury constructs from the testimony and evidence laid out during a trial
- A biography or an autobiography of a single character
- Explanations that people piece together at the scene of a grisly accident
- Histories that nationalists recount as they say why they have prior rights to a given territory
- Speeches of social movement leaders who are linking today's actions or demands to the movement's past

- The selective (and perhaps fanciful) account of his past with which a taxi driver regales his or her captive passengers during a long ride to the airport
- How people apologize for, or justify, their violations of other people's expectations: "I'm sorry, but . . ."
- What victims of a crime or a disaster demand when authorities say they do not know how or why it happened
- Conversations people carry on as they judge other people's sins, good deeds, successes, and failures
- How bosses and workers reply to the question "Why don't you folks ever hire any X's?"

Standard stories, in short, pop up everywhere. They lend themselves to vivid, compelling accounts of what has happened, what will happen, or what should happen. They do essential work in social life, cementing people's commitments to common projects, helping people make sense of what is going on, channeling collective decisions and judgments, spurring people to action they would otherwise be reluctant to pursue. Telling stories even helps people to recognize difficulties in their own perceptions, explanations, or actions, as when I tell a friend about a recent adventure only to remark—or to have my friend point out—a previously unnoticed contradiction among the supposed facts I have laid out.

Stories in Action

The sociological technique of interviewing (especially in the forms we call life histories or oral histories) benefits from the readiness of humans to package memory in standard stories. Although all of us have recollections we would prefer not to share with interviewers, in my own interviewing I have generally found people delighted to talk about past experiences and adept at placing those experiences in coherent sequences. Indeed, humans are so good at making sense of social processes after the fact by means of standard stories that skilled interviewers must spend much of their energy probing, checking, looking for discrepancies, and then reconstructing the accounts their respondents offer them.

In teaching sociology to North American and European students, I have been impressed by the ingenuity and persistence with which they pack explanations into standard stories. Whatever else we have learned about inequality, for example, sociologists have made clear that a great deal of social inequality results from indirect, unintended, collective, and environmentally mediated effects that fit very badly into standard stories. Yet, students discussing inequality tend to offer two competing variants on the same standard story: (1) that individuals or categories of individuals who differ significantly in ability and motivation arrive at various tests, judged by others, on which they perform with differential success, whereupon those others reward them unequally, *or* (2) that powerful gatekeepers follow their own preferences in sorting individuals or whole categories of individuals who arrive at certain choice points, thereby allocating them differential rewards.

Both variants respect the rules of standard stories—self-motivated actors in delimited time and space and conscious actions that cause most or all of the significant effects. Such a standard story shapes likely disagreements—over which variant is more accurate, over whether and why categories of people do differ significantly in ability and motivation, over whether existing performance tests measure capacities properly, over whether gatekeepers operate out of prejudice, and so on. Although many people in and out of sociology explain inequality in these ways, either variant of the story omits or contradicts major inequality-generating causal sequences well established by sociological research. Such a story conflicts, for example, with explanations in which inequality at work forms as a byproduct of hiring through existing, socially homogeneous personal networks of people already on the job, which happens to be the most common form of job recruitment through most of the contemporary capitalist world. That sort of confrontation between preferred standard stories and well-documented causal processes presents teachers and students of sociology with serious difficulties but also with great opportunities to rethink conventional explanations of social life. Later sections of this chapter examine the difficulties and opportunities in detail.

By no means does trouble with stories occur in pedagogy alone. It bedevils sociological analysis wherever that analysis takes place—in field observation, in historical reconstruction, in polling, on the editorial page, in everyday conversation, or in classrooms. Even veteran analysts of incremental, interactive, indirect, unintended, collective, and environmentally mediated causal processes in social life—I include myself—easily slip into interpreting new social situations as if standard stories adequately represented their causal structures. Although when discussing what we can do about weaknesses of stories I describe one sort of teaching that concentrates on the construction of more adequate stories, I see no yawning gulf between teaching and research; sophistication and effectiveness in one promotes sophistication and effectiveness in the other. At a minimum, teachers and researchers must learn the pitfalls of assuming that standard stories adequately represent causes and effects as they unfold in social processes.

For specialized purposes, of course, people often offer other sorts of accounts than the ones I have called standard stories. Novelists and poets occasionally write descriptions of humans who engage in inexplicable actions, respond to hidden forces, or experience all life as chaos. Patients reporting their medical histories commonly depart from standard stories to enumerate successions of mishaps. Religious and political doctrines often include great historical arcs that fulfill some powerful plan or immanent principle—progress, decline, destiny, or just retribution. A book titled *The Story of the Atom* may well include standard stories about Albert Einstein and Niels Bohr, but much of its account is likely to center on explications of physical principles. Standard stories stand out among all of the accounts we sometimes call stories by their combination of unified time and place, limited sets of self-motivated actors, and cause-and-effect relations centered on those actors' deliberated actions. Such stories predominate in everyday descriptions, explanations, and evaluations of human social behavior.

Why do standard stories occupy such central places in social life? I see two main possibilities that are not mutually exclusive. First, standard story structures might correspond closely to the ways in which human brains store, retrieve, and manipulate information about social processes. Brains seem to array objects, including social objects, in virtual spatial and temporal relations to each other; to assign objects attributes that are available as explanations of their behavior; and to assemble complex situations as interactions of self-motivated objects within delimited spaces and times. If so, then preference for standard story accounts and availability of storytelling as a wide-ranging social tool could spring from deep currents in the human organism.

Perhaps, however, brains and nervous systems do no more than accommodate storytelling as one of many possible ways of organizing social accounts. Perhaps people learn the structure of stories just as they learn maps of cities and melodies of favorite songs. In that case, we might reasonably expect different populations to vary in their emphases on storytelling and may well discover that Westerners acquired a preference for standard story packaging of social life through a long, distinctive history. Through that long history, we might find, people extended storytelling from an initial narrow invention to a wide range of applications.

Here, as always, the exact interplay between nature and nurture, between wired-in capacity and cultural immersion, and between genetic determination and historical transformation presents a great challenge to our long-term understanding and explanation of social life. But in the short run, we need only this conclusion: for whatever reasons, today's Westerners (and maybe all peoples) have a strong tendency to organize conversations about social processes in standard story form.

Disciplinary Stories

Each of the academic disciplines that concentrates on the explanation of some aspect of human behavior has made its own adjustment to the dominance of standard stories. Linguists, geographers, psychologists, historians, paleontologists, economists, anthropologists, political scientists, and sociologists all have characteristic ways of dealing with—or keeping their distance from—standard stories. Many historians, for example, insist that such stories accurately represent the causal structure of social life. They write their histories as tales of conscious, self-motivated actors. When they get to the large scales of wars, great transformations, and civilizations, however, historians split between those who refer to collective actors (e.g., classes, nations) in standard story form and those who resort to abstract causal forces such

as mentalities, cultures, technologies, and forms of power.

Psychologists take other approaches to stories. They divide among a dwindling number of storytelling analysts who continue to treat whole individuals as conscious acting entities and a variety of reductionists who trace observable human behavior to the operation of genes, neurons, hormones, and/or subconscious mental processes. Economists divide differently; many analysts of individual economic behavior adopt a highly stylized version of the standard story that centers on deliberate decision making within well-defined constraints, whereas analysts of macroeconomic processes introduce non-story-mediating mechanisms—impersonal markets, technologies, resource endowments, and flows of information, capital, goods, or labor. For all their differences in other regards, political scientists, anthropologists, and sociologists maintain similar relations to standard stories. Within each of the three disciplines, some specialists conduct almost all of their analyses in standard story form, whereas others reject stories in favor of explanations based on non-story structures and processes such as markets, networks, self-sustaining cultures, physical environments, and evolutionary selection.

What place should stories occupy in sociology? In ordinary circumstances, well-told standard stories convey what is going on far more forcefully than do the mathematical equations, lists of concepts, statistical tables, or schematic diagrams sociologists commonly chalk up on their blackboards. Why, then, should sociologists not turn to fiction and biography as models for their own efforts? After all, nonsociologists often reserve their highest praise for sociological work that "reads like a novel." Would a course in story writing not, therefore, provide the best introduction to sociological analysis?

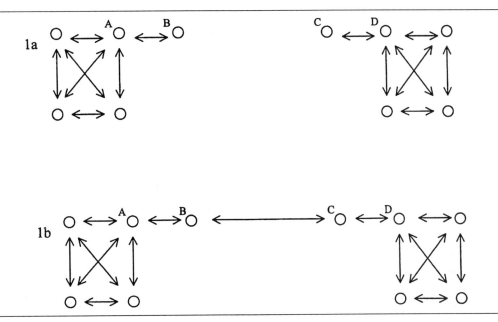

Figure 22.1. Changes in Centrality

No, it would not, at least not if the point of sociology is to describe and explain social processes. The difficulty lies in the logical structure of storytelling. Remember its elements: (1) limited number of interacting characters; (2) limited time and space; (3) independent, conscious, self-motivated actions; and (4) with the exception of externally generated accidents, all actions resulting from previous actions by the characters. Standard stories work that way, but on the whole social processes do not.

Consider some examples:

■ Within a high-fertility population, as improved nutrition or prevention of children's diseases reduces infant mortality, the population grows more rapidly and experiences a rise in life expectancy.

■ Job seekers who get their information about employment opportunities from other people who are already close to them do less well in the job market, on average, than do job seekers who get their information from more distant acquaintances.

■ Despite the sometimes sensational salaries of athletes, entertainers, and chief executive officers, the higher we go up the ladder of annual income in America, the larger looms inherited wealth and the smaller the share that wages of any type constitute current revenues.

■ In Figure 22.1, 1a, B and C obviously occupy peripheral locations, whereas A and D hardly differ from their neighbors in centrality. In Figure 22.1, 1b, however, the addition of a connection between B and C has made them much more central than any of their predecessors, whereas A and D also have gained in their access to others.

■ In American cities, children from low-income households often live in run-down, crowded housing where dust mites and cockroaches proliferate. Those pests trigger asthma attacks, which keep poorer children out of school or hamper their performance in school.

Each of these cases calls for qualifications and explanations. The rise in life expectancy as a consequence of declining infant mortality registers the passage of larger surviving cohorts into higher age groups and soon reaches a limit unless death rates start declining for those higher age groups as well. More distant acquaintances provide relatively effective news about available jobs not because individually they have better information but because collectively they connect job seekers with a wider range of opportunities than do close friends and kin. Inherited wealth actually places the bulk of rich Americans in their high positions and means that much of their income arrives as returns from capital rather than as salaries. Connecting apparently peripheral locations that possess complementary resources describes the work of effective entrepreneurs, brokers, and matchmakers; it frequently changes whole organizational configurations rapidly. Missing school and being sick in school not only reduce children's exposure to education but also promote children's confusion, inattention, and discouragement, which further damages learning.

The point of these obvious examples is twofold. In each case, strong, recurrent causal mechanisms are operating, but in none of them do the crucial causal mechanisms correspond to the structure of standard storytelling. Of course, we can tell standard stories about some aspects in each of these situations—how microbe hunters track down baby-killing diseases, how individual job seekers actually find employment, why parents bequeath wealth to their children, under what circumstances entrepreneurs notice good fits between unconnected locations, or how poor children experience schools. But these cases differ from the conventional matter of storytelling because central cause-and-effect relations are indirect, incremental, interactive, unintended, collective, or mediated by the nonhuman environment rather than being direct, willed consequences of individual actions. The standard stories we construct for such processes miss their central causal connections. Most significant social processes fall into a nonstory mode. Most of them do so because at least some crucial causes within them are indirect, incremental, interactive, unintended, collective, and/or mediated by the nonhuman environment.

Personally, I have nothing against standard stories. I read them eagerly, make arguments with them, remember things by telling myself stories, and gladly overhear stories people tell each other on the subway. I began this chapter with a standard story about Leacock. As a student of social processes, I have spent much of my career locating, transcribing, cataloging, analyzing, retelling, and pondering other people's standard stories. The pages of my books on popular contention overflow with stories in which ordinary people make collective claims. That massive effort to extract evidence concerning social processes from stories has brought me to appreciate the centrality of storytelling in human life, but it also has taught me the incompatibility in causal structure between most standard stories and social processes.

The Search for Causes

Refusal to recognize the limits of standard storytelling creates major problems for social analysts. In one light, the problems stem from distortion produced by forcing social processes into stories about self-motivated actors. In the opposite light, they consist of failures to specify causal mechanisms that actually drive social processes. To clarify what is at issue in the confrontation between standard storytelling and the social science explanation, we can use a rough distinction among the four dominant ontologies and explanatory strategies adopted by analysts of social life: methodological individualism, phenomenological individualism, systems realism, and relational realism. Let us review them and their connections with storytelling in turn.

Methodological individualism treats independent choice-making persons as the fundamental units and starting points of sociological analysis. Its explanations pivot on mental events—choices or decisions. People make choices that forward their interests, preferences, or utilities within constraints set by personal resources and environmental settings. What causes those choices? Other mental events in the form of calculations concerning the likely outcomes of different actions.

Methodological individualism has the great advantages of simplicity and generality—if and when it works. For the moment, it faces three large difficulties, two of them upstream and one of them downstream. Upstream (i.e., before the point of decision that constitutes its central object of explanation), (1) few actual human behaviors seem to fit its requirement of optimizing choices among well-defined alternatives and (2) supposedly fixed elements such as preferences and computations of outcomes actually wobble and interact in the course of social action. Downstream (i.e., once a decision supposedly is made), we confront difficulty in that (3) methodological individualism so far lacks a plausible account of the causal chains by which decisions produce their effects on individual action, social interaction, and complex social processes.

Methodological individualists, however, can take standard storytelling in their stride. They already are talking about self-motivated actors—the fewer, the better—within delimited times and places whose deliberated decisions produce all the effects worth mentioning. Their problem results not from intrinsic incompatibility of their causal accounts with storytelling but rather from the implausibility of the standard stories their causal accounts entail.

Phenomenological individualists, likewise, move easily on standard story terrain. They center descriptions and explanations of social processes on human consciousness. At the extreme of solipsism, indeed, the social world dissolves into individual consciousness, and systematic explanation of social processes faces an insuperable barrier—the impossibility of any observer's entering into his or her neighbor's awareness, much less explaining it. In less extreme forms, however, phenomenological individualists pursue a familiar variety of explanation. Through empathy, deduction, criticism, or some other means, they reconstruct the meanings, feelings, ideologies, and theories that presumably motivate social action. They can deal more easily than methodological individualists with collective actors such as churches, states, classes, or regions, to which they impute varieties and degrees of shared consciousness. At that point, nevertheless, phenomenological individualists confront the same explanatory obstacles as do methodological individualists—upstream, accounting for change and interaction of the conscious states that presumably produce social action; downstream, showing how those conscious states create their effects.

System realists have commonly prided themselves on escaping precisely those obstacles by recognizing the interdependence of individual actions, their constraint by previously existing social structure, and their coalescence into self-regulating systems. Structures sketched by system realists range in scale from friendships to civilizations, in content from fluid communications to evolutionary universals, and in structure from gossamer webs to iron cages. What unifies system approaches is their imputation of self-generating properties to social aggregates and their explanation of particular social events by connections to the larger social systems within which they occur. The great failures of systems theories lie in two main areas: (1) the absence of sturdy, well-documented causal mechanisms that actually are observable in operation and (2) the prevalence of poorly explicated functional explanations in which events, relations, institutions, or social processes exist because they serve some requirement of the system as a whole. Although they certainly describe their major actors—social systems—as self-propelling and sometimes describe social systems as having characteristic life histories, system realists usually avoid standard storytelling.

Relational analysis focuses on the transaction, interaction, information flow, exchange, mutual influence, or social tie as its elementary unit. For relational realists, individuals, groups, and social systems are contingent, changing social products of interaction. Relational realists vary greatly in the prominence they ascribe to culture—to shared understandings and their representations. At one extreme, hard-nosed network theorists treat the geometry of connections as having a logic that operates quite independently of the network's symbolic content. At the other extreme, conversational analysts treat the back-and-forth of social speech as inescapably drenched with meaning. In between, students of organizational processes who reject the idea that organizations are self-maintaining systems often trace webs of culturally conditioned interdependency among persons and positions within the organization.

At both extremes and in between, relational analysis maintains a curious connection with storytelling. It simultaneously denies the self-propulsion of a story's characters and affirms the centrality of mutual influences among characters that give standard storytelling its continuity. Relational analyses enjoy the advantages of providing excellent descriptive templates for social processes and of identifying robust regularities in social interaction. At least in principle, they offer the promise of treating standard stories not as descriptions or explanations of social processes but as changing, contingent *products* of social interaction. In fact, they could account for the production and use of nonstandard stories as well.

To be sure, in real life and in sociology, most attempts at explanation of social processes involve syntheses, amalgams, and compromises among some or all of our four basic approaches: methodological individualism, phenomenological individualism, system realism, and relational analysis. It is not hard, for example, to conceive of individuals as making rational choices within strict limits set by encompassing and self-regulating social systems, as in the model of a buyer or seller who enters a competitive market. Similarly, relational analysts often go on to argue that the structures created by interaction—hierarchies, paired categories, industries, and so on—have emergent properties, operate according to powerful laws, and shape social relations among their participants; to that extent, relational realists edge toward systems theories. Still, each of the four explanatory traditions generates some relatively pure and exclusive accounts of social life, each (even in compromised form) presents characteristically different difficulties, and at the limit all four cannot be valid. Furthermore, none of the four offers an explanatory structure that fits comfortably with the standard stories in which people ordinarily cast their social accounts.

In most circumstances, standard storytelling provides an execrable guide to social explanation. Its directly connected and self-motivated actors, deliberated actions, circumscribed fields of action, and limited inventory of causes badly represent the ontology and causal structure of most social processes. There are exceptions; some games, some battles, some markets, and some decision making within formal organizations approximate the ontology and causal structure of standard stories. But these are extreme cases, notable especially for the hidden institutional supports that make them possible. Most social processes involve cause-and-effect relations that are indirect, incremental, interactive, unintended, collective, and/or mediated by the nonhuman environment.

How to Confront Storytelling

Hence, a three-faced problem: how to cut through the limits set by prevalent stories on the explanation of social processes, how to convey valid explanations of social processes when audiences customarily wrap their own explanations in storytelling, and how to describe and explain the creation, transformation, and effects of existing standard stories.

The first is, surprisingly, the easiest. All well-versed practitioners of methodological individualism, phenomenological individualism, system realism, and relational analysis have at times learned to resist standard story interpretations of their subject matter and to adopt formalisms that assist them in imposing an alternative frame—mathematical models, diagrams, simulations, conceptual schemes, measurement devices, and more. It might be painful, and some skilled practitioners abandon their training, but such learned self-discipline comes with apprenticeship to the trade.

Communication with nonspecialists who customarily cast their social accounts in standard stories sets a greater challenge. Teachers of

mathematics' or chemistry's emphatically nonstory structures to novices have several advantages over sociologists; almost no one thinks mathematics or chemistry should or does follow the rules of storytelling, students have no previous training in mathematics or chemistry as a series of stories to shed before they can learn more adequate models, and students grudgingly or eagerly accept that learning the formal structure of mathematics or chemistry will give them future benefits. None of these, regrettably, applies to sociology.

On the contrary. Most people, including some teachers of sociology, think that social life actually does conform to the requirements of storytelling—self-motivated actors, deliberated actions, and the lot. In addition, people (or at least Western people) ordinarily carry on their moral reasoning in a standard story mode. They judge actual or possible actions by their conscious motives and their immediately foreseeable effects; this fact lies behind the frequent complaint that sociological explanations deny the responsibility, autonomy, and/or moral worth of individuals. In addition, people ordinarily join (1) moral judgments, (2) conceptions of what is possible, (3) ideas of what is desirable within that realm of possibility, and (4) causal accounts of social life. A discussion of what people should do presumes that they can do it, and the justification for their doing so usually includes judgments about the likely consequences of their doing so. As a result, people do not readily accept analysts' attempts to pry elements of moral thinking apart. (Perhaps for that very reason, young people who are beginning to question the moral systems within which they grew up develop greater receptivity to sociology than do their fellows.)

That is not all. Before they encounter sociology as a discipline, students and nonspecialist readers have had years of practice in constructing social explanations by means of storytelling; they do not cast off that practice easily. Finally, the benefits of doing so are much harder to discern than in the case of mathematics or chemistry; indeed, what most students and some professionals hope to find in sociology is the ability to construct more persuasive standard stories. Sociologists do not easily cut through the veil of resistance.

What can sociologists do about it? Here are some of the possibilities:

- Study the social processes that condition how and why similar stories strike one audience as quite authentic and strike another as utterly phony
- Teach competing ways of representing particular social processes, not only as storytelling and as alternative social scientific models but also as metaphor, machine, and political rhetoric; compare premises, procedures, and results of these competing representations, showing what is distinctive and valuable about the social scientific ones
- Dramatize the existence of social processes, configurations, or outcomes for which available standard stories offer implausible explanations, demonstrably false explanations, contradictory explanations, or no explanations at all and for which coherent sociological explanations exist
- More precisely and aggressively, create and use simulations of social processes (whether simple games or complex symbolic representations) that challenge available standard stories, embody sociologically plausible causes and effects, produce empirically verifiable outcomes, and allow participants to investigate the consequences of altering inputs or causal structures

- Trace standard story shadows of non-story processes, as by following a series of interdependent life histories, each itself in coherent standard story form, before examining the intersection and variation of those lives; how, for example, do variable relations to the same school system, firm, or labor market create contrasting trajectories and solidarities?
- Go even farther in the same direction and subvert storytelling; embed non-story explanations in ostensibly storytelling form, for example, by recounting the same social process—a military battle, flow of information through a hospital, or racial integration of a school system—from multiple perspectives, one standard story per participant, until the problem shifts to accounting for differences and connections among the experiences of participants
- Observe how the relationship and conversation between interviewer and respondent shape the responses that survey analysts later interpret as evidence of respondents' individual traits, preferences, intentions, and/or propensities
- Simulate and investigate what happens when participants in standard stories become aware of and respond deliberately to cause-and-effect relations that are indirect, incremental, interactive, unintended, collective, and/or mediated by the nonhuman environment, thus approximating what many theorists have advocated as "reflexive" sociology
- Tunnel under standard stories themselves by creating compelling explanations for both (1) the stories that participants in social processes tell about what is happening to them or others and (2) the stories that analysts, critics, ob-

servers, and even other sociologists tell about particular social processes, situations, and outcomes; using systematic knowledge of the social processes involved, for example, explain how and why police, criminals, judges, prosecutors, priests, social workers, and criminologists come to tell different stories about crime

From the last alternative unfolds a huge, promising program of sociological work. Analysts of social construction have generally contented themselves with demonstrating that entities that earlier interpreters have taken to be irreducibly real—identities, nations, states, genders, and more—consist of or depend on elaborate, contingent, but compelling cultural webs. They have not offered verifiable descriptions or explanations of the processes by which the relevant social construction takes place. They have taken social construction to be a blank wall, an opaque screen, or an impenetrable thicket, impossible to tunnel under. Because standard stories constitute one of the major zones of social construction, however, any systematic account of the processes by which people generate, transform, respond to, and deploy standard stories will serve as a model for tunneling under constructionist analyses in general, taking them seriously but identifying the social constructions involved as objects of explanation.

Here is a challenge to social science worthy of a lifetime's effort. To explain how, why, and with what effects people fashion standard stories will require a commodious, sophisticated theory. It will entail mapping the various contents, forms, and contexts of stories; tracing how they change; pinpointing the social work people do with them; and saying how some of them become fixed in laws, national traditions, or religious rituals, others form and flow like

jazz, and still others circulate as jokes, insults, potted biographies, excuses, moral pronouncements, and ad hoc explanations. Surely, hermeneutic and text-analytic methods will not suffice; attention will shift to the social processes that precipitate standard stories. We should enjoy the irony that a major obstacle to social explanation should become the object of social explanation.

We have some models for that sort of analysis. In the study of language, of art forms, of well-articulated ideologies, of contentious repertoires, of kinship systems, and of other phenomena where change in shared understandings clearly occurs and significantly affects participants' interactions, sociologists and other social scientists already have accumulated experience in tunneling under social construction. Not that they have reached high consensus or manufactured models that will easily export to the explanation of standard stories or other equally complex phenomena. However we evaluate the models currently available in these fields, their existence establishes the possibility in principle of taking the prevalence, variety, and power of standard stories as an explanatory challenge.

An even greater challenge lies farther along the same road. Sociologists eventually must reconcile three apparently contradictory features of social life:

- The recurrence of a limited set of causal mechanisms in a wide variety of situations
- The incessant improvisation that occurs in social interaction
- The great weight of particular histories, congealed as particular cultural configurations, on social interaction.

Each is so compelling that it has acquired its own advocates—advocates of general covering laws for human behavior, advocates of social life as nothing but piecemeal improvisation, and advocates of deep historical and cultural determinism cum particularism. In fact, all three operate and interact. The three features combine in producing path-dependent social processes that never quite repeat themselves, ceaseless flux in relations among participants, and strong but partial causal analogies from one iteration of a social process to the next.

We see the trio in the field of inequality, where similar processes of exploitation, resistance, and control recur in disparate circumstances, yet actual participants in any one of those circumstances negotiate, innovate, cheat, resist, and adapt without cessation, and all this improvisation occurs within strong limits, particular to the time and place, set by accumulated culture, so much so that within the same setting inequalities by gender, race, and citizenship operate as if they belonged to distinct idioms within a common language. We see the trio again in contentious politics, where an analyst of mobilization notices similar causal connections in a vast array of situations, where on the ground improvisation is not only prevalent but also essential, and where the forms of interaction themselves occur within or at the perimeters of previously established forms.

Although the production of standard stories surely conforms to causal principles and permits variation in storytelling style, storytelling lodges especially in the third category, in the social arrangements by which the accumulated collective past weighs on the present and the future. Social interaction generates stories that justify and facilitate further social interaction, but it does so within limits set by the stories people already share as a consequence of previous interactions. It would be a triumph of social analysis to tell the true story of how storytelling arises and how it affects our conduct of social life.

Enlightenment and Explanation

The prevalence of standard stories poses two significant problems for teachers and students of sociology. First, both teachers and students make choices, implicit and explicit, between conceiving of sociology as enlightenment or science, but for most people the paths to enlightenment pass through standard stories, substituting one standard story for another rather than complementing standard stories by means of science. Second, the actual causal structure of social processes, the indispensable core of any sociological explanation, usually contradicts the logical and causal structure of standard stories. As a consequence, teachers of sociology choose, however unconsciously, how to connect their presentation of the subject with standard stories.

Figure 22.2 schematizes the choice. At one extreme, teachers can emphasize sociology as enlightenment by formulating and telling superior stories. In what way superior? From a sociological viewpoint, superior stories have these qualities:

- They include all the major actors (including collective and nonhuman actors) that a valid causal account of the events in question would identify and relate.
- Within the social interactions they describe, they accurately represent cause-and-effect relations among actions of participants in the story, even if they neglect indirect, incremental, and other effects that are not visible in the participants' interactions.
- They provide effective means of connecting the story with times, places, actors, and actions outside its purview.
- They offer means of relating causes explicitly invoked by the story with other causes that are indirect, incremental,

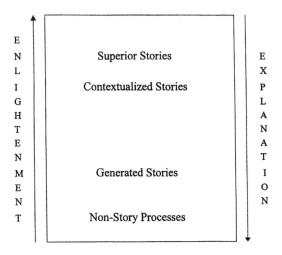

```
E                                              E
N          Superior Stories                    X
L                                              P
I          Contextualized Stories             L
G                                              A
H                                              N
T                                              A
E                                              T
N          Generated Stories                   I
M                                              O
E                                              N
N          Non-Story Processes
T
```

Figure 22.2. Ways of Presenting and Pursuing
Sociology

interactive, unintended, collective,
and/or mediated by the nonhuman environment.

Superior stories, that is, do not identify all the
relevant cause-and-effect relations, but they remain consistent with fuller, more adequate
causal accounts.

In the case of social movements, for example, an *inferior* but commonly credited story
says that people who have failed in fair, normal
competition vent their frustration in collective
complaints, to which right-thinking people respond by pointing to established channels for
the expression of political preferences. The
story is inferior because solid evidence concerning social movement recruitment and participation regularly contradicts its empirical implications and because the causal connections it
alleges—notably the chain from failure, to frustration, to collective action—do not hold up to
close observation.

A *superior,* sociologically validated story
says that people join social movements as a

consequence of their relations with other people who have already experienced injustice or
otherwise become aware of fellow humans'
experience with injustice. Neither story adequately represents the significance of network
connections in recruitment to social movements, but within the social interactions it does
represent, the second story comes much closer
to social processes actually governing social
movement activism. Thus, the superior story
makes a contribution to the teaching of sociology as enlightenment.

At the other extreme, nonstory processes,
we can decide to teach, learn, and use sociology
as a deliberate integration of social interaction
into causal chains, significant parts of which are
indirect, incremental, interactive, unintended,
collective, and/or mediated by the nonhuman
environment. Thus, we can construct, verify,
and communicate models of social movements
in which intentions, awareness, and deliberated
action take place in tight interdependence with
social processes that are not immediately visible
to social movement participants. This sort of
teaching, learning, and using is essential to the
discovery of new explanations and the full criticism of prevalent stories and, hence, is crucial
to the education of professional sociologists. It
is essential because cause-and-effect relations
within social processes do not, in fact, conform
to standard stories.

In between the two extremes, we also can
choose to pursue sociology as an effort to contextualize existing stories or to generate them.
Contextualizing stories involves identifying the
social situations in which certain types of stories
arise and tracing the consequences of adopting
those stories rather than others that are, in
principle, available. Thus, we might analyze the
conditions under which a connected but previously unmobilized population forms a story
about its distinctive national origins, makes
claims for political recognition on the basis of

that story, and then lives the consequences of having adopted that particular story rather than some other that may have been available.

The even more ambitious program of *generating* stories consists of analyzing the processes by which people actually create, adopt, negotiate, and alter the stories they employ in routine social life. Here, in principle, the analyst should be able to simulate and predict both form and content of stories as they enter the social interactions of juries, social movement activists, newscasters, coworkers, and people in general. Storytelling is such a fundamental, pervasive social process that it is hard to imagine effective generation of stories without deep understanding of nonstory processes. Thus, each rung in the ladder from explanation to enlightenment depends on those below it; construction of superior stories rests on some ability to contextualize them, contextualization requires some awareness of processes that generate stories, and the analysis of generation requires partial knowledge of the nonstory causal processes at work in social life.

To teach superior stories and the capacity to detect and criticize inferior stories, however, amply serves enlightenment. Sociology as enlightenment can profitably concentrate on critical examination and reconstruction of widely employed standard stories. Because most students of sociology go off into other walks of life, and because nearly all of them continue to conduct their lives by means of stories and responses to other people's stories, sociology as enlightenment should enrich and clarify social experience. An enlightenment-oriented sociological education can equip those nonspecialist citizens to identify, compare, classify, criticize, improve, or even deploy standard stories. On the presumption that knowing how powerful everyday processes actually work prepares the knowers for more effective encounters with social life, sociological teaching can serve well by concentrating on standard stories. If that sort of education then sensitizes nonspecialists to indirect, incremental, interactive, unintended, collective, and/or environmentally mediated causal links to the stories people tell, then so much the better.

References

Leacock, Stephen B. [1910] 1957. *Literary Lapses.* Toronto: McClelland and Stewart.
———. 1921. *Elements of Political Science.* Boston: Houghton Mifflin.

23

Challenging Assumptions of Human Diversity: The Teaching Imagination in Anthropology

Carole E. Hill

As we move into the 21st century and attempt, in some measure, to unlearn the 20th century, the expanding global knowledge produced by the interconnectedness of the world system certainly challenges essentialist thinking. Curricula are being "internationalized" and "culturalized." The garnering academic support for "multiculturalism" unquestionably promotes the addition of non-Western courses or course content across the curriculum, implying deletions or adjustments to traditional Western knowledge. Supporters of the "Western" approach to education view these changes as threats to the very foundations of the social arrangement between the middle class and universities. Viewed within the context of societal changes and related university changes, their informal social connections reflect the tensions, conflicts, and negotiations that are laying the foundations for the new formulations in anthropological teaching imaginations in the 21st century.

The current debate over the place of cultural diversity in higher education goes beyond the narrow parameters of political correctness to questioning definitions of knowledge, authority in knowledge transfer, and the basis for knowledge creation. The core issue involves *who* produces, reproduces, and transforms the canon. At stake in this debate are (1) the authority of the people who write books about their (and other) ethnic/racial groups; (2) the power of those who select the teaching faculty in universities; (3) the authority of faculty, departments, administrators, and cultural groups in the university to define the boundaries and content of what is taught about cultural diversity; and (4) the nature of linkages among departments that teach about other cultures. The key issues for all the stakeholders involve the relationship between the West and "the rest" within society and within academia and the power relationships among departments that teach about human diversity—the very core of the anthropological imagination. Anthropology's traditional knowledge system is, and always has been, controversial. Indeed, several of the key anthropological concepts are at the heart of the "culture wars." Weiner (1992) argues that anthropology has much to offer to advance the multicultural debate. Its history, theoretical framework, and objectivity make it difficult for anthropologists to legitimately take extreme positions on either side of the debate, whether fueling arguments that discredit the value of diversity or supporting arguments that equate all diverse groups.

The essence of the anthropological imagination in teaching is to compare, understand, and explain culturally and biologically diverse groups through space and time. It emphasizes similarities and differences in language, culture, society, and biological makeup of human populations. By challenging traditional assumptions of students about human diversity, anthropology opens the door to reflection on their own culture, society, and history in a relativistic and comparative manner. Studying other cultures operates as a mirror in that it brings "the other" close up and, at the same time, forces a distancing from the sense of "us" as the only way in which to live and think. A related learning goal of anthropology involves teaching students how to think about and relate to different cultures, particularly in ways that are less ethnocentric and judgmental. This goal requires teaching the inside perspective of the cultural and social worlds of diverse societies and groups. The fundamental aim of the teaching imagination in anthropology, then, is to teach students how to think comparatively and reflexively about their relationships with peoples from different cultures. It assumes that generalizations about human behavior cannot be made without a global examination of diverse human groups.

The anthropological approach to human diversity is both a product of and a rebellion against the academic knowledge systems present in the late 19th and early 20th centuries. The anthropological imagination challenges Western European (Western civilization) ideas that regard the intellectual traditions of other cultures as "uncivilized" and, for the most part, unworthy of having their literature, history, or culture included in university curricula. Until recently, students rarely were required to learn about the history and culture of Africa or Asia, for example, as they learned the history and culture of the West. In a true sense, higher education imagined the West and "the rest," lumping the latter into the study of non-Western cultures. The place to find courses in "the rest" was, for the most part, anthropology. It is a subject that most universities considered rather marginal to a student's education. The marginality of anthropology courses in university settings involves, according to Delbanco (1995), an informal social covenant between academia and U.S. society, particularly with the middle class. Under this agreement, the middle class assent to pay a large price to subsidize those who cannot pay for a college education. In return, academia agrees to teach the intellectual skills and expertise necessary to the youths to perpetuate middle-class society. Ideally, this ensures that it is what one knows and what one can do, not who one is, that is important to succeed in the society. Imagining other cultures had a low priority in this social arrangement; it was deemed unnecessary for the continuation of middle-class Western society. Indeed, thinking with an anthropological imagination often was regarded as a threat to civilization.

This chapter is broken down into four sections: a historical overview of the development of the anthropological imagination, the essential concepts that guide the imagination, the challenges to teaching the anthropological imagination, and the challenges to reconstituting the anthropological imagination in the 21st-century university.

The Teaching Imagination in Anthropology

From the beginning to the present, the major themes and concepts of the anthropological imagination have been constant in explaining cultural diversity. Although theoretical and methodological differences exist within the discipline, its imagination has, until recently, been the foundation of teaching cross-cultural understandings. This consistency is evident in the following description of the development of the anthropological imagination.

Anthropology is a very young discipline. Throughout its 125-year history, it has specialized in the exotic (Dimen-Schein 1977:19). Inspired by the Enlightenment, anthropology became a defined discipline in the 19th century. Its first theoretical paradigm, unilineal evolution (developed in North America and Britain), supported Western ideology about cultural and racial diversity. Consequently, the concepts of this fledgling discipline facilitated the legitimization of colonialism; evolution gave European countries a rationale for colonizing the "savages" and "barbarians" in an effort to help them evolve toward civilization. Fortunately, anthropologists at the turn of the century recognized the flaws in the assumptions of the 19th-century view of cultural evolution and developed more scientific and unbiased approaches to human diversity.

Franz Boas, the most influential anthropological scholar in the United States, challenged the 19th-century belief that race determined a person's intellect, physical characteristics, and behavior by insisting that anthropologists use science to study diverse groups. His definition of culture contested the widely accepted assumption that certain races or nationalities were superior to others. Before multiculturalism and the culture wars were issues in academia, Boas and his students helped establish that the insight of anthropology and the challenge to its practitioners was to teach students and the public about cultural diversity in the hope that such knowledge would enlighten people about the dangers of thinking and behaving ethnocentrically.

Working mostly in colleges and universities as part of an "arts and science education," anthropologists informed students about human diversity in other areas of the world. The anthropological imagination, in its earliest forms, traveled to the far reaches of the world and returned to report on its experiences with people who lived and thought quite differently from university students. Ironically, although similar to the rest of the university, those who chose to study the discipline were predominantly white. In their embrace of the exotic, anthropologists were a small tribe, rarely involved with large numbers of students or powerful positions in the university.

In the 20th century, anthropology built a framework—an imagination—for thinking about diverse human populations. The pedagogy does not teach students *what* to think about diversity; rather, it teaches them *how* to think about it. Anthropology has constructed four central concepts that lie at the hearts of its imagination: the culture concept, the cultural relativism concept, the comparative concept, and the adaptation concept. I am concentrating on the key components of the anthropological imagination in cultural anthropology. My comments, nevertheless, have implications for the other three subcategories of North American anthropology: biological anthropology, linguistic anthropology, and archaeology.

The Culture Concept

Although used and defined today by social scientists and nonacademic writers in a variety of ways, the concept of culture is a "child of anthropology" (Gamst and Norbeck 1976) with a long history and theoretical grounding in anthropology. Gamst and Norbeck state, "Unquestionably, anthropology has done the most to formulate the concept and use it to gain an understanding of man's nature and ways of life" than has any other discipline (p. 7). From the time of Boas, however, several hundred definitions of culture have been formulated by anthropologists. This abundance of definitions does not necessarily reflect a chaotic battle of many opinions. Kroeber and Kluckhohn (1952) demonstrated that the myriad of culture definitions can be reduced to a few categories with variation accounted for by the different theoretical orientations in the discipline.

Whatever the specific definition, anthropologists share several assumptions about the concept of culture. First, culture is learned through social interaction that clearly distinguishes it from those things that are not learned. Second, it assumes that every society has a culture or cultures that its members share to varying degrees. The fact that societies can be made up of different cultural groups allows anthropologists to speak about cultural variation between groups and within a group. People who frequently interact share a set of understandings about expected behavior and about their explanations of the world (belief systems). As Goodenough (1996) points out, culture is a product of learning and is the property of a society or group. "It is what the members of a human group have to know in order to function acceptably as members of that group in the activities in which they engage" (p. 293). It is the rules for and of behavior and their material manifestations within a society or group that give order and meaning to people's lives. Moreover, the rules are interconnected in intricate ways, making it necessary to understand the context of a particular rule or practice. Cultural practices must be contextualized within the framework of environmental and biological processes, making the study of culture a necessarily *holistic* enterprise.

Contemporary anthropologists generally take an active approach to the concept to incorporate its *transformational* properties. Furthermore, anthropologists no longer conceptualize culture exclusively on the local level. Indeed, Goody (1994) argues that culture no longer is encapsulated in local communities. The concept also is being applied to the impacts on societies and groups of the complex world system. Culture, then, is not a static concept. It is constantly changing vis-à-vis the globalization processes. This dynamic approach to the culture concept teaches students how to think about *intergroup* and *intragroup* commonness and diversity and how to recognize and solve cultural conflicts. Students are instructed on how to use these imaginary tools to live in societal diversity. It is conceivable that in the next century, they will be taught how to frame these thinking and practical tools within an imagination that attempts to transcend the "us-them" dichotomy.

One of the major strengths of the anthropology imagination in teaching is that it demands that students apply the theoretical assumptions of the concept of culture to their own lives. Through elucidating the complexity and holistic nature of the concept, including the dynamics of group or individual constructs and the historical and sociopolitical context of cultural systems, a pedagogy emerges that balances the dialectic of bringing diverse cultures that are far away "close up," and those close up can be framed as "far away."

Cultural Relativism

In reaction to 19th-century cultural evolutionism, Boas insisted that anthropologists inductively describe the details of cultures without judging the behavior and beliefs of other cultures. His teachings laid the foundation for the concept of cultural relativism, a key concept in the imagination of anthropological teaching.

Cultural relativism assumes that all cultures must be understood from the inside perspective. Cultural information can be understood only from the point of view of the people being studied, and "virtually all moral and epistemological authority derives from those people whose lives and worlds the anthropologist strives to understand" (Stein 1996:283).

Cultural relativism assumes that beliefs and behaviors of individuals in diverse groups have a rationale. There are meaningful reasons for diverse people to act differently. Therefore, there are at least two perspectives on every phenomenon, sometimes referred to as the inside and outside points of view. The concept assumes that value judgments about a society or group can be made only from within a particular cultural system—from the inside perspective. To do otherwise is to exhibit ethnocentric attitudes, that is, judging another society and culture by the values and standards of one's own society and culture.

Cultural relativism must be separated from ethical relativism. Hatch (1983) defines cultural relativism as understanding the values and worldviews of other groups but does not mean acceptance of all their practices and standards. Furthermore, in its extreme form, cultural relativism impedes the anthropological search for universals and can place anthropologists in awkward epistemological positions. Nevertheless, it is the driving force behind most undergraduate courses in anthropology, particularly introductory courses, as a counterbalance against ethnocentric thinking of students. Immersing students into the worlds and lives of other cultures provides a conceptual basis for understanding diversity and, often, for developing empathy, compassion, and respect for the context of how other groups and cultures create and experience life. Cultural relativism is a key concept in teaching the imagination of anthropology.

Comparative Concept

Understanding cultural diversity and its usefulness for survival of all human populations in the 21st century can be accomplished only by using the comparative approach to teaching. Anthropology assumes that generalizations about human behavior, beliefs, and values cannot be made without comparing them across a broad spectrum of societies. Generalizations based on studies that focus on the white middle class can only be made about that group, not about humans in general. In a general sense, then, comparing societies or groups in the classroom mitigates against students using their own knowledge and experiences to define normal beliefs, behavior, and institutions. Comparing the life ways of groups of people very different from their own allows them to put their lives in a comparative perspective.

The comparative approach is indispensable for generalizing beyond one society or group. As Ember (1996) points out, the phrases "cross-cultural comparison" and "cross-cultural research" are used almost synonymously. Cross-cultural research often is framed within the context of the comparative concept. Ember argues, however, that anthropologists who engage in cross-cultural research have more stringent requirements by narrowing the concept to the domain of scientific methodology and design. "Cross-cultural research has two main goals: to describe the range and distribution of the cultural variation that exists in the ethnographic record and to test theories and hypotheses that attempt to explain that variation" (p. 261). To teach students about similarities and differences in cultures, it is necessary to systematically compare the cultures of societies or groups. Anthropological teaching goes beyond the individual ethnographic case and searches for the distribution and causes of cultural variation through the comparative approach. To facilitate the comparison of diverse groups, a great deal of ethnographic data have been computerized in the Human Relations Area Files, also known as HRAF. These databases often are used in teaching students to assess the differences and similarities among human populations.

The Adaptation Concept

The anthropological imagination for teaching includes an appreciation for the adaptive nature of cultural diversity. Like biological diversity, cultural diversity is a prerequisite for human survival. It refers to the processes by which humans maintain themselves culturally, socially, and biologically in varying environments. Cultural and biological adaptation involves the interplay among culture, heredity, and biological plasticity (Kottak 1997). Through adaptation, the cultural and biological aspects of humans converge. The concept of adaptation implies evolution and the ability of populations to maintain a flexibility for change in response to environmental fluctuations. Bennett (1969) defines cultural adaptation as "the problem-solving, creative, or coping element in human behavior" (p. 13). The greater the number of adaptive strategies, the more likely a society is to survive change, no matter where a cultural group is placed in the social hierarchy of a society.

In 21st-century teaching, the adaptation concept will become more important in debates over human diversity. Greenbaum (1992) argues, "Cultural systems of disadvantaged ethnic groups collectively form the institutional and physiological basis for combating discrimination and its effects. These adaptive features are in part responsible for ethnic persistence" (p. 411). She extends her adaptive explanation for valuing cultural diversity by stating that in a pluralistic society, groups learn from one an-

other and can rely on resources beyond their own group. Contact with other cultural groups provides new ideas and alternative approaches and thus expands the repertoire of human ingenuity. Similarly, Rhodes (1991) suggests that cultural diversity is essential for continuing biological diversity. Vanishing cultural diversity weakens alternative agricultural and environmental knowledge systems that provide a balance to overspecialization of knowledge. Overspecialization of knowledge threatens universal human survival strategies.

Challenges to the Anthropological Imagination

Many of the traditional anthropological concepts currently are being expropriated by other disciplines, the media, and the public. Anthropologists are losing their assumed ownership of a concept and its assumptions and approaches that most believe their discipline pioneered. The traditional knowledge system of anthropology is increasingly becoming prominent within university instructional programs. Anthropology departments, nevertheless, rarely are leading this new surge of interest in "the other." Why? Perhaps anthropologists make "the other" too far away, continuing to perpetuate the "us-them" distinction.

Anthropologists have conceptually delineated cultural and biological group boundaries and, for the most part, the cultural content of the group. The major challenge for anthropologists in contemporary U.S. society is to collaborate with people who identify with diverse groups for the purpose of defining cultural boundaries and defining their cultural rules, categories, and behavior. From the 19th century, the definition of culture invented by "us" made sure that "we" were not "them" by placing all of "us" and "them" in an evolutionary model of cultural development. "We" decided cultural boundaries; that is, "we" decided which societies and groups belonged to "the other" and which belonged to "us" in an effort to define "ourselves" in terms of what "we" were not. This approach effectively laid the foundation for an "us-them" dialogue or, according to Goody (1977), the "grand dichotomy," which still permeates educational approaches to "the other."

It is clear, for whatever reason, that the little academic power and authority anthropology had over these concepts are shifting to other departments (Peacock 1997). Although anthropological concepts are being used extensively in other disciplines and other departments, their complex structural linkages within the anthropological knowledge system, particularly the link between cultural and biological, are lacking. Concepts often are presented as information to be used, not as a process of teaching an organized knowledge system to use for critical and responsible thinking.

Another impetus for the shifting imagination involves the people who anthropologists traditionally have studied ("the other"). They are demanding to be actively involved in collaborating on research projects, from defining the research objectives to developing research instruments. They also are demanding concrete and practical outcomes of the research, not just a publication. Groups are protecting their intellectual property and empowering themselves to participate in the research process (Posey 1991). The developing power of the traditional research subjects will have a far-reaching impact on the teaching imagination in the next century. This challenge to anthropology certainly will be reflected in the subjects of teaching materials.

Globalization processes and fascination with culture wars are rendering traditional concepts less obscure. The esoteric base of 20th-century anthropology is becoming everyday information. Anthropologists no longer are considered the only authorities on other cultures; they are losing the academic authority of their subject matter. These events of the late 20th century are having an impact on authority and control of anthropological knowledge and, consequently, on what constitutes the discipline's major concepts and research and what is taught within academia. They are precipitating new social contracts among anthropologists, universities, and the groups studied and taught about in the classroom. The anthropological paradigm in the 21st century will include ways in which to share the unique insights and approaches of anthropology with "others," whether inside or outside the university.

Reconstituting the Anthropological Imagination in the 21st-Century University

Although the anthropological imagination is, ideally, a key player in rebuilding higher education for the 21st century, the discipline has been, up until now, a faint voice in the reshaping of academy (Peacock 1997). It is as though anthropologists are waiting to be discovered, like some new exotic tribe. Perhaps anthropology is "imaginary challenged" for the 21st century and, at the same time, has a great deal to offer toward rebuilding a knowledge and skill base that students need to adapt to their lives in the 21st century. Without the integrative framework of the anthropological imagination, the information of the discipline may be transmitted but the knowledge system will be lost. The current trend is to emphasize "information" rather than "knowledge" in university curricula. Without the anthropological imagination as a partner in curricula development in the next century, the richness of "the other" is lost in the translation from a complex holistic knowledge system to information "bites."

Anthropology is in the process of recognizing the importance of praxis for developing its conceptual paradigms and in making its knowledge system useful for society. Practitioners are beginning to examine the dialectic between theory and practice, particularly the feedback from practice to theory building. In the 21st century, this approach will be embedded in the discipline. Students will learn the applications of anthropological knowledge for solving human societal problems. No longer can the bulk of anthropologists remain cloistered with their eyes on micro existence within academia. The changing nature of the discipline is compelling new alliances and collaborations with the public, industry, governmental and nongovernmental organizations, and universities. Anthropology is reaching out to the discipline's traditional "subjects" as a resource for survival in the 21st century. Critical contracts with minority and international populations, other disciplines, policymakers, and the public are essential for the continuation and transformation of the anthropological imagination.

The social connections resulting from collaboration with groups internal and external to the university certainly will affect the culture of anthropology and its imagination. Indeed, collaboration may be seen as a cultural process within the discipline—a type of adaptive strategy for the 21st-century university setting. Anthropology will reconstitute itself through forging new forms of alliances with the subjects and objects of their study and teaching and, at the same time, will maintain its imaginary goals. The resulting new forms of these collaborative efforts will create a type of "civil anthropology," one that reaches beyond the exotic tribe on university campuses. Anthropology will not be alone, however, in these endeavors; it will stand next to other related disciplines in forging these new social relationships (Hill 1988, 1994), extensively affecting the relationship between traditional anthropology and the university as well as relationships within the discipline. As anthropology becomes more practice oriented and as collaboration among anthropology, other disciplines, students, and the public increases, the image of the lone researcher in a far-off place will increasingly become antiquated.

The crucial questions for reconstituting anthropology in the social world of the university are as follows. How will the anthropological imagination be defined in the 21st century? Who will define it? How will it be transmitted and shared within university settings? My view is that these questions will be more narrowly defined within traditional anthropological knowledge and, at the same time, more broadly defined as the edges of its knowledge system converge with other academic and nonacademic groups. The concepts of culture, cultural relativism, comparative method, and adaptation are in the process of being reconstituted within the context of a collaborative culture. The emerging imagination, including its expanded networks of "others," will drive the core of anthropology in the 21st century. These new structural and intellectual collaborations link the discipline to the world. The anthropological imagination will continue as anthropological culture reconstitutes itself within the changing demands of the university and of society. New social covenants will be negotiated within the discipline and with the university, the public, and society in the 21st century.

References

Bennett, J. W. 1969. *Northern Plainsmen: Adaptive Strategy and Agrarian Life.* Chicago: Aldine.

Delbanco, A. 1995. "Contract with Academia." *The New Yorker,* May, pp. 7-8.

Dimen-Schein, M. 1977. *The Anthropological Imagination.* New York: McGraw-Hill.

Ember, Carol R. 1996. "Cross-Cultural Research." Pp. 261-65 in *Encyclopedia of Cultural Anthropology,* edited by David Levinson and Melvin Ember. New York: Henry Holt.

Gamst, F. C. and E. Norbeck. 1976. *Ideas of Culture: Sources and Uses.* New York: Holt, Rinehart & Winston.

Goodenough, Ward H. 1996. "Culture." Pp. 291-97 in *Encyclopedia of Cultural Anthropology,* edited by David Levinson and Melvin Ember. New York: Henry Holt.

Goody, J. 1977. *The Domestication of the Savage Mind.* Cambridge, UK: Cambridge University Press.

———. 1994. "Culture and Its Boundaries: A European View." In *Assessing Cultural Anthropology,* edited by R. Borofsky. New York: McGraw-Hill.

Greenbaum, S. D. 1992. "Multi-culturalism and Political Correctness: The Challenge of Applied Anthropology in Curricular Politics." *Human Organization* 51:408-12.

Hatch, E. 1983. *Culture and Morality: The Relativity of Values in Anthropology.* New York: Columbia University Press.

Hill, C. E. 1988. "Core Curriculum Issues." Pp. 37-46 in *Anthropology for Tomorrow,* edited by R. T. Trotter. Washington, DC: American Anthropological Association.

———. 1994. "Professional Organizations and the Future Practice of Anthropology." *Practicing Anthropology* 16:23-24.

Kottak, C. P. 1997. "Central Themes in the Teaching of Anthropology." In *The Teaching of Anthropology: Problems, Issues, and Decisions,* edited by C. P. Kottak, J. J. White, R. H. Furlow, and P. C. Rice. Mountain View, CA: Mayfield.

Kroeber, A. and C. Kluckhohn. 1952. "Culture: A Critical Review of Concepts and Definitions." In *Papers of the Peabody Museum of American Archaeology and Ethnology 7.* Cambridge, MA: Harvard University.

Peacock, J. 1997. "Anthropology in the South and the Southern Anthropological Society: Diversity, the South, Anthropology, and Culture." Pp. 190-99 in *Diversity in the U.S. South: A Region in Transition,* edited by C. E. Hill and P. Beaver. Athens: University of Georgia Press.

Posey, D. 1991. "Effecting International Change for Intellectual Property Rights." *Cultural Survival* 15:29-35.

Rhodes, R. E. 1991. "The World's Food Supply at Risk." *National Geographic* 179:74-105.

Stein, Howard F. 1996. "Cultural Relativism." Pp. 281-85 in *Encyclopedia of Cultural Anthropology,* edited by David Levinson and Melvin Ember. New York: Henry Holt.

Weiner, A. 1992. "Anthropology's Lessons for Cultural Diversity." *Chronicle of Higher Education* 38:1-2.

24

Teaching and Historical Understanding: Disciplining Historical Imagination with Historical Context

Harvey J. Graff

A democratic practice of history . . . encourages skepticism about dominant views but at the same time trusts in the reality of the past and its knowability. To collapse this tension in favor of one side or the other is to give up the struggle for enlightenment. An openness to the interplay between certainty and doubt keeps faith with the expansive quality of democracy. . . . Even in a democracy, history always involves power and exclusion, for any history is always somebody's history, told by someone from a partial point of view.

—Appleby, Hunt, and
Jacob (1994, p. 11)

AUTHOR'S NOTE: I thank Ron Aminzade for asking me to contribute to this volume and for his excellent comments on an earlier version. Both Ron and Bernice Pescosolido have been unusually encouraging editors. Michael Wilson also provided a very useful reading. My interest and my thinking (very much still in progress) on these concerns were influenced in part by a series of three panels on "historical literacy" that I organized for the annual meetings of the Social Science History Association in 1990, 1991, and 1993. In launching the first in 1990, none of us expected that our own and others' interest would lead to a long-running show. My thanks to the cast of participants, some of whom played multiple roles—Paul Adams, Kathy Biddick, Madonna Hettinger, David Mitch, Mark Poster, Jan Reiff, Marcia Sawyer, Peter Stearns, and Ian Winchester. My students also have played, and will continue to play, major parts. None of them bears any responsibility for what follows in this chapter.

History, in all its meanings, is no longer what it was once thought to be. It has been transformed over the course of the 20th century but most dramatically in the last generation. There have long been "new" histories, but never have they been so numerous, popular, or condemned and their recognition so divisive, both inside and outside of the academy. Recent works on the nature and practice of history reflect in their titles (and their pages) contemporary controversies and discomforts, from *Telling the Truth about History* (Appleby et al. 1994) to *The End of History and the Last Man* (Fukuyama 1992; see also Stearns 1993; Smith 1992; Jenkins 1991, 1995; Gagnon and the Bradley Commission on History in Schools 1989; Berkhofer 1995; cf. works from the preceding generation or two: Carr 1961; Hughes 1964; Bloch 1953; Berkhofer 1969; Hobsbawm 1972; Landes and Tilly 1971; Marwick 1970).

The sometimes contradictory impacts of these changes weigh heavily on the themes of this chapter, just as they do on various discourses about history as taught, practiced, and preached. A great revision of history, and major steps in rewriting history, came in large part from the democratizing (to some, the fragmenting or subverting) impact of the new social history and its fellow "new" histories. Together, they opened the pages of the past to different peoples and the practices of historians to different approaches, sources, and methods. Despite some signs of familiarity, the form, content, and practice of history have shifted. This includes changes in conceptualization and practice that came in viewing history as social science, critiques and reconstructions of historical (and other) forms of knowledge that followed from poststructuralist (including some feminist and postcolonial) perspectives, and debates about form, format, genre, and discourse stimulated by the domains of rhetoric, critical theory, and postmodernism (e.g., Ankersmit and Kellner 1995; Appleby et al. 1994; Berkhofer 1995; Burke 1992; Giddens 1990; Scott 1988, 1992; for critical responses to Appleby et al. 1994, see Bunzel, Smith, and Higham 1995; Martin, Scott, and Strout 1995).

The central argument of this chapter is deceptively simple, seemingly commonsensical, but subtly and subversively powerful. It begins with the claim that history is a distinctive discipline. Its distinction lies not only (or even primarily) in its subject matter or materials; rather, history is distinct as a form of inquiry and a mode of understanding.

After briefly exploring contemporary currents, this chapter centers on history's distinguishing characteristics—historical context and its discipline (or disciplining) of historical imagination and historical understanding. This discussion necessarily touches on both research and teaching and their interrelations. By way of conclusion, the chapter highlights selected needs for and uses of teaching and understanding history for social science and for society.

Changing History, History Teaching, and Crisis

To what extent history teaching has changed as a result of the discipline's shifts is unclear or hard to know with certainty. For some historians (including this author) trained in the heady days of novelty and excitement of the "new" histories, classroom practice changed in fairly direct relation to conceptual revision and research practice. Explicit interdisciplinary perspectives are one large cause and consequence. So too are more formal conceptualization and comparison and an awareness of the presence and uses of theory. The quantity and the quality of faculty, graduate programs, and student concerns about teaching have increased dramatically in the past two decades. If not synonymous, these are closely related developments that have stimulated many teachers to sharpen their own and their students' levels of self-conscious and self-critical awareness about their subjects. Key concerns that impinge on the classroom include discussion of the nature of disciplines, their development, functioning, and shifts over time; the various bases of knowledge and understanding and their changes; explicit comparison of alternative perspectives and closer attention to evidence and methodology as well as their possibilities and limits; and pluralistic efforts at inclusiveness. Reflecting disciplinary revision and research practice, a wider and more challenging range of primary sources, discrete examples, and case studies marks the curriculum.

Unsurprising, perhaps, is the criticism of virtually all of these developments by those who feel more loss than gain from the various "new histories" with their cross-disciplinary leanings (including emphases on "social studies" and "skills") or their high-tech aids. These outcries include claims that range from the putative loss of "synthesis" to the contamination of history by social science, quantification, theory, and ideology. To many today both within and outside the academy, the overall complex transformation is tantamount to a full-blown "crisis." Many, perhaps most, of the hand-wringers decry perceived negative consequences for formal teaching in the schools and in less formal modes of "public education." Shrilly proclaimed "losses" of dominating syntheses and canons, combined with assertions of a decline in "historical literacy" (especially, but not solely, in U.S. history), on the one hand, join with new levels of uncertainty about history's factual truths and truthfulness, meanings, and meaningfulness, on the other, to frame fears that go far beyond the basis of their evidence. Grist for these mills is easy to find, whether from results of standardized tests or from pseudo-scandalous incidents on college campuses over, say, "political correctness."[1]

Descriptions of the transformation, often framed in charged rhetorical discourse, take many forms. They range from turnings linguistic, poststructural, and postmodern to endings of history, objectivity, certainty, synthesis, canon, meaning or moral lessons, and even history itself. Narratives new and old, factual and speculative, litter the dustbin of history along with efforts at nonnarrative or nonlinear representations. Such charged language seldom is neutral or calm. Contested and combative, it typically either applauds uncritically or condemns unreflectively. The end of ideology, it seems, has been overtaken by a new war of ideologies.

Among the apparent ironies is a seemingly simple contradiction: as history as scholarly sphere or discipline has lost its idealistic innocence (and its popular audience, some also claim), its significance and its necessity for knowledge, understanding, and teaching in the late 20th century almost certainly have heightened. The reasons embrace the realms of scholarship, politics/ideology, and education—and their relationships. Therefore, it is no accident that all of the disciplines among the human sciences now embrace one or more historical or "historicist" subfields. Often, the subfield is proclaimed "new," as in the cases of the "new historicism" in literary criticism, the "new economic history" two or three decades ago, and "social science history" and "historical sociology" in the past two decades. These sub- or interdisciplines strive for standing and recognition within and beyond their parent or host domains, sometimes claiming the status of more autonomous interdisciplines, holding conferences, forming organizations, starting journals and book series, launching courses and creating course catalog subheads, and etching cross-disciplinary connections (now aided by electronic lists and World Wide Web sites) (Appleby et al. 1994; Bauman 1987; Bunzel et al. 1995; Calhoun 1995; Callinicos 1988; Gagnon and the Bradley Commission on History in Schools 1989; Harvey 1989; Hobsbawm 1993; Hunt 1990, 1991; Kramer, Reid, and Barney 1994; Martin et al. 1995; Scott 1988; Stearns 1993; White 1966, 1978).

Revising History and History Teaching

Although history is only one of many disciplines experiencing challenge and transformation, the terms of its conflicts are greater, reflecting at least in part its importance (and also its vulnerability). History's revision is neither easily accomplished nor easily accepted. Gains (some of them great) do not come without costs (some of them also great). Chief among the avowed casualties are two large costs for teaching and learning: the loudly proclaimed "decline of historical literacy" and the loss of encompassing "historical synthesis." As Kramer et al. (1994) report, "The most common critique of American education today stresses that the rising generation lacks even the most elementary knowledge of American history and the traditions of American culture" (p. 3). This situation is not new, they also note, a point insufficiently appreciated. The issue, of course, is not history and historical understanding in and of themselves but also national identity.

History has generally played a more fundamental role than literature in the creation and maintenance of national identities. . . . This traditional social function of historians has given way increasingly to another social function: the rediscovery of lost or ignored or excluded people who never entered the "canon" of events that constituted the collective national history and identity. (pp. 4-5)

The challenges to, and the implications for, teaching history across the curriculum and across the disciplines today are many. Old and more recent misunderstandings obstruct much needed clarification and revision. A renewed focus on historical context and historical imagination, as this chapter argues, is now demanded—a necessity whose pursuit has the potential to revise much social science as well as historical practice including the classroom.

Effective history telling and learning never are a matter of "all the facts"—or all the people's stories—"that fit." Nor are they a matter of a biased selection alone, no matter how inspiring or comforting they might be. Neither historical understanding nor history teaching is cumulative, itself a misleading approach to a more inclusive pluralism that requires more than revision through addition. No single canvas (to use one of history's common, if also misleading, metaphors) incorporates all peoples and their complex relationships that cut across lines of power, class, race, ethnicity, gender, generation, place, and the like about which history has so much to teach. Neither is learning an inclusive, relational history or a larger dimension of historical understanding mainly a matter of memorization for recall on testing or other confirming demand. Nor is there a singular or unitary historical canon of names, dates, events, texts, stories, and lessons—the stuff claimed for an inadequately conceptualized historical literacy, based on the fallacious model of Hirsch's (1987) "cultural literacy."[2] In such anachronistic and dangerous formulations, a comforting and nostalgic historical synthesis is meant to serve all manners of good, from socialization to integration and consensual understanding. That is not the only view of history or path to the past and back again.

History: Context, Understanding, and Teaching

History is a distinct form of inquiry and a mode of understanding. As Katz (1995) summarizes, "More than a set of stories about the past, 'history' signifies an epistemology; through constructing narratives that order experience into processes that occur over time, people explain everything from the mundane aspects of daily life to the great social institutions that channel their experience" (p. 10). From a different but related perspective, Tilly (1981) notes, "The integration of time and place into the very argument marks off historical analysis" (p. 7). Thus, history comprises a distinct approach or approaches that contribute to history's distinctiveness as a mode of thought, a way of knowing. These are hallmarks of history teaching as well, although perhaps not emphasized as explicitly or as formally as they might be.

More than a canon of facts, events/dates, texts, and stories, cognitively, history is a form of understanding; metaphorically, it is a way of seeing, a way of knowing.[3] History, moreover, is important not only in and of itself but also for other disciplines and outside the academy, as discussed later. The extent of its value, indeed the merit of its claim to a central place for and in teaching, might be clearer if history were not taught so commonly in ways that neglect, obstruct, or contradict the significance that derives from its distinctiveness.

Historical thinking is not easy to grasp. It requires practice and constructive criticism. It is tricky to learn and to teach, and it must be presented explicitly.[4] Far too often, an emphasis on memorizing facts whose origin, provenance, and significance are not effectively conveyed or challenged—names and dates, wars and presidents, generals and battles, "one damned thing after another"—or stories with their agreed-on meanings or lessons, negates any efforts to nurture a useful foundation for historical understanding. That history often is taught poorly, with the consequence of driving students of all ages away from any effort to know the past and value its continuing significance, is not exactly news.

Recently, a rhetoric of historical literacy (Gagnon and the Bradley Commission on History in Schools 1989) has emerged in the wake of cultural literacy. Stearns (1991) observes that the approach "converts history from analytic instrument to memorization enforcer" (p. 21). Not only is the rhetoric—and ensuing war of words—of historical literacy misleading; also compromised, if not lost entirely, is a more fully developed and expansive concept of historical literacy as a set of critical skills and abilities that contribute to the development of an encompassing and useful historical understanding. It is important to avoid adding to the ever lengthening lists of forms and brands of literacies that threaten to drown us. Nevertheless, such a historical literacy could be grounded in a notion of history as a distinctive form of thought and understanding based on a particular mode of

understanding in historical context. That might provide a novel approach to teaching history and judiciously using historical approaches and historical situations in other courses.

Despite the impact of the memorizing and canonizing movements, there does seem to be a growing awareness, at least, of the importance of teaching and cultivating historical thinking. Introducing the American Historical Association forum on "Thinking Historically in the Classroom," Blackey (1995) states,

Knowing that sooner or later much of the content we teach is forgotten . . . surely there is something more our discipline conveys. At the heart of that something is what we call thinking historically, a critical way of understanding and learning about the past that can be carried over into the study of other disciplines and beyond school walls, a way of thinking that can help our students to become better human beings. (p. 1)

Historical Imagination

Among the qualities that contribute directly to historical thinking and understanding, most important are historical context and historical imagination. Together, as they necessarily must be, they constitute much of the distinctiveness fairly claimed for a critical discipline of history. The work of historical context is to discipline what I call historical imagination. To put it too simply, we require the trained and practiced abilities of historical imagination to envision or imagine the realm of possible pasts that we never can know or experience directly. In acts of historical understanding, we then make our choices from that domain. How we fashion those choices, in turn, contributes to the possibilities open to us for communicating that knowledge to others via one medium or another, whether in spoken words or written words, still pictures or moving ones, nonfiction or "historical fiction." We can only know the past partially through its incomplete remains in the many forms of evidence that are themselves critically reviewed. The ways in which knowledgeable students of history reconstruct those pasts, and how well they do so, depend to a considerable extent on well-developed and critically tested abilities to imagine a past (or pasts) that fits within the terms of our larger understanding of and expectations for that particular historical time and place and the persons who lived then and there.

Historical imagination can and should be taught and fostered on all levels of instruction, both formally and informally, and should be taught explicitly. I have found the regular use of visual materials very effective—slides and transparencies of paintings, sketches, photographs, documentary films, historical films, docudramas, and material culture. When driven by questions that are regularly redefined, and when combined with an intelligent mix of primary and secondary sources, presentation of explicit conceptual and explanatory schemata (including alternative ones for students to consider), consideration of flexible and variable periodization and chronology, attention to the agency and constraints of historical persons and their circumstances, and classroom discussion (which encourages questioning and criticism), historical understanding is advanced by stimulating historical imagination (in conjunction with an appreciation of historical context). I also find rich case studies of particular places very useful in this effort, sometimes rivaling typically touted primary sources. The latter function best, I think, when they present multiple voices, viewpoints, and experiences.[5]

This is particularly useful in my urban history classes where the visual sense, on the one hand, and the importance of place, on the other, are so important in grasping the historical but also in courses in social history. I take the effort furthest in the interdisciplinary studies and graduate versions of a course on the history of growing up—children, adolescents, youth—in America in comparative perspective. A wide range of secondary source books and articles drawn from most disciplines across the human sciences accompanies primary source readings. Questions of theory and comparisons are raised from the outset. So too are problems in the relationship of past and present that impinge on both broad-based popular understanding and policy formulation—the play of the past in the present. First-person sources such as autobiographies, memoirs or semifictionalized life histories, and fiction join the mix of visual "texts." In class sessions and in short writing assignments, we explicitly probe the advantages and limits of various sources and their genres—how we can "read," assess, and use them—as well as the strengths and weaknesses of various disciplinary and interdisciplinary perspectives.[6]

Historical imagination, therefore, is needed to engage the past, to understand it so far as possible on its own terms as well as on those of today. We cannot fully escape the latter, although in the "cause" of "objectivity" we seek to "control" and/or enhance our own consciousness of its impacts and influences. Hunt (1991) elaborates, "History is a search for truth that always eludes the historian but also informs [his or] her work, but this truth is not an objective one in the sense of a truth standing outside the practices and concerns of the historian." Hunt defines history "as an ongoing tension between the stories that have been told and stories that might be told," concluding that "we cannot get at the 'real' truth and yet we must always continue to try to do so" (p. 109).

Historical thinking forms a mediation between our reconstructions of those times, places, and persons past and our own times (and our own selves as well). Necessarily, that mediation also reflects differences among us. Inseparable from the spirit or stuff of historical inquiry itself, this awareness mandates acknowledgment—and also real appreciation—of the contingent, probabilistic, and qualified objective basis of historical knowledge and historical understanding. Those qualities contribute centrally to an expansive and encompassing conception of historical context itself.

The Importance of Context

Historical thinking and historical understanding require not only historical imagination but also historical context. As already noted, together those elements constitute much of history's distinctiveness and undergird much of its achievement. Historical context serves to discipline what I call historical imagination. More than any other quality, the centrality of context distinguishes history—both rhetorically and substantively—from other modes of inquiry and understanding. Thompson (1972) also enunciates this principle: "The discipline of history is, above all, the discipline of context; each fact can be given meaning only within an ensemble of other meanings" (p. 45). Breaking free of the limiting boundaries of definitions rooted in dead facts of dead objects and dead subjects recounted in simple and certain story-telling form and other caricatures of history, Thompson also endorses an expansive but historically centered interdisciplinarity.[7]

There are many forms and levels of historical context and modes of contextualization. Contexts themselves are multiple and variable, as are historical voices and cultures. Occasionally a source of confusion, this variability and dynamism more often are sources of interpretive strength and flexibility. Thus, active conceptualizations of historical contexts can include the specificity of persons at risk and their cultural and physical resources and environments. Contexts also incorporate precedents, antecedents, influences, relationships, and (with great care) outcomes.

Historians, after all, often (if not always) have a good sense of how things came out and at least some of the impacts and implications. In this way, one key component of historical thinking lies in the special ability to look both backward and forward at once. Theoretical and comparative considerations, regardless of how formally or explicitly present, also contribute to an active and robust understanding and development of context and contextualization. These elements all have a place in teaching history and in using history appropriately in teaching in other disciplines. History provides a rich arena, a "laboratory" for many questions and topics. The specificity and the concreteness of the context, however, never can be neglected or slighted. Approaches that employ multiple and variable approaches to historical contextualization are especially useful, not only for advancing comparisons but also for recognizing and probing multivocal, multicultural histories.

Historical context and historical imagination, working inextricably and inseparably together, shift the possibilities for historical understanding in the direction of probabilities in the forming of historical knowledge rather than in the direction of the imaginary or the fictitious. Times and places, as well as their casts of actors and rosters of contingent possibilities, constitute a foundation that begins to define but certainly does not completely describe historical context.

In history's house, there are many types, levels, and uses of context. Levi (1992) declares, "Contextualization . . . can mean many things" (p. 106). He points to different ways of "reading" social context, for example, "as a place which imputes meaning to seemingly 'strange' or 'anomalous' particulars by revealing their hidden significance and consequently their fit with a system" or "discovering the social context in which an apparently anomalous or insignificant fact assumes meaning"

(p. 107). Levi denotes two other forms of contextualization. One, which has been popular and influential especially in intellectual and cultural histories—and their teaching—and in social theory, "understands cultural context as a process of collocating an idea within the boundaries prescribed by the languages available. . . . [It] sees context as being dictated by the language and idioms available and used by a particular group of people in a particular situation to organize, for example, their power struggles" (pp. 107-108). The other, which underlies a great deal of comparative history—and its teaching across disciplines—"consists of the formal, comparative placing of an event, form of behaviour, or concept in a series of others which are similar, though they may be separated in time and space" (p. 108). Here, the work of context involves identifying a series of things that share significant characteristics, but it also can function on the "level of analogy."

"The new cultural historians," Kramer et al. (1994) explain, "make the recurring and central points that historical writing depends on specific forms of cultural meaning (e.g., narrative traditions) and that historical knowledge carries the unavoidable traces of the cultural context in which it appears (i.e., its own historicity)" (p. 6). Influenced by literary criticism and cultural anthropology, recent cultural historians "stress that both the events of history and the writing about history are embedded in deep structures of linguistic and symbolic meanings that enable people to describe and organize the world." The slogan that all history is historiography is hardly a simplistic understanding; it can be a telling commentary and a guide. "This conception of historical knowledge places knowledge itself firmly within history and historical processes" (pp. 6-7).

This critical perspective on the construction of historical knowledge and historical understanding suggests an approach to teaching history based in a dynamic conceptualization of historiography itself. Such an approach might involve practice and criticism in "doing history" as historiography or, conversely, in historiography as "doing history." This enables students to approach history dynamically with questions and understandings that are repeatedly tested and critically discarded, refined, or redefined. That effort depends on searching for contingent human relationships and connections within the past but also within the present, explicit analytic and interpretive methodologies, and a firm appreciation of history's great strengths and its limits.

Among the instructional uses of history is the vitally important opportunity to test ideas, concepts, questions, interpretations, and the like in the richest laboratory the human sciences can offer—the laboratory of history. Thompson (1972) raises the question of the temporal limitations (i.e., historical context and historical imagination) of social science concepts across the epochs of historical time. Our related concern falls on testing questions, connections, interpretations, and understandings more generally. Thompson advises,

Where the influence of the social sciences is undoubtedly most fruitful, it is, at exactly the same point, most treacherous: in the comparative method. For it is precisely at the point where these 17th-century families become the nuclear family; where these 13th-century Russian peasants and those 19th-century Irish cottiers become the peasantry; where these Chartist Plug Rioters and those Communards become violence in industrial society; where, indeed, 18th-century Birmingham and a bazaar in 16th-century Persia and a village in 20th-century Ecuador become assimilated as pre-industrial society—it is at this point that the integument of the historical discipline comes under extreme strain and is in danger of being punctured to let in a gush of abstract typological air. (p. 46)

In the classroom, as in other forms of communication (all of them pedagogical), I strongly agree. The risks must be recognized and students must be explicitly forewarned, even to the point of sharing in the challenge. Thompson (1972) concludes, "Each new concept so gained must be thrust back into the ensemble of meanings of a specific historical context once again, and many of the concepts—perhaps the majority—will crumble to mere dust of irrelevancy in the immersion. Perhaps the continual making and breaking of the integument is the best that we can do" (p. 46). It is hard to imagine a more vital pedagogy or one we need more today.

Some Uses of Historical Understanding, or Why History Matters

In the place of a conclusion, I briefly identify a handful among the many areas in which historical understanding is urgently demanded more than ever before. If the larger point is granted, then the necessity of placing a renewed and revised historical discipline at the center of curricula across many subjects and disciplines needs to be confronted. And if that point is granted, then the next steps come in removing or reducing the many boundaries and constraints, institutional or otherwise, that obstruct the types of broadly interdisciplinary learning that students in the late 20th and 21st centuries undoubtedly and deeply need. Consider, as primary examples, these four dimensions: (1) the hermeneutic depth of historical specificity and the gains possible from embracing that depth, (2) the historical foundations of social research and the benefits that come from recognizing them, (3) the historical foundations of contemporary societies and history's usefulness in understanding them, and (4) the uses of history for foreseeing the future along with the past.[8]

With respect to the first dimension, Calhoun (1995) boldly and persuasively sounds a siren call for a thoroughgoing historical specification of social theory and social analysis more generally. "The issue of historical specificity arises at all levels of analysis. It also concerns all time periods" (pp. 86-87). It is historical changes that delineate the context in which theories are produced over time. For Calhoun, most important in this respect is "the demarcation of epochs in human history and the construction of conceptual frameworks adequate to epochal changes." Historical specificity is, therefore, especially significant "for debates about whether modernity is giving way to postmodernity, whether theories based on the economic strategies of individual capitalists explain much about contemporary capitalism" (pp. 86-87).

With respect to the second dimension, Tilly (1981) comments that from the 1960s, "history began to matter" (p. 38). Successful work by historians of a social scientific bent was one influence—demography and family, crime, voting, urban structure, and social mobility. So too was the "disillusion with models of modernization and development." Social scientists gave social research new historical foundations (if selectively) as they regained—at least in part—the historical foundations of social science. The benefits are many, "enlarging the place of historically grounded theories and challenging the place of theories that disregard time," "expanding the opportunities to formulate and test models of long-term change on reliable evidence concerning substantial blocks of time," and "increasing the numbers of sociologists who . . . detect what is problematic" (p. 44).

The work of Katz (1987, 1995) illustrates the third dimension, the historical foundations of contemporary societies and the benefits of recognizing them. Katz boldly articulates the view that understanding the historical origins and historical development of contemporary social structures and relationships is useful and necessary to understand their contemporary locations and operations. Both, in turn, are required if we seek to change them. In the effort to reconnect past and present—to the advantage of both—Katz advances a strong argument for the salience of history and the widest instruction in and dissemination of historical understanding. In his *Reconstructing American Education,* for example, Katz (1987) argues, "Contemporary concepts such as public education, modern organizational forms, especially bureaucracy, and institutional structures such as the multiversity originated as choices among alternative solutions to problems of public policy. They reflect circumstances at the time of their origin and the priorities of their founders" (p. 1).

Katz endorses White's (1966) declaration that historians' task is "less to remind men [and women] of their obligation to the past than to force upon them an awareness of how the past could be used to effect an ethically responsible transition from present to future" (p. 132). Although Katz (1995) recognizes that no concrete set of policy recommendations flows directly from historical analysis, he suggests that "understanding the origins and dimensions of a social issue can lead in very different policy directions" (p. 8). Maintaining that "history has meaning for women and men on the front line of social action," Katz emphasizes that historians and other scholars provide "reassurance and legitimation. . . . Academics validate their discontents, reassure them [that] they are not crazy or paranoid, and give them ammunition for their fights." Scholars "help them avoid blaming themselves by giving them the information to understand their situation better. They learn to locate themselves in time and space; they see the press of history and the web of connections that anchors their activities and constrains change" (p. 8).

To "transcend the past" means to take its powers seriously and to learn deeply from it.

Herein lies a need and a foundation for a renewed historical basis for pedagogy. Serving various levels of education and seizing varying modes for presentation and communication, the proper spheres for the contribution of historical context and historical imagination go well beyond the usual boundaries of venues labeled "history." Their proper place includes courses not only in history but in other curricular areas and other broadly instructional media across the human sciences, both inside and outside the academy. And herein lies a powerful motivation for linking pedagogically the valuable insights of Calhoun, Tilly, and Katz across the three dimensions.

Historical understanding also can provide a guide for the future as well as the past. Enunciating the fourth of these dimensions of history's pedagogical and public contributions, Hobsbawm (1981) proclaims that historians are superior forecasters because "all prediction about the real world rests to a great extent on some sort of inferences about the future from what has happened in the past, that is to say, from history" (p. 4). Historians' value as foreseers depends primarily on two qualities:

First, historians' forecasts, retrospective though they be, are precisely about the complex and all-embracing reality of human life, about the other things which are never equal and which are in fact not "other things" but [rather] the system of relationships from which statements about human life in society can never be entirely abstracted. And second, any historical discipline worthy of the name attempts to discover precisely those patterns of interaction in society, those mechanisms and tendencies of change and transformation, and those directions of the transformation in society which alone provide an adequate framework for forecasting. (pp. 8-9)

Unfamiliar, formally disavowed as antithetical to history as traditionally construed, and seldom admitted consciously, this dimension follows from, and in turn reiterates, history's relationships and responsibilities to the future as well as to the past. When taken with the first three dimensions and located on a foundation wrought of historical context and historical imagination, it completes the weaving of an extraordinarily rich and immensely useful web outlining the ways and uses of history. However formally or explicitly pursued—it ranges widely and flexibly from formal prescription to more diffuse orientation—this web constitutes at once an agenda for revising historical instruction and a historical core for revising the curriculum embracing the social and human sciences—for looking backward and forward; for the sake of the past, present, and future; for the young and the not so young.

Notes

1. See, for example, the responses, widely reported in the press, to the National Assessment of Educational Progress's 1994 U.S. History Report Card such as Nash (1995) and Loewen (1995). See also Stearns (1991, 1993), Bender (1986), Foner (1981), Gagnon and the Bradley Commission on History in Schools (1989), Gutman (1987), Hamerow (1987), Hirsch (1987), and Thelen (1987), among a huge outpouring. See, more generally, Wilson (1995), Williams (1995), Berman (1992), Bérubé, and Nelson (1995).

2. Such formulations also do a disservice to serious conceptualizations of literacy in historical contexts. The choice of words here derives from Gagnon and the Bradley Commission on History in Schools (1989). See Graff (1979, 1989, 1993); see also Stearns (1991, 1993) and Kramer, Reid, and Barney (1994). On synthesis, in particular, see Bender (1986) and Thelen (1987).

3. Much popular but sometimes academic confusion, too, follows from blurring the different meanings or "levels" of history, in par-

ticular, history as the past that has occurred before the present; history as the distinct discipline whose task is to record and study the past through its incomplete remains and typically (but not exclusively) by a special trained, certified, and practiced caste called historians; and history as the result or product of that study, usually in the form of written or printed words within a limited realm of formats and conventions but increasingly in different media and genres.

4. For example, I include in every undergraduate history course I teach an introduction to historical thinking that offers a quick sketch, literally a sketch or a simple "model" of the major cognitive steps—"baby epistemology," a good friend and philosopher called it. The model suggests how historians and students taking history classes move themselves from the incomplete remains of the past to question forming and testing, evidence and facts, probing, connection making, conclusion forming, interpretation making, and presenting those interpretations.

5. For the purpose of this chapter, I am using "primary" and "secondary" sources in conventional, normative ways. There are other approaches to sources that also are important. In the American Historical Association *Perspectives* discussion, see in particular the comments of Stearns (1991).

6. I cannot reproduce the syllabus here, but it appears in the March 1999 issue of *Journal of American History*. I also require a group project that involves researching past and present connections and results in an oral presentation to the class as well as a short research paper. In addition to historical and social science materials including my reader, *Growing Up in America* (Graff 1987), the readings include Douglass's *Narrative of the Life of . . . an American Slave,* Larcom's *A New England Girlhood,* Eggleston's *The Hoosier Schoolmaster,*

Crane's *Maggie: A Girl of the Streets,* Yezierska's *The Bread Givers,* Simon's *Bronx Primitive,* Wright's *Black Boy,* Doctorow's *World's Fair,* and Salinger's *The Catcher in the Rye.* Visual materials (e.g., films, photos, paintings) include *Lord of the Flies, The Retour de Martin Guerre, The Wild Child,* presentations from the American Social History Project and Canada's Visual Past, *The Molders of Troy, My Brilliant Career, Rebel without a Cause, High School, Street Wise,* and *Heathers.*

7. In addition to Tilly (1981) and Smith (1992), see in particular Sewell (1992) and Calhoun (1995). Smith (1992) warns against a contextualism that substitutes inadequately for periodization as history's defining temporal dimension. Yet, periodization and temporality also stand among the primary characteristics of historical context, along with place or space, historical processes and historical possibilities typically involving the centrality of the relationships between structure and agency. Calhoun (1995:35-36) is especially cogent on the varieties and importance of context and contextualization.

8. Other, no less significant areas and issues today comprise public and applied history, including policy history, and history's and historians' broad relationships to political and cultural power discursively, educationally, and institutionally, including the responsibilities of scholars and teachers. For now, I can only underscore that they too are worthy of notice. Among a large and diffuse literature, see Callahan, Caplan, and Jennings (1985), Neustadt and May (1986), Rothman and Wheeler (1981), Seixas (1983), Stearns (1991, 1993), Wertsch and O'Connor (1994), Wineburg (1994), and the journals *The Public Historian, Journal of Policy History,* and *Journal of Social History;* more generally, see Appleby et al. (1994), Bunzel et al. (1995), Burke (1992), Foner (1981), Gagnon and the Bradley Com-

mission on History in Schools (1989), Graff (1989, 1993, 1995), Gutman (1987), Hobsbawm (1993), Hunt (1990, 1991), Kramer et al. (1994), Martin et al. (1995), Scott (1988, 1992), Thelen (1987), and White (1966, 1978).

References

Ankersmit, Frank and Hans Kellner, eds. 1995. *A New Philosophy of History.* Chicago: University of Chicago Press.

Appleby, Joyce, Lynn Hunt, and Margaret Jacob. 1994. *Telling the Truth about History.* New York: Norton.

Bauman, Zygmunt. 1987. *Legislators and Interpreters: On Modernity, Post-modernity and Intellectuals.* Ithaca, NY: Cornell University Press.

Bender, Thomas. 1986. "Wholes and Parts: The Need for Synthesis in American History." *Journal of American History* 73:120-36.

Berkhofer, Robert F., Jr. 1969. *A Behavioral Approach to Historical Analysis.* New York: Free Press.

———. 1995. *Beyond the Great Story: History as Text and Discourse.* Cambridge, MA: Harvard University Press.

Berman, Paul, ed. 1992. *Debating P.C.: The Controversy over Political Correctness on College Campuses.* New York: Dell.

Bérubé, Michael and Cary Nelson, eds. 1995. *Higher Education under Fire: Politics, Economics, and the Crisis of the Humanities.* New York: Routledge.

Blackey, Robert, ed. 1995. "Thinking Historically in the Classroom." *Perspectives* (American Historical Association), October, pp. 1, 4, 23-35, 37.

Bloch, Marc. 1953. *The Historian's Craft.* Translated by Peter Putnam. New York: Vintage.

Bunzel, Martin, Bonnie G. Smith, and John Higham. 1995. "Truth, Objectivity, and History: An Exchange" [on *Telling the Truth about History,* with a "Response" by Joyce Appleby, Lynn Hunt, and Margaret Jacobs. *Journal of the History of Ideas* 56:651-80.

Burke, Peter. 1992. "Overture: The New History, Its Past and Its Future." In *New Perspectives,* edited by Peter Burke. University Park: Pennsylvania State University Press.

Calhoun, Craig. 1995. *Critical Social Theory.* Oxford, UK: Blackwell.

Callahan, Daniel, Arthur L. Caplan, and Bruce Jennings, eds. 1985. *Applying the Humanities.* New York: Plenum.

Callinicos, Alex. 1988. *Making History: Agency, Structure, and Change in Social Theory.* Ithaca, NY: Cornell University Press.

Carr, Edward Hallett. 1961. *What Is History?* New York: Vintage.

Foner, Eric. 1981. "History in Crisis." *Commonwealth* 18:723-26.

Fukuyama, Francis. 1992. *The End of History and the Last Man.* New York: Free Press.

Gagnon, Paul and the Bradley Commission on History in Schools, eds. 1989. *Historical Literacy: The Case for History in American Education.* New York: Macmillan.

Giddens, Anthony. 1990. *The Consequences of Modernity.* Stanford, CA: Stanford University Press.

Graff, Harvey J. 1979. *The Literacy Myth: Literacy and Social Structure in the Nineteenth-Century City.* New York: Academic Press.

———. ed. 1987. *Growing Up in America: Historical Experiences.* Detroit, MI: Wayne State University Press.

———. 1989. "Critical Literacy versus Cultural Literacy: Reading Signs of the Times— A Review of E. D. Hirsch, Jr., *Cultural Literacy.*" *Interchange* 20:46-52.

———. 1993. "Literacy, Myths, and Legacies: Lessons from the Past/Thoughts for the Future." *Interchange* 24:271-86.

———. 1995. *Conflicting Paths: Growing Up in America.* Cambridge, MA: Harvard University Press.

Gutman, Herbert. 1987. "Historical Consciousness in Contemporary America." Pp. 395-412 in *Power and Culture: Essays on the American Working Class,* edited by Ira Berlin. New York: Pantheon.

Hamerow, Theodore. 1987. "The Crisis in History." Pp. 3-38 in *Reflections on History,* edited by Theodore Hamerow. Madison: University of Wisconsin Press.

Harvey, David. 1989. *The Condition of Postmodernity.* Oxford, UK: Blackwell.

Hirsch, E. D., Jr. 1987. *Cultural Literacy: What Every American Needs to Know.* Boston: Houghton Mifflin.

Hobsbawm, E. J. 1972. "The Social Function of the Past: Some Questions." *Past and Present* 55:3-17.

———. 1981. "Looking Forward: History and the Future." *New Left Review* 125:3-20.

———. 1993. "The New Threat to History." *New York Review,* December, pp. 62-64.

Hughes, H. Stuart. 1964. *History as Art and as Science.* New York: Harper & Row.

Hunt, Lynn. 1990. "History beyond Social Theory." Pp. 94-111 in *The States of "Theory": History, Art, and Critical Discourse,* edited by David Carroll. New York: Columbia University Press.

———. 1991. "History as Gesture: Or, the Scandal of History." Pp. 91-107 in *The Consequences of Theory: Selected Papers from the English Institute,* edited by Jonathan Arac and Barbara Johnson. Baltimore, MD: Johns Hopkins University Press.

Jenkins, Keith. 1991. *Re-thinking History.* London: Routledge.

———. 1995. *On "What Is History?" from Carr and Elton to Rorty and White.* London: Routledge.

Katz, Michael B. 1987. *Reconstructing American Education.* Cambridge, MA: Harvard University Press.

———. 1995. *Improving Poor People: The Welfare State, the "Underclass," and Urban*

Schools as History. Princeton, NJ: Princeton University Press.

Kramer, Lloyd, Donald Reid, and William L. Barney, eds. 1994. *Learning History in America: Schools, Cultures, and Politics.* Minneapolis: University of Minnesota Press.

Landes, David S. and Charles Tilly, eds. 1971. *History as Social Science: The Behavioral and Social Sciences Survey—History Panel.* Englewood Cliffs, NJ: Prentice Hall.

Levi, Giovanni. 1992. "On Microhistory." Pp. 92-113 in *New Perspectives on Historical Writing,* edited by Peter Burke. University Park: Pennsylvania State University Press.

Loewen, James W. 1995. "The Politics of What We Tell Ourselves about the Past." *Radical Historians Newsletter,* November, pp. 1, 3-4, 13.

Martin, Raymond, Joan W. Scott, and Cushing Strout. 1995. "Forum: Telling the Truth about History." *History and Theory* 34:320-99.

Marwick, Arthur. 1970. *The Nature of History.* New York: Delta.

Nash, Gary. 1995. "There Goes the Republic." *Perspectives* (American Historical Association), December, pp. 29-30.

Neustadt, Richard E. and Ernest R. May. 1986. *Thinking in Time: The Uses of History for Decision Makers.* New York: Free Press.

Rothman, David J. and S. Wheeler, eds. 1981. *Social History and Social Policy.* New York: Academic Press.

Scott, Joan Wallach. 1988. *Gender and the Politics of History.* New York: Columbia University Press.

———. 1992. "Women's History." Pp. 42-66 in *New Perspectives on Historical Writing,* edited by Peter Burke. University Park: Pennsylvania State University Press.

Seixas, Peter. 1983. "Historical Understanding among Adolescents in a Multi-cultural Setting." *Curriculum Inquiry* 23:301-27.

Sewell, William H., Jr. 1992. "A Theory of Structure: Duality, Agency, and Transformation." *American Journal of Sociology* 98:1-29.

Smith, Daniel Scott. 1992. "Context, Time, History." Pp. 13-32 in *Theory, Method, and Practice in Social and Cultural History,* edited by Peter Karsten and John Modell. New York: New York University Press.

Stearns, Peter N. 1991. "The Challenge of 'Historical Literacy.'" *Perspectives* (American Historical Association), April, pp. 21-23.

———. 1993. *Meaning over Memory: Recasting the Teaching of Culture and History.* Chapel Hill: University of North Carolina Press.

Thelen, David, ed. 1987. "Roundtable: Synthesis in American History." *Journal of American History* 74:107-30.

Thompson, E. P. 1972. "Anthropology and the Discipline of Historical Context." *Midland History* 3:41-55.

Tilly, Charles. 1981. *As Sociology Meets History.* New York: Academic Press.

Wertsch, James V. and Kevin O'Connor. 1994. "Multivoicedness in Historical Representation: American College Students' Accounts of the Origins of the United States." *Journal of Narrative and Life History* 4:295-309.

White, Hayden V. 1966. "The Burden of History." *History and Theory* 5:111-34.

———. 1978. *Tropics of Discourse: Essays in Culture Criticism.* Baltimore, MD: Johns Hopkins University Press.

Williams, Jeffrey, ed. 1995. *PC Wars: Politics and Theory in the Academy.* New York: Routledge.

Wilson, John K. 1995. *The Myth of Political Correctness.* Durham, NC: Duke University Press.

Wineburg, Samuel S., ed. 1994. "The Teaching and Learning of History: Special Issue." *Educational Psychologist* 29, no. 2.

Doonesbury

BY GARRY TRUDEAU

Doonesbury

BY GARRY TRUDEAU

DOONESBURY

by Garry Trudeau

Section C

Professors in a Changing University and a Changing Society

Some debates are larger than the institution of higher education and go beyond its campuses. Here, the social world of higher education and the larger social world in which it exists sometimes cooperate and sometimes collide.

Colleges and universities always have had to negotiate fluid and shifting boundaries with the state, the marketplace, and the community. This negotiation process is evident in recurrent conflicts over the resources and demands of external patrons and constituents, from corporations and government agencies to sports-loving alumni, and in efforts to make our teaching relevant to contemporary issues. How we draw appropriate boundaries in negotiating or resisting external demands, in holding ourselves accountable to various constituencies, and in interacting with our students raises fundamental moral and pedagogical issues.

Specifically, the essays in this section focus on the nature of changes in society and the university and their impact on college teaching. They explore the shifting nature of boundaries between higher education and the outside world, the danger to the basic purposes and moral integrity of our educational communities posed by their permeability, and the role of tenure and academic freedom in maintaining appropriate boundaries. The authors write about the threats posed by corporatization and the marketplace, the growth of part-time exploited labor, attacks on tenure, and proposals for post-tenure review—again, all issues that Trudeau candidly observes. They also deal with issues of ethics and justice in admissions, hiring, and disciplinary procedures, which have been raised by recent controversies over affirmative action and sexual harassment. How we as individuals deal with these complex and controversial issues not only shapes what we do and how we define ourselves but also offers a model to those considering careers in tomorrow's universities.

Obstacles to innovative teaching, Howard Aldrich and Sølvi Lille-jord argue (Chapter 25), are created when the market-driven efficiency logic that dominates our economy permeates the academy and subordinates the logic of discovery. The goal-driven logic of control, which governs most administrative behaviors, focuses on efficient resource allocation, whereas the value-driven logic of discovery is primarily concerned with student learning. Faculty committed to innovative teaching, the authors suggest, need to work for greater cooperation among departments, more support for teacher training programs, and departmental leaders willing to challenge the logic of control. Recent developments, such as administrative efforts to introduce systems of responsibility-based budgeting that tie resource allocation to departmental and college enrollment levels, suggest that the logic of control continually threatens to subordinate the logic of discovery.

A strategy to counter this, improve the quality of our teaching, and respond to growing demands for relevance and accountability is offered by David M. Newman (Chapter 26). The proper response, he claims, is to connect our disciplinary knowledge to the "real world" and thus bridge the gaps that currently separate us from our students and the community. Newman's essay makes a persuasive case for the potential benefits of enhancing the personal, social, and process relevance of our courses. In other words, he argues that we need to draw the social worlds of the university and everyday life closer together. To the extent that we use common experiences and concerns to bring students to new, more complex understandings, this shrinks the generations and brings the experience of various cultures, "new majority" students, and other social worlds to enrich the classroom. However, the quest for relevance brings numerous potential dangers including the possibility that demands for relevance may produce a narrow utilitarianism. In addition, encouraging students to connect the materials we teach to their personal lives is likely to make some students very uncomfortable because it asks them to engage in intense critical scrutiny of what might be painful experiences. The success of such an endeavor presupposes a high level of trust between students and faculty; clear norms governing the disclosure of sensitive private information; recognition of the faculty's power over students; and an understanding of how student perceptions of that power are shaped by a professor's gender, race, and sexuality. Professors are forced to confront difficult ethical issues of privacy and disclosure when seeking the approval of human subject committees for their research. In teaching, this too often is a neglected consideration. We think that we are likely to confront such issues in teaching more frequently than in the past, with the increasing use of pedagogies aimed at promoting personal relevance via active and experiential learning.

At the other extreme, from concerns about the individual's personal history arises concerns about whether the large shadow cast by corporations should cover higher education. Lawrence C. Soley (Chapter 27) identifies this as a market-based threat to innovative, high-quality teaching—the growth of corporate- and Pentagon-sponsored research. In a strong statement, Soley documents the growing power of outside funders of research to set the agenda of universities and turn faculty into entrepreneurs and bureaucrats more concerned with acquiring large grants and meeting the needs of corporations than with teaching and learning. He believes that research and teaching are necessarily antithetical, in direct contrast to another often stated dictum that research and teaching go hand in hand, and that certainly the latter cannot be done by those who have abandoned the former. In his view, highly specialized research is unrelated to, and subversive of, our undergraduate teaching mission. More and more faculty time is devoted to research and is, therefore, largely responsible for higher tuition costs, reduced teaching loads, and low-quality teaching. Our own experiences and observations of excellent teachers suggest that neither extreme is accurate. There are instances in which research has enhanced graduate and undergraduate education, giving students valuable learning experiences and making important contributions to the larger community.

Finally, doing research may be less important to quality teaching in many instances than is keeping up with a broad understanding of new research in relevant fields. In between the personal experiences of our students and the larger structures of higher education lies the future of our own lives including issues of faculty governance, part-time or adjunct faculty, and the viability of tenure and necessity of post-tenure review as well as who is allowed to be members of the professoriate and how our personal lives intersect with those of our students. Linda Ray Pratt (Chapter 28) explores the high cost of allowing market relations to dominate higher education, but she focuses on deteriorating working conditions that have accompanied the rapid growth of part-time faculty employment. The exploitation of part-time faculty, she says, is a threat to faculty governance, academic freedom, and faculty economic welfare. In Pratt's view, effective responses to administrative efforts to reap the cost-cutting benefits of cheap part-time labor include faculty unionization, the enforcement of appropriate professional standards, and limitations on graduate school enrollments.

Although the institution of tenure has not prevented the growth of part-time faculty employment, it has prevented the further commodification of academic labor, protected academic freedom, and enabled faculties to resist growing incursions of the marketplace and the state. Erwin Chemerinsky (Chapter 29) asks the pointed question of whether tenure is necessary, at this historical juncture, to protect academic freedom. He argues that no reasonable alternative has presented itself and that the First Amendment does not provide an adequate substitute for tenure. Richard Edwards (Chapter 30) argues that tenure is necessary for academic freedom because it enables us to ask inconvenient questions and fosters a culture of critical inquiry. As a privilege, tenure implies corresponding responsibilities, to our students and the larger society, as well as mechanisms of accountability to ensure that these responsibilities are not abrogated. Although many institutions already have effective procedures in place for disciplining unethical or nonproductive faculty, the current controversy over tenure suggests to us that the best way in which to defend ourselves against attacks on academic freedom is to put our own house in order by creating effective post-tenure review procedures. William G. Tierney (Chapter 31) points out that an effective system of post-tenure review will require answers to difficult questions concerning who gets reviewed, how often, and with what consequences. The punitive tone of the current discussion, and accompanying negative portraits of the faculty, suggests the danger of costly procedures based on a bureaucratic logic of control rather than on faculty-initiated and controlled measures that help to rebuild community.

The debate over affirmative action highlights divisions among academics over the legitimate purposes of our institutions. Whether race and gender should be relevant selection criteria depends on how we define the goals of our institutions and whether we see durable inequalities as rooted in group-based processes or based on individual differences. The contributions of Steven M. Cahn (Chapter 32) and Amy Gutmann (Chapter 33) offer very different answers to these questions. Whereas Cahn emphasizes the promotion of individual merit and equality of opportunity, Gutmann highlights the goal of educating a group of officeholders who reflect the larger population. Cahn rejects what he labels "preferential affirmative action" because he is incapable of answering the question of why we should privilege certain differences, such as those based on race and gender, but not others based on regional background, marital status, or military experience. In his view, group-based policies of preferential treatment foster stereotypical thinking and create role models with questionable credibility because their success is not based solely on individual merit. Gutmann counters with what we think is an appropriate sociological response. She contends that we must situate admissions policies in the larger context of the history of social deprivations experienced by various groups and the multiple purposes of universities. Given these purposes, grades and test scores are not adequate indicators of all relevant qualifications for admission. Taking account of race, in her view, does not necessarily violate the principle of nondiscrimination because universities serve as gatekeepers and educators of officeholders, not just as vehicles of individual mobility. She suggests that we can distinguish between "mindless or trivial diversity" and meaningful diversity by asking whether various forms of discrimination exacerbate a serious social problem or threaten the realization of democratic values.

The final essays in this section highlight further divisions among academics concerning appropriate boundaries—in this case, those separating students and faculty. Whereas bell hooks (Chapter 34) is concerned with preserving the passion that energizes teaching and learning by breaking down barriers between students and professors, Jane Gallop (Chapter 35) stakes out a highly controversial position that is likely to provoke many readers. Her defense of consensual sexual relations between students and professors, and her attack on what she sees as an overly repressive view of sexual harassment that denies students' agency and sexuality, repeatedly asserts that her sexual relations with students did not affect her professional relations with students in the classroom or her ability to judge their work fairly. Many readers are likely to question whether her students shared this assessment. The remaining two essays in this section stake out different positions on this highly controversial issue. Patrick Dilger (Chapter 36) anchors the other side of the continuum, describing and defining Yale University's new strict policy against student-faculty relations. Whereas hooks warns that efforts to eliminate or suppress eros in the classroom threaten to create an apartheid of instruction and a mind-body split that inhibits student learning, Bernice A. Pescosolido and Eleanor Miller (Chapter 37) remind us of our professional responsibility to confront the dangers inherent in the unregulated expression of passion in relationships of unequal power. The harsh reality is that we often are drawn to some students and not to others and that this may affect our investment in how and what they learn and our evaluations of their work. They also argue that different situations call for different solutions, with problems avoided if discussions about ethics were part of graduate training.

25

Stop Making Sense!
Why Aren't Universities Better
at Promoting Innovative Teaching?

Howard Aldrich and Sølvi Lillejord

We begin with a paradox. Over the past several decades, many calls have been issued for better teaching at the research university level, but little sign of real systemwide change is evident on most campuses. Instead, students complain, faculty strain, administrators vacillate, and tradition rules. Research universities are touted as centers of teaching and learning where instructors are free to innovate behind the protective walls of the university system. Thus, one might think that the special atmosphere of universities would promote the ready adoption of innovative approaches such as cooperative and team-based learning, but change has come quite slowly. Indeed, the most innovative teaching practices tend to be found on smaller college campuses, particularly in the community college system. For example, the Network for Cooperative Learning in Higher Education originated and is run from California State University, Dominguez Hills, and a glance through its directory of practitioners shows that most are based at community colleges and small private and state institutions.

Why is there such a disjuncture between our image of universities as innovative places and the actual teaching practices found on most

of them? We believe that faculty are caught at the intersection of two conflicting logics: a logic of control and a logic of discovery. A logic of control governs most administrative behaviors, permeating administrators' relationships with their faculties, whereas a logic of discovery characterizes the behavior of faculty on the frontier of new teaching practices, engaging in practices that fit uneasily into the logic of control. Neither of these logics is "higher" or "lower" in the scheme of things. Both represent coherent ways of looking at the goals and practices of universities, with market-based and resource dependence-based pressures usually leading toward the subordination of the logic of discovery to the logic of control.

The two logics basically embody two different forms of rationality. The logic of control is mainly a logic for or of structure, whereas the logic of discovery is first and foremost a logic for or of content. We often find the logic of discovery in college and university policy reports and speeches, where officials write and speak *as if* the logic of discovery permeates the area of education. Nevertheless, the logic of control has shown an increasing tendency to rule the daily practices of authorities. Weber (1968, 1976) argued that the coordination of

TABLE 25.1 The Two Logics: Control and Discovery

	Control	*Discovery*
Form of rationality	For or of structure; goal driven	For or of content; value driven
Indicators of success	Generic indicators of efficient resource allocation	Specific indicators of student learning
Constraints	Norm of faculty autonomy	Competition between faculty and departments
	Offices are understaffed	Lack of support for teaching training
	Need for quantifiable indicators	Subunit officials accept logic of control

people's actions in modern societies increasingly occurs more through money and bureaucratic power than through rituals, religion, and tradition. He called this process *Die Entzauberung der Welt,* a demystifying process that ruins the poetic qualities of life. Weber made a distinction between *Zweckrationalität* (goal-driven rationality) and *Wertrationalität* (value-driven rationality). As society has become increasingly bureaucratized, and as pressures toward rationality and efficiency have increased, goal-driven rationality has strengthened its grip on behaviors typically governed by tradition and ritual. This Weberian perspective has been further elaborated by Habermas (Honneth and Joas 1991), through his concept of the "life-world," and by Bourdieu (1980).

We begin with the assumption that many, if not most, faculty *do* want to improve their teaching. In spite of almost no support from their professional disciplinary groups, most faculty profess at least a passing interest in improving their classroom performance. Although surveys have found that faculty see their professional rewards coming primarily from their research, studies also have found that faculty value good teaching and would like to improve their own. This chapter is about the context in which faculty operate and in which they are forced to deal with conflicts between the two logics at nearly every turn.

The Two Logics

The two logics are embedded in the culture of the university system and are a consequence of the many organizational and institutional constraints on universities, administrators, and faculty. Each logic has its own internal coherence, with a supportive ideology that justifies a variety of practices. The logics are carried by the members of universities, who enact the logics in their own behaviors and thus keep them alive. Individual faculty often find themselves at the intersection of the two logics, such as when a faculty member becomes an administrator, and the choices they make under those conditions keep alive the tension that we describe later. We are *not* arguing that the university is bifurcated into two opposing groups—administrators versus faculty—because the logics permeate the behavior of both. However, for ease of exposition, we often write as if the two logics have adherents divided into opposing camps. In Table 25.1, we summarize the differences.

The Logic of Control

University administrators, both public and private, work in an enrollment economy. In an enrollment economy, efficient allocation of resources is the paramount concern of administrators as they struggle to balance limited resources against unceasing demands from faculty who do not think in cost-benefit terms. What issues will administrators confront as they search for ways in which to create new policies regarding teaching practices?

In allocating resources, university administrators look for general generic indicators of faculty productivity that allow comparisons across departments. Departments, not faculty, are the operative budgeting units because it is simply too difficult for administrators to aim their control efforts directly at individual faculty members. Instead, they rely on their agents—department chairs and heads—to implement decisions made centrally.

Administrators seek measures that work for all departments rather than idiosyncratic ones that vary by department and discipline. Even though universities are not run as cooperatives, administrators still feel much more pressure than do executives in private businesses to articulate a rationale for their decisions. The rationale must carry at least the surface impression of being based on universalistic principles rather than on biased ones. Therefore, administrators often look to external indicators of productivity to justify their decisions as unprejudiced, such as reputational rankings of their departments by the national media. (This leads to a marked difference between the level of rhetoric and the level of practice.)

Strictly implementing the logic of control is extremely difficult for administrators because they face at least *three* serious constraints. First, administrators face a strongly entrenched norm of faculty autonomy. At the major research universities, faculty expect to be consulted about major decisions, and many universities have some sort of faculty governing body that tries to assert its rights vis-à-vis administrators. Faculty often object to the cold rationality of

the *logic of control,* arguing that universities should not be run like businesses. Administrators reveal their logic not only through their language and use of concepts but also through the way in which intentions are presented, such as calls for efficiency and quality evaluation.

So strong is the norm of faculty autonomy that nearly all administrators are drawn from the ranks of the faculty rather than from the private sector. Unlike just about every other major industry, universities recruit for administrators almost entirely within the population of colleges and universities rather than within private industry. The one exception to the rule is the population of business schools, which often recruit retired executives as deans. However, in those cases, the actual internal administration of the schools usually are in the hands of associate deans drawn from the ranks of the faculty. The logic of this selection process almost guarantees that most university administration, especially at the lower levels, is staffed with amateurs who must learn as they go and who are unusually dependent on the persons to whom they allocate resources, unlike the case in the private sector.

A second major constraint on the logic of control is that deans, provosts, presidents, and department heads work with vastly understaffed offices. In spite of faculty complaints that the number of university administrators is proliferating at an alarming rate, the ratio of administrators to faculty is really quite low, compared to the office staffs of most large corporations. Deans, for example, may have 15 or 20 departments reporting directly to them, with perhaps one or two associate deans who work part-time helping them in specialized areas such as personnel decisions. At the University of North Carolina at Chapel Hill, the new dean of the College of Arts and Sciences recently explained the dilemma she faced in allocating her time: "If I spent only 20 minutes with each department and curriculum chair each week, that activity would consume all my time, and I would have no time left for anything else."

One consequence of the understaffing of the offices of universities is that administrators spend a high proportion of their time on low value-added activities, doing for themselves many paper-processing activities that would be handled by lower level staff in private business. Low investments in information technology exacerbate the problem of understaffing, as deans work with outmoded budgeting and planning techniques. At a typical elite research university, about 6 percent of the university budget is spent on information technology, a figure unmatched by most of the other research universities and certainly not matched by four-year colleges. Low levels of information technology mean that administrators have very incomplete information on what departments are doing and, therefore, must rely on the governed—the departments and faculty—for performance indicators. Dependence on the governed creates a contest between the targets of control and the agents of control, as administrators search for generic indicators and departmental faculty try to make their own situations as idiosyncratic as possible.

Understaffing and poor information technology severely hamper administrators' abilities to implement new programs, such as initiatives to promote innovative teaching. If an administrator decides to adopt the "new" pedagogy, then departments and faculty must be induced to cooperate through strong incentives rather than through administrative fiat. Monitoring compliance with the new programs will be extremely difficult, and "control loss" will mean that resources allocated to the program are likely to be diverted to other issues.

A third constraint on the logic of control is that "teaching quality" is a very elusive thing.

How are we to reliably and validly measure it given the preceding constraints? Administrators, accustomed to a bureaucratic way of thinking, tend to view learning and knowledge as "information" and "production" and, therefore, to think of teaching quality as a *quantity* to be weighed, measured, and comparatively assessed. Most administrators have had little training in pedagogy, so their implicit models of learning and teaching are quite mechanical and linear. They transfer their mental maps of the control process to the teaching process, using very goal-rational, instrumental thinking.

Given the great difficulty of assessing teaching quality, as is well documented in the literature on educational psychology, administrators face strong temptations to find shortcuts. Even the most well-intentioned administrators might find themselves falling back on easily measured indicators, such as number of students per class, when they are faced with allocating resources across 20 highly diverse departments. Given faculty resistance to generic indicators, the logic of control leads administrators toward the simplest, most easily observable and incontestable indicators of teaching performance. Accordingly, the outcome is determined by the logic of structure, not the logic of content.

The problem we are discussing here has international implications. In his analysis of British reform policy in the 1990s, Ball (1995) writes of an "international circulation of ideas." The ideas to which he refers are manifested in concepts such as "market forces," "autonomy," "steering at a distance," and "management." Internationally, measurement and comparison have become key features of the management of organizations, as administrators attempt to tighten the coupling between individual efforts and the mission of the institution (Weick 1976). Tighter coupling is pursued through constant monitoring and surveillance.

The Logic of Discovery

In the logic of discovery, the faculty oriented toward helping their students learn must *discover* what techniques work best with the students in each of their classes and then find the resources needed to help the students learn. This "active" view of learning is based on a very different model of knowledge and learning from that used with the logic of control. Learning and knowledge are treated as process driven and search oriented rather than as "information" or "products" (Boice 1996).

Faculty adopting the new active learning and cooperative learning approaches, initially developed for elementary and secondary education but increasingly applied at the university level, adapt their teaching to the resources made available to them, including student preparedness and the difficulty of the material within the course's domain. Faculty must be extremely flexible because each class presents them with a different mix of students' readiness to learn and changes in the state of the art in the substantive topic.

In the logic of discovery, teaching effectiveness is based on an assessment of how much of an improvement over initial student understanding faculty achieve over the course of the term. In this very Deming-like view of teaching (Gartner 1993), faculty responsibilities are to their students, not to the administration, and faculty are held accountable to the extent that they adapt to what students know and then take students on from there toward a higher level of learning. We are using *higher* in the sense of the Bloom taxonomy of learning objectives (Bloom et al. 1956).

Faculty would like to vary things such as class size, type of meeting room, laboratory equipment, use of the library, and technological tools on the basis on what they discover students need and can profit from. A priori constraints on available resources make it more difficult for them to thoroughly apply an active or a cooperative learning approach in their classes.

Faculty also are guided by professional norms about what is to be covered in their classes. Sometimes, topical substance is spelled out in model curricula developed by professional associations. Departments also may have a developmental structure to their curricula in which higher level courses build on what is taught in lower level courses, thus constraining what innovations faculty can make in content but not in process. Finally, the logic of discovery also is affected by expectations of colleagues, but again the norm of faculty autonomy means that faculty have quite a bit of freedom to innovate if they so desire.

Constraints affect the operation of the logic of discovery, just as they affect the logic of control. In particular, we think that there are *three* constraints that drive the dynamics of the logic of discovery. First, the logic of control pits departmental colleagues against one another for resources and also pits departments against one another. Competition for resources, although perfectly understandable under the logic of control, disrupts the norms of cooperation needed for the sharing of scarce resources used in the logic of discovery. Sharing of resources is difficult because the question immediately arises as to who is to get credit for an outcome if shared resources are used. Competitive pressures also hamper topic-based versus discipline-based instruction, making it difficult for faculty to cooperate across departments. Although there are a number of examples of successful interdisciplinary curricula at research universities, faculty overwhelmingly identify with their departments, and departmental administrators place departmental needs above curriculum needs almost every time a decision is required.

Second, lack of organizational support for systematic and professional teacher training means that faculty are ill prepared to make wise choices in selecting resources. Pedagogical choices are made from within the resources available rather than from a plan designed from the beginning with discovery in mind. University accounting systems have no place for resource allocation that creates "public goods" such as better prepared teachers. After all, if teaching quality is hard to measure, then so is the quality of teacher training programs. Given the academic marketplace, administrators might believe that there is a strong likelihood that resources invested in teachers will be "wasted" as the teachers move to other schools. (The same decision, of course, faces administrators deciding to invest in research, but at least in that case they know that there is a measurable outcome that will turn up in the quantifiable indicators used by national ranking organizations.)

One consequence of the lack of support for teacher training means that departments allocate few resources to teacher training for graduate students. Teaching assistants are thrown into the classroom with minimal instruction, supervision is minimal, and monitoring and outcome assessment are almost nonexistent. Graduate students get the impression that departments do not value teaching very highly and that teaching is mostly a matter of intuition and imitation rather than being based on a large body of knowledge about effective teaching practices.

A long-term consequence of this lack of support is that universities produce incompetent new assistant professors, at least in terms of teaching skill. Those faculty who eventually adopt a more active and cooperative learning perspective, in keeping with the new pedagogical orientation advocated by teaching reformers, find that they must grope toward effective practices on their own. In an odd way, the logic of discovery supports this rather fragmented groping in that it emphasizes adopting practices to fit the situation as one encounters it, which will vary over classes and over semesters.

Third, with rare exceptions, departmental administrators have bought into university administrators' goals and measures and spend their time on those activities. Faculty pursuing the logic of discovery find that few resources are invested by departments in activities that are not "counted" by university administrators. Lack of departmental support means that faculty are isolated in their various departments if they decide to seek "better" teaching. They find that they must make common cause with faculty and other departments in spite of few rewards for doing so.

Whereas faculty would like to make decisions and plunge ahead, constructing rationales for their actions after they have made their discoveries, administrators resist such an irrational way of proceeding (Brunsson 1985). From the logic of control viewpoint, faculty who behave as opportunistic entrepreneurs, snatching up whatever loose resources are available, are simply impediments to rational planning. From the logic of discovery viewpoint, entrepreneurial behavior is essential or else faculty are liable to miss exciting opportunities at the frontiers of their fields. Each logic makes sense on its own terms, so each group—faculty and administrators—expresses outrage when the other behaves "irrationally."

Conclusion

The logic of control could be characterized as a spreadsheet placed over the seemingly chaotic and unpredictable world of teaching and education in an effort to make the creative chaos of the classroom measurable, predictable, and safe. The logic of control tends to colonize the logic of discovery because of its inherent drive toward assessing effectiveness via measurement and the possibility of putting a price tag on activities. Being able to price activities puts administrators at ease because they know what they are dealing with and quantitative data give them the tools they need to plan ahead.

The logic of control, as played out in universities, emerges as a model of very bureaucratically oriented management. Quality teaching is just one more product to be managed, and idiosyncratic variation across faculty is a nuisance factor in coming up with generic indicators of how "well" universities are doing. The logic of discovery, as played out in the lives of faculty who are socialized or converted into the "new" view of teaching and learning, leads to an emphasis on process and knowledge construction. Teaching-oriented faculty work with goal schemes, such as Bloom's taxonomy, that are process oriented, not content oriented. Accordingly, they find it difficult to justify their resource requests in terms of "information" and "knowledge."

When the two logics collide, agents of each have some resources on which to draw for gaining power and influence. University administrators argue that they are the persons best placed to ensure that resources are fairly allocated across colleges and departments. They also argue that they will be held accountable by the public and the other constituencies of the university. By contrast, the agents of the logic of discovery usually are faculty, and they justify their practices on the basis of serving the needs of students, who hold no allegiance to particular departments, even though they may well have declared majors. In the logic of discovery, bureaucratic constraints are simply a nuisance factor that complicate "professional" decisions.

The two logics coexist uneasily in most universities, and administrators and faculty often find themselves at odds because they are not speaking the same language when they talk about the principles for making decisions about resource allocation. Moreover, because most administrators are former faculty members, their decisions and pronouncements often contain a mix of the two logics, further complicating matters. Faculty, too, get many tastes of administration in their committee and staff work, so their decisions also often are couched in the two logics rather than single-mindedly based on only one.

Is there an easy resolution? No. But we note one practical implication. The survivors in this process are the people who are able to cope with both rationalities or logics and able to understand and identify the driving forces behind the complexities. Universities need people capable of recognizing that there are two logics at work and people capable of doing the analytic work required to explain the logics to others. Perhaps every university needs a vice provost of logics and rationalities?

References

Ball, Stephen. 1995. "Analyzing British Reform Policy in the 1990s." Plenary speech given at the Norwegian National Conference in Pedagogy, Aalesund, Norway, October.

Bloom, B. S., M. D. Engelhart, E. J. Furst, W. H. Hill, and D. R. Krathwohl. 1956. *Taxonomy of Educational Objectives: The Classification of Educational Goals, Handbook 1: Cognitive Domain.* New York: Longman.

Boice, Robert. 1996. *First-Order Principles for College Teachers.* Bolton, MA: Anker.

Bourdieu, Pierre. 1980. *Le Sens Pratique.* Paris: Éditions de Minuit.

Brunsson, Nils. 1985. *The Irrational Organization*. New York: John Wiley.

Gartner, Bill. 1993. "Dr. Deming Comes to Class." *Journal of Management Education* 17:143-58.

Honneth, Axel and Hans Joas, eds. 1991. *Communicative Action: Essays on Jürgen Habermas's Theory of Communicative Action*. Cambridge, MA: MIT Press.

Weber, Max. 1968. *Economy and Society; An Outline of Interpretive Sociology*. London: Bedminster.

———. 1976. *The Protestant Ethic and the Spirit of Capitalism*. 2d ed. London: Allen and Unwin.

Weick, Karl. 1976. "Educational Organizations as Loosely Coupled Systems." *Administrative Science Quarterly* 21:1-9.

26

Three Faces of Relevance: Connecting Disciplinary Knowledge to the "Real World"

David M. Newman

There was a time, in the not-so-distant past, when college professors taught their courses in a fairly insulated environment. Most universities were closed communities when it came to what instructors were teaching and what students were learning in the classroom. "Academic freedom" was a cherished, highly protected principle upon which most departments based their pedagogical policy. Since professors, especially tenured professors, were assumed to be learned experts, they were granted significant autonomy over what and how to teach. In many places, even colleagues were unaware of and uninterested in what went on in the classrooms of fellow professors. Only in extreme cases—suspected abuse of power, gross incompetence, extreme controversy, and the like —did constituencies outside the department or the university poke their collective noses into the classroom. In short, professors taught and learned with little outside interference. As long as they met basic requirements of their respective disciplines, no one bothered them much.

AUTHOR'S NOTE: This is a reprint of an article originally published as Newman, David M., "Three Faces of Relevance: Connecting Disciplinary Knowledge to the 'Real World'," *Journal of Sociology and Social Policy* 16 (11), 1996, pp. 81-94. Used with permission.

But all that has changed. In fiscally conscious times like these when budgetary streamlining and institutional retrenchment are the norm, universities are being forced, more than ever before, to account for themselves and clearly define their place within the larger society. Debates over such issues as multicultural education, core graduation requirements, and student outcomes—traditionally the stuff of departmental or curriculum committee meetings—have become "public property" pitting diverse moral, political, economic, and cultural interests against one another. With a firm grip on its pocketbook, the public is exposing the previously cozy and guarded college environment by demanding that universities provide evidence that they actually do what they say they do. The image of college as a mysterious, unseen, and ivy-covered community of higher learning is fast becoming obsolete.

Not surprisingly, many academic departments are being called upon by their respective *administrations* to prove their intellectual and perhaps even vocational utility. What is their niche within the overall university curriculum? What can they offer in terms of postgraduate career opportunity? What are their short-term goals and long-term contributions to the community? How do they aid in the rigorous development of the mind? How much "bang" do they provide for the "buck"?

Disciplines in the social sciences and humanities (for instance, sociology, anthropology, philosophy, history) are particularly susceptible to such outside scrutiny and demands for demonstrated relevance since they have traditionally been disciplines without well-defined postgraduate career paths. Sociology, in particular, has a reputation for being distantly critical of social problems without offering practical solutions or providing students with "marketable skills." Hence sociology departments are often placed in the unenviable position of continuously addressing the fiscal and substantive concerns of a skeptical community. These concerns are neither trivial nor harmless, as evidenced by highly publicized cases of massive cuts in sociology faculty (for example, San Diego State University), the actual or threatened liquidation of entire departments (for example, Yale University, Washington University), and the poorly rated quality of teaching compared to other disciplines (see February 1993 issue of *Footnotes*). In short, the crucial issue of academic relevance has become particularly urgent for departments around the country.

External demands for accountability don't stop at the level of the university or the department. Individual professors, too, are being challenged to show that they are both useful and necessary to the education process. In a cultural environment that places its highest premium on the efficient use of economic resources, recent technological trends such as distance learning and virtual universities are forcing professors to examine and justify their role within the institution. If a student can learn just as much about Weber or Durkheim through a course over the Internet [as] she or he can from sitting in a classroom three times a week listening to a professor talk about sociology, then why have professors at all?

These concerns over relevance and accountability—whether expressed by chairs, administrators, students, parents, politicians, media pundits, or the community at large—are not to be taken lightly, for they have a direct effect upon our professional lives. Warranted or not, motivated by good intentions or bad, such concerns will inevitably force us to carefully assess how and what we teach in our courses.

Let me say at the outset that I don't believe that our profession is completely under siege, and I certainly don't pine for a bygone era when, short of intellectual malpractice, professors were granted carte blanche to pretty much do what they pleased in their courses. But I do feel that as we approach the 21st century, all of us who teach college courses must face the fact that we will be playing to a much larger, and sometimes less trusting, audience than that to which we've grown accustomed. It is with this sociocultural backdrop in mind that I would like to examine how we, as instructors, can infuse our courses with material that has both contemporary relevance and social importance.

To that end, I identify three types of relevance that can be built into college teaching. Keep in mind that, like all typologies, this one is artificial. The boundaries between the different "types" of relevance are blurry. In fact, as you read this chapter, you will no doubt notice certain overlaps. The point of discussing each type of relevance separately is simply to describe three broad guiding principles that I feel can help us articulate the pertinence and applicability of our discipline and our teaching.

Personal Relevance

The first type of relevance I feel we should have in mind when we plan our courses directly connects the material we teach to the personal lives of our students. One of the changes I've noticed over the past 10 years or so is that more and more students come to our classes demanding that we teach them something they can use. Now granted, these demands may derive from their parents, who want to see a payoff for four years worth of a hefty financial and emotional investment in their children's educations. But students do seem to take a more "consumerist" and "consumptive" approach to their college educations than they did in the past (Edmundson, 1997). This is not an altogether bad thing. I believe that we, as educators, have an obligation to teach our students things they can use to understand, and maybe even to question, their own assumptions, beliefs, perceptions, and behaviors.

Consider, for instance, history. Historians know full well that history is not just about describing a past that appears strange and disconnected. However, students frequently arrive in these classes assuming that historical material is out of touch and irrelevant to their own lives. "What," they may ask, "does the industrial revolution have to do with [us]?" Only when they come to see that their own personal perspectives and ideas have their roots in perceptions, beliefs, and ideas of past centuries can they begin to understand the interconnectedness of their lives with the lives of their historical predecessors. They will come to see, for instance, that the industrial revolution's role in creating separate (and, more often than not, gendered) work and family spheres has a direct bearing on the things young people today expect and take for granted with regard to how they prioritize their work and family lives.

Sociology, in particular, is a discipline that is uniquely equipped to highlight the personal relevance of its theories and research. At its most basic level, sociology is about us. It in-

forms us about the forces that impinge on our personal day-to-day experiences while also providing insight into how those experiences are linked to the existence and maintenance of social institutions and social order. One of our goals as teachers, then, is to provide students with the tools to analyze the interconnectedess between their private lives and the social worlds they inhabit—to give them unimpeded access to the "sociological imagination." In so doing, our students can gain an awareness of the cultural, interactional, and institutional forces that influence that which is most intimate: their own behaviors, values, beliefs, attitudes, and self-concepts.

There are many methods that we can use to make students see themselves in the material they are studying. For instance, in my courses, I encourage students to write introspective papers in which they analyze personal experiences using sociological theories and concepts learned in class (for instance, instances of personal or institutional discrimination, the trajectory of their intimate relationships, experiences with failed impression management, breaches of everyday social norms, frustrations with bureaucratic inertia, and so on). The purpose of these papers is not simply to tell a story; nor is it to encourage students to use their individual lives to refute long-standing social theories. Instead, the purpose is to give students an opportunity to come to terms with their status as occupants of a social world and to see that their lives are constantly being influenced by other people as well as [by] the groups, organizations, institutions, and cultures to which they belong. As they begin to recognize the structural influences behind their private experiences, they come to understand the personal applicability of sociological theories.

Another method for drawing out the personal relevance of course material is the use of in-class demonstrations designed to make students explicitly acknowledge their own perceptions, stereotypes, and values. For instance, in a course on "Social Deviance," students meet in small groups in order to rank the perceived seriousness of a list of "deviant" or "criminal" acts. The ensuing discussions force them not only to come face to face with their own deeply held beliefs but [also] to try to understand the very different beliefs of fellow students. In "Sociology of Family," students write a short autobiography from the point of view of an elderly person looking back on her/his family life—an assignment which forces them to articulate their personal expectations for future relationships and family lives. In "Sociology of Madness," students write a short mini-essay on what mental illness "looks like" in everyday life. In [so doing], they must acknowledge their own attitudes toward difference and their own limited levels of tolerance. In all of these diverse exercises, students come to see how their values and presumptions strongly influence their perceptions of important social phenomena.

These exercises force students to critically examine how they perceive and understand important social issues and phenomena—something few of them have ever publicly articulated before. From there, it is a relatively short step to discussing where their ideas, beliefs, and perceptions come from. Students begin to see how their thoughts are, in part, the products of culture, history, and social institutions that are much larger than them. As a result, the "inevitability" and "inherent rightness" of their beliefs start to fade. As more and more students express their viewpoints, others can begin to see differences and similarities between the way they think and the way their peers think.

It often helps to show students how the breakdowns, problems, and injustices of society—both our own and others, past and present—are experienced by individual people.

For example, how are racism and sexism communicated and felt in face-to-face interaction? How do cultural definitions of age and beauty affect our perceptions and judgments of others? How do poverty and power influence self-concepts? Furthermore, how do we, as members of society, perpetuate certain social problems by our collective perceptions of them? For instance, can personal beliefs about the causes of poverty or sexual assault contribute to the very existence and perhaps even the exacerbation of these problems?

In using common personal experiences as a vehicle for understanding the interplay between individuals and society, the true value of sociology—as well as other social sciences—can be utilized. Granted, personal relevance may have less obvious market value than, say, learning the intricacies of the commodities market. But when students come to understand that the most private elements of their lives (personal characteristics, experiences, behaviors, and thoughts) affect, and are affected by, larger social historical and cultural phenomena, they gain a deeper appreciation of themselves and others, which will benefit them in any career they choose to pursue.

Drawing out personal relevance makes the familiar unfamiliar, forcing students to question the commonplace and the ordinary. Only when they are able to take a step back and examine the taken-for-granted aspects of their personal lives can they determine if there is some inherent, as yet unrecognized organization and predictability to them. This approach gives students the opportunity to recognize their own history-making potential and responsibility embedded in sociological understanding. As one sociologist puts it, "By seeing the human origins of social structures, the interests they reflect, the variety in human cultures, and the change that has characterized human history, students become aware of the precariousness of any society, social structure, or cultural practice and *its dependence on cooperation*" [emphasis added] (Davis, 1993, p. 237).

Making courses in the social sciences personally relevant to students is not without its problems, however. Insight into one's own life can be threatening in many ways. The tradition of benign disruption in the social sciences has a long history (Goldsmid and Wilson 1980), and it is true that "a gain in knowledge is a loss of innocence." Trying to induce students to see themselves in what they're studying or to face "inconvenient facts" (Weber, 1958) may lead them to question strongly held assumptions about how their lives and the world around them work.

This process can be uncomfortable and can provoke frustration among students. Some dearly held assumptions about common sense, or what they thought was common sense, may become head-scratchingly confusing. I think [that] any of us who teach want our students to somehow integrate course material into their lives. But rarely do we give our students a "safe" place in which to grapple with these important and sometimes threatening issues.

In my classes, I assure students that my task is not to preach or to make them change the way they think but simply to make them aware of how they came to think in that way and to acknowledge the existence of alternatives. It is crucial, then, that the instructor create a "low threat" environment (Billson 1986) which can make students comfortable enough to share this process of self-examination with others.

Social Relevance

In addition to helping them understand the trajectories of their personal lives, courses in the social sciences should also inform students about the larger world they inhabit. From local politics to national trends to international relations and the global economy, the social sciences provide insight into the psychological, political, social, and economic dynamics of life as we approach the 21st century. Students should be encouraged to see that a course in sociology or anthropology or political science can help them not only to understand their own private worlds but [also] to understand the important issues facing their neighborhoods, their communities, and their racial, religious, or ethnic groups.

One of the most effective ways of showing students the social relevance of course material is through an examination of current news stories and events. A glance at any newspaper on any given day will reveal many contemporary stories of social scientific importance. Some of my colleagues require that their students subscribe to a major national newspaper like the *New York Times* or the *Washington Post* and construct their writing assignments based on current issues being covered in the paper.

In my courses, I *always* devote the first ten minutes or so of each class period (which tends to be lost anyway because of late-arriving students and paper shuffling) to a current news story that relates either to specific topics being discussed in class or to sociology in general. The Internet is a particularly fruitful source of up-to-the-minute stories and events that can be linked to theories or concepts being discussed in class. The deaths of Princess Diana and Mother Teresa, for instance, were a useful example not just of celebrity and fame but [also] of how these things are linked to gender, economics and the media, politics, and cultural ideals of beauty.

Beyond illustrative applications, contemporary news stories can also be used as examples of the social construction of knowledge and the pitfalls of flawed research methodology. In my "Social Research Methods" course, for instance, we spend some part of each class period analyzing some "study" or "scientific claim" that has achieved widespread notoriety in the popular press. I believe it is essential that students begin to look critically at the kinds of "research facts" they are apt to see and examine the questions people in this society seem interested in addressing. Few of them are likely to become avid, regular readers of academic journals. So we focus on research published in newspapers and newsmagazines where results are usually reported uncritically.

Depending on the section of the course, I ask students to point out the flaws in the research (such as insufficient sampling, poor operationalization, or alternative interpretations of findings). Since the articles are likely to lack a detailed discussion of methodology, we also discuss what additional information would be important to know in order to assess the adequacy of the study. This is an effective way of determining whether students are developing their own hierarchy of criteria used for evaluating empirical research. Toward the end of the semester, the students become quite adept at picking apart studies that months earlier would have been accepted as objective truth. This usually leads nicely into a discussion of the sociology of knowledge. Students realize that we are all inclined to accept, as fact, that which appears in print. We discuss the tendency for information to become objectified (Berger and Luckmann, 1966) as we lose sight of the fact that the research was created by people. This is a powerful lesson for students as they become critical consumers of social information.

However, the issue of social relevance raises a larger disciplinary problem that goes beyond classroom dynamics to the very nature of our subject matter. It is my belief that we are doing our students a grave disservice if we don't make clear the vital role our discipline plays in understanding the important domestic and global issues of our time. Yet by stressing the applicability of sociology to *today's* social issues and problems, we place ourselves in the unavoidable trap of making our examples of application obsolete. This is particularly apparent in textbooks. Contemporary, "real world" examples bring our theories and concepts alive. Yet the examples will inevitably lose their topicality at some point in time (I recall the sea of eerily blank faces that awaited me when I once made a casual reference to the "Iran-Contra" hearings!). Hence we must be constantly on guard so that our course material does not become "dated." Just as textbooks must constantly be revised to account for the changing nature of society, so too must our courses.

A related problem associated with social relevance is the perceived "seriousness" of our courses and hence of our discipline. In the minds of many, social relevance is at odds with academic rigor. That is, those courses or those disciplines that are the most contemporary in their focus are sometimes seen as purveyors of "pop" culture—the university equivalent of a daytime talk show. All fluff, no substance. The "rigorous" courses are thought to be those based on classical theory, so-called "great works," time-tested postulates on the nature of things as they are or have always been.

As social scientists, we can avoid this criticism by moving beyond simply being commentators on contemporary social life to being analysts of it. For instance, it may be interesting to talk about the growing number of gay men and women who are starting their own families, but it becomes more informative and relevant if we also discuss why such a phenomenon is becoming more common, what accounts for the conservative backlash against it, and how it relates to our cultural and legal conception of what a family is or should be.

Process Relevance

The above two types of relevance orient students to life *outside* the classroom, informing them about their personal lives and their social world. The third type of relevance—what I call "process" relevance—is geared toward the students' pedagogical experiences *within* the classroom. In other words, it is designed to make the learning process itself relevant to the students by making them active "owners" of the course rather than passive recipients of a body of knowledge. It is my experience that students learn best when they feel they are valued co-participants in the process—that they are not simply students but are, in some instances, informants and teachers as well.

One way of showing students that they are part of the learning process is to allow them to evaluate the course *while it is in progress.* Mid-term course evaluations and periodic pauses for comments about the way the course is going and suggestions for improvement give students a sense of shared responsibility for the class. It is common practice at most institutions to hand out evaluation forms to students on or near the last day of class. Results usually are not received until well into the next semester. By then, however, it is too late to make adjustments in the evaluated course and too late to implement changes for the following term.

More important, this heavy reliance on end-of-term appraisals devalues feedback from students, who come to feel that their opinions and comments about the class are not taken seriously. Giving students the opportunity to offer suggestions for improving the course *during* the term, when it matters most, reinforces the belief that the course belongs to all involved, students as well as instructor. After I collect their evaluations, we usually spend some class time on their comments and suggestions.

Another way to give the course process relevance is to make students responsible for providing their peers with feedback—to play, if you will, the teacher role. One technique for accomplishing this is the use of peer critiques and evaluations of term paper drafts.

The procedure usually works like this. A few weeks into the semester, students submit a one-page description of their paper topic. They are free to choose any topic if it is relevant to course material. I ask them to pose a specific question that they will answer systematically in their paper. A rough draft of the paper is due about two-thirds of the way through the course.

At that point, the students hand in two copies of their draft; one goes to me and the other, which does not include the author's name, goes to another student in the class for critique. Before the exchange of papers, I hand out a three-page evaluation guide that students use to assess the paper they are reading. It consists of a series of Likert-type items pertaining to the clarity of expression and the content of the paper as well as to overall impressions (for instance: Did they like it? Did they learn anything new? Did it seem as if the author knew what he or she was writing about?). Students also are asked to provide additional comments and suggestions. A week or so after turning in their drafts, they receive two sources of feedback about their writing: one from a fellow student and one from me. They are then encouraged (or required, if the class is small enough) to meet with me to discuss the comments and suggestions that they received on their paper.

Although at first students don't think they will like this procedure—because it appears to them that they are writing two term papers instead of one—they soon realize that it helps their writing immensely. Because others, including their peers, are reading and judging their work *before* it is to be graded, they start to take more pride in their writing. As a side benefit, they derive a great deal of insight from their role as evaluator. Students rarely receive the opportunity to see what classmates are writing about and, more important, how they write. This exercise allows them to scrutinize a classmate's writing. Furthermore, they come to realize that writing is a *process,* which cannot be done well in a vacuum (i.e., without feedback from others), and that constructive criticism is *not* a sign of failure.

Although this method works quite well, I must point out that one problem is differences in students' critical abilities. Some students will be assigned a critic who offers in-depth analysis and valuable suggestions. Others, however, will have a critic who gives the paper only a cursory reading. Unfortunately, this problem is out of the instructor's control and is subject to the whims of random assignment. I deal with it as well as I can by stressing the importance of honest criticism and, as mentioned earlier, by providing instruction on how to evaluate papers.

Another technique I use to enhance process relevance is the group presentation. Students tend to learn material more effectively when they are responsible for presenting it to their peers. I always tell my students that the best indicator of their knowledge of some concept or idea is if they can explain it (that is, teach it) to someone else.

In my introductory course, for instance, the group presentation is in the form of a social issue panel discussion. Students choose a particular issue that is of interest to them (poverty, power, sexual or racial inequality, deviance, aging, and so on). Each panel is limited to five or six students. Students write a short, independent paper on some aspect of their issue. Then, along with the rest of their group, they orally present their paper to the rest of the class.

It is the group's responsibility to decide how to approach the topic and how to present it to the class.

A variation of the group presentation is the "feedback group." In my "Social Research Methods" course, students are required to do an independent piece of original research from start to finish—from literature review to development of hypotheses to collection and analysis of data. The project is divided up into several shorter papers, each paralleling a stage in the research process. Prior to handing in *each* paper, students meet with their groups and me to discuss their projects. Here, in an informal atmosphere, they report to the others on their progress, breakthroughs, roadblocks, frustrations, etc.

At these sessions, I try to do as little talking as possible. I want the students to be active participants in the learning process by helping one another. Frequently, a student will make a suggestion, only to have the shortcomings of the suggestion pointed out by another student who has an even better one. It is gratifying to see students thinking out loud and coming up with rather impressive ideas.

Moreover, as the semester progresses, they become more and more familiar with others' projects and initiate questions on their own. Some students even begin to refer to classmates' projects in their own papers. Furthermore, these small group discussions give students an opportunity to discover similar interests. On one occasion, a pair of students who were interested in the same population (adolescents) ended up coordinating their data collection strategies to make their use of time more efficient.

Maximizing the process relevance of a course often requires a modification of the traditional authority structure in the classroom. As instructors, it is tempting to claim a monopoly on wisdom. However, if we are to make our students co-owners of the pedagogical process, we must abandon the role as supreme "teller of truth." I usually tell my students at the beginning of a course that I am not the ultimate expert on the topic at hand and that I want to learn as much from them as I hope they want to learn from me. I also stress that learning is an interactive process, a give and take, a dialogue rather than a monologue.

Conclusion

The social sciences may never achieve the perceived status and marketability of business administration, biology, or chemistry. Yet no other disciplines are as well equipped to help students understand what is going on in the world today and why it is going on. Our very existence depends on this message getting out. Furthermore, one of the consequences of emphasizing personal social and process relevance in our courses is that it reduces the students' tendency to see society as inevitable and external. If we can offer them the intellectual tools to understand the dynamics of their lives—both personally and socially—then our disciplines cease to be merely "descriptive" or "critical" and be-

come something useful. In other words, if we enable our students to understand major national and international phenomena, we may also enable them to do something about them. Understanding must always precede action. Therefore, relevance cannot and should not be separated from empowerment.

References

Berger, P. & Luckmann, T. 1966. *The Social Construction of Reality.* Garden City, NY: Doubleday.

Billson, J. M. 1986. "The college classroom as small group: Some implications for teaching and learning." *Teaching Sociology* 14, 143-151.

Davis, N. J. 1993. "Bringing it all together: The sociological imagination." *Teaching Sociology* 21, 233-238.

Edmundson, M. 1997. "On the uses of a liberal education." *Harper's Magazine,* [September], 39-49.

Goldsmid, C. A. & Wilson, E. K. 1980. *Passing on Sociology.* Belmont, CA: Wadsworth.

Weber, M. 1958. *From Max Weber: Essays in Sociology.* Edited by H. H. Gerth & C. W. Mills. New York: Oxford University Press.

27

Underneath the Ivy *and* The Social Costs of Corporate Ties

Lawrence C. Soley

The Corporate Roots

Taking their cues from conservative critics, the media have also dwelled almost exclusively on a few stories about political correctness (PC) and in so doing have missed the real story about academe. The real story is about university physics and electrical engineering departments being seduced by Pentagon contracts; molecular biology, biochemistry, and medicine departments being wooed by drug companies and biotech firms; and university computer science departments being in bed with Big Blue and a few high-tech chip makers. The story about universities in the 1980s and 1990s is that they will turn a trick for anybody with money to invest, and the only ones with money are corporations, millionaires, and foundations. These investments in universities have dramatically changed the mission of higher education; they have led universities to attend to the interests of their well-heeled patrons rather than those of students.

AUTHOR'S NOTE: This is a reprint of chapters originally published as Soley, Lawrence C., "Underneath the Ivy" and "The Social Costs of Corporate Ties," in *Leasing the Ivory Tower* (South End Press), 1995, pp. 1-15, 145-53. Used with permission.

The University of California, Los Angeles (UCLA) typifies in many ways what has happened to universities in the real world. Corporations have contracted with the university for research, hired its professors as consultants, and endowed professorships. Foundations have established independently operating fiefdoms on the UCLA campus, and tycoons have become the advisers and namesakes of departments.[1] Moreover, several other universities have gone further than just naming professorships and departments after millionaires and corporations, as UCLA has. For example, Glassboro State College in Glassboro, New Jersey changed its name to Rowan College after receiving $100 million from industrialist Henry M. Rowan, the founder of a furnace company. Not since the Stalin era in the Soviet Union has a living individual had a monument of this size named after him.

When donations are made to higher education by corporations, the donors often receive massive benefits, even when strings aren't attached. In addition to tax write-offs, corporations get enormous public relations benefits from their donations. Philip Morris's Miller Brewing Company, for example, donates $150,000 annually to the Thurgood Marshall Scholarship Fund, which provides scholarships to African American students. But Miller also spends more than $300,000 a year to advertise the program and its contributions, and these advertisements carry the Miller logo. The corporation has also purchased time at professional basketball games to tout its donation.[2]

University administrators claim that such corporate and foundation money is accepted without strings. But this claim doesn't mean that universities are independent of their benefactors, according to Cal Bradford, a former fellow at the University of Minnesota's Humphrey Institute for Public Policy. Bradford should know. His contract wasn't extended after he criticized the university's ties to corporations. The outside funds "determine what universities will teach and research, what direction the university will take," Bradford says. "If universities would decide that they need an endowed chair in English and then try to raise the money for it, it would be one thing. But that's not what happens. Corporate donors decide to fund chairs in areas [where] they want research done. Their decisions decide which topics universities explore and which aren't [explored]."[3]

In some cases, the influence of donors is direct rather than subtle:

- At the University of Nevada at Las Vegas, the College of Hotel Administration negotiated a $2 million "gift" from the Japanese-owned ACE Denken Company, which manufactures slot machines. The arrangement ties the college to ACE Denken in perpetuity, pending a review every five years. The $2 million donation endowed a doctoral program in hotel administration. For the gift, university administrators promised to publish an annual monograph named for ACE on "issues facing the casino and gaming industry," to sponsor an annual seminar for ACE management and their friends on a topic picked by ACE, and to present ACE with an annual report on developments in gambling technology. The board of regents of the university initially rejected the deal, calling it a contract, not a gift. After some negotiations, however, they agreed to the deal with a few weak restrictions.[4]

- The $100 million gift to Glassboro State College from Henry M. Rowan in 1992 came with political strings explicitly attached. One part of the gift consisted of $3 million in scholarships for the children of Rowan's employees. However, the scholarships were only for children of Rowan's nonunion employees. Rowan stated that he would make scholarships available to employees "who have worked harmoniously with their company," not those who "won their contracts through threats and strikes."[5] Glassboro State College officials accepted this discriminatory policy, stating that they didn't "have any problem with an individual giving to defined groups as long as it's not in opposition to the interests of the institution." Union officials denounced the agreement as typical of Rowan's anti-unionism.[6] Eventually, pressures from unions, state legislators, and the media, not from the university, forced Rowan to reverse his anti-union stance and allow scholarships to be given to his union employees, too. Despite this reversal, Glassboro State's pronouncement indicates the unprincipled positions that universities are willing to embrace in order to get their hands on corporate and tycoon money.

Glassboro State is not an isolated case. Universities are constantly searching for new funding. One reason university administrators have strongly supported the emphasis on research and other non-instructional projects at their institutions—even at the expense of teaching—is that such projects are perceived to enhance a university's prestige and to have the potential of bringing in large sums of money. Universities are typically classified as to whether they are a "research institution," "liberal arts college," or another class of university.[7] Georgetown [University], Harvard University in Cambridge, Massachusetts, the Massachusetts Institute of Technology (MIT) also in Cambridge, Stanford [University], and Yale University in New Haven, Connecticut are classed as research institutions, and most administrators would like to see their universities described as being in the same class as these institutions.

In addition to prestige, research can potentially lead to direct economic benefits. The University and Small Business Patent Procedures Act of 1980 stimulated a race by universities to secure patents on their research discoveries in the belief that the patents might someday be valuable. Between 1986 and 1989, the number of patents issued to universities doubled from 619 to 1,145.[8] The number of patents that universities secure, rather than the success universities have in educating students, is now used as a measure by which university administrators demonstrate their accomplishments.[9]

Administrators see these patents as a long-run method for generating revenues, but this has so far proved to be an illusion. Universities typically have received little money from the research produced in their laboratories. The nation's biggest royalty recipient among universities is Stanford, which received $13 million in royalty revenues in 1990. This amounts to about 1 percent of Stanford's budget. Most universities received far less in royalties. The University of Pennsylvania, which is classed as a "research institution," received just $750,000 in royalties in 1989, and Penn's royalty revenues were higher than those of most universities.[10]

When universities do get large royalties, they usually come at a very high cost to the public, as Michigan State University's (MSU) cisplatin patent demonstrates. MSU received over $60 million in royalties from Bristol-Myers during the past decade for its patent on cisplatin, an anti-cancer drug used for treating bladder, testicular, and ovarian cancers. Bristol-Myers Squibb received an exclusive license to sell cisplatin (which means that only Bristol-Myers can produce the drug), even though MSU had developed cisplatin with federal funding.[11] Bristol-Myers's profits from the drug have been enormous because it has had a monopoly on production and sales.

When Bristol-Myers's exclusive licensing agreement came up for renewal, a half-dozen drug manufacturers expressed interest in also producing the drug. Some legislators favored ending the exclusivity agreement. However, a consortium of universities and representatives of Bristol-Myers lobbied the National Institutes of Health (NIH), which funded MSU's research, to extend the exclusivity agreement, despite the high prices that Bristol-Myers had been charging cancer victims for the drug. In the end, the NIH sided with the universities and Bristol-Myers, assuring that the drug would remain expensive.[12]

Government actions have promoted these increasing ties between business and universities. Although universities have always pandered to wealthy patrons, universities' toadyism intensified after President Reagan slashed spending on domestic programs. Reagan's cuts to student loans and funding for grant-giving agencies put the pinch on universities. For example, the college work-study program was cut by 26.5 percent, after adjusting for inflation. At the NIH, budget cuts resulted in the funding of just 20 percent of highly meritorious research proposals, as opposed to the 45-55 percent funded before Reagan took office.[13]

When grants to universities from agencies such as the NIH declined, universities began looking to the private sector and well-funded Pentagon programs for money. Today, some academic disciplines have become completely enslaved to corporations and the Pentagon for research dollars. For example, $1.8 billion was allocated to university research by the Defense Department in 1993. "That money accounts for more than 80 percent of all federal research funds for electrical engineering, more than 70 percent of those for materials and metallurgy, and more than 55 percent of those for computer science," the *New York Times* reported.[14]

Two federal laws—the previously mentioned 1980 University and Small Business Patent Procedures Act (P.L. 96-517), which was supplemented by a 1983 executive order extending the law to large corporations, and the 1981 Recovery Tax Act (P.L. 97-34)—helped cultivate the current relationship between universities and business. The 1980 law and later executive order allowed universities to sell patent rights derived from research to corporations, even if the federal government was the primary funder of research that led to the patents. The 1981 law increased corporate tax deductions for "donations" made to universities.

These laws have made it worthwhile for corporations to get involved with educational institutions. By sticking some of their dough into universities, corporations are able to buy the results of university research, even though much of the research is funded by the federal government. While federal tax dollars fund about $7 billion worth of research, corporate dollars are used to buy access to the results of

the research—at just a fraction of their actual cost. This subsidy to corporations has had a positive impact on corporate bottom lines, particularly in the fields of biotechnology and pharmaceuticals. Corporations have been able to shift part of their research and development costs to universities, thereby increasing corporate profits.

The costs of research and other work done at universities, however, are not all picked up by corporate dollars, government grants, or foundation monies. They also come from tuition-paying students who have been forced to subsidize projects that benefit multinational corporations. High research costs, which arise from the need for expensive, state-of-the-art research laboratories and from reduced teaching loads for faculty researchers, have caused tuition to skyrocket.[15]

At major research universities such as MIT, Harvard, and Stanford, the combined cost of tuition, student fees, and room and board now exceeds $25,000 annually. At public universities, tuition is lower but has been increasing at an even more rapid rate than at private institutions, as state legislatures have reduced their funding for higher education.[16] At public universities, tuition rates increased 170 percent between 1980 and 1992.[17] Increased tuition costs have had the greatest impact on the poor and minorities, particularly African American men, whose enrollment at universities has decreased rather than increased during the past decade. African American students comprised 9.8 percent of college enrollment in 1984 but only 9.2 percent in 1992.[18]

Given the benefits that corporations receive from pouring money into academia, it is little wonder that corporate dollars going to universities increased almost threefold between 1980 and 1986. Businesses spent about $235 million on university-sponsored research in

1980; by 1986, they were spending about $600 million. By 1991, the annual investment had increased to $1.2 billion.[19] For their money, corporations receive access to professors' research and offices, even though the professors' salaries are principally paid by students and taxpayers.

Corporate, foundation, and tycoon money has had a major, deleterious impact on universities. Financial considerations have altered academic priorities, reduced the importance of teaching, degraded the integrity of academic journals, and determined what research is conducted at universities. The social costs of this influence have been lower quality education, a reduction in academic freedom, and a covert transfer of resources from the public to the private sector.

Spurred on by corporations, universities encourage professors to abandon classrooms for research centers and laboratories, thereby dramatically reversing university priorities. Universities use research, grant-getting, and corporate contracts, not classroom teaching, as measures of academic performance. Today, successful professors are those who bring in contract and grant money; they are not necessarily good teachers, nor do they necessarily need to even step into the classroom. In fact, the more "successful" a professor is today, the less time she or he will spend teaching. This emphasis on research has reduced the importance and quality of undergraduate instruction while simultaneously boosting tuition costs for students, who are forced to help pay the salaries of professors who never teach.

Professors who cultivate corporate ties get perks, promotions, tenure, and endowed professorships, and [they] move up the university hierarchy. They determine whether other, younger professors will also get promoted and tenured. Thus young professors' academic records are evaluated by full professors, endowed chairs, administrators, and trustees whose [criterion] for granting tenure [is] whether the professor has brought in corporate or government grant monies, not whether the professor's scholarship is original or whether she or he is an effective teacher.

As this process continues, more and more tenured faculty at universities will be indentured servants to corporations rather than independent scholars. The indentured servants will make sure that more of their kind are hired and tenured and that even fewer free-thinkers are hired. In the end, universities will be as intellectually stimulating as a GM assembly plant.

Although the relationship is not as clear as the one between corporate research and poor undergraduate instruction, corporate investments in universities have had another, more subtle impact on universities. At most campuses, disciplines that cultivate close contacts with industry have large budgets and good facilities. Other disciplines, particularly the arts and humanities, languish in substandard facilities. This not only produces two classes of faculty—the haves and the have-nots—but also [produces] two classes of students. Students in the arts and humanities not only receive instruction in shabbier facilities but [also are] short-changed because their tuition dollars are diverted to the disciplines that do research for corporations.

Corporate funding has also had a deleterious effect on faculty morale and ethics. The emphasis on contract- and grant-getting at universities, and the two-tier pay system, has reduced the morale of professors in fields—such as literature and fine arts—in which corporations have little interest. Through their actions, university administrators have told professors in these fields that their work and contributions are less valued than the work of professors in

TABLE 27.1 Expenditures of Major State Universities: Main Campuses (in millions [of dollars])

	1980			1990		
	Total	Instruction	Research	Total	Instruction	Research
University of Colorado (Boulder)	141.9	39.8	24.2	352.5	111.3	82.5
University of Florida	318.3	106.1	64.2	772.7	229.0	220.0
University of Georgia	200.0	62.1	39.9	497.5	106.6	130.6
University of Maryland	183.9	63.3	24.4	524.0	152.1	85.6
University of Michigan	598.4	153.2	83.8	1,759.2	304.7	244.4
University of Minnesota	542.4	156.3	85.7	1,418.9	329.4	276.3
University of North Carolina (Chapel Hill)	292.3	117.4	44.2	686.4	241.1	103.1
Penn State University	285.3	84.3	40.0	685.2	166.1	179.2
University of Wisconsin (Madison)	457.4	111.6	127.9	1.188.0	227.8	303.1

SOURCE: *American Universities and Colleges,* 12th and 14th editions.

areas like business and computer science, which have cultivated close ties with corporations. This lack of respect, in turn, has made professors in these fields place increasing emphasis on "research" and publication, rather than [on] teaching, in the tenure and promotion process. By emphasizing research, professors in literature and the arts have attempted to demonstrate that they are "just as good" as professors of business, medicine, and computer science. This shift in focus has lowered the quality of teaching in these fields as well.

The Financial Impact of Corporate Research

Since the early 1980s, the largest increase in university expenditures has been for research. At most universities, research expenditures more than doubled between 1980 and 1991. At many large state universities, research expenditures tripled in the same period, as did tuition. As Table 27.1 shows, research expenditures at the University of Colorado in 1991 were over three times what they were in 1980. At the University of Michigan, research expenditures tripled between 1980 and 1991, whereas instructional expenditures didn't quite double. As a result, Michigan spent nearly as much on

research in 1991 as on instruction. Similar increases in research expenditures occurred at large private universities, such as Harvard and MIT, so that their research expenditures now equal or even exceed instructional expenditures.

The primary beneficiaries of these increases in university R&D spending have been corporations, which receive the benefits of the research at a subsidized cost. But it is students and taxpayers who pick up the bill for most of it. At the University of Michigan, for example, corporate grants and contracts during fiscal year 1993 funded about a tenth of the university research, from which corporate interests benefited most. Tuition, federal agencies, state allocations, and university investments paid for the rest. Overall, the university contributed more money to research than did industry.[20]

The research expenditures presented in Table 27.1, and [as] described above, greatly underestimate actual university research expenses because they do not include indirect costs, such as the salaries of university bureaucrats—grants officers, development experts, and lawyers— who secure research contracts and grants. This class of university employee increased more rapidly during the 1980s than [did] any other. Other indirect, hidden costs of university research include constructing expensive, state-of-the-art facilities and equipping laboratories. When these hidden costs are added to direct research expenditures, it becomes clear that universities are R&D, not instructional, centers.

Another hidden cost is the increasing diversion of state funds to lure research centers from one university to another. For example, the state of Florida appropriated $66 million to lure a magnet-studying lab from MIT to Florida State University. The lab was brought to Florida in the hopes that it would stimulate more research there and thus bring in additional corporate and government grants.[21] Florida taxpayers will undoubtedly have to pour millions more into the laboratory after it arrives at Florida State.

Another indirect effect of the emphasis on research at universities—one that has contributed to higher tuition and inferior undergraduate instruction—is that universities emphasizing research tend to have expensive, labor-intensive Ph.D. programs, which produce research assistants to work on the R&D projects. At some universities, such as the University of Minnesota, graduate courses are often taught with just two or three Ph.D. students in them. Because professors are teaching these small graduate classes, fewer undergraduate classes are taught, and this scarcity increases the number of students in each undergraduate class.

Sometimes universities hire additional professors to reduce growing class sizes. This strategy simply increases universities' expenditures and thus, ultimately, tuition. Some universities employ graduate students as teaching assistants to provide undergraduate instruction. These teaching assistants, however, usually receive tuition reimbursement, which eliminates tuition dollars that would go to pay professors to teach graduate courses. The professors' salaries

must therefore be paid by undergraduates, even though the undergraduate students are not taught by professors.

And when universities face budget cuts, it is undergraduate educational programs, not research laboratories, that face the most draconian cuts. For example, after the state of Wisconsin forced the University of Wisconsin–Milwaukee to trim its budget by $1.85 million, administrators announced that the university would hire more part-time instructors, increase the size of classes, and cut tutorial programs.[22] The university didn't announce any cuts to its research program.

Moving from the Boardroom to the Classroom

University research has produced a downward spiral in instructional quality and an upward spiral in tuition at most universities. The only way that this cycle can be broken is by forcing professors back into classrooms and out of laboratories—by cutting university-corporate ties.

A first step in reversing the downward educational spiral would be the enactment of state laws that require professors at state universities to teach a minimum number of courses (e.g., three) each semester. All professors—including department chairs, endowed professors, and grant-funded researchers—should be required to teach the minimum. This requirement would place more emphasis on teaching, decrease class sizes, and remove the incentive for professors to pursue corporate contracts. It would also make it more likely that teacher-scholars would move into administrative posts rather than having such posts filled by professional administrators who have little regard for teaching or scholarship.

Another step to reverse this spiral would be to mandate that teaching, not research contracts and grant-getting, be given the greatest weight in the tenure and promotion process. Thus professors who have neglected their classroom responsibilities for consulting, contract research, and other corporate work would be penalized rather than rewarded.

To accomplish these goals, reformers must change the composition of universities' boards of trustees, which are now dominated by corporate CEOs. Trustees of state universities need to represent their populations rather than business.[23] One way to accomplish this change in representation would be to enact legislation mandating that these boards of trustees mirror their state's population.

Another step—one that would help reverse the shift of public money to the private sector—would be to change the tax code. City, county, and state governments need to revoke the tax-exempt status of centers, institutes, and laboratories that conduct corporate research at private universities. Because these centers function as corporate R&D laboratories, they should be taxed as though they were corporate, rather than instructional, facilities. The taxes collected from these centers could be used for bona fide educational programs such as student scholarships.

On a national level, the 1980 University and Small Business Patent Procedures Act needs to be rescinded. It is this law that allows universities to virtually hand over to corporations research funded by taxpayers, providing a major incentive for corporations to cultivate close ties to universities.

Moreover, academic organizations need to change their assumptions, as the American Psychological Association recently did, and require professors to disclose their consulting, contracts, stock ownership, and other conflicts of interest in published research articles. [Not only should] professors' conflicts of interest be disclosed in articles, but readers should also be warned that the findings are to be viewed as tentative until independently replicated. Academic organizations also need to establish stiff sanctions such as the expulsion of members who violate their conflict-of-interest rules.

Universities need to adopt similar, but much more strenuous, policies such as prohibiting professors from publishing research in which they have any financial stake. Professors who violate these policies should be fired.

Notes

1. In UCLA's College of Engineering and Applied Sciences, there is the Rockwell International Chair of Engineering, the Northrop Chair in Electrical Engineering, the TRW Chair in Electrical Engineering, the Hughes Aircraft Company Chair in Manufacturing Engineering, and the Nippon Sheet Glass Company Chair in Materials Science. UCLA also houses the John E. Anderson School of Business, named for the tycoon who gave it $15 million in 1987, and the Olin Center for Policy, an on-campus advocacy center that is funded by a million-dollar grant from the John M. Olin Foundation.

2. Julie L. Nicklin, "Philip Morris Boosts Aid to Colleges, but Critics Question Tobacco Company's Motives," *Chronicle of Higher Education,* October 13, 1993, pp. A37, A39.

3. Telephone interview of February 12, 1992.

4. "Across the USA," *USA Today,* March 9, 1993, p. A8; Goldie Blumenstyk, "Philanthropy Notes," *Chronicle of Higher Education,* May 12, 1993, p. A35. According to these reports, Janet MacDonald, the deputy treasurer of the University and Community College System of Nevada, said that the regents initially rejected the ACE "gift" because a company cannot contract for "research and count it as a charitable donation." Two months later, after University of Nevada at Las Vegas officials re-

negotiated the agreement with ACE Denken, the board of regents approved the "gift." The new agreement still called for the university to hold an annual seminar on gambling, but it did not allow ACE management to choose the topic or determine the invitation list. However, the new agreement did not prohibit ACE from suggesting topics for the seminar or a list of people who should be invited. The agreement still called for the university to publish a journal, albeit with fewer restrictions than called for in the original agreement. Finally, the new agreement called for ACE and the university to review their collaboration every five years rather than having the agreement last indefinitely. The board of regents approved the new agreement, stating that it was not without strings. "The ambiguities are gone," Janet Mac-Donald said of the new agreement.

5. "Give and Take," *Chronicle of Higher Education,* November 25, 1992, p. A21; "$100 Million Donated to New Jersey College," *Washington Times,* July 7, 1992, p. A5.

6. "School Aid on One Condition," *Philadelphia Inquirer,* November 13, 1992, p. A1; "NJ Legislators and Unions Assail Henry Rowan's Scholarship Rule," *Philadelphia Inquirer,* November 14, 1992, p. A1.

7. For example, this classification, first employed by the Carnegie Foundation, is used in "Pay and Benefits of Leaders at 190 Private Colleges and Universities," *Chronicle of Higher Education,* May 5, 1993, pp. A17-A24.

8. L. Stuart Ditzen, "Colleges Learn Price of Patents," *Orlando Sentinel Tribune,* May 6, 1990, p. D1.

9. University of Minnesota president Nils Hasselmo typifies the atitude of university administrators. Although student satisfaction at his university was rated 122nd among major universities in a *U.S. News & World Report* survey, Hasselmo lauded his university's accomplishments in a *Star Tribune* commentary, writing that "we have become one of the nation's leading universities in patents secured." See Nils Hasselmo, " 'U' Ties to Industry Result in Private, Public Benefits," *Minneapolis Star Tribune,* June 7, 1998, p. A25.

10. Ibid.

11. Linda Williams, "Academia Wises Up on Patents," *Los Angeles Times,* March 16, 1990, p. A1.

12. Felicity Barringer, "Drug Patent Debate Turns on Risks, Costs," *Washington Post,* May 13, 1983, p. A17; "Bristol-Myers' License for Anti-Cancer Drug Is Extended," *PR Newswire,* January 15, 1988.

13. Ernest Hollings, "The Ruins of Reaganism," *Washington Post,* April 30, 1989, p. C2.

14. Eric Schmitt, "House Battle Threatens Big Research Universities with Loss of Millions," *New York Times,* August 17, 1994, p. A9.

15. Jim Glassman, "University Research: Private Investment and Public Interests," *At the Crossroads* (Northern Tier Land Grant Accountability Project), July 1993, pp. 1-2, 7.

16. William Honan, "Cost of 4-Year Degree Passes $100,000 Mark," *New York Times,* May 4, 1994, p. A13.

17. *The World Almanac and Book of Facts 1994* (Mahwah, NJ: Funk & Wagnals, 1993), p. 200.

18. "Financial Aid: Attempts at Diversity Create Bidding Wars," *Daily Political Report* (American Political Network), October 7, 1992; Rhonda Reynolds, "Doctorates Up . . . but to What Degree?," *Black Enterprise,* June 1994, p. 40.

19. Philip Stevens, "Universities Find a New Partner," *World Press Review,* October 1986, p. 37; Anthony DePalma, "Universities' Reliance on Companies Raises Vexing Questions on Research," *New York Times,* March 17, 1993, p. B9.

20. Most statistics in this chapter are from the university self-reports published in *American Council on Education, American Universities and Colleges,* 14th ed. (New York: Walter de Gruyter, 1992). The 1980 data came from the 12th edition of this publication. The University of Michigan statistics are from "UM Research Outlays at an All-Time High," *Michigan Today,* March 1995, p. 6. Just as tuition has helped pay for university research, patient fees at academic hospitals have been used to subsidize research. Many academic hospitals admit this but deny that their research spending has contributed to the increased costs of medical care. For a discussion of patient subsidies to medical research, see Elisabeth Rosenthal, "Elite Hospitals in New York City Are Facing a Major Crunch," *New York Times,* February 13, 1995, p. A13.

21. William Celis, III, "The Big Stars on Campus Are Now Research Labs," *New York Times,* December 4, 1994, pp. 1, 18.

22. Tom Vanden Brook, "UWM Meets Mandate to Cut $1.85 Million," *Milwaukee Journal,* December 30, 1994, p. B1.

23. This doesn't simply mean that high school dropouts should be appointed as trustees but that social workers, psychologists, educators, and others who can address the needs of the poor and disadvantaged and can represent them should be. The same can be said for other constituencies.

28

Disposable Faculty: Part-Time Exploitation as Management Strategy

Linda Ray Pratt

A passage in a song by the group Meatloaf captures succinctly part of the daily reality for part-time faculty. "I want you, I need you," the song begins, but there's no way, the passage continues, "I'm ever gonna love you." Don't be sad, the song advises, "'cause two out of three ain't bad." Of course, if the bill of particulars were to continue, it would not be love alone that's missing in the contract for part-time faculty; respect, a fair salary, benefits, and a role in governance are often equally unavailable.

Part-time faculty employment is one of those abusive situations that is just too convenient for institutions to give up if they don't have to. There are some who argue the value of an inexpensive temporary faculty to institutional flexibility, and some who insist that many people—they especially like to point to women—are really served by the possibility of part-time teaching, but none of these apologists can wash out the undeniable exploitation that accompanies the job, even for those who want only part-time work. "Part-time teaching" often is a slow track to nowhere if you want anything more than the pleasures of having a class and

an affiliation with a college or university.[1] The pay scale has been static for several years, the jobs hardly ever convert to regular tenure-track lines, and a record of part-time faculty employment damages one's prospects in the job market. No one who is employed part-time or who employs a part-time faculty will be startled by these statements. The thorny question is why things don't seem to change when everyone knows what the problems are and what might make them less painful to the people and the profession as a whole.

Not only are solutions not taking hold, but the number of people affected keeps escalating. Nationally, the number of part-time workers throughout the economy increased by 88.9 percent between 1969 and 1992. Statistics about the number of new jobs filled suggest that as many as 75 percent of them are part-time. Still, the percent of faculty who are part-time is more than double the 16.9 percent overall figure for the U.S. workforce.[2] Statistics can only hint at the human costs, but they are compelling measures of the marginalized state of academic employment. According to the most recent data collected by the United States Department of Education, the percentage of faculty members holding part-time positions has risen from 22 percent in 1970 to nearly 45 percent in 1992.[3] The percentage of part-time faculty in commu-

AUTHOR'S NOTE: This is a reprint of an article originally published as Pratt, Linda Ray, "Disposable Faculty: Part-Time Exploitation as Management Strategy," in *Will Teach for Food*, edited by Cary Nelson (University of Minnesota Press), 1997, pp. 264-77. Used with permission.

nity colleges has risen to almost 65 percent. Percentages in the range of 40 to 45 percent of all faculty translate as something close to four hundred thousand people. Constricted funding for higher education, the downsizing of the tenure-track faculty in many institutions, and an increase in the number of Ph.D. degrees granted each year are likely to send these figures higher every year for the foreseeable future.

In the field of English, for example, which employs large numbers of part-time faculty, the number of Ph.D.'s awarded in 1995 rose to 1,080 from 943 in 1994, while the number of tenure-track jobs fell to 234 from 249 the year before; the number of listed positions of all kinds in 1995 was 605, down from 679.[4] If we assume that new Ph.D.'s remain viable in the market for at least three years, the compounding number of job-seekers must be reaching about ten people for each tenure-track position. Put another way, if things continue unchecked, about 90 percent of the English Ph.D.'s on the market in the next few years will not find a tenure-track job. More than 40 percent of recent Ph.D.'s in English won't secure any full-time position. The numbers of recent Ph.D.'s who then seek part-time employment to survive in the profession create an ever-larger pool of cheap labor that only an administrative saint could resist.

In terms of the numbers of aspiring faculty members who will be shoved out of the profession, the situation is desperately bad and getting worse. In terms of those who continue as part-time or temporary full-time faculty, the market will be more flooded with overqualified applicants, though in a few places there are small signs of improving conditions that help to make long-range underemployment more palatable. In terms of the profession, the growing use of non-tenure-track faculty is diminishing the influence of the faculty by reducing the number of tenure-track jobs, the role of faculty in governance, and the general prestige of the academy. From an administrative point of view, these patterns may facilitate the new pathways that administrative organizations such as the American Association of Higher Education want to create. These new pathways include reduced emphasis on research and more emphasis on undergraduate teaching; post-tenure review; erosion of the tenure system; increased evaluation of teaching, especially by peers in the classroom; and greater responsiveness to external communities.[5]

In the presence of efforts to reduce the size of the tenure-track faculty, expand non-tenurable positions, and institute post-tenure review, the power of tenure to protect faculty from assaults on their academic freedom and economic stability is under severe attack. Many administrators and their organizations openly expect eventually to eliminate tenure, and the replacement of full-time faculty with part-time faculty is one strategy in this effort. Some tenure-track faculty callously accept the professional advantages that arise from employing an underpaid cadre of part-time teachers, but growing numbers of them are troubled because the link between increased use of part-time faculty and administrative redesign of faculty roles is more apparent now that post-tenure review is an open strategy. Faculty members see their own departments shrinking and their work changing. They are also confronted with their own inability to successfully assist their graduate students in securing a place in the profession.

Areas such as English, math, and modern languages that are typically required for a liberal arts degree have traditionally relied most heavily on part-time faculty to cover beginning-level courses. However, in an era of "downsizing" in which such departments have lost as much as 10, 20, and 30 percent of their tenure-track lines,[6] the part-time faculty is increasingly called on to teach upper division courses. The failure of most institutions to provide any kind of support for faculty development for part-time faculty is less acceptable as those faculty members take on a wider role in teaching an advanced curriculum. Ten years ago, only about 30 percent of part-time faculty held the Ph.D. degree, and only about 20 percent of part-time faculty sought full-time employment.[7] The increasing number of unemployed Ph.D.'s, the overwhelming majority of whom want tenure-track jobs, has changed all that.[8] Aspiring faculty with the terminal degree, teaching experience, and scholarly activity, often with a list of publications, crowd a part-time market that was once predominantly made up of people with master's degrees and limited credentials beyond graduate course work.

The better the credentials of prospective part-time faculty members, the more apparent the professional debasement of them becomes. Many a graduate assistant, reasonably supported and mentored while in the degree program, has found herself with degree in hand teaching the same courses at the same institution for less pay and no benefits as a part-time faculty member. Many departments provide travel money for Ph.D. students to give papers at conferences as part of the effort to provide responsible graduate training but offer nothing to part-time faculty for the same activity. About half of the institutions provide some medical benefits to employees who work half-time or more, but almost none provides retirement benefits. The future impact of a number of years in the workforce without accruing retirement cannot readily be calculated, but it is potentially an employment liability from which one can never fully recover. After several years of staying alive in the profession through part-time teaching, one of three things usually happens: a few people find a full-time job of some sort and move on with their careers; a larger proportion settles into long-term part-time teaching if another source of family income makes it affordable to work this way; [or] a substantial number, faced with the need for more income and some opportunity to advance, leave the profession. Even those who choose to teach part-time because of partner relationships or other personal considerations are demoralized when performance goes largely unnoticed or faithful service over time does not merit stability of appointment. Eventually, a profession that offers nothing better than marginal employment to those who have met the standards will not attract the most promising young minds.

Stories of the "highway flyers" or "scholar gypsies" who combine two or three part-time jobs in order to make a living are legend, but they are not representative of the large numbers of people for whom multiple academic jobs—even part-time ones—are not a possibility. Many of the biggest universities and best private colleges are not in urban areas where numerous other campuses exist, and many part-time faculty members find themselves in a one-employer market where wages face no competition and an oversupply of degrees floods the local pool. What is "the profession" like for them?

The letter of appointment will also contain the notice of termination. The salary is on a per-course basis, typically somewhere between one thousand and three thousand dollars per section. The average is closer to sixteen hundred dollars. Perhaps you are earning twenty-eight hundred dollars per section in math, but your friend in Spanish is getting eighteen hundred dollars per section. You are teaching six courses a year but are still called "part-time," even though full-time faculty members typically teach three courses per semester—the explanation for what differentiates the two is that the latter also have time assigned to research and service. For teaching six to eight courses in an academic year, the income may be less than ten thousand dollars and rarely more than twenty-five thousand dollars. Private colleges, which often tout themselves as places where students receive personal attention, will probably pay you less than the state university to provide that special care. You will be required to turn in student teaching evaluations, but no one will read them or evaluate your work. Your rank will have nothing to do with your credentials. Many of the people in the department will not know who you are, even as you begin your fifth year with them. The governance structure will provide for student members on committees, but not for the presence of part-time faculty. You will share a small office with three other part-time faculty who are also teaching three or four classes a semester. No typewriter or computer is in the office, and the department does not supply voice mail since the telephone is shared and maybe not in the office at all. When you set up appointments for all the students in a class, you move to a table in the student union for the day since it will be quieter to talk with them there. When the students ask about nominating you for a teaching award, you have to tell them you are not eligible. You give a paper at your own expense at a conference, and the department lists it as evidence of its productivity. Next year, you will have to apply all over again for this job and wait until summer to know if you have it. The final blow is that after a few years of working under these conditions, you'll find yourself stigmatized on the job market as a "part-timer" by those who know perfectly well what the market is like but wonder what was wrong with you that you didn't get a job.

Those close to the world of part-time employment know that this profile, while it varies some from place to place [and from] person to person, is not exaggerated. With pay so low, professional considerations so few, demeaning conditions so prevalent, and unanimity among the professional associations and teachers unions about the need for change, how can this situation go on year to year with so little improvement? First, the profit to the institution is outrageously advantageous. To illustrate, if a full professor in math, English, or modern languages with a salary of $69,750 retires and the department loses the tenure-track line, the equivalent number of courses may be taught by a part-time faculty member for a "replacement" cost of two or three thousand per section.[9] By replacing the tenured line with part-time instruction, the institution may spend ten thousand to fifteen thousand dollars to cover the same number of classes. This is a savings of fifty-five thousand to sixty thousand dollars in salary instead of the thirty thousand to thirty-five thousand dollars that would have been saved had a new tenure-track position been approved. Exact figures will vary in each institution, of course, but the pattern is that replacing a retiring member of the tenure track with part-time faculty will often save as much as three-quarters of the salary, as opposed to half or less of it if a new tenure-track hire is approved. Since the part-time faculty member will not get start-up costs or a full benefits package, the savings are in fact even greater than just from salary.

Beyond its utility for stretching the budget and subsidizing the reallocation of salary money to other purposes, the use of part-time faculty is also valued as a deliberate management strategy. This is more reprehensible than the practice of using part-time employment as a means to balance the budget. Exploitative employment situations are bad enough when they are an unfortunate but necessary budget restriction. Exploitative employment practices as a tactic to redesign—or "re-engineer"—the academy are worse because they coolly calculate the use the institution can make of the economic desperation and despairing ambitions of its potential workers. Higher education is indeed on a tighter budget; state appropriations in the 1990s were down over the increases of the 1980s, and many institutions had zero increases or increases below the inflation rate. But except in a few states, funding was not down as much or as uniformly as some accounts imply. The disastrous cuts in California distort the national figures for funding in the 1990s, which tend to hold at about the rate of inflation when California is left out of the picture (Lively 1993, A29). Many states had small but steady increases over the rate of inflation, and some, especially in the South, had significant increases in funding.

With a generally static budget picture on many campuses, the bruising pinch for funds in part came from changing priorities within the institutions. Higher education now reflects a definition of what colleges and universities must offer students and external communities *in addition* to faculty and classes. At the state universities, reallocation has transferred resources away from academic programs and into expanding management personnel and student services and extending connections to the corporate and civil communities, known in administrative jargon as the "stakeholders." Within the academic programs, classes have gotten larger, the tenure-track faculty smaller, and the part-time faculty and graduate assistant instructors more numerous. A recent sampling of departments around the country for the American Association of University Professors found it was not uncommon for as much as 65 percent or more of instruction in math, English, and modern languages to be in the hands of part-time faculty and graduate students.[10] At the state level, shifts in resources were often away from the more costly four-year institutions to the two-year colleges where instruction is cheaper because it is mainly in the hands of low-paid part-time and non-tenure-track faculty.

Administrators who hire part-time and non-tenure-track faculty at wages less than beginning public school teachers would make have the insulation of not having to see the human situation at the other end of their management objectives. Part-time faculty appointments are largely a hidden problem above the level of the department administration. The department chair may be the only person in the institution who knows how many part-time faculty [and who] are carrying out what work in the department. Since the non-salary academic costs of making fewer full-time commitments are largely hidden, delayed, or shifted elsewhere in assessing the real fiscal and educational impact, the immediate profit for an administration in using part-time faculty is an expediency that seemingly outweighs the harm that comes with the gains. The biggest costs are to the overall stability of the academic programs, especially in curricular development and research activity. Some other kinds of costs, unemployment compensation for example, can add up to a considerable sum in places where part-time faculty are hired in an off-and-on pattern. Part-time faculty can usually qualify for up to twenty-six weeks of unemployment compensation after working for the institution [for] four months. Twenty-six weeks of unemployment compensation may cost the institution as much as it would have paid in salary to keep the employee. I have known part-time faculty members who sustained themselves between appointments in just this way. In metropolitan areas with a large turnover in part-time faculty, these costs can be substantial. Professional employees, because they are an expensive investment in training, increase costs to an institution in numerous ways when it has a high rate of turnover, not the least of which is the cost of expensive graduate programs to train people for nonexistent jobs. But these kinds of cost issues are not usually much considered when making decisions about faculty. Administrators on the fast track to bigger things are more often measured by their ability to cut budgets and produce more with less than by the long-term stability and quality of the academic programs for which they were responsible. Strengthening tenure, investing more in faculty resources, and improving the status of the lowest ranking instructors are not the values that secure career moves for administrators. Studies of "administrative bloat" indicate that proximity is one important factor in determining an administrator's sense of priorities.[11] Just as this bloat produces in them a greater felt need for more midlevel administrators, so, too, does it make the conditions of an almost wholly invisible part-time faculty less real and pressing.[12]

Recognizing that part-time employment is a management tool as well as a budgetary strategy means that merely exposing the wrongs will not lead to remedy. The very attractiveness of part-time faculty for institutions depends on maintaining the status quo. Thus, despite their growing numbers and the open concern expressed about the conditions of part-time employment by nearly every disciplinary and professional organization, part-time faculty remain largely unseen and unheard in their institutions, which allows the exploitation to go unchecked. Only those strategies that can alter the institutional self-interest are likely to be effective. Faculty members in general, [and] the most vulnerable and powerless faculty in particular, cannot influence institutional directions as long as they are silent, uninformed, or unorganized. The conditions of part-time employment conspire, however, to create a climate in which fear for one's tenuous appointment curbs dissent. One's marginalized position in the profession makes it difficult to know what is happening before it's done, and one's isolation within the

workforce makes it difficult to identify others in the same situation. Despite these barriers, some progress has been made. Part-time faculty members at Rutgers and Kent State have successfully organized unions. After an intense and protracted struggle, the Rutgers union negotiated its first contract. *The Adjunct Advocate,* under the editorship of P. D. Lesko, has given a national voice to part-time faculty. The American Association of University Professors (AAUP), the American Federation of Teachers (AFT), and the National Education Association (NEA) have all published thoughtful status reports and position papers that lend credibility to the critical analysis of part-time employment and offer viable guidelines that could improve it. A few institutions, such as New Mexico State, have approved plans that provide nontenure-track faculty with adequate notice, renewable appointments, equivalent rank, and professional evaluation. In still fewer cases, the institution has agreed to a limit on the number of part-time faculty and a plan for the eventual conversion of such appointments to full-time permanent positions.

The most effective way for part-time faculty to act in their own behalf is through a union, but that is not a possibility in many cases and not a probability in many others. Part-time faculty unions are most likely to succeed where the full-time faculty unions have set a precedent for faculty organizing. Often the part-time faculty will be represented by the same union that negotiates for the full-time faculty, but just as likely, part-time faculty will have a parallel organization. Unions are the best way to take the cheapness and convenience out of part-time employment because they raise the institution's monetary costs and time investment through both the contract and the act of negotiating it. That, of course, is why institutions will fight tooth and nail to defeat unions that may curtail the degrees of flexibility and savings that make part-time faculty desirable. Although collective bargaining offers the only legally protected way for employees to negotiate the terms of their employment, part-time teachers must have other strategies. Whole regions of the country, such as the South and much of the Southwest, deny faculty the right to collective bargaining. Even in states where the right of teachers to bargain is enabled by legislation, the right of part-time employees may be restricted. Faculty members in private institutions have been denied the right to collective bargaining by the Supreme Court's *Yeshiva* decision, which argues that faculty are essentially managers and thus not entitled to unionize.[13] States such as New York, New Jersey, Connecticut, Michigan, and California have extensive faculty collective bargaining, but the majority of U.S. professors are not unionized, unlike their counterparts in much of the rest of the world. Part-time faculty members may find significant legal barriers to unionizing, but there are no laws against organizing, even under the name of an association that may function as a union elsewhere (e.g., the AAUP, AFT, and NEA). An organization of part-time faculty members, armed with the policy recommendations from the disciplinary and professional associations, can give voice to their concerns and purpose to their agitation.

The goal of part-time faculty strategies must be to take the cheapness and convenience out of current practice. This means forcing administrations to put more money into it and more stability behind it, two conditions that negate the attractiveness of part-time over full-time positions. In the long term, this means either restructuring the funding priorities in favor of faculty resources or reversing the marketplace by eliminating the surplus of Ph.D.'s. In the short term, a number of objectives can advance these goals and ameliorate the present situation. One crucial strategy is to establish professional considerations that protect the quality of higher education and the standards appropriate to the profession. These include the use of job descriptions to structure responsibilities and rewards; a formal evaluation of job performance; acceptable standards for working conditions (office space, supplies, basic technology); adequate notice of renewal and termination; access to benefits; rank commensurate with credentials; resources for professional development; participation in faculty governance; and the state-sanctioned protections of affirmative action, equal pay for equal work, due process, and nondiscrimination. In the long term, the profession must balance the supply of Ph.D. degrees with the opportunities for employment, which means limiting graduate school enrollments.

Many of the changes listed above do not require a major financial investment and are patently in the interest of quality education. Yet most institutions have doggedly avoided implementing them. One reason administrations oppose affordable improvements for part-time faculty, such as assigning rank according to credentials or requiring annual evaluation of performance, is that written records of quality work and acknowledgments of credentials legitimize professional status. Recognition of professional accomplishment raises expectations on both sides about the conditions of employment. Written recognition of professional accomplishment opens the door to advancement where merited and grievance where merit is denied. In blunt terms, institutions do not want to be responsible for providing professional situations for part-time faculty, and thus they avoid changes that encourage professional expectations. Administrations may feel that they are acting in the most pragmatic sense of institutional interests in holding down the expectations of temporary faculty. It is, however, a rationale that few would want to defend in a public forum, especially to parents and politicians who think that higher tuition should produce an improved quality of college education. An institution cannot buy instruction on the cheap and still convince the public of its commitment to the high quality of its education, at least not unless we let [it].

As long as the academic labor supply far outstrips the number of positions available, the profession will be vulnerable to the use and abuse of part-time faculty. As long as institutions need the savings and want the management implications derived from a large number of underemployed faculty, they will continue to hire them. Those who worry about creating a two-tier faculty should recognize that it is already here and begin to focus on closing up the distances that harm both tiers and the institutions themselves. Nothing can place at greater risk the status of full-time faculty or the importance of tenure than withholding professional treatment from almost half the members of the profession. The lyrics from Meatloaf's song speak of having the need and the desire but withholding the love. If "love" translates in the world of work as respect, fairness, and interest in the collective welfare of one's colleagues, then the treatment of part-time faculty members today withholds that necessary component to professional soundness. In practice, if not in rhetoric, institutions use part-time faculty as an inexpensive and consumable commodity. The disposable faculty. A consumer-oriented society invests in and protects those things it considers too valuable to replace easily. The future academic environment will determine whether faculty members—full- and part-time—are to be disposed of, recycled, or protected. The haunting emotion of Meatloaf's lyrics is that they play their meagerness off the promise of fullness in the original song by Elvis where want, need, and love hold equal stanzaic importance. Unlike that original expression of wholehearted commitment, the revision illustrates the cold

miscalculation that unravels all. As members of the profession, we, too, can invalidate all in the denial of essential parts of the whole. If higher education miscalculates its own best interests that badly, it, too, will lose the respect that is its coin of value. And no one needs to remind us what's down at the end of that lonely street.

Notes

1. "Part-time faculty" is not a fully accurate term since many faculty work full-time some semesters and part-time others, often in the same year for the same institution. Some work on full-time temporary contracts for one to three years and then find themselves back to part-time employment. "Temporary faculty" is also an inaccurate term since the average length of time a part-time faculty member teaches at an institution is almost seven years. I shall use the term "part-time faculty" because the problems associated with the most exploitative aspects of faculty underemployment affect those who do not have full-time permanent positions, even though their appointment in any given year may vary. In that sense, though they may wind up with a "full-time equivalent" (FTE) assignment of courses in any given semester or year, they are situationally part-time in terms of pay, security, status, and, in most cases, benefits.

2. These figures, drawn from several government sources, are published in Robinson 1994, 4.

3. Department of Education data from Fall 1992 are the most recent national figures. The data supplied by the National Center for Education Statistics cited herein were presented at the annual meeting of the AAUP in June 1996 by Ernest Benjamin of the national staff. The 1992 national survey of postsecondary faculty estimated the number of part-time faculty at 43 percent. Benjamin's analysis notes that these

figures do not include part-time faculty replacements for faculty on leave. He argues for adjusting the figures upward to 45 percent. I cite his figures because his analysis recognizes more of the variables in how and when part-time faculty are employed.

4. See Modern Language Association of America (MLA) 1996. The MLA chart cites the positions advertised in the English-language edition of the October 1995 *Job Information List* (*JIL*) and the National Council on Research Report 1995. Not all the positions listed are either definite jobs or new ones, and not all positions get advertised nationally. Some jobs advertised are contingent on funds that do not materialize, and others are positions that were carried over from the year before. Some term contract positions that materialize after the spring publication of *JIL* are advertised only regionally or in the *Chronicle of Higher Education*. I have no statistics about jobs that open after the close of the traditional academic year, but observation and experience indicate that most of these positions will be filled by part-time faculty. These jobs are usually designed to cover enrollment overflow or last-minute changes in the assignment of permanent faculty.

5. The American Association of Higher Education's new pathways project includes publications, workshops, and meetings designed to advance these and other ideas. The Pew Charitable Trust is funding much of this work.

6. My own department has undergone about a 20 percent reduction in the number of tenure-track lines in the last decade; Cary Nelson reports that his department dropped 30 percent in the number of tenure-track lines between 1970 and 1990. Neither institution nor department has had a significant decline in enrollments.

7. Figures from National Center for Educational Statistics of the Department of Educa-

tion 1987. The data in this survey were extensively analyzed in the "Report on the Status of Non-Tenure-Track Faculty" 1992.

8. Lomperis's study of Ph.D.'s from 1975 to 1985 indicated that two-thirds of them sought full-time work (see Lomperis 1990).

9. For purposes of this example, I took the average salary for full professors in Category I (doctoral) public institutions as reported in the 1995-96 salary survey of the AAUP (see "Not so Bad" 1996). Given the salary and the kind of institution behind this data, I then estimated the average range of starting salaries in these disciplines and the most frequently reported range of stipends per course for part-time replacement.

10. The sample was part of the work of the AAUP's Committee G on the status of part-time and non-tenure-track faculty. The committee published its extensive "Report on the Status of Non-Tenure-Track Faculty" with policy recommendations in 1993.

11. The term "administrative bloat" derives from Bergmann 1991.

12. Perhaps a similar sense of proximity of interests explains how administrative salaries in 1995-96 increased by 4.2 percent while faculty salaries increased by 2.9 percent. It was the fourth year in a row that administrative salaries exceeded the rate of inflation (College and University Personnel Association figures as printed in "Administrators' Salaries Outstrip Inflation" 1996, 11).

13. The court's absurd interpretation of faculty governance as the evidence of manager status must seem even more bizarre when extended to non-tenure-track faculty.

References

"Administrators' Salaries Outstrip Inflation." 1996. *Academe* 82, no. 2: 11.

Bergmann, Barbara. 1991. "Bloated Administration, Blighted Campuses." *Academe* 77, no. 6: 1216.

Lively, Kit. 1993. "State Support for Public Colleges Up 2% This Year." *Chronicle of Higher Education* (October 27): A29.

Lomperis, Ana Maria Turner. 1990. "Are Women Changing the Nature of the Academic Profession?" *Journal of Higher Education* 61, no. 6: 643-77.

Modern Language Association. 1996. Materials distributed at the Association of Departments of English meetings. Summer sessions.

National Center for Educational Statistics of the Department of Education. 1987. *National Survey of Post-secondary Faculty, 1987*.

———. 1992. Unpublished data from 1992 presented at the annual meeting of the [American Association of University Professors] in June 1996.

"Not so Bad: The Annual Report on the Economic Status of the Profession." 1996. *Academe* 82, no. 2: 14-108.

"Report on the Status of Non-Tenure-Track Faculty." 1992. *Academe* 78, no. 6: 3948.

Robinson, Perry. 1994. *Part-Time Faculty Issues*. Washington, D.C.: American Federation of Teachers.

Steinman, Jim. 1977. "Two Out of Three Ain't Bad." *Bat Out of Hell*. Vocals by Meatloaf. New York: CBS Inc.

The Tenure Debate

29

Is Tenure Necessary to Protect Academic Freedom?

Erwin Chemerinsky

The Role of Tenure in Protecting Academic Freedom

The institution of tenure is under serious attack. New schools, such as the soon-to-open Florida Gulf Coast University, are being created without the possibility of tenure for faculty members.[1] Some universities, such as Vermont's Bennington College, have abolished tenure.[2] In fact, it is estimated that nationally, about 20 percent of all independent four-year colleges no longer offer their faculty tenure.[3]

In addition, there are efforts in many places to significantly weaken the traditional protections accorded to tenured faculty members. A national debate over tenure was triggered by a proposal by the regents of the University of Minnesota to allow the university to fire tenured faculty members whose departments are eliminated and to permit the university to cut the salaries of tenured faculty members for reasons other than a financial emergency.[4] At the University of Southern California, tenured faculty members in the Basic Sciences Department of the Medical School sued when the

university decreased their salaries by 25 percent.[5]

Apart from all of these individual events, criticism of tenure is increasingly common by political officials and in the popular press. Attacks on tenure are prompted by a desire to increase the accountability of faculty members and to enhance the quality of their performance. Tenure is challenged as protecting the lazy faculty member who no longer engages in scholarship or effective teaching. The perception is that, safeguarded by a job for life, faculty members are insulated from scrutiny and pressure for enhanced performance.

Moreover, tenure is an anomaly; other than federal judges, who have their positions for life unless they are impeached, tenure is virtually unheard of in the American workplace. It is not surprising that politicians and the public question why academics should have a form of job security that is available to almost no one else.

Perhaps most important, the attack on tenure is a reflection of the lack of a recent systematic threat to academic freedom. During and soon after the McCarthy era, it was easy to explain the need for tenure to safeguard the ability of professors to speak and write in politically unpopular ways. Likewise, during the Vietnam War, tenure was understood as necessary to protect faculty members from reprisals

AUTHOR'S NOTE: This is a reprint of an article originally published as Chemerinsky, Erwin, "Is Tenure Necessary to Protect Academic Freedom?" *American Behavioral Scientist* 41(5), 1998, pp. 638-51.

for their political activities. But now those threats seem remote, and the need for tenure appears more abstract. A reflection of this is that a recent survey by the Higher Education Research Institute at UCLA found that 43 percent of all faculty members younger than age 45 believe that tenure is an outmoded concept, compared with about 30 percent of faculty members older than age 55.[6]

All of these attacks on tenure raise a basic question: is tenure necessary to protect academic freedom? Few would deny that it is imperative that faculty members be protected from adverse employment actions because of the content of their teaching, writing, or political activities. Protecting faculty members' freedom in these areas is both instrumentally and intrinsically desirable.

From an instrumental perspective, academic freedom ideally leads to better and more creative teaching and scholarship. Without the assurance of academic freedom, many faculty members might be chilled from taking novel or unpopular positions. Potentially important ideas might not be advanced, and intellectual debate and advancement would suffer. The late Chief Justice Earl Warren wrote,

The essentiality of freedom in the community of American universities is almost self-evident. . . . To impose any straitjacket upon the intellectual leaders in our colleges and universities would imperil the future of our nation. No field of education is so thoroughly comprehended by man that new discoveries cannot yet be made. . . . Scholarship cannot flourish in an atmosphere of suspicion and distrust. Teachers and students must always remain free to inquire, to study and to evaluate, to gain new maturity and understanding; otherwise, our civilization will stagnate and die.[7]

From an intrinsic perspective, tenure safeguards the freedom of faculty members to speak, write, and associate however they choose. Justice Thurgood Marshall observed

that "the First Amendment serves not only the needs of the polity but also those of the human spirit—a spirit that demands self-expression."[8] Freedom of speech is regarded in our society as an essential liberty, basic to autonomy. Professor Baker said that

to engage voluntarily in speech is to engage in self-definition or expression. A Vietnam War protester may explain that when she chants "Stop this war now" at a demonstration, she does so without any expectation that her speech will affect continuance of the war; . . . rather, she participates and chants in order to *define* herself publicly in opposition to the war. The war protester provides a dramatic illustration of the importance of this self-expressive use of speech, independent of any effective communication to others, for self-fulfillment or self-realization.[9]

Thus, academic freedom is highly valued.[10] It is not surprising that the Supreme Court has declared that "our nation is deeply committed to safeguarding academic freedom, which is of transcendent value to all of us and not merely to the teachers concerned."[11]

Tenure is a key mechanism for protecting academic freedom. Once a faculty member receives tenure, he or she cannot be subjected to adverse employment actions, such as firing, without proof of cause.[12] The American Association of University Professors, in a famous 1940 Statement of Principles on Academic Freedom and Tenure, declared,

Tenure is a means to certain ends, specifically: (1) freedom of teaching and research and of extramural activities and (2) a sufficient degree of economic security to make the profession attractive to men and women of ability. Freedom and economic security, hence tenure, are indispensable to the success of an institution in fulfilling its obligations to its students and to society.[13]

Tenure has an obvious role in protecting academic freedom.[14] By limiting the ability of the university to fire or otherwise take adverse actions against faculty members, tenure provides protection for faculty members to teach and write as they choose. As professors Brown and Kurland explained, "A system that makes it difficult to penalize a speaker does indeed underwrite the speaker's freedom."[15] A tenured faculty member can take a position, in the classroom or in scholarship or in the public arena, knowing that it is unpopular without worrying that it will lead to reprisals.

Often overlooked is that tenure offers both procedural and substantive protections. Procedurally, tenure means that a faculty member has continuing employment unless the university initiates an action against the faculty member and succeeds in proving "cause" for termination. The university must begin the proceedings to terminate a tenured faculty member and must bear the significant burden of proving the justification for its proposed action.

Substantively, tenure means that only specific, narrowly defined circumstances will constitute cause sufficient for termination or other adverse employment actions. Although the definition of *cause* varies by university, in general, there must be serious violations of the law or of principles of academic honesty to meet the standard.

The focus of this chapter is on whether alternatives to tenure can succeed in protecting academic freedom. My conclusion is that no alternative yet described is likely to succeed in providing both the procedural and the substantive protections accorded by tenure. In general, the inadequacy of alternatives is evidenced by their motivation. Those who seek alternatives to tenure do so because of a desire to weaken the current protections accorded to faculty members. Although the motivation behind these reforms is the laudable desire to increase accountability for faculty members, by definition, this entails a lessening of the safeguards embodied in the concept of tenure. Thus, any

alternative to tenure is likely to mean a substantial decrease in the protection afforded faculty members and consequently of academic freedom. The better approach is to devise ways to improve performance and accountability within the tenure system.

However, those who challenge tenure argue that alternatives might succeed in adequately protecting academic freedom, even if less so than the institution of tenure. Two primary alternatives have been advanced. One possibility is to protect faculty members from adverse actions that are in retaliation for the content of their teaching, writing, or political activity. The Supreme Court, in a series of cases, has provided protection for the First Amendment rights of government employees and limited the power to punish them for their speech activities.[16] Some argue that academic freedom can be adequately safeguarded by applying these principles to faculty members.

Another alternative is to provide faculty members with long-term contracts, such as for five or seven years, and to create a grievance procedure that would need to be followed before a faculty member could be terminated. This approach would seek to provide job security in the form of contractual protections and procedural safeguards in the nature of grievance hearings and decisions by faculty panels.[17]

I believe that neither of these alternatives is likely to succeed in protecting academic freedom. Neither provides the substantive protections that tenure accords in that neither limits the situations in which adverse actions can be taken to those that constitute cause. In addition, neither provides the procedural protection of tenure requiring that the university initiate proceedings and prove cause. The second section of this chapter discusses the former proposal of applying First Amendment protections accorded government employees to faculty members, and the third section analyzes the latter suggestion for replacing tenure with long-term contracts and grievance hearings.

Would First Amendment Protections Be an Adequate Substitute for Tenure?

Those who seek to weaken tenure generally do not argue against the concept of academic freedom or advocate the elimination of all protections for faculty members' speech. Rather, the argument is often made that academic freedom can be adequately protected by applying First Amendment principles. The claim is simple: tenure is valued because it protects the academic freedom of faculty members to speak and write without fear of reprisal. Therefore, tenure can be replaced by protections that limit the ability of a university to act against a faculty member because of his or her speech.

An analogy is often drawn to a series of decisions in which the Supreme Court has protected the free speech rights of government employees. Stated generally, the Court has held that the First Amendment prevents the government from acting against its employees because of their speech. The argument is that the application of these precedents to faculty members would suffice to safeguard academic freedom. In evaluating the desirability of this alternative, I first review the law concerning the First Amendment protections for government employees and then explain why this standard is insufficient to protect academic freedom.

The Law Concerning First Amendment Protections for Government Employees

The Supreme Court has held that the government may not punish the speech of public employees if it concerns matters of public concern unless the state can prove that the needs of the government outweigh the speech rights of the employee. In other words, speech by public employees is clearly less protected than other speech; First Amendment protection does not exist unless the expression is about public concern, and even then the employee can be disciplined or fired if the government can show, on balance, that the efficient operation of the office justified the action. It should be noted that these protections apply only for government employees, not for employees in the private sector. The Constitution applies only to government conduct, not to private action.

Pickering v. Board of Education is an important case in holding that speech by government employees is protected by the First Amendment.[18] A teacher was fired for sending a letter to a local newspaper that was critical of the way school officials had raised money for the schools. The Supreme Court held that the firing violated the First Amendment. Justice Marshall, writing for the Court, said that its task was to balance the free speech rights of government employees with the government's need for efficient operation. Justice Marshall wrote,

The state has interests as an employer in regulating the speech of its employees that differ significantly from those it possesses in connection with regulation of the speech of the citizenry in general. The problem in any case is to arrive at a balance between the interests of the teacher, as a citizen, in commenting upon matters of public concern and the interests of the State, as an employer, in promoting the efficiency of the public services it performs through its employees.[19]

The Court emphasized that there was no indication that Pickering's statements in any way interfered with the teacher's ability to perform or the operation of the school district. The Court also stressed that the speech concerned a matter of public concern: the operation of the school district. Indeed, the Court said that a teacher is likely to have unique and important insights as to the adequacy of educational funding. Although there were some factual inaccuracies in the statement, the Court held that "absent proof of false statements knowingly or recklessly made by him, a teacher's exercise of his right to speak on issues of public importance may not furnish a basis for his dismissal from public employment."[20]

In *Mt. Healthy City School District Board of Education v. Doyle,*[21] the Court articulated a test to be used in applying *Pickering.* An untenured teacher was not rehired after several speech-related incidents including arguing with another teacher, making an obscene gesture to students, and informing a local radio station about the principal's memorandum on teacher dress and appearance. The Court reiterated that speech by public employees is protected by the First Amendment. The Court said, however, that a public employee who otherwise would have been fired does not deserve special protection because of the speech.

Thus, the Court said that a public employee challenging an adverse employment action must initially meet the burden of showing that "his conduct was constitutionally protected and that this conduct was a 'substantial factor'—or, to put it in other words, that it was a 'motivating factor'" for the government's action.[22] If this is done, the burden shifts to the government to show by a "preponderance of the evidence that it would have reached the same decision . . . even in the absence of the protected conduct."[23]

In *Connick v. Meyers,*[24] the Court added [another] requirement to the *Pickering/Mt. Healthy* approach. An assistant district attorney, angry over a transfer to a different section in the office, circulated a memorandum soliciting the views of other attorneys in the office concerning the transfer policy, the level of morale, and the need for the establishment of a grievance committee. When the attorney was fired, she sued, alleging a violation of the First Amendment.

The Supreme Court ruled against the attorney, emphasizing that the speech was not protected by the First Amendment because it did not involve comment on matters of public concern. The Court, in an opinion by Justice White, said,

The repeated emphasis in *Pickering* on the right of a public employee as a citizen, in commenting upon matters of public concern, was not accidental. . . . [When] employee expression cannot fairly be considered as relating to any matter of political, social, or other concern to the community, officials should enjoy wide latitude in managing their offices without intrusive oversight by the judiciary in the name of the First Amendment.[25]

The Court said that "whether an employee's speech addresses a matter of public concern must be determined by the content, form, and context of a given statement."[26] Although Meyers' statements related to the performance of supervisors and policy in a public office, the Court said that it did not concern matters of public concern, especially because she was not seeking to inform the public.

However, the Court also has expressly ruled that private statements that are not made publicly are protected by the First Amendment so long as they involve matters of public concern. In *Givhan v. Western Line Consolidated School District,* the Court unanimously held that the school district violated the First Amendment [when it fired] a teacher because of her speech that privately communicated grievances about racially discriminatory policies.[27] The Court said that no First Amendment freedom "is lost to the public employee who arranges to communicate privately with his employer rather than to spread his views before the public."[28]

In *Rankin v. McPherson,* the Court applied *Connick* and found that a public employee's statement was protected by the First Amendment when she declared, after hearing of an assassination attempt directed at President Ronald Reagan, "If they go for him again, I hope they get him."[29] The Court held that the firing of the employee because of the statement violated the First Amendment because it concerned a matter of public concern. The Court, in an opinion by Justice Marshall, said that

the statement was made in the course of a conversation addressing the policies of the president's administration. It came on the heels of a news bulletin regarding what is certainly a matter of heightened public attention: an attempt on the life of the president. The inappropriate or controversial character of a statement is irrelevant to the question of whether it deals with a matter of public concern.[30]

The Court said that if a statement is of public concern, then a court must balance the public employee's First Amendment rights with the state's interest in the "effective functioning of the public employer's enterprise."[31] The Court found that the speech was protected by the First Amendment because there was no evidence that it interfered with the efficient functioning of the office.

The specific content of the employee's speech is obviously crucial in applying this test. Often, of course, there will be a dispute between the employer and employee over exactly what was said. How is this dispute to be resolved? The Court addressed this issue in *Waters v. Churchill.*[32] A nurse was disciplined and ultimately fired from a public hospital for her speech, but there was a dispute between her and the employer over what she actually said.

Justice O'Connor, writing for a plurality of four, said that the trier of fact should accept the employer's account of what was said so long as it is reasonable to do so. Justice O'Connor said

that there is no violation of the First Amendment when a government employer reasonably believes that speech does not involve matters of public concern. The plurality said that a court should side with the employer so long as the employer acted reasonably in obtaining information about what was said and so long as the employer's belief is reasonable.

Justice Scalia wrote an opinion concurring in the judgment, joined by two other justices, and said that the employee was protected by the First Amendment only if she could prove that the firing was in retaliation for constitutionally protected speech.[33] Scalia objected to the plurality's requirement that employers use reasonable procedures to ascertain what was said.

Justice Stevens dissented, in an opinion joined by Justice Blackmun, and argued that the content of the speech was a question of fact that should be tried like any other factual issue.[34] Justice Stevens said that the issue is not whether the employer followed reasonable procedures or even whether the employer had a reasonable belief. The question is whether the speech is protected by the First Amendment, and that can be ascertained only by first deciding what was said.

Thus, a three-step analysis can be derived from the cases: (1) the employee must prove that an adverse employment action was motivated by the employee's speech (if the employee does this, the burden shifts to the employer to prove by a preponderance of the evidence that the same action would have been taken anyway); (2) the speech must be deemed to be a matter of public concern; and (3) the Court must balance the employee's speech rights against the employer's interest in the efficient functioning of the office. Phrased another way, the employee can prevail only if he or she convinces the Court that speech was the basis for the adverse employment action, if the Court concludes that the speech concerned matters of public concern, and if the Court decides that, on balance, the speech interests outweigh the government's interests in regulating the expression for the sake of the efficiency of the office.

The First Amendment Is Not an Adequate Substitute for Tenure

For many reasons, it would be undesirable to replace tenure with the protections that are accorded government employees. At the outset, it should be noted that faculty members employed by public colleges and universities already have the First Amendment safeguards described above. A faculty member at a government institution now has both the protections of tenure and those of the Constitution. Abolishing tenure would not substitute new protections for these individuals but [would] only decrease the current safeguards of academic freedom.

Procedurally, a First Amendment approach would be far inferior from a faculty member's perspective when compared with tenure. Under the First Amendment approach, the burden would be on the faculty member to initiate an action claiming that the university acted improperly in retaliation for speech activity. In contrast, under the tenure system, the university has the burden of starting the proceedings to terminate a tenured faculty member. At the very least, the need to bring formal proceedings is a disincentive for the university to act. The easier it is for the university to terminate a faculty member, the more likely it is to act in retaliation for unpopular teaching or writing.

More important, a First Amendment approach puts the burden on the faculty member to show that the university's motive was a reprisal for speech activities. In many cases, this can be an insurmountable obstacle for the faculty member. Proving motive is often elusive,

and many faculty members may be discouraged from even initiating proceedings because of doubts about meeting this burden. When the faculty member protests the university's action, showing an improper motive for the adverse employment action may not be possible, even in some cases when the university's action actually was in retaliation for speech. In contrast, under the tenure system, the university must prove cause for termination. There is no burden on the faculty member to demonstrate improper purposes on the part of the university; the only issue is whether the university can prove just cause for termination.

From a substantive perspective, a First Amendment approach provides much less protection than the current tenure system. Now a tenured faculty member can be terminated only if there is proof of a limited number of circumstances that constitute cause. But under a First Amendment approach, the university is not restricted to just these narrow situations for taking an adverse action. Under the First Amendment approach, the university can act for any reason so long as it is not in retaliation for speech. This distinction is crucial: tenure means that a very narrow set of circumstances will be sufficient for terminating a faculty member; a First Amendment approach means that a virtually limitless set of circumstances will be sufficient for terminating a faculty member so long as the action is not a reprisal for the content of teaching or writing. For example, under the First Amendment approach, a university might try to fire a tenured faculty member for insubordination if he or she disobeys an order from a senior administrator. Under the tenure system, only in the most extreme cases could this be cause for termination.

Moreover, the First Amendment approach that is used to protect government employees would not even provide adequate safeguards for faculty members against reprisals for speech activities. If the government employee precedents were applied to faculty members, then only speech about matters of public concern would be protected.[35] Currently, all speech by tenured faculty members—whether or not of public concern—is protected from being the basis for reprisals unless it meets the narrow standard for cause. Moreover, the requirement that the speech be of public concern can be questioned because the First Amendment generally has no such limitation. In *Connick,* for example, the Court found that the employee's speech was not of public concern, even though it pertained to the functioning of an important public office.

Even more important, under current law, the government may act against an employee because of his or her speech if it demonstrates that, on balance, the expression interfered with the efficient functioning of the office. Under this approach, a faculty member could be terminated if the university demonstrated that the speech was disruptive and that, on balance, the university's interests outweighed the faculty member's interests in academic freedom. This is far less protection than faculty members have under the tenure system. Now a faculty member can be terminated only under the restrictive standards found in the definition of cause. But under the First Amendment approach, the university would just have to demonstrate that, on balance, its action was justified.

This simple balancing test—weighing speech interests against the government's interest in administrative efficiency—can be questioned as failing to place sufficient weights on the free speech side of the scale. The balance would seem to be specific to each case as to whether the university's interest in that instance outweighed the faculty member's speech interests. But the proper balance should be more general, weighing the overall effect on academic freedom of allowing the termination for the speech against the university's interests.

At the very least, a balancing test as used in *Pickering* and its progeny would leave faculty members uncertain as to when their speech would be protected and when it could be the basis for adverse employment actions. The high degree of protection embodied in tenure would be lost. Many faculty members might be chilled by this uncertainty, and academic freedom would be seriously compromised.

Thus, protecting faculty members' speech through a First Amendment approach would provide neither the procedural nor the substantive safeguards accorded by tenure. The First Amendment approach seems far inferior as a way of ensuring academic freedom.

Can Academic Freedom Be Adequately Protected through Long-Term Contracts and Grievance Procedures?

An alternative possibility for safeguarding academic freedom would be to provide faculty members with long-term contracts, such as for five or seven years, and require that the university succeed in grievance proceedings to terminate a faculty member. In a recent article, professor J. Peter Byrne [advocates] this approach.[36] In fairness to Byrne, he does not propose that this replace the institution of tenure. Rather, he argues for this as an alternative in those universities that do not have a tenure system. However, Byrne concludes that these "measures would fully protect the familiar terrain of academic freedom."[37]

It is this conclusion that I wish to challenge. I focus on Byrne's proposal, in part, because it is representative of this approach and, in part, because it is a particularly well-conceived version of this approach.

The Alternative Described

Byrne's proposal seeks to protect academic freedom through the combination of a number of devices. He suggests that faculty contracts should make explicit the protection of academic freedom. He says that "an institution that wants to respect academic freedom should bind itself to do so through an explicit promise that it will not violate the academic freedom of the faculty."[38] In fact, Byrne offers a model definition for faculty contracts. He offers the following proposed language:

Academic freedom includes the following rights and duties:
1) Faculty members have the right to pursue chosen research topics and to present their professional views without the imposition or threat of institutional penalty for the political, religious, or ideological tendencies of their scholarship, but subject to fair professional evaluation by peers and appropriate institutional officers.
2) Faculty members have the right to teach without the imposition or threat of institutional penalty for the political, religious, or ideological tendencies of their work, subject to their duties to satisfy reasonable educational objectives and to respect the dignity of their students.
3) Faculty members may exercise the rights of citizens to speak on matters of public concern and to organize with others for political ends without the imposition or threat of institutional penalty, subject to their academic duty to clarify the distinction between advocacy and scholarship.
4) Faculty members have the right to express views on educational policies and institutional priorities of their schools without the imposition or threat of institutional penalty, subject to duties to respect colleagues and to protect the school from external misunderstandings.[39]

Byrne proposes that "an institution provide a fair internal appeals mechanism to challenge adverse personnel decisions on the grounds that they violate the faculty member's academic freedom."[40] He suggests a grievance system in which the majority of the appeals panel should be professors and in which the hearing procedure should "make extensive use of the familiar legal devices of the prima facie case and shifting burdens of proof."[41] In addition, Byrne recognizes the importance of long-term contracts as part of any alternative to tenure.[42]

Although Byrne concludes that this alternative could suffice in protecting academic freedom, he also acknowledges that this could vary depending on the institution. He notes that

the benefits to academic freedom that will accrue by replacing tenure with the described procedures will vary depending on the mission of a particular school, and the administrative costs of adopting the procedures could be high, particularly the extensive procedures required for not renewing a contract. The administrative costs will not be as high, of course, as they would be in any individual case of dismissing a tenured professor.[43]

The Inadequacy of Byrne's Proposal

Byrne's proposal provides neither the substantive nor the procedural protections contained in the current tenure system. From a substantive perspective, Byrne's approach would accord faculty members much less protection than that provided by tenure. Each part of his statement of academic freedom gives the university substantial discretion to be able to dismiss the controversial teacher or scholar. The first part of his definition, as quoted above, says that faculty members have the freedom to engage in their chosen research "but subject to fair professional evaluation by peers and *appropriate institutional officers.*" This language would seemingly open the door for university officials to exercise control over faculty members' research. This permits university administrators to exercise control over faculty members' research and provides no limits on the permissible grounds for evaluation other than the very vague word *fair*.

The second part of the definition protects the right of faculty members to teach without the imposition or threat of institutional penalty, "subject to their duties to satisfy reasonable educational objectives and to respect the dignity of their students." The latter phrase is obviously vague and certainly provides less protection than the current definition of cause. Conceivably, any unusual method of teaching or discussion of any controversial viewpoint could be seen as showing insufficient respect for the "dignity of the students."

More seriously, the third part of Byrne's statement only provides protection for speech on "matters of public concern" and protects faculty members' speech only if they obey the "distinction between advocacy and scholarship." As expressed above, there is no reason why the protection of speech should be limited to matters of public concern. Furthermore, a distinction between advocacy and scholarship, even if it exists, is incredibly difficult to define and apply. Undoubtedly, universities would attempt to use this language to terminate faculty members taking unpopular positions, claiming that the writings were "advocacy" and not "scholarship." In many fields, faculty members take and defend positions in their scholarship. This is most likely to be dismissed as advocacy when the viewpoint is unpopular or the reader disagrees with the author.

The fourth part of Byrne's definition protects the right of the faculty member to criticize the university, "subject to duties to respect colleagues and to protect the school from external misunderstandings." The latter phrase is very troubling. Universities could use it to discipline faculty members who are perceived as embarrassing the university in the eyes of the public.

Faculty members who take unpopular positions, especially those who criticize the university's administration, can be easily disciplined under this standard for failing "to protect the school from external misunderstandings." A faculty member who publicly criticized the university and embarrassed it might be terminated for failing to adequately prevent "external misunderstandings." At the very least, the vague language of the rule likely would chill faculty members from engaging in public criticism of their university and risking punishment under this rule.

Comparing Byrne's proposal as a whole to tenure, it provides far less substantive protection. Under tenure, the university may terminate a faculty member only under the few circumstances that constitute cause. Under Byrne's approach, the university could terminate a faculty member under any circumstances, except for those delineated under his statement of academic freedom. Even these are far less protective than tenure because, as explained above, each has vague language that could be exploited by the university.

From a procedural perspective as well, Byrne's proposal is inferior to the current tenure system. Five-year contracts are no substitute for a lifetime position. Knowing that their employment is uncertain, some faculty members are much less likely to take positions that are unpopular or that might anger university officials. At the very least, in the last year or two of a contract, a faculty member facing a renewal decision might behave much differently [from] one who has a lifetime position.

Byrne recognizes that his approach provides less in the way of procedural protection than the tenure system. He writes that "under the described procedures, the school would need to be prepared only to prove that it did not act for forbidden motives. Not only would the institution's range of action be broader, its burden of proof would be lighter and procedural hurdles lower."[44] The result inevitably would be that faculty members would feel less protected and academic freedom would suffer.

Notes

1. Dennis Kelly, "New University Becomes Setting for Tenure Debate," *USA Today,* 17 July 1996.

2. David Fischer, "Taking on Tenure: A Job for Life? More Schools Are Just Saying No," *U.S. News & World Report,* 3 March 1997, 60.

3. Id. at 62.

4. Jon Sanders, "Debate over College Tenure Dividing America, the Public, and the Professorate," *Greensboro News & Record,* 8 February 1997, F6.

5. The suit [was] pending in Los Angeles County Superior Court as of May 1997.

6. Fischer, supra note 2, at 62.

7. *Sweezy v. New Hampshire,* 354 U.S. 234, 250 (1957) (plurality opinion).

8. *Procunier v. Martinez,* 416 U.S. 396, 427 (1974).

9. Edwin C. Baker, "Scope of the First Amendment Freedom of Speech," *UCLA Law Review* 25 (1978): 994.

10. For an excellent exploration of the meaning of academic freedom, see J. Peter Byrne, "Academic freedom: A Special Concern of the First Amendment," *Yale Law Journal* 99 (1989): 251.

11. *Keyishian v. Board of Regents,* 385 U.S. 589, 603 (1967).

12. An important question is what types of adverse employment actions, short of dismissal, constitute a violation of tenure. For example, cutting a person's salary by 90 percent surely has the same effect as firing the individual. Protecting the existence of a person's job means little if the person could be effectively fired by eliminating his or her salary. The difficult question, and one beyond the scope of this [chapter], is the point at which an adverse employment action is inconsistent with tenure. In evaluating the importance of tenure for academic freedom, this [chapter] focuses primarily on dismissals from employment. Obviously, if alternatives to tenure are adequate in providing protection from termination, they are likely to be sufficient as to less extreme adverse employment actions.

13. Reprinted in "Freedom and Tenure in the Academy: The Fiftieth Anniversary of the 1940 Statement of Principles," *Law and Contemporary Problems* 53 (1990): 407, Appendix B; see also Walter P. Metzger, "The 1940 Statement of Principles on Academic Freedom and Tenure," *Law and Contemporary Problems* 53 (1990): 3.

14. For an excellent discussion of the relationship of tenure to academic freedom, see Ralph S. Brown and Jordan E. Kurland, "Academic Tenure and Academic Freedom," *Law and Contemporary Problems* 53 (1990): 325.

15. Id. at 329.

16. These are summarized in Richard H. Hiers. "New Restrictions on Academic Free Speech: Jeffries v. Haleston," *Journal of College and University Law* 22 (1995): 227-49; see also text accompanying notes 18-26, infra.

17. This approach is described in J. Peter Byrne, "Academic Freedom without Tenure?" American Association for Higher Education, Working Paper Series, Inquiry No. 5 (1997).

18. 391 U.S. 563 (1968). See also *Perry v. Sinderman,* 408 U.S. 593, 597 (1973) (holding that the First Amendment limits the ability of the government to fire or discipline employees because of their speech activities).

19. Id. at 568.

20. Id. at 574.

21. 429 U.S. 274 (1977).

22. Id. at 287.

23. Id. This is the same approach the Court uses with regard to proof of discriminatory intent under the Fourteenth Amendment. See *Village of Arlington Heights v. Metropolitan Housing Dev. Corp.*, 429 U.S. 252 (1977).

24. 461 U.S. 138 (1983).

25. Id. at 143.

26. Id. at 147-48.

27. 439 U.S. 410 (1979).

28. Id. at 415.

29. 483 U.S. 378 (1987).

30. Id. at 386-87.

31. Id. at 388.

32. 114 S.Ct. 1879 (1994).

33. Id. at 1893 (Scalia, J., concurring in the judgment).

34. Id. at 1898 (Stevens, J., dissenting).

35. See, for example, *Connick v. Meyers,* 461 U.S. 138 (1993), discussed above at text accompanying notes 24-26.

36. Byrne, "Academic Freedom without Tenure?"

37. Id. at 13.

38. Id. at 4.

39. Id. at 6.

40. Id. at 7.

41. Id. at 8.

42. Id. at 11. Indeed, Byrne notes that "it is not surprising that most alternatives to tenure embrace long-term contracts."

43. Id. at 14.

44. Id. at 15.

30

Why Tenure Is Worth Protecting

Richard Edwards

What is it we value about tenure? Undoubtedly for most of us (we who are tenured, anyway), the economic security associated with tenure is an enormous boon; yet we must recognize that this benefit, at least in an economy that does not guarantee job security for most other employees, fails to be a sufficient reason to maintain the tenure system in higher education. As Gene Rice, who heads a project examining alternatives to tenure for the American Association for Higher Education (AAHE), pointed out, "The professorate has not effectively articulated the social meaning of tenure—the protection of the university as a place where inconvenient questions can be asked, and not as job protection for a specially sheltered status group."

More nobly, we assert that tenure is essential to guarantee our academic freedom. Yet even academic freedom seems an increasingly problematical basis for defending tenure. Administrators at the Gulf Coast campus of the State University System of Florida, which opened with a faculty hired on non-tenurable term contracts, assure us that academic freedom will be guaranteed by a provision in the campus's faculty code. Georgetown University law

AUTHOR'S NOTE: This is a reprint of part of an article originally published as Edwards, Richard, "Why Tenure Is Worth Protecting," *Academe*, May-June, 1997, pp. 28-31. Used with permission.

professor J. Peter Byrne proposes in an AAHE paper, "Academic Freedom without Tenure?," that faculty grievance procedures and similar mechanisms can ensure academic freedom. C. Peter Magrath, in "Eliminating Tenure without Destroying Academic Freedom" (*Chronicle of Higher Education,* February 28, 1997), argues that the First Amendment already provides ample protection for academic freedom. Magrath, who is president of the National Association of State Universities and Land Grant Colleges, asks if it isn't true that "untenured assistant professors or adjuncts enjoy the same protections of speech and inquiry as tenured full professors" and thunders his answer: "As I understand the laws and the Constitution of the United States, they do. We must acknowledge that academic freedom and tenure, in fact, have been uncoupled."

If neither economic security nor academic freedom is sufficient to justify continuing the tenure system, what's left? What's left is what has always been true: Tenure is required to nurture in individual faculty members the habit of critical inquiry regardless of inconvenience or consequences and to sustain on campuses a culture that values and upholds such inquiry. Academic freedom is not mainly about individuals and isolated acts—the case where a professor, perhaps impetuously, makes a bold, controversial statement and then, when he is threatened with dismissal, defends himself by filing a grievance or invoking the First Amendment. Rather, tenure is the foundation for an institutional system organized to promote critical inquiry.

Academic freedom is a habit of the scholarly or scientific mind, a way of approaching all questions large and small in which the only point of raising the question is to get at the truth, whether convenient or not. Moreover, academic freedom requires a campus culture in which not only are punishments for inconvenient opinions avoided, but critical inquiry is fostered and rewarded. Thus academic freedom does not just provide an immunity bath for fringe professors or the overly impetuous; it is the sea in which all scholars swim. What is needed to understand academic freedom is not legal case reasoning about individuals but rather a cultural and social-organizational analysis: What social and institutional circumstances most favor the flourishing of a passion for learning, free debate, a fierce determination to pursue even inconvenient truths, and the actual discovery of new knowledge? There is no simple answer, but tenure would appear to be central for sustaining critical inquiry on campus.

31

Academic Community and Post-Tenure Review

William G. Tierney

In Texas, the state legislature has taken up the issue of "post-tenure review"; had the proposed policy been enacted in its original form, it would have had dramatic consequences for how tenure is defined in Texas. At a private institution thousands of miles away, administrators have agreed to the need for periodic review and have begun discussing how to implement post-tenure evaluation. Last year in North Dakota, the state board for higher education initiated a committee to investigate various tenure-related issues including post-tenure review. In Kansas, each public institution has been at work on a post-tenure review policy with remarkably different tenors of discussion and policies. Last year, the University System of Georgia's board of regents approved a post-tenure review policy. And in the most celebrated controversy over the last few years, the University of Minnesota's regents sought to change tenure and post-tenure review, which prompted faculty to file a petition for collective bargaining in an effort to derail any changes to the university's Tenure Code.

AUTHOR'S NOTE: This is a reprint of an article originally published as Tierney, William G., "Academic Community and Post-Tenure Review," *Academe*, May-June, 1997, pp. 23-25. Used with permission.

Post-tenure review is hot. Although the hue and cry for evaluation of tenured faculty comes from various groups—state legislators, regents, administrators, state boards, public citizens—the desire for a policy revolves around a few key complaints. The overriding perception of those who favor post-tenure review is that accountability is essential. They maintain that faculty members are employees and, whether tenured or not, there is a need to document that each professor delivers valued services in exchange for his or her salary.

Over the last two years, I have interviewed close to ninety individuals on public and private campuses in the United States, as well as state legislators and members of coordinating boards, about issues surrounding faculty productivity. I have received about 500 e-mail messages from faculty and administrators about what is happening on their campuses. Interviewees consistently gave three reasons for post-tenure review: to root out "deadwood" faculty, to counter new retirement policies, and to make all faculty members more accountable for how they allocate their workload. Some individuals raised all three issues when they discussed the need for post-tenure review, and others concentrated on only one. Deadwood, for example, seems to be a concern at all campuses, whereas faculty workload is most often discussed in relation to publicly funded institutions.

The Need for Post-Tenure Review

Deadwood

Perhaps the most prevalent complaint I heard is that a certain segment of tenured faculty do little, if any, work. In general, "deadwood" pertains to faculty who do no research or scholarship and who therefore are not even attempting a significant part of their assignment. In effect, critics say, we are paying [individuals] full-time for a part-time job. The concern is that colleges and universities have personnel who would be fired in any other organization but who maintain jobs simply because they have tenure. At a time when postsecondary institutions face fiscal crises, critics argue, we can no longer afford to carry unproductive individuals. While the business world is going through dramatic reorganization to remain competitive, academia appears tied to outmoded ways of structuring organizational life.

Retirement

A second concern has to do with all tenured faculty in the wake of the uncapping, or removal, of a mandatory retirement age. The assumption is that a certain cadre of faculty will hang around the institution and never retire. Unlike "deadwood" professors who may be lodged at the associate level and have a relatively meager salary, uncapping raises the ante because faculty members who may once have been productive, were thus promoted, and now earn a sizable salary will remain on the faculty until their dying days while providing little benefit to the institution. Once again, what I hear is a worry that, with the fiscal stress in which institutions find themselves, they cannot become a retirement home for faculty. And too, analogies to the business world are made; critics question why we cannot be more organized and strategic in our approach to personnel issues, in the way corporate America is.

Faculty Accountability

Although fiscal stress and comparisons to the business world drive discussions about deadwood and uncapping, such concerns are not the sole force behind the desire for post-tenure review as a means of accountability. Accountability pertains to all tenured faculty, not merely the aged or the incompetent. The assumption here is that all faculty members need to be held accountable to those who pay their salaries—the state, the general citizenry, consumers, families, and students.

The last decade has seen a parallel concern about how faculty members spend their time. Research has shown that in all institutions except community colleges, faculty are more rewarded for doing research than for teaching. In addition, critics argue, once someone is tenured there is nothing anyone can do to change professorial prerogatives. If a post-tenure review policy were put in place, the thinking goes, then at least the possibility would exist to shift priorities as external contexts and demands change. Accountability is not so much a concern with lazy or incompetent faculty [as] with the idea that even hardworking professors may not be performing in ways that are most helpful to the organization.

Framing Post-Tenure Review

Time Frame

Some argue that post-tenure review ought to occur on an annual basis and be tied to merit pay. Others suggest more formalized and structured reviews that are akin to the promotion and tenure process. Post-tenure review, for example, might occur once every three or five years. The intent here is quite different from an annual review. Untenured faculty also have annual reviews that are tied to pay increases, proponents suggest; what is needed is a different analysis that will do for tenured faculty what the tenure process does for untenured faculty: provide a formalized assessment of an individual's work over a specific time horizon.

Who Gets Reviewed?

Interviewees delineated two specific responses: everyone or the deadwood. If everyone is reviewed, the argument goes, the process is equitable and ensures that all faculty members remain productive and accountable. Those who favor reviewing only the deadwood argue that the formalized review of all tenured faculty will be remarkably cumbersome and time-consuming. Why, they ask, should an institution force someone who has won a Nobel Prize to undergo post-tenure review? Instead, they suggest that the institution define chronic low performance and then implement an annual review process for those who meet these criteria. One phrase that has been used is a "red flag review." When an individual receives one or perhaps a series of low annual performance reviews, a formalized process would come into play to analyze, rectify, and resolve the problem.

Intensity of Review

Obviously, discussions in colleges and universities about how they will undertake the review process vary widely. On the one end of the spectrum is a self-report that is reviewed by the individual's department chair or perhaps a departmental or schoolwide committee. The report may be open-ended, a survey where individuals check off number of publications, advising load, and the like; or perhaps the narrative is divided into different sections that deal with one's scholarship, broadly defined.

At the other end of the spectrum is a review process that mirrors what takes place for tenure review. Outside letters of reference might be requested, and the post-tenure review candidate assembles a dossier not unlike that of an assistant professor. Multiple levels of evaluation occur, and ultimately the provost, president, and board provide some form of judgment.

Ramifications of Post-Tenure Review

Unlike the awarding of tenure upon successful review of an assistant professor, in general I have not heard any discussion in the interviews about the positive results for faculty of post-tenure review. That is, no one has suggested that we implement post-tenure review in order to reward faculty. Rather, such policies are geared toward sanction.

For those who advocate faculty accountability, the desired outcome is to reassign a professor from one task to a more efficient and effective one. Most often what critics expressed was that many faculty members do not do any research, and, if post-tenure review proves that to be the case, then they ought to be given higher teaching loads. The possibility also exists that someone who has fallen by the wayside may find his or her way back to productivity through a review process, but in general the discussion has focused less on restoration and more on penalty.

The more serious consequences that have been proposed are reduction of salary or removal of tenure and dismissal from the institution. A professor, for example, who has undergone a series of "red flag reviews" and has not improved might lose his or her tenure or face a pay cut.

From Bureaucracy to Community

Reacting to Post-Tenure Review

The criticism that has surrounded post-tenure review has been voluminous and severe. One individual commented, "Post-tenure review is not about the dead souls. It's about intimidation, about raising the ante and destroying community." Further, no research justifies the claim that senior tenured faculty are significantly less productive than their younger counterparts or that numerous senior faculty hang on so long that the academy is becoming a nursing home for the senile. Others point out that, although a handful of faculty on any campus are "deadwood," no research indicates that colleges and universities have any more deadwood than do business and industry. Further, procedures already exist to rectify problems or dismiss clearly unproductive faculty.

Accountability is perhaps a more serious issue because it goes to the heart of what tenure stands for—academic freedom. We instituted tenure with a rigorous review system precisely so that we would have confidence that productive, creative individuals would be immune from the vagaries and whims of outside interference. Accountability is essential, argue the critics of post-tenure review, but the faculty members—not the legislature, not the board of regents, not an administrator—should be those who define accountability and set academic priorities.

A rigorous post-tenure review that occurs every three to five years is not a post-tenure review; in effect, such a system will destroy the fundamental concept of tenure insofar as what it actually will offer is a series of long-term contracts. What does tenure mean if every five years an individual may lose it? Whither academic freedom?

Anyone who is familiar with the tenure review process knows how time-consuming and involved the activity is for one candidate in a department. Having all individuals undergo such scrutiny will consume an inordinate amount of organizational time and effort. The results are also problematic. "If such evaluations did not result in many dismissals," note Michael S. McPherson and G. Winston in *Paying the Piper: Productivity, Incentives, and Financing in U.S. Higher Education,* "they would be largely wasted. If they did, the university would bear the costs of greater turnover." Thus, we are devising a system that seems either untenable because of its unwieldiness and potential consequences or illogical because it ultimately will be useless.

Perhaps the most troubling and criticized aspect of the post-tenure review debate is the tenor of the discussion. In a 1996 book based on 300 interviews, *Promotion and Tenure: Community and Socialization in Academe,* E. M. Bensimon and I point out the amount of time, energy, and effort that faculty expend in their jobs. To cast post-tenure review as something that needs to be done in order to penalize lazy or unconcerned faculty members is both uncalled for and ineffective. It is uncalled for because the vast majority of faculty members are hardworking and serious intellectuals. It is ineffective, and in no small part ironic, because organizational literature consistently points out that the path to high performance, total quality, and continuous improvement is through the encouragement of employees, not through the bureaucratic implementation of mechanisms to monitor them. If we seek to mimic the business world, why develop policies that promote job insecurity and lower morale? Post-tenure review, bureaucratically framed, offers little, if anything, of positive benefit to the individual who undergoes it other than the relief that he or she is safe for another few years.

Rebuilding Community

I must admit to a high degree of discomfort not only with the negative portrait of faculty that has been drawn but also with our reaction to the portrait. The faculty response usually succeeds in stymieing any change so that often the most draconian measures of post-tenure review are not enacted; quite often, the policies are so watered down that they will not impact our daily lives in the least. And yet, what troubles me is that we have been forced into a defensive posture where one side defines the problems—and the solutions—and then we react.

Privately, informally, we all have our own stories that underscore institutional problems and challenges. Although I reject the pejorative language that has framed this discussion—deadwood, tenured senility—we must recognize that problems exist, and we must seek creative solutions. A small number of tenured faculty no longer perform their jobs, if I am to believe my interviewees. Some individuals would be more productive if they were not stuck within the holy trinity of "research-teaching-service." Our knee-jerk response is to claim that we can and do dismiss inadequate performers and that we can and do counsel people to retire early, to shift into other positions, or to assume other responsibilities. In reality, however, all too frequently we faculty do not take great enough responsibility for one another, and the kinds of difficult conversations that need to take place are studiously avoided. We ought not to implement a post-tenure review policy merely because a state board, a legislator, or an administrator on our campus has pointed out ill-defined problems and ill-conceived solutions. We ought to consider post-tenure review as a form of faculty development, as an intellectual undertaking that seeks to bolster bonds of social obligation, as opposed to a bureaucratic process that seeks to penalize and sanction. In *Restructuring American Education,* Michael Katz writes that the ideal university

should be a community of persons united by collective understandings, by common and communal goals, by bonds of reciprocal obligation, and by a flow of sentiment which makes the preservation of the community an object of desire, not merely a matter of prudence or a command of duty. Community implies a form of social obligation governed by principles different from those operative in the marketplace and the state.

The idea of community moves us away from an "us-them" struggle, where "we" (external constituencies) seek to exert authority and control over "them" (the faculty). Instead, faculty members—by bonds of reciprocal obligation—should seek to develop one another's performance. Further, performance "review" is retrospective; we review, evaluate, and judge what someone has done. We should develop a more prospective system that looks at what we have done and what we intend to do. No one—my dean, department chair, or colleagues—can offer suggestions, critiques, or advice about how I might improve, and how they might help me, if they do not have a clear idea of what I am attempting to do. Conversely, I have an obligation to outline how I intend, through my work, to aid my institution and my colleagues. Evaluation from this perspective becomes more of a formative and dialogical undertaking and moves away from a punitive, retrospective position. To be sure, some of our colleagues may need to rethink priorities and efforts, but the manner in which we help one another think through these possibilities occurs in a cultural milieu, as Katz says, "different from those operative in the marketplace." The path to high performance is through an ongoing informalized and formalized structure that enables each individual to delineate what he or she intends to do and how we as a collective can support and evaluate this work. The challenge, then, is not to engage in intellectual ping-pong where one group lobs a critique and suggestion our way and we fire back our response so that the status quo is maintained. In a community where responsibility is shared, the role of the collective is to develop a self-regarding culture that fosters a climate of intellectual creativity and responsibility. Who could ask for more?

The Debate on
Affirmative Action

32

Two Concepts of Affirmative Action

Steven M. Cahn

In March 1961, less than two months after assuming office, President John F. Kennedy issued Executive Order 10925, establishing the President's Committee on Equal Employment Opportunity. Its mission was to end discrimination in employment by the government and its contractors. The order required every federal contract to include the pledge that "the contractor will not discriminate against any employe[e] or applicant for employment because of race, creed, color, or national origin. The contractor will take affirmative action to ensure that applicants are employed and that employe[e]s are treated during employment without regard to their race, creed, color, or national origin."

Here, for the first time in the context of civil rights, the government called for "affirmative action." The term meant taking appropriate steps to eradicate the then widespread practices of racial, religious, and ethnic discrimination.[1] The goal, as the president stated, was "equal opportunity in employment."

In other words, *procedural* affirmative action, as I shall call it, was instituted to ensure that applicants for positions would be judged without any consideration of their race, reli-

AUTHOR'S NOTE: This is a reprint of a chapter originally published as Cahn, Steven M., "Two Concepts of Affirmative Action," *Academe*, January-February, 1997, pp. 14-19. Used with permission.

gion, or national origin. These criteria were declared irrelevant. Taking them into account was forbidden.

The Civil Rights Act of 1964 restated and broadened the application of this principle. Title VI declared that "no person in the United States shall, on the ground of race, color or national origin, be excluded from participation in, be denied the benefits of, or be subjected to discrimination under any program or activity receiving federal financial assistance."

But before one year had passed, President Lyndon B. Johnson argued that fairness required more than a commitment to such procedural affirmative action. In his 1965 commencement address at Howard University, he said, "You do not take a person who for years has been hobbled by chains and liberate him, bring him up to the starting line of a race and then say, 'you're free to compete with all the others,' and still justly believe that you have been completely fair."

And so several months later, Johnson issued Executive Order 11246, stating that "it is the policy of the government of the United States to provide equal opportunity in federal employment for all qualified persons, to prohibit discrimination in employment because of race, creed, color, or national origin, and to promote the full realization of equal employment opportunity through a positive, continuing program in each department and agency." Two years later, the order was amended to prohibit discrimination on the basis of sex.

While the aim of Johnson's order is stated in language similar to that of Kennedy's, Johnson's abolished the Committee on Equal Employment Opportunity, transferred its responsibilities to the Secretary of Labor, and authorized the secretary to "adopt such rules and regulations and issue such orders as he deems necessary and appropriate to achieve the purposes thereof."

Acting on this mandate, the Department of Labor in December 1971, during the Nixon administration, issued Revised Order No. 4, requiring all federal contractors to develop "an acceptable affirmative action program" including "an analysis of areas within which the contractor is deficient in the utilization of minority groups and women, and further, goals and timetables to which the contractor's good faith efforts must be directed to correct the deficiencies." Contractors were instructed to take the term "minority groups" to refer to "Negroes, American Indians, Orientals, and Spanish-surnamed Americans." (No guidance was given as to whether having only one parent, grandparent, or great-grandparent from a group would suffice to establish group membership.) The concept of "underutilization," according to the revised order, meant "having fewer minorities or women in a particular job classification than would reasonably be expected by their availability." "Goals" were not to be "rigid and inflexible quotas" but "targets reasonably attainable by means of applying every good faith effort to make all aspects of the entire affirmative action program work."[2]

Such *preferential* affirmative action, as I shall call it, requires that attention be paid to the same criteria of race, sex, and ethnicity that procedural affirmative action deems irrelevant.

Is such use of these criteria justifiable in employment decisions?[3]

Return to President Johnson's claim that a person hobbled by discrimination cannot in fairness be expected to be competitive. How is it to be determined which specific individuals are entitled to a compensatory advantage? To decide each case on its own merits would be possible, but this approach would undermine the argument for instituting preferential affirmative action on a group basis. For if some members of a group are able to compete, why not others? Thus, defenders of preferential affirmative action maintain that the group, not the individual, is to be judged. If the group has suffered discrimination, then all its members are to be treated as hobbled runners.

But note that while a hobbled runner, provided with a sufficient lead in a race, may cross the finish line first, giving that person an edge prevents the individual from being considered as fast a runner as others. An equally fast runner does not need an advantage to be competitive.

This entire racing analogy thus encourages stereotypical thinking. For example, recall those men who played in baseball's Negro leagues. That these athletes were barred from competing in the major leagues is the greatest stain on the history of the sport. But while they suffered discrimination, they were as proficient as their counterparts in the major leagues. They needed only to be judged by the same criteria as all others, and ensuring such equality of consideration is the essence of procedural affirmative action.

Granted, if individuals are unprepared or ill equipped to compete, then they ought to be helped to try to achieve their goals. But such aid is appropriate for all who need it, not merely for members of particular racial, sexual, or ethnic groups.

Victims of discrimination deserve compensation. Former players in the Negro leagues ought to receive special consideration in the arrangement of pension plans and any other benefits formerly denied them due to unfair treatment. The case for such compensation, however, does not imply that present black players vying for jobs in the major leagues should be evaluated in any other way than their performance on the field. To assume their inability to compete is derogatory and erroneous.

Such considerations have led recent defenders of preferential affirmative action to rely less heavily on any argument that implies the attribution of noncompetitiveness to an entire population.[4] Instead, the emphasis has been placed on recognizing the benefits society is said to derive from encouraging expression of the varied experiences, outlooks, and values of members of different groups.

This approach makes a virtue of what has come to be called "diversity."[5] As a defense of preferential affirmative action, it has at least two advantages. First, those previously excluded are now included not as a favor to them but as a means of enriching all. Second, no one is viewed as hobbled; each competes on a par, although with varied strengths.

Note that diversity requires preferential hiring. Those who enhance diversity are to be preferred to those who do not. But those preferred are not being chosen because of their deficiency; the larger group is deficient, lacking diversity. By including those who embody it, the group is enhanced.

What Sorts of Diversity Matter?

But what does it mean to say that a group lacks diversity? Or to put the question another way, would it be possible to decide which member of a ten-person group to eliminate in order to decrease most markedly its diversity? So stated, the question is reminiscent of a provocative

puzzle in *The Tyranny of Testing,* a 1962 book by the scientist Banesh Hoffman. In this attack on the importance placed on multiple-choice tests, he quotes the following letter to the editor of the *Times* of London:

> Sir.—Among the "odd one out" type of questions which my son had to answer for a school entrance examination was: "Which is the odd one out among cricket, football, billiards, and hockey?" [In England, "football" refers to the game Americans call "soccer," and "hockey" here refers to "field hockey."]

The letter continued:

> I said billiards because it is the only one played indoors. A colleague says football because it is the only one in which the ball is not struck by an implement. A neighbour says cricket because in all the other games, the object is to put the ball into a net. . . . Could any of your readers put me out of my misery by stating what is the correct answer?

A day later, the *Times* printed the following two letters:

> Sir.—"Billiards" is the obvious answer . . . because it is the only one of the games listed which is not a team game.

> Sir.— . . . Football is the odd one out because . . . it is played with an inflated ball as compared with the solid ball used in each of the other three.

Hoffman then continued his own discussion:

> When I had read these three letters, it seemed to me that good cases had been made for football and billiards and that the case for cricket was particularly clever. . . . At first I thought this made hockey easily the worst of the four choices and, in effect, ruled it out. But then I realized that the very fact that hockey was the only one that could be thus ruled out gave it

so striking a quality of separateness as to make it an excellent answer after all—perhaps the best.

Fortunately for my piece of mind, it soon occurred to me that hockey is the only one of the four games that is played with a curved implement.

The following day, the *Times* published yet another letter, this from a philosophically sophisticated thinker:

> Sir.—[The author of the original letter] . . . has put his finger on what has long been a matter of great amusement to me. Of the four—cricket, football, billiards, hockey—each is unique in a multitude of respects. For example, billiards is the only one in which the colour of the balls matters, the only one played with more than one ball at once, the only one played on a green cloth and not on a field. . . .
>
> It seems to me that those who have been responsible for inventing this kind of brain teaser have been ignorant of the elementary philosophical fact that every thing is at once unique and a member of a wider class.

With this sound principle in mind, return to the problem of deciding which member of a ten-person group to eliminate in order to decrease most markedly its diversity. Unless the sort of diversity is specified, the question has no rational answer. In searches for college and university faculty members, we know what sorts of diversity are typically of present concern: race, sex, and certain ethnicities. Why should these characteristics be given special consideration?

Consider, for example, other nonacademic respects in which prospective faculty appointees can differ: age, religion, nationality, regional background, economic class, social stratus, military experience, bodily appearance, physical soundness, sexual orientation, marital status, ethical standards, political commitments, and cultural values. Why should we not seek diversity of these sorts?

To some extent, schools do. Many colleges and universities indicate in advertisements for faculty positions that they seek persons with disabilities or Vietnam War veterans. The City University of New York requires all searches to give preference to individuals of Italian American descent.

The crucial point is that the appeal to diversity never favors any particular candidate. Each one adds to some sort of diversity but not another. In a department of ten, one individual might be the only black, another the only woman, another the only bachelor, another the only veteran, another the only one over 50, another the only Catholic, another the only Republican, another the only Scandinavian, another the only Socialist, and the tenth the only Southerner.

Suppose the suggestion is made that the sorts of diversity to be sought are those of groups that have suffered discrimination. This approach leads to another problem, clearly put by John Kekes, who argues in *Affirmative Action and the University*:

> It is true that American blacks, Native Americans, Hispanics, and women have suffered injustice as a group. But so have homosexuals, epileptics, the urban and the rural poor, the physically ugly, those whose careers were ruined by McCarthyism, prostitutes, the obese, and so forth. . . .
>
> There have been some attempts to deny that there is an analogy between these two classes of victims. It has been said that the first were unjustly discriminated against due to racial or sexual prejudice and that this is not true of the second. This is indeed so. But why should we accept the suggestion . . . that the only form of injustice relevant to preferential treatment is that which is due to racial or sexual prejudice? Injustice occurs in many forms, and those who value justice will surely object to all of them.

Kekes's reasoning is cogent. But another difficulty looms for the proposal to seek diversity only of groups that have suffered discrimination. For diversity is supposed to be valued not as compensation to the disadvantaged but as a means of enriching all.

Consider, for example, a department in which most of the faculty members are women. In certain fields such as nursing and elementary education, such departments are common. If diversity by sex is of value, then such a department, when making its next appointment, should prefer a man. But men as a group have not been victims of discrimination. So, to achieve valued sorts of diversity, the question is not which groups have been discriminated against but which valued groups are not represented. The question thus reappears as to which sorts of diversity are to be most highly valued. I know of no compelling answer.

Not a Temporary Solution

Seeking to justify preferential affirmative action in terms of its contribution to diversity raises yet another difficulty. For preferential affirmative action is commonly defended as a temporary rather than a permanent measure.[6] Yet preferential affirmative action to achieve diversity is not temporary.

Suppose it were. Then once an institution had appointed an appropriate number of members of a particular group, preferential affirmative action would no longer be in effect. Yet the institution may later find that it has too few members of that group. Since lack of valuable diversity is presumably no more acceptable at one time than another, preferential affirmative action would have to be reinstituted. Thereby it would in effect become a permanent policy.

Why do so many of its defenders wish it to be only transitional? They believe the policy was instituted in response to irrelevant criteria for appointment having been mistakenly treated as relevant. To adopt any policy that

continues to treat essentially irrelevant criteria as relevant is to share the guilt of those who discriminated originally. Irrelevant criteria should be recognized as such and abandoned as soon as feasible.

Some defenders of preferential affirmative action argue, however, that an individual's race, sex, or ethnicity is germane to fulfilling the responsibilities of a faculty member. They believe, therefore, that preferential affirmative action should be a permanent feature of search processes, since it takes account of criteria that should be considered in every appointment.

At least three reasons have been offered to justify the claim that those of a particular race, sex, or ethnicity are particularly well suited to be faculty members. First, it has been argued that they would be especially effective teachers of any student who shares their race, sex, or ethnicity.[7] Second, they have been supposed to be particularly insightful researchers due to their experiencing the world from distinctive standpoints.[8] Third, they have been taken to be role models, demonstrating that those of a particular race, sex, or ethnicity can perform effectively as faculty members.[9]

Consider each of these claims in turn. As to the presumed teaching effectiveness of the individuals in question, no empirical study supports the claim.[10] But assume compelling evidence were presented. It would have no implications for individual cases. A particular person who does not share race, sex, or ethnicity with students might teach them superbly. An individual of the students' own race, sex, or ethnicity might be ineffective. Regardless of statistical correlations, what is crucial is that individuals be able to teach effectively all sorts of students, and it is entirely consistent with procedural affirmative action to seek individuals who give evidence of satisfying this criterion. But knowing an individual's race, sex, or ethnicity does not reveal whether that person will be effective in the classroom.

Common Views and Distinct Perspectives

Do members of a particular race, sex, or ethnicity share a distinctive intellectual perspective that enhances their scholarship? Celia Wolf-Devine, in *Affirmative Action and the University,* has aptly described this claim as a form of "stereotyping" that is "demeaning." As she puts it, "A Hispanic who is a Republican is no less a Hispanic, and a woman who is not a feminist is no less a woman." Furthermore, are Hispanic men and women supposed to have the same point of view in virtue of their common ethnicity, or are they supposed to have different points of view in virtue of their different sexes?

If our standpoints are thought to be determined by our race, sex, and ethnicity, why not also by the numerous other significant respects in which people differ such as age, religion, sexual orientation, and so on? Since each of us is unique, can anyone else share my point of view?

That my own experience is my own is a tautology that does not imply the keenness of my insight into my experience. The victim of a crime may as a result embrace an outlandish theory of racism. But neither who you are nor what you experience guarantees the truth of your theories.

To be an effective researcher calls for discernment, imagination, and perseverance. These attributes are not tied to one's race, sex, ethnicity, age, or religion. Black scholars, for example, may be more inclined to study black literature than [are] non-black scholars. But some non-black literary critics are more interested in and more knowledgeable about black literature than [are] some black literary critics. Why make decisions based on fallible racial generalizations when judgments of individual merit are obtainable and more reliable?

Perhaps the answer lies in the claim that only those of a particular race, sex, or ethnicity can serve as role models, exemplifying to members of a particular group the possibility of their success. Again, no empirical study supports the claim, but in this case it has often been taken as self-evident that, for instance, only a woman can be a role model for a woman, only a black for a black, only a Catholic for a Catholic. In other words, the crucial feature of a person is supposed to be not what the person does but who the person *is.*

The logic of the situation, however, is not so clear. Consider, for example, a black man who is a Catholic. Presumably he serves as a role model for blacks, men, and Catholics. Does he serve as a role model for black women, or can only a black woman serve that purpose? Does he serve as a role model for all Catholics or only for those who are black? Can I serve as a role model for anyone else, since no one else shares all my characteristics? Or perhaps I can serve as a role model for everyone else, since everyone else belongs to at least one group to which I belong.

Putting aside these conundrums, the critical point is supposed to be that in a field in which discrimination has been rife, a successful individual who belongs to the discriminated group demonstrates that members of the group can succeed in that field. Obviously, success is possible without a role model, for the first successful individual had none. But suppose persuasive evidence were offered that a role model, while not necessary, sometimes is helpful, not only to those who belong to the group in question but also to those prone to believe that no members of the group can perform effectively within the field. Role models would then both encourage members of a group that had suffered discrimination and discourage further discrimination against the group.

To serve these purposes, however, the person chosen would need to be viewed as having been selected by the same criteria as all others. If not, members of the group that has suffered discrimination as well as those prone to discriminate would be confirmed in their common view that members of the group never would have been chosen unless membership in the group had been taken into account. Those who suffered discrimination would conclude that it still exists, while those prone to discriminate would conclude that members of the group lack the necessary attributes to compete equally.

How can we ensure that a person chosen for a position has been selected by the same criteria as all others? Preferential affirmative action fails to serve the purpose, since by definition it differentiates among people on the basis of criteria other than performance. The approach that ensures merit selection is procedural affirmative action. By its demand for vigilance against every form of discrimination, it maximizes equal opportunity for all.

The policy of appointing others than the best qualified has not produced a harmonious society in which prejudice is transcended and all enjoy the benefits of self-esteem. Rather, the practice has bred doubts about the abilities of those chosen while generating resentment in those passed over.

Procedural affirmative action had barely begun before it was replaced by preferential affirmative action. The difficulties with the latter are now clear. Before deeming them necessary evils in the struggle to overcome pervasive prejudice, why not try scrupulous enforcement of procedural affirmative action? We might thereby most directly achieve that equitable society so ardently desired by every person of goodwill.

Notes

1. A comprehensive history of one well-documented case of such discrimination is Dan A. Oren, *Joining the Club: A History of Jews and Yale* (New Haven and London: Yale University Press, 1985). Prior to the end of World War II, no Jew had ever been appointed to the rank of full professor in Yale College.

2. 41 C.F.R. 60-2.12. The order provides no suggestion as to whether a "good faith effort" implies only showing preference among equally qualified candidates (the "tie-breaking" model), preferring a strong candidate to an even stronger one (the "plus factor" model), preferring a merely qualified candidate to a strongly qualified candidate (the "trumping" model), or canceling a search unless a qualified candidate of the preferred sort is available (the "quota" model). A significant source of misunderstanding about affirmative action results from both the government's failure to clarify which type of preference is called for by a "good faith effort" and the failure on the part of those conducting searches to inform applicants which type of preference is in use. Regarding the latter issue, see my "Colleges Should Be Explicit about Who Will Be Considered for Jobs," *The Chronicle of Higher Education* 35(30), 1989, reprinted in *Affirmative Action and the University: A Philosophical Inquiry*, Steven M. Cahn (ed.) (Philadelphia: Temple University Press, 1993), pp. 3-4.

3. Whether their use is appropriate in a school's admission and scholarship decisions is a different issue, involving other considerations, and I shall not explore that subject in this [chapter].

4. See, for example, Leslie Pickering Francis, "In Defense of Affirmative Action," in Cahn, *op. cit.*, especially pp. 24-26. She raises concerns about unfairness to those individuals forced by circumstances not of their own making to bear all the costs of compensation as well as injustices to those who have been equally victimized but are not members of specified groups.

5. The term gained currency when Justice Lewis Powell, in his pivotal opinion in the Supreme Court's 1978 *Bakke* decision, found "the attainment of a diverse student body" to be a goal that might justify the use of race in student admissions. An incisive analysis of that decision is Carl Cohen, *Naked Racial Preference* (Lanham, Md.: Madison Books, 1995), pp. 55-80.

6. Consider Michael Rosenfeld, *Affirmative Action and Justice: A Philosophical and Constitutional Inquiry* (New Haven and London: Yale University Press, 1991), p. 336:

"Ironically, the sooner affirmative action is allowed to complete its mission, the sooner the need for it will altogether disappear."

7. See, for example, Francis, *op. cit.*, p. 31.

8. See, for example, Richard Wasserstrom, "The University and the Case for Preferential Treatment," *American Philosophical Quarterly* 13(4), 1976, pp. 165-170.

9. See, for example, Joel J. Kupperman, "Affirmative Action: Relevant Knowledge and Relevant Ignorance," in Cahn, *op. cit.*, pp. 181-188.

10. Consider Judith Jarvis Thomson, "Preferential Hiring," *Philosophy and Public Affairs* 2(4), 1973, p. 368: "I do not think that as a student I learned any better, or any more, from the women who taught me than from the men, and I do not think that my own women students now learn any better or any more from me than they do from my male colleagues."

33

Distributing Higher Education

Amy Gutmann

This chapter focuses on the issue of how higher education within selective universities should be distributed. Although they constitute a minority of the over 3,000 American universities, selective universities raise, for reasons I explore below, some very important issues concerning the distribution of democratic education above the threshold, the most obvious being how universities should decide whom to admit.[1]

Nobody doubts that the freedom to decide "who may be admitted to study" is essential to a university's ability to maintain its own academic and associational standards, but many doubt how absolute this "essential freedom" should be.[2] This doubt raises some of the hardest and most controversial questions concerning the distribution of higher education: Should a university admissions committee have the discretion to discriminate for or against members of disadvantaged groups? In discussing this issue, I focus on the case of blacks. The form of my argument can be extended to other disadvantaged minorities and women, although the discretion available to admissions committees will vary depending on the differing social deprivations of each group and the policies of other universities.

AUTHOR'S NOTE: This is a reprint of a chapter originally published as Gutmann, Amy, "Distributing Higher Education," in *Democratic Education* (Princeton University Press), 1987, pp. 194-211. Used with permission.

Nondiscrimination

The principle of nondiscrimination as it applies to university admissions has two parts. The first stipulates that the qualifications or standards set for university places must be relevant to the legitimate purposes of the university. The second is that all applicants who qualify [for] or satisfy these standards should be given equal consideration for admission.[3] The simplicity of the principle masks the complexity of applying it to judge particular admissions programs.[4] In trying to establish what qualifications are relevant to being admitted to a university and what constitutes equal consideration of those who meet those qualifications, the hard work begins.

Relevant Qualifications

What qualifications are relevant for being considered for a place in a university? No one doubts that academic ability is relevant. Unless its title is a mere pretext for tax exemption, the primary purpose of a university is higher education. Students who lack adequate academic ability cannot benefit themselves, their university, or society by attending a selective university. Some critics argue that academic ability therefore is all that is relevant. Universities should pick the *most* academically able applicants among those sufficiently able to qualify for consideration. On this argument, the first part of the nondiscrimination standard—the standard of relevant qualification—completely specifies the second part—the standard of equal consideration. To give every applicant equal consideration entails judging who among the applicants is the most academically able.

The simplest rationale for counting academic ability as the sole qualification is that the pursuit of higher learning is the singular purpose of universities, and the smartest students best enable universities to achieve their purpose. But this rationale is an incomplete understanding of the legitimate purposes of universities. It neglects the significant role of universities as academic communities and educators of officeholders.

A more compelling reason for counting only academic ability as a qualification would be that the most academically able derive the greatest benefits for themselves, their university, and society from a university education. We have, however, little reason to think that the most academically able actually do derive the greatest benefits from higher education for themselves, their university, and their society. Students who are academically able enough to benefit from a college education may learn more by being in college than more academically able students who learn more on their own. Some of the most academically able may not contribute most to the academic life of universities. They may be less academically stimulating than some less able students. As for benefiting society, academic ability is, by the best accounts, a very poor predictor of social contribution, however it is measured.[5]

More accurately, one should say that academic ability "seems" to be a poor predictor of social contribution because it is not clear how either academic ability or social contribution can be measured. Let me focus here on the problems of measuring academic ability. When universities speak of selecting the academically most able, they generally mean choosing those applicants with the highest weighted average of high school grades and test scores. This weighted average is the best statistical indicator now available for predicting a student's first-year grades. But these predictions are far from accurate even for the first year (the weighted average accounts for between 5 and 30 percent of the variance in first-year grades), and the correlation between weighted average and grades diminishes substantially over subsequent years,[6] suggesting that grades and test scores do not measure all that there is to academic ability, that academic ability is not all that it takes to succeed in college (or in later life), or that the academic ability of students changes in college, some becoming relatively better and others relatively worse academically. All these inferences are surely correct, and widely accepted when so simply stated, but the implications of these inferences for the admissions policies of universities are not widely appreciated, perhaps because many people consider nonacademic qualifications more subjective and therefore less legitimate grounds for favoring one applicant over another.

Leave the charge of subjectivity aside for a moment and consider the implications of these inferences for university admissions. Being academically able is a relevant qualification, arguably the most relevant qualification given that the pursuit of higher learning is what defines a university. It does not follow that academic ability is best measured by high school grades and test scores or that it is the only relevant qualification that universities should consider. Even if some universities conceived of themselves solely as "knowledge factories," aiming only to maximize their "intellectual product," they would consider in addition to test scores and grades: evidence of creativity, perseverance, emotional maturity, aesthetic sensibility, and motivation to learn. These qualities are either aspects of academic ability or qualities that support academic success in some fields. They are measured, if at all, only very imperfectly by high school grades and test scores.[7] It is possible that they cannot be measured or even discerned by admissions committees (a problem to which I return in a moment).

The vast majority of universities self-consciously serve as more than knowledge factories and should be free to consider more than academic ability and its related qualities as qualifications for admission. Most universities legitimately aim to contribute not only knowledge to society but also people who will use their knowledge to serve society well. Evidence of motivation to help people, honesty, reliability, leadership, and a capacity to work well with others are among the qualifications relevant to a university's purpose as educator of office-holders. Virtually nobody argues that good character is a sufficient qualification for pursuing a professional career.[8] The assumption that all anyone needs is academic ability is almost as absurd.[9]

It is not absurd, however, to argue that judgments of character generally are extremely difficult to make or at least to make accurately. Members of admissions committees, moreover, may disagree in their evaluation of what constitutes good character or in their interpretation of what the evidence implies about a student's character. Were the College Board to offer a standardized test for character, we would do well to doubt what it measured other than the ability to take a test. Admissions committees must rely upon evidence that cannot be found in test scores or grades: recommendations written by teachers (most of whom they do not know), evidence of extracurricular activities and accomplishments reported mostly by students themselves, a personal essay (written with

the help of a student's parents or teachers), and sometimes a short personal interview. These pieces of evidence are obviously incomplete, the product of varying standards of assessments, and subject to differing interpretations. So are high school grades. It does not follow that admissions committees therefore should rely exclusively on test scores. It would follow only if test scores gave complete evidence or if all other factors gave no evidence of the qualities that universities legitimately seek in their students. Neither is the case.

It was the case, however, that admissions committees of some of the most selective American universities used subjective standards such as potential social contribution and ability to get along with others as rationales—or rationalizations—for keeping out "socially undesirable" minorities, Jews in particular, despite their high test scores. One way of countering this prejudice was to pressure those committees to rely on grades and test scores rather than judgments of character and potential social contribution. The legitimate purpose of such pressure was to counter prejudice against Jews, not to institute a meritocracy based on testing. A meritocratic system cannot be based on grades and test scores because grades and test scores cannot measure many of the qualities relevant to the academic life of a university or to the offices for which universities serve as gatekeepers. Grades and test scores cannot measure intellectual creativity, honesty, aesthetic sensibility, perseverance, motivation to help others, leadership, and many other qualities that would "merit" a student's entry into a university, assuming entry can be merited.

If the best reason for pressuring universities to rely more heavily on grades and test scores was to prevent them from perpetuating prejudice against Jews, then we might reconsider whether the same pressure is warranted today—now that it may prevent universities from overcoming prejudice against blacks, who (unlike Jews) have disproportionately low test scores. The discretion inherent in assessing nonacademic qualifications does not counsel exclusive reliance on test scores and grades. It does warrant making admissions committees more accountable to a larger community for explaining their standards and the results of their deliberations. Admissions committees are generally so unaccountable to larger communities of faculty, scholars, students, or citizens that it is almost impossible for an outsider to get good evidence of the criteria they use to make their decisions. Many critics suspect that admissions committees often give weight to the wrong nonacademic characteristics—conformity rather than creativity, ambition rather than motivation to help others, lust for power rather than leadership, good manners rather than good character. Unlike academic ability, these characteristics should not be considered qualifications (and perhaps would not be so considered were admissions committees more accountable).

The simplest—and the strongest—reasons for insisting that selective universities rely exclusively on test scores and/or grades are to minimize the use of such irrelevant nonacademic considerations and to maximize the average academic achievement of student bodies. Substantially higher test scores and high school grades usually correspond to substantially higher grades during [the] freshman year.[10] Were a university's sole purpose to maximize the academic contribution of its student body, its admissions committee might be well advised to rely exclusively on test scores and high school grades. I say "might" for two reasons. First: test scores and high school grades predict only freshman, not upper class, grades. Second: were test scores and grades also good predictors of upper class grades, grade-point average still would be an incomplete measure of a student's academic contribution. Students also contribute to a university's intellectual life by participating in academically oriented extracurricular activities such as editing the student newspaper and debating, often to the detriment of their grade-point averages. Some students create more intellectual stimulation on campus by challenging ways of thinking that would otherwise be taken for granted, without themselves being the most successful students. Universities therefore may be able to maximize the academic contribution of their student [bodies] not by maximizing the standard academic indicators but by admitting a more intellectually diverse group of students with less than the highest average test scores and high school grades.

More critically, universities have aims other than maximizing the academic contribution of their student [bodies], aims that offer additional reasons for not resting admissions decisions exclusively on quantifiable academic qualifications. As gatekeepers of office and educators of officeholders, many nonacademic characteristics of students are relevant qualifications for admissions: motivation to learn and to help others, leadership, honesty, and so on. Most of these qualities are impossible for admissions committees to measure and difficult—but probably not impossible—for them to discern. The same can be said about intellectual creativity, aesthetic sensibility, perseverance, and other significant components of academic ability. The limited ability of admissions committees to judge the character and intellectual aptitude of applicants counsels uncertainty, humility, and even skepticism, but not skepticism selectively directed at nonquantifiable, nonacademic qualifications, since test scores and high school grades are only partial measures of what universities legitimately value.

Many characteristics of applicants are relevant to the role of universities as communities, depending on the purposes to which they are dedicated. Some private universities aspire to being religious communities and may therefore consider religious identification as a qualification for admission. Most universities legitimately aspire to diversity, although diversity can be illegitimately invoked to justify a questionable range of admissions policies. Mindless or trivial diversity does not constitute a legitimate goal of university admissions. Such diversity could be achieved considering penmanship style and taste in stereo systems as qualifications. One might wonder whether more commonly considered characteristics—such as athletic talent and place of residence—border on the mindless or trivial. Universities more sensibly seek economic, sexual, racial, religious, and cultural (which only sometimes correlates with geographical) diversity for the sake of significantly enriching their intellectual life.

In considering the qualifications relevant to a university's associational purposes, admissions committees must remember that universities are, above all, *academic* communities. None of the characteristics relevant only to its *associational* purposes should therefore be considered either necessary or sufficient to *qualify* a student for membership. Qualification follows social purpose in this quite specific sense: since the necessary purpose of a university is academic inquiry, a necessary qualification for admission into a university must be academic ability. Insofar as academic inquiry need not completely constitute the social purpose of any university, academic ability need not be a sufficient qualification for admission. Universities therefore should be constrained to consider academic ability as a necessary or primary qualification for admission yet free to consider as additional qualifications nonacademic characteristics that are relevant to their social purposes.

Admissions committees therefore can exercise discretion in determining qualifications that are relevant to the particular purposes to which their universities are dedicated. Discretion leaves room to consider a variety of qualifications as relevant, but it does not leave room to neglect academic qualifications, which are relevant to the primary purpose of a university. Nor does discretion leave room for setting qualifications that are irrelevant to those university purposes that can be publicly defended, nor for acting arbitrarily, which effectively precludes the pursuit of any purpose. An admissions committee is free to set nonacademic qualifications within three principled bounds. Each nonacademic qualification must be (1) publicly defensible, (2) related to the purposes to which the university is publicly dedicated, and (3) related to associational purposes that are themselves consistent with the academic purposes that define a university as such. These three criteria leave ample room for different universities to count different characteristics as qualifications (and to weigh the same characteristics differently), depending on their particular associational purposes.

Equal Consideration

Having set qualifications that are relevant to [their] legitimate social purposes, universities then must give equal consideration to all qualified candidates. What does equal consideration entail? The most basic requirement of equal consideration is that similar cases must be treated similarly. Two students who have the same qualifications must both be admitted or both be rejected. If they are both accepted, an applicant whose qualifications all are better must also be accepted. And so on. This logic is very simple, but it is not very useful if few applicants have the same qualifications and [if] most rank high on some qualifications but low on others. Many of the disagreements over who should be admitted concern the relative weight that should be given to different qualifications. How should an admissions committee compare Student A with high test scores but few extracurricular interests to Student B with low (but adequate) test scores but many extracurricular interests including a great deal of community service? My characterization of the two students is deceptively simple because it is sorely incomplete. Most admissions committees would want to judge, if they could, whether either student had to work against economic, social, or physical hardships. The fact that Student B was physically handicapped or from a poor family or black might make a difference in the committee's judgment of her intellectual and moral motivation. The fact that Student A was a farm boy from Kansas and very interested in becoming a scholar might make a difference in the committee's judgment of his potential contribution to the intellectual life of the university. The subjectivity and discretion involved in making such judgments is not a good reason to restrict them as long as they are relevant to the social functions of universities.

The two most significant practical requirements of equal consideration are that (a) admissions committees read the folders of *all qualified applicants* and consider their relative qualifications as prospective students and [that] (b) they take *all relevant qualifications* of each applicant into account in making their decisions. Equal consideration entails considering all the relevant qualifications of every qualified candidate. Neglect of the first requirement leads admissions committees to overlook some qualified applicants, often because they have generalized, perhaps correctly, from their previous experience that applicants of a certain social "type"—farm boys from Kansas, say— are less likely to get admitted than other, easily "typed" applicants. Farm boys from Kansas who are exceptions to this (presumed) rule are

therefore denied equal consideration. Neglect of the second requirement often results in overly restrictive definitions of relevant qualifications, designed to perpetuate the university as it presently exists rather than its purposes. An admissions committee from a predominantly white male university may count being from Kansas but not being black or a woman as a relevant qualification, even though racial and sexual diversity are as essential as geographical diversity to satisfying the university's professed purposes.

These two requirements are simple but far from trivial, as we can see upon considering preferential admissions for blacks. Although they constrain the way that admissions committees must deliberate, these requirements do not determine who among the many qualified applicants must be admitted. The determinate answer results from the undoubtedly difficult and subjective deliberations of admissions committees—constrained by the requirements of relevant reasons and equal consideration.

Racial Discriminations

Do the constraints of relevant reasons and equal consideration justify efforts by the state to prevent universities from discriminating either in favor of or against blacks in their admissions policies? The most common liberal answer, based on a commitment to nondiscrimination, is "yes": the state should prevent universities from discriminating both against and in favor of blacks because both policies violate the nondiscrimination standard. This common conclusion is a mistaken inference from the commonly agreed-upon principle. The nondiscrimination standard precludes discrimination *against* blacks but does not preclude all ways of discriminating *in favor of* blacks. It rules out the use of racial *quotas*—strictly understood—that favor blacks, but it does not rule out the most common ways in which many universities now give preference to blacks over otherwise equally qualified applicants. Although the empirical details of this argument are specific to the situation of blacks in the United States today, the form of the argument applies equally well to the case of other disadvantaged minorities and women.

Discriminating against Blacks

Consider first the case of a fundamentalist Christian university that does not admit blacks because "the sponsors of the university genuinely believe that the Bible forbids interracial dating and marriage."[11] Should the university be allowed to discriminate against blacks on the basis of a sincere religious doctrine that regards "cultural or biological mixing of the races . . . as a violation of God's commands"?[12] The argument of the university's sponsors—that its policy of racial discrimination is relevant to, indeed required by, its religious and associational purposes—is correct but incomplete. It ignores the other social functions that every university serves by virtue of being a university.

Like all universities, fundamentalist Christian universities serve not just as religious communities but also as gatekeepers to the professions and other high-status jobs. If they count being black as a disqualification for admission, they violate the principle of nondiscrimination in carrying out their function as gatekeepers.[13] The problem is not discrimination per se— Catholic universities may legitimately discriminate against non-Catholics [and] women's colleges against men in their admissions policies. We must question the social impact of different discriminations before arriving at a conclusion concerning their legitimacy. In the case of university admissions that discriminate against

non-Catholics or men, discrimination by a few universities does not create or perpetuate a problem of religious or sexual discrimination in the distribution of office (if anything, such universities have helped overcome problems of religious and sexual discrimination).

The case of blacks is special in this sense: discrimination against *blacks* by any university *in our society* exacerbates an already egregious social problem. Blacks are underrepresented in professional life as a result not of cultural choice but of a very recent history of economic, social, political, and educational discrimination following a far from ancient history of slavery. The connections between underrepresentation in the professions and discrimination are not at all remote. For example, "it was not until 1968 that the American Medical Association banned racial bars to membership in its state and local affiliates." We should not be surprised to learn that "in 1970, as in 1950, slightly over 2 percent of the country's physicians were black, and the ratio of black doctors to the black population was about one-seventh that of white doctors to the white population."[14] More than half of the black doctors, moreover, were educated in two black medical schools (Howard University and Meharry Medical College). One need not therefore support a scheme of proportional group representation in the professions to recognize the problem of perpetuating past discrimination against members of a group, all of whom have suffered in some significant respect from a history of degradation and discrimination.

In the context of such a history, no university can perpetuate racial discrimination and still serve its proper social function as a university. Freedom of association provides universities with a prima facie defense against state regulations that violate [their] associational purposes, but that defense is inadequate to sustain the case of any American university that discriminates against blacks today. When we imagine a society in which it might be permissible for a university to favor whites over blacks on religious grounds—a society, say, in which whites are the oppressed minority—we recognize immediately how radically different that society would be from ours. Taking account of race is not what constitutes a violation of the nondiscrimination standard. Rather, the standard is violated by taking race into account in order *to exclude blacks* from a university education in a society in which being black means being a member of a severely disadvantaged minority.

The nondiscrimination standard rules out discrimination against blacks not because race is an ascriptive or unearned human characteristic but because counting race as a disqualification is incompatible with the gatekeeping function that universities fulfill in our society.[15] The same reasoning that justifies preventing a fundamentalist Christian university from discriminating *against* blacks therefore does not also justify preventing a professedly liberal university from discriminating *in favor of* blacks in its admissions policy.[16] To decide whether a democratic government should prevent preferential treatment for blacks, or what is commonly called (by its critics) "reverse discrimination," we need to begin again and ask whether policies favoring blacks violate the nondiscrimination standard.

Discriminating in Favor of Blacks

Consider two hypothetical but not extreme cases, both of which entail preferential treatment for blacks. The admissions committee of Queenston University considers individually all applicants who meet [its] minimum academic requirements (the weighted average of grades and test scores judged necessary for doing acceptable academic work). Whether an applicant is black is one among many additional characteristics that the admissions committee regards as a qualification. During [its] final deliberations, the committee decides to admit 100 black applicants, 50 of whom have lower grades and test scores than any of the white applicants whom they have admitted with the exception of 25 football and hockey players, who also meet the minimum academic standards.

Kingston University—otherwise identical to Queenston—sets its academic requirements considerably higher (higher, therefore, than what is necessary to do acceptable academic work). As a result, its regular pool of qualified applicants contains very few blacks or athletes. Kingston therefore sets aside 50 places in its incoming class for the most qualified black students, regardless of whether they satisfy the minimal academic standards set for the rest of the applicant pool. It also sets aside 25 places for athletes. During [its] final deliberations, Kingston's admissions committee admits 100 black students—50 from [its] regular [pool] and 50 from [its] special, all-black applicant pool.

Should the state prevent either Queenston or Kingston from continuing its preferential admissions program for blacks? Both universities prefer blacks over otherwise better qualified white students. Both also prefer athletes [over] otherwise better qualified students. Are these preferences per se illegitimate? Although universities are often criticized for admitting athletes with relatively lower academic qualifications, most critics agree that universities have the right to do so (assuming the academic qualifications of athletes are high enough to do acceptable academic work). Yet many of the same critics argue that universities should be prevented from giving blacks preferential treatment on grounds that racial preferences—whatever their effect or intent—are invidious. Is the apparent inconsistency of the critics' position sustainable?

Both Queenston and Kingston universities think that athletics enhances university life and serves as a way of keeping alumni loyal to the university. They regard the outlook of athletes as complementary to the generally more intense academic outlook of other students (but they would not admit athletes just for this reason). Since the nondiscrimination standard does not require universities to admit the most academically qualified students, preferring athletes to more academically qualified students is a legitimate policy that the state should not prohibit.

But the ways in which Queenston and Kingston universities give preference to athletes differ, and the differences matter from the standpoint of equal consideration. Queenston admits athletes from its general pool of applicants, all of whom meet minimal academic standards and all of whom are individually considered. Kingston admits athletes from a special pool consisting only of athletes. The different procedures might make a difference in the results of the admissions process, since in its deliberations Queenston might discover, say, a talented violinist whose academic ranking was lower than the cutoff point set by Kingston for its regular applicant pool but higher than the academic ranking of five of Kingston's athletes. Because Kingston has a special pool reserved for athletes, it ignores the violinist, while Queenston admits her. The athletes and blacks that Kingston admits could also have significantly lower academic qualifications than those [who] Queenston admits, since Kingston's special pool, unlike Queenston's regular pool, has no lower limit on academic qualifications.

A utilitarian might try to calculate whether the greater efficiency of Kingston's quota policy makes it "worth" overriding the principle of nondiscrimination. But the nondiscrimination standard is meant to block just this kind of (impossible?) consequentialist calculation. Nondiscrimination still remains a partly conse-

quentialist standard. One reason to consider every qualified applicant is to avoid having any qualified applicant turned down merely by virtue of having been ignored. The use of a special athletic pool indicates either that Kingston admits athletes who are not academically qualified or that it refuses even to consider other potential applicants with similar academic qualifications and similarly relevant nonacademic qualifications. Kingston's special pool for athletes makes its policy of preferential admissions for athletes suspect by the standard of nondiscrimination, while Queenston's is not.

We may judge the policies of preferential admissions for blacks in a similar manner. If being black is also a legitimate qualification, then we must reach the same conclusion: Kingston's procedure of creating a special pool for blacks violates equal consideration, while Queenston's procedure of giving equal consideration to every applicant who meets minimal standards does not, despite the fact that both prefer blacks over applicants who are otherwise better qualified. I say "otherwise" because what remains at issue is whether being black is a legitimate qualification. It is obviously not the same kind of personal characteristic as is being athletic or musically talented. No one does anything to become black, just as no one does anything to be born to an alumnus of Kingston or to become a farm boy in Kansas, and so to be preferred over more qualified applicants. But as these examples may indicate, the *kind* of characteristic that being black, athletic, musically talented, the son of an alumnus, or a farm boy from Kansas is—whether it is, for example, an earned or unearned attribute—is not what matters for the purposes of nondiscrimination. What matters is whether the characteristic is a qualification. Is being black relevant to the legitimate social purposes of universities?

Suppose that the administrators, faculty, and students of Queenston largely agree that it is: "in a country where racial problems and misunderstandings are so prominent, all students stand to benefit from the chance to live and work with classmates of other races who can offer differing attitudes and experiences that will challenge and inform others and increase the understanding and tolerance of everyone concerned."[17] Queenston also thinks it can best serve its function as a gatekeeper to the professions by admitting more blacks, as long as they can do acceptable work, because the United States needs more professional blacks both to serve its underserved black communities and to serve as role models for the next generation of blacks who may not otherwise think it reasonable to aspire to professional office. Bringing more blacks into the [medical], law, and other professions, moreover, will make white doctors, lawyers, and other professionals more aware of the special problems and needs of blacks.[18] To recognize its right to give preference to blacks, we need not think that Queenston's priorities are correct, only that they are relevant to one of its legitimate social functions—which they clearly are.

Why, then, is there so much public resistance to preferential admissions (untied to quotas) for blacks? The simplest, and I think strongest, explanation is historical: we have learned from our history to be suspicious of racial classifications because they have been used almost exclusively to subvert rather than to support democratic justice.[19] In this country, racial discrimination has historically preserved the political power, social status, [and] economic and educational advantage of already privileged white males. Discrimination against blacks after the Civil War added injury to injury. This historical explanation should not prevent us from supporting a racial classification when it is justly used for a just cause, as in the case of Queenston's preferential admissions policy, which

aims to create a racially integrated society by means of equal consideration.

A commitment to equal consideration also provides a way around the worry, well expressed by Robert Fullinwider, that preferential policies will become entrenched even after they have outlived their justification:

Thirty-five years after V-J Day, veterans of World War II are still enjoying employment preferences in state and federal governments. Because of this, women are effectively barred from holding many top-level civil service jobs. Here is a preferential program that tolls a substantial cost in the frustrated aspirations of many nonveterans and which effectively discriminates against women; yet, although once given by a majority, the program is a privilege the majority cannot now easily eliminate. The danger that racial preferences will become similarly entrenched should be taken seriously.[20]

This danger is mitigated by (a) making preferential treatment the result of a series of autonomous decisions by universities rather than of a centrally imposed governmental policy and (b) requiring the procedures of all universities to satisfy the standards of nondiscrimination. This would mean that every year, the admissions committees of [all universities] would have to defend their preferences not only for blacks but also for alumni children, athletes, and farm boys from Kansas above otherwise more qualified applicants. It also means that as our society becomes more egalitarian and the experience of being black becomes less relevant to the educational and social purposes of universities, the case that members of admissions committees make for preferring black applicants over more academically qualified white applicants will become weaker. Taking the problem of entrenchment seriously means taking university autonomy and the demands of nondiscrimination seriously, not opposing preferential treatment on grounds that it may be abused.

Notes

1. This discussion applies to both public and private universities. The limits of legitimate state regulation vary, according to my argument, not with the form of ownership but with the (legitimate) purposes to which a university is dedicated. Insofar as publicly owned universities may not be sectarian, the state may prevent them from preferring Protestants, say, to Catholics and Jews. But the same criteria that would make it illegitimate for a public university to discriminate against blacks would also make it illegitimate for a private university to do so.

2. See Justice Frankfurter's often-quoted summary of the "four essential freedoms" of universities in *Sweezy v. New Hampshire,* 354 US 234 at 263: "It is the business of a university to provide that atmosphere which is most conducive to speculation, experiment, and creation. It is an atmosphere in which there prevail 'the four essential freedoms' of a university—to determine for itself on academic grounds who may teach, what may be taught, how it shall be taught, and who may be admitted to study."

3. For nonselective universities, only the first part of the nondiscrimination standard is relevant. Nondiscrimination demands that every qualified applicant be admitted.

4. This discussion of nondiscrimination is taken from Amy Gutmann and Dennis F. Thompson, eds., *Ethics and Politics: Cases and Comments* (Chicago: Nelson-Hall, 1984), ch. 7 ("Equal Opportunity"), p. 171. See also Walzer, *Spheres of Justice,* pp. 143-47, on which my discussion here also relies.

5. "Numerous studies reveal that even substantial differences in grades and test scores explain very little of the variations in the success students achieve after graduation, whether success is measured by salary or status or by more refined criteria of accomplishment. It is true that high grades and scores may have a significant bearing on the ability to succeed in research or a few other callings that make unusual intellectual demands. Since universities are legitimately interested in preparing students for such careers, they may well decide to enroll an ample number of applicants who possess exceptional academic aptitude. . . . But universities are also interested in preparing students for many occupations, and in most of them a host of other factors play an important role in determining achievement in later life." Bok, *Beyond the Ivory Tower,* pp. 96-97.

6. See William H. Angoff, *The College Board Testing Program* (New York: College Entrance Examination Board, 1971), p. 53. In *Beyond the Ivory Tower,* Bok cites this evidence to support a similar conclusion that "such measures are the best we have to meet the threshold goal of screening out applicants who are likely to have trouble meeting the academic standards of the institution. . . . But grades and test scores are much less helpful in deciding whom to admit from a large number of well-qualified applicants" (p. 96). Compare Klitgaard, *Choosing Elites,* pp. 104-53.

7. For some examples of how standardized tests may devalue intellectual creativity, see David Owen, *None of the Above: Behind the Myth of the Scholastic Aptitude* (Boston: Houghton Mifflin, 1985), pp. 33-88. Owen also discusses a method by which some students have been successfully coached to "beat" the tests (pp. 113-40).

8. [However,] most professionals—whether in medicine, law, or business—cite nonacademic along with academic qualifications as important to success in their fields. See Klitgaard, *Choosing Elites,* pp. 132 and 240, n. 1.

9. Almost, I say, because a few professional careers, in theoretical mathematics, for example, require almost exclusively intellectual ability. Although universities are the primary source of education in such fields, a very small proportion of college students concentrate in them.

10. The increase in freshman grades is even more substantial when increases in high school grades are included along with increases in test scores. See Klitgaard, *Choosing Elites,* pp. 104-15, 195-209.

11. This language is taken from *Bob Jones University v. United States* and *Goldsboro Christian Schools, Inc. v. United States,* 461 U.S. 574 (1982) at 580: "To effectuate these views, Negroes were completely excluded until 1971. From 1971 to May 1975, the university accepted no applications from unmarried Negroes but did accept applications from Negroes married within their race. . . . Since May 29, 1975, the university has permitted unmarried Negroes to enroll, but a disciplinary rule prohibits interracial dating and marriage" (ibid. at 2022-23). Although the details of the *Bob Jones* case are different, the issue is the same. Prohibiting interracial dating and marriage is different only in degree from excluding blacks entirely.

12. Ibid. at 582 (referring to the religious doctrine of *Goldsboro Christian Schools*).

13. If serving a social function does not imply serving it "well," then the nondiscrimination standard would not be a moral standard.

14. Allen P. Sindler, *Bakke, DeFunis, and Minority Admissions: The Quest for Equal Opportunity* (New York: Longman, 1978), p. 48.

15. [Compare] Chief Justice Burger's opinion in *Bob Jones University v. United States:* "The institution's purpose must not be so at odds with the common community conscience as to undermine any public benefit that might otherwise be conferred" (587). The Court may find it more convenient to rely upon the "common community conscience," but the right (indeed the duty) of the state to prevent universities from discriminating against blacks would be just as strong were the community's conscience less well developed.

16. [Compare] Justice Powell's argument in the *Bakke* case: "The guarantee of equal protection cannot mean one thing when applied to one individual and something else when applied to a person of another color. If both are not accorded the same protection, then it is not equal." *Regents of the University of California v. Bakke,* 98 S.Ct. 2733 at 2748 (1978).

17. Bok, *Beyond the Ivory Tower,* p. 99. As a thought experiment, one might substitute "regional" for "racial" and [substitute] "regions" for "races." The case for diversity seems to me to become much less persuasive.

18. For a lucid defense of such reasoning, see Richard A. Wasserstrom, "Preferential Treatment," in *Philosophy and Social Issues: Five Studies* (Notre Dame, IN: University of Notre Dame Press, 1980), pp. 55-61. Wasserstrom uses these reasons as a basis for making a more thoroughly consequentialist argument for preferential treatment.

19. See Dworkin, "DeFunis v. Sweat," pp. 82-83.

20. Robert K. Fullinwider, *The Reverse Discrimination Controversy: A Moral and Legal Analysis* (Totowa, NJ: Rowman and Littlefield, 1980), p. 249.

References

Anghoff, William H. *The College Board Testing Program.* New York: College Entrance Examination Board, 1971.

Bok, Derek. *Beyond the Ivory Tower: Social Responsibilities of the Modern University.* Cambridge, Mass.: Harvard University Press, 1982.

Dworkin, Ronald. "DeFunis v. Sweatt." In *Equality and Preferential Treatment,* ed. by Marshall Cohen, Thomas Nagel, and Thomas Scanlon, 63-83. Princeton, N.J.: Princeton University Press, 1977.

Fullinwider, Robert K. *The Reverse Discrimination Controversy: A Moral and Legal Analysis.* Totowa, N.J.: Rowman & Littlefield, 1980.

Gutmann, Amy, and Dennis F. Thompson, eds. *Ethics and Politics: Cases and Comments.* Chicago: Nelson-Hall, 1984.

Klitgaard, Robert. *Choosing Elites.* New York: Basic Books, 1985.

Owen, David. *None of the Above: Behind the Myth of the Scholastic Aptitude.* Boston: Houghton Mifflin, 1985.

Sindler, Allan P. *Bakke, DeFunis, and Minority Admissions: The Quest for Equal Opportunity.* New York: Longman, 1978.

Walzer, M. *Spheres of Justice.* New York: Basic Books, 1983.

Wasserstrom, Richard. "Preferential Treatment." In *Philosophy and Social Issues: Five Studies,* 51-82. Notre Dame, Ind.: University of Notre Dame Press, 1980.

The Debate on
Student-Faculty Relations

34

Eros, Eroticism, and the Pedagogical Process

bell hooks

Professors rarely speak of the place of eros or the erotic in our classrooms. Trained in the philosophical context of Western metaphysical dualism, many of us have accepted the notion that there is a split between the body and the mind. Believing this, individuals enter the classroom to teach as though only the mind is present and not the body. To call attention to the body is to betray the legacy of repression and denial that has been handed down to us by our professorial elders, who have been usually white and male. But our nonwhite elders were just as eager to deny the body. The predominantly black college has always been a bastion of repression. The public world of institutional learning was a site where the body had to be erased, go unnoticed. When I first became a teacher and needed to use the rest room in the middle of class, I had no clue as to what my elders did in such situations. No one talked about the body in relation to teaching. What did one do with the body in the classroom? Trying to remember the bodies of my professors, I find myself unable to recall them. I hear voices, remember fragmented details, but very few whole bodies.

AUTHOR'S NOTE: This is a reprint of an article originally published as hooks, bell, "Eros, Eroticism, and the Pedagogical Process," in *Teaching to Transgress: Education, the Practice of Freedom*, copyright © 1994 Gloria Watkins. Reproduced by permission of Routledge, Inc.

Entering the classroom determined to erase the body and give ourselves over more fully to the mind, we show by our beings how deeply we have accepted the assumption that passion has no place in the classroom. Repression and denial make it possible for us to forget and then desperately seek to recover ourselves, our feelings, our passions in some private place—after class. I remember reading an article in *Psychology Today* years ago, when I was still an undergraduate, reporting a study which revealed that every so many seconds while giving lectures many male professors were thinking about sexuality—were even having lustful thoughts about students. I was amazed. After reading this article, which as I recall was shared and talked about endlessly in the dormitory, I watched male professors differently, trying to connect the fantasies I imagined them having in their minds with lectures, with their bodies that I had so faithfully learned to pretend I did not see. During my first semester of college teaching, there was a male student in my class whom I always seemed to see and not see at the same time. At one point in the middle of the semester, I received a call from a school therapist who wanted to speak with me about the way I treated this student in the class. The therapist told me that the students had said I was unusually gruff, rude, and downright mean when I related to him. I did not know exactly who the student was, could not put a face or body with his name, but later when he identified himself in class, I realized that I was erotically drawn to this student. That my naive way of coping with feelings in the classroom that I had been taught never to have was to deflect (hence my harsh treatment of him), repress, and deny. Overly conscious then about ways such repression and denial could lead to the "wounding" of students, I was determined to face whatever passions were aroused in the classroom setting and deal with them.

Writing about Adrienne Rich's work, connecting it to the work of men who thought critically about the body, in her introduction to *Thinking through the Body,* Jane Gallop comments,

Men who do find themselves in some way thinking through the body are more likely to be recognized as serious thinkers and heard. Women have first to prove that we are thinkers, which is easier when we conform to the protocol that deems serious thought separate from an embodied subject in history. Rich is asking women to enter the realms of critical thought and knowledge without becoming disembodied spirit, universal man.

Beyond the realm of critical thought, it is equally crucial that we learn to enter the classroom "whole" and not as "disembodied spirit." In the heady early days of women's studies classes at Stanford University, I learned by the example of daring, courageous women professors (particularly Diane Middlebrook) that there was a place for passion in the classroom, that eros and the erotic did not need to be denied for learning to take place. One of the central tenets of feminist critical pedagogy has been the insistence on not engaging the mind/body split. This is one of the underlying beliefs that has made women's studies a subversive location in the academy. While women's

studies over the years has had to fight to be taken seriously by academics in traditional disciplines, those of us who have been intimately engaged as students or teachers with feminist thinking have always recognized the legitimacy of a pedagogy that dares to subvert the mind/body split and allow us to be whole in the classroom and as a consequence wholehearted.

Recently, Susan B., a colleague and friend whom I taught in a women's studies class when she was an undergraduate, stated in conversation that she felt she was having so much trouble with her graduate courses because she has to come to expect a quality of passionate teaching that is not present where she is studying. Her comments made me think anew about the place of passion, of erotic recognition in the classroom setting because I believe that the energy she felt in our women's studies classes was there because of the extent to which women professors teaching those courses dared to give fully of ourselves, going beyond the mere transmission of information in lectures. Feminist education for critical consciousness is rooted in the assumption that knowledge and critical thought done in the classroom should inform our habits of being and ways of living outside the classroom. Since so many of our early classes were taken almost exclusively by female students, it was easier for us to not be disembodied spirits in the classroom. Concurrently, it was expected that we would bring a quality of care and even "love" to our students. Eros was present in our classrooms, as a motivating force. As critical pedagogues, we were teaching students ways to think differently about gender, understanding fully that this knowledge would also lead them to live differently.

To understand the place of eros and eroticism in the classroom, we must move beyond thinking of those forces solely in terms of the sexual, though that dimension need not be denied. Sam Keen, in his book *The Passionate*

Life, urges readers to remember that in its earliest conception "erotic potency was not confined to sexual power but included the moving force that propelled every life-form from a state of mere potentiality to actuality." Given that critical pedagogy seeks to transform consciousness, to provide students with ways of knowing that enable them to know themselves better and live in the world more fully, to some extent it must rely on the presence of the erotic in the classroom to aid the learning process. Keen continues,

When we limit "erotic" to its sexual meaning, we betray our alienation from the rest of nature. We confess that we are not motivated by anything like the mysterious force that moves birds to migrate or dandelions to spring. Furthermore, we imply that the fulfillment or potential toward which we strive is sexual—the romantic-genital connection between two persons.

Understanding that eros is a force that enhances our overall effort to be self-actualizing, that it can provide an epistemological grounding informing how we know what we know, enables both professors and students to use such energy in a classroom setting in ways that invigorate discussion and excite the critical imagination.

Suggesting that this culture lacks a "vision or science of hygeology" (health and well-being), Keen asks, "What forms of passion might make us whole? To what passions may we surrender with the assurance that we will expand rather than diminish the promise of our lives?" The quest for knowledge that enables us to unite theory and practice is one such passion. To the extent that professors bring this passion, which has to be fundamentally rooted in a love for ideas we are able to inspire, the classroom becomes a dynamic place where transformations in social relations are concretely actualized and the false dichotomy between the world

outside and the inside world of the academy disappears. In many ways, this is frightening. Nothing about the way I was trained as a teacher really prepared me to witness my students transforming themselves.

It was during the years that I taught in the African American studies department at Yale (a course on black women writers) that I witnessed the way education for critical consciousness can fundamentally alter our perceptions of reality and our actions. During one course, we collectively explored in fiction the power of internalized racism, seeing how it was described in the literature as well as critically interrogating our experiences. However, one of the black female students who had always straightened her hair because she felt deep down that she would not look good if it were not processed—were worn "natural"—changed. She came to class after a break and told everyone that this class had deeply affected her, so much so that when she went to get her usual "perm," some force within said no. I still remember the fear I felt when she testified that the class had changed her. Though I believed deeply in the philosophy of education for critical consciousness that empowers, I had not yet comfortably united theory with practice. Some small part of me still wanted us to remain disembodied spirits. And her body, her presence, her changed look was a direct challenge that I had to face and affirm. She was teaching me. Now, years later, I read again her final words to the class and recognize the passion and beauty of her will to know and to act:

I am a black woman. I grew up in Shaker Heights, Ohio. I cannot go back and change years of believing that I could never be quite as pretty or intelligent as many of my white friends—but I can go forward learning pride in who I am. . . . I cannot go back and change years of believing that the most wonderful thing in the world would be to be Martin Luther King, Jr.'s wife—but I can go on and find the strength I need to be the revolutionary for myself rather than the companion and help for someone else. So no, I don't believe that we change what has already been done, but we can change the future, and so I am reclaiming and learning more of who I am so that I can be whole.

Attempting to gather my thoughts on eroticism and pedagogy, I have reread student journals covering a span of ten years. Again and again, I read notes that could easily be considered "romantic" as students express their love for me, our class. Here an Asian student offers her thoughts about a class:

White people have never understood the beauty of silence, of connection and reflection. You teach us to speak and to listen for the signs of the wind. Like a guide, you walk silently through the forest ahead of us. In the forest, everything has sound, speaks. . . . You too teach us to talk, where all life speaks in the forest, not just the white man's. Isn't that part of feeling whole—the ability to be able to talk, to not have to be silent or performing all the time, to be able to be critical and honest—openly? This is the truth you have taught us: all people deserve to speak.

Or a black male student writing that he will "love me now and always" because our class has been a dance, and he loves to dance:

I love to dance. When I was a child, I danced everywhere. Why walk there when you can shuffleball change all the way. When I danced, my soul ran free. I was poetry. On my Saturday grocery excursions with my mother, I would flap, flap, flap, ball change the shopping cart through the aisles. Mama would turn to me and say, "Boy, stop that dancing. White people think that's all we can do anyway." I would stop, but when she wasn't looking, I would do a quick high bell kick or tow. I didn't care what white people thought, I just loved to dance-dance-dance. I still dance, and I still don't care what people think, white or black. When I dance, my soul is free. It is sad to read about men who stop dancing, who stop being foolish, who stop letting their souls fly free. . . . I guess for me, surviving whole means never to stop dancing.

These words were written by O'Neal LaRon Clark in 1987. We had a passionate teacher/student relationship. He was taller than six feet; I remember the day he came to class late and came right up to the front, picked me up and whirled me around. The class laughed. I called him "fool" and laughed. It was by way of apologizing for being late, for missing any moment of classroom passion. And so he brought his own moment. I, too, love to dance. And so we danced our way into the future as comrades and friends bound by all we had learned in class together. Those who knew him remember the times he came to class early to do funny imitations of the teacher. He died unexpectedly last year—still dancing, still loving me now and always.

When eros is present in the classroom setting, then love is bound to flourish. Well-learned distinctions between public and private make us believe that love has no place in the classroom. Even though many viewers could applaud a movie like *The Dead Poets Society*, possibly identifying with the passion of the professor and his students, rarely is such passion institutionally affirmed. Professors are expected to publish, but no one really expects or demands of us that we really care about teaching in uniquely passionate and different ways. Teachers who love students and are loved by them are still "suspect" in the academy. Some of the suspicion is that the presence of feelings, of passions, may not allow for objective consideration of each student's merit. But this very notion is based on the false assumption that education is neutral, that there is some "even" emotional ground we stand on that enables us to treat everyone equally, dispassionately. In reality, special bonds between professors and students have always existed, but traditionally they have been exclusive rather than inclusive. To allow one's feelings of care and will to nurture particular individuals in the classroom—to expand and embrace everyone—goes against the notion of privatized passion. In student journals from various classes I have taught, there have always been complaints about the perceived special bonding between myself and particular students. Realizing that my students were uncertain about expressions of care and love in the classroom, I found it necessary to teach on the subject. I asked students once, "Why do you feel that the regard I extend to a particular student cannot also be extended to each of you? Why do you think there is not enough love or care to go around?" To answer these questions, they had to think deeply about the society we live in, how we are taught to compete with one another. They had to think about capitalism and how it informs the way we think about love and care, the way we live in our bodies, the way we try to separate mind from body.

There is not much passionate teaching or learning taking place in higher education today. Even when students are desperately yearning to be touched by knowledge, professors still fear the challenge, allow their worries about losing control to override their desires to teach. Concurrently, those of us who teach the same old subjects in the same old ways are often inwardly bored—unable to rekindle passions we may have once felt. If, as Thomas Merton suggests in his essay on pedagogy "Learning to Live," the purpose of education is to show students how to define themselves "authentically and spontaneously in relation" to the world, then professors can best teach if we are self-actualized. Merton reminds us that "the original and authentic 'paradise' idea, both in the monastery and in the university, implied not simply a celestial store of theoretic ideas to which the Magistri and Doctores held the key, but the inner self of the student" who would discover the ground of [his or her] being in relation to [himself or herself], to higher powers, to community. That the "fruit of education . . . was in the activation of that utmost center." To restore passion to the classroom or to excite it in classrooms where it has never been, professors must find again the place of eros within ourselves and together allow the mind and body to feel and know desire.

35

Consensual Amorous Relations

Jane Gallop

Just last week, I was gossiping with a friend of mine about the department she teaches in. My friend, who is a feminist, confessed that she supported a junior colleague "even though he is a sexual harasser." Being pretty sensitive about the issue, I confronted her: "Is he really a sexual harasser, or does he just date students?"

She only meant that he dated students. Thanks to an administrative stint, my friend is very familiar with academic policy. Her casual use of the term "sexual harasser" was not aberrant but, in fact, represents a new sense of sexual harassment operative in the academy today.

Nowadays, most campus sexual harassment policies include a section on "consensual relations" between teachers and students. These range from outright prohibitions of teacher-student relationships to warnings that a consensual relationship will not protect the teacher from the student's claims of harassment. Although the range suggests some uncertainty about the status of consensual relations, *their very inclusion within harassment policies* indicates that consensual relations are themselves considered a type of sexual harassment.

Sexual harassment has always been defined as *unwanted* sexual attention. But with this expansion into the realm of consensual relations, the concept can now encompass sexual attention that is reciprocated and very much welcome. This reconfigures the notion of harassment, suggesting that what is undesirable finally is not unwelcome attention but sexuality per se. Rather than some sexuality being harassing because of its unwanted nature, the inference is that sexuality is in and of itself harassment.

I have reason to be sensitive to this slippage in meaning. When I was accused of sexual harassment by two students, my relation to one of the complainants was deemed to be in violation of the university's policy on "consensual relations."

The two students charged me with classic quid pro quo sexual harassment. They both claimed that I had tried to get them to have sex with me and that, when they rejected me, I had retaliated by withdrawing professional support (in one case with negative evaluations of work, in the other with a refusal to write letters of recommendation). The university's affirmative action office conducted a lengthy investigation which resulted in a pretty accurate picture of my relations with these students. I had not tried to sleep with them, and all my professional decisions regarding them seemed clearly based

AUTHOR'S NOTE: This is a reprint of an article originally published as Gallop, Jane, "Consensual Amorous Relations," in *Feminist Accused of Sexual Harassment* (Duke University Press), 1997, Chapter 2. Used with permission.

in recognizable and consistent professional standards. No evidence of either "sexual advances" or "retaliations" was to be found.

What the investigation did find was that I indulged in so-called sexual behavior that was generally matched by similar behavior directed toward me on the part of the students. Not only did they participate in sexual banter with me, but they were just as likely to initiate it as I was. With one of the students, this banter was itself so minimal that the case was dismissed. But because my relationship with the other complainant was much more elaborate, it was determined that this mutual relationship of flirtatious banter and frank sexual discussion violated the consensual relations policy.

The woman who conducted the investigation thought that because I had a consensual "sexual relation" with a student, I should be considered guilty of sexual harassment. My lawyer argued that if this were a consensual relation, I was at most guilty of violating a university policy, not of breaking the federal law prohibiting harassment. While campus harassment policies increasingly encompass consensual relations, the laws that make harassment illegal not only do not concern themselves with such mutual relations but would seem specifically to exclude them.

This confrontation between my lawyer and the university investigator (both specialists in the area of discrimination) demonstrates the gap opening up between a general understanding of harassment as unwanted sexual attention and this new sense of harassment operating in the academy today—which includes all teacher-student sexual relations, regardless of the student's desires.

After the investigation had been conducted, but before the findings were released, the university hired a lawyer from off-campus to head the affirmative action office. It was she who wrote the final determination of my case. This lawyer found no probable cause to believe that I had sexually harassed anyone. But her determination does go on to find me guilty of violating university policy because I engaged with one of my students in a "consensual amorous relation."

The document explains the choice of "amorous" (a word that appears in the policy) as denoting a relation that was *"sexual" but did not involve sex acts*. Much less serious than quid pro quo harassment (trading professional support for sexual favors), less serious than hostile environment harassment (discrimination by emphasis on sexuality), less serious even than consensual *sexual* relations, the precise finding of "consensual amorous relations" is, in fact, the slightest infraction comprised within the policy.

It was as if I had been accused of "first-degree harassment" and the charge had been reduced to something like "fourth-degree harassment." The distinction between sexual harassment and consensual relations becomes not a difference in kind but merely a difference in degree. The university found no evidence of compromised professional judgments or of discrimination, unwanted sexual attention, or any sort of harassment; it found I wasn't even having sex with students. But the investigation revealed that I did not in fact respect the boundary between the sexual and the intellectual, between the professional and the personal. It was as if the university, seeing what kind of relations I did have with students, felt I must be *in some way* guilty and was able, through this wrinkle in the policy, to find me *slightly guilty of sexual harassment.*

The presumption on campuses today is that any sexual relation between a teacher and a student constitutes sexual harassment. One of our most esteemed universities explains, "What might appear to be consensual, even to the parties involved, may in fact not be so." The contrast here between "appearance" and "fact" suggests that so-called consensual relations policies are *not in reality* about consensual relations but about relations that are only *apparently* consensual. The policies assume that there is, in fact, no such thing as a consensual relation between a teacher and a student.

The policy of another major university elaborates: "The respect and trust accorded a professor by a student, as well as the power exercised by the professor in giving praise or blame, grades, recommendations, etc., greatly diminish the student's actual freedom of choice. Therefore, faculty are warned against even an apparently consenting relationship. The administration involved with a charge of sexual harassment shall be expected to be unsympathetic to a defense based upon consent when the facts establish that a professional power differential existed within the relationship."

Students do not have full freedom of choice; thus their consent is not true consent but merely the appearance of consent. The very existence of "a professional power differential" between the parties means a relationship will not be treated as consensual, regardless of whether consent was in fact granted. Because students cannot fully, freely, and truly consent, all teacher-student relations are presumed to be instances of sexual harassment.

As a teacher of feminist theory, I recognize this critique of consent. It is based on a radical feminist critique of heterosexuality. Students cannot "really" consent to sex with professors for the same reasons that women cannot "really" consent to sex with men. Feminists saw that economic arrangements make heterosexuality generally "compulsory" for women. In a society where women are economically disadvantaged, most women must depend upon sexual relations with men (ranging from legal marriage to literal prostitution) for economic survival. If women need to have sex with men

in order to survive, their consent to these sexual relations is not freely given.

There has been a good deal of confusion about what this critique of compulsory heterosexuality means. A few feminists have taken it to mean that no women *really want* to have sex with men. This then slides into the injunction that any woman who wants to be free *should not* have sex with men. Although only a very small number of feminists have ever taken this position, a lot of people have mistaken this extreme opinion for *the* feminist line. This confusion has resulted in widespread outrage at the idea that feminism would deny women the right to desire and enjoy men.

The feminist critique of compulsory heterosexuality was not meant to be a condemnation of heterosexuality per se but only of the way society forces men upon women without regard for our desire. Most feminists, in fact, understand this critique as an attempt to distinguish between socially coerced heterosexuality and women's actual desires for men. The crucial question is whether women are treated as mere sex objects or whether we are recognized as desiring subjects.

University administrators who piously intone against teacher-student sex, citing the student's impossibility to freely grant consent, would be shocked if they knew their position was based in a critique of the institution of marriage. And I don't think [one] could get them to agree to policies likewise prohibiting heterosexuality on the grounds that the power differential means a woman's consent is always to some extent coerced. Yet campuses around the country are formulating and enforcing policies that are the equivalent of the much-decried and seldom-embraced fringe feminist injunction against women sleeping with men.

As a feminist, I am well aware of the ways women are often compelled to sexual relations with men by forces that have nothing to do with our desire. And I see that students might be in a similar position with relation to teachers. But as a feminist, I do not think the solution is to deny women or students the right to consent. Denying women the right to consent reinforces our status as objects rather than desiring subjects. That is why I believe the question of whether sexual advances are *wanted* is absolutely crucial.

Prohibition of consensual teacher-student relations is based on the assumption that when a student says yes, she really means no. I cannot help but think that this proceeds from the same logic according to which when a woman says no, she really means yes. The first assumption is protectionist; the second is the very logic of harassment. What harassment and protectionism have in common is precisely a refusal to credit women's desires. Common to both is the assumption that women do not know what we want, that someone else, in a position of greater knowledge and power, knows better.

I think back to that jubilant feminist dance I attended in 1971. Although sexual harassment was not a phrase we used in those days, unwanted sexual attention would pretty well describe the behavior of the guys who came to crash the party. They had, in fact, come with the explicit purpose of harassing us. Yet today, the notion of sexual harassment more likely would be applied to the mutually desirable relation between my women's studies teacher and the student who was her date to the dance.

When I think of that dance, I balk at the idea that teacher-student sex is synonymous with harassment. I remember the feminist student I was, what I wanted and what I didn't want, and I remember that it was precisely my sense of knowing what I did and didn't want that made me feel strong.

A year or so after that dance, I began graduate school. My first semester there, feminist graduate students and faculty in the department recognized that I was a feminist and invited me to join a consciousness-raising group they were forming. It was in many ways a typical consciousness-raising group; in comparing our experiences, we began to see them as not merely individual but as the shared experience of women. But in our case, there was even greater similarity because we were all women in the same department.

A student in the group was dating a professor while two of us were taking his graduate seminar. When we discussed our sex lives, I listened to what she said with more than the usual curiosity. No one in that feminist group thought their relationship inappropriate and, although it was titillating to have this access to private information about him, I don't believe it substantially added to or undermined his professional authority.

The group functioned not only politically, intellectually, and personally; it also became the core of our social life. I became close friends with two of the women in the group, women who remained my closest friends all through graduate school—one was a graduate student, the other a young professor. Around the group proper, a larger social circle formed as we socialized not only with each other but [also] with each other's friends and lovers.

This larger social circle brought together graduate students and junior faculty, women and men of both statuses. Our clique included two of the teachers who most mattered to me at the time. Both men in their thirties, not long out of graduate school themselves, these two turned me on to the latest ideas in the field I was studying—this was the cutting edge. These guys were brilliant; I wanted to do work that would impress them, and I wanted more than anything to be like them.

I was fortunate to have both of them on my dissertation committee. I pursued and developed personal relations with each of them. At the time, one was single, the other divorced; both were socially available. I met each of them frequently for lunches and dinners, coffees and drinks. I helped one move into a new apartment; I spent the day at the other's house watching a tennis tournament on TV. I wanted ever so badly to sleep with these guys. And I did my utmost to seduce them.

Both of them turned me down, more than once. But over the years, I did what I could to sway them. Trying not to be too obnoxious, I watched for opportunities that might present themselves, prepared to take advantage and press my suit. During my last year of graduate school, the year I was writing my thesis, I finally managed to have sex with them (each separately, to be sure, but oddly, coincidentally, in the same week).

I had sex but once with each of them. Neither of these became "relationships." It was just what is called "casual sex," although there was nothing casual about my relation to either of them. Their opinion of me already mattered profoundly; their teaching had forever changed the way I understood the world.

To be honest, I think I wanted to get them into bed in order to make them more human, more vulnerable. These two had enormous power over me; I don't mean their institutional position but their intellectual force. I was bowled over by their brilliance; they seemed so superior. I wanted to see them naked, to see them as like other men. Not so as to stop taking them seriously as intellects (I never did) but so as to feel my own power in relation to them.

Screwing these guys definitely did not keep me from taking myself seriously as a student. In fact, it seemed to make it somewhat easier for me to write. Seducing them made me feel kind of cocky, and that allowed me to presume I had something to say worth saying.

It never occurred to me to worry that sex would prevent them from responding profes-

sionally to my work. Both men continued to serve on my dissertation committee. And they continued to serve me well, to offer vital criticism as well as encouraging praise, devoting considerable time and effort to responding to my writing. In other words, these men did not treat my work any differently than before we had sex.

Sexual harassment creates an environment that is hostile to a student's education. My experience was the opposite. I was in an environment extremely conducive to my education, a heady atmosphere where close personal contact intensified my desire to learn and my desire to excel. I learned and excelled; I desired and I fucked my teachers.

And they taught and challenged me, criticized and praised me; they let me see them as men and never stopped taking me seriously as a student. I felt that in their eyes I was both a desirable woman and a serious scholar. And thus I believed I could be both; I didn't feel I had to choose one at the expense of the other.

Fifteen years later, when I became aware that campuses were "protecting" students by banning student-teacher relations, I felt my desire erased and the way it had made me feel powerful denied. Although I am aware that not all such liaisons are so empowering for the student, I also know that my experience was far from unique. Lots of other smart, ambitious young women, many of them likewise feminist academics today, have felt powerful because they seduced their teachers.

Experience like mine is currently invisible. In the general consensus that student-teacher relations demean and debase the student, an entire stretch of women's experience is being denied, consigned to silence. And it just happens to be women's experience of feeling powerful and sexy, smart and successful.

After graduate school, I got a job at a medium-sized state university in a small college town. In the late seventies, the academic job market was tight; one took whatever job one could get (such is very much the case again today). I moved to this dinky little town where there wasn't really anything else but the university. It seemed like everyone in town was either under twenty-two or married; it didn't look like there would be much in the way of romantic possibilities.

My first year there, I taught a summer course; a graduate student from another department enrolled. He happened to live in the same apartment complex as I did, and sometimes I ran into him out by the pool. He was two years older than me and going through a divorce. A couple weeks into the term, he asked me if I wanted to go out on Friday night. Living in that town, I hadn't had a date in quite a while, so I was happy to accept his invitation.

We dated for the rest of the summer term. I don't think it affected my judgment of his work or my treatment of the other students in the class. But I will admit both of us found our secret titillating: it was a perverse thrill to treat him in class just like the other students though all the while we also had this sexual relation outside of class.

We continued dating through the fall. I enjoyed spending time with him, but he wanted a more serious relationship and began pressuring me to live with him. By January, I gave in and let him move into my apartment. In April, I went out of town for the weekend to present a paper at an academic conference. While I was gone, he started sleeping with another woman. Although I was not in love with him, I was very attached to his companionship and desperate to hang on to him. I couldn't do it; by the time classes ended in May, he had moved out of my apartment and in with her.

I felt rejected and quite alone. One day, shortly after he moved out, I ran into an under-grad who had been in my class during the spring semester. This cute kid was intense and eccentric and one of the students most keyed into my teaching. He was excited to run into me off-campus. I was pretty down; it did me good to feel admired. During the semester, I had invited his class to my place for a party; so he had met the grad student who lived with me and now asked [about] him. I blurted out that he had just dumped me for another woman. That evening, the undergrad stopped by my apartment. His idea was to cheer me up by sleeping with me. I was glad he had come by and immediately took to the idea.

We had sex on several other occasions over the course of the next year or so. This was, however, not at all a romantic relationship; all the sex was very casual. For example, about a year later, he stopped by in just the same way he had the first time; it was my birthday, and in view of the occasion, he wanted to make sure I got laid. The thought was sweet; I appreciated and accepted his offer.

But his real devotion to me was intellectual. He took every course he could with me during the rest of his time in college, began to read my scholarly articles, and generally tried to learn what I was trying to teach. He even went so far as to take a women's studies course from me, although he had never shown any interest in feminism. This was my first women's studies course, and although I was touched dear Scott signed up, he was not the audience it was actually aimed at.

As expected, most of the students in that class were women, many of whom were feminists, a rarity among the conservative students at that school. A lesbian couple enrolled, the first out lesbians I had run into in my three years there. The two of them were delightful; it wasn't just that they both were smart, hip, and really good-looking, but they enjoyed performing their relationship in public, flaunting their sexuality to the discomfiture of the very straight student body.

The couple adopted me as their pet teacher, and as I thoroughly admired [the couple], I was tickled to be so chosen. On weekends, [the two] would take me with them to the nearest lesbian bar, an hour's drive from the college town. Or they would come by in the evening with a bottle of wine, and the three of us would talk til the wee hours, as the atmosphere thickened with unspoken fantasies of transgressive possibility. One night, they giddily confided that every time they passed my apartment building, they would jokingly suggest "SBFJ." After making me beg repeatedly for explication, one of them finally whispered that the joke's abbreviation stood for "Stop By, Fuck Jane."

In the middle of that semester, they broke up. Late one weekday evening soon after, the tough, curly-haired one showed up at my apartment with the express purpose of seducing me. I didn't know they'd broken up and was surprised both by her visit and by her intentions. But since I found her very sexy, I was thrilled to let her seduce me. We spent the night enacting the unspoken fantasies of months of heady conversations. She was even sexier than I'd imagined.

It was morning when she left my place. That afternoon, I was giving a public lecture on campus, previewing the book I was then writing, a book whose publication would soon make my career as a feminist theorist (a book called, incidentally, *The Daughter's Seduction*). The lecture was a triumph; the large room was full, [and] the assembled colleagues and students were quite enthusiastic about my new work.

Sitting right up in the front row was Micki, my brash young seducer. Not herself a very serious student, caring rather more about her career as a singer/guitarist, Micki was not, in fact, particularly interested in my work. But she was turned on by the crowd's response to my presentation. Bursting with the sense of having possessed me but a few hours earlier, she looked like the proverbial cat who'd eaten the canary.

Her aim had been conquest; she had gotten what she wanted and given me a lot of pleasure in the process. It was a classic one-night stand, intensely tied to the moment. Although that was the extent of our sexual connection, we remained friendly. A month or so later, she invited me to come hear her perform at a local coffeehouse; it was my turn to be in her audience, my turn to be proud to know her.

Whatever role Micki's dalliance with me might have played in her breakup with Diane, it didn't seem to have any negative effect on Diane's relation to me. A year later, Diane found occasion to invite me to spend the night with her. Diane was soulful and very beautiful; I was extremely flattered and more than happy to accept her invitation.

With Diane too, sex was a one-night affair, but I remained her teacher well past that encounter. In contrast [to] Micki, Diane was a serious student. During her last semester of college, two years after her first class with me, she enrolled in the senior seminar I taught for graduating women's studies students. She did excellent work in that seminar, we worked together productively, and our relation both in and out of class seemed, as far as I could tell, unaffected by our erotic history.

By the time I taught that senior seminar in the spring of 1982, I no longer was having affairs with students. And I haven't slept with a student since then. Not, however, because of any change in my views about teacher-student liaisons. The reason lies rather in a change in my personal situation; by 1982, I was madly in love with the man I'm still happily with today.

Over the years we've been together, he's taught me ever so much and been more than willing to learn from me, but he was never, strictly speaking, either my teacher or my student.

The stories I have just told portray human relations. In these affairs, my motivations as well as the motivations of the students are profoundly—sometimes sadly, sometimes sweetly—human. They span the usual range of reasons why people make contact: loneliness, sympathy, rebounding from a recently failed relationship, and, of course, admiration. I hope this gallery can give a sense of the diversity and humanity of such relations.

The stories also run the gamut of teaching relations: from intense, serious connections where the student's way of thinking is centrally transformed by the teaching to very casual encounters where the teaching is pretty much marginal to the student's concerns. In my experience, the teaching relation remained essentially the same after sex; the casual students continued not to care particularly about the teaching, [and] the serious students continued to take the teaching seriously and to be taken seriously as students by the teacher.

As I gather these experiences together—and place them in proximity to my seduction of my own teachers—I notice one consistency. In every instance, it was the student who made the first move; it was always the student who initiated sexual activity. This certainly runs counter to the cliche of the lecherous professor putting the moves on innocent young things. To be sure, I'm not trying to claim that teachers never make the first move, but that is not my experience. And I've had my share of experience, both as student and as teacher.

Although I no longer actually have sex with students, I still embrace such relations in principle. I resist the idea that what I did was wrong and persist in seeing these liaisons as part of the wide range of sexual opportunities that I sampled as fully as possible in my younger days.

As someone who came of age during the sexual revolution, my teens and twenties were full of short-term serious romances and an even larger number of casual sexual encounters. This variety of experience was particularly good for me as a young intellectual woman, making me feel bold and forceful as well as desirable, helping me view the world as a place of diverse possibility. Especially for women pursuing the life of the mind, desire is a blessing rather than an insult. My desire gave me drive and energy; being an object of desire made me feel admired and wanted, worthy and lovable. Now long past my twenties, I am still convinced that desire is good and that when mutual desire makes itself felt, it is a very fine thing indeed.

Prohibitions against teacher-student relations seem based in a sense of sex as inherently bad. Sex for me is not some wholly separate, nasty, debased thing, but belongs more to the world of conversation and friendship, where people make contact with others who seem interesting, forceful, attractive. Because I value human connection above all else, I regard sex as a considerable good.

I think of my students primarily as people. As with people in general, I don't like some of them, I'm indifferent to many, and I find some of them especially admirable, congenial, or engaging. Although an awareness of our institutional roles definitely gave my affairs with students a certain pleasurable edge of transgression, I slept with students for essentially the same reasons I slept with other people —because they engaged me as human beings, because a spark of possibility lit between us.

It is ironic that relations between teachers and students have been banned as part of the fight against sexual harassment. We fight against sexual harassment precisely because it's dehumanizing, but the ban on consensual relations is dehumanizing too. Telling teachers and students that we must not engage each other sexually ultimately tells us that we must limit ourselves to the confines of some restricted professional transaction, that we should not treat each other as human beings.

Around 1990, I began to take loud and public exception to the new consensual relations policies. I felt free to do so precisely because I hadn't been having sex with students since long before these policies came into existence. I thought I could risk opposing these policies because I was not in fact violating them.

This was, of course, before I found myself charged with sexual harassment. Two years after I started protesting these policies, the complaints against me were filed. A year after that, the university officially declared that I had violated its consensual relations policy. Thus, I was found in violation of the very policy I had set about to protest.

I thought I was protesting a policy banning the sort of relations I used to have. I had not realized it was possible to apply the policy to the sorts of relations I still have with students.

Back in the days when I was sleeping with students, all the sex had taken place within a larger context of social and personal relations. For example, in that summer school class where I started dating the grad student, there was another student, a female undergrad, that I used to hang out with. She had great style, and I loved to go shopping for clothes with her. Or we'd go drinking and compare notes on the difficulties of dating men. The next year, while I rarely had sex with Scott, I often went uptown to a bar with him and his friends to play pinball. And my relation to Micki and Diane began as a friendship with a couple; at the time, none of us expected the couple to break up. The drink-

ing and talking, or going out on a weekend, was not unlike relations I had with other students.

I have such relations with students to this day, although now mainly with graduate students. I socialize with students in groups and singly; we might go out to dinner, play tennis, or see a movie. Or one of my graduate advisees will tell me about his love life while I thoroughly enjoy giving him advice. Some of my best friends are students. Even though I no longer have sex with students, my relations with students have not really changed at all.

Some of these personal relations remain pretty casual; but others get intense, complicated, and sticky. The intense relations involve students who take me very seriously as a teacher. These are students who want, in some way, to be intellectuals or academics like I am. And these are the students I most care about as a teacher.

It was indeed just such a relation that landed me in violation of the school's consensual relations policy. When this graduate student took her first course from me, immediately after the second class meeting, she came up and asked if we could talk. I told her to come to my office hours the next morning, but she didn't want to wait and pressed me to meet with her right then. Seeing how important it was to her, I relented and went with her to my office, despite the fact that it was 9:30 p.m. When we got there, she didn't even sit down but blurted out that she wanted me to be her adviser. She was jittery with excitement, and I was tickled to see someone who wanted that much to work with me. I immediately agreed to be her adviser; she was overjoyed and asked if we could go to the bar across the street to talk. Flattered by the ardor of her desire to work with me, I again agreed. And so began a relationship that involved not only working together in class and in my office but [also] going out for drinks and dinners, sometimes with other students or with her girlfriends, sometimes just the two of us.

Right from the start, the relationship was not just professional, not even just social, but intensely personal and personally intense. She was, by her own admission, enamored of my work before she even met me. An ambitious woman with a flair for outrageous performance, she identified with me and thought I'd be the ideal teacher for her. I responded strongly to her desire for a career like mine. The relationship was charged with energy [and] was, as such crucial relations often are, difficult. Because I believe that the most powerful educational experiences occur in an atmosphere of such intensity, I welcomed it, even though I often found it personally challenging.

I have had other teaching relationships that were as or more personal and intense. Although always tricky, they generally produce excellent results. I see the students consistently learn a lot, work really hard, and clearly benefit from working with me; I also learn a lot in such relationships and derive real satisfaction from seeing the difference I can make in the quality of their thinking and their work.

But in this case, the relationship failed. Not because of its adventurous style but in the way so many teaching relations fall apart: more than once, I told the student her work was not satisfactory; she did not accept my judgments and became increasingly suspicious and angry. And because so much passion had been invested in our relationship, the failure was particularly dramatic. The student felt let down, became outraged, and charged me with sexual harassment.

And because she did, the university had occasion to investigate my teaching practices. Although no evidence was found of the harassment the student claimed, the university looked at the pedagogical relation we had and decided it was against university rules.

As upsetting as it was to have someone I had worked so hard to help turn against me and accuse me of a loathsome crime, I am much more disturbed by the implications of the university's determination. Seeing a relation between a student enamored of a teacher's work, a student who wanted to be like that teacher, and the teacher who responded deeply to the student's desire to work with her, who wanted profoundly to help her do what she desired, the university deemed such a connection, passionate and involving so many personal hopes and dreams, an amorous relation.

And indeed it was.

In my formal response to the student's complaint, I used the psychoanalytic notion of "transference" to explain her relation to me. In psychoanalytic theory, transference is the human tendency to put people in the position our parents once held for us. It is a nearly universal response to people whose opinions of us have great authority, in particular doctors and teachers. Since our feelings about our parents include an especially powerful form of love, transference is undoubtedly an "amorous relation." But transference is also an inevitable part of any relationship we have to a teacher who really makes a difference.

In the official report on my case, the university recommends that in the future I should stop working with any student who has such a transference onto me, [which] means that I would not work with any student who really believed I had something important to teach her. I would be forced to turn away precisely those students most eager to work with me, including those graduate students who come to the university where I teach expressly in order to work with me.

While I had vociferously opposed the consensual relations policies before I was accused, I never dreamed how dangerous these policies could be. My case suggests the way the category of "amorous relations" can snowball. By moving from the restricted field of romantic love to the exceedingly wide field of relationships that are social [or] personal or involve intense feelings, what was originally a policy about sexual relations could become a policy restricting and chilling pedagogical relations.

At its most intense—and, I would argue, its most productive—the pedagogical relation between teacher and student is, in fact, a "consensual amorous relation." And if schools decide to prohibit not only sex but [also] "amorous relations" between teacher and student, the "consensual amorous relation" that will be banned from our campuses might just be teaching itself.

36

Putting an End to Risky Romance

Patrick Dilger

Over the past year or so, allegations of sexual impropriety have stained the sanctity of the Catholic priesthood, rattled the upper echelons of the U.S. military, and even threatened the presidency. Nor has academia been immune. In the face of embarrassing public revelations, a succession of leading universities across the country have been forced to take an uncomfortable look at their own regulations on sexual relationships. Just last month, the Yale Law School hosted a three-day conference on sexual harassment that focused on the pathbreaking scholarship of Catharine MacKinnon, who as a student did much to frame the debate that is now so widespread.

The conference came in the wake of a major change in Yale's own policy on the subject. Following a year-long review, a ten-member campus committee in late November recommended that, instead of merely discouraging romantic contacts between professors and their students as had been the case in the past, the university should ban them outright. "Any such relationship jeopardizes the integrity of the educational process by creating a conflict of interest," the committee wrote in its report to the university's provost, Alison Richard. After

AUTHOR'S NOTE: This is a reprint of an article originally published as Dilger, Patrick, "Putting an End to Risky Romance," *Yale Alumni Magazine,* April, 1998, pp. 30-33. Used with permission.

receiving administrative approval, a new policy based on the committee's recommendations will likely take effect later this year.

The review followed a ruling in late 1996 by the Yale College Grievance Board for Student Complaints of Sexual Harassment. After investigating a complaint by a female undergraduate, the board found that a mathematics professor had violated university regulations by having a "nonconsensual" sexual relationship with the woman, who was 17 at the time.

The board found that the relationship was "seriously inappropriate to the dealings between a teacher and a student" and recommended that the faculty member be dismissed at the end of the fall 1996 semester. Instead, he received a "stern reprimand" because he was already scheduled to take up a teaching post at Ohio State University the following January. But in December 1996, Ohio State rescinded its offer, leaving the professor's career in apparent limbo.

The mathematician had fallen afoul of a Yale policy that at the time considered sexual relations between professors and their students "potentially coercive," even when they were apparently founded on mutual consent. The faculty handbook warned that "the faculty member will bear the burden of overcoming a presumption that the activity was not consensual on the part of the student."

In the wake of the committee's ruling, however, many faculty members criticized the policy as well intentioned but ambiguous, muddied by the fact that it was incorporated into a broader policy on sexual harassment. The accuser, for example, had described the two-month relationship as consensual at first, although she said it later left her "confused and distraught." She said she did not consider her teacher's actions to be sexual harassment and "an abuse of his authority" until several months after the relationship had soured.

Yale College dean Richard Brodhead was one of those who called for a review of the policy. "In an area that can't entirely be rescued from the ambiguities of human nature and human conduct," he wrote, "the least we can do is to give as clear a message as we can about the university's expectations. If the teacher's actions can be judged wrong in hindsight, then perhaps we ought to say upfront: 'Just don't.' Having sexual relations with one's students is just not something teachers should do."

The committee agreed. The new policy, which is published in the faculty handbook, explicitly states that teachers—whether professors or teaching assistants—may not have a sexual relationship with a student over whom they have direct supervisory responsibilities, "regardless of whether the relationship is consensual." According to Calhoun College master William Sledge, who chaired the committee, "The main rule is now crystal clear. Teachers and [their] students cannot have sex, period."

The policy has met with general approval on the campus. "We can be friendly, we can be social, we can be personable, but there's also a line that can never be crossed," history professor Jay Gitlin told the *Yale Daily News.*

But some feel that the restriction borders on the draconian, particularly because it applies to graduate students, who are generally older and, presumably, wiser in the ways of the world

than undergraduates are likely to be. "If two people are genuinely attracted to each other, why would anyone interfere, especially an institution?" Pascale Teysseire, a doctoral candidate in Near Eastern languages and civilizations, asked.

Sledge counters that Yale is not attempting to "moralize about people's sexual involvement and behavior." Rather, it is seeking to "change the milieu" by encouraging professors and students to assume responsibility for their actions when an affair of the heart presents a conflict of interest. The hope is that the policy will allow both parties to protect themselves against the fallout of a relationship gone bad. "There'll be no 'sex police' reporting what's going on," says Sledge. "We're not looking to control whether people fall in love. We're just saying that, if they do, they can't be in a teacher-student relationship."

Although Yale was in the vanguard on such matters when it introduced its policy discouraging student-faculty relationships in the mid-1980s, it has been relatively slow to impose a total ban on sexual contact between professors and their students. Indeed, the Sledge committee found in a review of 15 peer institutions that more than a quarter of them had adopted such a policy in recent years.

According to many, the harder line can be traced to the heightened awareness of sexual harassment issues since the highly publicized Anita Hill-Clarence Thomas hearings that followed Thomas's nomination to the U.S. Supreme Court. But other factors are involved. A series of studies such as that recently conducted by Yale psychologist Suzanne Swan have found that most women suffer sexual harassment in the workplace. Of 300 female university employees surveyed by Swan in her study, 68 percent reported an unwanted sexual experience, and of 447 women in the private sector, 63 percent had experienced at least one incident of sexually harassing behavior in the past 24 months.

As it turns out, private universities have somewhat more leeway than public institutions in attempting to restrict faculty-student affairs. According to Jonathan Alger, associate counsel with the American Association of University Professors, public institutions face various potential legal challenges regarding the right to privacy and free association. "If the university is saying who I can and cannot go out with, [it] can be accused of violating my constitutional rights," Alger argues.

Yale's approach to the issue rests largely on the conviction that a professor's responsibilities toward students are little different [from] those of a doctor or psychiatrist. Just as those in medical professions are held accountable for their actions toward patients, this position holds, so too should professors be in their dealings with students. Moreover, say proponents of the Yale policy, professors can have a major impact on a student's academic career and future prospects, whether through grades, letters of recommendation, or simple personal influence over colleagues' decisions. This imbalance of power is particularly evident in relationships with undergraduates, given the typical gap in age and worldly experience between most professors and their students. "Some students are to professors what groupies are to rock stars," says Rosalyn Amenta, co-coordinator of women's studies at Southern Connecticut State University. "The potential for exploitation is enormous."

Perhaps so, but faculty members who find themselves accused of misconduct might argue that the system is weighted against them. The former Yale mathematician's attorney, John Stewart, decried the lack of due process during his client's Yale hearing (the professor was allowed no legal representation) and the basic presumption that he was "guilty until proven innocent."

Stewart points out that the teacher denied all the allegations made by the student, saying that he never so much as held her hand. "Yet he's been punished twice: Yale gave him a reprimand, and Ohio State withdrew a job offer. If other institutions take the same attitude, then this man will never teach again, and his career in math is probably over."

Mary Gray, a mathematics professor at American University who has worked with the American Association of University Professors on its guidelines for handling sexual harassment, takes a different tack. She argued in a recent issue of the *Chronicle of Higher Education* that if academics took harassment as seriously as they do other forms of professional misconduct like plagiarism, then such career-threatening situations would be less likely to occur. "The notion of institutions acting in a parental capacity for students is old, but I still think that institutions have some obligation not to put someone who has a propensity to harass in a situation where he can do it easily," said Gray. She believes that warning other universities about an accused harasser should be compared to notifying communities when convicted sex offenders move into a neighborhood.

Others say that is going too far. "The attitude seems to be that this is some kind of pedophelia, some child molestation business, some kind of compulsion that's bound to recur," argued Roger Howe, a Yale mathematics professor and one of 15 faculty members who issued a letter supporting the accused teacher. In most sexual harassment cases, Howe told the *Chronicle,* "my instincts would be that you're dealing with intelligent people who crossed some kind of gray line without understanding where they were, and they understand that now and will not repeat it."

Indeed, no one is saying that it is a crime to fall in love. And there certainly have been faculty-student relationships that have prospered and even some that have developed into happy, lasting unions. But as the writer Jeffrey Toobin put it in an article entitled "The Trouble with Sex," published in *The New Yorker:* "Between students and their teachers at Yale, there is now, officially, no sex without harassment." Toobin went on to note that "it is worth pausing to consider the costs of policing consensual sex. They include expanding the university's responsibility for private, intimate conduct; they institutionalize the university's role as a bedroom snoop; and, perhaps most important,

they apply the rules of sexual harassment—a law that is supposed to concern discrimination—to what are often victimless crimes."

Whatever the merits of that argument, Southern Connecticut's Rosalyn Amenta observes that the mathematician's case and others like it should serve as a warning. "Certainly, seduction can be a two-way street," she says. "But the bottom line is: 'Who's going to pay the biggest price if the relationship unravels?' The answer is: the faculty member."

37

Of Nerds, Ardent Suitors, and Lecherous Professors

Bernice A. Pescosolido and Eleanor Miller

The issue of the relationship between public responsibility and private morality first came to the forefront in the 1980s as the result of a series of well-publicized and controversial cases in politics, business, religion, and medicine. At that time, professionals and those concerned with professional ethics both within and outside academe made "professional responsibility" a major topic of inquiry. Since that time, a number of cases have emerged within higher education itself that have kept interest in this area alive and forced the professoriate to turn the spotlight on the professional practices of its own members (e.g., Bloom's [1987] *Closing of the American Mind;* Smith's [1990] *Killing the Spirit;* Sykes's [1988] *Profscam*).

In this chapter, we seek, first, to use a sociological approach to socioethical aspects of the professoriate to shed light on a number of conceptual and pedagogical issues at three distinct but interconnected levels: individual (moral-philosophical), communal (professional), and social (societal). Second, we argue that a sociological approach establishes the centrality and unavoidability of conceiving ethical issues as professional rather than simply personal matters. Third, we try to demonstrate that the framework we have outlined provides a useful way in which to analyze ethical issues particularly salient in teaching, research, and graduate training generally. We focus on teaching because it seems the area in which graduate students seem to be given the least formal guidance. It is also, not unrelatedly, an area in which many feel that a professionally responsible professoriate emerges naturally from the personal moral decision making of the individual instructors who people its ranks. We focus specifically on "social relations" between faculty and students, primarily a myriad of issues that include classroom atmosphere, friendship, romantic relationships, and sexual harassment, because efforts to regulate same have been vigorously debated of late and because ethical issues in this area so clearly illuminate the concerns we have just enumerated.

Fourth, and finally, we conclude that training new and current members of the professoriate to think legalistically about whether or not

AUTHOR'S NOTE: Three points deserve mentioning. First, since the main issue in our perspective is power, what happens within groups at the same level or rank may raise other issues but is not relevant here. Second, given that there are numerous examples of "successful" couples who met under these conditions, the focus is better placed on patterns of repeated behavior that are troublesome. Third, in response to this, many academic departments and institutions have drafted and approved policies that do not prohibit such relationships but which require that the senior person remove themself from all supervision and evaluation of the junior one.

their behavior might be deemed sexual harassment is a less useful and informative way of formulating guidelines for a professional community's behavior in the area of student-faculty relations than is socializing them to conceive of decision making in this area as guided by the ethical considerations that bind the members of this and any profession more generally.[1]

The Relevance of Sociology to the Issue of Professional Responsibility

Sociologists have analyzed the importance of sociocultural background, shared normative standards, and formal ethical codes on the social position, training, behavior, and punishment of the members of "consulting" professions such as law, medicine, and even business. They also have studied the ways in which the cultural beliefs of the members of a profession about their work, their mandate, and their status, as well as their beliefs about those they serve, shape both the way in which they do their work and the effect it has on those served (e.g., Abbott 1983; Becker et al. 1961; Berry 1990; Crane 1975; Freidson 1970; Shapiro 1984; Anspach 1993). Yet as Cahn (1986) points out, there has been little scholarly discussion of a major domain of higher education's enterprise, the professoriate.

This is particularly unfortunate because social science analysis in general and sociological analysis in particular, with their emphases on the relationship between the sociocultural and the personal, provide a powerful tool to help make sense of debates on professional responsibility, understanding what problems arise as inevitable features of the work of academics, and determining which issues need to be addressed in the professional socialization of members of a profession.

Professional Responsibility: Analytic Levels and a Sociological Theory

Three distinct levels are involved in the idea of professional responsibility. The first resides with the individual practitioner of a profession wrestling with moral choices and ethical standards in dealing with the everyday, real-life situations. At this moral-philosophical level, abstract normative standards are translated, consciously and unconsciously, into personal decisions and behaviors. This level, where philosophers and ethicists usually direct their attention, has to date been the one most often addressed in discussion of issues such as the right to die, insider trading, and the like, that is, the personal responsibility of the individual professional (e.g., Jennings, Callahan, and Wolf 1987). The second level focuses on the profession as an occupation group designated as "expert" and possessing substantial autonomy over its activities, the training of future members of the profession, and the regulation of colleagues. At this group level, the site of most sociological research, it is the social responsibility of the profession to confront ethical dilemmas and to set standards for practice central to the profession's duties and important for its privileges. The third level of professional responsibility targets the larger society, both state and civil sectors. It addresses the societal responsibility to oversee the professions in order to assist or pressure both individual practitioners and professions as bodies of practitioners to attend in practice to publicly defined socioethical responsibilities. This third level involves the public, other professions, and the state, all of which influence a societal context through formal and informal norms and sanctions including legal regulation, resource allocation, and the conveying or withholding of both trust and prestige. Much of the discussion in this chapter is situated at the second, sociological level as it bears on ethical issues in higher education. It is important, therefore, to distinguish this level clearly from the others.

The first level of professional responsibility requires that members of a profession hold (or at least be aware of) expectations to develop a moral philosophy. It calls on individual professionals to consider explicitly both the range and the nature of ethical responsibilities. Questions on the specific meaning of "protection of human subjects," "appropriate relations with students," and "suitable service activity" cannot be answered or illuminated by scientific inquiry, on the one hand, or by empirical scrutiny of how the real world works, on the other. These questions fall within the realm of right and wrong, good and bad, where moral reasoning adjudicates among potential solutions. Ethical and moral principles represent a conscious and systematic way in which to work through specific situational dilemmas in practice (particularly in the face of very general standardized professional or legal codes).

The second level of professional responsibility focuses on professions in their sociological definition as particular types of collectivities, raising the consideration of ethics above the individual to the level of the group. These privileged occupations, by virtue of their unique societal position, possess a heavy measure of rights and responsibilities including monopoly of practice, autonomy, and self-regulation (Berlant 1975; Freidson 1970). Even if we cannot agree on the essential properties of a profession that distinguish it from other occupations, we can agree with Becker (1970) that "profession" is an honorific symbol identifying a morally praiseworthy type of occupational organization. Studies of the rise to occupational dominance of the scholarly professions (e.g.,

the clergy, the professoriate) in the Middle Ages or of the consulting professions (e.g., law, medicine) in the "Great Transformation" indicate quite clearly that professions historically have viewed the consideration and regulation of ethical behavior part of their responsibility or at least as a necessary tool in obtaining public trust (Abbott 1983; Carr-Saunders and Wilson 1933; Larson 1977). As Jennings et al. (1987) observe, professions "embraced the language of ethical responsibility and have made that language an integral part of their own cultural identity" (p. 5).

One of the major ways in which specific professions have concretized their societal obligations (and ensured their privileged social status) is in canons of professional ethics (Abbott 1983:856). Whether they do so on the basis of ethical dedication or economic self-interest or because of the need to distance themselves from other contenders with differing views, the collective nature of these obligations has two important implications: that an individual practitioner's status depends entirely on membership in the profession and that because the profession demands more autonomy than do other occupational groups, it must "make good" its claim to regulate its members' practice and behavior (see Abbott 1983:868). It is clearly within the purview of the profession, indeed it is part of its social contract with society, to provide standards of practice, to ensure that practitioners understand them, and to see to their enforcement. Even if individual practitioners have well-considered standards for their actions, their right to practice can be limited or revoked by the profession if their behaviors do not correspond in significant ways with professional standards. Professional associations can deny membership and access to related benefits, but it is that state (e.g., in medicine) and/or specific work organizations (for professors) that can terminate employment.

The third level of professional responsibility deals with the larger society itself. Society represents the context that places cultural, legal, and political expectations on the profession. These standards of practice are imposed from the outside on both the profession and individual professionals. From civil society come normative standards, albeit often vague, for the practice of the profession. In some cases, these standards find expression in public policy (including regulations and legal statutes) developed, implemented, and enforced by members of other professions that dictates ethical standards to which a particular profession must adhere.[2] Bayles (1981) remarks, "Professions do not have a right to practice; it is a privilege conferred by the state" (p. 14). The state provides both direct and indirect means of setting ethical limits on professional work. For example, the social, cultural, legal, and bureaucratic attachments to the notion of a "right to health care" in the United States and the United Kingdom placed different ethical burdens on the American Medical Association (AMA) and the British Medical Association, respectively, and on the physicians who were their members (Hollingsworth 1986). In similar fashion, insider trading was defined as a discrete ethical issue in the United States only with the passage of the Securities Exchange Act in 1934; it remains undefined in Japan. Addressing this third level, which is not a focus in the sections that follow, requires a multidisciplinary approach that links micro and macro phenomena and connects societal arenas.[3]

Although disentangling the multiple dimensions of professional responsibility analytically is crucial both for our argument and for the individual professional, it does not negate the importance of understanding that these dimensions are, indeed, intertwined. Thus, despite the individualistic nature of the first level of professional responsibility, the ability of practitioners to develop a moral philosophy requires at least a basic awareness of professional and societal standards for practice.

Codes developed by professional associations (e.g., American Sociological Association [ASA] 1997; American Association of University Professors [AAUP] 1984) are of central concern, as are codes specific to the institutions in which individual scholars practice (e.g., department and university policies). These codes are not deterministic because their very general language requires practitioners to translate their meanings into guides for specific and often complicated individual actions. In addition to these formal codes of ethics, societal standards exist, often in the form of legal proscriptions or requirements. For example, the detailed, explicit, and systematic review of relevant scholarly research by human subjects committees was instituted across the board at the not-so-gentle suggestion of the federal government, which held the fiscal resources necessary to ensure institutional compliance. While individual practitioners may set a standard of practice and behavior consistent with their own values or needs, as members of a profession they cannot form their moral-philosophical code independently of their obligations to the profession and to society. As Bayles (1981) points out, "Individual professionals have obligations to assist the professions in improving skills and maintaining a position that enables them to fulfill their professional roles" (p. 110).

The second level of professional responsibility is likewise influenced both by individual practitioners and by larger societal structures. Codes of ethics, as Veatch (1981:89) remarks, are essentially profession-generated documents. Practitioners themselves create and revise the codes of their professional associations, usually with the approval of a majority of the membership. But society, either through the state or through civil sectors, can alter even these agreements by shaping and sanctioning professional standards of practice and conduct. Colombotos and Kirchner's (1986) research, for example, documents the action of the state in pressuring at least some sectors of the medical profession to assist in responding to the perceived large-scale societal responsibility of providing medical care to the elderly. Although the AMA threatened a boycott if Medicare legislation passed, it was unable to follow through on its threat for several reasons: because more of its general membership agreed with the legislation than the AMA leadership had estimated, because the passage of the legislation itself changed the attitudes of some practitioners and made others unwilling to violate societal proscriptions, and because such a challenge posed a threat to the very legitimacy and trust on which the status of medicine as a profession rests.

We conclude, then, that professional ethics is not simply the purview of ethical theory. Neither is it a matter of individual morality. It requires a consideration of legal, social, cultural, and professional factors in addition to moral philosophy at either theoretical or individual levels (Bayles 1981).

Professionalization, as documented in both sociological studies and social histories, involved the transfer of expertise in particular tasks from the general population to a specialized group that claimed expertise in an esoteric body of knowledge and thus demanded as right and proper a high degree of autonomy over its work. With the imposition of or acquiescence to a profession's cultural authority came a transfer of social power and, with it, social responsibility (Starr 1982). Therefore, these privileged occupations have responsibilities as professions to establish guidelines and codes for the socialization of their practitioners, for determining key elements of practice, and for monitoring and sanctioning their members. Ethics no longer is an individual matter only; a sense of collective responsibility exists on the part of the individual practitioner, the professional group, and members of other professions charged with overseeing, in some way, the common good marked out by the professions as their terrains. In the remaining sections, the chapter employs this sociological analysis as a framework for rethinking faculty-student relations, especially in the area of teaching.

In the next section, we describe the central role of social relations in any discussion of professional responsibility.

Power in the University: Professional Responsibility and Social Relations

The distinction between scholarly and consulting professions traditionally has been based on the latter's fee-for-service arrangement, which calls for a personal relationship between client and practitioner (Bayles 1981:61). The scholarly professions have been regarded as more removed, having an "audience" rather than individual clients and, in the case of the sciences, including sociology, following a tradition of remaining at sufficient distance to sustain value neutrality in the Weberian tradition. Even if we argue that researchers can remove themselves from what they study (which sociologists of science say is not possible and some feminists say is not desirable), current ideas on what constitutes high-quality teaching for undergraduates and training for graduate students call this distinction into question.

Lowman (1984) states, "In theory, the college classroom is strictly an intellectual and rational arena. In reality, a classroom is a highly emotional interpersonal arena" where perceived or actual interpersonal relations between students and teachers strongly affect students' morale, motivation, and learning (pp. ix, 12). Both intellectual excitement and interpersonal rapport create what Lowman terms "masterful teaching"; this occurs when teachers provide their students a sense of incorporation into the learning enterprise. The very nature of this enterprise, with its tension between independent scholarship and "mentoring" and with personal commitment by both students and teachers, makes all too real the possibility of misinterpretation or misuse of the student-teacher relationship for unselfish or selfish, unconscious or conscious, reasons. Moreover, as hooks points out in this section (Chapter 34), the classroom is inevitably an erotic space. She says, "Understanding that eros is a force that enhances our overall effort to be self-actualizing, that it can provide an epistemological grounding informing how we know what we know, enables both professors and students to use such energy in a classroom setting in ways that invigorate discussion and excite the critical imagination" (p. 384).

In short, the issue of social relations between faculty and students is central to the teaching mission and is a touchstone for ethical issues in the classroom.

Ethical Guidelines for Social Relations between Faculty and Students: The Contributions of Sociology

The lists of general codes, specific admonitions, and detailed interpretations of policies with regard to student-faculty relations is a long one that demonstrates the wide variation in specificity, means, and proscriptions for dealing with the tensions inevitable in teaching or graduate training (e.g., Cahn 1986; Lowman 1984; and various policies generated by professional organizations, the AAUP, and specific institutions of higher education; see also Dilger in this section [Chapter 36] for Yale University's recent decision). Adequate professional socialization requires, at the very least, that members of the profession and those aspiring to membership should be exposed to these codes and encouraged to discuss them. Simply receiving copies of relevant codes constitutes more preparation for handling professional responsibilities than most members of the professoriate have undergone in their graduate training or postgraduate years. Perhaps many potential dilemmas could be avoided if the professoriate did not allow its next generation to face inevitably difficult situations as ethics "innocents," asking them to pick this up on their own or to glean standards (correctly or not) from those of their mentors. However, a sociological framework based on an analysis of the operation of professions and knowledge of the various levels of professional responsibility discussed heretofore, combined with an understanding of organizations as systems of stratification or hierarchy, illuminates ethical issues related to teaching in a most informative way and helps inform readings of these codes.

If we regard the university or college as an organization or, mindful of hooks's (Chapter 34, this volume) insight that the classroom always is a site in which eros dwells, as a community unto itself, then one of the primary factors to consider sociologically is that it is a stratification system as well. Adapting Mills's (1956) view of power and stratification, it can be argued that the role of professionals in higher education has three features. First, the teaching-learning process involves three major sets of actors: faculty (the professionals), undergraduates (the clients), and graduate students (both clients and professionals in training). Second, each of these groups represents, in essence, a stratum of like-situated individuals approximately equal in social position. Ethical expectations within strata are clearly different from ethical expectations between strata. Third, the relationship among professors, graduate students, and undergraduates is first and foremost a power relationship. Teaching-learning and training are social processes set within a context of deference, authority, and power.

Baseline Implications for Professorial Responsibility within a Stratified System

This framework carries some baseline implications for professional responsibility. In view of the power differential, general proscriptions that "condemn the use of professional skills for selfish purposes" (Becker 1970:95) are unlikely to meet opposition. With regard to teaching-student relations, for example, few would agree that "sex for grades" (quid pro quo sexual harassment) is ethically acceptable. Yet, as Elbe (1976) and Lowman (1984:69) point out, this coercive behavior "is much less common and less problematic than other dilemmas which involved generally willing but discrepantly powerful participants." Dziech's (1984) truly "lecherous professors" are by no means extinct or less troubling, but the tolerance of colleagues, universities, and the law has changed over the past 20 years. Using the classroom to work out life problems and insecurities, pro-

moting one's personal views and acquiring "disciples," using students to air one's employment difficulties, and using the classroom as a "supply center" for relationships or errands all represent misuse of professional power. Having said this is not to deny that the faculty's right to academic freedom (professional autonomy) often is strained in this regard. Academic freedom is the "right of professionally qualified people to discover, teach, publish the truth as they see it within their fields of competence" (Cahn 1986:5). However, this right does not extend to the belief, a legitimate position, that "what I do in my classroom or personal life is my own business" if that personal life is played out to a large extent or even moderately in one's role as teacher, in the classroom, or in any way that negatively affects the morale or affective life of a department or a university community.

Implications for Professorial Conduct of the Professional Standard of Expertise

As argued earlier, the social contract that a profession has with the members of society who grant its members autonomy and honor is in large part based on their claim to have expertise in particular tasks that are informed by an esoteric body of knowledge. With the acceptance of a profession's cultural authority and concomitant bestowal of power comes certain social responsibilities (Starr 1982). This relationship helps to illuminate gray areas associated with the appropriate scope of professional responsibility and expertise. For example, if professors are charged with guiding students, then their sphere of influence does not include the personal problems of students that interfere with learning. Expanding professional obligations beyond the guidance of learning puts one at risk of the "generalization of expertise" (Veatch 1973:29), which arises when individuals with scholarly/technical expertise in other areas are assumed, consciously or unconsciously, to have (or assume themselves to have) expertise in other areas. So, for example, even if good teaching has a substantial interpersonal component (and even a "kinship with therapy" [Cahn 1986:34-35]), faculty do not generally have the power, expertise, professional legitimacy or mandate, or obligation to deal with students' socioemotional problems. Even when they do have such training, the wisdom of acting in this role is questionable because of obligations to the profession; it sets up aprofessional standards for other professors and unnecessarily clouds student expectations. Cahn (1986) says, in the regard, "It is both foolish and dangerous for a person with an advanced degree in English, economics, or engineering to attempt to act as a clinical psychologist" (p. 36). This principle removes the often-mistaken ethical obligation to be involved in the lives of, and always helpful to, students in every way possible and protects faculty from some (or even most) students' inability to understand the nature of intellectual interest and passion that is (potentially) inclusive of all students and that which is particularistic and exclusive and often assumed to be amorous (again, see hooks, Chapter 34).

Implications for Professorial Behavior of the Professional Mandate of Universalism

Another aspect of the social contract between a profession and the society concerns the social expectation that professionals will render their services equitably to those clients who seek them, that they will treat all clients with wisdom, respect, and concern without regard to the social standing of the client and irrespective of any personal biases they might hold. This mandate derives from the principle of circumscribed expertise in that it is assumed that a professional knowledge and practice does not vary from client to client except in ways that derive from inadequacies in the knowledge base itself. In short, it is assumed that a professional employs universalistic standards in the application of knowledge and expertise. This mandate flies in the face of what little we know about the ethical training of professionals—their general beliefs, values, and standards of practice. What limited information exists is primarily based on studies of the medical profession and seems to indicate that in the absence of agreed-on professional solutions to specific ethical dilemmas, individual practitioners' solutions have systematic nonprofessional social biases. In short, these studies suggest that professionals tend to report their own experiences as the source of ethical guidelines. Crane (1975) finds, for example, that in general, physicians' decisions on whether or not to withdraw treatment in cases of terminal illness are patterned systematically by religious backgrounds; Protestant physicians are the most likely and Catholic physicians the least likely to agree to patients' requests to withhold or terminate care. Nevertheless, universalism is assumed on the part of members of a profession including members of the professoriate. This standard is thought to guide teachers as they evaluate students' work and, despite the fact that it sometimes is challenged, it is the assumption that permits university instructors to engage in all sorts of assessments of students that are potentially fraught with opportunities for personal bias, with very little risk of students' withdrawing the trust they have been taught to have that teachers, as professionals, will grade their work on its merits.

The mandate of universalistic treatment also extends to the issue of "client competence." It suggests that a professional should neither patronize a client nor take advantage or slight a naive or uninformed client. The burden of making sure that the terms of the professional relationship and its nature are clear to the client, and that in rendering service the professional at least "does no harm," rests fully on the shoulders of the professional.

Rethinking Student-Faculty Relations: From Friendship to Sexual Harassment

In her recent book *Feminist Accused of Sexual Harassment* (Gallop 1997; see excerpt in Chapter 35, this volume), University of Wisconsin–Milwaukee distinguished professor of English and comparative literature and feminist Jane Gallop explores a contradiction that she says placed her in a position to be accused of sexual harassment. As a teacher dedicated to feminist pedagogy and in keeping with the feminist maxim that "the personal is the political," she sought to make her teaching highly personal, but as a result of this effort, which involved intensely personal relationships with her students, she was accused of sexual harassment (Gallop 1994:18). The details of her case have been widely discussed (e.g., Gallop 1994, 1997; Harris 1997; Himmelfarb 1997; Lane 1997; Leatherman 1997; Talbot 1994) and do not concern us here, but her arguments with regard to the relationship between pedagogy and faculty-student relations illuminate the argument we have been making to this point.

Gallop (1997) describes the sexual relationships she had as a graduate student with members of her dissertation committee. She argues that those experiences were empowering in that they humanized and made vulnerable those who had power over her. This made it easier for her to write, to presume that she had something to say, and to feel that she was in some way the intellectual equal of her mentors. She argues that these men "continued to serve her well, to offer vital criticism as well as encouraging praise, helping to make the thesis as good as possible. . . . In other words, these men did not treat my work any differently than before we had sex" (pp. 41-42). As a faculty member, Gallop admits to having had sex with students who successfully seduced her and continues to socialize with her students and give them advice on personal matters including their love lives (p. 57). She admits that some of her relationships with students get "intense, complicated, and sticky," but she argues that these relationships are a testament to the fact that these particular students take her "very seriously as a teacher" (p. 53).

These are "students who want, in some way, to be intellectuals or academics like me. . . . And these are the students I most care about as a teacher" (p. 53). In her formal response to a student who filed a sexual harassment complaint against her, Gallop argues that the most intense and productive teaching is of this sort; it involves "transference" that a skilled teacher may manipulate to promote learning. In short, it is a "consensual amorous relation." She concludes that "if schools decide to prohibit not only sex but [also] 'amorous relations' between teacher and student, the 'consensual amorous relation' that will be banned from our campuses might just be teaching itself" (p. 45). That such a relationship cannot be sexual harassment, Gallop argues, hinges on the fact that sexual harassment promotes an environment hostile to learning, whereas the consensual amorous relations she describes do the opposite.

Gallop's theory of pedagogy highlights some of the considerations that we argued earlier constitute historically grounded and sociologically sound ways of thinking about professional ethics for the professoriate. First and foremost, there is no acknowledgment that members of the professoriate operate at the level of the group. They derive their status and authority from their membership in a community of professionals, not from particularistic qualities inherent in who they are as individuals.

Second, her pedagogical stance is interesting when compared to that of bell hooks, who also highlights the status of the classroom as an erotic space, as opposed to the teacher as an erotic object, but argues that it often is necessary to help students understand the difference between the two. Gallop's theory of pedagogy also ignores the importance of the professional standard of universalism. Because the impetus to learning is transference to her as an individual rather than, as hooks claims, a passion "fundamentally rooted in a love for ideas," it is profoundly disabling for the student for whom the teacher holds no personal appeal and is in no way a role model but in whom a passion for the ideas might be stirred in a pedagogical space within a more universalistic culture. Even if some indescribably charismatic teacher should appeal to all students, carrying the idea of universalism to its logical conclusion, as Gallop describes it, would be unfathomable. The irony is that such a person would likely be more savvy, more socially skilled, and less likely to hold such a stance. As Gallop readily admits, her experi-

ences as a girl considered to be too smart but not attractive enough for her frank and rude peers shaped her response to the electric pairing of sexuality and intellect. No one has ever contended that those who end up in the professoriate were those most likely to have stood at the pinnacle of the social hierarchy in high school (see, e.g., the recent study [Laumann 1994] reporting an inverse relationship between educational degrees and frequency of sexual activity). Perhaps, then, more than for some other occupational groups, the "nerd" factor might be considered as an impetus to discussing (1) the power of intellectual authority and ideas, (2) its frequent confusion with sexual attraction, and (3) the responsibility of professors to understand inappropriate admiration as part of students' struggle to confront this "awakening."

Conclusion

If the finding described here that suggests that, as least in medicine, much ethical decision making on the part of the professional is based on the idiosyncratic, although no doubt patterned, personal experiences of the professional, rather than on acquaintance with the substance of relevant professional codes and thoughtful discussion with other professionals, then what might be done to change this situation? Focusing our sociological lenses on the professional tasks of the professoriate, especially in training future professionals, brings into sharper focus the need to convey to graduate students that they have professional responsibilities to themselves, to students, to their departments, to the institutions within which they work, to the profession, and to the larger society. Professional ethics form the backbone of the public's trust in professions (Jennings et al. 1987). The practical concern is how to pass along a sense of rights and obligations if informal socialization processes do not provide adequate preparation or discussion. Graduate school provides not only formal training but also an arena in which "university faculty members participate in the process of ensuring that entering students undergo a transformation of identity. The student is expected to learn to perceive and think as faculty members do—both technical and nontechnical values" (Egan 1989:200). If we assume (correctly, we think) that "most people most of the time want to do what is ethically correct" (Bayles 1981:3), then graduate training must provide some direct contact with and discussion of the ethics of practice involved in this transformation of identity and instillation of values. To do so, we must begin with and pass on a basic understanding of relevant professional codes, the strength and binding force of which ultimately depend on the continuing active discussion, reflection, and use by members of the profession.

Students and colleagues, at a minimum, must be familiar with the formal standards of practice, at least as echoed in formal codes; with the meaning of academic freedom and its appropriate applications; and with their rights as well as their responsibilities. As Cahn (1986) writes, "To enumerate these obligations is not to guarantee their fulfillment. But the first step toward discharging duties is to know what they are" (p. 7). These codes, written in general language, do not provide day-to-day guidelines. Without explicit discussion about these matters as a systematic part of graduate training, it is likely that professionals will fail to see the ethical questions surrounding a course of action (Bayles 1989:3). Students and faculty must bring to this discussion an analytic under-

standing, not simply personal opinions about morals or ethical behavior. Becker (1970) points out that codes of ethics are not, in some ways, realistic descriptions when he states that "educators might perform a great service by working out a symbol more closely related to the realities of the work life practitioners confront, a symbol which could provide an intelligible and workable guide in problematic situations" (p. 100). Whether in specific courses, integrated into various substantive courses, or as the result of role modeling, we need to bring people's attention to the problems they are likely to encounter in practice and give them some sense of "customary values, habits, and written or unwritten rules" (Hodges 1989:3).

In concluding, we must issue a note of caution. Students need to learn from us what ethical theories are, how they could or should make decisions, and what unvarying and immutable rules should be followed. They also should learn what scholarship (from philosophy to social science) has to contribute to ethical decision making. As sociologists, we have attempted to lay out in this chapter how the very private issues and troubles of individual practitioners and clients (in our case, professors and students) are related to larger public issues and social structures (a form of analysis laid out in the work of Mills 1959). Graduate students must recognize that we do not expect them to avoid ethical problems; in fact, by the very social nature of our teaching and research tasks, they inevitably will face them. They must understand, however, that in their position as scholarly professionals, they do not act solely as individuals; they have both rights and obligations to themselves, to their clients (research participants or students), to the community of professionals (both disciplinary and institutional), and to the larger society. As previous experience indicates, if they do not take these obligations seriously, then they may well find them imposed.

Notes

1. This is a revised, expanded, and updated version of "The Sociology of the Professions" (1991). Much of the revision should be credited to the second author and profits from five or more years of service of both authors on the American Sociological Association's (ASA) Committee on Professional Ethics, during which the ASA's *Code of Ethics* was revised. The second author also has experience at the university and national levels on issues of professional responsibility.

2. Adoption of this view should avoid the commonsense notion that "society" needs to reach some agreement on ethical standards if laws or policies are to be enacted. This notion belies what we know about how public policies form, how laws are passed, and how they influence members of society. Law and public policy can be proactive or reactive (Black 1976; Colombotos and Kirchner 1986; Lowi 1964).

3. See, for example, frameworks developed by Coleman (1990), Etzioni (1988), and Giddens (1984), which provide plausible ways in which to approach analytically this third level of professional responsibility.

References

Abbott, Andrew. 1983. "Professional Ethics." *American Journal of Sociology* 88:855-85.

American Association of University Professors. 1984. *Policy Documents and Reports*. Washington, DC: American Association of University Professors.

American Sociological Association. 1997. *Code of Ethics*. Washington, DC: American Sociological Association.

Anspach, Renee R. 1993. *Deciding Who Lives: Fateful Choices in the Intensive Care Nursery*. Berkeley: University of California Press.

Bayles, Michael D. 1981. *Professional Ethics*. Belmont, CA: Wadsworth.

Becker, Howard S. 1970. *Sociological Work: Method and Substance*. New Brunswick, NJ: Transaction.

Becker, Howard S., Blanche Geer, Everett C. Hughes, and Anselm L. Strauss. 1961. *Boys in White: Student Culture in Medical School*. Chicago: University of Chicago Press.

Berlant, Jeffrey L. 1975. *Professions and Monopoly*. Berkeley: University of California Press.

Berry, Bonnie. 1990. "The Sanctioning of Physicians: A Theory of Response to Professional Threats." Paper presented at the annual meeting of the American Sociological Association, Washington, DC.

Black, Donald. 1976. *The Behavior of Law*. New York: Academic Press.

Bloom, Alan. 1987. *The Closing of the American Mind*. New York: Simon & Schuster.

Cahn, Stephen. 1986. *Saints and Scamps: Ethics in Academia*. Totowa, NJ: Rowan & Littlefield.

Carr-Saunders, A. M. and P. A. Wilson. 1933. *The Professions*. Oxford, UK: Clarendon.

Coleman, James S. 1990. *The Foundations of Social Theory*. Cambridge, MA: Belknap.

Colombotos, John and Corinne Kirchner. 1986. *Physicians and Social Change*. New York: Oxford University Press.

Crane, Diane. 1975. *The Sanctity of Life*. New York: Russell Sage.

Dziech, Billie Wright. 1984. *The Lecherous Professor: Sexual Harassment on Campus*. Boston: Beacon.

Egan, Janet Malenchek. 1989. "Graduate School and the Self: A Theoretical View of Some Negative Effects of Professional Socialization." *Teaching Sociology* 17:200-8.

Elbe, Kenneth E. 1976. *The Craft of Teaching: A Guide to Mastering the Professor's Art*. San Francisco: Jossey-Bass.

Etzioni, Amitai. 1988. *The Moral Dimension: Toward a New Economics*. New York: Free Press.

Freidson, Eliot. 1970. *The Medical Profession*. New York: Dodd, Mead.

Gallop, Jane. 1994. "Sex and Sexism; Feminism and Harassment Policy." *Academe,* September-October, pp. 17-23.

———. 1997. *Feminist Accused of Sexual Harassment*. Durham, NC: Duke University Press.

Giddens, Anthony. 1984. *The Constitution of Society: Outline of the Theory of Structuration*. Berkeley: University of California Press.

Harris, Elise. 1997. "Jane's Addiction." *Out,* June, pp. 82ff.

Himmelfarb, Gertrude. 1997. "Professor Narcissus: In Today's Academy, Everything Is Personal." *The Weekly Standard,* June 2, pp. 17-21.

Hodges, Louis. 1989. "Comments." In *Professional Ethics in Higher Education: Methods, Theories, Practices*. Report of a conference held at the Poynter Center, Indiana University.

Hollingsworth, J. Rogers. 1986. *A Political Economy of Medicine: Great Britain and the United States*. Baltimore, MD: Johns Hopkins University Press.

Jennings, Bruce, Daniel Callahan, and Susan M. Wolf. 1987. "The Professions: Public Interest and Common Good." *Hastings Center Report,* February (special supplement).

Lane, Ann J. 1997. "When Power Corrupts." *Women's Review of Books,* September, pp. 8-9.

Larson, Magali S. 1977. *The Rise of Professionalism*. Berkeley: University of California Press.

Laumann, Edward O. 1994. *The Social Organization of Sexuality: Sexual Practices in the United States*. Chicago: University of Chicago Press.

Leatherman, Courtney. 1997. "A Prominent Feminist Theorist Recounts How She Faced Charges of Sex Harassment." *Chronicle of Higher Education,* March 7, pp. A12-A13.

Lowi, Theodore. 1964. "American Business, Public Policy, Case Studies, and Political Theory." *World Politics* 16:677-715.

Lowman, Joseph. 1984. *Mastering the Techniques of Teaching*. San Francisco: Jossey-Bass.

Mills, C. Wright. 1959. *The Sociological Imagination*. New York: Oxford University Press.

Shapiro, Susan. 1984. *Wayward Capitalists*. New Haven, CT: Yale University Press.

Smith, Page. 1990. *Killing the Spirit: Higher Education in America*. New York: Penguin.

"The Sociology of the Professions and the Profession of Sociology: Professional Responsibility, Teaching, and Graduate Education." 1991. *Teaching Sociology* 19:351-61.

Starr, Paul. 1982. *The Social Transformation of American Medicine*. New York: Penguin.

Sykes, Charles. 1988. *ProfScam*. Washington, DC: Regenery.

Talbot, Margaret. 1994. "A Most Dangerous Method." *Lingua Franca*, January-February, pp. 24-40.

Veatch, Robert. 1973. "Generalization of Expertise." *Hastings Center Studies* 1:29-40.

———. 1981. *A Theory of Medical Ethics*. New York: Basic Books.

DOONESBURY

by Garry Trudeau

Doonesbury © G. B. Trudeau. Reprinted with permission of Universal Press Syndicate. All rights reserved.

Section D

The Personal Worlds of Professors: Past, Present, and Future

The final section of Part II forces us to consider the private social world in which college teachers live as individuals. Again, we face a series of myths and contradictions: great teachers are born, not made; we must bring in our personal life or stoically leave it out entirely; personality does or does not matter; we cannot be simultaneously friendly and objective assessors. To discuss teaching and higher education without bringing in issues of "self" provides a safe but unrealistic examination of the key resource of any profession. Faculty must be concerned with the pressures that confront them as individuals and as those charged with training the future professorate. Teaching forces us to struggle with a variety of deeply personal issues concerning our identities, whether realistic or not, as Trudeau remarks in his comment on our Latin professor, and how they are implicated in our relationships with students, colleagues, and course materials. As committed teachers, we are forced to ask how to improve the quality of our teaching despite personal limitations, how our preferences and teaching styles affect students' ability to learn, how we can educate students very different from ourselves (including those who resist our messages), and how we can justify our authority to impart knowledge about sensitive issues beyond the realm of our own personal experiences. Answering these questions requires that we use our social science imaginations to situate ourselves and our students within the social locations and processes that shape our lives. The first set of essays in this section asks these difficult questions, offering a variety of concrete suggestions about how to achieve excellence, build trust, prevent our personal convictions from silencing students who do not share our views, and grapple with the contradictions inherent in teaching.

What makes a good teacher? Although it is difficult to pinpoint a specific set of skills or techniques, the authors of the essays in this section highlight the importance of self-knowledge. Daniel F. Chambliss (Chapter 38) also emphasizes the importance of knowing our own strengths and weaknesses as well as those of our students. Excellence in teaching, he argues, can be achieved by doing what works to improve students' abilities and performances, building on our own individual strengths, fostering social worlds that support learning and excellence, and setting high standards and expectations for all students. He believes that mundane actions can produce significant learning experiences and result in qualitative leaps in student accomplishments. Chambliss also suggests that we organize our classes to benefit the best students, which for him means those who really want to learn, rather than aiming to the middle. The danger, in our view, is that we will too readily define "the best" students as those who respond well to our own teaching and learning styles, thereby failing to appreciate adequately and respond appropriately to the diversity in our classrooms. Given Gerald T. Powers' (Chapter 39) evidence that the teaching styles of professors often contrast with the learning styles of their students, this danger is very real. It suggests, as Powers contends, that faculty need to reorganize their courses to cater to a diversity of student learning styles to accomplish Chambliss's goal.

Teachers can earn the trust that facilitates student learning, claims Stephen Brookfield (Chapter 40), by demonstrating a willingness to admit error, modeling behaviors we wish to encourage in our students, being explicit about our expectations, and making our words and actions congruent. The task is more difficult when we encounter students who resist the messages we send them or do not respect our authority. Peter Elbow (Chapter 41) discusses yet another challenge facing teachers: how to reconcile their contradictory roles as allies and judges, rooted in conflicting obligations to students and to society and knowledge. The solution, he argues, is not to deny the inherent contradictions of our teaching tasks but rather to acknowledge and creatively navigate them. We can do so by carefully distributing support and judgment over time and space and, via cooperative learning, across many individual students. Marilyn R. Schuster and Susan R. Van Dyne (Chapter 42) trace the history of women in higher education, examining how and when the curriculum changed.

In the next set of essays in this section, Elizabeth Higginbotham (Chapter 43) argues that we have a responsibility to try to get all of our students to listen. Meeting this responsibility, she suggests, means planning for resistance and understanding its character and scope. We must be attentive to our own social location and how it affects the classroom, to student silences and absences, and to power dynamics within the classroom. Thomas J. Gerschick (Chapter 44) also discusses student resistance, in this case to his authority to teach about forms of oppression he has not directly experienced. His solution is to earn students' trust by openly discussing his own personal characteristics and privileged position, encouraging students to challenge him, inviting "other voices" into the classroom, and acknowledging that he is a learner as well as a teacher. Elizabeth Ellsworth (Chapter 45) takes critical pedagogy to task for failing to move beyond criticism toward real curriculum reform. Finally, Brian Ault (Chapter 46) attacks the myth of graduate student failure, pointing out that individualist assumptions about the declining quality of students permit faculty to evade responsibility for graduate programs that produce high rates of failure among students.

One way in which to see how the personal affects the professional is to travel throughout the academic career. The final set of essays in this section traces personal journeys into the classroom, documenting the problems and opportunities facing teachers at different points in their careers. According to Parker J. Palmer (Chapter 47), knowing and trusting who we are, rather than mastering certain techniques, is critical. In his view, good teachers are a diverse lot, but all share in common a strong sense of personal identity, which infuses their work. Sara C. Hare, Walter R. Jacobs, and Jean Harold Shin (Chapter 48) explore the marginal location, anxieties, and challenges facing graduate associate instructors and discuss the strategies they have developed to maintain their authority and credibility within the classroom. Kent L. Sandstrom (Chapter 49) reflects on his unsuccessful initial effort as a beginning junior professor to engage students in participatory learning. The experience prompted him to realize that he had to learn more about his students and about the cultural, regional, institutional, and departmental contexts shaping his classroom experiences. This knowledge led him to adopt a more flexible repertoire of teaching styles, acknowledge his authority, and embrace more modest hopes. Diane Gillespie (Chapter 50) reminds us that teaching also is a learning experience by recounting an episode in which a student's challenge forced her to realize that generational and racial differences may impede our understanding of students' lives and thus our own teaching effectiveness. In the final essay in this section, Howard Aldrich (Chapter 51) reflects on the career trajectories of academics as teachers, tracing a distinctive socialization process marked by shifting social networks that shape our understandings and identities.

38

Doing What Works: On the Mundanity of Excellence in Teaching

Daniel F. Chambliss

Mark Schubert is a great teacher or, to be more precise, a great swimming coach. He has been a member of six Olympic team staffs and has coached several dozen Olympic gold medalists and many scores of national champions. He has helped a number of athletes set world records. He probably is the most successful coach currently in competitive swimming and perhaps is the most successful swimming coach ever. I asked him a few years ago what makes him a great coach. He answered, to my surprise (for he is a very ambitious man), "I never wanted to be a great coach. I've never thought much about it. *I just wanted to have the best program.*"

Schubert is concerned not with his own place or status or even his abilities but rather with the results he gets, that is, with the success of the programs he has built for training great athletes. In practice, this means that, for example, he hires excellent assistant coaches and uses them; he will even hand over world record

holders to his assistants if he thinks they will help the athletes more than he can. He spends time on details of financing the program, getting the right equipment in the weight room, even getting the locker room showers properly cleaned. (I have seen him chew out the cleaning man for a maintenance company for not making the floors shine and then thank the man for his help and let him know that he was a part of a great team.) He can be very difficult to work for, demanding that his subordinates pay close attention to very small details—how loose cords are wrapped around false start poles, for example—but they *do* work for him. They want to be part of a great program, and Schubert builds great programs.

Schubert's example provides, I think, a counterweight to the fetishism of teaching that pervades public, and even academic, discussions of education. We glorify the great teachers—Jaime Escalante of the movie *Stand and Deliver*; Chipping, the beloved prep school hero of the classic *Goodbye, Mr. Chips;* or Mr. Holland of *Mr. Holland's Opus* fame. At our own universities, we have the local charismatic lecturers, the innovators, the in-your-face challengers, and the boundless enthusiasts of the classroom. All of these teachers garner public attention, attract crowds of students (and journalists), and drive the search for "how to be a

EDITORS' NOTE: For more discussion and some ideas on improving teaching, see Angelo's "A Teacher's Dozen: Fourteen General, Research-Based Principles for Improving Higher Learning in Our Classrooms"; Sherwin's "The Continuum of the 'Educational Self' "; Lowman's "A Table of Roles for Effective College Teaching"; and all of the pieces in the Developing an "Effective" Approach subsection in the *Fieldguide*.

great teacher." And charismatic teachers can be valuable, certainly. But great teaching is not the same as great learning, and as Schubert's comments suggest, what really matters is not who the teacher is but rather what results he or she can produce. The great teachers in this sense—that is, those who get great results—are, I think, pragmatists. *They focus on getting results. They do what works.*

In practice, we can see that many different styles of teaching "work" in this sense. Some teachers are great in the lecture hall, engaging students, conveying huge amounts of difficult material in accessible form, or transforming students' perspectives on the world. Others are masters of the discussion group, sitting back and saying little, only a word here or there to turn the students' thoughts in a new direction. Still others employ the bullying interrogations of Socratic method and force their students, in law school *Paper Chase* style, to lift their intellectual standards and powers of concentration to a far higher plane than they had achieved before. One of the best teachers I have ever known had none of these skills. She was a mediocre lecturer, a passable discussion leader, not a Socratic type at all, nothing of a leading figure in her discipline, and (frankly) not even as smart as a fair number of her students. But she was a great teacher and attracted good students who did first-rate work for her because *she never held them back.* As a professor, she did not know envy and so was not afraid of the best students. They loved her for it. That was her strength, and she applied it magnificently.

What all the great teachers—again, "great" not in the sense of being charismatic or innovative but rather in the sense of getting results—share is that they have made significant changes for the better in their students. They make what we can call *qualitative changes* in their students—marked changes in skills or knowledge, in love of a subject or of learning, in the ability

to see beauty, in perspective or point of view. There are many ways in which to do this. The idea that "great teachers are born, not made" assumes a few models of greatness, a handful of settings in which teaching is done, and a limited flexibility of techniques. My approach here looks instead for ways in which virtually anyone can become a great teacher in the sense of achieving significant, qualitative improvements in their students' ability and performance. The rest of this chapter presents a method for developing teaching excellence with the aim of achieving such qualitative changes.

The Mundanity of Excellence

This chapter is based on personal experience in teaching and on earlier theoretical work, derived from a field study of world-class competitive swimming (Chambliss 1988, 1989). I call the theoretical approach the "mundanity of excellence" argument. The basic argument falls into four parts:

1. Excellence, defined as "consistent superiority of performance," is a qualitative phenomenon. Different levels of achievement result from very different ways of behaving. In a sense, world-class performers are not playing in the same game as are lower level participants.

2. Excellent performance typically is accomplished in distinctive social worlds. Far from being isolated loners, excellent performers are in fact closely connected with others who also perform at very high levels.

3. "Talent" is useless as an explanation of varying degrees of achievement, being simply a reification of the performance it purports to explain.

4. Excellence, for the excellent, is mundane. It is "accomplished through the doing of actions, ordinary in themselves, performed consistently and carefully, habitualized, compounded together, added up over time" (Chambliss 1989:85). There is no magic to becoming an Olympic gold medalist, a Nobel Prize winner, or a great lawyer. In the colloquial phrase, "anyone can do it."[1]

In the rest of this chapter, I try to apply these four ideas to the world of college and university teaching, working them together with some other semirandom observations and perhaps prejudices I have about that subject. Here, I am going beyond hard evidence and rigorous testing. I expect the reader to be skeptical but willing to consider what might be some new ideas.

First, consider how the four principles just listed apply directly to education.

Changes in Student Accomplishment Result from Qualitative Leaps

Student intellectual development in college rests less on the mass of experiences in classrooms, and certainly less on the average teacher's performance, than on *a small number of significant experiences* that make major differences in the students' skills, perspectives, sense of standards, and so on. Years after graduation, one remembers the few outstanding classes or teachers, the few critical discussions, or perhaps the four or five books that changed one's life. Most of what happens in college is a humdrum background, a time filler that students pass through in search of the few great experiences that really matter. Taking a few more literature courses and reading a few more books provide few benefits unless combined with real qualitative changes.

If this is true, then some of our standard course design techniques are misguided. For example, having "writing-intensive" courses in which students are given a large volume of papers to write is not—barring marked changes in the quality of writing made at the same time—a good way in which to improve composition skills. Reading more books in the same inefficient way only reinforces reading inefficiency. Practice does not make *perfect;* rather, it makes *permanent.* Volume of work per se only drills in one's own (perhaps bad) habits. To use an athletic example, for a mediocre basketball player to take 100 foul shots a day, sloppily done, without upgrading his or her technique is simply to practice the wrong way of doing things; it would be far better not to practice at all. Similarly, too often we teachers have our students do more work, without attention to its quality, in the name of rigor or from a misplaced belief in the intrinsic value of hard work. We should not ask them to do more; rather, we should ask them to do *better.*

This also suggests that, in college, the few great teachers matter more than the many average ones. I would even argue that poor teachers do little damage because students usually can avoid them. This does not mean that colleges and universities should provide a comfortable haven for poor teachers or that deans should not care about incompetence in the classroom. But the top priority should be to support the great teachers first because they create the small number of significant positive experiences that shape students' experience.

Student Achievement Occurs in Social Worlds

Students learn best in a socially supportive environment. To put it differently, most people act the way in which most other people act, and when the setting supports learning, most people will learn. For example, we already know in detail the importance of family background to one's intellectual and academic capabilities. Families differ dramatically in their attitudes about school, about learning, and about reading and books and ideas. Families with more books in the home produce children who read and learn; the childhood setting supports learning. Different cultural and ethnic groups also reinforce varying notions of the value of ideas, of critical thinking, and of listening to authority or challenging received wisdom. Different ethnic, class, religious, and occupational groups have different cultures of work, different habits and styles, and different relations to intellectual life. All of these are major predictors of an individual person's ability and willingness to learn.

At the micro level, I suspect that most students learn at roughly the level of their friends. They work as hard as their friends think is appropriate, and they talk about classes with people who want to talk about classes. Good students tend to hang out with good students, and uninvolved students tend to hang out with uninvolved students. So, students are either helped or hurt by those around them. Many are, in fact, held back by families who will say "You think you're getting too smart for us" or by friends who tease them about staying in the dorm to study rather than going out for pizza. Overall, in some colleges, the social atmosphere for learning is good; in others, it is quite bad.

That is why the old platitude "You can get a good education anywhere if you want to" is, quite simply, ridiculous. It is wrong because, first, even the most motivated student will not learn if he or she is taught the wrong things or is taught bad information, as happens when teachers are not knowledgeable. Second, it is wrong because the conditional "If you want to . . ." is dramatically shaped by one's friends and

colleagues. Few 18-year-olds can completely disregard their peers' reaction to how they spend their time and what they talk about at dinner. You cannot get a good education if your friends will not let you. That is why, whatever the quality of classroom teaching there, Harvard is a great university and a great college. There are lots of smart people there who value thinking; there are great bookstores, newspapers, and active research programs; really smart professors are paid lots of money and have their whims indulged; the admissions office values high SAT scores, creative thinking, and unusual achievement; and esoteric lectures by obscure foreign professors often are well attended. Harvard caters to learning and makes it socially acceptable.

A basic lesson of sociology (my own discipline) is that who you spend time with shapes who you are. So, our success in helping students depends in large measure on creating for them *social worlds* of excellence in individual courses, in departmental majors, and in colleges. Anytime we can put good students together so that they can support each other, we do more for learning; anything we do to support students eager to learn is more positive than all the lecture preparation in the world.

Talent Is a Useless Concept

"Talent" is the layperson's term for "unexplained variance in performance." When an athlete performs beautifully, with skill and grace and an apparent lack of effort, we speak of talent. When a student understands a difficult idea quickly and then casually moves to a sophisticated criticism of it, we speak of talent. When actions seem effortless, we speak of talent. In all of these cases, we see excellence and then infer behind it an inner ability, discrete from the performance itself, that has caused the performance. But there is no measure of that talent apart from the performance it purportedly causes. Talent is a reification, an imputation of a thing where there is really only the abstract, invisible cause of a concrete, visible result. In academia, talent "explains" a quick answer, a clever analysis, or a brilliant lecture. In our casual efforts to explain ability, talent is really just a sloppy way of saying that "We don't know how they do it."

Applied to teachers, reliance on the idea of talent means that we look at the teacher's personality, believing that teaching excellence is a radiated function of personality that cannot be changed. Certainly, teaching is a deployment of one's personality. The vivacious, outgoing teacher can do well in large lectures; the thoughtful, quiet type might prefer small seminars. Our schools and universities have forms (e.g., classes, lectures) that favor certain personalities. Those teachers with a dramatic flair (or who have, as I do, actual theater training) generally have an advantage in those settings. If American colleges relied more on tutorials, as do those in Great Britain, then different teachers would be seen as "talented." And the superb teachers in graduate programs have nothing of the personality of the great introductory lecturers. So, although the personality of a teacher is important, more important is how one's personality is deployed—how it is used.[2]

Applied to students, talent and related notions—"disability," for example—reify performance, making it the outcome of a concrete cause, a thing lying in the student's head. We act as if ability is a set thing, given once and for all. But it is not. Several years ago, I had a student I will call Jason in my introductory sociology course. Jason had a problem in that he froze into silence when confronting oral examinations. My introductory course uses these examinations exclusively. There are three of them in the course, 15 minutes each, with essay questions given to the students a week in advance and picked at random for the exam. At the first exam, one-on-one in my office, Jason sat in silent terror for 15 minutes, barely speaking a word. He flunked. Later, a dean called to tell me that Jason had been diagnosed in high school with a two-pronged "learning disability"; he could not handle time pressure, and he could not handle oral work. My oral exam was Jason's nightmare. "We have a stack of reports this high from counselors," said the dean. "It's diagnosed." He suggested written exams, more time in the orals, easier questions, and perhaps extra work that Jason could do rather than the exams. I declined and suggested, to the student, detailed preparation and verbatim rehearsal of answers. On the final exam, Jason got a B. When I asked how he had prepared differently, he said, first, "Well, I did all the reading" and then went on to explain his careful, targeted studying; preparation of detailed, clearly outlined answers; and rehearsal of all the answers. Certainly, he had been afraid, but he had learned with some effort to perform despite his fear.

I am afraid that too often a "disability" is just an observer's reification of a pattern of poor performance. Jason never had done well in oral examinations, so people said he *could not* do well. Likewise, "talent" is simply a reification of good performance. In each case, rather than trying to find such inborn dispositions, we would do better to simply teach the skills and information necessary to improve.

Excellence Is Achieved through Mundane Actions

Excellence is achieved through mundane actions; small, doable actions, added up and compounded, produce major results. Two examples might make the case here, one from a colleague in my field (sociology), and the other from a student.

Randall Collins is an excellent sociologist who might tell us about what produces excellence. Collins is a leading synthetic thinker who has organized and made sense of large areas of sociology and presented their results in clear and powerful ways. He is very well known in the discipline, a leading theorist who at the same time has written some of the finest introductory-level works ever produced. I once asked Collins what made him so successful. I expected an analysis of his intellectual roots and cognitive capacities. He said two things, which I quote loosely. "First," he said, "I think of Marx and Weber as real people; they were smart guys but not gods. Second, when I get up in the morning, I work on my book." He does not fix some coffee, read the newspaper, or answer the mail; he works on his book. "It's not because I'm smarter than anybody else," said Collins. "There are people much smarter than I am who haven't published much significant work." (He then named one or two such people.)

Collins was saying that excellence is achieved through mundane actions—getting up in the morning and doing the things that matter, the things that produce big results. Being a successful sociologist involves not genius but rather painstaking craftsmanship, self-discipline, and persistence. It requires that one do the research and write the book—organizing, editing, rewriting. These mundane tasks are done, in part, because one believes in the "mundanity" of the people who have done great things. As Collins said, Marx and Weber were *real* people, a couple of guys who got up in the morning and worked on their books. And some of their ideas were wrong. They were pretty smart guys, yes, but probably not the smartest. They were consistent workers, focused on their projects, workmanlike in their approach to scholarship and writing, and self-disciplined.

They surrounded themselves with other people who were intelligent and did good work, and they read important books. They used their limited resources (limited by a badly damaged psyche, in Weber's case, and by near poverty and some political impediments, in Marx's case) carefully. Certainly, both benefited from superb educations in one of the best systems yet created for intellectual excellence, that of Germany in the 19th century. But that system was created; it did not just wait for the talent of individuals to emerge. The creation of excellent work is, in this sense, mundane. Anyone can do these things; there is no magic involved.

So, too, for teaching. Some years ago, I asked a small group of junior high school students, whom I coached on a swim team, who their best teacher was. They named a social studies teacher. I asked, "What makes him good?" They thought a minute, and one of them said, "He never yells at us." They all eagerly agreed. At first, I thought their response was silly or trivial—the way in which nurses sometimes think patients' concern with getting injections is trivial—but I realized then that whether it was trivial or not (and it really is not) did not matter. *Not yelling worked.* Yelling, I think, would have distracted them from the message and made our relationship problematic, it would have made practice time unpleasant, and they heard me no better when I yelled than when I did not. Not yelling showed respect, and the respect was reciprocated. I resolved at that point, as a swimming coach, never to yell at the kids. Similarly, in college teaching, learning and using all of your students' names seems a small thing, but it really does matter; it works. Again, small actions can have big results.

If excellence can be gained through mundane actions, then one needs to determine what actions are best leveraged, what skills really matter, and what concrete behaviors produce major results. It may be, as with learning students' names, that we are surprised by the smallest of the effective techniques. Very easy actions might work very well. And it may be that we do not realize our own strengths. Both of these make sense in light of the "different worlds" principle described earlier. People at lower levels really do not understand what makes better performers better; they live in different worlds. One can passively agree with Collins' comment about "working on my book," but few of us actually take his advice to heart and do it. So we should (1) make qualitative leaps, (2) create social worlds of learning, (3) forget talent, and (4) find the doable actions that matter. The basic analytic technique always will be to ask what actions produce the best results—not what should or what we would like to, what students "should care about," or what we "need to work on" but rather what works— and then to *do* those things that get results.

So, How Do We Make Major Improvements?

How does a single professor implement these ideas? Does this program require dramatic changes to one's personality, abandonment of old methods, and denial of one's natural gifts or limitations?

Not at all. In fact, the underlying tone of my chapter should be that excellent work need not be difficult. In fact, it may well be *easier* to be excellent than to be mediocre. If you are doing excellent work, then you can get your social rewards from people who are doing great things—students doing exciting projects, colleagues responding to your writings—rather than struggling along with bored sophomores who are just filling distribution requirements. Excellence, I suggest, involves not much more work (if any) than mediocrity, but the work is

targeted differently. You need not change your personality, only how it is deployed.

At its heart, teaching is a deployment of personality, and personality is hard to change by the time one is an adult. Some teaching guides suggest that one should "be enthusiastic," develop a sense of humor, or learn to really listen to one's students. Shy teachers want to become theatrical, and awkward teachers want to be graceful. But these changes are very unlikely to happen. So, what can one do?

I suggest two steps. First, analyze your own strengths and weaknesses. This requires an empirical study, something any trained researcher should be able to do. I suggest looking over your old student evaluations and your old teaching reviews from colleagues and then conducting a handful of interviews with former students to determine where (in their view) you shine and where you do not. Several years ago, swamped with work and facing a physical collapse (I was working 60 to 70 hours a week, according to my time log, and I was rereading all the books for every course every semester), I devoted one week of spring break to this type of analysis. I reviewed all of my old evaluations and then called about 10 former students from a range of past years. Applying my best interview techniques, I found that what mattered in my best courses was that I listened to students, respected them, and challenged them intellectually. In fact, they said that I was one of the few teachers who truly paid attention to students and took them seriously. Obviously, this was nice to hear. On the other hand, no one complimented the detail of my lectures, my level of class preparation, or the fact that I had mastered the assigned reading. But those were the things on which I was spending tremendous amounts of time and effort. I was wasting my energy on tasks that I was not good at and that no one seemed to care about anyway. (I'll share my solution to this shortly.)

It is good to learn these weakness, not so much to eliminate them as to make them irrelevant. I once had a visiting colleague who was a very fine scholar but a bit dry in the classroom. He would come to me periodically and say, "Give me a joke. I need a joke. The students say I'm boring in class. Do you have any jokes?" I suggested that jokes were not the way for him to go. He *was* boring in class, but the solution was to stop droning through masses of material that neither he nor they enjoyed and rather to jump to the intellectually sophisticated issues he loved and hope then to at least engage the high-level students who would find the sheer challenge exciting. His department had made the great mistake of putting him in the introductory course (on the theory that "everyone should teach 'intro' "). He had great weaknesses, as we all do; the department had made those weaknesses his most visible characteristics. His strength as a scholar was wasted, the students were bored, and the poor man was utterly demoralized.

So, the first step is to recognize your strengths and weaknesses; the second step is to redesign your work to take advantage of your strengths. If you are a great lecturer, then drop those small seminars and do lectures. If in-class experiments provide the best learning that students take from your courses, then do in-class experiments. If you are strong at teaching social survey analysis, then do not keep struggling along trying to explain ethnography. Better that the students learn survey methods well, do some memorable experiments, or hear a riveting lecture than for you to marginally improve a technique you do not do well. In my own "redesign your work" project, I reduced my time on class preparation, stopped rereading old texts, and stopped covering the blackboard with detailed outlines. I began sleeping more, reading interesting new books, and getting myself into a good mood before class so that I could really pay attention to the students. I asked them more questions, argued with them in class, and challenged their ideas. My evaluations went way up, I was happier, and the students got more out of the class. I worked less, and they profited—because I was giving them what I could give. And when students want great lectures, they go to my colleague, Doug Ambrose, who gives wonderful, fascinating, detailed lectures that I heartily recommend to students; that is one of several settings in which he is great.

The trick is to find the few things—perhaps the one thing—that you are really good at and then spend your time doing that. You need not be good at everything. Remember, it is the few great experiences that benefit students—the set of oral examinations you do in your economic statistics class that challenge them to new heights of concentration and precision of ideas, the criminology field trips to night court that open their eyes to the criminal justice system, the intellectual power of your 20th-century history seminar, or even the scintillation of your *son et lumière* postmodernist theory lectures, complete with slides and sound tracks and visiting "refugee professor" speakers. Each of these can be a major contribution; the key is in finding what your contribution can be.[3]

But these still are suggestions for the teacher. How can we get students to make great strides in their work? Return for a moment to Schubert, the Olympic swimming coach who built a great program without worrying about whether he was a great coach. I asked how he had achieved such success, and he said simply, "I built the program around the best people." He financially supported swimmers who made Nationals more than those who did not, he assigned the best coaches to the most serious swimmers, and he designed rules to benefit the most committed athletes. You build the program (your policies, grading, reading loads, intellectual level, etc.) to benefit the best students, however you define that. (In my own case, I ask of each policy decision, "How will this affect the students who really want to learn?")

Of course, this is very different from how we usually do things. Most teachers design classes around the average students in the class—what amount of reading they will complete, what level of vocabulary and intellectual challenge they will understand, what demands on class participation they will satisfy. We usually aim to the middle. Class discussions revolve around people in difficulty rather than around those with sharp questions, and workloads are designed for average rather than superior students. Some professors, in fact, even aim to the low end, spending their efforts trying to help the needy, engage the uninterested, and motivate the slackers. They regard teaching as a form of intellectual evangelism and believe that their task is to save lost souls. But as a result, the good students too often are left to fend for themselves, are not challenged, and end up bored. In the long run, such teachers become demoralized and "burned out." Instead of playing to the bottom or even to the middle, I think you do better to "feed the hungry," those students who want your help; you should challenge the best students and support them. Go and ask your best students what you can do to help them. This approach will (1) keep you enthusiastic as you see real results for your work and attract more good students to your classes; (2) engage the vast middle, who will respond to the greater challenge; and (3) possibly even wake the near-dead, who might come to realize they are now in real trouble.

"Building around the best" actually means *not* focusing on the weak students. This comes hard for many of us. Reaching out to those in trouble sounds ennobling; it makes one feel virtuous. But if you build a college around weak students, then you will, naturally enough, attract more and more weak students. They will be drawn to your sympathy and attention. The good ones, however, will feel neglected (rightly so) and, having other options, will choose another school or at least another teacher. Remember that learning occurs in social worlds; if you build a world that supports good students or students who want to learn, then you will attract those students. The great mass of average students, who are driven by the prevailing winds, will move more swiftly, and you will discover, mirabile dictu, that *the weaker students did not have to be weak; they have been rewarded for it.*

Realize, finally, that in the simple sense you cannot motivate people; that door, it has been said, is locked from the inside. But you can structure your program to benefit those who are motivated (by supporting and challenging them, supporting the teachers they like, etc.) and learn what does motivate them. The key to motivating people is to find out what motivates them—what they want—and then offer it to them. Let me recall two personal examples. When I was a little boy, I loved playing army; military things attracted me. I had an arsenal of toy guns, hundreds of toy soldiers, and even a modest library of books on military strategy and tactics. My father, a fine teacher, took full advantage of my interests; he tapped into my motivation. When I wanted to build a tank, he used that (eventually unfulfilled) project to teach me about engines, steering mechanisms, and axle differentials (so that the tank could drive around corners). When I wanted to build a cannon, he taught me the geometry used in range finders, and we bought potassium nitrate to mix some (pretty weak) gunpowder. When my young squadmates and I wanted walkie-talkies, my dad bought me an electronics kit and taught me about resistors and circuit boards. (For readers who see in war toys a harbinger of violence, I should add that I never joined the military and never wished to do so. I burned my draft card. And I still enjoy war games.) Similarly, a teenage passion for competitive swimming led me, in my desire to eventually become a great coach, to study exercise physiology, group dynamics, and even some elementary fluid mechanics and, years later, to write a book about swimming. Again, tapping into a strong motivation can further learning in surprising ways. So, spend a few days in talking with your students and doing some quiet thinking, uncover what really motivates your students (especially the good ones), and then design your program and courses around those needs.

A Few Words for Administrators and Department Chairs

So, teachers should find and deploy their own strengths, building their work to benefit the type of students they want to teach. But if you are a department chair or dean, then what can you do to raise the quality of teaching—in terms of results—among your faculty?

Again, I think that traditional beliefs about the importance of talent and individual ability can easily lead to administrative quiescence around teaching. We seem to believe that one either is or is not a good teacher and that not much can be done about it. And the solutions we do sometimes propose involve workshops; little sets of "techniques," tips, or gimmicks; or sending old Joe off to a conference. The aim throughout is to change Joe's abilities as a teacher. That is all right, but it is hard to do, and besides, you can get good results without actually changing Joe.

We also should recognize that there is very little public or professional support for good teaching. Although some star professors are in fact wonderful teachers, professors rarely are promoted for being great teachers. Obviously, the major prestigious figures in our field are not there for their teaching abilities. This actually can be an advantage for the department that does want good teachers. Because many prestigious institutions downplay teaching in their hiring, you can grab some great people who are dying for the right job. And if you actually support good teachers (with pay, promotion, visibility, influence, supplies, etc.), then you will keep them or at least will always be able to attract good new ones.

So, here is how to get great teaching in your college or department:

1. *Hire great teachers.* Don't laugh. In most departments and colleges, such hiring is not the top priority. Instead, we water it down with preconceptions about "the areas we need to cover,"[4] the identity groups we need represented, how candidates must have a strong publication record, or how the chosen one should be a good departmental colleague. If you hire people to be friends with you, then you will have some friendly people, not great teachers. If you want good researchers, then hire researchers. But do not think that this is hiring teachers. If there are 3 great teachers in your pool of 300 at the beginning of the search, then you will eliminate at least 2 of them with all these other considerations. In the sociology department at Hamilton College, we say that we want "excellent teachers for high-quality undergraduates." Now in fact, the second part of that statement means that we typically hire strong scholars. Most applicants with the intellectual horsepower we want are serious about research. But research excellence per se is not our goal. Hiring great teachers is.

And how do you spot a great teacher? Look for a person with a record of great teaching, not "potential" for teaching or "interest" in teaching. Ignore those brilliant "philosophy of teaching" statements unless you are hiring someone to write "philosophy of teaching" statements. Writing about teaching is not the same as doing it. Similarly, being impressive in an interview is not the same as being a great teacher, nor is having an impressive vita. So, if you want a great teacher, then take the candidate with a record of great teaching.

2. *Support great teachers.* Once you have hired a great teacher, give the teacher whatever he or she needs to do the work. When you are redesigning the curriculum, ask the best teachers how to do it. When you have extra money for office supplies, get requests from your best teachers first. Make sure they are not driven out by jealous colleagues. Again, this might seem obvious, but in fact conscientious administrators too often think first of helping weak performers, not supporting strong ones. Remember that the strong teachers are producing your results.

3. *Learn your faculty's strengths.* Then, place professors in courses and projects in which their strengths are used. One of my colleagues, a brilliant thinker, recently moved to our advanced Social Theory course, where his intellectual power can be fully exerted. And one of my junior colleagues loves, and excels at, working one-on-one with research students; she manages our senior project seminar, in which students carry out field research studies. The visiting professor mentioned earlier (who had no jokes to tell) never should have taught an introductory-level course. Try to place people where their strengths will show. This is how to handle old Joe, who is not very exciting in the big lectures but is good at teaching archival research techniques, statistics, or writing.

4. *Protect the great opportunities.* Remember, students forget most of their college experiences but remember the few really outstanding ones. A few great classes, the one or two professors who really cared, a series of wonderful conversations, a challenging and rewarding time spent in community service—these will be formative experiences, the few qualitatively different moments that matter. As the old saying goes, 20 percent of your people (and experiences) produce 80 percent of your results. So, you must protect those 20 percent of faculty who do great things, the 20 percent of programs that work. The disproportionate productivity—the huge results—of those 20 percent is the best argument, I believe, for retaining tenure in higher education. Tenure gives your best people freedom to try new things that some colleagues think are silly or suspicious; it can let them experiment, take risks, or be outrageous. Soon after receiving tenure, I could dare to try using oral examinations in my introductory classes despite the misgivings of some faculty colleagues; the exams worked marvelously. True, tenure protects mediocre faculty, but the mediocre do not matter that much in college. They are mostly irrelevant because students usually can avoid their classes. But your excellent faculty—the superb 20 percent who produce 80 percent of the educational results—do matter a lot. It is far more important to keep and support the great teachers (and tenure does that) than to eliminate a few weak performers.[5]

Conclusion

When college administrators talk about improving the quality of education, they typically look first to quality of teaching. Faculties debate systems of evaluating teaching, student evaluation forms of teaching are revised, and periodic post-tenure reviews are established. Deans host workshops on teaching, prizes for teaching are awarded, and books on teaching (such as this one) are written. This approach to improving education suggests that it is the *teacher* who matters and that the teacher's ability is crucial to the learning process. And what I have just said about supporting great teachers acknowledges their important role. But perhaps we should focus more on discovering which techniques or practices get results in student learning and worry less about the quality of teaching per se. Again, as Schubert might point out, the goal is not great *teaching* but rather great *learning*.

The "mundanity of excellence" concept suggests that in teaching and in learning, excellence is not something magical or mysterious; rather, it is achievable with a little analysis, some steady effort, and application of a few basic principles. As a teacher, find out what works for you and do more of it. You need not do everything for your students if you can do one thing really well. And if you are in a position to hire or promote other teachers, then try to do so based on what they actually accomplish, not on what they say about teaching (their "philosophy"), on how they fit preconceptions about good teaching (lecture style), or on how "innovative" they are.

The good news is that if you want to foster good teaching in this sense, then there is little competition. Yes, some colleges give teaching prizes—a one-time, usually small, recognition that some professor does good work. In some large universities, faculty have begun to talk more about teaching. Some state legislators are giving speeches about higher education's need to reemphasize undergraduate education, and some college presidents are discussing it at their conferences. Some of our better community colleges always have valued good teaching and learning. But these are small gestures in a professional reward system that is infatuated with scholarly productivity. In the large research universities that dominate the academic world, the professional prestige system generally relegates

teaching to a secondary status at best. So, if you actually care about educating students, supporting teachers who are the catalysts for learning, or creating a department or college in which students enjoy those qualitative leaps that make for a wonderful college experience, then I think you have a relatively easy task, achievable through a simple, effective technique. It is not mysterious at all: *find out what works, and do more of it.*

Notes

1. Well, perhaps not anyone. But what is striking in the history of world-class sports is how many successful people had huge obstacles to overcome. If there is a base level of ability necessary, then it is hard to say where it is because there are such visible exceptions.

2. Until our colleges and universities understand this and begin to deploy faculty to maximize their strengths, we will continue to waste the abilities they bring to our programs. Elite small colleges tell faculty they should do well in "teaching, scholarship, and service." Gifted teachers, then, are reminded that they need to publish more; serious scholars are warned to spend more time on teaching; and all teachers are told, against their better inclinations, to serve on committees. At the end of the day, no one is spending their energy in their field of excellence. We should instead use people where they can excel, with different people filling different needs.

3. Of course, you do need to find a strength. I am not offering an easy excuse to avoid big lectures and then sit around playing computer games. If the dean gives you free rein to teach from your strengths, whatever they are, then you need to do it well.

4. This is the fastest way in which to eliminate large numbers of the best teachers or schol-

ars from consideration. An ad that says "must be able to teach statistical research methods" immediately disqualifies two-thirds of the finest teachers in any social science applicant pool. Certainly in some disciplines and in some departments, area coverage is necessary—but perhaps not so much as academic conservatives believe.

5. For other organizations, such as hospitals, this logic does not apply. Bad doctors kill people; bad professors just bore them.

References

Chambliss, Daniel F. 1988. *Champions: The Making of Olympic Swimmers.* New York: William Morrow.

———. 1989. "The Mundanity of Excellence: An Ethnographic Report on Stratification and Olympic Athletes." *Sociological Theory* 7:85.

39

Teaching and Learning:
A Matter of Style?

Gerald T. Powers

Instruction begins when you, the teacher, learn from the learner, put yourself in his place so that you may understand what he learns and the way he understands it.

—Søren Kierkegaard

For someone who has labored in the vineyards of academe for more than 30 years, it can be very humbling to come face-to-face with the disconcerting realization that one of the most important lessons to be learned as a teacher is that you really have not understood what it means to be a learner. This chapter provides an account of how I serendipidously discovered a "truth" about the teaching-learning process that apparently has been self-evident to folks such as Kierkegaard for more than a century.

Some background might help to set the stage for how I arrived at this newfound, personal "age of enlightenment." For several years, I had been teaching a graduate-level seminar on human behavior and the social environment in a school of social work. Motivated in part by a research project I had been working on at the time, it occurred to me that it might be interesting to have my students complete a personality inventory as one means of helping them to gain

an appreciation of human behavior—especially their own. The experience elicited a good deal of excitement on the part of the students, who were instrumental in encouraging me to incorporate the exercise as a regular part of subsequent seminars.

After having collected data on three additional groups of students, I realized that many of these same students had enrolled in a research course I also taught the following semester as part of the core curriculum. My inquisitive research assistant, who had enrolled in both of these classes, wondered aloud one day whether her personality type might be functionally related in some way to her performance in the research course. On the face of it, the question seemed to pose an intriguing possibility, one that I naively assumed had more to do with the student's capacity to *learn* than my own ability to *teach*.

The Painful Discovery

Until that time, the process I had been using to evaluate students was guided in large part by a set of assumptions that I believed to be both objective and fair. Indeed, I took a certain amount of pride in my efforts to remove personal bias from the grading process. I later discovered that my apparent preoccupation with "objectivity" may well have been driven more by my own personality than by any clear understanding of the phenomena I was attempting to evaluate. I took for granted that the distribution of grades that resulted from my evaluation procedures accurately reflected real differences in the students' intellectual capacities to handle the demands of the course. That assumption seemed entirely reasonable to me at the time, if for no other reason than probability theory alone. It seemed obvious to me that some students were innately more intellectually talented than others. After all, this was a research course, and not all students could be expected to perform equally well with respect to handling the rigors of "empirical science." Therefore, it seemed entirely plausible that my well-conceived evaluation procedures should produce a performance distribution that would more or less approximate the normal curve. When this occurred, it served to reinforce the very assumptions with which I had begun. As I later discovered, much to my chagrin, that is not quite how the learning process works.

Psychological Types According to Jung

The personality inventory I had been using in the human behavior course was the Myers-Briggs Type Indicator (MBTI) (Myers and McCaulley 1985). The MBTI is a personality preference instrument developed by Isabel Myers and her mother, Katherine Briggs. It is based on Jung's ([1921] 1971) theory of psychological types. In essence, Jung maintained that what appears to be the random nature of most human behavior actually can be explained in terms of patterned variations with respect to how people tend to *perceive* and make *judgments* about the world in which they live.

According to Jung, all conscious mental activity (including teaching and learning) derives from an individual's preferences with respect to how information is permitted to enter one's consciousness, and once having arrived there, how that information is then processed for purposes of decision making. Both of these mental processes, *perception* and *judgment,* are viewed within a dialectical perspective, the various dimensions of which are captured in the four bipolar scales comprising the MBTI: Extraversion-Introversion (E/I), Sensing-Intuition (S/N), Thinking-Feeling (T/F), and Judgment-Perception (J/P). Although there is evidence to suggest that one's preferences on all four axes affect learning (Lawrence 1991), this chapter focuses solely on the two processes Jung considered to be the most important with respect to problem solving: the way in which people *perceive* reality and the way in which they make *judgments* about it.

The Perceiving Axis: Sensing versus Intuition

With respect to *perception,* according to Jung, individuals may be classified as being either *sensing* or *intuitive.* The sensing types tend to be very practical, and as such, they rely heavily on their senses to inform them about what appears to be going on in the real world. Preferring a sequential approach to learning, they are naturally attracted to educational opportunities that enable them to master factual information as well as pragmatic ways in which to solve problems. They often are very attentive to details and are willing to engage in repetitive exercises that promise to lead to the mastery of tangible skills. They are more likely to appreciate the big picture when provided opportunities to engage in repetitive hands-on experiences that inductively permit them to systematically link prior experiences with present realities.

Because of their attentiveness to detail, sensory types often develop skills that rely more on observation than on imagination.

The major strength of the intuitive types, on the other hand, is creativity. They are more interested in general *ideas* than in specific *facts.* Because of their speculative nature, they are open to varying interpretations of reality. They tend to be more concerned with future possibilities than with present realities. Their propensity to dwell on abstractions leads them to prefer discussions that are informed by theory, permitting the more sensing types to figure out and apply the practical implications of the theory. Unlike their sensing counterparts, the intuitive types often are impatient with repetitive or routine activities. They are likely to be more intrigued by creating solutions than by implementing them in practice.

The Judging Axis: Thinking versus Feeling

Perception may be thought of as a gatekeeping function in the sense that it provides the means by which we become aware of people, places, and things including ideas and emotions. It provides the means by which we access new information and new possibilities. The *judging* function, on the other hand, refers to all the cognitive and emotional processes that enable us to make decisions about the products of our perceptions. Our natural inclination when functioning in a *judging attitude* is to plan operations, organize activities, and ultimately come to closure (i.e., make decisions).

According to Jung, the manner by which we interact with the world around us reflects the relative strength of our preference for one of two contrasting ways of making decisions. Those whose judgments are primarily informed by appeals to reason are classified as *thinking* types, whereas those whose judgments are pri-

marily influenced by the emotional content of the situation are classified as *feeling* types.

Individuals who rely on *thinking* as their primary mode for making decisions tend to prefer objective and rational approaches in most problem-solving situations. They confront each new set of circumstances in an organized and analytical manner, carefully weighing the available evidence before arriving at a conclusion. They typically appeal to principles of justice and fairness in their efforts to resolve ambiguous situations including situations involving the human condition. They seek consistency and order in a world that is believed to function according to principles of cause and effect. Because of their reliance on "impersonal logic" and their natural tendency to be critical and skeptical, thinking types sometimes appear to be somewhat cold, detached, and enigmatic. They can appear to be insensitive to the complexities of interpersonal relations. Although there is very little evidence to suggest that *thinking* types are any less emotional than their *feeling* counterparts, it probably is fair to say that they are less likely to permit personal and subjective considerations to influence their judgments.

The hallmark of individuals who rely on *feeling* as their primary mode for making decisions is an acute awareness of the ultimate impact that judgments have on real people. Feeling types are genuinely concerned about attaining and maintaining harmony. They do not typically view the world as operating in accordance with a set of impersonal, immutable rules. Instead, consideration for personal and group values are at the heart of the decision-making process. Given the personal and subjective nature of values, those who base their judgments on feeling are more likely to be aware of and comfortable in dealing with value issues, both their own and those of others. Within this context, the people who are affected by decisions are considered to be more important than the empirical facts on which those decisions are based.

Jung considered the two major functions of *perceiving* and *judging* to be independent but dynamically related. When combined, they create unique pathways for the gathering and processing of information—pathways, I suggest, that not only affect the way in which students learn but also affect the way in which faculty teach. At one time or another, everyone uses both perceiving functions (sensing and intuition) as well as both judging functions (thinking and feeling). Not unlike our natural tendency toward right- or left-handedness, each of us is inclined to rely more heavily on one of the two options within each function most of the time.

These paired preferences create four possible type combinations: Sensing-Perception (S/P), Sensing-Feeling (S/F), Intuition-Thinking (N/T), and Intuition-Feeling (N/F). Each combination, in turn, reflects a different orientation to consciousness, differences that, according to Jungian theory, help explain seemingly chance variations in human behavior. Myers (1992) suggests that each of these combinations produces a different type of personality, characterized by the *interests, values, needs, habits of mind, and surface traits that naturally result* from the combination. Combinations with a common preference will share some qualities, but each combination has qualities all its own, arising from the *interaction* of the preferred way of looking at life and the preferred way of judging what is seen.

Keirsey and Bates (1984), building on the work of Kretschmer (1925), characterize various preference combinations on the MBTI as "temperaments." They suggest that one's temperament "places a signature on each of one's actions, making it recognizably one's own" (p. 27). Temperament determines the way in which we behave in our efforts to fulfill *our*

needs. Their characterizations of the temperaments helped sensitize me to how entrenched my attitudes had become with respect to what I considered to be "good teaching."

I discovered that my "teaching style" reflected *my* "interests" and "needs," and I realized that I inadvertently had been designing my classes the way in which I learned best, that is, the way in which I thought courses should have been taught to me. As a result, I assumed that what worked for me should work equally well for my students. As an N/T type, I was naturally and unwittingly attracted to pedagogical approaches that started with and emphasized the paramount importance of theory. I took seriously Lewin's (1951) admonition that "nothing is as practical as a good theory." I approached my subject in a logical and organized manner, emphasizing the exploration of ideas, the development of models, and the building of conceptual systems. My goal was to develop in students not only the capacity to think but also to think critically and comparatively in ways that would enable them to understand and control, and to explain and predict, phenomena in the world in which they lived. It was my assumption that such skills required keen analytical abilities and a well-developed capacity for abstract thinking. My evaluation techniques were designed to test those abilities, and it was not surprising to discover that the results of my assessment efforts only served to reinforce my impression that students who demonstrated such competencies were somehow innately more intelligent than those who did not.

Using the MBTI to Identify Student Preferred Learning Styles

With the help of the MBTI, I discovered that a large percentage of the social work students were S/F types, in stark contrast to the percentage of the faculty teaching them (including myself), who were largely N/T types. What this suggested with respect to teaching and learning was somewhat disconcerting. Apparently, the modes of learning that would best reach our students mismatched the modes of teaching "naturally" developed by the faculty. Specifically, individuals with the combined S/F preference (i.e., the majority of our students) perceive reality and process information differently from their N/T counterparts. They tend to be more concrete and practical in their orientation to life in general. By virtue of this preference, they learn best experientially, preferring educational opportunities that emphasize inductive reasoning, hands-on experience, and the liberal use of examples directly related to issues involving personal values and the human condition. They learn from the "bottom up," piecing together examples in an effort to arrive at the general picture.

However, N/T types (i.e., the majority of our faculty) have a more global, impersonal orientation to life. Their natural propensity is to view "reality" in terms of the big picture, a perspective that enables them to deductively generate a wide variety of theoretical alternatives. Unlike S/F types, who tend to be action oriented and people centered, N/T types are attracted to the more contemplative life of the world of ideas and possibilities. N/T faculty prefer to teach from the "top down," offering general theories peppered with an occasional example or two for illustrative purposes. Taking this new insight one step further, I was intrigued by the possibility of discovering whether the differences between students and faculty really mattered.

Because I had earlier gathered MBTI profiles on virtually all of my students, I was able to test the teaching-learning style premise with my research class. Had the students whose MBTI profiles were similar to mine (i.e., N/T) performed better than those whose profiles

TABLE 39.1 Comparison of Grades by Combined Type (percentages and N's)

Type	Grading Distribution			
	A	B	C	Total
Intuitive-Thinking	11 (17)	5 (8)	2 (3)	18 (28)
Intuitive-Feeling	12 (19)	21 (33)	6 (9)	39 (61)
Sensing-Thinking	2 (3)	6 (10)	4 (7)	13 (20)
Sensing-Feeling	3 (5)	16 (25)	11 (18)	30 (48)

NOTE: Percentages are rounded to the nearest whole number, $\chi^2 = 29.26$, $df = 6$, $p < .001$, Cramer's $V = .305$.

contrasted with mine (e.g., S/F)? The pattern that emerged was at once sobering and disconcerting. It was immediately apparent that the students who had earned the highest grades in my research class were, for the most part, those who were most like me with respect to their preferences on both the perceiving and judging axes. Table 39.1 summarizes the grading differences among all four of the combined types.

Fully 61 percent of the 28 N/T types in my classes attained grades in the A range, whereas only 10 percent of the 48 S/F types were seen as performing equally well. Conversely, 38 percent of the S/F types attained grades of C, whereas only 11 percent of the N/T temperament group did that poorly. Although the grading differences between the N/T and S/F types were the most dramatic among the four type combinations, it was apparent that even students with whom I shared only one of the two preferences also may have been significantly disadvantaged. For example, students whose personality types included *intuition* as their preferred mode for perceiving reality were seen as clearly outperforming students whose type relied on the *sensing* preference. Intuitive types earned more than four times as many A's and nearly three times fewer C's compared to their sensing type counterparts. Performance differences of this magnitude are unlikely to have occurred by chance.

Although the percentage of N/T types among my research students was slightly higher (just under 18 percent) than that found in the general population (approximately 12 percent), more than four out of five of my students differed from me with respect to one or both of their preferences on the perceiving and judging axes. This disparity in preferred teaching-learning styles might help explain why some of my students had indicated in course evaluations that they felt frustrated in their attempts to master the content being covered in class. It also might help explain why the students whose learning styles mirrored my preferred teaching style tended to earn higher grades.

Teaching Old Dogs New Tricks: Could Changing Teaching Styles Improve Learning?

Confronted with these unsettling yet compelling "facts," as an N/T type, I was forced to rethink not so much *what* I was teaching as *how* I should be presenting and processing information with students so that they could learn. Was it possible for me to modify my approach to teaching in ways that would prove to be more responsive to the diverse set of learning styles represented among the students? My initial concern, when faced with this prospect, was the fear that in the process I may have to sacrifice rigor and compromise learning objectives. What I discovered was quite the opposite. As I struggled to teach the subject matter in ways that offered a better "fit" to a wider range of student learning styles, I was forced to stretch the boundaries of my own comfort zone. Presenting the same material in different ways (i.e., in ways that would be responsive to both S/F

and N/T types) required me to *think* and *act* in different ways. As this occurred, the students began to play with ideas in ways that generated a new level of critical thinking. I spent less time repeating material for those I had assumed were the "slower" learners in the group, and they in turn seemed to be having more fun. Having been forced to reverse my own mind-set helped me better appreciate what it must be like for students when I expected them to do the same. At some point in this process, I realized that a subtle and important transformation had taken place in the way in which I was approaching the course. *Learning* began to replace *teaching* as the driving imperative for how I organized the course. This pedagogical shift enabled me to gain insights into the subject matter that never had occurred to me before. Changing my teaching style was benefiting not only the S/F types but also the N/T types—including me.

I discovered that it was possible to "retool" my own N/T teaching style to better accommodate the idiosyncratic learning styles of a wider range of students. For example, I decided to involve the students in the creation and implementation of a research project designed to evaluate their own attitudes and feelings about research. The project had an immediate appeal for virtually all of the students. The sensing types had a concrete task to work on, whereas the intuitive types were challenged to speculate about how such attitudes originate. The thinking types contributed their analytical skills in designing the research process, whereas the feeling types identified the appropriate attitudes and feelings to be explored. By mixing and matching personality types into interactive task groups that included both S/F and N/T types, I was able to maximize the learning opportunities for all students. The process demonstrated well Lawrence's (1991) argument: "Opposite types can supplement each other in any joint undertaking. When two people ap-

Intuitives Need Sensing Types, Sensing Types Need Intuitives
    To bring up pertinent facts, To bring up new possibilities
    To apply experience to problems, To supply ingenuity on problems
    To read the fine print, To read the signs of coming change
    To notice what needs attention, To see how to prepare for the future
    To have patience, To have enthusiasm
    To keep track of essential details, To watch for new essentials
    To face difficulties with realism, To tackle difficulties with zest
    To remind that the joys of the present are important, To show that the joys of the future are worth looking for
Feeling Types Need Thinkers, Thinkers Need Feeling Types
    To analyze, To persuade
    To organize, To conciliate
    To find the flaws in advance, To forecast how others will feel
    To reform what needs reforming, To arouse enthusiasm
    To hold consistently to a policy, To teach
    To weigh "the law and the evidence", To sell
    To fire people when necessary, To advertise
    To stand firm against opposition, To appreciate the thinker

Figure 39.1. Lawrence's Matrix of Interactive Types
SOURCE: Lawrence (1991).

proach a problem from opposite sides, each sees things not visible to the other" (p. A-5). By helping the students to understand their differences in type, they were able to appreciate each other's unique contributions and exploit the learning opportunities they presented. These opportunities are captured in Lawrence's matrix of interactive types (Figure 39.1).

Once I engaged the students in this process, their performance improved dramatically. To my amazement, the earlier observed performance differences between S/F and N/T students (as measured by both objective tests and analytical assignments) completely disappeared without compromising the level of performance of the latter group. Reaching more students did not mean *teaching down,* as many critics of higher education fear; rather, it meant *teaching differently.* In addition, the MBTI was found to be a useful diagnostic tool that could be employed not only for purposes of improving the "goodness of fit" between teaching-learning styles but also as a vehicle for stimulating valuable discussion concerning how individual differences among social work prac-

titioners might be best exploited in relation to both research and practice.

As this occurred, independent measures of student *interest* in research increased, and their associated *anxiety* concerning my expectations regarding a generally dreaded subject decreased. The negative mind-set that many social work students bring to learning experiences involving research can be modified substantially if the subject is taught in a manner that is compatible with their individual learning styles. To the extent to which this is true, it suggests that the difficulties many students encounter in learning may have much more to do with how the subject is taught than with the student's innate capacity to comprehend it. If this is true for our social work students, then it also might be true for students in general.

Faculty and Their Teaching Styles

I suspect that my experience is not unique. Indeed, only about 12 percent of the general population are N/T types like myself. It is by far

Table 39.2. Percentages of N/T Type Teachers at Various Levels of Education

Educational Level	N/T Teachers
Elementary	10.31
Middle school	15.15
High school	16.17
Junior college	23.17
College/university	31.20

NOTE: N/T = Intuition-Thinking.

the smallest of the four type combinations. More important, however, is the fact that N/T types are disproportionately represented among college and university teachers (approximately 31 percent). In fact, the proportion of N/T teachers in the classroom, as seen in Table 39.2, increases at each educational level (Myers and McCaulley 1985).

Regardless of our personal preferences as teachers, by chance alone, it can be expected that there always will be a variety of different learning styles represented in our classes. The secret to effective teaching is to employ what Butler (1987) refers to as *style differentiated instruction,* "the process of selecting the most appropriate style response for the learning situation." Style differentiated instruction implies more than merely accommodating to each student's preferred learning style. Faculty also must know when the achievement of the learning task requires the development of abilities that run counter to the student's style. Both situations require a flexible teaching strategy, knowing when and how to accommodate the student's needs as well as how and when to challenge the student's natural tendencies. Obviously, there is no one right way in which to accomplish this goal. The specific techniques that are most appropriate for any given course will vary widely depending on the profession or discipline in question, the nature of the subject matter under consideration, and style variations within the class itself. The most challenging

aspect of this task, however, is likely to involve the development of learning experiences that cater to the needs of students whose learning styles contrast most sharply with those of the instructor. In my case, that included the students whose S/F temperaments threatened my weaker, less used mental processes.

The task of adapting one's teaching style to a variety of different learning needs inevitably involves adjustments in both *attitudes* and *activities* on the part of the instructor. Butler (1987) refers to this process as *bridging.* "We apply attitudinal bridging when we recognize the perceptions of others and reach out to them as individuals. We use activity bridging when we offer suggestions to students to help them through a learning difficulty or a style mismatch for which they have no alternative but to accomplish the task." Obviously, we cannot compromise our educational objectives simply because certain students typically encounter difficulty in their efforts to master them. The ultimate litmus test of effective teaching might be the ability to devise learning experiences that enable all of our students to achieve the identified course objectives. When we accomplish that task in a creative and flexible manner, we are engaged in the bridging process.

In an effort to rectify the situation, I made several pedagogical changes that were specifically designed to adapt my teaching style to a wider range of students. As an N/T type, I had to work at providing more concrete examples, especially examples that involved people and their feelings. I had to spend less time lecturing and more time involving students in interactive activities that provided them with hands-on experiences. In effect, I had to become less controlling of the classroom environment and place my trust in the students' capacity to learn from one another. Intellectually, I understood the value added by having opposite types working together. Now, all I had to do is exactly what

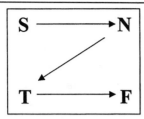

Figure 39.2. Lawrence's Zig-Zag Process

the sensing types would have had me do all along—translate theory to practice.

I assumed that any adjustments in teaching style that I could make to better accommodate the idiosyncratic needs of the students whose type preferences (e.g., the S/F types) were alien to my own would enable me to encompass the widest possible range of student learning styles. I had no doubt that my natural inclinations as an N/T type would continue to meet the needs of the students who always had succeeded in my classes. The challenge was to be more inclusive and flexible.

Lawrence (1991) suggests a useful technique for organizing learning experiences in a way that ensures the involvement of all four processes: sensing, intuition, thinking, and feeling. He refers to the technique as the "zig-zag" process (Figure 39.2), a formula that ensures that all four mental processes are involved in the solving of any problem.

Lawrence (1991) describes the process as follows:

When faced with a problem, we properly start by gathering relevant, concrete data through the senses. The raw data by themselves do not settle the problem. The meaning of the data, their relationships to prior experience, are given by intuition—so the arrow goes from S [sensing] to N [intuitive]. Intuition also asks: What are the possibilities in these data for solving the problem? The arrow moves from N to T [thinking] when we engage thinking to analyze and decide the logical consequences of acting upon each of the possibilities. And finally, the possibilities are also weighed by the feeling-judgment to assess how deeply we care about the effects of each option; we test the human consequences, the harmony with basic personal values, or the values of others. (p. 58)

The more I was able to involve all four mental processes in the development of course content, the more animated and involved the students became. It was as if I had validated the importance of all four modes of "knowing." All the students felt that they had something to contribute. The *thinking* types were able to pursue the logical order of things, whereas the *feeling* types ensured that content was viewed within the context of personal and societal values. The *intuitive* types explored the big ideas and new possibilities, whereas the *sensing* types attended to the more concrete realities and reminded the group of the importance of mastering practical skills. Once the process was set in motion, it seemed to take on a life of its own, creating a synergistic effect that enabled all of us to better appreciate both the strengths and limitations of our preferred style. As students began to feel comfortable debating issues from a position of strength, some very intriguing exchanges took place including a spontaneous discussion into the nature of knowledge itself. I realized that they were fully immersed in the subject when they began to hypothesize about the possible association between a person's preferred learning style and his or her propensity to view reality from a "logical positivist" or "constructivist" point of view. It is unlikely that students would have engaged in such a discussion in the same way had they not felt empowered to press the issue from a position of personal strength. I knew then that something very important and very different was happening in my class. I just did not know how important or how different until I later realized that the performance differences I had observed the previous year apparently had vanished.

Additional Factors Related to Learning Styles

My purpose is not to promote any particular frame of reference with respect to assessing teaching-learning styles. The MBTI is illustrative. It happens to be the assessment tool with which I am most familiar, but it certainly is not the only (or necessarily the most effective) way in which to capture the most critical variables affecting learning. Indeed, there is an extensive and impressive literature that explores a variety of biological, social, psychological, and environmental factors believed to be functionally related to various facets of the learning style phenomenon (Reiff 1992).

There also is a growing number of useful instruments on the market designed specifically to measure individual learning styles. The Dunns have developed a multimodal Learning Style Inventory that targets a variety of environmental, emotional, sociological, and physical factors that collectively are believed to affect the learning process (Dunn, Dunn, and Price 1985). Kolb's (1985) Learning Style Inventory instrument attempts to describe how information is *taken in* and then *processed for use.* It classifies people in relation to four interactive styles: converger, diverger, assimilator, and accommodator. The Gregorc Adult Transactional Ability Inventory differentiates individuals along two major dimensions (Gregorc 1982). Gregorc (1982) maintains that individuals think either abstractly or concretely, and depending on their preferred style, they organize their thoughts either sequentially or randomly. This combination creates four distinct thinking styles, each of which has important learning implications: Abstract-Sequential, Abstract-Random, Concrete-Sequential, and Concrete-Random. Soloman's (1992) Inventory of Learning Styles is yet another instrument designed to assess learning styles. Like the MBTI, it classifies learning styles along four major axes, each of which constitutes a bipolar scale designed to identify a different characteristic of the learning process: sensing or intuitive *perception,* active or passive *processing,* visual or verbal *input,* and sequential or global *understanding.* Finally, Witkin (1973) has been assessing cognitive styles in relation to what he characterizes as *field-dependent/field-independent* learners. Although both types of students are assumed to possess comparable intellectual capacities, they differ widely with respect to how they process and use information (Witkin et al. 1977). Field-dependent students typically are more global and flexible in their approach to problem solving and the way in which they attack new learning challenges. They tend to be more sensitive to social cues and thus are more likely to rely on external validation before proceeding with a learning task. Field-independent students, on the other hand, tend to be more focused and task oriented. They exhibit an analytical ability that enables them to direct their attention to issues that we teachers often consider to be the more relevant aspects of a given task. Because of their independent nature, they are more inclined to proceed with assignments and new challenges without having to rely on external validation.

In addition to these general theories, a number of developmental theories attempt to identify stages of intellectual growth that typically occur in the college years. Each stage would appear to have important implications for how students learn. The best known of these are based on the longitudinal studies of Perry (1970) and his associates at Harvard University in the 1950s and 1960s. Building on the work of Perry, Belenky and her colleagues argue persuasively that women and men differ in their intellectual development and that some of the changes that students go through in their efforts to achieve intellectual independence are gender based (Belenky et al. 1986).

There certainly is no dearth of published research concerning the way in which people process and use information in the teaching-learning process. A search of the World Wide Web generates literally thousands of references and links to subjects related to learning styles. St. John's University in Jamaica, New York, has established a Learning Style Center that serves as a repository for learning style research and its application to the classroom (Learning Style Network). In addition, Rita and Kenneth Dunn have established the *Learning Styles Network Newsletter*, designed to facilitate communication among individuals interested in teaching practices related to learning styles.

Although many people are writing about the subject from a variety of different perspectives, many of their theoretical constructs and conclusions seem to be very similar. It is probably less important that we settle on a particular way of classifying different learning styles than that we recognize the fact that differences exist. In the final analysis, it might be as simple as asking the students. They generally know how they learn best. Our job is summarized well by Armstrong (1987):

The role of the professional educator is to be familiar with those factors affecting learning and to design educational experiences that maximize the learning that occurs. If students are to gain the most from education, they must have the opportunity to work within a style that facilitates their own learning. (p. 157)

References

Armstrong, C. 1987. "On learning styles." *The Clearing House* 61:157-61.

Belenky, M., B. Clinchy, N. Goldberger, and J. Tarule. 1986. *Women's Ways of Knowing: The Development of Self, Voice, and Mind.* New York: Basic Books.

Butler, K. A. 1987. *Learning and Teaching Style in Theory and Practice.* 2d ed. rev. Columbia, CT: Learner's Dimension.

Dunn, R., K. Dunn, and G. Price. 1985. *Learning Styles Inventory (LSI).* Rev. ed. Lawrence, KS: Price Systems.

Gregorc, A. 1982. *An Adult's Guide to Style.* Maynard, MS: Gabriel Systems.

Jung, C. [1921] 1971. *Psychological Types.* Translated by H. G. Baynes. Revised by R. F. C. Hull. Princeton, NJ: Princeton University Press.

Keirsey, D. and M. Bates. 1984. *Please Understand Me: Character and Temperament Types.* 4th ed. Del Mar, CA: Prometheus Nemesis.

Kolb, D. 1985. *Learning Style Inventory.* Rev. ed. Boston: McBer.

Kretschmer, E. 1925. *Physique and Character.* New York: Harcourt Brace.

Lawrence, G. 1991. *People Types and Tiger Stripes: A Practical Guide to Learning Styles.* 2d ed. Gainsville, FL: Consulting Psychologists Press.

Lewin, K. 1951. *Field Theory in Social Science.* New York: Harper.

Myers, I. 1992. *Gifts Differing.* Palo Alto, CA: Consulting Psychologists Press.

Myers, I. and M. McCaulley. 1985. *Manual: A Guide to the Development and Use of the Myers-Briggs Type Indicator.* 2d ed. Palo Alto, CA: Consulting Psychologists Press.

Perry, W. 1970. *Forms of Intellectual and Ethical Development in the College Years: A Scheme.* New York: Holt, Rinehart & Winston.

Reiff, J. C. 1992. *Learning Styles: What Research Says to the Teacher.* Washington, DC: National Education Association.

Soloman, B. S. 1992. *Inventory of Learning Styles*. Raleigh: North Carolina State University.

Witkin, H. 1973. *The Role of Cognitive Style in Academic Performance and in Teacher-Student Relations*. Research Bulletin 73-11. Princeton, NJ: Educational Testing Service.

Witkin, H., C. Moore, D. Goodenough, and P. Cox. 1977. "Field Dependent and Field Independent Cognitive Styles and Their Educational Implications. *Review of Educational Research* 47:1-64.

40

Building Trust with Students

Stephen Brookfield

Underlying all significant learning is the element of trust. Trust between teachers and students is the affective glue binding educational relationships together. Not trusting teachers has several consequences for students. They are unwilling to submit themselves to the perilous uncertainties of new learning. They avoid risk. They keep their most deeply felt concerns private. They view with cynical reserve the exhortations and instructions of teachers. The more profound and meaningful the learning is to students, the more they need to be able to trust their teachers.

The importance of trust is highlighted time and again in students' critical incident responses and in studies of the experience of learning. In speaking of transformative learning events, students often make explicit mention of how teachers' actions, and the trust these inspire or destroy, are crucial to learning. At the center of the cluster of characteristics that make teachers more trustworthy in students' eyes are two components that might be described as teacher credibility and teacher authenticity. These are connected but, as we shall see, they are not necessarily complementary.

AUTHOR'S NOTE: This is a reprint of an article originally published as Brookfield, Stephen, "Building Trust with Students," in *The Skillful Teacher: On Techniques, Trust, and Responsiveness in the Classroom* (Jossey-Bass), 1990, pp. 163-76. Used with permission.

Teacher Credibility

Teacher credibility refers to teachers' ability to present themselves as people with something to offer students. When teachers have this credibility, students see them as possessing a breadth of knowledge, depth of insight, and length of experience that far exceeds the students' own. Freire (Shor and Freire, 1987, p. 172) describes credibility as the "critical competence" that students have a right to expect of their teachers. Students continually stress their desire to be in the presence of someone whose knowledge, skill, and expertise mean that they can help students come to grips with some of the contradictions, complexities, and dilemmas they are experiencing. Although teacher education programs often stress process skills above content mastery, students still attach great importance to teachers' having subject and skill expertise; without intellectual and experiential credibility, process skill is ultimately empty.

Teacher Authenticity

Authentic teachers (Moustakas, 1966) are, essentially, those [who] students feel they can trust. They are also those who students see as real flesh-and-blood human beings with passions, frailties, and emotions. They are remembered as whole persons, not as people who hide behind a collection of learned role behaviors appropriate to college teaching. In more specific terms, students see four behaviors as evidence of authenticity: (1) teachers' words and actions are congruent; (2) teachers admit to error, acknowledge fallibility, and make mistakes in full public view of learners; (3) teachers allow aspects of their personhood outside their role as teachers to be revealed to students; and (4) teachers respect learners by listening carefully to students' expressions of concern, by taking care to create opportunities for students' voices to be heard, and by being open to changing their practice as a result of students' suggestions.

Taking Steps to Build Trust

Trust is not given to teachers as a right, and teachers cannot assume that it exists a priori. It must be earned. In particular, the teachers' right to challenge students is not a given. Only if teachers have first displayed a public willingness to be learners themselves by adopting a critical stance toward their own actions and ideas can they legitimately ask for the same critical stance to be demonstrated by their students.

You must remember that not only can you not expect students to trust you from the outset, you may also have to face accumulations of mistrust nurtured by the actions of cynical and arrogant teachers in the past. When you face students for the first time, you also face their accumulated educational histories and their memories of all the teachers they have experienced in the past.

Building trust is neither quick nor easy. It can be very dispiriting to realize that your efforts to build trust may often bring little immediate result. But remember that, in Carl Rogers'

words (1980, p. 273), "Students have been 'conned' for so long that a teacher who is real with them is usually seen for a time as simply exhibiting a new brand of phoniness." With persistence, however, and [with] attention to some of the factors and processes described in this chapter, it is possible to build trust where none has existed before. If you do this, students will remember the time they spent with you as a time when they were valued and affirmed.

Don't Deny Your Credibility

One of the most erroneous and damaging beliefs held by some college teachers concerns the best way to show that they value students' experiences. There is a tendency among these teachers to try to dignify the validity of students' experiences by belittling their own. This is a serious mistake. Teachers may believe that if they say to students, "Look, my own experiences have no greater innate validity than yours—you'll teach me as much as I teach you," they are recognizing and affirming students' life experiences. In fact, the reverse can be true.

Teachers' protestations that they don't really know any more than students do and that they are simply there to help students realize that they already possess the knowledge and skills they need sound supportive and respectful. But such protestations from teachers who are demonstrably more skillful, more intellectually able, and possessed of a much greater range of experience than that of students will be perceived as false. Instead of students warming to what teachers believe to be admirably humane and respectful attitudes, students may conclude that if teachers' experiences have left them with no greater skill, knowledge, or insight than that possessed by students, then there is nothing useful students can learn from them. So in your desire to affirm the validity of your students' experiences and abilities, be careful not to undermine your own credibility in their eyes.

Be Explicit about Your Organizing Vision

Teachers cannot avoid having visions that guide their practice. This is quite normal. What is problematic for students, however, is when teachers deny having any visions yet through their actions make it apparent that such visions exist and are highly influential in determining what happens in the classroom.

I have an educational agenda, and I always try to acknowledge this fact plainly to students. Instead of pretending that I have no power in the classroom, that anything goes as far as curricula, methods, or evaluative criteria are concerned, I try to make explicit at the outset what my expectations and organizing principles are. In interviews with applicants for degree programs, in consultations with students who are interested in finding out about my courses, and in all the course descriptions I circulate, I state the evaluative criteria that inform my teaching.

On the first meeting of any new course, I advise students to regard their attendance as a provisional sampling, a testing of the water. If they object to my agenda and concerns, then they can leave after this first meeting with no ill feeling. I will make sure that I say something like the following at this meeting:

If you decide to join this class, you must expect to be asked to be critically reflective about your own practice as educators. You must also anticipate being asked to analyze critically the congruences and discrepancies between your experiences and the pronouncements of theorists and researchers who are regarded as experts. These features are nonnegotiable, and you should know this right from the beginning. If you don't like them, or if you feel you're not ready to do these things, then you should think seriously about not coming to the second meeting of class. If you do show up next week, then I'll take this as indicating that you accept these fundamental purposes. If you don't show up, that's fine—you'll have saved yourself a lot of needless anxiety. I know that critically reflective education is hard to understand and anticipate until you find yourself immersed in it, so let's take some time now to discuss some of the queries and uncertainties that I'm sure you have about what staying in this class involves.

Having said this, I can then negotiate in good faith with students about possible changes in methods, areas of content, and evaluative indicators by which the development of critical reflection can be recognized. Not to make explicit right at the outset the fact that I have an organizing vision and not to inform students of the form that vision takes in the class would be fundamentally dishonest.

Make Sure Your Words and Actions Are Congruent

The congruence of words and actions is absolutely paramount. Few things destroy students' trust in teachers more quickly than teachers who say they will do one thing and then proceed to do something quite different or teachers who espouse one set of philosophical aims and guiding principles and then proceed to practice in ways that render these null and void. One of the most frequently described examples of dissonance between teachers' words and actions concerns those teachers who claim they are fully committed to democratic principles. Such teachers will declare that the classroom is a collaborative learning laboratory in which students will have a full and equal role in determining what happens. Yet, subtly and manipulatively, teachers override students' concerns and expressed wishes to do what they, as teachers, feel is important.

Such spuriously democratic teachers will tell students at the outset of a class that the curriculum, methods, and evaluative criteria are in students' hands. As matters progress, however, it becomes apparent that the teachers' preferences and judgments are prevailing. This can happen explicitly and overtly but is more likely to be done insidiously. Indeed, there are some teachers (I have sat in their classes) who vigorously deny that any subtle manipulation of events is occurring, even as they express surprise that the "collaborative" curricula to be studied and the methods to be used coincidentally happen to match those that they prefer.

Be Ready to Admit Your Errors

Learners seem to warm to teachers who acknowledge that they don't have all the answers and that, like their students, they sometimes feel out of control. So be prepared to admit to being plagued by occasional feelings of anxiety and unease about the inadequacies you perceive in yourself. Such admissions will help reduce the tension students feel about their own need to be seen as perfect by their peers and teachers.

Remember, however, that your admissions of error have some kind of releasing effect on students [only] when they are made after you have already established a degree of credibility. The timing of such admissions of error is all important. If you walk into a classroom and begin immediately to assert your inadequacy without having previously established that you have something to offer students, you will probably be perceived as overwhelmingly weak or inept. In fact, the typical reaction from most students will be annoyance at having found themselves in a class where they obviously aren't going to learn anything.

So, whereas public declarations of fallibility from teachers who have clearly earned credibility are prized by students, these same declarations from teachers who are unknown quantities may produce an effect exactly opposite to the one intended. Instead of releasing students from the self-imposed burden of needing to be exemplars at whatever activities they are exploring, it increases their burden of anxiety. In response to teachers' ill-timed avowals of inadequacy, students might quite legitimately ask, "Well, if you have so little to offer me, then why on earth am I here?"

Reveal Aspects of Yourself Unrelated to Teaching

Be ready to refer to enthusiasms, passions, and concerns outside your teaching role. When you reveal aspects of your personhood, it gives students a sense that they're dealing with a flesh-and-blood human being. Tarule (1988) calls this the autobiographical metaphor in teaching and points out how women, in particular, warm to teachers who are willing to bring evidence of their own extracurricular enthusiasms into the classroom.

For many years, I steadfastly refused to refer to anything to do with my life outside the classroom. To me, personal disclosure smacked of amateur psychotherapy and indicated only that the teacher was using the learning group as a dumping ground for unresolved personal issues. There is no doubt that this can sometimes happen, but the authentic disclosure that students appreciate is very far from this. It is seen in teachers using incidents from their own daily lives to illustrate general principles, in their talking about the passions that led them to develop an interest in their fields, and in referring to the enthusiasms that currently sustain and renew these interests.

Show that You Take Students Seriously

Listen carefully for any concerns, anxieties, or problems voiced by students. If none [is] forthcoming, arrange opportunities and provide encouragement for students to speak out about what's on their minds. When concern is expressed on an issue—no matter how misplaced or trivial it seems to you—don't give a quick and polished response and then move on to something else. Give students plenty of time to express their thoughts. Don't finish their sentences for them. Don't rephrase what they've just told you as a way of benevolently interpreting their anxieties for them. You may feel that you're saving them some embarrassment by doing this, but in reality you're sending them the humiliating message that you don't think they are capable of speaking intelligently for themselves.

Be wary of your actions unwittingly reinforcing students' belief that they are incapable of contributing to discussion at any serious level. Even if you're confused about what someone is saying or impatient to ask a series of sharp, quick questions for clarification, resist these temptations. Hold yourself back, and the chances are that another class member will jump in and state the same concern in a way that is clearer to you. Here is Ira Shor's attempt to show students he takes them seriously:

I modulate my voice to conversational rhythms rather than didactic, lecturing tones. I listen intently to every student utterance and ask other students to listen when one of their peers speaks. I don't begin my reply after the student ends his or her *first* sentence but ask the student to say more about the question. If I'm asked what I think, I say I'd be glad to say what I think, but why don't a few more people speak first to what the student just said, whether you agree or not. If I don't have a reply to what a student said or don't understand a series of student comments and can't invent on-the-spot questions to reveal the issue, I go home and think about it and start a next class from what a student said before, to keep

signaling to students the importance of their statements. (Shor and Freire, 1987, p. 117)

Be ready to explain, clearly and frequently, why you wish students to do the things you are asking. If students propose alternatives to your carefully thought-out plans, don't dismiss them out of hand. If you need time to think about a student's suggestion, then say this and promise to respond at the next class—and keep this promise. Be open to change. Show your readiness to negotiate and to adapt what you had planned to [use] some other format. When students suggest themes, exercises, and issues they wish to explore, even if these are outside the scope of your original activities, consider very seriously how you can make some compromise to include some of these. If, in good faith, your own convictions or external constraints make these inclusions impossible, be prepared to explain and justify your decisions. Don't fall back on your presumption of authority as a way of winning the day, and don't imply that students lack the sophistication needed to understand your reasoning by refusing to discuss it with them.

Don't Play Favorites

In every class, there are students whom you like more than others, people whose work you look forward to receiving, and people whom you would welcome as personal friends. Conversely, there are those whom you dislike personally, whom you think boorish and insensitive, and whom you believe are sliding through a course with a minimum of effort and a maximum of cynical contempt. You wouldn't be human if you didn't warm to some students as people and freeze in the presence of others. But if you are ever to be trusted by students, it is absolutely essential that you don't allow yourself the luxury of exercising these personal dislikes, that you avoid playing favorites.

Playing favorites—showing that you regard some people's work more favorably because of their appealing personalities and that you are prejudiced against others' efforts for their personal failings—destroys your credibility in students' eyes very quickly. So watch out that in discussions you don't slip into the habit of giving automatic preference to the contributions of those you like, while only acknowledging as a last resort the contributions of those you dislike. Try not to let your nonverbal gestures communicate how you feel about the personalities of contributors to discussions. Be alert to students' picking up your nonverbal messages about which students you like or dislike personally. When you see students making scapegoats of people whom you personally dislike, ask yourself how much your attitude is coming through to the group. When you see scapegoating happening, send a strong symbolic message by explicitly creating a space in the discussion where the person who was made the scapegoat has the chance to contribute—fully and freely—without intimidation. You are bound to have likes and dislikes regarding the different students in your classes. The important thing is to avoid letting these influence your public actions as a teacher.

Realize the Power of Your Own Role Modeling

Teachers sometimes shy away from acknowledging the significance of their own actions to students. They believe that regarding their own actions as particularly significant within a learning group indicates an unpleasant egoism. They like to think that they are at one with students and that their own actions have no more significance than those of any other member of the learning group. This is patently not the case. As Jackson (1986) acknowledges, the role modeling undertaken by teachers is the most important element in transformative teaching. What we do as teachers is invested with enormous symbolic significance by students. So recognize the inevitable symbolic significance of your actions and make a virtue of necessity by ensuring as far as you can that these actions are perceived as authentic by students.

Let me give an example from my own practice of how seriously I take role modeling as a contributing component to trust building. My primary function as a teacher is to encourage critical thinking—something I suspect is an organizing principle for teachers across many academic disciplines and subject boundaries. More than any other factor, it is a teacher's willingness to display the habits of critical questioning toward his or her own ideas and actions that encourages these same habits in students.

From my own practice, I know that the position of institutional authority I possess as a professor at Teachers College or as the "expert" consultant invited to give a keynote speech or conduct a workshop means that most people will be reluctant to criticize publicly any of my pronouncements. The risk of doing this is perceived as just too great. When they recall how such criticism has been received by leaders in the past, they may conclude that silence is the best policy or that, if they do speak, it should be to affirm the validity and accuracy of the leaders' insights.

Knowing this, I usually critically scrutinize my own ideas in front of my students or conference audiences. I will talk about mistakes I have made, about errors in my work, or about times when I wrote about something before fully understanding the phenomenon. I will discuss the areas of my work most in need of refinement. I will identify the issues I wish I had paid attention to or the most problematic areas for future inquiry. I talk about my confusions as much as my certainties. It is easier for me to do this without damaging my credibility than for someone just beginning in the field. Because of my writings and speeches and the credibility that accrues to published authors (regardless of whether what they published actually made any sense), I can move very quickly to this critical role modeling. Were I back in 1970 teaching my first classes, I would be much more cautious about this approach.

One thing I am very careful to do is to encourage the first hesitant critical comments of students, even if I think their criticisms are wholly misconceived. Despite my annoyance at being personally criticized, I try to make sure that the giver of this criticism is not silenced by other members of the group anxious to observe what they see as the pedagogical proprieties of the college classroom. A very powerful symbolic action for me is to distribute to students copies of reviews critical of my books and to point to the valid points in such reviews. This is a difficult thing for me since I react to such reviews personally and with a sense of injured martyrdom. But if it were easy for me to distribute critical reviews, then the symbolic power of doing this would be diminished. Because it's obvious that I'm hurt by these reviews, students are that much more convinced that I mean what I say about being open to criticism.

Shor describes, in similar terms, how he acts carefully to model the critical thinking he tries to encourage in students:

What I try . . . is to demonstrate that there is no punishment for disagreeing with me, and also there is no reward for simply agreeing with me. I do this in several ways. In class, I react blankly to any student who mimics my ideas in his or her own voice. I do not model approval of mimicry. Then, I raise questions about my very own position, phrased by the student, to challenge [his or her] manipulation of me for a grade. If students write papers mimicking my ideas, I do the same thing but in written response on their essays, asking leading questions about the ideology they "psyched out." I don't give automatic A's to the mimic papers, and my written questions urge

the students to reason out the issues in depth next time. From the reverse point of view, if a student writes a paper or makes a statement antagonistic to my views, I don't pounce on him or her in a one-to-one debate. Instead, I reproduce the paper for class reading and discussion or re-present the statement as a problem theme for our inquiry. (Shor and Freire, 1987, p. 184)

Teachers who declare that they are running critical or liberatory classrooms in which everything is open to critical scrutiny cannot expect students to breathe an immediate sigh of relief and release at inhaling this heady air of intellectual freedom. The more likely reaction is for students to wonder exactly which particular game the teacher is playing and when his or her agenda will start to emerge. So if you're trying to encourage critical thinking, you must expect a period in which students will scrutinize very carefully to what degree your protestations are congruent with your actions.

Balancing Credibility and Authenticity

Credibility and authenticity are elusive concepts, made the more so by the fact that they cannot be easily standardized. It is impossible to develop training packages to tell people how to be credible or authentic, since contextual features affect so strongly how students and teachers define credible and authentic behaviors. The most one can do is offer some of the general guidelines discussed in this chapter, give examples of how teachers in different settings try to build trust, and urge teachers to pay attention to the necessity for doing this. However, although these concepts evade precise definition, students sense when they are and are not present. In fact, it is usually much easier to say when these elements are absent, since students are mistrustful and uneasy, and their awareness of these feelings is sharp and disturbing. When students trust teachers, they cross new intellectual terrain with a tread that is firm and confident. When they mistrust teachers, each step is filled with trepidation and taken with the ever-present fear that it will be the one to send them sinking into quicksand or hurtling into a ravine.

The problem with pursuing authenticity and credibility (aside from the fact that neither of these concepts can be standardized in behavioral terms) is that the actions associated with these ideas often seem contradictory. In pursuing one, you risk threatening the other. On the one hand, in striving to establish your credibility with students, you risk seeming to show off your knowledge and experience in a manner that appears authoritarian, arrogant, and inauthentic. On the other hand, however, in striving to be authentic, you risk weakening your credibility if you overdo your readiness to admit to error; students can be left with a perception that your most distinguishing characteristic is your ineptness. You also strain your credibility when you make students squirm in embarrassment because you are too personally revealing about your life outside the classroom. No student likes a teacher to use a class as a therapy group for the exorcising of his or her personal demons. So overemphasizing or mistiming can destroy the very trust you are working so hard to create.

This problem has no easy solutions, and most of the time you will probably feel you are erring too much on one side or the other. The only comfort I can give is this. If you don't make the effort to build credibility or act authentically, then you will do more harm than good. Better to try and achieve some sort of balance, knowing this will always remain elusive, than to neglect this trust building entirely. Teaching is never easy, and of all the complex balances we try to attain, being credible and authentic in the right proportions is one of the most difficult. But if you neglect entirely the need to build credibility in students' eyes, then they will have little confidence in the value of what you ask them to do. And if you behave inauthentically, they will regard your asking them to do it as a self-serving confidence trick.

References

Jackson, P. *The Study of Teaching.* New York: Teachers College Press, 1986.

Moustakas, C. *The Authentic Teacher: Sensitivity and Awareness in the Classroom.* Cambridge, Mass.: Howard A. Doyle, 1966.

Rogers, C. R. *A Way of Being.* Boston: Houghton Mifflin, 1980.

Shor, I., and Freire, P. A. *Pedagogy for Liberation: Dialogues on Transforming Education.* Granby, Mass.: Bergin & Garvey, 1987.

Tarule, J. M. "Voices of Returning Women: Ways of Knowing." In L. H. Lewis (ed.), *Addressing the Needs of Returning Women.* New Directions for Continuing Education, No. 39. San Francisco: Jossey-Bass, 1988.

41

Embracing Contraries
in the Teaching Process

Peter Elbow

My argument is that good teaching seems a struggle because it calls on skills or mentalities that are actually contrary to each other and thus tend to interfere with each other. It was my exploration of writing that led me to look for contraries in difficult or complex processes. I concluded that good writing requires, on the one hand, the ability to conceive copiously of many possibilities, an ability which is enhanced by a spirit of open, accepting generativity; but on the other hand, good writing also requires an ability to criticize and reject everything but the best, a very different ability which is enhanced by a tough-minded critical spirit. I end up seeing in good writers the ability somehow to be extremely creative and extremely critical, without letting one mentality prosper at the expense of the other or being halfhearted in both.

In this frame of mind, I began to see a paradoxical coherence in teaching where formerly I was perplexed. I think the two conflicting mentalities needed for good teaching stem from the two conflicting obligations inherent in the job; we have an obligation to students, but we also have an obligation to knowledge and

society. Surely we are incomplete as teachers if we are committed only to what we are teaching but not to our students, or only to our students but not to what we are teaching, or halfhearted in our commitment to both.

We like to think that these two commitments coincide, and often they do. It happens often enough, for example, that our commitment to standards leads us to give a low grade or tough comment, and it is just what the student needs to hear. But just as often we see that a student needs praise and support rather than a tough grade, even for her weak performance, if she is really to prosper as a student and a person—if we are really to nurture her fragile investment in her studies. Perhaps we can finesse this conflict between a "hard" and "soft" stance if it is early in the semester or we are only dealing with a rough draft; for the time being, we can give the praise and support we sense is humanly appropriate and hold off strict judgment and standards til later. But what about when it is the end of the course or a final draft needs a grade? It is comforting to take as our paradigm that first situation where the tough grade was just right and to consider the trickier situation as somehow anomalous and, thus, to assume that we always serve students best by serving knowledge, and vice versa. But I now

AUTHOR'S NOTE: From *Embracing Contraries* by Peter Elbow. Copyright © 1986 by Peter Elbow. Used by permission of Oxford University Press, Inc.

think I can throw more light on the nature of teaching by taking our conflicting loyalties as paradigmatic.

Our loyalty to students asks us to be their allies and hosts as we instruct and share: to invite all students to enter in and join us as members of a learning community—even if they have difficulty. Our commitment to students asks us to assume they are all smart and capable of learning, to see things through their eyes, to help bring out their best rather than their worst when it comes to tests and grades. By taking this inviting stance, we will help more of them learn.

But our commitment to knowledge and society asks us to be guardians or bouncers; we must discriminate, evaluate, test, grade, certify. We are invited to stay true to the inherent standards of what we teach, whether or not that stance fits the particular students before us. We have a responsibility to society—that is, to our discipline, our college or university, and to other learning communities of which we are members—to see that the students we certify really understand or can do what we teach, to see that the grades and credits and degrees we give really have the meaning or currency they are supposed to have.

A pause for scruples. Can we give up so easily the paradigm of teaching as harmonious? Isn't there something misguided in the very idea that these loyalties are conflicting? After all, if we think we are being loyal to students by being extreme in our solicitude for them, won't we undermine the integrity of the subject matter or the currency of the credit and, thereby, drain value from the very thing we are supposedly giving them? And if we think we are being loyal to society by being extreme in our ferocity —keeping out *any* student with substantial misunderstanding—won't we deprive subject matter and society of the vitality and reconceptualizations they need to survive and grow?

Knowledge and society only exist embodied— that is, flawed.

This sounds plausible. But even if we choose a middle course and go only so far as fairness toward subject matter and society, the very fact that we grade and certify at all—the very fact that we must sometimes flunk students—tempts many of them to behave defensively with us. Our mere fairness to subject matter and society tempts students to try to hide weaknesses from us, "psych us out," or "con us." It is as though we are doctors trying to treat patients who hide their symptoms from us for fear we will put them in the hospital.

Student defensiveness makes our teaching harder. We say, "Don't be afraid to ask questions," or even, "It's a sign of intelligence to be willing to ask naive questions." But when we are testers and graders, students too often fear to ask. Toward examiners, they must play it safe, drive defensively, not risk themselves. This stunts learning. When they trust the teacher to be wholly an ally, students are more willing to take risks, connect the self to the material, and experiment. Here is the source not just of learning but also of genuine development or growth.

Let me bring this conflict closer to home. A department chair or dean who talks with us about our teaching and who sits in on our classes is our ally insofar as she is trying to help us teach better, and we can get more help from her to the degree that we openly share with her our fears, difficulties, and failures. Yet insofar as she makes promotion or tenure decisions about us or even participates in those decisions, we will be tempted not to reveal our weaknesses and failures. If we want the best help for our shortcomings, someone who is merely fair is not enough. We need an ally, not a fair judge.

Thus we can take a merely judicious, compromise position toward our students only if we are willing to settle for being *sort of* committed to students and *sort of* committed to subject matter and society. This middling or fair stance, in fact, is characteristic of many teachers who lack investment in teaching or who have lost it. Most invested teachers, on the other hand, tend to be a bit passionate about supporting students or else passionate about serving and protecting the subject matter they love—and thus they tend to live more on one side or the other of some allegedly golden mean.

But supposing you reply, "Yes, I agree that a compromise is not right. Just middling. Muddling. Not excellence or passion in either direction. But that's not what I'm after. My scruple had to do with your very notion of *two directions*. There is only one direction. Excellence. Quality. The very conception of conflict between loyalties is wrong. An inch of progress in one direction, whether toward knowledge or toward students, is always an inch in the direction of the other. The needs of students and of knowledge or society are in essential harmony."

To assert this harmony is, in a sense, to agree with what I am getting at in this [chapter]. But it is no good just asserting it. It is like asserting, "Someday you'll thank me for this" or "This is going to hurt me worse than it hurts you." I may say to students, "My fierce grading and extreme loyalty to subject matter and society are really in your interests," but students will still tend to experience me as an adversary and undermine much of my teaching. I may say to knowledge and society, "My extreme support and loyalty to all students is really in your interests," but society will tend to view me as a soft teacher who lets standards down.

It is the burden of this [chapter] to say that a contradictory stance is possible—not just in theory but in practice—but not by pretending there is no tension or conflict. And certainly not by affirming only one version of the paradox, the "paternal" version, which is to stick up for standards and firmness by insisting that to do so is good for students in the long run, forget-ting the "maternal" version which is to stick up for students by insisting that to do so is good for knowledge and society in the long run. There is a genuine paradox here. The positions are conflicting, and they are true.

Let me turn this structural analysis into a narrative about the two basic urges at the root of teaching. We often think best by telling stories. I am reading a novel and I interrupt my wife to say, "Listen to this, isn't this wonderful!" and I read a passage out loud. Or we are walking in the woods and I say to her, "Look at that tree!" I am enacting the pervasive human itch to share. It feels lonely, painful, or incomplete to appreciate something and not share it with others.

But this urge can lead to its contrary. Suppose I say, "Listen to this passage," and my wife yawns or says, "Don't interrupt me." Suppose I say, "Look at that beautiful sunset on the lake," and she laughs at me for being so sentimental and reminds me that Detroit is right there just below the horizon—creating half the beauty with its pollution. Suppose I say, "Listen to this delicate irony," and she can't see it and thinks I am neurotic to enjoy such bloodless stuff. What happens then? I end up not wanting to share it with her. I hug it to myself. I become a lone connoisseur. Here is the equally deep human urge to protect what I appreciate from harm. Perhaps I share what I love with a few select others—but only after I find a way somehow to extract from them beforehand assurance that they will understand and appreciate what I appreciate. And with them I can even sneer at worldly ones who lack our taste or intelligence or sensibility.

Many of us went into teaching out of just such an urge to share things with others, but we find students turn us down or ignore us in our efforts to give gifts. Sometimes they even laugh at us for our very enthusiasm in sharing. We try to show them what we understand and love, but they yawn and turn away. They put their feet up on our delicate structures; they chew bubble gum during the slow movement; they listen to hard rock while reading *Lear* and say, "What's so great about Shakespeare?"

Sometimes even success in sharing can be a problem. We manage to share with students what we know and appreciate, and they love it and eagerly grasp it. But their hands are dirty or their fingers are rough. We overhear them saying, "Listen to this neat thing I learned," yet we cringe—because they got it all wrong. Best not to share.

I think of the medieval doctrine of poetry that likens it to a nut with a tough husk protecting, a sweet kernel. The function of the poem is not to disclose but rather to conceal the kernel from the many, the unworthy, and to disclose it only to the few worthy (Robertson, 1963, 61ff.). I have caught myself more than a few times explaining something I know or love with a kind of complexity or irony such that only those who have the right sensibility will hear what I have to say—others will not understand at all. Surely this is the source of much obscurity in learned discourse. We would rather have readers miss entirely what we say or turn away in boredom or frustration than reply, "Oh, I see what you mean. How ridiculous!" or "How naive!" It is marvelous, actually, that we can make one utterance do so many things: communicate with the right people, stymie the wrong people, and thereby help us decide who are the right and the wrong people.

I have drifted into an unflattering portrait of the urge to protect one's subject, a defensive urge that stems from hurt. Surely much bad teaching and academic foolishness derive from this immature reaction to students or colleagues who will not accept a gift we tried generously to give (generously, but sometimes ineffectually or condescendingly or autocratically). Surely I must learn not to pout just because I can't get a bunch of adolescents as excited as I am about late Henry James. Late Henry James may be pearls, but when students yawn, that doesn't make them swine.

But it is not immature to protect the integrity of my subject in a positive way, to uphold standards to insist that students stretch themselves til they can do justice to the material. Surely these impulses are at the root of much good teaching. And there is nothing wrong with these impulses in themselves—only *by themselves*. That is, there is nothing wrong with the impulse to guard or protect the purity of what we cherish so long as that act is redeemed by the presence of the opposite impulse also to give it away.

In Piaget's terms, learning involves both assimilation and accommodation. Part of the job is to get the subject matter to bend and deform so that it fits inside the learner (that is, so it can fit or relate to the learner's experiences). But that's only half the job. Just as important is the necessity for the learner to bend and deform himself so that he can fit himself around the subject without doing violence to it. Good learning is not a matter of finding a happy medium where both parties are transformed as little as possible. Rather, both parties must be maximally transformed—in a sense deformed. There is violence in learning. We cannot learn something without eating it, yet we cannot really learn it either without being chewed up.

Look at Socrates and Christ as archetypal good teachers—archetypal in being so paradoxical. They are extreme, on the one hand, in their impulse to share with everyone and to support all learners, in their sense that everyone can take and get what they are offering; but they are extreme, on the other hand, in their fierce high standards for what will pass muster. They did not teach gut courses, they flunked "Gentleman C" performances, they insisted that only "too much" was sufficient in their protectiveness toward their "subject matter." I am struck also with how much they both relied on irony, parable, myth, and other forms of subtle utterance that hide while they communicate. These two teachers were willing in some respects to bend and disfigure and, in the eyes of many, to profane what they taught, yet on the other hand, they were equally extreme in their insistence that learners bend or transform themselves in order to become fit receptacles.

It is as though Christ, by stressing the extreme of sharing and being an ally—saying "suffer the little children to come unto me" and praising the widow with her mite—could be more extreme in his sternness: "unless you sell all you have" and "I speak to them in parables, because seeing they do not see and hearing they do not hear, nor do they understand" (saying in effect, "I am making this a tough course *because* so many of you are poor students"). Christ embeds the two themes of giving away and guarding—commitment to "students" and to "subject matter" in the one wedding feast story: the host invites in guests from the highways and byways, anybody—but then angrily ejects one into outer darkness because he lacks the proper garment.

Let me sum up the conflict in two lists of teaching skills. If, on the one hand, we want to help more students learn more, I submit we should behave in the following four ways:

1. We should see our students as smart and capable. We should assume that they *can* learn what we teach—all of them. We should look *through* their mistakes or ignorance to the intelligence that lies behind. There is ample documentation that this "teacher expectation" increases student learning (Rosenthal and Jacobson, 1968, 33-60).

2. We should show students that we are on their side. This means, for example, showing them that the perplexity or ignorance they reveal to us will not be used against them in tests, grading, or certifying. If they hide their questions or guard against us, they undermine our efforts to teach them.

3. Indeed, so far from letting their revelations hurt them in grading, we should be, as it were, lawyers for the defense, explicitly trying to help students do better against the judge and prosecuting attorney when it comes to the "trial" of testing and grading. ("I may be able to get you off this charge, but only if you tell me what you really were doing that night.") If we take this advocate stance, students can learn more from us, even if they are guilty of the worst crimes in the book: not having done the homework, not having learned last semester, not *wanting* to learn. And by learning more—even if not learning perfectly—they will perform better, which in turn will usually lead to even better learning in the future.

4. Rather than try to be perfectly fair and perfectly in command of what we teach—as good examiners ought to be—we should reveal our own position, particularly our doubts, ambivalences, and biases. We should show we are still learning, still willing to look at things in new ways, still sometimes uncertain or even stuck, still willing to ask naive questions, still engaged in the interminable process of working out the relationship between what we teach and the rest of our lives. Even though we are not wholly peer with our students, we can still be peer in this crucial sense of also

being engaged in learning, seeking, and being incomplete. Significant learning requires change—inner readjustments, willingness to let go. We can increase the chances of our students being willing to undergo the necessary anxiety involved in change if they see we are also willing to undergo it.

Yet if, on the other hand, we want to increase our chances of success in serving knowledge, culture, and institutions, I submit that we need skill at behaving in four very different ways:

1. We should insist on standards that are high in the sense of standards that are absolute. That is, we should take what is almost a kind of platonic position that there exists a "real world" of truth, of good reasoning, of good writing, of knowledge of biology, whatever—and insist that anything less than the real thing is not good enough.

2. We should be critical-minded and look at students and student performances with a skeptical eye. We should assume that some students cannot learn and others will not, even if they can. This attitude will increase our chances of detecting baloney and surface skill masquerading as competence or understanding.

3. We should not get attached to students or take their part or share their view of things; otherwise, we will find it hard to exercise the critical spirit needed to say, "No, you do not pass," "No, you cannot enter in with the rest of us," [or] "Out you go into the weeping and gnashing of teeth."

4. Thus we should identify ourselves primarily with knowledge or subject matter and care more about the survival of culture and institutions than about individual students—even when that means students are rejected who are basically smart or who tried as hard as they could. We should keep our minds on the harm that can come to knowledge and society if standards break down, or if someone is certified who is not competent, rather than on the harm that comes to individual students by hard treatment.

Because of this need for conflicting mentalities, I think I see a distinctive distribution of success in teaching. At one extreme, we see a few master or genius teachers, but they are striking for how differently they go about it and how variously and sometimes surprisingly they explain what they do. At the other extreme are people who teach very badly, or who have given up trying, or who quit teaching altogether; they are debilitated by the conflict between trying to be an ally as they teach and an adversary as they grade. Between these two extremes, teachers find the three natural ways of making peace between contraries: there are "hard" teachers in whom loyalty to knowledge or society has won out; "soft" teachers in whom loyalty to students has won out; and middling, mostly dispirited teachers who are sort of loyal to students and sort of loyal to knowledge or society. (A few [members] of this last group are not dispirited at all but live on a kind of knife edge of almost palpable tension as they insist on trying to be scrupulously fair both to students and to what they teach.)

This need for conflicting mentalities is also reflected in what is actually the most traditional and venerable structure in education: a complete separation between teaching and official assessment. We see it in the Oxford and Cambridge structure that makes the tutor wholly an ally to help the student prepare for exams set and graded by independent examiners. We see something of the same arrangement in many European university lecture-and-exam systems which are sometimes mimicked by American Ph.D. examinations. The separation of teaching and examining is found in many licensing systems and also in some new competence-based programs.

Even in conventional university curricula, we see various attempts to strengthen assessment and improve the relationship between teacher and student by making the teacher more of an ally and a coach. In large courses with many sections, teachers often give a common exam and grade each other's students. Occasionally, when two teachers teach different courses within each other's field of competence, they divide their roles and act as "outside examiner" for [each] other's students. (This approach, by the way, tends to help teachers clarify what they are trying to accomplish in a course, since they must communicate their goals clearly to the examiner if there is to be any decent fit between the teaching and examining.) In writing centers, tutors commonly help students improve a piece of writing which another teacher will assess. We even see a hint of this separation of roles when teachers stress collaborative learning; they emphasize the students' role as mutual teachers and thereby emphasize their own pedagogic role as examiner and standard setter.

But though the complete separation of teacher and evaluator is hallowed and useful, I am interested here in ways for teachers to take on both roles better. It is not just that most teachers are stuck with both; in addition, I believe that opposite mentalities or processes can enhance each other rather than interfere with each other if we engage in them in the right spirit.

References

Robertson, D. W. *A Preface to Chaucer.* Princeton. 1963.

Rosenthal, Robert, and Lenore Jacobson. *Pygmalion in the Classroom: Teacher Expectation and Pupils' Intellectual Development.* New York. 1968.

42

Stages of Curriculum Transformation

Marilyn R. Schuster and Susan R. Van Dyne

Charting the Change Process

Outlining the evolution of curriculum change efforts reveals many parallels with the directions of the last twenty years of scholarship on women; the insights from that research have altered the content of many academic disciplines. Accumulation of [these] new data, in turn, generates new questions about the nature of women's experience and that of other groups not currently represented in the traditional syllabus. Because of the important landmarks in that scholarship, and because of the examples of curriculum change projects across the country, we can begin to identify the interactions between research questions and classroom practice that stimulate the transformation of the curriculum.

Our description suggests that teachers move through a sequence of stages, trying a variety of strategies to represent women and minorities adequately in their courses.[1] Yet these stages have fluid boundaries, and individuals may not experience them as a strictly linear progression. It is also unlikely that different groups of teachers within a single institution will move through the same stages at the same

AUTHORS' NOTE: This is a reprint of an article originally published as Schuster, Marilyn R. and Susan R. Van Dyne, "Stages of Curriculum Transformation," in *Women's Place in the Academy* (Rowman & Littlefield), 1985, pp. 13-29. Used with permission.

time. By organizing the description as a series of stages, we illustrate that a range of phenomena are often associated, that raising a particular set of questions leads to similar kinds of curricular outcomes. Even more important, the more the commitments that lead teachers to ask these questions are understood, the more can continued growth among our colleagues be encouraged.

Table 42.1 highlights the major characteristics of the six stages of the change process. Included for each stage are the operative perspective for seeing women's experience, the questions raised about women in order to reconstruct the syllabus, the incentives that motivate faculty and govern their intellectual inquiry and teaching, the means or strategies they use to represent women on the syllabus, and the curricular outcomes, including the types of courses typically generated and the changes in the student's role in her education. In analyzing the sources of resistance to change at each level, we've focused on the obstacles for the teacher and for the student. Our observations are derived from listening to teachers involved in faculty development projects and to those who drop out or refuse to join them.

Stage 1: Invisible Women

In the curriculum of some institutions, the absence of women is simply not noticed. Although

TABLE 42.1 Stages of Curriculum Change

Stage	Questions	Incentives	Means	Outcomes
1. Invisible women	Who are the truly great thinkers/actors in history?	Maintaining "standards of excellence"	Back to basics	• Pre-1960s exclusionary core curriculum • Student as "vessel"
2. Search for missing women	Who are the great women, the female Shakespeares, Napoleons, Darwins?	Affirmative action/compensatory	Add to existing data within conventional paradigms	• "Exceptional" women on male syllabus • Student's needs recognized
3. Women as disadvantaged, subordinate group	Why are there so few women leaders? Why are women's roles devalued?	Anger/social justice	Protest existing paradigms but within perspective of dominant group	• "Images of women" courses • Women's studies begins • Links with ethnic, cross-cultural studies
4. Women studied on own terms	What was/is women's experience? What are differences among women? (attention to race, class, cultural difference)	Intellectual	Outside existing paradigms; develop insider's perspective	• Women-focused courses • Interdisciplinary courses • Student values own experience
5. Women as challenge to disciplines	How valid are current definitions of historical periods, greatness, norms for behavior? How must our questions change to account for women's experience, diversity, difference?	Epistemology	Testing the paradigms; gender as category of analysis	• Beginnings of integration • Theory courses • Student collaborates in learning
6. Transformed, "balanced" curriculum	How can women's and men's experience be understood together? How do class and race intersect with gender?	Inclusive vision of human experience based on difference and diversity, not sameness and generalization	Transform the paradigms	• Reconceptualized, inclusive core • Transformed introductory courses • Empowering of student

this phenomenon was much more common in the 1950s, it is hardly rare today. In fact, it may be the most harmful outcome of the recent push for curricular "coherence" that has moved many faculties in the mid-'80s to reinstate a central core of required courses as the heart of a liberal education. To the extent that their search for coherence is nostalgic, faculties may simply reproduce the old orders and alleged civilities of their own undergraduate education rather than undertake a revision of the curriculum that would reflect the state of current knowledge.

A curriculum in which the experiences of women and of nonwhite cultures are entirely absent is not, of course, perceived as regressive or exclusionary by its supporters. Teachers arrested at this stage often claim the existence of indisputable "standards of excellence" and their moral, as well as intellectual, responsibility to maintain them. Excellence, in their definition, implies greatness; and their expectation is that we will all know and recognize greatness when we are exposed to it. The questions posed at this stage in structuring a syllabus focus on the incomparable individual: "Who are the truly great thinkers, or writers, or actors in history?" Such criteria acknowledge no relativity in these judgments nor any ideological context surrounding them.

If these values are reminiscent of Matthew Arnold and his father, their most recent incarnation in the American educational system was also influenced by the specific historical and social circumstances following World War II. The core curriculum most of us grew up on, Rhoda Dorsey reminds us, was designed for the predominantly male population returning to college on the G.I. Bill.[2] What was regarded as essential knowledge was substantially shaped by both the producers and primary consumers of that education—the influx of fresh male Ph.D.'s who began teaching, even at women's colleges, in the 1950s and the return of male students in great numbers to the college classroom.

Certainty and simplicity explain the popularity, in current debates, of plans to return to what is, in effect, an exclusionary definition of essential knowledge. The rallying cry "back to basics" rejects the last two decades of curriculum change as frivolous. Proponents of the old core would dismiss as confusing fragmentation the proliferation of women's studies and the diversification of ethnic and cultural studies and would disparage student-centered learning as a misguided notion of "relevance." Serious students, they maintain, need sterner stuff, which they usually equate with the subjects, and often the very books, they themselves studied twenty or forty years ago. This definition distrusts education as process and prefers fixed principles of value and judgment and supposedly timeless products.

It is not surprising that teachers who want to provide the "truly great" or "the best that has been thought and known" tend to conceive of their students as waiting vessels. Although the female (or male) student's passivity in this kind of curriculum is often very real, the professor does not imagine himself as exercising power in determining what is valued or regarded as "best" and would probably never admit or even understand that his choices on the syllabus or in the classroom are political or gendered. More likely, he sees himself as the vehicle for transmitting knowledge he imagines to be immutable and apolitical. Many male professors do not notice the absence of women; when a system of priorities, a set of values, or a syllabus serves a group's interests or at least does not constrain them, members of that group find it very difficult to become aware of the inadequacies of these designs. The number of female professors who still see no inequity or omissions in the male-defined curriculum is even more startling and serves to underscore dramatically how thoroughly women students may be deceived in believing these values are congruent with their interests.

Stage 2: Search for the Missing Women

The search for women figures good enough to be included on the syllabus may be well meaning but risks being short-lived because of the way questions are raised at this stage: "Who are the great women, the female Shakespeares, Napoleons, Darwins?" The missing women are assumed to resemble the men already present in the traditional curriculum; the criteria by which greatness and excellence are defined remain unexamined. A few women turn up when the syllabus is revised with these expectations, but they exist in isolation from each other, apparent anomalies within their gender.

Those "women worthies" who appear are usually actors in the public sphere—queens, martyrs, suffragists, female novelists with male pseudonyms—women whose outstanding characteristic is their similarity to men. Adding these women to the existing order on the syllabus provides students with the distorted view that women have participated only occasionally in the production of history or culture or [have] expressed themselves only eccentrically in their writing or behavior. The courses that emerge at this stage of attempted curriculum transformation show women's experience as the "special case" of the larger topic, which is still considered ungendered.

The fair-minded faculty member whose search for worthwhile women to study is guided by resemblances to the established male examples may find less than he had hoped. Most women's histories, recovered in such a search, will not measure up to the preeminent male model. As writers, their production will seem minor in form or scope; as political activists, their participation in the sweep of history will appear sporadic; as representatives of a culture, their significance will seem subordinate or muted; as biological or moral beings, they will appear derivative or flawed. It is important to notice that the "minor status" of most women, considered from this perspective in the change process, is attributed to an individual fault or inadequacy, a personal inability to achieve prominence, genius, or "universal" value. "If only Emily Dickinson had written longer poems or Jane Austen broader novels; if only that reformer could have championed more than her specifically female causes" are the reasons we hear at this stage for not devoting more days of the semester to women's experience. In other words, the more women's experience and production have differed from men's, the less [they] will seem worth including in a survey of knowledge structured by male norms. The very differences that could illuminate the study of both genders bar the admission of all but a few women to the traditional syllabus.

Stage 3: Women as a Subordinate Group

These questions are often provoked by the frustrating search for the missing women. Rather than opting out of the transformation endeavor because of the initially disappointing results, concerned faculty members find themselves moved by extra-academic concerns. Women teachers raise such questions for their women and men students to enable them to seek social justice. Women and men teachers also begin redefining their intellectual responsibility. Rather than a narrowly defined responsibility to a disciplinary canon of great works or great acts, they broaden their inquiry to the historical and cultural context as the means for understanding the results they found at Stage 2. Such a comprehensive understanding of what constitutes their legitimate subject matter is liberating, yet it may create new sources of anxiety. As teachers begin a program of interdisciplinary reading and teaching, they often question their ability to judge work in fields outside their own specialty.

Both teachers and students often report that they feel angry discussing the new questions of Stage 3. The classroom heats up because the material introduced about women begins to reveal the "invisible paradigms" on which the old syllabi rest. The multiple structures of the culture that define women as a disadvantaged or subordinate group begin to emerge. We can readily understand that women students in late adolescence regard as extremely unwelcome the news that their opportunities may be in any way limited; likewise, young male students are uncomfortable with the possibility that male-defined cultural values or systems are unfair. Because most young women and young men have relatively little experience in the adult work world,[3] and because both groups are relatively unconscious of their gender socialization, they are skeptical of a structural analysis that suggests their behavior is either constrained (female) or culpable (male).

Student resistance to courses that focus on a structural analysis of gender asymmetry is quite high. Students, rather than faculty, are more likely to take flight at this stage in the change process. For women students especially, the temptation is great to disassociate themselves from the disadvantages they perceive as defining women as a group. As protection, they may cling to a faith in an "individual solution," the belief that their own merit or worth will be sufficient to overcome the disability of gender. Another reaction may be that such a picture of social reality may be historically true but irrelevant to their own future. Contemporary women students, whether or not they represent a "postfeminist" generation, may believe that the equality of their aspirations will be matched by an equality of opportunities as a result of the women's movement. Instead of becoming mobilized to examine the remaining persistent and pervasive gender inequalities and to work to change them, as their teachers might have hoped, these students, both male and female, may deny that the problem exists.

Stage 4: Women Studied on Their Own Terms

Fortunately for us, the history of women's studies and of black studies offers proven strategies for overcoming both the anger and disbelief of Stage 3. Black studies gave women's studies another perspective that has made possible the kind of curriculum transformation we are currently envisioning. We have learned from black studies that slavery was the most salient feature of black experience only from the narrow perspective of the dominant group and in a North American context. To study black experience in its own terms, it was necessary to step outside the paradigms of the dominant group or the framework of the androcentric, white, Western syllabus and attempt to adopt an "insider's" perspective. What became visible was the range and diversity of black experience, including forms of resistance to oppression and various sources and strategies for exercising power. Rather than focusing on cultural subordination, the evolution of black studies demonstrated that the multicultural realities of black experience could be articulated on their own terms.

The second major movement in women's studies courses and in feminist scholarship, especially in the humanities and the social sciences, has been to delineate the character of women's experience as women themselves have expressed it. This stage is crucial to successful transformation of traditional courses because only through developing women-focused courses do we discover the data we need to draw a full picture of human experience. This stage takes as its premise the eye-opening declaration of Gerda Lerner that "to document the experience of women would mean documenting all of history; they have always been of it, in it, and making it. . . . Half, at least, of the world's experience has been theirs, half of the world's work and much of its products."[4] Rather than disappointment, disbelief, or anger, the participants in this stage of the change process, teachers and students alike, experience a liberating intellectual excitement, a sense of expanding possibilities.

For teachers, whole new fields of inquiry are opened; new areas for research, publication, and professional renewal become available. The compelling motivation most frequently described by teachers who have entered this stage is a voracious intellectual appetite: "What was and is women's experience, known as a subject rather than object? What differences among women, such as race, class, and culture, have contributed to their identities?" This stage produces the careful cross-cultural comparisons that will complicate the questions we ask about the dimensions of women's experience and that will enable us to avoid inaccurate generalizations about "all women" derived from a limited sample. Attention to race and class also brings into view the experience of most men who had been absent from the syllabus. As Peggy McIntosh argues, the determination to recover the experience of subordinate groups will give us access not just to women but to "about nine-tenths of the world's population . . . who, for

reasons of sex, race, class, [or] national or religious background, were defined as lower caste."[5]

Stage 5: Women as a Challenge to the Disciplines

What we learn in Stage 4 is too important to keep to ourselves or to study with only a limited group of self-selected students in women-focused courses. The accumulation of data gathered from the insider's perspective causes us to question in profound ways the frameworks that organize our traditional courses: "How valid are current definitions of historical periods, standards of greatness or excellence, [and] norms for behavior? How must the organizing questions of each academic discipline change to account for the diversity of gender, race, and class?" Teachers who have spent some time developing women-focused courses or who have read extensively in the scholarship on women are the most likely to undertake the most thorough form of curriculum transformation: testing the paradigms that have conventionally organized knowledge on the syllabus to exclude or marginalize women and other subordinate groups. In personal terms, the move from women-focused study to transformation of the conventional curriculum is inevitable, because most of us as teachers inhabit both worlds and must necessarily question how what we learned by studying women bears on the other courses we teach.

In institutional terms, the movement from women's studies to integrating or transforming the core curriculum is rarely seen as a natural or necessarily welcome outgrowth. When faculty members who have enjoyed a Stage 1 curriculum for most of their professional lives are asked the questions typical of Stage 5, they often feel that not only their own credentials are in doubt but [also] the worth and integrity of their academic disciplines. Perhaps because questioning the paradigms we use to perceive, analyze, and organize experience pointedly asks not only what we know but how we came to know it, the intellectual investment on both sides of the debate may be higher than at earlier points in the process of change. Even those who are willing to admit the validity of the feminist critique of the disciplines—that periodization in history does not mark the significant changes in women's estates, that canons of great art and literature are derived from and reinforce male practice as most valuable, that the scientific method defines objectivity in androcentric rather than gender-neutral terms—may resist the deconstruction of their own discipline.

Underneath the wide variety of expressions of resistance is a residual fear of loss, a reluctance to give up what had seemed most stable, efficient, authoritative, transcendent of contexts, and free of ideological or personal values—in short, a fear that feminist criticism means a loss of subject matter and methodology with no compensating gain. "If the current systems are flawed," we often hear, "they at least serve us better than no system at all. When feminists can offer us a workable alternative, then we'll consider reconceiving the total design of the syllabus."

In 1980, Catharine Stimpson characterized the first five years of scholarship in *Signs* as "the deconstruction of error" and identified the next major task as "the reconstruction of theory."[6] Yet the very tools that allowed us to document the errors have already provided the strategies for an alternative construction of the syllabus. To allay the fears of wholesale loss, and to

demonstrate that feminist theory has moved beyond merely offering a critique, those engaged in curriculum transformation need to be explicit about the ways that gender as a category of analysis enriches and illuminates traditional subjects, including the experience of elite white men. Using gender, race, and class as primary categories of analysis will transform our perspective on familiar data and concepts as well as reveal new material to be studied.

Stage 5 unequivocally means a loss of old certainties, but the gains are the recovery of meaningful historical and social context, the discovery of previously invisible dimensions of the old subjects, and access to instruments of analysis (gender, race, and class as significant variables) that expose strata of formerly suppressed material.

Stage 6: The Transformed Curriculum

What paradigms would make it possible to understand women's and men's experience together? What would a curriculum that offers an inclusive vision of human experience and that attends as carefully to difference and genuine pluralism as to sameness and generalization actually look like? Although we possess the tools of analysis that allow us to conceive of such an education, we can't, as yet, point to any institution that has entered the millenium and adopted such a curriculum.

What would exist there would depend on the recognition that any paradigm is historical and that no one framework is likely to serve for all time. This stage promotes process rather than immutable products and fixed principles.

Our descriptions so far resemble an ideal frame of mind, a hypothetical state, more than they promise a syllabus we could distribute to classes next term. Perhaps the greatest danger at this stage is the impatience for a concrete product. Administrators and teachers who are persuaded that the curriculum could be improved by more equitable representation of gender, race, and class often underestimate the time it will take. Gerda Lerner has suggested that if patriarchy his held sway for more than 2,000 years, we should not be surprised if, in a discipline like history, it takes several dozen women scholars, fully funded for the length of most grants, even to imagine the categories that would have to change to bring this curriculum into being.[7]

While the goal of a Stage 6 curriculum is often readily assented to, the means may seem too costly or cumbersome. Many well-meaning college presidents and deans wish to move directly from Stage 1 to Stage 6 with no allocation of resources [or] enduring, clear commitment to women-focused study. They are tempted to believe that the promised land can be attained without passing through the difficult terrain of women's studies. Some curriculum change projects risk foundering because good intentions, especially of administrators who want to sponsor programs that will be perceived as apolitical, are substituted for the expertise developed by those who have taught and contributed to the scholarship on women. It would be an intellectual mistake of monumental proportions to believe that we can do without or bypass women-focused study in the name of the greater good of the transformed or "gender-balanced" curriculum. The vital work of Stage 4, studying women on their own terms, generates the transformative questions that stimulate the change process as well as provide the data and alternative paradigms that inform the whole continuum of curriculum transformation we have described.

Notes

1. We are indebted, in developing our description of the stages of curriculum transformation, to the work of Gerda Lerner, who detailed the new questions raised by the study of women's history in her 1975 essay, "Placing Women in History: Definitions and Challenges," in *The Majority Finds Its Past: Placing Women in History* (New York: Oxford University Press, 1979); to Peggy McIntosh, who analyzes the effect of a changing curriculum on women's lives in a moving narrative, *Interactive Phases of Curricular Re-Vision: A Feminist Perspective* (Working Paper No. 124, Wellesley College Center for Research on Women, 1983); and to Mary Kay Tetreault, Elizabeth Arch, and Susan Kirschner of Lewis and Clark College, whose scale of disciplinary change reflects interviews with participants in their 1981 faculty seminar, "Measuring the Impact of Faculty Development in Women's Studies" (unpublished paper presented at the conference of the National Women's Studies Association, Humboldt, Calif., 1982).

2. Goucher College President Rhoda Dorsey, in her remarks at the opening panel of college presidents at the Skidmore College Conference, "Towards Equitable Education for Women and Men: Models from the Last Decade," 11 March 1983.

3. Of course, some students have always worked; students at public institutions are more likely than the privileged, mostly white population of elite schools to have experienced firsthand the gender inequalities in the workplace. Such experience may ready them for a feminist structural analysis or only reinforce their sense that these pervasive inequalities are "natural."

4. Gerda Lerner, *The Female Experience: An American Documentary* (Indianapolis, Ind.: Bobbs-Merrill, 1977), p. xxi.

5. Peggy McIntosh, "The Study of Women: Implications for Reconstructing the Liberal Arts Disciplines," *Forum for Liberal Education* 4, no. 1 (October 1981): 3.

6. Catharine Stimpson, originally in a talk for the Smith College Project on Women and Social Change, Smith College, Northampton, Mass., 12 March 1980.

7. Gerda Lerner, in a comment at the Wingspread Conference, "Liberal Education and the New Scholarship on Women: Issues and Constraints," sponsored by the Association of American Colleges, October 1981.

The Debate on the Ownership of Knowledge

43

Getting All Students to Listen:
Analyzing and Coping
with Student Resistance

Elizabeth Higginbotham

In the last two decades, there has been an explosion of new scholarship that raises critical questions about race, gender, and social class. Also many institutions in higher education have introduced courses that directly address diversity and multiculturalism. This area of scholarship is fast becoming a key part of the curriculum. The introduction of more inclusive materials is welcomed by many students who are eager to learn more about the historical backgrounds, literature and arts, and social circumstances of the many peoples who populate this nation and the world (Sidel, 1994). However, this new material can be a challenge to some students who find the material foreign, question its inclusion in the curriculum, and may be deeply disturbed by the implications it has for thinking about themselves. Anticipating varied student responses to curricula changes and examining the nature of possible resistance

AUTHOR'S NOTE: This is a reprint of an article originally published as Higginbotham, Elizabeth, "Getting All Students to Listen: Analyzing and Coping with Student Resistance," *American Behavioral Scientist*, 40(2): November-December, 1996, pp. 203-11.

EDITORS' NOTE: See the Opening Up New Roads: Diversity Issues section in the *Fieldguide*.

can help a faculty member scale such hurdles and promote a positive classroom setting.

Too often a faculty member will be energized by new perspectives in his or her field and revise a course to be more inclusive, only to have this excitement dashed as a few students voice their dissatisfaction with the altered nature of the course. If done well, these changes seek to present gender, race, class, sexual identity, and other multicultural categories as sources of social stratification and dimensions of analysis that speak to us all rather than [as] concepts reserved only for discussion of disadvantaged groups (Higginbotham, 1990). This innovative teaching may be applauded, even if only with smiles or nods, from students generally ignored or marginalized in the traditional curriculum. Yet these same curricular modifications can represent major changes for the more privileged students in the classroom. Privileged students are not by any means a monolithic group, because many may welcome the opportunity to explore major sources of inequality in our society. However, others may be steeped in an educational experience in which sexist, racist, classist, homophobic, and other ideological messages have supported their positions as right and proper. These privileged students may feel committed to a sense of entitlement and operate in a system in which their privileges and power are not acknowledged. As faculty, our goal is to provide an environment in which all students can reflect on and entertain various perspectives, if only during the class. To prepare for that task, we must plan for resistance and do what we can to understand its character and scope. Issues of power and privilege, in the content of our teaching and classroom dynamics, are key to that understanding.

Planning Courses to Address Power and Privilege

Essential to planning multicultural courses is to use course materials that make the best case for our subject matter: materials that present gender, race, social class, and other dimensions of inequality as structural inequalities that relate to power differentials in the society. In my experience, much of the traditional teaching in the social sciences has been focused on the majority group experience, postponing until the end of the term and presenting as different or deviant the cases of women, people of color, the working class, and other marginal groups. For example, traditional teaching of the family focuses on White, middle-class, two-parent families with a clear division of labor with men in paid employment and women working at home. Such courses were likely to present Black and Latino families as culturally different and single-parent families as problematic. Within this framework, attention would be directed toward how these latter families were different, disadvantaged, or deviant from the normative case. However, missing is an investigation of structural inequalities relevant to race, class, and heterosexuality that give some families enhanced access to resources as well as the ideological advantages of being defined as "proper."

The new scholarship seeks to explicitly address how gender, race, social class, and other dimensions of inequality structure major systems of advantages and disadvantages in social relationships and how the understanding of those relationships is often obscured from those who are privileged along specific dimensions. This approach moves us beyond looking at those who are not privileged as lacking critical characteristics that can be held accountable for their lack of success. For example, for decades the slow pace of Black achievement has been attributed to low levels of educational attainment. Yet we now have to recognize that African Americans still face racial discrimination in the labor market even when they have secured college and advanced degrees (Hochschild, 1995). This structural approach also helps us move beyond simple victim-oppressor explanations. When we consider how gender is structured in many institutions, our thinking moves from a focus on women as victims and men as the source of their problems. Thus the selection of appropriate course materials is critical, because our selection sends a message about our interpretation of issues of inequality and suggests answers to the students' unasked questions of "who is to blame." Ideally, we want students to move beyond blaming to understanding the complexity of the social order and how we all have to contribute to solving major social ills.

In teaching multicultural courses, we cannot rely solely on course materials. One's pedagogical style, ability to communicate a vision of the course, and ability to engage students in the learning process can result in cooperative dynamics. Teaching to a diverse student population requires attention to classroom interactions. Our classrooms are part of the larger social world; thus structural inequalities in the larger society are reproduced in the classroom in terms of power and privilege. Classrooms are places in which "members of privileged groups are more likely to talk, have their ideas validated, and be perceived as making significant contributions to group tasks" (Weber Cannon, 1990, p. 129).

As faculty, we have to attend to our own social location and its impact an the classroom. Our own race, gender, social class background, and sexual identity will influence the power dynamics between us and students. For example, faculty of color challenge the status quo by their mere presence in front of the class, but they might have to actively and repeatedly demonstrate their right to define the subject matter they teach (Williams, 1991). Faculty from working-class backgrounds teaching privileged students may find that these students question their circumstances and their legitimacy as teachers (Dews & Law, 1995). Awareness of power dynamics can help faculty work to personally resolve these conflicts, because the classroom is one place where all faculty do have power and many students look to the faculty to use that power to establish a comfortable place to learn (Meacham, 1995; Weber Cannon, 1990). Sometimes the power of faculty is most obvious to working-class students, who are intent on upward mobility, whereas middle- and upper-class students may not see their performance or any particular course grade as critical to their success. This is not to say that there are ironclad rules of interaction but to suggest that we must wrestle with how our own status as [faculty members] is a variable in the equation of classroom dynamics.

The implications of power differentials are very pronounced for students, especially in multicultural or diversity classes in which there is explicit discussion of inequality. In these settings, faculty can challenge the normative power arrangements and give students equal opportunities to be active participants in the class. We can do so because "teachers are given authority and control in the college classroom by virtue of their social role to prepare and credential people to occupy middle-class positions in the social structure" (Weber Cannon, 1990, p. 129). There are many teaching strategies. For example, timing students' introductions on the first day of class ensures that all students get equal space to present themselves to their peers. In my undergraduate courses, all students read a letter of introduction to the class during our second meeting. These letters answer a series of questions including their own social class background and particular interest in the subject matter. Group projects can also give students opportunities to work together, to learn respect for each other, and to share their learning with other students (Institute for the Study of Social Change, 1991). In addition, one can establish ground rules for interaction that foster an open atmosphere in the classroom, in which students are expected to respect the points of views of others and to be committed to new learning (Weber Cannon, 1990). Ground rules can reassure students that they will not be attacked by others for having different opinions.

As a group, faculty can be more sensitive to the impact of various curriculum changes on the classroom. Attention to power differences among students can help us navigate these shifting shoals. Courses change when faculty modify the curriculum and when elective courses in women's and racial and ethnic studies are designated as required diversity courses. This change means the entrance of new populations of students into what were previously safe settings for women and students of color. Frequently, the new students are likely to want to question the very premise of the courses rather than explore their own privilege (Deay & Stitzel, 1991), for example, when a student raises the question, "Why do we have to study gender or race when we are all people?"

At the same time, the women and students of color may resent the presence of more privileged students, as this course is now similar in its student makeup to many others in the college or university, and as a consequence, these students have lost one of the few safe spaces to talk about their issues without a fight over basic assumptions and terms. In most cases, a few or even one vocal student can change the dynamics of a class, even though the majority of students are willing or even eager to learn the new material. These are times when it is clear who feels secure in the privilege to challenge faculty and take up other students' time with his or her protests during the class. Systematic thinking about interactions between faculty and students, including the nature of the materials selected for presentation by the faculty, and student-to-student interactions in light of the major dimensions of inequality in our society can help us unravel the dynamics such as these at work in our classrooms.

Faculty often interact with students in the classroom, office, and other settings in the college and university, but in doing so they fail to realize that students do not treat all faculty the same. Students can behave very differently depending on whether a course is an elective, required as part of the core curriculum, or required in their major. Thus a student might use a general education or elective course as the place to challenge trends in higher education, whereas the same student will not question the political science professor who might be the source of a letter of recommendation. Similarly, those students whose futures the faculty have greater control over are also less likely to challenge their authority in the classroom. The nature of resistance varies, but more critical are the teaching strategies that faculty develop to confront resistance and ensure respectful dialogue in the classroom.

Resistance from Students: Vocal, Silent, and Absent

When considering student resistance to multicultural materials, we often think at first that White males are the major culprits. Yet the dynamics of resistance are far more complex. For example, the way that gender issues are introduced in traditional and even women's studies courses may be suspect to some women and men of color. Students may decide to be vocal, silent, or absent in their resistance. Vocal resistance is the open questioning or challenging of the premise of the course or information that is presented as facts or the truth. Such a stance should not be confused with having a difference of opinion with the teacher. Discussions with my graduate students opened my eyes to how we as faculty often focus on vocal resistance and may not recognize other forms.

We may be aware as teachers that there are several students who disagree with us but [who] remain silent throughout the semester. This behavior can be problematic, because such students might listen but not become engaged in the ideas. Structuring feedback into the course can help the teacher to make contact with the silent students. For example, asking students to keep journals in which they reflect on course material can give students an outlet for voicing their opinions. Many teachers read these journals but do not grade them; instead, they comment on, and encourage, deeper thinking about issues. Over time, students who would otherwise be silently resistant become more comfortable talking in class and learn that the classroom is a place for the exploration of a range of ideas.

Faculty often pay too little attention to student absence from class as a strategy by resistant students for avoiding learning. For example, on my campus, the sociology of gender is a popular course, but not all faculty teach this from a feminist perspective. Often students are uncomfortable with the courses designed by feminist faculty. A privileged student may ask the department chair to transfer him or her to a different section of the same course in which the faculty member does not hold views that are contrary to the student's. My graduate student informants told me about a social inequality class that explored social class, race, and gender. In this class, the students of color were very positive about the attention to race. However, they were less interested in gender issues. Thus, on the days when *women* were discussed, many elected to skip class. Absence as a form of resistance is less visible to faculty, and indeed, it might seem easier to teach without the presence of students who will raise many questions. Yet we do have to acknowledge such behaviors as unwillingness to learn.

It is sometimes possible to engage these students, who already have their minds made up about the material, by communicating a vision of the course that challenges their initial thinking. Faculty can plan to talk with their students at the beginning of the course and make explicit how this teaching approach may differ from other presentations of the material the students have experienced in the past (Morgen, 1985). The first class of the semester is critical, because faculty have the floor and can make their best case rather than expecting a syllabus and initial readings alone to do this for them. The first class is also an opportunity to let students see the overview of the course and become familiar with the learning objectives, such as being exposed to different perspectives, so that after receiving this information they can develop informed opinions. Faculty do not have to be defensive, but as specialists in our disciplines, we can claim this expertise, present a rationale for our teaching decisions, and discuss how this transformed curriculum represents new developments in our disciplines. In making our case, we might also speak directly to ease students' anxieties that a course on gender might attack men, that a course on race might put down White people, and so forth.

Vocal resistance arises most often from students who are members of privileged groups. What constitutes a privileged status can be situational. White, middle-class men who are heterosexual and the normative age of the student population might enjoy the most privilege. In a typical class, where there are few people of color and between 50% and 65% women, such a student would generally feel privileged and might even dominate class discussions. In classroom situations where there are greater numbers of students of color, as on predominantly racial/ethnic campuses and in specialty courses, members of these groups may feel privileged. Yet the middle-class men among these students of color might still dominate these classroom settings. In the same way, on single-sex campuses where women are in the majority, internal rankings among them can create a hierarchy. Often middle-class women are privileged, even women of color from these ranks, whereas the working-class women find it hard to take the floor in discussions. Thus faculty need to think about the various statuses of students on their campus and the unique composition of different classrooms.

Faculty (and the media) have attended most to resistance from White, middle-class, heterosexual men, who are likely to feel challenged when discussions turn to examining the very sources of their privilege. When teachings challenge their expectations, these men can be vocal regardless of the setting, even in women's studies and racial/ethnic courses. For many White, middle-class men, the social facts of structural inequality can make them uncomfortable. In response, they might want to talk about the "exceptions." For example, it is clear that the majority of employed women earn less than employed men, but a male student may want to talk about how *he* is paid less than women in the same workplace. His experience is not confirmed by the data presented in the class, but his sense of entitlement gives him the liberty to challenge the validity of those data, even when they are supported by government statistics.

When confronting the "exception," faculty can explain the difference between individual experiences and larger social trends. For example, in one class I spoke about how deindustrialization and downsizing have meant an increase in the number of people in poverty, as many people who formerly had high-wage jobs have been unable to replicate their previous employment circumstances. During the following class, one student told me that her boyfriend said that was not true. He had been laid off and was able to find an even better job, and so he believed that other people could do the same if they really tried. I first acknowledged that, of course, there can be exceptions to larger social trends but then asked this student to ask her boyfriend if everyone who was laid off with him had been able to not only find *another* job but also improve themselves. Young White men might not recognize that it is easier for them to find new employment than [it is for] older White men when they have been laid off. It is critical that we attend to the experiences of the group, not just the individual, in order for the students to learn about larger social trends. In a highly individualized society where most students are not even introduced to the concept of social structure until college, it is frequently difficult to get students to think about life be-

yond their own experiences, especially the students who enjoy privilege and are reluctant to examine it.

I should note here that although privilege is often obscured from those students who enjoy the most advantages, these same privileges can be quite glaring to nonprivileged students. Often women and students of color may see privilege reflected in the very questioning of social facts that are at odds with one's experiences, because the nonprivileged are more accustomed to being marginalized and even invisible in the curriculum. Thus, in our classrooms, the women and students of color may resent expressions of the very privileges that advantaged students are reluctant to acknowledge. For faculty, the task of managing a diverse student population in the classroom involves balancing the needs and perspectives of all the students rather than attending primarily to the White male students.

Members of less privileged groups are often accustomed to silence and avoidance as resistance strategies unless they are in a safe setting, for example, when their numbers are greater as in women's studies and racial/ethnic courses. Yet these students may carry scars of years in classrooms where teachers' perspectives differed from their own. Thus faculty seeking to address multicultural issues, even in presumably safe settings, must do so with care. Here is where the nature of materials and the presentation by the teacher become critical. Listening to long lectures that describe women and people of color as oppressed might not suit all women students and students of color, especially those who believe firmly that hard work and determination are the keys to success. These students, like the more privileged ones, have also been exposed to individualistic ideologies that support the status quo and might actually believe explanations that blame victims for their circumstances. We can anticipate resistance from women and students of color, but it can often be avoided by using materials that balance discussions of oppression with careful attention to resistance. For example, in teaching one can also address not only how oppression can limit individuals' options but also how individuals can challenge the imbalance of power and overcome apparent barriers to their achievement.

Conclusion

As we learn about the new scholarship that reveals gender, race, and class as critical dimensions of inequality, it inspires many of us to change the content of what we teach. We want to bring new and exciting material to our students. We also want to open up the classroom for significant discussions as students incorporate this new leaning into their own thinking about their lives. Teaching cutting-edge scholarship is important for all students, because it enables the faculty to present critical social issues in a balanced way that can open up the learning experience for all students, male and female. Indeed, a major contribution of gender and race scholarship has been to broaden the definition of resistance and to encourage explorations into the nature and importance of empowerment and cultural maintenance. Yet attention to issues of power and privilege also has to be part of our preparation for teaching in order for this transformational process to take place properly in the classroom.

Selecting course materials that present gender, race, class, sexual identity, and other multicultural categories as sources of social stratification can help initiate and guide a discussion of structural issues. However, one also has to attend to the power dynamics in the classroom, beginning with the faculty member's interactions with the students and also extending to the students' interactions with each other. Ef-

forts can be made to shift the normative balance of power, but one should still anticipate resistance from students who find their assumptions challenged. Being aware of the diversity of resistance can help us develop teaching strategies for engaging students. However, students who challenge the premises of a class cannot be permitted to circumvent the teaching and learning objectives for the course. We have to respect our students' experiences and what they can contribute to our classes but still [must] be willing to carefully analyze their comments and identify instances in which the thinking is not logical or is not supported by the facts.

Most important, as teachers we should strive to keep in mind our own statuses in the United States, including the sources of our own power in the classroom, and how this can contribute both positively and negatively to classroom dynamics. In addition, we need to remember that in our society examining the realities of social inequality and injustice is not easy. Many otherwise good citizens have avoided these challenges for decades. Thus our students are to be appreciated for the difficult task they are undertaking. Our major responsibility as faculty is to strive to create a learning environment in which all of our students can explore issues of diversity and learn critical lessons that will have significance for them and for our society.

References

Deay, A., & Stitzel, J. (1991). Reshaping the introduction to women's studies courses: Dealing up front with anger, resistance, and reality. *Feminist Teachers, 6*(1), 29-33.

Dews, C. L. B., & Law, C. L. B. (1995). *This fine place so far from home: Voices of academics from the working class.* Philadelphia: Temple University Press.

Higginbotham, E. (1990). Designing an inclusive curriculum: Bringing all women into the core. *Women's Studies Quarterly, 18*(1-2), 7-23.

Hochschild, J. (1995). *Facing up to the American dream: Race, class and the soul of the nation.* Princeton, NJ: Princeton University Press.

Institute for the Study of Social Change. (1991). *Diversity project: Final report.* Berkeley: University of California Press.

Meacham, J. (1995). Conflict in multi-cultural classes: Too much heat or too little? *Liberal Education, 81*(4), 24-29.

Morgen, S. (1985). *To see ourselves, to see our sisters: The challenge of re-envisioning curriculum change.* Memphis, TN: University of Memphis, Center for Research on Women.

Sidel, R. (1994). *Battling bias: The struggle for identity and community on college campuses.* New York: Viking.

Weber Cannon, L. (1990). Fostering positive race, class, and gender dynamics in the classroom. *Women's Studies Quarterly, 18*(1-2), 129-134.

Williams, P. (1991). *The alchemy of race and rights.* Cambridge, MA: Harvard University Press.

44

Should and Can a White, Heterosexual, Middle-Class Man Teach Students about Social Inequality and Oppression? One Person's Experience and Reflections

Thomas J. Gerschick

Tom felt completely comfortable lecturing on the women's movement and on the issues of rape and rape culture which some would consider as intrinsically outside of a man's ability to truly understand. Even beyond this is the incongruity of a straight man lecturing on radical lesbian politics with the incredible assumption of authority. . . . Is it only me, or is something really strange, not to say really sexist, about this situation?[1]

As the above quote indicates, some of my students have had strong feelings about whether a white, heterosexual, middle-class man could and should teach others about op-

AUTHOR'S NOTE: From "Should and Can a White, Heterosexual, Middle-Class Man Teach Students about Social Inequality and Oppression? One Person's Experience and Reflections," in *Multicultural Teaching in the University*, edited by David Schoem. Copyright 1993 by Praeger Publishers. Reproduced with permission of Greenwood Publishing Group, Inc., Westport, CT.

EDITORS' NOTE: See the Opening Up New Roads: Diversity Issues section in the *Fieldguide*.

pression. This chapter describes my experiences teaching an Introductory Sociology course focusing on social inequality. I taught this course at the University of Michigan over the past three academic semesters.[2] The class consistently drew 125 students, approximately 35 percent of whom were students of color. The class tended to be evenly distributed between men and women. We addressed the issues of racism, sexism, ableism, homophobia/heterosexism, and classism. The format of the course was two fifty-minute lectures a week in addition to a two-hour small group discussion session. In this chapter, I focus on the issues that concerned students raised about me personally and the larger issues that arose as a result of our dialogue.

There is a small, but growing, body of literature that addresses the question of who is appropriate to teach whom or who is appropriate to teach what at the university level (Shoe 1988; Beauchamp and Wheeler 1988). The National Association of Scholars (1988) argues that entertaining the question of who can teach whom unnecessarily politicizes the academy. It argues that "academic freedom is based on disciplinary competence and entails a responsibility to exclude extraneous political matters from the classroom" (Short 1988: 7). Thus, according to the association, one's gender, class, sexual orientation, and race do not have an effect on an instructor's ability to teach; only one's competency matters.

However, studies have shown that in addition to competence and enthusiasm, an instructor's personal characteristics do have an effect on the teaching process *for some* students (see Dukes and Victoria 1989: 448-50 for a review of this research). Most often, these are the same students who tend to be marginalized by the educational system.

Today's students increasingly come from diverse backgrounds, with different needs, expectations, identities, and beliefs. As instructors, we must pay attention to these differences and seek to understand the experiences of diverse groups if we are going to be able to build truly multicultural universities in the future. Attention to these dynamics allows for the development of rapport, which is a necessity for effective teaching (Dukes and Victoria 1989). "If we cannot communicate, we cannot teach or learn. If students' and instructors' worlds are galaxies apart, prospects are poor for effective instruction" (Goldsmid and Wilson 1980: 55). Lack of identification with instructors by students of color; by lesbian, bisexual, and gay students; and by women students often leads them to feel underappreciated, discouraged, disenfranchised, and alienated. Following W. I. Thomas's (1931: 189) prescription that "if human beings define situations as real, they are real in their consequences," I maintain that an instructor's gender, class, sexual orientation, and race do matter. Yet, students' perceptions, needs, and concerns involving these issues are rarely taken into account when instructors plan their courses and develop their teaching styles (Chasteen 1987).

In order to determine the effect of my personal characteristics on my ability to reach students, each term I asked them about this issue directly. Not surprisingly, the responses varied considerably. Many of the students felt that if I were committed to the issues, enthusiastic, and knowledgeable about the subject matter, they would have no problem learning with me. However, every term there was a significant minority of concerned students for whom my personal characteristics had an effect on their ability to identify and learn with me. Their concerns raise important questions about my ability, and the ability of instructors like me, to teach courses on inequality and oppression.

Conflict over My Personal Characteristics

> Tom, as a white, straight (tell me if I'm making an assumption there) male, only needs to think about the issue of racism, heterosexism, sexism, etc. only three to four hours a week, while a lesbian teaching about lesbian issues is thinking about and living heterosexism. A person of color needs to deal with this racist society every day. I guess I am not sure how a white male can relate to the oppression of others.

To me, this quote captures the lack of trust and the doubts about legitimacy I have often experienced as a white male teaching about inequality and oppression. These are two central dynamics of this issue that I confronted when teaching the course.

Trust

As a heterosexual, white, middle-class man, I am a representative of a social structure that oppresses other groups of people. Hence, from some students' perspectives, I have no business teaching others about being oppressed. Simply put, because I benefit from the current status quo, I am not to be trusted. It was difficult for me to hear such statements from students without feeling attacked and defensive. Yet, the questions and challenges regarding my personal characteristics are important because education relies, in large part, on trust. Trust cannot be expected, given the long history of relations between oppressed people and white academe. Trust must be earned, and there are particular practices that, if used, can help establish it. The following are some of the things that I used in the course to create or build upon incipient trust.

First, my willingness to discuss my characteristics helped to create a classroom environment where students were not afraid to challenge the instructor. To me, this indicated a nascent sense of trust, which allowed us to continue to explore these questions and issues throughout the term. It also indicated that students were thinking critically, which was one of the expressed goals of the course. For me not to entertain these questions would have had long-term ramifications for openness and trust. Through my willingness to discuss these issues, students' concerns were validated.

By taking students' challenges and concerns to heart, and by making it one of the expressed goals of the course [to openly] discuss these issues, I encouraged students to challenge me, each other, and themselves. Although this seemed to be outside the realm of experience for many students, over time I found that they grew more comfortable with the practice and learned that they could trust me and the other students not to get defensive or become punitive. In doing so, my commitment to their concerns became more apparent and the bases for trust were furthered.

Implicit in our ongoing dialogue was the question of whether I could transcend the interests of my own group to understand and empathetically identify with the experiences of other people. The students also questioned whether I was willing to confront my own privilege and power as both a white male and a professor. These are important questions to ask. I think the answers provide insight into determining whether white men are appropriate for teaching such courses. In class, I stressed that although white males of this generation may not have created the oppressive social system, we benefit from it and, as a result, must be held accountable and responsible to help bring about change. To me, the process of confronting this requires critical reflection on the ways in which I benefit from the current social structure. It also requires becoming conscious of the oppressive roles I have taken on and actively resisting the differential power and rewards that accompany such roles (Pease 1990). Confronting other men, especially white men because I am a white man, also becomes essential to this process and provides others with an excellent indication of where one's commitment lies.

However, I also realized that my words were not enough to satisfy some students. They wanted further proof to demonstrate my commitment. Similar to what Bob Pease (1990) experienced, my anti-oppression activities on campus indicated to students over time that I was not as suspect as they thought. However, that is not to say that all students came to trust me or were convinced, by the end of the course, of my convictions and abilities to teach the course.

Credibility or Legitimacy

The second major issue that I faced in teaching the course was credibility or legitimacy. The way in which concerned students in the course understood legitimacy meant that if one had experienced and, as a result, understood oppression such as sexism, only then was one capable of understanding other forms of oppression such as racism. As the following quotes indicate, some students felt that I was not appropriate to teach a course on oppression because, as a white, heterosexual, middle-class man, I have not experienced any of these forms of oppression.

In my opinion, Tom, you can teach the course from a technical standpoint, but you cannot relate to the situations or understand exactly how the oppressed and discriminated against feel.

I feel that you can be empathic, but you can never fully understand or relate to the oppressed, let alone sufficiently explain feelings, frustrations, and a variety of other emotions. Anyone can be technical, but only the oppressed group can better explain their standpoint, for they are the ones who are being oppressed.

The issue of credibility and legitimacy presents a more difficult problem than the lack of trust. It is impossible for me to experience systematic oppression. Hence, there was no way for me to become legitimate in some students' eyes. Knowing that I could not change this situation, I was challenged to try to mitigate the lack of credibility. I chose to start by being honest about my life experiences, especially the privileges I have encountered. This acknowledgment contributed to building trust within the classroom. I also stressed my belief that different people have different experiences and, as a result, have different perspectives. These different perspectives reflect our different realities. Hence, I noted that in order for us to learn from one another, all perspectives must be acknowledged and understood. This made room for a white male perspective and became a norm in the course for all students.

Second, I tried not to play the role of "expert"; rather, I continually stressed that we all had something to learn from each other. This action resulted in reducing the hierarchy of the classroom. It also alleviated any responsibility students might have thought that I had to convey everything about the different forms of oppression. Moreover, it meant that they had the responsibility to contribute what they knew about the subject matter. Three other related strategies were guest speakers, films, and literature. Through the use of "other voices," my legitimacy became a less significant issue.

Additionally, we changed the organization of the course over the three semesters to incorporate a diverse teaching team so that we differed by race, class, sexual orientation, and gender. This allowed students to identify with different members of the teaching team, thus alleviating some of the credibility issues.

Thus, people with characteristics such as mine face two (and from some perspectives, intractable) issues when teaching courses of this nature. The issue of trust seems to be a more easily overcome problem than the issue of legitimacy. Hence, different strategies need to be used to mitigate the latter's deleterious effects.

Larger Issues

There are larger considerations apart from the personal concerns of students. As part of the ongoing dialogue with the class, I challenged students to think in other ways about the questions they raised. This reinforced the practice of critical thinking and the belief that there are multiple perspectives on every issue. Given the concerned students' reasons that white males should not teach these types of courses, the following is my list of reasons why they should.

To begin by placing this in context, I firmly believe that more faculty representing oppressed groups are needed in academe. The situation presented by the course is clearly exacerbated by the limited number of such people teaching at universities. Having been traditionally marginalized by the academic profession, oppressed people have pursued other fields. For instance, according to a recent National Research Council report, the number of African Americans earning Ph.D.'s dropped 23 percent between 1979 and 1989 (Thurgood and Weinman 1990). Our department reflects this trend in the limited number of faculty of color whom we have. Despite our attempts, we have had a difficult time hiring faculty who represent oppressed groups. Recent labor market trends have placed such faculty in high demand. Consequently, it is also difficult to retain them once they are hired.

In addition, we need to confront the expectation that traditionally oppressed people should teach classes about inequality and oppression. This expectation places an undue burden on these instructors for several reasons. First, although it is often true, we should not assume that faculty representing oppressed groups strongly identify with their group. Second, why should these faculty be pressured to teach courses of this kind at the expense of their other teaching agendas? As a white instructor, I do not face the same expectations or burdens. I have always been allowed to teach in the areas in which I am interested rather than ones determined by the color of my skin, my sex and gender, my sexual orientation, or my social class. Third, because of their small numbers on college campuses, these individuals tend to be in high demand as role models, advisers, guest speakers, members of committees, and so on. These are extremely time-consuming obligations. Adding preconceived teaching expectations only exacerbates this problem. Fourth, to have only such faculty teach these classes lets

white faculty, especially white male faculty, off the hook. It sends a message that oppression is not a white problem and that white men do not have to confront the issues and problems raised in this chapter. However, oppression is not solely the problem of oppressed people; it is a white problem, too (Katz 1988; Chesler and Crowfoot 1990; McDavid 1988). White instructors, especially white male instructors, need to show more initiative in this area to reinforce the idea that oppression is everyone's problem and that we are all responsible for eradicating it. We thus have an opportunity to become role models for other white students and instructors who are trying to understand, take responsibility, and challenge their privileged positions (Beauchamp and Wheeler 1988; Pease 1990; Chesler and Crowfoot 1990; Folsom 1983; McDavid 1988).

My experience has been that another reason for white males to teach such courses is that my personal characteristics tended to lessen some white students' resistance to discussing these issues. In this regard, my viewpoint was seen as less threatening and was less easily dismissed by them. As Audre Lorde (1981) has noted, white people challenging other white people evokes much less guilt and defensiveness on the part of whites, and as a result they get a better hearing. This dynamic is evidenced by the following two quotes from students:

Another thing I liked that other people complained about was having a white male professor and teaching assistant (T.A.). It made me feel like the opinions were not biased. I think I would have had the attitude that, of course, you are going to say what you are saying. Since you are black, a woman, a homosexual, or whatever, you would tell me you are oppressed since you would have something to gain by making myself and others believe that. Which, when I look at it, is probably a racist, sexist, and homophobic thing to say, but that is how my thinking was when the class started.

Although he is a white, young, upper class, heterosexual man, I believe that fact may actually serve to somewhat validate his claims to some students, who are used to learning and accepting what comes from people with those same characteristics.

The above quotes suggest that white students may have difficulty relating to faculty who are different from themselves. While I am glad that I was able to reach these students, I am also troubled by the fact that my co-teachers may have been seen as biased. As Peggy McIntosh (1988) and Jack Folsom (1983) have reported, I did not totally succeed in creating an environment where persons of color, women, lesbians, bisexuals, and gay men could speak with as much credibility as a white male. I will continue to struggle with this, knowing that it is a reflection of a larger societal dynamic but an important one to continue to challenge.

Finally, teaching a course on oppression provides white faculty, especially white men, an opportunity to grow as instructors and as people. As Louis Kampf and Dick Ohmann (1983) report, participation in teaching about oppression can be a process of self-education and consciousness raising. Richard Bach once said, "You teach best what you need most to learn" (Bach 1977: 48), and this course will continue to provide me with an excellent opportunity to challenge myself and the values and beliefs that I have internalized. In addition, it will provide me with the stimulation and the environment necessary to question and challenge the privilege and power that accrue to me solely on the basis of my personal characteristics.

Summary

These are some of the salient issues surrounding instructor orientation, the learning process, and

courses on social inequality and oppression. The issues I raise were raised in the course as we struggled with the question of who should teach whom about what. Some, but not all, of the concerned students agreed with me at the end of the course that white men could and should teach such courses. Despite the lack of consensus, we were much more informed about the different perspectives that exist on this issue, and much learning occurred. To me, this has remained an important outcome of the course.

To return to the first question in the title of this chapter, namely, whether white, heterosexual, middle-class men should teach about social inequality and oppression, I argue strongly yes. In doing so, white men indicate that oppression is also a white male problem, they become role models for other white faculty and students, they challenge the belief that only oppressed people should teach about oppression, and they are provided with an ongoing opportunity to explore and confront the privilege that accrues to them on the basis of their sex, sexual orientation, skin color, and class. As to whether white, heterosexual, middle-class men can teach students about oppression, I give a more qualified yes. If a white man is willing to confront his status and privilege and to continue to challenge himself as well as the class, then he is in a position to teach such a course. This entails the use of numerous strategies aimed at creating trust and mitigating the lack of legitimacy that white males tend to encounter based on their lack of experience of oppression.

Notes

I am indebted to Tracy Ore, Mark Freyberg, and Kim Simmons for the many insights that came out of our conversations as we struggled with how best to teach this course. Additionally, I am indebted to Lynda Duke, Mark Chesler, and David Schoem, who reviewed earlier drafts of this chapter and helped shape its ideas.

Notes

1. All quotes come from course critiques or from the course computer conference.

2. I did not teach this course alone. I taught with two other persons, who were responsible for the small group meetings. Because my responsibilities included the large lecture section, I was identified by the students as the primary instructor.

References

Bach, Richard. 1977. *Illusions*. New York: Delacorte Press.

Beauchamp, Bill and Bonnie Wheeler. 1988. "From Achilles to the Heel: Teaching Masculinity." *Women's Studies Quarterly,* Fall/Winter, Volume XVI, Numbers 3 & 4, pp. 100-111.

Chasteen, Ed. 1987. "Balancing Cognitive and the Affective in Teaching Race Relations." *Teaching Sociology,* January, Volume 15, pp. 80-81.

Chesler, Mark and James Crowfoot. 1990. "Racism in Higher Education. I: An Organizational Analysis." Program in Conflict Management Alternatives, Working Paper #21, University of Michigan.

Dukes, Richard L. and Gay Victoria. 1989. "The Effects of Gender, Status, and Effective Teaching on the Evaluation of College Instruction." *Teaching Sociology,* October, Volume 17, pp. 447-457.

Folsom, Jack. 1983. "Teaching about Sexism and Language in a Traditional Setting." *Women's Studies Quarterly,* Spring, Volume XI, Number 1, pp. 12-15.

Goldsmid, Charles A. and Everett K. Wilson. 1980. *Passing on Sociology*. Washington, D.C.: American Sociological Association.

Kampf, Louis and Dick Ohmann. 1983. "Men in Women's Studies." *Women's Studies Quarterly,* Spring, Volume XI, Number 1, pp. 9-11.

Katz, Judith. 1988. "Facing the Challenge of Diversity and Multiculturalism." Program in Conflict Management Alternatives, Working Paper #13, University of Michigan.

Lorde, Audre. 1981. "An Open Letter to Mary Daly," in *This Bridge Called My Back,* edited by C. Moraga and G. Anzaldua. Watertown, MA: Persephone Press, pp. 94-97.

McDavid, Alex. 1988. "Feminism for Men: 101 Educating Men in 'Women's Studies'." *Feminist Teacher,* Fall/Winter, Volume 3, Number 3, pp. 25-33.

National Association of Scholars. 1988. *Is the Curriculum Biased? A Statement of the National Association of Scholars*. Princeton, N.J.: National Association of Scholars.

Pease, Bob. 1990. "Challenging Domination in Social Work Education." Paper presented at the 25th International Conference of Schools of Social Work, Lima, Peru, August 16-20.

Short, Thomas. 1988. " 'Diversity' and 'Breaking the Disciplines': Two New Assaults on the Curriculum." *Academic Questions,* Summer, Vol. 1, No. 3, pp. 6-29.

Thomas. W. I. 1931. "The Relation of Research to Social Process," in *Essays on Research in the Social Sciences*. Washington, D.C.: Brookings Institute, pp. 186-197.

Thurgood, Delores M. and Joann W. Weinman. 1990. *Summary Report 1989, Doctorate Recipients from United States Universities*. Washington, D.C.: National Academy Press.

45

Why Doesn't This Feel Empowering? Working through the Repressive Myths of Critical Pedagogy

Elizabeth Ellsworth

Have We Got a Theory for You!

As educators who claim to be dedicated to ending oppression, critical pedagogues have acknowledged the socially constructed and legitimated authority that teachers/professors hold over students.[1] Yet theorists of critical pedagogy have failed to launch any meaningful analysis of or program for reformulating the institutionalized power imbalances between themselves and their students or of the essentially paternalistic project of education itself. In the absence of such an analysis and program, their efforts are limited to trying to transform negative effects of power imbalances within the classroom into positive ones. Strategies such as student empowerment and dialogue give the illusion of equality while in fact leaving the authoritarian nature of the teacher-student relationship intact.

"Empowerment" is a key concept in this approach, which treats the symptoms but leaves

AUTHOR'S NOTE: This is a reprint of an article originally published as Ellsworth, Elizabeth, "Why Doesn't This Feel Empowering? Working through the Repressive Myths of Critical Pedagogy," in *Feminism and Critical Pedagogy*, edited by Carmen Luke and Jennifer Gore (Routledge), 1992. pp. 98-105. Used with permission.

the disease unnamed and untouched. Critical pedagogies employing this strategy prescribe various theoretical and practical means for sharing, giving, or redistributing power to students. For example, some authors challenge teachers to reject the vision of education as inculcation of students by the more powerful teacher. In its place, they urge teachers to accept the possibility of education through "reflective examination" of the plurality of moral positions before the presumably rational teacher and students.[2] Here, the goal is to give students the analytical skills they need to make them as free, rational, and objective as teachers supposedly are to choose positions on their objective merits. I have already argued that in a classroom in which "empowerment" is made dependent on rationalism, those perspectives that would question the political interests (sexism, racism, colonialism, for example) expressed and guaranteed by rationalism would be rejected as "irrational" (biased, partial).

A second strategy is to make the teacher more like the student by redefining the teacher as learner of the student's reality and knowledge. For example, in their discussion of the politics of dialogic teaching and epistemology, Shor and Freire suggest that "the teacher selecting the objects of study knows them better than the students as the course begins, but the teacher re-learns the objects through studying them with their students."[3] The literature explores only one reason for expecting the teacher to "re-learn" an object of study through the student's less adequate understanding, and that is to enable the teacher to devise more effective strategies for bringing the student "up" to the teacher's level of understanding. Giroux, for example, argues for a pedagogy that "is attentive to the histories, dreams, and experiences that . . . students bring to school. It is only by beginning with these subjective forms that critical educators can develop a language and set of practices"[4] that can successfully mediate differences between student understandings and teacher understandings in "pedagogically progressive" ways.[5] In this example, Giroux leaves the implied superiority of the teacher's understanding and the undefined "progressiveness" of this type of pedagogy unproblematized and untheorized.

A third strategy is to acknowledge the "directiveness"[6] or "authoritarianism"[7] of education as inevitable and [to] judge particular power imbalances between teacher and student to be tolerable or intolerable depending upon "towards what and with whom [they are] directive."[8] "Acceptable" imbalances are those in which authority serves "common human interests by sharing information, promoting open and informed discussion, and maintaining itself only through the respect and trust of those who grant the authority."[9] In such cases, authority becomes "emancipatory authority," a kind of teaching in which teachers would make explicit and available for rationalist debate "the political and moral referents for authority they assume in teaching particular forms of knowledge, in taking stands against forms of oppression, and in treating students as if they ought also to be concerned about social justice and political action."[10] Here, the question of "empowerment for what" becomes the final arbiter of a teacher's use or misuse of authority.

But critical pedagogues consistently answer the question of "empowerment for what?" in ahistorical and depoliticized abstractions. These include empowerment for "human betterment,"[11] for expanding "the range of possible social identities people may become,"[12] and "making one's self present as part of a moral and political project that links production of meaning to the possibility for human agency, democratic community, and transformative social action."[13] As a result, student empowerment has been defined in the broadest possible humanistic terms and becomes a "capacity to act effectively" in a way that fails to challenge any identifiable social or political position, institution, or group.

The contortions of logic and rhetoric that characterize these attempts to define "empowerment" testify to the failure of critical educators to come to terms with the essentially paternalistic project of traditional education. "Emancipatory authority"[14] is one such contortion, for it implies the presence of, or potential for, an emancipated teacher. Indeed, it asserts that teachers "can link knowledge to power by bringing to light and teaching the subjugated histories, experiences, stories, and accounts of those who suffer and struggle."[15] Yet I cannot unproblematically bring subjugated knowledges to light when I am not free of my own learned racism, fat oppression, classism, ableism, or sexism. No teacher is free of these learned and internalized oppressions. Nor are accounts of one group's suffering and struggle immune from reproducing narratives oppressive to another's—the racism of the women's movement in the United States is one example.

As I argued above, "emancipatory authority" also implies, according to Shor and Freire, a teacher who knows the object of study "better" than do the students. In fact, I understood racism no better than my students did, especially those students of color coming into class after six months (or more) of campus activism and whole lives of experience and struggle against racism—nor could I ever hope to. My experiences with and access to multiple and sophisticated strategies for interpreting and interrupting sexism (in white middle-class contexts) do not provide me with a ready-made analysis of or language for understanding my own implications in racist structures. My understanding and experience of racism will always be constrained by my white skin and middle-class privilege. Indeed, it is impossible for anyone to be free from these oppressive formations at this historical moment. Furthermore, while I had the institutional power and authority in the classroom to enforce "reflective examination" of the plurality of moral and political positions before us in a way that supposedly gave my own assessments equal weight with those of students, in fact my institutional role as professor would always weight my statements differently from those of students.

Given my own history of white skin, middle-class, able-bodied, thin privilege and my institutionally granted power, it made more sense to see my task as one of redefining "critical pedagogy" so that it did not need utopian moments of "democracy," "equality," "justice," or "emancipated" teachers—moments that are unattainable (and ultimately undesirable, because they are always predicated on the interests of those who are in the position to define utopian projects). A preferable goal seemed to be to become capable of a sustained encounter with currently oppressive formations and power relations that refuse to be theorized away or fully transcended in a utopian resolution— and to enter into the encounter in a way that both acknowledged my own implications in those formations and was capable of changing

my own relation to and investments in those formations.

The Repressive Myth of the Silent Other

At first glance, the concept of "student voice" seemed to offer a pedagogical strategy in this direction. This concept has become highly visible and influential in current discussions of curriculum and teaching, as evidenced by its appearance in the tides of numerous presentations at the 1989 American Educational Research Association Convention. Within current discourses on teaching, it functions to efface the contradiction between the emancipatory project of critical pedagogy and the hierarchical relation between teachers and students. In other words, it is a strategy for negotiating between the directiveness of dominant educational relationships and the political commitment to make students autonomous of those relationships (how does a teacher "make" students autonomous without directing them?). The discourse on student voice sees [students] as "empowered" when the teacher "helps" students to express their subjugated knowledges.[16] The targets of this strategy are students from disadvantaged and subordinated social class, racial, ethnic, and gender groups—or alienated middle-class students, without access to skills of critical analysis, whose voices have been silenced or distorted by oppressive cultural and educational formations. By speaking, in their "authentic voices," students are seen to make themselves visible and [to] define themselves as authors of their own world. Such self-definition presumably gives students an identity and political position from which to act as agents of social change.[17] Thus, while it is true that the teacher is directive, the student's own daily life experiences of oppression chart her/his path toward self-definition and agency. The task of the critical educator thus becomes "finding ways of working with students that enable the full expression of multiple 'voices' engaged in dialogic encounter,"[18] encouraging students of different race, class, and gender positions to speak in self-affirming ways about their experiences and how they have been mediated by their own social positions and those of others.

Within feminist discourses seeking to provide both a place and power for women to speak, "voice" and "speech" have become commonplace as metaphors for women's feminist self-definitions—but with meanings and effects quite different from those implied by discourses of critical pedagogy. Within feminist movements, women's voices and speech are conceptualized in terms of self-definitions that are oppositional to those definitions of women constructed by others, usually to serve interests and contexts that subordinate women to men. But while critical educators acknowledge the existence of unequal power relations in classrooms, they have made no systematic examination of the barriers that this imbalance creates for the kind of student expression and dialogue they prescribe.

The concept of critical pedagogy assumes a commitment on the part of the professor/teacher toward ending the student's oppression. Yet the literature offers no sustained attempt to problematize this stance and confront the likelihood that the professor brings to social movements (including critical pedagogy) interests of her or his own race, class, ethnicity, gender, and other positions. S/he does not play the role of disinterested mediator on the side of the oppressed group.[19] As an Anglo, middle-class professor, I could not unproblematically "help" a student of color to find her/his authentic voice as a student of color. I could not unproblematically "affiliate" with the social groups my students represent and inter-

pret their experience to them. In fact, I brought to the classroom privileges and interests that were put at risk in fundamental ways by the demands and defiances of student voices. I brought a social subjectivity that has been constructed in such a way that I have not and can never participate unproblematically in the collective process of self-definition, naming of oppression, and struggles for visibility in the face of marginalization engaged in by students whose class, race, gender, and other positions I do not share. Critical pedagogues are always implicated in the very structures they are trying to change.

Although the literature recognizes that teachers have much to learn from their students' experiences, it does not address the ways in which there are things that I, as a professor, could *never know* about the experiences, oppressions, and understandings of other participants in the class. This situation makes it impossible for any single voice in the classroom—including that of the professor—to assume the position of center or origin of knowledge or authority, of having privileged access to authentic experience or appropriate language. A recognition, contrary to all Western ways of knowing and speaking, that all knowings are partial, that there are fundamental things each of us cannot know—a situation alleviated only in part by the pooling of partial, socially constructed knowledges in classrooms—demands a fundamental retheorizing of "education" and "pedagogy," an issue I will begin to address below.

When educational researchers writing about critical pedagogy fail to examine the implications of the gendered, raced, and classed teacher and student for the theory of critical pedagogy, they reproduce, by default, the category of generic "critical teacher"—a specific form of the generic human that underlies classical liberal thought. Like the generic human, the generic critical teacher is not, of course, generic at all. Rather, the term defines a discursive category predicated on the current mythical norm, namely: young, white, Christian, middle-class, heterosexual, able-bodied, thin, rational man. Gender, race, class, and other differences become only variations on or additions to the generic human—"underneath, we are all the same."[20] But voices of students and professors of difference solicited by critical pedagogy are not additions to that norm but oppositional challenges that require a dismantling of the mythical norm and its uses as well as alternatives to it. There has been no consideration of how voices of, for example, white women, students of color, disabled students, white men against masculinist culture, and fat students will necessarily be constructed in opposition to the teacher/institution when they try to change the power imbalances they inhabit in their daily lives in schools.

Critical pedagogues speak of student voices as "sharing" their experiences and understandings of oppression with other students and with the teacher in the interest of "expanding the possibilities of what it is to be human."[21] Yet white women, women of color, men of color, white men against masculinist culture, fat people, gay men and lesbians, people with disabilities, and Jews do not speak of the oppressive formations that condition their lives in the spirit of "sharing." Rather, the speech of oppositional groups is a "talking back," a "defiant speech"[22] that is constructed within communities of resistance and is a condition of survival.

In [the class], the defiant speech of students and professor of difference constituted fundamental challenges to and rejections of the voices of some classmates and often of the professor. For example, it became clear very quickly that in order to name her experience of racism, a Chicana student had to define her voice in part through opposition to—and rejection of—definitions of "Chicana" assumed or taken for granted by other student/professor voices in the classroom. And in the context of protests by students of color against racism on campus, her voice had to be constructed in opposition to the institutional racism of the university's curriculum and policies—which were represented in part by my discourses and actions as Anglo-American, middle-class woman professor. Unless we found a way to respond to such challenges, our academic and political work against racism would be blocked. This alone is a reason for finding a way to express and engage with student voices, one that distances itself from the abstract, philosophical reasons implied by the literature on critical pedagogy when it fails to contextualize its projects. Furthermore, grounding the expression of and engagement with student voices in the need to construct contextualized political strategies rejects both the voyeuristic relation that the literature reproduces when the voice of the professor is not problematized and the instrumental role critical pedagogy plays when student voice is used to inform more effective teaching strategies.

The lessons learned from feminist struggles to make a difference through defiant speech offer both useful critiques of the assumptions of critical pedagogy and starting points for moving beyond its repressive myth.[23] Within feminist movements, self-defining feminist voices have been understood as constructed collectively in the context of a larger feminist movement or women's marginalized subcultures.

Feminist voices are made possible by the interactions among women within and across race, class, and other differences that divide them. These voices have never been solely or even primarily the result of a pedagogical interaction between an individual student and a teacher. Yet discourses of the pedagogy of empowerment consistently position students as individuals with only the most abstract of relations to concrete contexts of struggle. In their writing about critical pedagogy, educational researchers consistently place teachers/professors at the center of the consciousness-raising activity. For example, McLaren describes alienated middle-class youth in this way:

These students do not recognize their own self-representation and suppression by the dominant society, and in our vitiated learning environments they are not provided with the requisite theoretical constructs to help them understand why they feel as [bad] as they do. Because teachers lack a critical pedagogy, these students are not provided with the ability to think critically, a skill that would enable them to better understand why their lives have been reduced to feelings of meaningless, randomness, and alienation.[24]

In contrast, many students came into "Media and Anti-Racist Pedagogies" with oppositional voices already formulated within various antiracism and other movements. These movements had not necessarily relied on intellectuals/teachers to interpret their goals and programs to themselves or to others.

Current writing by many feminists working from antiracism and feminist poststructuralist perspectives recognizes that any individual woman's politicized voice will be partial, multiple, and contradictory.[25] The literature on critical pedagogy also recognizes the possibility that each student will be capable of identifying a multiplicity of authentic voices in her/himself. But it does not confront the ways in which any individual student's voice is already a "teeth-gritting" and often contradictory intersection of voices constituted by gender, race, class, ability, ethnicity, sexual orientation, or ideology. Nor does it engage with the fact that the particularities of historical context, personal biography, and subjectivities split between the conscious and unconscious will necessarily render each expression of student voice partial and predicated on the absence and marginalization

of alternative voices. It is impossible to speak from all voices at once, or from any one, without the traces of the others being present and interruptive. Thus the very term "student voice" is highly problematic. Pluralizing the concept as "voices" implies correction through addition. This loses sight of the contradictory and partial nature of all voices.

In [the class], for example, participants expressed much pain, confusion, and difficulty in speaking, because of the ways in which discussions called up their multiple and contradictory social positionings. Women found it difficult to prioritize expressions of racial privilege and oppression when such prioritizing threatened to perpetuate their gender oppression. Among international students, both those who were of color and those who were white found it difficult to join their voices with those of U.S. students of color when it meant a subordination of their oppression as people living under U.S. imperialist policies and as students for whom English was a second language. Asian American women found it difficult to join their voices with other students of color when it meant subordinating their specific oppressions as Asian Americans. I found it difficult to speak as a white woman about gender oppression when I occupied positions of institutional power relative to all students in the class, men and women, but positions of gender oppression relative to students who were white men and, in different terms, relative to students who were men of color.

Finally, the argument that women's speech and voice have not been and should not be constructed primarily for the purpose of communicating women's experiences to men is commonplace within feminist movements. This position takes the purposes of such speech to be survival, expansion of women's own understandings of their oppression and strength, sharing common experiences among women, building solidarity among women, and political strategizing. Many feminists have pointed to the necessity for men to "do their own work" at unlearning sexism and male privilege rather than looking to women for the answers. I am similarly suspicious of the desire by the mostly white, middle-class men who write the literature on critical pedagogy to elicit "full expression" of student voices. Such a relation between teacher [and] student becomes voyeuristic when the voice of the pedagogue himself goes unexamined.

Furthermore, the assumption present in the literature that silence in front of a teacher or professor indicates "lost voice," "voicelessness," or lack of social identity from which to act as a social agent betrays deep and unacceptable gender, race, and class biases. It is worth quoting bell hooks at length about the fiction of the silence of subordinated groups:

Within feminist circles, silence is often seen as the sexist defined "right speech of womanhood"—the sign of woman's submission to patriarchal authority. This emphasis on woman's silence may be an accurate remembering of what has taken place in the households of women from white Anglo-Saxon Protestant (WASP) backgrounds in the United States, but in black communities (and in other diverse ethnic communities) women have not been silent. Their voices can be heard. Certainly for black women, our struggle has not been to emerge from silence to speech but to change the nature and direction of our speech. To make a speech that compels listeners, one that is heard. . . . Dialogue, the sharing of speech and recognition, took place not between mother and child or [between] mother and male authority figure, but with other black women. I can remember watching, fascinated, as our mother talked with her mother, sisters, and women friends. The intimacy and intensity of their speech—the satisfaction they received from talking to one another, the pleasure, the joy. It was in this world of woman speech, loud talk, angry words, women with tongues sharp, tender sweet tongues, touching our world with their words, that I made speech my birthright—and the right to voice, to authorship, a privilege I would not

be denied. It was in that world and because of it that I came to dream of writing, to write.[26]

White women, men and women of color, impoverished people, people with disabilities, gays and lesbians, are not silenced in the sense implied by the literature on critical pedagogy. They are not talking in their authentic voices, or they are declining/refusing to talk at all, to critical educators who have been unable to acknowledge the presence of knowledges that are challenging and most likely inaccessible to their own social positions. What they/we say, to whom, in what context, depending on the energy they/we have for the struggle on a particular day, is the result of conscious and unconscious assessments of the power relations and safety of the situation.

As I understand it at the moment, what got said—and how—in our class was the product of highly complex strategizing for the visibility that speech gives without giving up the safety of silence. More than that, it was a highly complex negotiation of the politics of knowing and being known. Things were left unsaid, or they were encoded, on the basis of speakers' conscious and unconscious assessments of the risks and costs of disclosing their understandings of themselves and of others. To what extent had students occupying socially constructed positions of privilege at a particular moment risked being known by students occupying socially constructed positions of subordination at the same moment? To what extent had students in those positions of privilege relinquished the security and privilege of being the knower?[27]

As long as the literature on critical pedagogy fails to come to grips with issues of trust, risk, and the operations of fear and desire around such issues of identity and politics in the classroom, their rationalistic tools will continue to fail to loosen deep-seated, self-interested investments in unjust relations of, for example, gender, ethnicity, and sexual orientation.[28] These investments are shared by both teachers and students, yet the literature on critical pedagogy has ignored its own implications for the young, white, Christian, middle-class, heterosexual, able-bodied man/pedagogue that it assumes. Against such ignoring, Mohanty argues that to desire to ignore is not cognitive but performative. It is the incapacity or refusal "to acknowledge one's own implication in the information."[29] "[Learning] involves a necessary implication in the radical alterity of the unknown, in the desire(s) not to know, in the process of this unresolvable dialectic."[30]

Notes

1. Nicholas C. Burbules, "A theory of power in education," *Educational Theory,* 36 (Spring 1986), pp. 95-114; H. Giroux and P. McLaren, "Teacher education and the politics of engagement: The case for democratic schooling," *Harvard Educational Review* 56 (1986), pp. 213-227.

2. D. P. Liston and K. M. Zeichner, "Critical pedagogy and teacher education," *Journal of Education* 169 (1987), p. 120.

3. I. Shor and P. Freire, "What is the 'dialogical method' of teaching?" *Journal of Education* 169 (1981), pp. 11-31.

4. Henry Giroux, "Radical pedagogy and the politics of student voice," *Interchange* 17 (1986), pp. 48-69.

5. Ibid., p. 66.

6. Shor and Freire, "What is the 'dialogical method' of teaching?," p. 22.

7. Burbules, "A theory of power in education"; Giroux and McLaren, "Teacher education and the politics of engagement," pp. 224-227.

8. Shor and Freire, "What is the 'dialogical method' of teaching?," p. 23.

9. Burbules, "A theory of power in education," p. 108.

10. Giroux and McLaren, "Teacher education and the politics of engagement," p. 226.

11. Walter C. Parker, "Justice, social studies, and the subjectivity/structure problem," *Theory and Research in Social Education* 14 (Fall 1986), p. 227.

12. R. Simon, "Empowerment as a pedagogy of possibility," *Language Arts* 2 (1987), pp. 370-382.

13. Giroux, "Literacy and the pedagogy of voice," pp. 68-69.

14. Giroux and McLaren, "Teacher education and the politics of engagement," p. 225.

15. Ibid., p. 227.

16. Shor and Freire, "What is the 'dialogical method' of teaching?" p. 30; Liston and Zeichner, "Critical pedagogy," p. 122.

17. Simon, "Empowerment as a pedagogy of possibility," p. 380.

18. Ibid., p. 375.

19. S. Aronowitz, "Postmodernism and politics," *Social Text* 18 (Winter 1987/1988), pp. 99-115.

20. L. Alcoff, "Cultural feminism versus post-structuralism: The identity crisis in feminist theory," *Signs* 13 (1988), pp. 405-436.

21. Simon, "Empowerment as a pedagogy of possibility," p. 372.

22. bell hooks, "Talking back," *Discourse* 8 (Fall/Winter 1986/1987), pp. 123-128.

23. bell hooks, "Pedagogy and political commitment: A comment," in *Talking back: Thinking feminist, thinking black,* ed. bell hooks (Boston: South End Press, 1989), pp. 98-104.

24. Peter McLaren, *Life in schools* (New York: Longman, 1989), p. 18.

25. Alcoff, "Cultural feminism versus post-structuralism"; G. Anzaldua, *Borderlands/La Frontera: The new mestiza* (San Francisco: Spinster/Aunt Lute, 1987); T. de Lauretis, ed., *Feminist studies/critical studies* (Bloom-

ington: Indiana University Press, 1986); hooks, *Talking back;* Trihn T. Minh-ha, *Woman, native, other* (Bloomington: Indiana University Press, 1989); C. Weedon, *Feminist practice and post-structuralist theory* (New York: Basil Blackwell, 1987).

26. hooks, *Talking back,* p. 124.

27. Susan Hardy Aiken, Karen Anderson, Myra Dinerstein, Judy Lensink, and Patricia MacCorquodale, "Trying transformations: Curriculum integration and the problem of resistance," *Signs* 12 (Winter 1987), pp. 225-275.

28. Ibid., p. 263.

29. Shoshana Felman, "Psychoanalysis and education: Teaching terminable and interminable," *Yale French Studies* 63 (1982), pp. 21-44.

30. S. P. Mohanty, "Radical teaching, radical theory: The ambiguous politics of meaning," in *Theory in the classroom,* ed. Cary Nelson (Urbana: University of Illinois Press, 1986), p. 155.

46

View from the Inside: The Disabling Structures of Graduate Education

Brian Ault

Research university faculty looking for reasons why their chosen discipline at times might seem in disarray, or why it is not quite as "good as it used to be," frequently target graduate programs as the source of malaise. Too often, they believe that a decline in the quality of graduate students over time has been the primary reason for disciplinary decline (Lipset 1994; Blalock 1987). As a graduate student, I would like to take issue with the individualistic assumption about the poorer quality of contemporary graduate students, their lack of "success," and the implications for teaching and training.

It is my contention that this line of reasoning is nothing more than a canard, a simplistically convenient and consistently used piece of explanatory overstatement. It fails to consider the process or structure of graduate education, which I would like to examine as a grad student in the midst of this professional training. To be sure, there might be students admitted who are comparatively "marginal" depending on the chosen evaluative standards (just as there are "marginal" faculty depending on the gauge, e.g., teaching evaluations). However, if success is defined as completion of one's program, then a recent study suggests that graduate record exam scores and grade point averages have little predictive power in explaining success relative to other factors (Wood and Wong 1992).

In light of this, it might be argued that faculty admissions committees are performing poorly and that the array of criteria employed by committees is insufficient to determine who has the best potential to succeed.

Despite what I am sure have been good faith and inventive efforts to perfect the analytical process of evaluating applicants, I maintain that the focus and analytical energies have been misapplied. The "poorer" student line of argumentation is an example of teleological reasoning. Proponents jump from an empirical outcome (lack of graduate student success) to a seemingly plausible, causally antecedent condition (the decline in the quality of graduate students themselves). This "causality" ignores the intervening process, namely *graduate education.*

The structural realities of graduate programs are, at best, very quietly acknowledged or, at worst, completely ignored in this debate. A worst-case speculation would hold that the vested interests of all scholars produced by "the system" mitigate against critical structural self-evaluation. I would like to think more kindly that most faculty are too busy with the myriad demands on their time to rigorously scrutinize the structure of their own graduate programs.

A more compelling argument suggests that the causal explanation for graduate student failure is more complex, owing to an interaction between individual student and the structural realities of the research university. In contrast to more individualistic explanations, I argue that the structure of graduate programs at research universities constitutes the *major* source for graduate student failure. Specifically, factors such as the demographic and experiential mismatch between faculty and students, the organizational and professional realities of departments within research universities, and insufficient training foster the success of some and set up expectations of failure for others. Furthermore, by extension, it produces scholars—the stars rising above the mass of "marginal" students—who in turn contribute to the perceived disciplinary decline. What are the structural dynamics that fuel graduate student dropout rates and produce atomized scholars with seemingly little concern beyond their own research agendas? In what follows, I explore some of the modal aspects of this structural reality as I perceive them. I use my chosen discipline of sociology as an example.

The Mismatched Social Worlds of Faculty and Students

In the past 15 years, the usual entering cohort to a sociology grad program has been increasingly more female, rising from 50 percent female in 1980 to 55 percent in 1987, to 59 percent in 1991. In addition, the percentage of full-time graduate students in doctorate-granting institutions reported as being "foreign" increased from 17 percent in 1980 to 27 percent in 1987. The percentage of minority students receiving sociology Ph.D.'s fluctuated between 10 and 12 percent from 1977 to 1988.

What is the composition of the sociology professorate? Although I do not have data on the professorate by race/ethnicity, I can offer some on gender by rank. Kulis (1988) reports data in 1984 showing that the percentages of full, associate, and assistant professors in sociology who were female were 9, 23, and 40 percent, respectively (p. 209). More recent data have these same percentages at 18, 30, and 46 percent (American Sociological Association 1992). I suspect that data for sociology faculty by race/ethnicity would reveal even smaller percentages of "faculty of color" in the higher ranks, with the best representation being found in the rank of assistant professor. These numbers, however, have been changing and should continue to do so into the next century (Eitzen 1991).

Thus, demographic changes in the composition of sociology graduate students have not been paralleled as quickly by those in the professorate. Given that tenured faculty more often closely "guide," "direct," or "mentor" graduate students through their programs and theses (in most departments, untenured faculty are not allowed to serve as committee chairs), we have had, and currently still have, a compositional, experiential disjuncture between many faculty and graduate students.

A number of accounts have been written about being a minority student within grad program structures that are "gendered," "raced," and "classed" to privilege the dominant group (cf. Cuadraz and Pierce 1994; Rendon 1992; Paludi 1991; Reinharz 1984; Blackwell and Janowitz 1974). From their marginalized positions within this process, these student stories shed light on the interaction between a student's "being," however constituted, and a particular program's structural demands. Any new graduate student who falls outside the boundaries of the dominant groups is almost immediately "at risk." Egan (1989) maintains that, in contrast to a belief that graduate education in sociology is "add-on" socialization, what happens is actually resocialization. The institutional forces of graduate programs subjugate all other personal statuses, orientations, and belief systems (e.g., mother, activist, African American) to that of graduate student, professional scholar-in-training. From this vantage point, the resocialization process is fraught with potential negative social psychological ramifications, depending on a student's expectations, self-image, and prior experiences.

Whatever the field, graduate education is not, by and large, different in this respect. Even in medical school, the identity-shaping processes of such "total" institutions share commonalities (for a balanced appraisal of how "total" graduate school is as an institution, see Goodman 1989). The very important contribution Egan (1989) has made seems to me to be in expanding the insights first made by minority students recounting their experiences of graduate school. Egan argues that anyone who by necessity, belief, and the like must embrace several cogent identities (some of which might not be labeled "minority" as such) might be at odds with the structured, monolithic, unidimensional status of graduate student. As a result, those "at risk" and those "at odds" are more prone to failure.

Organizational Imperatives and the Implicit Tournament Model

Another set of forces at work are those of an organizational nature, where professional standards intersect with the bureaucratized context of departments existing within American research universities in the late 20th century (Rau and Baker 1989). Crothers (1991) maintains

that "university departmental structures remain distinctly feudal." This view is only partially correct because it ignores significant historical developments in the evolution of research universities.

Universities *have* changed over time in respect to adopting certain corporate qualities, techniques, and strategies that are to function to make the university-as-organization more efficient in times of scarce resources. This organizational isomorphism (Dimaggio and Powell 1983) is not surprising given that the university, for all that it is, does exist in part as an economic entity within a capitalist economy. How do the organizational factors related to these larger social forces work to impede graduate student success?

Faculty reward structures, the departmental generation of adequate numbers of graduate "FTEs"[1] (full-time equivalents), and the amount and duration of graduate student funding all structurally may come together to produce high rates of failure among students in successive cohorts. Aldous (1989) addresses some of these factors in the context of graduate education.[2] The two most salient factors she cites are the "number of students in each year's graduate cohort" and the "evaluation criteria used for faculty advancement" (p. 215). I say more about evaluation criteria in a later section on training, but first, I discuss cohort size. For Aldous, larger cohorts benefit graduate students by (1) increasing the chances of finding other students with similar interests, thus creating long-lasting support networks; (2) enhancing students' departmental power in taking stands on particular issues of concern; and (3) lessening the pressure and demands that students in small cohorts feel in working many hours fulfilling stipend requirements. Aldous maintains that from a departmental perspective, the ability to recruit large cohorts decreases the political infighting and jockeying for those students identified as outstanding or especially promising.

This particular factor relates to the "departmental generation of FTEs" cited earlier. Although it may be true that students have a greater chance to find fellow students of like persuasions, what about finding professors of the same ilk with the time, energy, and willingness to engage yet another new student? With a constant stream of 13 to 15 new faces per year, each looking for quality (and quantity) mentoring time, a finite faculty (a shrinking or static number in these economic times) will have difficulty adequately and properly mentoring an ever increasing advisee load (especially given that the number of years to completion has crept upward to somewhere in the 8- to 10-year range).

A grad program, any program of considerable size, must have sufficient graduate bodies to "make ends meet" and to justify its program offerings. This pressure is most often external to the department, with top-level administrators (e.g., deans, vice presidents) as the source. As a result, some number of graduate students are sacrificed through this organized economic imperative as "FTE fodder." In sum, there are not enough professors with enough time to provide each and every graduate student with an intensive research apprenticeship opportunity.

Sacrificing of students is consonant with a "tournament" model of graduate education (Rosenbaum 1986; Turner 1960). Admission and retention programs often are based on "survival of the fittest," with an assumption that the wheat will separate from the chaff. This model provides more students with the initial opportunity to compete, with many fewer to be "chosen" for the Ph.D. and even fewer for the professorate. More troubling, perhaps, is that although this model may be implicitly or explicitly assumed by faculty, it rarely is publicly presented to graduate students in such honestly stark terms. Most graduate students, as a result of gaining admittance, feel academically worthy and assume that equal structural opportunity and sufficient mentoring will ensure their success. Counter to the faculty tournament model, with its connotation of graduate school as a game, most graduate students sincerely believe that a more intimate and intensive apprenticeship model will be operative for all given that they have made this significant life choice.

The Issue of Adequate Funding

A related organizational factor is the structure of graduate student funding via research and teaching assistantships. It is debatable whether current research assistant or teaching assistant wages are sufficient to pay all the bills that graduate students have, especially those students who may have family obligations. Funding is not as abundant as it once was, and it usually is not guaranteed beyond three or four years, depending on the department. What most students have to do is piece together an economic existence, which slows down their program progress and leads to the steadily rising statistic of "years to completion" (whether expressed as a mean or median). In fact, I have known a number of students who have engaged in "stopping out" after course work and preliminaries because they needed a job with more money. This sort of behavior can be structurally induced by funding inadequacies.

Lagging behind Undergraduate Improvements

A final element in this "iron cage of structured failure" is the programmatic context of training. The revolution in undergraduate education, away from lecture and reading assignments to collaborative active learning, does not seem to have penetrated the graduate seminar. Core course work in most departments prepares students to actually *do* . . . nothing. Students, as Egan (1989) points out, must be taken from passive receptor to proactive, functioning practitioner. This can only happen in on-the-job training via a rigorous apprenticeship with one or a few faculty members for a lengthy period of time. Some will say that is what the thesis/dissertation is designed to be, but by this point a considerable number of graduate students already have been lost, in part due to the absence of rigorous engagement in an actual research setting where veteran scholars are able and willing to transmit not only the technical know-how but also the passion that fuels their curiosity. Through these experiences, students actively confront the exciting and messy world of real research and teaching.

Many programs have something akin to a sequence in which a student signs up with a professor for a "research experience," where the end requirement is a research paper. Although better than nothing, the duration of this is too short, and the parameters of the experience are too circumscribed to qualify as rigorous, intensive immersion in a full-blown research program. Moreover, research assistant slots, if they are a panacea, never have been abundant, plentiful, or available for everyone.

Efforts at "downsizing" graduate student cohorts might increase the possibility for intensive mentoring and rigorous training. It might even improve the academic market in the long run by creating a smaller yet higher quality (i.e., better trained) supply of candidates in competition for scarce jobs. Restructuring efforts might be problematic and conflict with a departmental/university economic desire to have an expanding group of relatively inexpensive graduate instructors to teach many lower level courses and to support a faculty of a given size.

Compounding this problem of too few professors and/or professors with too little time is the research university reward structure, what Aldous (1989) calls "evaluation criteria used for faculty advancement." At most research universities, "grantsmanship" and "publication records" may be of overriding concern and disproportionate weight in promotion and tenure decisions, vis-à-vis teaching and service. The rank-order priority given to rewarding research might fall more acutely on untenured faculty, who, given their relative "closeness" to graduate students (in composition as well as experience), are structurally dissuaded from attending to too many students for too long a period of time (Aldous 1989:216). Employing a rational choice lens, most faculty (especially untenured ones) faced with this structural demand would be expected to opt to prioritize their research commitments, lest they imperil their careers. This is not to say that there are not dedicated faculty who struggle valiantly in altruistic fashion in service to as many students as possible. They are just too few and usually spread too thin. What these forces produce, I believe, is an appreciable number of graduate students on the outside in the early stages of their careers, in limbo, feeling alienated and detached from the discipline that had captivated them previously.

The Social Creation of Failure

All told, from the social psychological to the organizational, from the micro to the macro, graduate students are in some very real respects set up to fail. From a moral and humanitarian perspective, if it is true that appreciable numbers of students are tacitly assumed, expected, or structurally predisposed to fail, then graduate programs are, at a minimum, misleading graduate students to believe that each and every one of them will be afforded sufficient structural opportunity to "succeed." In this vein, the individualist ideology that "the cream rises to the top," which has been seized on consistently, serves the purpose of masking very real mitigating structural factors.

This raises a related question: why are faculty so willing to stop at individual-level psychologizing when it comes to graduate students and graduate education? In the context of an accepted tournament model of graduate education, this psychologizing has utility and is expedient as a "natural" explanation. To question the model itself and to lay bare its structure might be disconcerting for too many faculty, whose core value of egalitarianism might be contradicted in the analytical process.

In sum, an array of significant structural forces work against graduate students that have little to do with their native intellect. These factors, although acknowledged only here and there in the literature, have not been sufficiently examined. These larger structural forces are fundamentally at odds with the noble intentions and sincere efforts of many faculty. These forces are rooted in the organized professional culture and reward structures embedded in departments at the research university. This chapter is a small first step toward beginning a dialogue between graduate students and faculty focused on these issues.

Notes

1. FTE is a fiscal administrative measure relating student bodies to university/departmental revenue.

2. Rau and Baker's (1989) piece certainly is akin to my structural analysis, but their context is the crisis in undergraduate instruction.

References

Aldous, Joan. 1989. "Graduate School and the Self: A Response to Egan." *Teaching Sociology* 17:215-17.

American Sociological Association. 1992. *Survey of Sociology Departments and Divisions.* Washington, DC: American Sociological Association.

Blackwell, James E. and Morris Janowitz. 1974. *Black Sociologists: Historical and Contemporary Perspectives.* Chicago: University of Chicago Press.

Blalock, H. M. 1987. "Providing Tough Intellectual Challenges: The Issue of Quality Training." *American Sociologist* 18:19-22.

Crothers, Charles. 1991. "The Internal Structure of Sociology Departments: The Role of Graduate Students and Other Groups." *Teaching Sociology* 19:333-43.

Cuadraz, Gloria H. and Jennifer L. Pierce. 1994. "From Scholarship Girls to Scholarship Women: Surviving the Contradictions of Class and Race in Academe." *Explorations in Ethnic Studies* 17:25-41.

Dimaggio, Paul J. and Walter W. Powell. 1983. "The Iron Cage Revisited: Institutional Isomorphism and Collective Rationalization in Organizational Fields." *American Sociological Review* 48:147-60.

Egan, Janet Malenchek. 1989. "Graduate School and the Self: A Theoretical View of Some Negative Effects of Professional Socialization." *Teaching Sociology* 17:200-8.

Eitzen, D. Stanley. 1991. "The Prospects for Sociology into the Twenty-First Century." *American Sociologist* 22:109-15.

Goodman, Norman. 1989. "Graduate School and the Self: Negative Resocialization or Positive Developmental Socialization—And for Whom?" *Teaching Sociology* 17:211-14.

Kulis, Stephen. 1988. "The Representation of Women in Top-Ranked Sociology Departments." *American Sociologist* 19:203-17.

Lipset, Seymour M. 1994. "The State of American Sociology." *Sociological Forum* 9:199-220.

Paludi, Michele A. 1991. *Ivory Powers: Sexual Harassment on Campus.* Albany: State University of New York Press.

Rau, William and Paul J. Baker. 1989. "The Organizational Contradictions of Academe: Barriers Facing the Next Academic Revolution." *Teaching Sociology* 17:161-75.

Reinharz, Shulamit. 1984. *On Becoming a Social Scientist: From Survey Research and Participant Observation to Experiential Analysis.* New Brunswick, NJ: Transaction Books.

Rendon, Laura. 1992. "From the Barrio to the Academy: Revelations of a Mexican American 'Scholarship Girl'." *New Directions for Community Colleges* 80:55-64.

Rosenbaum, James. 1986. "Institutional Career Structures and the Social Construction of Ability." Pp. 139-71 in *Handbook of Theory and Research for the Sociology of Education,* edited by J. Richardson. New York: Greenwood.

Turner, Ralph. 1960. "Sponsored and Contest Mobility." *American Sociological Review* 25:855-67.

Wood, James L. and Amy C. Wong. 1992. "GRE Scores and Graduate School Success." *American Sociological Association Footnotes* 20 (9): 6.

The Forgotten Journey to the Classroom

47

The Heart of a Teacher:
Identity and Integrity in Teaching

Parker J. Palmer

Now I become myself It's taken
Time, many years and places;
I have been dissolved and shaken,
Worn other people's faces . . .

—May Sarton,
"Now I Become Myself"[1]

Teaching beyond Technique

Not long before I started this book, as summer took a slow turn toward fall, I walked into a college classroom and into my third decade of teaching.

I went to class that day grateful for another chance to teach; teaching engages my soul as much as any work I know. But I came home that evening convinced once again that I will never master this baffling vocation. Annoyed with sorties of my students and embarrassed by my own blunders, I pondered a recurring question:

might it be possible, at my age, to find a new line of work, maybe even something I know how to do?

The students in my first section were silent as monks. Despite my shameless pleading, I could not buy a response from them, and I soon found myself sinking into one of my oldest phobias: I must be very boring to anesthetize, so quickly, these young people who only moments earlier had been alive with hallway chatter.

In the second section they talked, but the talk flared into conflict as one student insisted that the concerns of another student were "petty" and did not deserve attention. I masked my irritation and urged open listening to diverse views, but the air was already polluted, and the dialogue died. That, of course, sank me into another ancient angst: how awkward I am at dealing with conflict when my students decide to start talking!

I have taught thousands of students, attended many seminars on teaching, watched others teach, read about teaching, and reflected on my own experience. My stockpile of methods is substantial. But when I walk into a new class, it is as if I am starting over. My problems are perennial, familiar to all teachers. Still, they take me by surprise, and my responses to them—though outwardly smoother with each

AUTHOR'S NOTE: This is a reprint of part of a chapter originally published as Palmer, Parker J., "The Heart of a Teacher: Identity and Integrity in Teaching," in *The Courage to Teach* (Jossey-Bass), 1998, pp. 9-13. Used with permission.

EDITORS' NOTE: See Lantos's "Principles of the Motivating Professor" and Pavela's "Faculty and Academic Integrity" in the *Fieldguide*.

year—feel almost as fumbling as they did when I was a novice.

After three decades of trying to learn my craft, every class comes down to this: my students and I, face to face, engaged in an ancient and exacting exchange called education. The techniques I have mastered do not disappear, but neither do they suffice. Face to face with my students, only one resource is at my immediate command: my identity, my selfhood, my sense of this "I" who teaches—without which I have no sense of the "thou" who learns.

This book builds on a simple premise: *good teaching cannot be reduced to technique; good teaching comes from the identity and integrity of the teacher.*

The premise is simple, but its implications are not. It will take time to unfold what I do and do not mean by those words. But here is one way to put it: in every class I teach, my ability to connect with my students, and to connect them with the subject, depends less on the methods I use than on the degree to which I know and trust my selfhood—and am willing to make it available and vulnerable in the service of learning.

My evidence for this claim comes, in part, from years of asking students to tell me about their good teachers. Listening to those stories, it becomes impossible to claim that all good teachers use similar techniques; some lecture nonstop and others speak very little, some stay close to their material and others lose the imagination, some teach with the carrot and others [teach] with the stick.

But in every story I have heard, good teachers share one trait: a strong sense of personal identity infuses their work. "Dr. A is really *there* when she teaches," a student tells me, or "Mr. B has such enthusiasm for his subject," or "You can tell that this is really Prof. C's life."

One student I heard about said she could not describe her good teachers because they differed so greatly [from one] another. But she could describe her bad teachers because they were all the same: "their words float somewhere in front of their faces, like the balloon speech in cartoons."

With one remarkable image, she said it all. Bad teachers distance themselves from the subject they are teaching—and in the process, from their students. Good teachers join self and subject and students in the fabric of life.

Good teachers possess a capacity for connectedness. They are able to weave a complex web of connections among themselves, their subjects, and their students so that students can learn to weave a world for themselves. The methods used by these weavers vary widely: lectures, Socratic dialogues, laboratory experiments, collaborative problem solving, creative chaos. The connections made by good teachers are held not in their methods but in their hearts—meaning *heart* in its ancient sense, as the place where intellect and emotion and spirit and will converge in the human self.

As good teachers weave the fabric that joins them with students and subjects, the heart is the loom on which the threads are tied, the tension is held, the shuttle flies, and the fabric is stretched tight. Small wonder, then, that teaching tugs at the heart, opens the heart, even breaks the heart—and the more one loves teaching, the more heartbreaking it can be. The courage to teach is the courage to keep one's heart open in those very moments when the heart is asked to hold more than it is able so that teacher and students and subject can be woven into the fabric of community that learning and living require.

If teaching cannot be reduced to technique, it is both good news and bad. The good news is that we no longer need suffer the boredom many of us feel when teaching is approached as a question of "how to do it." We rarely talk with each other about teaching at any depth—and why should we when we have nothing more than "tips, tricks, and techniques" to discuss? That kind of talk fails to touch the heart of a teacher's experience.

The good news gets even better. If teaching cannot be reduced to technique, I no longer need suffer the pain of having my peculiar gift as a teacher crammed into the Procrustean bed of someone else's method and the standards prescribed by it. That pain is felt throughout education today as we glorify the method du jour, leaving people who teach differently feeling devalued, forcing them to measure up to norms not their own.

I will never forget one professor who, moments before I was to start a workshop on teaching, unloaded years of pent-up workshop animus on me: "I am an organic chemist. Are you going to spend the next two days telling me that I am supposed to teach organic chemistry through role-playing?" We must find an approach to teaching that respects the diversity of teachers and subjects, which methodological reductionism fails to do.

The good news is very good, but the bad news is daunting. If identity and integrity are more fundamental to good teaching than technique—and if we want to grow as teachers—we must do something alien to academic culture; we must talk to each other about our inner lives—risky stuff in a profession that fears the personal and seeks safety in the technical, the distant, the abstract.

I was reminded of that fear recently as I listened to a group of faculty argue about what to do when students share personal experiences in class—experiences that are related to the themes of the course but that some professors regard as "more suited to a therapy session than to a college classroom."

The house soon divided along predictable lines. On one side were the scholars, insisting that the subject is primary and must never be compromised for the sake of the students' lives. On the other side were the student-centered folks, insisting that the lives of students must always come first, even if it means that the subject gets shortchanged. The more vigorously these camps promoted their polarized ideas, the more antagonistic they became—and the less they learned about pedagogy or about themselves.

The gap between these views seems unbridgeable—until we understand what creates it. At bottom, these professors were not debating teaching techniques. They were revealing the diversity of identity and integrity among themselves, saying, in various ways, "Here are my own limits and potentials when it comes to dealing with the relation between the subject and my students' lives."

If we stopped lobbing pedagogical points at each other and spoke about who we are as teachers, a remarkable thing might happen: identity and integrity might grow within us and among us instead of hardening as they do when we defend our fixed positions from the foxholes of the pedagogy wars.

Note

1. May Sarton, "Now I Become Myself," in *Collected Poems, 1930-1973* (New York: Norton, 1974), p. 156. Copyright © 1993, 1988, 1984, 1947 by May Sarton. Reprinted by permission of W. W. Norton & Company, Inc.

48

Entering the Classroom from the Other Side: A Conversation on the Life and Times of Graduate Associate Instructors

Sara C. Hare, Walter R. Jacobs, and Jean Harold Shin

Graduate associate instructors (GAIs) are a valuable resource at many colleges and universities because they often can shoulder a sizable portion of the teaching load. GAIs frequently are able to gain a great deal of practical firsthand experience as teachers of their own courses during the span of their graduate school careers. However, they do so while simultaneously balancing the rigorous demands of being full-time students. In this sense, they enter the classroom from another side than the faculty members who train them—a side that is filled with different circumstances, statuses, anxieties, and expectations. This chapter is a dialogue on pedagogical issues among three experienced GAIs at Indiana University. It is designed to represent three somewhat distinct philosophies on teaching as a GAI but at the same time brings up common concerns that they face daily in the classroom.

The chapter is organized into three sections. The first, "Thinking about Teaching,"

explores the place of GAIs in the larger academic community. Next, "Mastering Course Preparation" focuses on the unique anxieties of GAIs as they prepare to teach, especially for the first time. Finally, "Facing Classroom Challenges" discusses the construction of authority and rapport in the classroom. The theme of each section is generated and developed by one of the authors, followed by elaboration from the other two. Together, the voices of the three authors truly reflect the challenging yet exhilarating life and times of GAIs.

Thinking about Teaching

Walt

I am located in the margin. I make a definite distinction between marginality which is imposed by oppressive structures and that marginality one chooses as a site of resistance—as location of radical openness and possibility.

—bell hooks, *Yearning* (1990:153)

EDITORS' NOTE: See Preparing the Curriculum subsection and other subsections in the *Fieldguide* to get started on planning courses.

GAIs are strange animals. On the one hand, we have undergraduate degrees and, thus, are one step above the undergraduates we teach. On the other, we have not finished the Ph.D. and, thus, have not fully completed the life of the student. We are, in sum, marginal individuals, betwixt and between the worlds of the undergraduate and the professor.

Because teaching is tough enough without the distraction of status obtainment, many GAIs try to downplay their marginality. They might, for example, never mention that they are graduate students, letting their undergraduates assume that they are professors and implementing strategies to maintain this illusion. Others, going a step further, do not think about the issue at all, telling themselves that status does not really matter in the end. We, however, believe that an active negotiation with GAI marginality can be empowering. Following hooks (1990, 1994), we believe that the margin can be a space of possibility, a space that facilitates active and engaging teaching and learning on the part of students and GAIs alike.

The key lies in the recognition that marginality need not be purely negative, as it is commonly understood (Jacobs 1994). A marginality that is chosen has both positives and negatives; our task is to optimize the mix of positives and negatives (Brooks and Jacobs 1996). This does not, however, mean that we seek a "middle ground" where some sort of neutral objectivity exists; rather, it means that we be willing to read power-laden social worlds and create temporary understandings of our teaching environments. Giroux (1996) argues,

The issue for teachers is not to abandon judgments in the name of a false neutrality that suggests they simply be priests of an unproblematic truth; on the contrary, teachers and other cultural workers need to try to understand how the values that inform their work are historically conditioned and institutionally produced. (p. 179)

As part of a more thorough understanding of the historical and institutional production of the life and times of graduate students, we must be active in national debates about whether or not we are "employees" of the university or "students" (e.g., Nelson 1997a, 1997b). If we are to embrace the margin, however, then we must resist an either/or perspective. For one thing, our "bigger siblings" frequently oppose our efforts at improving our position (Robin and Stephens 1997). We cannot swing to the other extreme either because undergraduates are either indifferent or similarly hostile to the plight of graduate students (Newmann 1997). We must, rather, combine memories of our days as students with understandings about expectations about our desired slots as professors to avoid alienating either our students (our "customers" in the language of today's view of the academy as market) or the faculty (our "managers").

In one form or another, this enters the minds of most GAIs when we learn that we have been slotted to teach a class for the first time. Many, however, do not spend any time seriously thinking about the implications of that tension of our position betwixt and between undergraduates and professors, and they move on to more pressing issues of decisions about books, grading scheme, topics, and the like. I argue that GAIs *should* spend time on the larger issue of inhabiting a marginal status. This will lead to both theoretical and practical manifestations.

On the theoretical side, an explicit engagement with impending marginality leads to the development of a strong teaching philosophy. GAIs who desire to maintain an empowering marginality will cultivate relationships with professors, other graduate students, and undergrads to traverse multiple tensions among these groups. They are constantly thinking about past, present, and future realities to create selves that will be able to negotiate ever fluctuating classroom environments. This takes us into the practical side. GAIs who spend time thinking about marginality beforehand will not be surprised when the classroom throws up challenging situations. They will be prepared to connect with students without compromising their authority or selling out to demands of higher-ups. They become critical subjects with intact agency.

As agents, students and others need to learn how to take risks, to understand how power works differently as both a productive and a dominating force, to be able to "read" the world from a variety of perspectives, and to be willing to think beyond the commonsense assumptions that govern everyday experience. (Giroux 1994:133)

In essence, entering the margin means taking risks. With pressures concerning accountability rising along with the marketization of the academy, professors and GAIs alike no longer can passively "play the game" and hope to succeed. They must actively play it, evaluating and taking risks when necessary. When thinking about the classroom, envisioning its shape and our roles within it, GAIs must enter the margin, becoming aware of and willing to negotiate multiple and sometimes contradictory tensions on us as students *and* as academics.

Jean

I agree with Walt that a GAI's marginal status can be empowering, especially when you view it as part of a very valuable professional socialization process. Unlike other professions in which one is thrown into a new daily work routine only after finishing school, college professors have the unique privilege of being gradually trained for years in graduate school to balance teaching, research, and service responsibilities. In the transition from undergraduate student to college professor, associate

instructors spend countless hours in the margin between these statuses learning how to be contributing professional members of a scholarly community.

Where does teaching fit into this gradual learning process? I have had to think a lot about the role that it plays in the framework of my own graduate education, especially as I near the academic job market. A major benefit of a gradual professional socialization process is the trial and error GAIs get to experience as they first mix teaching responsibilities with course work and then later with their dissertation research. I think that GAIs get a really good sense of what type of academic institution they are best suited for—one that prizes good teaching and makes it the main professional focus or one that looks for frequent high-level research and has a lesser teaching load. Developing this sense helps when filling out job applications, shoring up perceived shortcomings on the vita, and preparing new courses to teach. As we cross the wide span of the academy from one side to another, the experience of being a GAI is invaluable to making the trip a smooth one.

Sara

The world of marginality as Walt describes it, of being betwixt and between the worlds of the undergraduate and the professor, will not disappear when we are hired as professors or research sociologists. The locus of marginality simply will shift. Then we will find ourselves occupying the slot between senior faculty and students or between senior researchers and staff. Thus, I think we find ourselves betwixt and between for most of our professional careers. And, as Walt suggests, we need to acknowledge and actively negotiate this position.

I agree with Walt that we need to seriously consider our position in academia and in our local departments. I think that most graduate students here are politically savvy in that way. We realize that we need to cultivate working relationships with our peers and professors. In fact, those who do not do this are at risk of pursuing an orphan dissertation or of being isolated and out of the loop. In this way, we must actively "play the game."

Whereas Walt contends that, having contemplated our marginality beforehand, we will not be surprised when students challenge or resist information, I explore, in the third section, the full ramification of this. I agree that we should be prepared for the possibility of challenges. But it is altogether a different matter when you are confronted with these challenges in the midst of teaching. I explore how GAIs work to preempt challenges and discuss two specific challenges I have encountered.

Mastering Course Preparation

Jean

Looking back at my career so far as a GAI, it sometimes is hard to believe how worried I was about the preparation of my first course. The routine and necessary tasks seem pretty intuitive and natural to me now, and like many seasoned teachers, I think I often take them for granted. But I have come to realize that growing and learning are just as much a part of good teaching as is teaching itself. Part of this process as a teacher involves mastering the anxieties and problems that invariably come up before, during, and after every semester and realizing that you have gained from the experience. Another part is recognizing that your outlook can change over time and that previous assumptions and ideas can give way to new ones. For me, this is exactly what has happened to my view of course preparation. It has become a task that involves a blend of fresh ideas and time-tested

strategies. But what it also involves is an open recognition that there is not always one correct approach, particularly when a course is being "prepped" for the first time.

The thing that I remember most vividly about preparing to teach for the first time is the nervousness I felt about appearing and acting young (I was 24 years old). I was only three years removed from being an undergraduate myself, and I was determined to do things "by the book" to establish authority and credibility. I turned to what I felt were established sources on teaching for guidance, particularly Lowman's (1984) *Mastering the Techniques of Teaching* and Eison's (1990) "Confidence in the Classroom: Ten Maxims for New Teachers." Lowman's (1984) book and others like it offer various strategies on course preparation using very generalized terms, fit for creating "master teachers." Eison's (1990) article suggests tips on how to maximize course readiness and awareness of tricky issues as you plan your first course. I looked to both of their suggestions as a collective, official model for how to meet the challenge of course preparation.

What I found was somewhat of a surprise. Although extremely detailed and comprehensive, Lowman's (1984) book did not deal very much with the course preparation issue that I was dreading the most—my position on the "margin" between the undergraduate students and faculty. Eison's (1990) article was a bit more help but still did not quell some of my anxieties. So, I just figured that the best strategy would be to follow an extremely strict, very controlled, tightly structured, and highly organized style as I prepared my course so as to maximize my authority and credibility to the students. After all, I thought, this is a job, and I have got to live up to the high professional standards of Indiana University. The course I was assigned was a lower level sociology course with mostly freshmen and sophomores, and I figured this to be the best way in which to prepare for it. The readings that I chose, the assignments and tests that I devised, the order of topics to be covered, the format of class periods, and the amount of material presented all reflected my goal of being super-rigid and ultra-prepared. I wanted to make my course not only informative but also challenging and deliberate. Although I consider myself to be fairly laid back, creative, and open-minded in social settings, I wanted my classroom to be as strictly professional as possible, and this showed in the organization of the course.

What finally changed my perspective on course preparation? It was a realization that most of my concerns about authority and credibility were based on a false pretense about what a course taught by an GAI (or any teacher, for that matter) was supposed to be. I went through about a month of implementing my extremely structured teaching style, even going so far as to wear a jacket and tie (not my usual preference of clothing, trust me), carrying a briefcase, and referring to myself as "Mr. Shin" in the third person. One day in my office hours, I had a conversation with a student about course-related matters. Outside of the classroom, I had let my "strict" persona fade a bit and was comfortably chatting like I would to anyone else. When I asked how things were going in the course, he responded somewhat positively but asked me, out of curiosity, whether my preparation style for the course and in-class demeanor also were applicable outside of the classroom. To him, I seemed very different interacting in my office hours than in the classroom. For the first time, I realized I was possibly creating an atmosphere that was confusing students and was actually contrary to how I handled other interpersonal interactions in daily life. I did not really respond to my student's

question right then, but that night I decided that I was done with trying so hard to be credible and authoritative. I had to be more myself in preparing and implementing my course, not some conjured image of how I thought a teacher should look and act. I had completely taken my personality out of teaching in my quest for credibility and authority. I suppose that I never will really know how my old strategy was working, but since that first month of teaching I have let my natural instincts dictate the types of activities I plan in class and the way in which I interact with students. And I think it has worked out extremely well in semesters since then.

This valuable lesson learned in my first semester of teaching keeps getting reinforced every time I prepare a course, old or new. It is nice to have an idea of how you want to operate in class, whether this idea is based on a "how to" teaching book or article, memories of your own undergraduate experience, or mental pictures of how you think a class should be taught. In my case, I had developed such a firm, unwavering picture of what I thought a teacher should be like that I created all types of cognitive dissonance for myself. It has taken a bit more fine-tuning (and it still does from time to time), but I have tried to create a balance between basing course preparation on my instincts for confident interaction and still retaining an acceptable level of organization and structure.

Ultimately, I believe that this is a good way in which to center your teaching around your students' learning and not around your own anxieties or preoccupations with the "rules" of masterful teaching. I have found that it also makes preparing to teach more fun and not just merely like the tasks of a job. As simple as it may sound, I feel that being yourself is the key to being comfortable in the classroom and that this then creates a positive, effective learning environment for everyone. Although it is not always feasible to prepare a course completely around your personality, even just being able to relax and take your natural teaching instincts into consideration can benefit both you and your students.

Sara

I have to smile in thinking that Jean referred to himself as "Mr. Shin" in front of his class. Jean's vivacious and interactive style is engaging for students and is quite the opposite of a rigid, formal, distanced presentation. In explaining his initial demeanor in class, Jean initially was worried about whether students would see him as credible and competent, which is the topic that my essay covers, but he also worried that he would not be able to "live up to the high professional standards of Indiana University." I think that we are writing about two aspects of the same phenomenon. We have a huge respect for the responsibilities that professors undertake, and we wonder (as shown in this section) whether we are capable of filling those large shoes and worry (as shown in the third section, "Facing Classroom Challenges") that students will not accept our attempts at doing so. It is not an easy balance, but it can be done through consideration of pedagogy in general and issues surrounding individual course preparation.

Walt

I, too, have much respect for the responsibilities that professors and GAIs have, but unlike Sara and Jean, I had very few doubts about living up to those standards. This, I think, is due to my privileged set of social locations. Whereas Jean was worried about reduced authority due to his age and perhaps his ethnicity (Korean American), and Sara was concerned about gender and age, when I first entered the classroom as a 6-foot 5-inch, deep-voiced, heterosexual,

27-year-old male, I had no doubt that I would command a high level of respect. This has turned out to be the case in each of the six courses I have taught. The only potential problem is my race (African American), but that is handled by a presentation of self in which I establish myself as "safe," as someone who is not an "irrational angry black man" but rather a more complex individual straddling several communities (Brooks and Jacobs 1996).

When thinking about their first teaching assignments, then, I would concur with Jean and Sara that GAIs should consider how social location (e.g., age, gender, race, sexual orientation, class) should affect presentation of self and the establishment of authority. I would add that GAIs should examine consequences of their unique *combination* of locations and work to actively effect a display of identities that enhances an empowering authority. As Jean demonstrates, however, GAIs should be wary of creating an artificial combination that runs counter to their natures. Rather, GAIs should consider highlighting some identities and downplaying others, based on their philosophies and course objectives and goals. This is a first step toward the creation of a dynamic and enjoyable course.

Facing Classroom Challenges

Sara

I will use the concept of "margins" in another sense because I leave the margins of this chapter to respond to the chapters that follow. In the following chapter in this volume, Sandstrom (Chapter 49) reminisces about his first classroom experiences as a junior faculty member. He wanted a classroom climate in which students helped decide the class focus and content rather than developing a strongly hierarchical classroom culture. In a sense, he did not want to play the "heavy" as the overriding authority figure. Gillespie (Chapter 50), in the subsequent chapter, discusses her realization of losing a sense of students' frames of reference as she ages. She and the students no longer share common experiences or worldviews. I want to respond to these thoughts as I describe some common graduate students' thoughts on "authority" as we begin our teaching careers.

Whereas Sandstrom hoped to have a less hierarchical relationship with students, we often deal with pre-teaching fears from the opposite end of the spectrum; we commonly fear that students will consider us impostors. Colleagues tell me that "they will realize that I don't know enough to teach this class . . . they will sense that I'm only a graduate student . . . they will feel ripped off that they paid for knowledgeable instruction and they are stuck with me." From this, we worry that students will challenge our qualifications or abilities to teach our classes. For most GAIs, this is a fleeting fear; our classroom experiences have been quite positive. Nevertheless, many of us have, on occasion, had our knowledge or authority challenged in the classroom. Graduate students discuss these incidents endlessly as we advise and commiserate with each other.

One common theme we discuss is whether students' challenges are related to the GAI's physical and social characteristics. That is, do students challenge our authority because we do not resemble the imposing, white, male, middle-aged professor? Most of us do deviate from this image in some way, being female, young-looking, short, ethnic, and/or shy. We develop hypotheses about this, arguing that students give female GAIs a harder time, do not respect young-looking instructors, or dismiss ethnic GAIs as teaching their "personal agendas." Moore (1996) calls these student responses "inappropriate challenges" because they suggest incompetence based solely on professors' social characteristics, especially gender and race.

Moore finds that, whereas many professors experience these inappropriate challenges as isolated incidents, young-looking female professors experience them as persistent problems. I argue that any trend of this sort is magnified for GAIs. That is, if young-looking female professors' authority is persistently challenged, then young-looking female GAIs must constantly be on guard.

We respond to these challenges by altering our physical appearances. Some GAIs begin the semester by dressing in a more professional manner, wearing ties, sports jackets, skirts, or dresses. Female GAIs have been advised to wear makeup to look more mature. For my first teaching semester, I spent a sizable chunk of my meager graduate student salary on more conservative clothes. I also bought a large leather briefcase, which I plop on the front desk in class and from which I pull out many manila folders. I hope the briefcase and the clothes convey the message that I am organized, efficient, and well versed in running college classes.

Other GAIs, particularly those who look young, also respond to challenges by limiting the information they reveal about themselves. First, they do not provide any clues that would reveal their ages. So, whereas I, as an older graduate student, feel comfortable mentioning where I was when President Kennedy was assassinated, young GAIs are careful not to release any information that might date them. Thus, they consciously avoid doing precisely what Gillespie (Chapter 50) regrets that she no longer can do. Gillespie mentions that as she ages, she no longer can connect as well with students' frame of reference. Young-looking GAIs, who do share students' worldviews, are careful not to use these connections. They avoid using examples that reveal their shared experiences with students. Second, most GAIs during their first semester of teaching do not reveal to students that they have no prior teaching experience. I evaded this disclosure with the following subterfuge: I mentioned previous semesters' classes without explaining that I had assisted the instructor rather than having *been* the instructor. Now that I have taught for several semesters, I continue to mention incidents from previous semesters so that students know that I have teaching experience.

Whereas the challenges and fears discussed heretofore resonate with new instructors in all disciplines, sociology instructors face challenges that are specific to our discipline. The sociological approach dismantles many of the fundamental beliefs that students hold, asking them to rethink their worldview. They have, after all, been socialized into our very individualistic society, and those without an understanding of the sociological perspective feel threatened when asked to question their taken-for-granted daily lives.

Students are particularly resistant to sociology's teachings on the structural and political roots of stratification. In my "Sociology of the Family" class, students express this resistance in two ways. First, they use the buzzword "male-bashing," and both males and females have accused me of this. Undergraduate males do not feel themselves to be advantaged, and similarly, undergraduate females do not feel disadvantaged. In fact, the relative status of men and women in college may well be more equal than at any other point in their lives (Neitz 1985:340). Thus, both males and females resent being told that women are systematically disadvantaged in our society.

Students also resist stratification information by evoking the "Dark Ages" comment. They often think that any information more than four years old is outdated and obsolete, particularly when discussing media, sex and gender roles, and family issues. "Things have changed," they commonly claim. Neitz (1985) comments on this phenomenon: "The women

acknowledge that things used to be bad for women, but they believe the cigarette ads— 'You've come a long way, baby'—and anticipate no difficulty in combining romance and companionship, motherhood and a career, in their lives" (p. 339).

Although I suspect that most sociology instructors encounter this resistance to stratification information, GAIs may have to be more careful in how we respond to these challenges. In the students' eyes, we do not have the claims of legitimacy that professors do because we do not have doctorates or other accomplishments. Thus, they might read the situation differently, suspecting that we are wrong or simply "pushing our political agendas."

Although I paint quite a daunting picture of the world of GAIs, I think that the overwhelming majority of us enjoy teaching. We feel that we are providing students with tools to critically assess our society and our taken-for-granted lives. Although we are more likely to remember the students' challenges, the moments in which we truly reach them are much more frequent.

Walt

Sara provides interesting strategies on how we GAIs deal with issues of authority. In a sense, however, these are strategies of displacement in that we use them to hide or overcome challenges to our status as legitimate teachers. As GAIs gain experience and comfort, I would suggest that they begin to actively *use* authority: "By allowing their own forms of authority to be held up to critical scrutiny, authority itself becomes an object of social analysis and can then be viewed as central to the conditions necessary for ownership and production of knowledge" (Giroux 1996:136). Many students feel that they can relate to GAIs better than they can to professors. Building on this connection, GAIs can demonstrate how *they* fit into webs of stratification and encourage students, similarly, to investigate their complicities and resistances within systems of power. So, in addition to having a ready store of information to convey to students, if instructors are willing to open themselves up for analysis—and, in the process, to open up for analysis the concept of authority itself—then students might form a more complete understanding of their social worlds (for a more complete discussion, see Jacobs 1998).

Of course, all instructors will not be willing or able to attempt this strategy. At the very least, experienced GAIs should consider this strategy. Even if the strategy itself is not operationalized, an analysis of why *not* may productively inform the use of alternative strategies for dealing with authority.

Jean

Once you have thought about what you are going to do when you get up in front of your class, actually doing it is a big step. Presenting your course material and interacting with your students brings about a lot of anxieties that seem to change in nature from day to day. Sara's concern about authority in the classroom is a particularly salient one for GAIs, especially when you consider that we are fully responsible for everything that happens during the course of a semester—good or bad. I always have felt a strange sense of internal conflict when evaluating my role in educating undergraduates—on the one hand, I am eternally grateful for the opportunity to gain teaching experience as a graduate student. But at the same time, I sometimes look at myself in front of a classroom and wonder whether the parents of these students are aware that their tuition dollars are being spent so that their kids can be taught by someone with barely a master's degree and relatively

little else. Exactly what makes me a qualified authority to teach?

The answer seems to be that we never can really know in some respect. I can only put extreme faith in my training thus far as a scholar and then actively find ways in which to channel my relative youth and working knowledge into making my students excited about sociology. I have found that students respond well when they perceive that a teacher is not only knowledgeable about the course topic but also genuinely enthusiastic about it. Because this enthusiasm often is assumed by students to be lost when one becomes a faculty member, I try to use my GAI status to my advantage. At Indiana University, we are lucky that a culture has developed among undergraduates that values GAIs for their exuberance and ability to relate well to students in the classroom. My hope is that I do not ever lose these traits as my teaching career progresses because they are the foundation on which classroom interaction should be based.

Conclusion

Together, our voices reflect just a portion of the diverse backgrounds and philosophies that characterize GAIs. However, given that the three of us have different teaching interests and views on the GAI experience, we hope that we have provided some firsthand insight into the potential concerns that GAIs deal with every day. The life and times of GAIs are filled with rewards as well as challenges, and in tandem these create not only effective teachers for the present but also empowered, sensitive, and responsible faculty for the future.

References

Brooks, Dwight and Walter R. Jacobs. 1996. "Black Men in the Margins: Space Traders and the Interpositional Strategy against

B[l]acklash." *Communication Studies* 47:289-302.

Eison, James. 1990. "Confidence in the Classroom: Ten Maxims for New Teachers." *College Teaching* 38:21-25.

Giroux, Henry. 1994. *Disturbing Pleasures.* New York: Routledge.

———. 1996. *Fugitive Cultures.* New York: Routledge.

hooks, bell. 1990. *Yearning.* Boston: South End.

———. 1994. *Teaching to Transgress.* New York: Routledge.

Jacobs, Walter R. 1994. "Off the Margin: The Interpositional Stranger." *Symplokē* 2:177-94.

———. 1998. "The Teacher as Text: Using Personal Experience to Stimulate the Sociological Imagination." *Teaching Sociology* 26:222-28.

Lowman, Joseph. 1984. *Mastering the Techniques of Teaching.* San Francisco: Jossey-Bass.

Moore, Valerie Ann. 1996. "Inappropriate Challenges to Professorial Authority." *Teaching Sociology* 24:202-6.

Neitz, Mary Jo. 1985. "Resistances to Feminist Analysis." *Teaching Sociology* 12:339-53.

Nelson, Cary. 1997a. "Between Crisis and Opportunity: The Future of the Academic Workplace." Pp. 3-31 in *Will Teach for Food: Academic Labor in Crisis,* edited by Cary Nelson. Minneapolis: University of Minnesota Press.

———. 1997b. *Manifesto of a Tenured Radical.* New York: New York University Press.

Newmann, Kathy M. 1997. "Poor, Hungry, and Desperate? Or Privileged, Histrionic, and Demanding? In Search of the True Meaning of the 'Ph.D.' " Pp. 81-123 in *Will Teach for Food: Academic Labor in Crisis,* edited by Cary Nelson. Minneapolis: University of Minnesota Press.

Robin, Corey and Michelle Stephens. 1997. "Against the Grain: Organizing TAs at Yale." Pp. 44-79 in *Will Teach for Food: Academic Labor in Crisis,* edited by Cary Nelson. Minneapolis: University of Minnesota Press.

49

Embracing Modest Hopes: Lessons from the Beginning of a Teaching Journey

Kent L. Sandstrom

Although seven years have passed, I still remember how I felt as I prepared to teach my first course. Above all, I felt excited. I was getting a chance to do what I always had wanted to do—teach at a college level. In addition to feeling excited, I felt a certain measure of confidence. I thought that I could do fairly well as a college teacher, even as a beginner. After all, I had plenty of preparation. I had worked at professional jobs that required me to engage in educational and public speaking responsibilities. I had served as a teaching assistant for a variety of college classes, gaining experience in lecturing, leading group discussions, writing examinations, and grading course work. I had taken graduate courses such as "Teaching Sociology" that allowed me to develop my pedagogical knowledge, values, and skills. Given this background, I was about as ready as I could be to tackle the challenges of teaching.

Yet, beneath my excitement and confidence, I wrestled with doubts and anxieties. At times, I wondered whether I was truly prepared

EDITORS' NOTE: See Preparing the Curriculum subsection and other subsections in the *Fieldguide* to get started on planning courses.

to assume the role of a college instructor. I worried about what would happen when I walked into the classroom and began teaching more than 90 students. I asked myself the following questions. Will any of these students feel as excited about this course as I do? Will they find the topics and readings interesting? Will they get involved in discussions? Will they see the course as useful and worthwhile? Will they think that I am a good teacher?

As the first day of the course approached, my worries intensified. For better or worse, classes were going to start and I would have to put my teaching philosophies and skills on the line. I tried to allay these anxieties by reminding myself that I had spent hours preparing a thoughtful, engaging, and student-centered course. This course, "Sociology of Everyday Life," would give students an opportunity to discuss and reflect on the issues they faced in their daily social worlds. It would revolve around carefully formulated discussions and assignments that would enable students to better understand their social contexts and relationships. The course also would offer students choices about what they wanted to study and how they wanted to be evaluated. Given this structure, I thought that it would provide students with an interesting, rewarding, and successful learning experience.

Once the course began, my "well-laid plans" quickly crashed against the realities of a large, general education classroom. In fact, my goals and strategies were challenged as early as the first couple of class sessions. To illustrate this, I briefly recount a few events that took place. In describing these events, I highlight some key difficulties I encountered as a beginning teacher and how I learned to better understand and address them through using a sociological perspective.

The First Days in the Classroom

Like many professors, I began my first class session by passing out copies of the syllabus and asking the students to look it over. Next, I described my teaching goals and philosophy, stressing my belief that classes should be discussion-centered so that students could have a meaningful "voice." To demonstrate this, I decided to get our first discussion underway. In setting it up, I asked the students to pair off and interview each other, making sure to learn some things about each other's interests, backgrounds, and everyday lives. This went well. The students talked openly with one another and, when asked to share a few details of their conversations, several did so.

Given how favorably this first discussion proceeded, I decided to go ahead with my plans for a second, more difficult exercise. It required the students to make decisions about the course contents. In kicking this off, I again emphasized my belief that students should have meaningful input in their courses. To show my sincerity, I pointed out that I had not yet selected topics or readings for some class sessions. They had been left open-ended, I explained, because I wanted

to give class members an opportunity to choose a few of the topics they would study. I then asked them to tell me what topics they might like to consider and I walked to the chalkboard, waiting eagerly to write down suggestions. A deadly silence filled the room. I tried not to feel unnerved by what was happening, remembering that I had to wait patiently to get students to say something in a large class. After 30 to 40 seconds (which seemed like hours), not a single student uttered a word. They looked at me with what I can only describe as "dead fish eyes." Not knowing how to deal with this, I repeated my request, making it clear that I genuinely wanted to hear their ideas and give them input in course planning. So, I asked again what topics they might like to add, sounding as sincere and enthused as I possibly could. This succeeded only in eliciting more silence, along with some annoyed looks. I started to panic. Assuming they would find it easier to respond to a list of options, I offered several topics that had not been included on the syllabus and asked which they might like to learn more about. Alas, this strategy did not work either. The students remained deafeningly silent.

I decided to cut my losses and move on, temporarily abandoning my hopes for student input. Instead, I outlined the basic course requirements and assignments, stressing the opportunities that class members would have to reflect on their everyday lives. As I finished, three or four students raised their hands. "All right," I thought, "a few of them are warming up." I nodded eagerly toward the first student. She remarked, "The syllabus doesn't say what kind of exams you'll be giving or how you'll be grading us. Will you be giving multiple choice or essay exams? Also, are you going to be grading us on a curve?" My heart sank. I had hoped she would comment on the course topics or opportunities. Nevertheless, I tried to appreciate her concerns and politely answered her questions. As I did so, other students who had raised their hands quickly put them down. Apparently, I had answered their questions as well. I decided to end the class for the day.

After dismissing the students, I gathered my notes and reflected on what had happened in the class. "What a disaster!" I thought. "I need to regroup and rethink my plans to make the course discussion centered." I spent several of the following hours reflecting on my plans for upcoming class sessions. I decided to adopt a new approach that would blend elements of traditional, lecture-oriented pedagogies with elements of more recent, interactive pedagogies. This approach, consisting of a combination of mini-lectures, videos, and topical discussions, would place less emphasis on class discussion while still encouraging it. Feeling confident that students would respond favorably to this, I looked forward to the next class session.

My confidence and optimism did not last long. The second class session unfolded as problematically as the first. I encountered a problem even before I entered the classroom. As I walked up to the door, I discovered representatives from a note-taking business handing out flyers to my students. The flyers announced that students could buy a packet of "high-quality course notes taken by a graduate student" and, thus, would not have to attend class if they were "too busy" or had "other obligations." A number of students took the flyers and walked away from the classroom. As the second class meeting began, I looked out on a classroom that contained fewer than two-thirds of the enrolled students. I felt deeply discouraged given the time and energy I had put into preparing that session. Nonetheless, I pushed forward, focusing on the students who had attended class and intent on engaging them in a lively analysis of the day's topic: culture and everyday life. I briefly lectured about the concept of culture

and then invited the students to identify and discuss examples of its key components (e.g., symbols, values, norms). Although they knew examples of these components, I again had made a naive and faulty assumption about their participation. They responded with silence. The only exception was one student who, either out of pity for me or irritation with long silences, offered a brief description of a norm. No one else uttered a word, despite my repeated attempts to elicit responses.

Perplexed about how to respond to the students' ongoing silence, I chose the path of least resistance and lectured for the remainder of the class period. Although I had prepared a provocative lecture, it certainly did not lead to the type of class session I envisioned. The students dutifully took notes but, overall, looked bored and disengaged. I left feeling frustrated and confused. After class ended, I let out an exasperated sigh and asked myself, "Why is this class getting off to such a poor start? Is it because I'm a bad teacher? Or, is it because the students are alienated, apathetic, or unreachable? Or, is it because of structural factors such as the size and context of the class?"

A couple of friends who were experienced teachers happened to call after that class. When I told them about the difficulties I had been encountering, they helped me to modify my expectations for student participation given the large class size. At the same time, they offered me a helpful strategy for generating and facilitating better discussions in a class of this size: having students first address questions in pairs or small groups and then asking them to respond in the context of the larger class.

After I employed this strategy, the course improved. Still, I felt uneasy and frustrated by my experiences, especially as the semester drew to a close. I wondered why so few students had shown enthusiasm about the course or participated actively in class discussions. I felt like the course had failed in important ways, even though several students told me that they had enjoyed it. I came to realize that the frustrations and difficulties I had experienced in teaching this course were not simply attributable to the size of the classroom, the motivations of the students, or my "rookie" teaching skills. Other forces also were at work. To make sense of these forces, I needed to learn more about the dynamics of teaching and higher education, not only in terms of what happens inside of the classroom but also in terms of the larger realities and contexts that influence the classroom experience. In other words, to develop a deeper understanding of my struggles as a beginning teacher, I needed to draw on the lessons of my own discipline and make use of the "sociological imagination."[1]

Learning about the Context of Teaching: Applying the Sociological Imagination

Like most teachers, I implicitly assessed the context within which I began to teach. For example, I thought about the mission and values of the university that employed me, the backgrounds and aspirations of the students I taught, the priorities and practices of my departmental colleagues, and the nature of the community within which the university was located. Yet, in spite of my sociological training, I did not explicitly examine how my teaching experiences were shaped by these and other contextual factors. As time passed and I taught more courses, I started to recognize how I could better understand the challenges I faced in the classroom by thinking more sociologically about my contexts. In turn, I developed a series of analytic questions about the interrelated contexts—cultural, regional, institutional, and de-

partmental—that influence the dynamics of classroom teaching.

Questioning and Assessing Teaching Contexts

Questions about Cultural and Regional Contexts

What is the moral, political, and economic climate of the region? What beliefs, values, and norms prevail among the members of this region and its constituent communities? What types of racial, ethnic, class, and gender relations characterize these communities? What forms of popular culture and leisure are prominent in these settings? What educational priorities and "schooling practices" are widely accepted? How do community leaders define and measure "successful" education? Do they emphasize mechanics, techniques, and standardized outcomes (including traits desired by the corporate world), or do they focus on the processes, conditions, and qualities of learning experiences? How do these conceptions of successful education influence the outlooks and actions of students? On a more general level, what is the relationship between your university or college and surrounding communities? Which segments of these communities are closely allied to your university or college? Which are alienated from it? Which are relatively indifferent? Which segments provide you with most of your students? Why?

Questions about Institutional and Departmental Contexts

What is the primary focus of the university, college, or department? What priority is given to teaching in the key decisions of your university, college, or department? What types of resources (e.g., time, funding, training, technologies) are made available for teaching purposes? What types of support networks are offered? Do senior faculty serve as teaching mentors to beginning faculty? Do faculty meet regularly to discuss teaching issues, philosophies, frustrations, or successes? Do they emphasize and recognize "good" teaching? Do they offer rewards and recognition to one another for this type of teaching? Also, how do faculty define good teaching? Do university or college administrators have a similar definition? How do these administrators conceive of educational success? What assumptions and measures do they rely on? Do they consult with faculty about these assumptions and measures?

In addressing the set of questions about cultural and regional contexts, I found the literature in the sociology of education useful, particularly the literature written by conflict theorists.[2] This literature highlights important features of education in the United States. First, the educational process is strongly influenced by *credentialism,* the belief that educational degrees should serve as the basis for evaluating people (Collins 1979). In many ways, schools have become "credentials factories" or institutions geared toward providing people with degrees that give them access to various jobs and statuses. In turn, schools have developed into powerful gatekeepers; they distinguish "capable" from "incapable" individuals, granting credentials to the capable ones (Henslin 1996). Employers rely on these credentials as sorting devices in hiring decisions, using diplomas or degrees to determine people's eligibility for jobs, even if these degrees have little relevance for the work to be performed. Given this characteristic of the job market, it is not surprising that many students conceive of education as a (somewhat irrelevant) process they have to endure to get the credentials necessary for desired employment. It also is not surprising that some students choose to engage in behavior such as buying lecture notes and otherwise minimizing their involvement in large, anonymous, general education courses. They learn that what matters most is getting the credits and credentials they need to become employable, not participating actively in courses.

In addition to revealing the effects of credentialism, conflict theorists have highlighted how the schooling process teaches students both a formal and "hidden" curriculum (Apple 1971, 1979; Bowles and Gintis 1976; Giroux 1981, 1988a; Giroux and Aronowitz 1993). The latter consists of the unstated norms and values that students learn through the social context, interpersonal relations, and organizational structure of the classroom, beginning with their first days in kindergarten (Dreeben 1968; Giroux 1981; Gracey 1997; Jackson 1968). These include the following:

1. Being punctual and complying with clock-oriented, bureaucratic regimens

2. Acting in a disciplined and independent manner, that is, engaging in work independent of intrinsic task motivations

3. Achieving goals and rewards through competitive rather than cooperative relationships with others

4. Submitting to authority and "knowing one's place" in existing systems of hierarchy and inequality

5. Conforming to the practices, standards, and linguistic styles of the dominant culture[3]

6. Learning for the sake of extrinsic rather than intrinsic rewards (Kohn 1993)

Through these features of the hidden curriculum, students learn that their exposure to the contents of the formal curriculum is much less important than the "nonacademic" traits they develop through the schooling process. These traits—punctuality, discipline, competitiveness, conformity, subordinacy, and extrinsically motivated work habits—prepare them to fit into the corporate workplace and to reproduce the larger social and economic order.[4] In fact, classrooms themselves serve as miniature workplaces "in which time, space, content, and structure are fixed by others [besides students]; rewards are extrinsic; and all social interactions between teachers and students are mediated by hierarchically organized structures" (Giroux 1981:53). Thus, through their classroom experiences, students learn to embrace passive and subordinate roles and, more generally, to accept the legitimacy of pedagogies that (1) give little credence to their needs, interests, or understandings and (2) exclude them from meaningful participation in classroom decisions and discussions.[5]

Given the disposition that students learn as a part of the hidden curriculum, especially through their primary and secondary schooling, it becomes easier to understand why they hesitate to participate in classroom discussions or decisions, even when their instructors welcome such participation. Students have been encouraged to remain relatively passive in their classes, avoiding participation in ways that might challenge the authority or expertise of their teachers. In most cases, they have had little opportunity to make decisions about the content or structure of their curriculum. As a result, they have not acquired the skills, experiences, or knowledge base that would enable them to trust that they can and should do this. Moreover, they have not developed a basis for trusting that an instructor would truly want them to become involved in making decisions about a course.

Guided by these insights, I better understood some of the resistance I had encountered in getting students to participate in the classroom, even in small courses. Students had learned (all too well) not to speak up in class, especially in creative and critically reflective ways. Yet, although the students' internalization of the hidden curriculum could account for some inhibitions about participation, I sensed that other cultural factors also were influential such as the norms and values they had learned within their families and communities. Most of my students at the University of Northern Iowa (UNI) were raised in rural and predominantly Scandinavian communities that emphasized the values of hard work, stoic endurance, humility, taciturnity, and conflict avoidance (Honnold 1997). Through the socialization process, the students learned to embrace these values and, consequently, were not inclined to challenge or question the traditional structures and outcomes of schooling. Most important, they learned to avoid engaging in interactions characterized by open conflict or disagreement. They also learned to see garrulousness and passionate verbal displays as immodest and undesirable. Given their internalization of such dispositions, I could better see why these students had not eagerly responded to my invitations to engage in reflective discussions—discussions that required them to share their ideas and perspectives and to critically evaluate the ideas and perspectives of others including those who had authority.

As I became more aware of why my students had hesitated to engage in discussion, I felt troubled about what I could realistically hope for and accomplish as a teacher. Could I counter the impact of the students' prior socialization experiences and effectively use an interactive and democratic pedagogy? Fortunately, when I assessed the *institutional and departmental* contexts at UNI, I found reasons to feel more optimistic about my prospects as a teacher. Overall, UNI emphasized and took pride in its reputation for "teaching excellence." It gave priority to teaching in its key policies and decisions including tenure and promotion decisions. In addition to this, UNI provided faculty members with substantial fiscal and social support for pedagogical and curricular development. For example, it established a Center for the Enhancement of Teaching, which offered faculty a variety of helpful pedagogical resources and encouraged them to engage in innovative teaching activities. This general emphasis on teaching quality and innovation was bolstered by a similar orientation within my department. I quickly discovered that my departmental colleagues were committed to practicing high-quality teaching and to pedagogical creativity. They were willing to help me improve my teaching skills and knowledge. When I consulted with colleagues, most offered me helpful feedback about a range of topics including course preparations, discussion exercises, lecturing techniques, and the use of new or alternative pedagogies.

Although I found support for teaching in my department and university, I also discovered that beginning faculty did not receive some badly needed forms of guidance. University administrators did not offer us any clear-cut ideas about what they defined as good teaching or as desirable educational goals. Neither did they provide us with any definitive criteria or rationales for how they assessed the quality of teaching. The only pedagogical direction they offered was implicit; that is, through their resource allocations, they encouraged us to embrace teaching strategies that relied heavily on multimedia technologies. They did not, however, explain how and why this would enhance teaching and learning at UNI. Perhaps most significant, administrators demonstrated little interest in engaging in discussions with faculty about how to define and assess pedagogical success.

On the departmental level, beginning faculty received no clearer guidelines regarding the meaning of or method to successful teaching. Senior faculty did not explicitly define good teaching, nor did they engage in open discussion about the desired qualities or outcomes of teaching. Thus, to talk about pedagogical issues and get needed direction, beginning faculty had to take the initiative. Some did not feel comfortable doing this, primarily because of concerns about alienating people who had power over them. As a result, they did not find the mentoring and support they needed to address their teaching concerns. Instead, they struggled with feelings of isolation, confusion, and frustration. Fortunately, I opted to seek out guidance from my senior colleagues and, as a result of my conversations with them, built a network of support. This network enabled me to cope effectively with the challenges and uncertainties that I experienced in beginning my teaching journey. It also prompted me to learn more about the most important component of teaching—*students*.

Learning about One's Students

Learning about the contexts of teaching provided me with an understanding of the common backgrounds, values, and behavioral dispositions of my students. It did not, however, give me insight into their individual attributes, interests, or potentials. Nor did it inform me of the personal meanings that they gave to college education or the classes I taught. To learn more about these things, I needed to interact directly with my students.

Through my research training as an ethnographer, I had learned the importance of "taking the perspective" of those whose lives and experiences you wish to understand. Guided by this assumption, I developed a variety of pedagogical techniques that gave students safe opportunities to share their perspectives. For example, at the beginning of each course, I asked students to break into small groups and talk with each other about four themes: their personal interests, their goals for the course, their expectations of me as a professor, and their ideas about evaluation procedures (e.g., tests, grades, papers, styles of feedback). After the students completed this group task, I asked them to summarize their discussions for the larger class. This exercise worked very well because students openly discussed their interests, goals, expectations, and perspectives on evaluation. In the process, they raised some interesting issues and learned that I would listen to them in designing class sessions and assignments.

Using this successful exercise as a springboard, I developed other strategies that enabled me to learn about students and avoid repeating the mistakes I made during my first teaching experience. These included involving the students in role-playing exercises, classroom experiments, interactive games, dramatic skits, and group analyses of case studies.[6] In addition to using these classroom-based strategies, I designed assignments that allowed students to share their perspectives more privately. For instance, at the beginning of each course, I asked students to write a personal essay about a central theme addressed in that course such as the "nature of individuality" in social psychology or the "meaning of personal freedom" in freedom, community, and social control. Through reading these essays and subsequently discussing them with the students, I gained a better understanding of their outlooks. I also felt more connected to them in my teaching endeavors. When lecturing, leading discussions, or planning course sessions, I could keep specific individuals in mind such as Matt, the creative thinker who dreamed of becoming a novelist, or Kristy, the witty extrovert who hoped to become a counselor in student services, or Michelle, the cynical marketing major who

doubted she could learn much useful in sociology. This was far more engaging than trying to teach to a sea of anonymous faces (Beidler 1986).

Most important, through employing these pedagogical strategies, I offered my students opportunities to participate actively and meaningfully in my courses—opportunities that were not as dull, problematic, or threatening for them as large, open class discussions. In the process, I learned how to better draw on and celebrate students' voices and experiences. As Giroux (1988a) proposes, this is a critical component of teaching. We fail to truly teach if we do not celebrate students' voices, recognize the meanings they give to their experiences and selves, and make them a central part of our pedagogical endeavors (Freire 1970). By focusing on how students construct meaning, what categories they draw on in this process, and how they bring these categories into play in their encounters with us, we become their collaborative allies in the practices of teaching and learning (Freire 1970, 1995; Giroux 1988a, 1993).

Learning about Oneself as a Teacher

As I built stronger alliances with my students and learned about who they were, I gained a better understanding of who I was and wanted to be as a teacher. This understanding grew and deepened through my unfolding struggles with three key pedagogical issues: (1) what teaching style to employ in my classes, (2) how to use my authority as a teacher, and (3) how to sustain a sense of hope in the teaching process.

The Issue of Style

When I talked with colleagues, I often was advised to "find a style that fits your personality." If I did this, they assured me, I would experience success as a teacher. Although I appreciated their intentions in offering this advice, I quickly learned how and why it was flawed. The problems I encountered as I started to teach did not result from my failure to find a teaching style that fit my "personality." Instead, these problems resulted from the fact that I tried to employ an unorthodox style that fit my personality but that did not fit with the characteristics of my teaching contexts or students.

Thus, my colleagues' advice to find a style that fit my personality did not help me much as a beginning teacher. In offering this advice, they assumed that I would be adopting a fairly conventional pedagogical approach. They also assumed that the issue of pedagogical style was primarily a matter of learning a professional role. They made the mistake of downplaying the significance of the context of teaching. Although I had made a similar mistake in choosing a dialogic style for a large, general education course, I learned that the question of style could not be separated from one's context. The appropriateness and effectiveness of a particular style depends on a number of widely varying factors including the nature of one's cultural, regional, institutional, and situational contexts.

As I became more aware of how contextual factors influenced the effectiveness of a pedagogical style, I recognized the importance of not getting locked into a specific style. By cultivating a flexible repertoire of teaching styles, I could adjust my methods in response to the particular characteristics of my contexts and students. In turn, I could find a variety of ways in which to pursue and realize the pedagogical goals I regarded as essential—active learning, critical thinking, and democratic classroom relations.

In experimenting with various styles and methods, I learned that a certain consistency exists between pedagogical means and goals.

Lectures are unlikely to foster classroom democracy. However, I also learned that teaching is a dialectical process that works best when it involves students in divergent and sometimes contradictory moments. That is, good teaching not only encourages students to think critically and creatively but also offers them moments to "let their guard down" and uncritically "fall in love with" a subject (Elbow 1986). Guided by this insight, I developed a teaching style that gave students opportunities to engage in both of these dimensions of learning.

Ultimately, through my struggles with the issue of pedagogical style, I have discovered that I need to show students, above all else, that I am committed to teaching them in the best ways I can. For me, this means using methods that tell the students I am (1) interested in both teaching and learning from them, (2) willing to help them pursue or develop their "itch" for learning, (3) ready to take the time to carefully evaluate their learning efforts while holding them to high standards, and (4) unwilling to coerce them into learning, even if they want me to do this.

The Issue of Authority

When I started to teach, I thought of authority as primarily negative. I had suffered under a number of ineffective teachers who "played the heavy" in the classroom, trying to intimidate their students into learning. I did not want to teach like them. Instead, I wanted to emulate the effective teachers who had inspired me and others to learn. These teachers had invited their students to join them in exploring challenging questions and in thinking imaginatively. They also had listened thoughtfully to students' ideas and treated them more like allies than adversaries. Because of this, students rarely thought of them as exercising authority.

I began my teaching career with the assumption that if I adopted a similar approach, I could sidestep the issue of authority. But my first days in the classroom revealed the flaws in this assumption. In spite of my attempts to use invitational and democratic methods, the students saw me as an authority figure who would evaluate their classroom participation and academic performance. Whether I liked it or not, I was located in an institutionalized power relationship with them, and I carried the weight of authority. To try to avoid or deny this was to be naive and deceptive (Elbow 1986; Giroux 1988a).

In turn, rather than evading the issue of authority, I developed a broader and more positive conception of authority, recognizing how it could serve as an enabling force in student-centered pedagogies. As I gained more teaching experience, I became increasingly aware of how I could use my authority to promote conditions that encouraged students to participate actively in discussions, to grapple with challenging issues, to think creatively and critically, to understand and appreciate diverse perspectives, and to form thoughtful and just relationships with one another.

In discerning how to use my authority in positive and student-centered ways, I struggled with the problem of how to serve simultaneously as a nurturing ally and a challenging evaluator of my students. In addressing this problem, I drew on a "solution" offered by Elbow (1986); that is, I chose to become an ally to my students in meeting the challenging standards of thinking, writing, and communicating I held them to in my courses. In forging this alliance, I clearly communicated my standards as a teacher and gave students more than one chance to meet them (e.g., by allowing them to take practice exams and to submit preliminary drafts of papers before getting graded evaluations). I also found ways to negotiate and share

authority with students in the evaluation process. This meant engaging them in reflection and dialogue about what criteria should be applied in assessing their exams, papers, or classroom participation. Through asking students to evaluate each other's papers and to identify and explain the criteria they used in their evaluations,[7] they became more aware of what standards to aspire to in their own work. They also had a chance for input in the evaluation process. This allowed the students to see that I could not be perfectly fair or objective in assessing their work. Doubts, questions, ambivalences, and biases inevitably would come into play in my assessments because I—like them—was "engaged in learning, seeking, and being incomplete" (Elbow 1986:149).

The Issue of Hope

The most vexing issue I faced as a beginning teacher was how to sustain a sense of hope. As I started teaching, I held ambitious visions of and goals for teaching, defining it as a true vocation that, at its best, "calls" practitioners to be involved and dedicated, inquisitive and creative, critically reflective of themselves and their world, and willing to promote understandings that contribute to the construction of a more humane world. Inspired by Freire (1970), I also believed that teaching should be a "practice of freedom"—a means that enables people to "deal critically and imaginatively with reality and to discover how to participate in the transformation of their world" (p. 15). I thought that one of the key goals of teaching should be "citizenship education" (Dewey [1918] 1967) or the fostering of political visions, social hopes, and critical thinking skills that would prepare students for active and socially responsible citizenship. I wanted to enhance students' abilities to understand and participate effectively in the decision-making processes that affected their lives. I also wanted to assist them in developing the intellectual and emotional resources that would allow them to transform oppressive social practices and to create more just, nonviolent, and democratic forms of community life.

After teaching a few courses, I became painfully aware of how difficult it was to realize these teaching ideals. This did not lead me to abandon my visions or hopes, but it did force me to come to terms with four key obstacles I encountered in pursuing them. The first and most prominent of these obstacles was the power of the "hidden curriculum." Given their internalization of the lessons of the hidden curriculum, many of my students had difficulty accepting or responding to pedagogical methods that offered more participatory, transformative, and intrinsically rewarding educational experiences. The second major obstacle was the impact of social and economic trends such as credentialism, the globalization of the economy, the increase in corporate downsizing, and the decline occurring in "real" wages. In responding to these trends, a growing number of students viewed a college education primarily as a means to enhance job prospects, not as preparation for democratic citizenship. The third obstacle was the combination of cultural values and existential propensities that led students to place a premium on conformity, predictability, conflict avoidance, and quiescence rather than on my goals of creativity, ambiguity, critical reflection, dialogue, and transformation. The fourth obstacle was my own growing realization that any pedagogical strategy I used had domesticating as well as liberating features (Freire 1970). In my efforts to become an effective and provocative teacher, I had to address the reality that all pedagogical models and visions construe the world in a manner that limits their adherents' capacities to imagine and construct it in other ways.

As I grappled with these four obstacles, I began to modify my pedagogical ambitions. Although I did not give up my visions of teaching as a practice of freedom, I started to see how difficult it was to engage in this practice. I also began to appreciate the unpredictable and sometimes fleeting moments when students and I successfully enacted freedom in the classroom. In addition to this, and perhaps most essentially, I became more aware and appreciative of the "small accomplishments" I experienced as a teacher—those moments of joy, grace, and wonder when my students fell in love with an idea, gained an interesting insight, asked a provocative question, felt excited about learning, or looked at themselves and their world in new ways.

So, as I reflect on the beginnings of my teaching journey, I realize that the most important lesson I have learned is to embrace modest hopes and appreciate the small pleasures that arise in the teaching process. Although I continue to believe that teaching is a special calling that should foster critical thinking, reflective action, and democratic relationships, I have learned to temper my hopes for fully realizing these goals, especially given the effects of larger social conditions and relations on the educational process.

Notes

1. In short, the sociological imagination is a way of thinking that allows one to see how the intimate realities of one's life are influenced by broader social structures, contexts, and processes (Mills 1959).

2. Conflict theorists concentrate on the patterns of inequality and corresponding dynamics of conflict and change that characterize social structures. When analyzing the educational system, these analysts tend to focus on how it reproduces and legitimates the patterns

of inequality that characterize the larger social and economic order. They also consider how educational institutions serve as sites of conflict and contestation among members of unequal groups and how oppressed groups can challenge and transform prevailing power relations within and through critical pedagogies.

3. Schools often see conformity to the dominant cultural practices and standards as evidence of the development of "good citizenship skills." Ironically, students who rate high on these skills also rate "significantly below average on measures of creativity and mental flexibility" (Bowles and Gintis 1976:41). Thus, schools define citizenship in a way that measures how well they serve as agents of social control rather than how well they enable students to think critically and act ethically in their daily worlds.

4. In making these points, I am drawing on Bowles and Gintis's (1976) argument that a structural correspondence exists between the social relations of the educational system and the social relations of production. However, this correspondence cannot be understood in mechanistic or one-dimensional terms. Although schools often legitimate and reproduce the social relations of production, they do so in complex and often contradictory ways (Giroux 1981, 1988b). Schools do not simply impose legitimating ideologies and behavioral routines on powerless students. As Willis (1977) emphasizes, students are "not passive bearers of ideology but active appropriators who reproduce existing structures only through struggle, contestation, and partial penetration of those structures" (p. 175).

5. This is particularly true for students from working-class or lower middle-class backgrounds. As Bowles and Gintis (1988) propose, "Predominantly working-class schools emphasize behavioral control and rule-following" (p. 3) and allow for less student participation and decision making than do schools in well-to-do suburbs.

6. In addition to helping teachers better understand their students, these group-oriented strategies allow students and teachers to explore and experience democratic relationships in the classroom. Moreover, they give students the experience of learning with and from each other and provide students with a context that stresses social responsibility and solidarity. All of these dynamics help the students to counteract the effects of the hidden curriculum. For an insightful discussion of how group work is an integral aspect of a critical and democratic pedagogy, see Giroux (1981).

7. When asking students to evaluate one another's papers, I take steps to ensure that (1) the authors and the evaluators remain unknown to one another and (2) the evaluators offer encouraging and constructively critical feedback rather than negative judgments.

References

Apple, Michael. 1971. "The Hidden Curriculum and the Nature of Conflict." *Interchange* 2:27-41.

———. 1979. *Ideology and Curriculum.* London: Routledge.

Beidler, Peter. 1986. *Distinguished Teachers on Effective Teaching.* San Francisco: Jossey-Bass.

Bowles, Samuel and Herbert Gintis. 1976. *Schooling in Capitalist America: Educational Reform and the Contradictions of Economic Life.* New York: Basic Books.

———. 1988. "The Correspondence Principle." Pp. 1-4 in *Bowles and Gintis Revisited,* edited by Mike Cole. London: Falmer.

Collins, Randall. 1979. *The Credential Society: An Historical Sociology of Education.* New York: Academic Press.

Dewey, John. [1918] 1967. *Democracy and Education.* New York: Free Press.

Dreeben, Robert. 1968. *On What Is Learned in Schools.* Reading, MA: Addison-Wesley.

Elbow, Peter. 1986. *Embracing Contraries: Explorations in Learning and Teaching.* New York: Oxford University Press.

Freire, Paulo. 1970. *The Pedagogy of the Oppressed.* New York: Seabury.

———. 1995. *Pedagogy of Hope: Reliving Pedagogy of the Oppressed.* New York: Continuum.

Giroux, Henry. 1981. *Ideology, Culture, and the Process of Schooling.* Philadelphia: Temple University Press.

———. 1988a. *Schooling and the Struggle for Public Life.* Minneapolis: University of Minnesota Press.

———. 1988b. *Teachers as Intellectuals: Toward a Critical Pedagogy of Learning.* Granby, MA: Bergin & Garvey.

———. 1993. *Living Dangerously: Multiculturalism and the Politics of Difference.* New York: Peter Lang.

Giroux, Henry and S. Aronowitz. 1993. *Education Still under Siege.* Granby, MA: Bergin & Garvey.

Gracey, Harry L. 1997. "Learning the Student Role: Kindergarten as Academic Boot Camp." Pp. 376-88 in *Down to Earth Sociology,* 9th ed., edited by James Henslin. New York: Free Press.

Henslin, James. 1996. *Essentials of Sociology: A Down to Earth Approach.* Boston: Allyn & Bacon.

Honnold, Donovan. 1997. "Yep, Nope: Professor Studies Why Midwesterners Don't Talk Much." *Northern Iowan Today,* Spring, p. 1.

Jackson, Philip N. 1968. *Life in Classrooms.* New York: Holt, Rinehart & Winston.

Kohn, Alfie. 1993. *Punished by Rewards: The Trouble with Gold Stars, Incentive Plans, A's, Praise, and Other Bribes.* Boston: Houghton Mifflin.

Mills, C. Wright. 1959. *The Sociological Imagination.* New York: Oxford University Press.

Willis, Paul. 1977. *Learning to Labor.* Aldershot, UK: Gower.

50

Carl's Story: Narrative as Reflective Teaching Practice

Diane Gillespie

I cannot remember the day or really even the year, but I remember how Carl's hand shot up from the back of the class where he often sat alone, away from the other African American students who usually sat together. The suddenness of his movement startled me. And as our eyes met, before I could even speak his name, he blurted out loudly, "All this socialization stuff is just not true—it's all bullshit." Stunned by his directness, I remember his words exactly . . . and the way his smile covered the intensity of his feelings. The class fell silent. Usually Carl entertained the class—if he participated at all—by making funny remarks on the side, just beyond the range of hearing. I remember distinctly noticing his hair as he spoke out—he had just tinted the front of it orange. Momentarily locked in his gaze, I suspected that this was his first public commitment to ideas—this "socialization stuff" mattered to him deeply.

I recall putting on my "look." It's really more like a holding position, a gesture toward something. I want my students to read my face this way: "She's really thinking about what he said; this is important and interesting to her. We

all need to take note." Usually I feel this way, but that day it hid impatience and irritation fed by my fatigue. I have always taught nontraditional students, many from ethnic minority groups. Until Carl, I had found teaching this unit easy. Most of them "got" socialization like the Pepsi can that drops down from the vending machine. I was behind in the syllabus, and the subject of most interest to me lay just ahead in the next readings. I wanted to be there already, and so I had dropped the coins in the socialization slot. But there sat Carl with his newly tinted orange hair and defiant hand protesting all my tacit expectations and assumptions.

In recollecting Carl, I feel myself being pulled back even further in time, to myself as the young teacher who had easy access to the world of her students. When I started teaching as a graduate student in the late 1960s, my African American students, most from the south side of Chicago and some from Menard State Penitentiary, knew firsthand about civil rights. Almost all had read parts, if not all, of Malcolm X's autobiography, for example, or had seen him on television. I had used their knowledge of politics and civil rights as a bridge into courses and syllabi that excluded their perspectives. And right on through the 1970s and early '80s, I tacitly held a frame of reference, a perspective about my students and myself, based

AUTHOR'S NOTE: Adapted from Gillespie, Diane, "Memory: From Storehouse to Dramatic Event," in *The Minds We.* Copyright © 1992 by the Board of Trustees, Southern Illinois University. Reprinted by permission of the publisher.

on the 1960s. Sitting in my class fifteen years later, Carl had little experience with or knowledge of the civil rights movement, and caught up in committee work and research, I had grown distanced from the daily experiences of my students.

I remember, perhaps most vividly, how Carl came up to me the day after I finished reteaching the socialization unit through a simulation. All the other students had left the classroom. He told me that all his brothers were in prison and that his father, an alcoholic, had left his family. He fought theories of socialization because, he said, "I thought it meant I would wind up like all the other men in my family. I've always seen myself as an individualist, but now I see that these ideas are more complex and that things aren't one way or the other. How do you think like this without getting mixed up and scared?" What I didn't apprehend then, but know now, in this act of recollection is that, like Carl, I was scared. His actions were essential to my development as a teacher. Looking back, I realize it was my first serious encounter with being a middle-aged teacher. I had lost contact with some of the lifeworld of my students, with the backstage of our classroom. For the first time, I questioned my tacit knowledge about my students' frames of reference and began to wonder how I would remain connected to them as I grew older.

Reflections on Carl's Story

I share this story because it was a turning point in my teaching. I had always known that it was important to create bridges between my students' life experiences and the conceptual abstractions that so often intimidate them. If they can feel personally connected to the concepts and theories they study, then they can begin to feel a sense of belonging to the academic world.

The diversity in my classrooms provides a reservoir of experiences from which to draw, but the multidimensionality can overwhelm us too. For example, sitting next to Carl was Lien, an Asian American refugee, who, well socialized, memorized every chapter in the book (including the one on socialization). I try to get my students to stay with a new concept long enough for it to have meaning in an increasingly expanding conceptual network. Where I see a broad highway between experience and ideas, my students often perceive the chasm with the flimsy footbridge in *Indiana Jones*. Carl had resisted the concept of socialization itself in a way that I had never experienced before. In the process of reteaching it through a simulation, I began to recognize how much my students' lives had changed, including their concrete experiences of socialization. As Carl heard the discussion about socialization in the debriefing of the simulation, he began to think about how some of his life experiences might fit socialization theory. It was not, however, just the experience that transformed his ability to be receptive to new information; nor was it my particular method or even the particular simulation. Rather, it was our ability to trust each other and to listen attentively to the other in public and private dialogues. As he began to *frame his concerns* in light of the concepts from the chapter, I more directly connected him with real, ongoing academic debates about responsibility and choice in traditional socialization.

The story reveals Carl's vulnerability as an African American man in a family system where he perceives the other men to have failed. But the story also reveals my vulnerabilities as a white female teacher becoming aware of her own age. As a result of seeing this broader context, I find myself quite naturally seeking to uncover on a much more regular basis what exactly my students are thinking about when they think about "subject matter."

References

Gillespie, D. (1991). "The case of Carl and the concept of socialization." In R. Edgerton, P. Hutchings, & K. Quinlan (Eds.), *The Teaching Portfolio: Capturing the Scholarship of Teaching.* Washington, DC: American Association for Higher Education.

Gillespie, D. (1992). *The Mind's We: Contextualism in Cognitive Psychology.* Carbondale, IL: Southern Illinois University Press.

51

Promise, Failure, and Redemption: A Life Course Perspective on Teaching as a Career

Howard Aldrich

In a chapter I wrote a few years ago about my teaching career, I described myself as passing through three stages: promise, failure, and redemption (Aldrich 1997). I used the term "promise" to describe my successes in high school and college at playing the academic game—being dazzled by my instructors, getting high grades, and taking pleasure from the learning experience. Graduate school was more of the same, causing me to look forward with anticipation to my first job, even though I had very little teaching experience as a graduate student. I used the term "failure" in describing my teaching performance as an assistant professor because I failed to live up to the role models I had seen as a college student. My ignorance of the fundamentals of good teaching was compounded by my total absorption in the publishing game, and my colleagues did not help much. Intellectual arrogance, lack of a support system, and a reward system focused on research and publication rather than on teaching nearly consigned me forever to the ranks of poor teachers. Fortunately, I was able to use a third label, "redemption," to describe what happened next. Dealing with renewal and promotion decisions, designing new courses, and moving to a new university finally brought me up to the standard that I originally had imagined for myself. In-

deed, I improved to the point where I am currently in charge of the teaching seminar that all of our graduate students must take. So, my story had a happy ending.

My narrative was, I thought, idiosyncratic. At least, I thought the phases through which I passed and the emotional roller coaster I rode were unique to me. However, I learned otherwise when Bernice Pescosolido asked me to rewrite my experiences to tell a more general tale. She referred me to an article of hers (Pescosolido 1986), in which I found the precise cycle I had described. Not only did her three-stage model of role assimilation mirror the one I thought was unique to me, it also reminded me of an article I had recently worked on concerning boundaryless careers (Baker and Aldrich 1996).

In this chapter, I adopt the general life course model used by Pescosolido (1986) and use it as a framework to describe the careers of academics as teachers. To her model, I add two additional components. First, I draw on Baker and Aldrich (1996) to describe how people have the potential for gaining cumulative knowledge and enhancing their sense of identity over their life course. Second, I point out some factors peculiar to universities that somewhat modify the model proposed by Pescosolido (1986). In

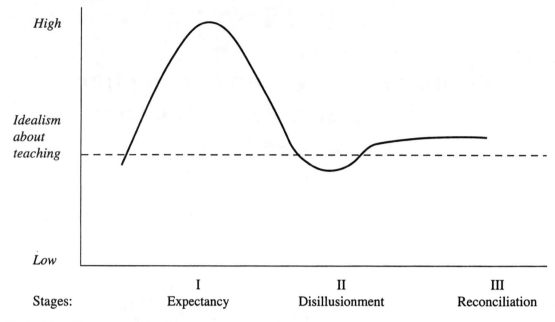

High

Idealism
about
teaching

Low

| Stages: | I | II | III |
| | Expectancy | Disillusionment | Reconciliation |

Figure 51.1. Three Stages of Role Assimilation for Teachers in Their Academic Careers
NOTE: Dotted line refers to average level of idealism.

using ideas from the life course perspective, I explicitly recognize that my portrayal of college instructors' experiences is historically specific. The social context of teaching is evolving, and seeds of change are apparent in the current system. Although much of my analysis depicts conditions hampering professors' abilities to improve teaching, I also describe several encouraging developments likely to increase the standing of teaching in academic work. I conclude by listing reasons why we ought to care more about helping junior faculty achieve what Pescosolido calls the "reconciliation" stage of their careers.

A Network Theory of Role Assimilation

A life course perspective on careers highlights the changes that occur as people voluntarily enter new social positions over their lifetimes. Pescosolido (1986:523) points out that *sociali-*

zation and *assimilation* theories can be combined to illuminate a predictable pattern of changes in attitudes, values, and behaviors as people prepare for an occupation and then gain experience in it. Contact with others in the occupation leads to socialization via social learning, and voluntary choice of new roles results in assimilation by veterans already in the roles.

Three broad stages of role assimilation have been found in studies across a variety of occupations: expectancy, disillusionment, and reconciliation (as shown in Figure 51.1). In the first stage, *expectancy,* new entrants view their chosen occupation in very idealistic terms, expressing high levels of commitment and enthusiasm. As they go through training and preparatory education, their idealism actually increases. These early days are a time of anticipatory socialization in which the initiates "say and feel what they think they are supposed to as incumbents of their new status" (Pescosolido 1986:525).

The second stage, *disillusionment,* occurs when the initiates' expectations do not live up to the reality they encounter on the job. "Initiates inaccurately perceive the role, their place in it, and member reactions" (Pescosolido 1986:524). Veterans are amused by the rookies' idealism and might make fun of them. New entrants also find that the veterans do not give them the respect they think they deserve given their training. The third stage, *reconciliation,* occurs for those initiates who remain in the occupation and experience somewhat of a return to the commitment and idealism with which they initially entered the occupation. Regardless of the rebound in idealism experienced, veterans in the occupation never return to the level of idealism they showed as initiates, and so in Figure 51.1, in Stage III the curve for idealism is shown as rising from Stage II but remaining below its peak of Stage I.

Pescosolido (1986) argues that this pattern of role assimilation results from three stages in the formation of social networks in which new entrants become embedded: anticipated networks, networks of initiates, and networks of members. In the first stage, rookies are relatively isolated from veterans in their occupation and so have few tangible guidelines as to what the occupation actually involves. They use their ideal-typical projection of what the occupation must be like to fashion the norms and values they believe characterize the occupation.

In the second stage, when they actually encounter veterans in the occupation, they find that their earlier views were incorrect and, therefore, revise their expectations downward. In this second stage, they form networks with other initiates in similar circumstances and may even develop a subculture that is in opposition to the occupation's dominant culture. These networks of strong ties with other initiates may provide emotional support, but they do not assist the entrants with their role assimilation into the occupation.

Finally, in the third stage, new entrants become involved in networks of veterans in the occupations and learn more about what the occupation is really like. They also learn how veterans have adapted to occupational demands, and they take on a more favorable image of the occupation. The picture painted by Pescosolido (1986) has been documented for students in medical school, nursing school, and dental school and also has been seen among police recruits and prison guards. More to the point, the pattern of idealism, cynicism, and the rebirth of idealism fits perfectly the picture I painted of my own career.

However, the model needs to be modified, not only by a recognition that people experience continuous change over an their entire life course but also by incorporating factors that are somewhat unique to the college or university setting. The norms and values affecting college or university teachers vary with the historical context, and the current senior faculty who earned their Ph.D.'s in earlier eras had an academic experience very different from that of graduate students earning Ph.D.'s today. The generic process might be the same, but certainly the content of norms and the context is different.

A Life Course Perspective on Careers

A life course perspective on careers studies people over the long term rather than just the stages immediately before and after they enter an occupation. Theorists look not only at people preparing to enter an occupation and their postentry experiences but also more generally at how they develop in their careers over their lifetimes.

The life course perspective has developed over the past several decades and "refers to the social patterning of events and roles over the life span, a process ever subject to the interaction of individual behavior with a changing society"

(Elder and Caspi 1990:205). This perspective directs our attention to historical influences that affect processes of identity formation and expression within careers and to how knowledge is accumulated and put to use. In my work with Ted Baker (Baker and Aldrich 1996), we identify three dimensions along which people change in their careers: number of employers, extent of knowledge accumulation, and the role of personal identity.

The first dimension is simply the number of employers included in a person's work history. Some academics, especially those who entered their profession in the 1960s or 1970s, might work in three or four colleges or universities over their lifetimes. The academic labor market has fragmented somewhat in the 1990s, and many younger scholars have not been able to find permanent jobs. Thus, they will experience even more job changes over their careers.

The second dimension is the extent to which the knowledge and competencies gained are cumulative over the course of a career. *Knowledge* can be divided into two types: explicit and implicit (or tacit). Explicit knowledge can be codified, formalized, and passed on through routinized training. Implicit or tacit knowledge comprises the unwritten and difficult to articulate information held by occupational incumbents that must be learned on the job, through apprenticeships and mentoring. For academics, at least insofar as their research careers are concerned, cumulative knowledge development is facilitated by formalized graduate education and postdoctoral positions, complemented by informal practices in mentoring relationships that pass on tacit knowledge. Knowledge accumulation on the teaching side of an academic career is more problematic, as I will point out.

The third career dimension is the extent to which employees themselves play an instrumental role in structuring their work histories through their personal identities. The identity concept draws on social psychological notions of authenticity and self-efficacy. Authenticity denotes the belief that people have some sense of an "essential self" to which they are motivated to remain true (Gecas and Burke 1995). Self-efficacy "refers to the perception or experience of oneself as a causal agent in one's environment" (p. 47). The development of an identity-enhancing career is facilitated by circumstances allowing people to set and work toward challenging but nonetheless attainable goals. Achieving their goals provides personal evidence to people that their unfolding careers are coherent reflections of how they understand themselves. People whose job tasks fit in with their sense of core identity, and who are able to take a lead role in setting and accomplishing challenging goals, will develop careers that are high on the identity scale. Success in setting and achieving personally meaningful goals will enhance attempts to express identity through work activities (Hall 1971).

The Three Stages: Knowledge and Identity

Our careers as teachers are a result of our abilities to make choices and influence our own lives in the context of changing structures of constraints and opportunities. Using Pescosolido's (1986) model of the three stages of socialization and role assimilation, as shown in Figure 51.1, we can examine more closely the stages of a career in academia.

Expectancy: Anticipated Networks

Future college teachers almost always are recruited into the profession as undergraduates; few doctoral programs recruit their new entrants from other occupations. One of the most endearing qualities of undergraduates, even among "Generation X'ers," is their idealism. Lowman (1995), McKeachie (1994), and Boice (1996) write about the emotional impact of college professors and emphasize the strong role that interpersonal skills play in outstanding teaching. Excellent college teachers motivate and inspire their students and spend a great deal of time with students who express an interest in learning more about their field. Faculty are flattered to have such students around, and students are awed by the worldliness and seeming omniscience of their favorite professors.

In my own case, I remember being incredibly impressed, even enthralled, by the patience and understanding of my professors. They worked in their offices, with their doors open, and almost never turned me away, no matter when I appeared. In conversations with graduate students in my teaching seminar, I find that nearly all of them recall one or two outstanding professors who took a special interest in them and planted in them the idea of one day playing the same role for other students.

At this early stage, all that a potential new entrant knows about the occupation of college teacher is its glamorous side—intellectual freedom, apparent large blocks of free time in which to pursue esoteric interests, and a lifestyle that includes frequent travel and long holiday breaks. Professors have no incentive to disabuse undergraduates of these notions, and in their honors classes, they might even heighten the allure of the profession by praising students' work.

Graduate school is a rude awakening for many would-be college teachers, as they encounter the realities of the academic world. Students find that building cumulative explicit knowledge about their disciplines requires long hours in the library and laboratory and the sacrifice of leisure and family time. Many are assigned immediately to teaching assistantship duties, for which they are ill prepared, and they may find that senior faculty take little interest in them unless they agree to work on the faculty members' projects. In the social sciences and humanities, more than half the entering students drop out before earning their degrees.

Graduate student stipends, at most universities, allow a lifestyle not much above the subsistence level, but because their peers are in the same situation, most do not seem to mind at first. Some students even find that their penurious existence heightens the romance of being a scholar, and they become fond of the role. For example, universities in the Boston and San Francisco Bay areas are famous for their cadres of nth-year graduate students, unable to cut their ties to a style of life they have grown to love.

Unlike Stage I in Pescosolido's (1986) model, the socialization process for initiates in the academic profession is confounded at the start by a two-track socialization process. Almost immediately on entering graduate school, students are taught the importance of research productivity for their careers. In the social sciences, there might be separate theory and research tracks, and in the physical sciences, students might be assigned to a lab or an apprenticeship. Mentors are chosen for the students on the basis of research compatibility, and initiates are expected to begin their own project with an eye toward publishing before they leave graduate school. By contrast, very few graduate departments have courses specifically on preparation for teaching, and very little attention is paid to the formal preparation of initiates as teacher.

For those students establishing good relationships with mentors, graduate school can be a pleasant experience. Mentoring relationships, however, almost always are based on scholarly research, not teaching. Few students decide to work with a faculty member because of that person's reputation as an excellent teacher. Instead, they pick a person who can advance their career or who will indulge their idiosyncratic work habits.

As graduate students construct their identities as scholars, from the very beginning research assumes a more important role than does teaching. Because they have been thrown into the teaching assistantship role without training, they come to share the general faculty prejudice that teaching requires no special preparation. Their departments typically do not require courses on pedagogy taught by scholars doing research in the area, such as from psychology departments or schools of education, and therefore graduate students get the impression that teaching skills can be learned on the job. In short, teaching skills belong in that gray area of tacit knowledge that will somehow be learned by watching others.

Curiously enough, few students question the imbalance in their training. Most still expect to take academic jobs in which they will be contractually paid for their teaching and expected to fund their research out of grants and contracts. Although on its face this seems like an odd arrangement, students take it for granted. Even though they have seen many of their professors insulate themselves from their students and denigrate them, the saliency of teaching as a part of the college professor role remains undiminished.

Over the past decade, the harsh portrait I have just painted has softened somewhat as colleges and universities have developed teaching and learning centers. Although small and often underfunded, these centers have made great strides in inspiring departments to do more for their students. For example, at the University of North Carolina–Chapel Hill, the Center for Teaching and Learning runs workshops for graduate students and has succeeded in convincing the administration to conduct regular inventories of what departments are

doing to prepare their graduate students to teach. Moreover, at that university, several departments have semester-long courses for their graduate students on teaching, and many others have shorter orientations to the topic. Nonetheless, most departments invest far more resources in preparing students to do research than to teach.

Disillusionment: Networks of Initiates

Disillusionment with the teaching side of the college professor role begins for many people in graduate school, when they encounter seasoned veterans with particularly jaundiced views about their own teaching. Students learn in graduate school that teaching is not to be taken seriously, as they observe the actual incentive system in their profession. Time and resource allocation in graduate programs also conveys a strong message to students that they should not waste too much time preparing to teach.

On their first job, disillusionment deepens as the reality of trying to produce enough to earn tenure sinks in. Pescosolido (1986) noted that initiates form networks with other initiates in most occupations in this period of initial entry, but universities are unique in that a large entering cohort at a university does *not* mean that a junior faculty member will have a large network of initiates. The networks of departmental initiates available to beginning college teachers are extremely thin, as many junior professors will have had larger graduate student cohorts than peer cohorts on their first jobs.

Departments typically hire only one or two faculty members per year, and potential networks of initiates in colleges and universities are fragmented by departmental and college barriers. Indeed, departmental boundaries often impede efforts at organizing joint activities with other initiates. Senior faculty will counsel junior faculty that they need to get to know their own departmental culture, learning local tacit knowledge, and thus going outside the department requires special initiative. The tenure system exacerbates the problem because it introduces an element of competition among peers for the small number of tenure slots available. Competition heightens junior faculty anxiety about their careers and may lead to further neglect of their teaching in favor of trying to produce enough to escape their current situations. Within departments, the networks of members into which young scholars are assimilated are very heterogeneous. Rather than the single coherent set of norms and values implied by Pescosolido's (1986) model, initiates in colleges and universities find groups of cynics, groups of agnostics, and groups of true believers regarding the value of teaching. Some of the cynics still pay lip service to quality teaching, but many simply reject the notion that their self-worth/identity has anything to do with how well they teach. By contrast, some of the committed members play an active role in the department, often not appreciated, and are active in creating cross-university networks. Needless to say, heterogeneity in the culture causes some confusion for the initiates but also leaves an opening for eventual reconciliation.

Another confusing factor stems from the incentive system of most universities, which is a classic example of "rewarding A while hoping for B" (Kerr 1975). Although department chairs, deans, and college presidents vigorously defend the importance of quality teaching, resource allocation decisions are made almost strictly on the basis of a department's prestige in national reputational rankings, based on research productivity. Another consideration might be the number of students taught, but that typically is not tied to the *quality* with which those students are taught. Rewards honoring excellent teaching are increasingly a feature of colleges and universities, but they are given on an individual rather than a departmental basis. So, a colleague's outstanding teacher award does nothing for the department's share of university resources, whereas a colleague's large research grant means additional overhead for the department and perhaps a boost in the department's national standing. That boost, in turn, can translate into more positions and perhaps lower teaching loads in the future.

Reconciliation: Networks of Members

The situation to this point, as I have described it, looks rather bleak. Given the context I have described, with idealism crushed by encounters with the reality of winning a place in the academic system, how and why do some faculty go on to once again value their teaching? Several concepts from life course studies help us to understand how reconciliation occurs given the cultural heterogeneity I have described: control cycles, situational imperatives, and accentuation (Elder and O'Rand 1995). Loss of control often is brought on by situational imperatives, which are circumstantial changes resulting in a reduction in personal control. Change often creates a disparity between goals and accomplishments, with the corresponding loss of control prompting efforts by people to regain control. In stressful periods, prominent individual characteristics tend to become even more pronounced, a process labeled the "accentuation principle." In particular, when long-established identities are threatened, people tend to rely heavily on what has worked in the past rather than on changing their sense of self, although if social support is available, then they also might search for new ways of coping.

Junior faculty face many situational imperatives that threaten loss of personal control. They get the worst teaching assignments, the most inexperienced teaching assistants, the smallest offices, and the worst committee assignments. Depending on the strength of identity they carried into graduate school and through their graduate careers, some might become even more disillusioned when confronted with loss of control. However, for others, the situation is an opportunity that reawakens their earlier sense of idealism. For example, many junior faculty throw themselves into their teaching in spite of warnings that such efforts will not enhance their tenure prospects.

If they do this on their own, in a solo effort, then they face an uphill battle. However, academic culture is neither coherent nor monolithic. Heterogeneity in the veterans' group presents junior faculty with alternative role models, and mentoring by veterans gives many junior faculty the adaptive tools they need to persevere. A few strong ties with helpful veterans can give junior faculty the emotional support they need to reassert their buried idealism.

Thus, junior faculty might discover that there are groups of senior faculty who value teaching a great deal, but they also might discover that the rewards of good teaching are almost entirely local. By contrast, they already had learned that the rewards for excellent research are national or international in scope, and this lesson is reinforced as the tenure clock ticks away. My sense is that reconciliation is not fully achieved until after the tenure process is finished, when faculty have a clearer idea of the road ahead.

The tenure review gives junior faculty a realistic, albeit possibly brutally frank, assessment of their prospects for achieving high visibility in their profession. For those earning tenure, it also gives them the freedom to re-express the idealism—although in reduced form—that brought them into the field in the first place. The viability of the norm of good teaching is sustained by the senior scholars who not only carry a national reputation of excellent research in their field but also attend diligently to their teaching. These veterans are role models who offset the more cynical message conveyed by other departmental members.

Reconciliation also is more likely these days because of the much larger network of teaching-friendly veterans into which faculty may now move. People interested in teaching excellence have formed a small but growing national community with journals, conferences, newsletters, and a network of consultants who offer training courses and seminars on improving teaching. University centers for teaching and learning work with junior faculty in their first year, getting them off on the right foot, and many have set up sites on the World Wide Web that make their expertise available worldwide. These networks have been reinforced by the accountability pressures universities are experiencing, in the private and public sectors, from their constituencies. Publishers now advertise books, aimed at administrators, on how to create teaching assessment programs.

Thus, unlike the rather one-sided environment I experienced in the 1970s, junior faculty today might find that their interest in teaching is rewarded by positive feedback at the local and national levels. The picture of initiate socialization and role assimilation painted earlier probably is too one-sided as well. Networks of veterans certainly are a powerful socializing influence on new entrants. However, junior faculty who have taken teaching seminars and short programs as graduate students have the ability to affect departmental veterans in positive ways. Their enthusiasm and aura of confidence regarding teaching might even inspire some of the cynics in their new departments to try something different.

Why Should We Care about Reconciliation?

Why should we care about increasing the number of junior faculty who survive the period of disillusionment and go on to the stage of reconciliation? I get this question fairly regularly from graduate students in my teaching seminars who want to know whether it is all worth it. I point out three things to them. First, academic productivity is highly stochastic, driven by many forces only partially under one's control. The interaction of various situational imperatives gives rise to a highly unpredictable future. It is extremely hard to please peer reviewers, and the competition for scarce journal space is fierce. Second, the real story for academic life, for most people, is that publishing in the top journals is extremely difficult. Most people do not publish very much, and what they do publish never is cited. If one's identity is totally invested in being a productive and prestigious researcher, then a shortfall is inevitable.

Third, the sources of *real* job satisfaction, for most of us, are local in origin, not national. Teaching is a daily round, with weekly and monthly rhythms of its own, whereas articles and books are produced in much more irregular cycles. External validation of one's efforts from external peers occurs fairly infrequently. Teaching well, by contrast, results in immediate feedback, with an emotional impact unmatched by occasional acceptance letters from publishers and journal editors.

References

Aldrich, Howard E. 1997. "My Career as a Teacher: Promise, Fall, Redemption." Pp. 14-26 in *The Teaching Experiences,* edited by Rae Andrè and Peter Frost. Thousand Oaks, CA: Sage.

Baker, Ted and Howard E. Aldrich. 1996. "Prometheus Stretches: Identity, Knowledge Cumulation, and Multi-employer Careers." Pp. 132-49 in *The Boundaryless Career: A New Employment Principle for a New Organizational Era,* edited by Michael B. Arthur and Denise M. Rousseau. New York: Oxford University Press.

Boice, Robert. 1996. *First-Order Principles for College Teachers.* Bolton, MA: Anker.

Elder, Glen H., Jr. and A. Caspi. 1990. "Studying Lives in a Changing Society: Sociological and Personological Explorations." Pp. 201-47 in *Studying Persons and Lives,* edited by A. I. Rabin, R. S. Zucker, R. A. Emmons, and S. Frank. New York: Springer.

Elder, Glen H., Jr. and Angela M. O'Rand. 1995. "Adult Lives in a Changing Society." Pp. 452-75 in *Sociological Perspectives on Social Psychology,* edited by Karen S. Cook, Gary Alan Fine, and James S. House. Boston: Allyn & Bacon.

Gecas, Viktor and Peter J. Burke. 1995. "Self and Identity." Pp. 4-67 in *Sociological Perspectives on Social Psychology,* edited by K. S. Cook, G. A. Fine, and J. S. House. Boston: Allyn & Bacon.

Hall, Douglas T. 1971. "A Theoretical Model of Career Subidentity Development in Organizational Settings." *Organizational Behavior and Human Performance* 6:50-71.

Kerr, Steven. 1975. "On the Folly of Rewarding A While Hoping for B." *Academy of Management Journal* 18:769-83.

Lowman, Joseph. 1995. *Mastering the Techniques of Teaching.* 2d ed. San Francisco: Jossey-Bass.

McKeachie, Wilbert J. 1994. *Teaching Tips: A Guidebook for the Beginning College Teacher.* 9th ed. Lexington, MA: D. C. Heath.

Pescosolido, Bernice. 1986. "Migration, Medical Care Preferences, and the Lay Referral System: A Network Theory of Role Assimilation." *American Sociological Review* 51:523-40.

PART III

Charting the Landscape of Higher Education in the 21st Century

The final task that remains is to consider the shape and substance of higher education in the future, a challenge of momentous importance if Allan Bloom is correct. Such a vision requires that we recognize both the nature of future trends and the power of individuals within higher education to forge changes and protect the critical value in colleges and universities. This part is forward looking—charting out likely directions and alternative possible futures for teaching and learning.

Although some scholars have argued that prediction of the future is an important criterion for evaluating social research, social scientists never have been very good at crystal ball gazing. At our best, we offer plausible visions of alternative possible futures and map out the opportunities and obstacles to their realization. In this final part, the essays describe the possible future landscape of higher education based on extrapolations from current trends, speculations about the likely outcome of current contradictions, and identification of possible agents of change.

For example, Craig Calhoun (Chapter 52) identifies economic and demographic trends that are likely to alter the job market, student enrollments, curriculum content, graduate and undergraduate instruction, institutional differentiation, and prospects for multicultural, international, and interdisciplinary education. He notes that the precise form these changes will take depends on the outcome of conflicts and will vary across institutions. R. Eugene Rice (Chapter 53), following up on his agenda-setting work with Ernest Boyer, outlines possibilities for the future of college teaching.

Robert B. Barr and John Tagg (Chapter 54) outline their vision for an alternative possible future based on a learning paradigm that will transform colleges and universities. Such a transformation would require a thorough reorganization of higher education to retrain faculty, grapple with coordination problems, redesign reward structures and evaluation criteria, and promote greater faculty and departmental collaboration.

In the final essay, Elizabeth Grauerholz, Brett McKenzie, and Mary Romero (Chapter 55) bring their considerations into the day-to-day life of the classroom. They present a vision of the classroom of the future. The technological revolution, student and faculty diversification, and increased demands for quality teaching, they say, are likely to produce more interdisciplinary, multicultural, collaborative, and electronically enhanced classrooms, less constrained by temporal and physical boundaries. Although their relatively optimistic scenario is filled with new opportunities for improved teaching and learning, it also contains serious challenges including the need for more administrative coordination, greater time demands on faculty (especially female and minority professors), increased student questioning of faculty authority, and less face-to-face contact with students. These opportunities and challenges will require us to creatively rethink our relationships with students, colleagues, and the curriculum as well as to the world outside academia.

The Debate: The Student and the University

Allan Bloom

Our problems are so great and their sources so deep that to understand them we need philosophy more than ever, if we do not despair of it, and it faces the challenges on which it flourishes. I still believe that universities, rightly understood, are where comunity and friendship can exist in our times. Our thought and our politics have become inextricably bound up with the universities, and they have served us well, human things being what they are. But for all that, and even though they deserve our strenuous efforts, one should never forget that Socrates was not a professor, that he was put to death, and that the love of wisdom survived, partly because of his *individual* example. This is what really counts, and we must remember it in order to know how to defend the university.

This is the American moment in world history, the one for which we shall forever be judged. Just as in politics the responsibility for the fate of freedom in the world has devolved upon our regime, so the fate of philosophy in the world has devolved upon our universities, and the two are related as they have never been before. The gravity of our given task is great, and it is very much in doubt how the future will judge our stewardship.

AUTHOR'S NOTE: Adapted and reprinted with the permission of Simon & Schuster from *The Closing of the American Mind* by Allan Bloom. Copyright © 1987 by Allan Bloom.

52

Continuing Trends or Future Transformations?

Craig Calhoun

By the 1990s, as we know too well, the trends discussed throughout this volume had contributed to public pronouncements of a "crisis" in higher education. Calls proliferated for faculty to spend more time in the classroom and for more undergraduate classes to be taught by senior faculty. Quality teaching was a central concern for parents, students, trustees, state legislators, journalistic critics, administrators, and indeed faculty members themselves as they talked and wrote about this crisis. That it was perhaps *the* basic issue was obscured, however, by the rise of a politically charged debate over "political correctness" (PC) and academic freedom. That is, a public rightly concerned about the quality of education provided by America's colleges and universities was told wrongly by many commentators to look for the sources of the problem in the ideologies of professors and not in the social organization of higher education. Accusations about "tenured radicals" (which were, for the most part, poorly supported by the evidence) distracted attention from much more basic questions about whether professors—including tenured ones—taught well, taught enough, and taught the right students. One reason was that the critical discussion focused almost entirely on what went on in the most elite and selective schools (the ones in which "liberal arts" predominated). Fights

over the place of Shakespeare in the canon, or of world cultures versus Western civilization, had much more to do with Stanford University and the Ivy League than with community colleges and four-year schools dominated by applied majors. This was so precisely because the dispute was largely, if not explicitly, about how to construct and certify an elite. Certainly, other sorts of institutions have experienced the effects and the intellectual changes, if fewer of the rancorous quarrels.

As often happens, the argument became most heated shortly before social changes would render it obsolete. It was never the case (even in sociology, one of the fields most stereotyped as left wing) that there was any preponderance of "tenured radicals." By the time the anti-PC argument found its full voice, conservatism was gaining ground in much of the academy. Perhaps more important, a long-standing glut of Ph.D. holders was beginning to turn to shortage. The shortage so far has been very selective; the job market has opened up dramatically, but there still is a backlog of the underemployed, and the demand is greatest in certain subfields and at certain sorts of institutions (reflecting the general trends discussed in Part I of this volume). The earlier glut had left academics on the defensive when faced with an onslaught of criticism, demands that senior faculty teach more beginning courses, questions about the role of research, and other challenges. The growing scarcity of faculty, combined with a highly unequal "star" system, mitigates against this. But never mind; the argument will recur, as it has for more than 100 years. It is endemic to the basic structural differentiation and ambiguity of mission that characterizes American higher education. The specifics continue to shift, but neither characteristic is likely to disappear any time soon.

So what is likely to happen? With apologies for the sketchy character of what follows, here are some likely possibilities.

1. *The currently strong job market will temporarily—but only temporarily—reduce calls for an end to tenure.* These have flourished recently not only because conservatives thought tenure was protecting left-wing opinions, foolish PC, or the replacement of classics by cultural studies but also because the abolition of a mandatory retirement age allowed many senior professors to continue to hold positions while talented younger scholars were denied them. The relative ease of gaining tenure during the rapid expansion of the 1960s and early 1970s exacerbated the problem by leaving in place an unusually large number of tenured scholars, many of whom had been chosen with relatively low selectivity. These scholars constituted a kind of demographic bulge, blocking job opportunities and mobility for the large cohorts of talented graduate students attracted to fields such as sociology in the 1960s and 1970s. A downturn in employment opportunities exacerbated this, turning many of the newer Ph.D.'s into a kind of enduring academic underclass. Members of this generation who considered themselves underplaced have constituted competition for new Ph.D.'s for 20 years. In the same period, simple financial pressures encouraged challenges to tenure at many institutions

(famously Bennington College in 1994).[1] Calls to rethink tenure also flourished because of the extraordinary freedom and opportunities for self-regulation afforded academics, at least those with tenure in relatively elite schools. It was (and remains) easy to find examples of scholars who do little teaching, no research, and much gardening—even while studies show that, overall, academics work quite long hours. Colleges and universities added to the problem both by offering the public extremely poor explanations of what professors do and by failing to implement effective systems of post-tenure review and continual performance monitoring.

Elite academics have worn blinders in considering the issue of tenure. Many have relied on the crutch of arguments about academic freedom that are both self-interested and (often) irrelevant. Keeping protections against dismissal for unpopular political views seems important. So does (but with more qualifications) protecting against dismissals that reflect short-term fluctuations in the popularity of different scholarly fields. Both of these can be addressed through good labor law, due process, and other institutional mechanisms as well as tenure. Moreover, simply citing academic freedom as the basis for protecting tenure ignores the transformations that have changed the professorate since that argument was developed.[2] First, compared to the earlier institutions in which the academic freedom argument was classically developed, today's American colleges and universities pioneered a less hierarchical structure of ranks (but not salaries) in which the range of protected "professors" was expanded to include a majority of teachers. Second, the growth and differentiation in American higher education discussed heretofore meant that most faculty protected by tenure worked outside the elite institutions committed to the production and transmission of original knowledge and perspectives. Third, at least between the late 1970s and mid-1990s, tenure may have worked to inhibit free speech and intellectual diversity. It did this both by reducing the number of positions available for younger scholars and by holding the younger faculty lucky enough to get tenure-track positions in an extended purgatory subject to intense scrutiny and review with ever elevated standards. These standards tended toward the production of a high volume of relatively routine publications rather than toward the encouragement of radical differences from established views of the senior faculty. Fourth, and following from the same demography, in this period tenure became manifestly a system privileging an older professorate against younger would-be entrants. This older professorate was disproportionately white and male, which meant not only that it was harder for minorities and women to get in but also that when affirmative action measures were used, they were more likely to provoke resentment because competition was limited to a reduced range of openings.[3]

The current relative shortage of faculty probably will continue for several years, at least so long as the economy remains strong. It will mitigate inflation of standards. But it will not change the fundamentals. If anything, it probably will exacerbate bidding wars over stars (which now operate, to some extent, at all stages of scholarly careers). At the same time, colleges and universities will continue their drives toward increasing productivity and efficiency.[4] Willingly or under external pressure, more and more will adopt post-tenure reviews, and more of these will come to have real teeth. Which forms of faculty productivity they favor will be a matter of struggle and will vary among institutions. Colleges and universities also will continue to employ large numbers of temporary and adjunct faculty. If anything; the proportion of faculty in these positions will increase. It is bad faith for those protected by tenure not to recognize that this means that a large percentage of university teachers already work outside the protection or even potential protection of tenure. There will be mounting pressures for colleges and universities to develop better employment practices for these faculty and career paths for non-tenure-track faculty that offer them reasonable, if limited, job security and opportunities for promotion or recognition. In addition, there should be efforts to incorporate these faculty more fully into the intellectual and collegial life of colleges and universities. Indeed, it is arguable that at least those in potentially long-term non-tenure-track positions should be represented in faculty senates and similar institutions of self-governance.

2. *Enrollments will remain strong based on demographic momentum but subject to economic cycles; however, there is no reason to expect a return to the growth in resources and enrollments characteristic of the postwar period.* Stagnation or retrenchment already have affected institutions differently. This probably will harden distinctions in the kinds of education and teaching and intellectual environments they offer. In particular, less selective schools will be much more dramatically tied to economic factors. This means fluctuating enrollments (an incentive for administrators to continue to rely on temporary faculty). It also means that the shift toward courses sold on the basis of their job market advantages will not be reversed (as some liberal arts advocates fondly hope). If anything, job-related courses will become more clearly the staple offerings of most nonselective or minimally selective schools. Thus, the distinction between sociology set in predominantly liberal arts settings and sociology set in more applied contexts is likely to continue to grow. In the absence of major intel-

lectual changes producing an increased theoretical unification of the field, this is likely to mean differences not only in practical dimensions of teaching but in what is actually taught. It will be the basis for continuing splits within the field. An increase in adult students will bring some seeking liberal arts courses as "life enrichment" but more seeking retraining to compete in the job market.

Enrollments in predominantly liberal arts schools will be likely to remain approximately constant. The good news for advocates of the kinds of education they offer is that these schools are more shielded from economic pressures (directly on them and indirectly on students' choice of fields). The bad news (for those same advocates) is that outside those schools, liberal arts teaching probably will shrink and applied teaching probably will grow. To understand this, we should set it in the context of recent shifts in fields of study.

Analysts have noted three important flaws in many accounts of decline in the liberal arts (Turner and Bowen 1990; Oakley 1992). First, partly because of the conservative cultural agenda of many authors, these are commonly written as though the heart of the matter is a decline in the humanities. In fact, the issue is better understood as a decline in numbers of students pursuing liberal arts degrees; indeed, the natural sciences and, to a lesser extent, the social sciences also have given way to other choices of majors. Second, the location of transformation during and after the late 1960s has led commentators to exaggerate political and content dimensions and to fail to grasp a key underlying dynamic. There was a dramatic growth in arts and sciences majors in the years of university expansion. Curricula at new schools largely mirrored those at older ones. Expanding campuses attempted to upgrade their statuses by upgrading the place of arts and sciences in their curricula. The increase was

short-lived, however. Turner and Bowen (1990) cite Ball State University as an example. There arts and sciences degrees grew from 2.5 percent of the total in 1954 to 29.9 percent in 1970, before failing back to 13.3 percent in 1986. Third, commentators have missed a crucial difference between male and female enrollment patterns. Male enrollment in the humanities, for example, had already declined dramatically *before* the 1960s. This did not translate into significant effects on aggregate course enrollments because women were entering colleges and universities in growing numbers and disproportionately choosing humanities courses. Women's choices of majors began to shift away from the humanities later than did men's; in the 1970s and 1980s, women moved out of the humanities in a trend similar to that of men a generation earlier. This occurred largely because many professional careers became increasingly open to women, and women began to place more emphasis on preparation for employment. It resulted, however, in a specious conclusion about the "crisis of the humanities."

3. *The increasing inequalities of American society will bring further differentiation within higher education as well as between those who attend college and those who do not; these will have direct implications for how sociology is taught.* How any individual school pursues its educational mission and what it is able to offer its students is shaped not only by internal policy decisions but also by its position in the larger field of higher education.

Already, competition to attend highly selective schools is intense and has increased compared to that a few years ago. This represents, in part, an accurate recognition on the part of parents and students that elite degrees pay off substantially more than do nonelite degrees. At the same time, schools struggle with each other, not only to attract numbers of students but also, in the case of the more selective schools, to attract the best students. If schools are not able to maintain a high level of selectivity, then they become vulnerable to loss of their elite status, devaluation of their degrees, increasing price competition, commoditization of faculty work, and other potential transformations. Many will cease to be centered on the arts and sciences. Although private schools figure prominently in this top rung of American higher education, so do some public universities and colleges. These include both the most selective research universities and the increasingly prominent publicly funded liberal arts colleges. The latter sometimes are designated "honors colleges" of their state systems (e.g., College of New Jersey, New College of the University of South Florida).

4. *Growth in graduate education is likely to continue, with implications for the place of undergraduate teaching in the overall professorate.* The growing prevalence of postbaccalaureate degrees is as dramatic a development of the postwar years as the internal differentiation of undergraduate institutions and curricula. The majority of graduates of highly selective liberal arts colleges and universities now go on to graduate or professional school, and there is every reason to expect that growth to continue. Grumbling about it—and its consequences—also is likely to continue. Nonetheless, graduate education has emerged as just as much a normal stage of personal development today as undergraduate education was in the prewar period.

It is undergraduate education that defines the American public conception of both college and university. In the case of universities, however, graduate students are at least as basic to the character of campus life. Graduate education is, however, poorly understood. In particular, there is little appreciation of why majors in arts and science subjects are not more closely

tied to employment, leaving many students to seek either professional credentials or more advanced academic study in a research and/or scholarly field. This might reflect credentialism, but I do not think it reflects only that. There also have been genuine increases in knowledge and in the skill bases for many lines of work. Much of the confusion has to do with the more general pattern of institutional differentiation that leaves schools pursuing different educational mandates under the common names "college" and "university."

Growth in graduate education is an important strategy for institutional reputation building, although it works differently at different levels of the status hierarchy. Whereas adding a master's program or two would do little to enhance the standing of the most elite and selective liberal arts colleges, it is a productive investment for many schools in which applied majors dominate. The basic distinction lies between high-status professional fields in which professional degrees are exclusively or primarily postgraduate and lower status fields in which undergraduate credentials predominate (or in which college degrees are not yet required). The elite liberal arts colleges offer relatively general educations that prepare students for specialization in high-status professional schools or Ph.D. programs (or for jobs that do not require highly specialized training or credentials but that reward general learning, social status, and/or networks). By contrast, less selective or nonselective schools emphasize applied programs at the bachelor's level (although, of course, they also may, in varying proportions, offer "arts and science" degrees, the holders of which may seek entrance to elite professional or graduate schools). Some fields—notably business—straddle the distinction. By and large, the more elite and selective business schools avoid undergraduate instruction, and those on the way up have incentives to minimize their work with undergraduates. This leaves the field of under-graduate studies in business largely open to less selective schools. The latter, in turn, have an incentive to develop graduate programs. This not only serves faculty interests but also might make undergraduate degrees more valuable and help to recruit students. The presence of a graduate program enables the school to develop better connections to employers and makes it more likely that those who receive bachelor's degrees will be able to claim a connection to people placed higher in the administrative hier-archies of prospective and actual employers.

In the professional fields where under-graduate credentials remain prominent, there is apt to be a growing differentiation among prac-titioners that correlates with a growing role for graduate degrees. Development of graduate nursing programs, for example, reflects the ex-pansion of nursing into new domains (e.g., clinical assessments for schools or courts), the growing proportion of nurses who work in large institutional settings rather than small clinics or patients' homes, and the introduction of increased managerial and planning responsi-bility in the context of a changing health care system. A number of sociologists teach in nurs-ing programs (and/or those programs require sociology courses). This might be only a transi-tional pattern, however, because there is a ten-dency for each field to seek to educate its own future faculty members. Hence, holders of doc-torates in nursing who have specialized in re-search on social dimensions of the field may increasingly replace sociologists on nursing fac-ulties.

This is not the place to take on the larger questions about the nature of graduate educa-tion (as distinct from professional programs). I simply want to make five more specific points.

First, graduate education is not growing at the expense of undergraduate education.[5] The two can flourish together. It is true that small colleges offer undergraduates a level and kind of contact with faculty members that large uni-versities seldom can match. This is partly be-cause of the presence of graduate students but more so because of the numbers of under-graduates and the different expectations for research productivity. In addition, such a view fails to take seriously the contributions of graduate students as teachers. It is not a failing for research universities to put graduate stu-dents into the classroom if they are advanced students and are well trained and appropriately monitored. On the contrary, it provides some of the continual infusion of new ideas and diverse perspectives that is one of the distinctive advantages of attending a research university. This is less apparent partly because of the way in which graduate student teachers are com-monly used. They often are misleadingly called teaching assistants even when they have full course responsibility. They also typically are assigned to teach the broadest and most basic courses (e.g., introductory sociology). These courses are, in fact, among the most difficult to teach well and are among the courses in which years of experience (combined with continued effort) pay off well. These also are courses in which graduate students have the least chance to offer their special advantage as teachers—ex-posure for undergraduates to active, vital, en-gagement in research. It would make more sense for many graduate students to be assigned to teach in their areas of research specialization, where they know the literature well and can bring some of the excitement of their own research to their undergraduate students.

Second, the institutional setting of graduate education matters. Just as undergraduate edu-cation is very different in a residential liberal arts college, a research university, or a four-year commuter campus, so too does the experience and, to some extent, the intellectual content of graduate education vary with context. I already have mentioned the advantages any one graduate program draws from being embedded within a graduate school offering a panoply of such programs. These advantages are centrally intellectual but also extend outside the curricula. Graduate students benefit from the presence of, and opportunity to interact with, other graduate students and from specialized support services that are available only where there is a critical mass to use them (e.g., special language programs, centers for development of teaching).

Third, work with graduate students also is teaching and deserves attention as an important part of teaching. Graduate students are, after all, not different people but unusually talented and serious former undergraduate students. Courses and seminars for them may be taught better or worse. Advising and mentoring can be strong and enriching or minimal. They may have opportunities for research apprenticeships or lack them. Professors (and programs) may create settings in which groups of graduate students with similar interests learn from each other over extended periods of time or leave each graduate student in relative isolation. Graduate programs can be well planned, with strong teaching of basic courses such as theory and methods, or collective efforts to ensure the strength of such teaching can be minimal because of notions of professorial privilege. Similarly, there may be a hierarchy of graduate courses in which some cover the range of work in a field, whereas others follow up on specific aspects. Or, all instructors may simply assume the right to teach their own research or their own biases, obliterating the distinction between a more basic course and an idiosyncratic seminar. Not least of all, departments may choose to have graduate students systematically evaluate the instruction they receive—or choose to hide—from the information such evaluations would provide.

Fourth, one of the important tasks of graduate programs is to educate the future professorate. Whereas teaching assistants are widely decried as cheap labor, they also are teachers in training. Failure to make clear the distinction of roles and to make good on the promise of really providing training for teaching puts many American universities in a difficult situation. It is not surprising that teaching assistants have begun to form unions. Viewed simply from their contributions of labor power, they are indeed paid low salaries and subjected to exploitation. It is not at all uncommon for students to be paid 20 percent of what senior faculty members are paid to take on at least superficially similar responsibilities. The problem is more complex than this account would make it seem. In principle, faculty members also take on many other responsibilities including supervision of graduate students, undergraduate advising, and participation in collegial duties and administration—not to mention research. Most faculty members spend many working hours on these tasks. But, and here is a key feature of the problem, institutions generally apply few, if any, negative incentives to those who fail to perform these roles. Faculty who do not advise undergraduates, mentor graduate students, serve on committees, take on administrative tasks, or publish research might not receive raises, but they are not fired or subjected to loss of income. Indeed, doing all these things badly (except perhaps research) works surprisingly well as a way in which to gain free time within the context of university employment.

Fifth, the majority of graduate students, including Ph.D. holders, will not become college teachers. In thinking about how we teach at the graduate level, it is vital to pay attention to the multiple career tracks for which we prepare students. As with so much else, this is likely to be reflected in a differentiation of institutional roles. Educating students as researchers is likely to remain the dominant strategy for those who wish to be among the most elite Ph.D. programs. Expansion into applied research might grow, but expansion into nonresearch fields (e.g., marriage and family counseling) is likely to be rare. The elite graduate departments would do well to think explicitly about how they can best prepare students for jobs in selective liberal arts colleges, where research continues to flourish alongside a strong emphasis on undergraduate teaching. Development of applied programs outside the research emphasis may take place more at other universities and may offer them distinctive niches. In all settings, it is important to keep in mind that graduate education is, at least ideally, not simply "training" but a much broader intellectual and scholarly enterprise. Students are not simply developing technical skills; this may be more or less important depending on their career aspirations. They are continuing an education. If this works well, then they may become business executives, journalists, politicians, or even college administrators but still remain, in important ways, sociologists.

5. *The internationalization of American higher education will continue and will pose both opportunities and challenges.* There might be debate about how to understand increasing global integration, but there can be little doubt that it is a basic fact of life in the contemporary world. Barring the catastrophic scenarios of science fiction novels, there is good reason to think that global integration will continue to grow in the next century as it has grown in the past five centuries. This holds direct implications for the teaching of sociology.

First, of course, there is a challenge to the actual substantive content we teach. For example, American sociology is struggling to break free from constraints that have impaired its otherwise great ability to speak to the processes and concerns of globalization. A simple ethnocentrism is the first. The vast majority of American sociological research has been about America (even if often presented as discoveries of universal truth). In introductory textbooks, "cross-cultural" examples have been commonly drawn from older anthropological studies of "exotic" or "primitive" peoples, not from contemporary social contexts other than America. The recent growth of international research is a welcome countertrend; so is the growing introduction of sociological research from other countries into the teaching and scholarship of Americans. In addition to ethnocentrism, there is the extent to which sociology has taken its very notion of society from the rise of the nation-state (Tilly 1984; Calhoun 1995). This has made a taken-for-granted assumption out of a question that needs to be explored, with attention to all the different scales and manners in which collectivities and social relations are constructed. Thus, bringing international content more fully into our teaching is not simply a matter of comparative sociology in which the units of comparison are presumed to be "whole societies," that is, nation-states. It also is a matter of studying transnational processes— movement of people, flows of culture or capital, corporate organization, and other nongovernmental organizations. Taking internationalization seriously also means seeing the internal heterogeneity of each allegedly "whole" society—cultural diversity, regional distinctions, different forms of ties to other societies around the world, and different relations to the international activities of the government. All of this implies that what is needed is not only more courses on explicitly international topics but also an introduction of more globally diverse content into all sorts of courses.

Beyond the desirability of better scientific content, institutional transformation makes internationalization an issue for teaching. Close to half a million international students study in U.S. colleges and universities.[6] This does not include foreign-born residents of the United States, who have become a rapidly growing proportion of the student population. Both groups are distributed unevenly among schools; close to 10 percent of all foreign students attend colleges and universities in metropolitan New York. In general, foreign students are more prominent at schools in large metropolitan areas but attend a wide variety of kinds of schools in those areas. Courses need to change not only to better educate these students but also to better take advantage of the diversity their presence brings to classrooms. Much of the growth in international students has been in graduate students, and of course, this also calls for attention. Too many programs have been slow to meet the interests of the students they attract; too many treat international students as a separate category, subject to different expectations and monitored for signs as to whether they will return to their home countries after graduation or make careers in the United States. Many do the latter, of course, and contribute to a growing presence of international faculty in American colleges and universities. This too is a transformation with implications for teaching. These faculty have much to contribute, but both employing schools and students are ambivalent about them (e.g., quick to criticize accents).

The flow of students in the other direction also is important. Some 89,000 American students studied abroad in 1995-1996. Study abroad programs, however, are prominent only among students at the more selective colleges and universities. This is partly a reflection of students' aspirations and choice of courses of study, but it also is largely shaped by financial resources.[7] This suggests all the more need to bring international content into a wide range of

teaching. Study abroad is growing and increasingly being encouraged in liberal arts programs (and in a few more applied programs, mainly at selective schools). A weak link, however, is the development of opportunities for returning study abroad students to integrate their international experiences into their curricula, to reflect on what they learned and see it in intellectually deeper ways. Students evaluate study abroad experiences extremely favorably, but except for language majors, these remain largely cut off from the rest of what they do in school, and "reentry" sometimes is a letdown.

6. *Student populations will continue to grow more diverse.* As college and university education has become less exclusively the prerogative of an elite, as women have been included in growing numbers, and as religious and racial exclusions have been eliminated, student bodies have become more heterogeneous. This has been true on nearly every campus, but diversity also has been unevenly distributed among campuses. The changes reflect not only higher education policies but changes in the demography and stratification of American society.

Increasing enrollments of students outside dominant groups has brought recurrent resentments, regardless of whether the newly admitted or expanding groups were Jews, Blacks, Asians, or women. The affirmative action policies adopted in and after the 1960s have produced especially widespread resentment and criticism including from some of their intended (and actual) beneficiaries. In the late 1990s, attacks on such programs began to enjoy more success in courts and referenda. It seems likely that the extent of affirmative action in college and university admissions will be reduced. Certainly in some states such as California, dramatic changes in policy have been adopted. But it is not likely that there will be an even rollback to such programs; rather, the level of effort made to attract various minorities will likely vary from school to school and from state to state.

Cutbacks in affirmative action will most adversely affect blacks and Hispanics. They will benefit whites and Asians, and in states with large Asian populations, they will benefit Asians the most.[8] The main impact will be not on the overall numbers of each group attending college but rather on which colleges they attend. Where affirmative action is relaxed, the most selective schools will become more white and Asian, the less selective more black and Hispanic. The impact probably will be greater on public schools than on private ones. The impact is likely to be more extreme in some states such as California. In general, it will work to increase the implications of the differentiation of institutions we already have noted.

Whatever happens with affirmative action, however, diversity is likely to grow—and to grow even at highly selective schools. High levels of immigration in the past decade are a key reason and are reinforced by the relatively young ages of most immigrants and the relatively high fertility of immigrants (and nonimmigrant minorities). Teachers will need to be attentive to the different backgrounds and interests of a much wider range of groups than were present in American higher education even a couple of decades ago. Already, teachers in major metropolitan areas are dealing with such changes in student bodies. Recent immigrants figure especially prominently in community colleges and some public four-year schools. These are attractive not only because of low cost and open admissions but also because of programs that meet these students' needs and convenience for living at home (which many such students and/or their families prefer). Wherever minority students are, there also will

be demand for teaching that bears directly on the distinctiveness of their lives and communities.[9]

The goal of having faculty populations broadly reflecting the composition of student bodies is becoming even harder to attain. This is likely to be a source of continuing controversy. The problem is not that there are few talented members of minority groups but that there are many such minority groups. Asian students might think it a good thing to have black and Hispanic as well as white faculty, for example, but it hardly overcomes a lack of Asian faculty. South Asian students might feel poorly represented by Chinese faculty members, although both are "Asian." Pakistani and Indian students might not feel equally well represented by faculty of either national background—and, as the example suggests, religion is likely to play a role (uncomfortable for many American sociologists) alongside race, language, and national origin. Many of these also are categories of potential faculty that current department members, even those favorable to affirmative action for blacks, have a hard time conceptualizing as important for increasing diversity and representativeness. To this, add the question of whether women of ethnic and racial minorities are hired as often as men. In any case, more different minority group members will compete (with each other as well as with whites) for open positions. Foreign students figure in some groups, such as Asians, alongside immigrant or longtime Americans. Many such groups are coming to be prominent in graduate student populations while still poorly represented in faculty positions.

To the extent that departments successfully recruit a range of minority faculty, they will have to pay attention to the shortage of co-ethnic senior mentors for these new junior faculty. They also will need to deal well with situations in which senior faculty are over-whelmingly white and junior faculty are over-whelmingly people of color. Recruiting diverse junior faculty is, after all, only one step in a longer process of adjusting to change. Not least of all, senior faculty will need to be prepared to work with students of various ethnicities, including white and black Americans, to minimize their prejudices against members of other groups, for example, Asians with strong accents.

7. *Within colleges and universities, there will be opportunities to achieve stronger intellectual communities across disciplinary divisions, but there also will be resistance.* One of the great changes in higher education institutions has been a reduction in the embeddedness and membership of each individual faculty member in his or her home institution. This has come partly as a result of growth in scale. It has come largely as a result of interinstitutional mobility. As faculty move from school to school, they have reduced cross-unit ties within each school. A crucial dimension of all of this is the development of highly distinct academic disciplines. This is not just—or perhaps even crucially—a matter of intellectual distinctions (Calhoun 1992). It is a matter of power and turf control. It also is largely a matter of the creation of sociometric universes within which reputations and careers are formed.

Different disciplines are supported by separate professional associations, scholarly journals, and periodic conventions. There also are interdisciplinary associations, journals, and conventions. These typically play smaller roles in job markets, but they are not altogether different. As we discussed earlier, the rising importance of research facilitated the creation of supralocal job markets and career opportunities. These are of greatest importance, not

surprisingly, for those scholars and institutions that most emphasize research. The more invested academics are in research, the greater their opportunities for mobility and the more differentiated their career patterns are likely to be. At the same time, the proliferation of temporary faculty also works against the construction of strong intellectual community.

Among the impacts of this pattern is a strong compartmentalization of intellectual life. Not only is each discipline an intellectual in-group suspicious of outsiders, so are many subdisciplines. The jokes about scholars knowing more and more about less and less have bite. Specialization is a path to certain forms of success. It is, however, a path antithetical to strong local intellectual community. It also encourages a differentiation, and sometimes even an alienation (of teaching scholars, especially those focused mainly on undergraduates), from those playing the most powerful roles in the elite research institutions.

Continuing reductions in research funding, especially government support for scholar-initiated "basic science," will narrow the range of schools and the range of scholars who can depend heavily on this kind of research. Most other schools and scholars will have greater reasons to strengthen their local ties. Proprietorial research has grown rapidly, although only minimally in sociology. Where this is rooted in local university-industry connections rather than in the discrete funding of individual scholars' research, this enhances local ties. Growth in applied research also furthers local ties and frequently is less closely controlled by disciplinary concerns than is basic science. Last, but not least, as government funding is cut and tied to special programs, foundations play a larger role. These, however, seldom are set up on disciplinary bases and commonly set up their programs on the basis of cross-cutting thematic concerns. Ease of long-distance communication (e.g., by e-mail and the Internet) also facilitates formation of cross-disciplinary subgroups. As more graduate students seek employment outside universities, the hold of disciplines on them (and thus on those who pay for their education and employ their teachers) may be reduced. Two-career couples have become more prominent, and geographic mobility is harder for them.

Among the implications of low levels of local interdisciplinary ties is a tendency for teachers in any one field to know relatively little about what their students are studying in other departments. A valid but not altogether novel criticism of contemporary college educations is that there is little coherence to the overall package of courses a student takes and that there are few opportunities for students to reflect on how the whole fits together. Instructors who have weak knowledge of and ties to colleagues in other fields are poorly placed to help students make the relevant connections. Colleges and universities recently have responded to this line of criticism with a renewed emphasis on inter-disciplinary general education at the "founda-tions" level and on "capstone" courses, usually within majors, at the immediate pre-graduation stage. The latter have commonly been discipli-nary and often oriented especially toward stu-dents continuing toward disciplinary graduate programs. Some, however, have addressed the needs of students headed toward postbacca-laureate professional schools or making the transition from college to employment. There remains, however, a tension between the strong interdisciplinary interests of many students and the extent to which disciplines continue to con-trol the turf of academic employment.

Intense competition over research stars on the part of elite graduate institutions is likely to continue. This will lead to more interinstitu-tional mobility and reductions in local integra-tion across disciplines in those institutions. The more open the job market, the greater will be the reward attaching to disciplinary prestige compared to local cross-unit ties. On the other hand, many stars are hired on the basis of interdisciplinary reputations and engagements. In many universities, moreover, disciplinary de-partments are the primary defenders of the status quo. Conservative against most forms of change (except growth in their own resources), they resist curricular reform, the introduction of new fields, and investment in interdiscipli-nary scholarship and teaching, even when these are intellectually exciting and/or attractive to students.

It is at least possible that the hold of discrete disciplines over academic employment and other resources will be attenuated. This is per-haps least likely in the largest research univer-sities. But if interdisciplinary education be-comes more attractive to potential employers, then there will be some incentive for graduate schools to provide it. This coincides with a strong set of intellectual challenges to disci-plines. Sociology, for example, has relatively weak internal coherence, and this is closely related to an intellectual diversity and openness that many of us find among its principal attrac-tions. But this also limits the hold of any puta-tive center on a wide range of nominal members of the discipline. Excitement in interdiscipli-nary fields from social history to cultural stud-ies, science studies, and the intersecting worlds of theory is palpable. Both research funding and employment opportunities for students draw other sociologists toward criminology, medical sociology, family studies, and other more "ap-plied" fields. This seems likely to continue, along with disciplinary resistance and varying levels of accommodation.

Changes continue. Some are welcome, like the current opening up of the job market. Even such welcome changes demand action as it becomes crucial to attract talented students, especially minority students, to graduate education and teaching careers. We must be careful not to vocalize excessively the frustrations and cynicism forged in years when there were virtually no jobs in this changed era. At the same time, even the opening up of the job market has different implications for different sorts of institutions. It does not come with a simple elimination of fiscal stringency, for example, and it does not erase the enormous movement toward temporary employment that has deeply affected academic careers and intellectual life in recent years. There also is more and more attractive nonacademic employment for graduate students. But both this and the effective education of future college teachers call for deeper examination of graduate curricula—beyond the goal of training researchers—and for a recognition that graduate teaching is an increasingly important kind of teaching (not something else that some undergraduate teachers happen to do).

A major concern is the extent to which institutional differentiation is giving way to polarization. For schools heavily invested in liberal arts education, the most basic issue is whether they are able to attract more qualified applicants than they can accept. This means paying the bills without growing beyond the high-level applicant pool (and, in most cases, maintaining both diversity and intellectual quality by providing scholarships for a sizable number of students). Being able to keep undergraduate programs focused on the arts and sciences also means securing graduate or professional school placement for most graduates and offering sufficient general prestige to help others without job-specific credentials in the market for middle-class jobs. Schools that cannot meet these requirements will be pressed to focus increasingly on applied subjects and direct ties to labor markets and will face different competitive and fiscal pressures.[10]

For all the criticisms of American colleges and universities that have been offered in recent years, it is important to keep in mind that we offer higher education to an unprecedented proportion of our population. We welcome international students in large numbers and attract them partly because of the quality of our schools. There is much to be proud of. This has made it all the more frustrating when critics—insiders as well as outsiders—have claimed that teaching was being utterly neglected or ideologically subverted. Equally frustrating, our leaders in higher education have done a strikingly poor job in explaining colleges, universities, the work of their faculties, and the education of their students to the public and to interested groups such as parents and, indeed, students themselves. Reporters might understand us poorly, but because they are our graduates and the readers of our press releases, we should not simply blame them for this.

It has been harder to develop strong approaches to the teaching of sociology when these are pursued without attention to the differentiation of students and institutions. To measure up to the tasks of educational excellence before us, we need to be clear-sighted about the transformations we have experienced and those we still are working through.

Notes

1. Larger institutions were not immune. Under financial pressure in 1991, the University of California introduced not only economic incentives for retirement but also procedures that could lead to termination of tenure for low-productivity faculty who did not volunteer. See Brubacher and Rudy (1997:402-4).

2. O'Brien (1997) offers a useful discussion of some of the background and arguments, and he concludes that tenure is not a necessary condition of academic freedom.

3. One of the continuing obstacles to appointing more minority faculty, at least in the research universities, is that their records are compared primarily to their age mates. The inflation of publication standards in an era of few jobs makes this a tough comparison. But hardly anyone is willing to admit the extent to which many minorities denied jobs because their research records were not "up to par" in fact have stronger records than already tenured faculty.

4. Institutions will continue to experience fiscal pressures, even in good economic times. Many of the factors that already have driven up costs will continue to do so. These include not only labor costs but also expenditures on libraries, physical plant, and laboratory facilities (for teaching as well as research). At the same time, competition for students will center partly on cost (in the form of scholarships at elite institutions and directly in the form of tuition and fees at less elite ones).

5. One would generally not say that college education has grown at the expense of high school. There might be at least one grain of truth in such a statement, however, as in the notion that graduate education has in some way sapped undergraduate education. In our very hierarchical educational field, prestige and material rewards typically are greater at higher levels. This will tend to draw strong teachers away from lower levels of the system. The fact remains, in the case of high school as in that of college, that the biggest change in character of education has had to do with extension of entrance to a much larger percentage of the population.

6. The total was 457,984 in 1996-1997, according the Institute for International Education. This is an increase of about 1 percent over the year before. The most rapid growth in numbers of foreign students took place in the 1980s. The recent crisis of Asian economies might actually reduce the numbers, but probably only temporarily.

7. The financial resources in question include not only those of the student and his or her parents but also those of the school itself. Operating study abroad programs is expensive; encouraging students to attend programs operated by others and offering transfer credit means losing tuition revenue. It also should be noted that the impact of class on study abroad is not limited to financial resources; it also includes the effect of parents' "cultural capital" including whether they have traveled abroad, are aware of international issues, and so on.

8. California is the paradigm for this. It should be noted, however, that "Asian" is not a single and internally homogeneous category. Asian groups vary in their economic standing and in the extent to which their children will benefit from admissions policies emphasizing grades and test scores alone.

9. Such teaching might, in fact, be one of the most important exceptions to the tendency for "applied" courses to dominate in less elite schools.

10. Among other things, alumni giving and other private benefactions go very disproportionately to the more selective schools. This is only partly because their alumni are better off. It also is because donors like to back winners and be associated with elite institutions. And it might be because students who attend less selective schools feel more like they have bought educational goods in a pure market transaction and less like they have been admitted to membership in a privileged status group. Those who attended schools without a strong (usually residential) community also might have developed weaker loyalties. The primary exception to this pattern is corporate donors. These often back elite institutions with either the students or researchers of which they wish to have a connection. But they also back local schools as a

part of their involvement in local communities, economies, and labor markets.

References

Brubacher, John S. and Willis Rudy. 1997. *Higher Education in Transition: A History of American Colleges and Universities.* New Brunswick, NJ: Transaction Publishers.

Calhoun, Craig. 1992. "Sociology, Other Disciplines, and the Project of a General Understanding of Social Life." Pp. 137-95 in *Sociology and Its Publics,* edited by T. Halliday and M. Janowitz. Chicago: University of Chicago Press.

———. 1995. *Critical Social Theory.* Cambridge, MA: Blackwell.

Oakley, Francis. 1992. *Community of Learning: The American College and the Liberal Arts Tradition.* New York: Oxford University Press.

O'Brien, George Dennis. 1997. *All the Essential Half-Truths about Higher Education.* Chicago: University of Chicago Press.

Tilly, Charles. 1984. *Big Questions, Large Processes, Huge Comparisons.* New York: Russell Sage.

Turner, Sarah E. and William G. Bowen. 1990. "The Flight from the Arts and Sciences: Trends in Degrees Conferred." *Science,* October 26, pp. 517-21.

53

Rethinking Faculty Careers

R. Eugene Rice

Just as the established view of scholarship is rooted in a particular epistemology, it also assumes a particular kind of faculty career—both narrow and limited. The prevailing conception of what constitutes a valued academic career begins with a Ph.D. (based primarily on research in a discipline) and leads to a tenure-track appointment, achieving tenure in a prescribed time, and advancing on a short, three-rung ladder from assistant to associate to full professor, all turning in large part on one's research performance. Many faculty take other paths, and there are wide variations, but this is the legitimate and honored career pattern. It is a career path growing out of a set of priorities cultivated in a different time—the assumptive world of the academic professional.

Faculty priorities as we have known them are now being challenged and, in many colleges and universities, substantially changed. The contexts in which faculty work—the financial constraints, the technological environment, the basic assumptions about work itself—are being transformed. But we are only now beginning to rethink the ways in which faculty careers are arranged. Many accommodations are being patched together to permit individual faculty

AUTHOR'S NOTE: This is a reprint of part of an article originally published as Rice, R. Eugene, "Rethinking Faculty Careers," American Association for Higher Education, Working Paper Series No. 1, 1996, pp. 19-24. Used with permission.

and institutions to make it through this turbulent time. We have not, however, addressed the serious organizational implications of these changes for the patterning of faculty careers.

In this effort to reexamine faculty careers, I want us to consider more than the way in which the career is sequenced and the policy implications, more than tenure and its alternatives, as important as these are. Instead, the tenure issues need to be placed within a larger context that relates to the kinds of working lives people who choose academic careers are able to live. I want us to think about careers that, in the future, will attract the best of a new generation into the profession. We need careers that will be more resilient and self-renewing for individual faculty, but ones that are also aligned with the central missions of our colleges and universities, enabling our institutions to lead in a society where the priorities and needs are changing in an environment of growing constraints.

Changes in the Academic Workplace

As we move into a new century, we are already grappling with the front edges of difficult [and] challenging changes in the academic workplace. An enlarged vision of the scholarly work of faculty promises to ease the difficulty of negotiating this critical transition period by opening the way for a richer variety of choices for individual faculty and providing appropriate and adaptive options for institutions. Taking full advantage of this multidimensional approach to scholarly work will require, however, significant changes in the way in which we organize and support the careers of faculty.

The major shifts in the future of the academic workplace impinging directly on our assumptions about faculty careers are these:

From	To
• Maintaining a primary focus on faculty–who we are and what we know	• A primary focus on learning
• An emphasis on the professional autonomy of faculty	• Increased faculty involvement in academic institution building
• Highly individualistic ways of working ("my work")	• Greater collaboration ("our work")
• Career dependence	• Career resilience
• A perception of colleges and universities as worlds set apart	• Greater faculty responsibility for public life and the quality of democratic participation

Toward a Complete Scholar

Faculty in the early stages of their careers and the graduate students interviewed in our "Heeding New Voices" inquiry express a longing for academic careers that, over the years, would lead to a more complete sense of what it meant to be a scholar. Young faculty who love their specializations and enjoy research regretted that what counted as serious scholarship was too narrowly circumscribed. One faculty member complained that if her writing "was accessible to a broader public, it was devalued." Another in the social sciences lamented that if his scholarly work "was too applied," it would be regarded as of questionable quality.

In the report from the distinguished Presidential Young Investigator Colloquium on "America's Academic Future," new faculty in the sciences, engineering, and mathematics set forth as their first [principle]: "Encourage and reward teaching excellence, instructional scholarship, and public service as well as research." And, they concluded, "In short, there is a strong need to promote a higher quality of faculty life that more fully recognizes and develops the diverse talents and interests of all the faculty" (1992, p. 2).

This is what is envisioned for the new American scholar, that over a lifetime one could, in fact, become a complete scholar. This would involve the cultivation of a multidimensional sense of the professional self.

Reference

America's Academic Future: A Report of the Presidential Young Investigator Colloquium on U.S. Engineering, Mathematics, and Science Education for the Year 2010 and beyond. Directorate for Education and Human Resources, National Science Foundation, January 1992.

54

From Teaching to Learning: A New Paradigm for Undergraduate Education

Robert B. Barr and John Tagg

The significant problems we face cannot be solved at the same level of thinking we were at when we created them.

—Albert Einstein

A paradigm shift is taking hold in American higher education. In its briefest form, the paradigm that has governed our colleges is this: a college is an institution that exists *to provide instruction.* Subtly but profoundly, we are shifting to a new paradigm: a college is an institution that exists *to produce learning.* This shift changes everything. It is both needed and wanted.

We call the traditional, dominant paradigm the "Instruction Paradigm." Under it, colleges have created complex structures to provide for the activity of teaching conceived primarily as delivering 50-minute lectures—the mission of a college is to deliver instruction.

Now, however, we are beginning to recognize that our dominant paradigm mistakes a means for an end. It takes the means or method—called "instruction" or "teaching"—

AUTHORS' NOTE: *Change,* November-December, 1995, pp. 13-25. Reprinted with permission of Helen Dwight Reid Educational Foundation. Published by Heldref Publications, 1319 Eighteenth St., N.W., Washington, D.C. 20036-1802. Copyright © 1995.

and makes it the college's end or purpose. To say that the purpose of colleges is to provide instruction is like saying that General Motors' business is to operate assembly lines or that the purpose of medical care is to fill hospital beds. We now see that our mission is not instruction but rather that of producing *learning* with every student by *whatever* means work best.

The shift to a "Learning Paradigm" liberates institutions from a set of difficult constraints. Today it is virtually impossible for them to respond effectively to the challenge of stable or declining budgets while meeting the increasing demand for postsecondary education from increasingly diverse students. Under the logic of the Instruction Paradigm, colleges suffer from a serious design flaw: it is not possible to increase outputs without a corresponding increase in costs because any attempt to increase outputs without increasing resources is a threat to quality. If a college attempts to increase its productivity by increasing either class sizes or faculty workloads, for example, academics will be quick to assume inexorable negative consequences for educational quality.

Just as important, the Instruction Paradigm rests on conceptions of teaching that are increasingly recognized as ineffective. As Alan Guskin pointed out in a September/October 1994 *Change* article premised on the shift from teaching to learning, "The primary learning environment for undergraduate students, the fairly passive lecture-discussion format where faculty talk and most students listen, is contrary to almost every principle of optimal settings for student learning." The Learning Paradigm ends the lecture's privileged position, honoring in its place whatever approaches serve best to prompt learning of particular knowledge by particular students.

The Learning Paradigm also opens up the truly inspiring goal that each graduating class learns more than the previous graduating class. In other words, the Learning Paradigm envisions the institution itself as a learner—over time, it continuously learns how to produce more learning with each graduating class, each exiting student.

For many of us, the Learning Paradigm has always lived in our hearts. As teachers, we want above all else for our students to learn and succeed. But the heart's feeling has not lived clearly and powerfully in our heads. Now, as the elements of the Learning Paradigm permeate the air, our heads are beginning to understand what our hearts have known. However, none of us has yet put all the elements of the Learning Paradigm together in a conscious, integrated whole.

Lacking such a vision, we've witnessed reformers advocate many of the new paradigm's elements over the years, only to see few of them widely adopted. The reason is that they have been applied piecemeal within the structures of a dominant paradigm that rejects or distorts them. Indeed, for two decades the response to calls for reform from national commissions and task forces generally has been an attempt to address the issues *within the framework of the Instruction Paradigm*. The movements thus generated have most often failed, undone by the contradictions within the traditional paradigm. For example, if students are not learning to

solve problems or think critically, the old logic says we must teach a class in thinking and make it a general education requirement. The logic is all too circular: what students are learning in the classroom doesn't address their needs or ours; therefore, we must bring them back into another classroom and instruct them some more. The result is never what we hope for because, as Richard Paul, director of the Center for Critical Thinking, observes glumly, "Critical thinking is taught in the same way that other courses have traditionally been taught, with an excess of lecture and insufficient time for practice."

To see what the Instruction Paradigm is, we need only look at the structures and behaviors of our colleges and infer the governing principles and beliefs they reflect. But it is much more difficult to see the Learning Paradigm, which has yet to find complete expression in the structures and processes of any college. So we must imagine it. This is what we propose to do here. As we outline its principles and elements, we'll suggest some of their implications for colleges—but only some, because the expression of principles in concrete structures depends on circumstances. It will take decades to work out many of the Learning Paradigm's implications. But we hope here that by making it more explicit, we will help colleagues to more fully recognize it and restructure our institutions in its image.

That such a restructuring is needed is beyond question; the gap between what we *say* we want of higher education and what its structures *provide* has never been wider. To use a distinction made by Chris Argyris and Donald Schön, the difference between our espoused theory and our theory-in-use is becoming distressingly noticeable. An "espoused theory," readers will recall, is the set of principles people offer to explain their behavior; the principles we can infer from how people or their organizations actually behave is their "theory-in-use." Right now, the Instruction Paradigm is our theory-in-use, yet the *espoused* theories of most educators more closely resemble components of the Learning Paradigm. The more we discover about how the mind works and how students learn, the greater the disparity between what we say and what we do. Thus so many of us feel increasingly constrained by a system increasingly at variance with what we believe. To build the colleges we need for the 21st century—to put our minds where our hearts are and rejoin acts with beliefs—we must consciously reject the Instruction Paradigm and restructure what we do on the basis of the Learning Paradigm.

The Paradigms

When comparing alternative paradigms, we must take care; the two will seldom be as neatly parallel as our summary chart suggests (see Chart 54.1). A paradigm is like the rules of a game; one of the functions of the rules is to define the playing field and domain of possibilities on that field. But a new paradigm may specify a game played on a larger or smaller field with a larger or smaller domain of legitimate possibilities. Indeed, the Learning Paradigm expands the playing field and domain of possibilities, and it radically changes various aspects of the game. In the Instruction Paradigm, a specific methodology determines the boundary of what colleges can do; in the Learning Paradigm, student learning and success set the boundary. By the same token, not all elements of the new paradigm are contrary to corresponding elements of the old; the new includes many elements of the old within its larger domain of possibilities. The Learning Paradigm does not prohibit lecturing, for example. Lecturing becomes one of many possible

methods, all evaluated on the basis of their ability to promote appropriate learning.

In describing the shift from an Instruction Paradigm to a Learning Paradigm, we limit our address in this [chapter] to undergraduate education. Research and public service are important functions of colleges and universities but lie outside the scope of the present discussion. Here, as in our summary chart, we'll compare the two paradigms along six dimensions: mission and purposes, criteria for success, teaching/learning structures, learning theory, productivity and funding, and nature of roles.

Mission and Purposes

In the Instruction Paradigm, the mission of the college is to provide instruction, to teach. The method and the product are one and the same. The means is the end. In the Learning Paradigm, the mission of the college is to produce learning. The method and the product are separate. The end governs the means.

Some educators may be uncomfortable with the verb "produce." We use it because it so strongly connotes that the college takes *responsibility* for learning. The point of saying that colleges are to *produce* learning—not provide, not support, not encourage—is to say, unmistakably, that they are responsible for the degree to which students learn. The Learning Paradigm shifts what the institution takes responsibility for: from quality instruction (lecturing, talking) to student learning. Students, the co-producers of learning, can and must, of course, take responsibility for their own learning. Hence, responsibility is a win-win game wherein two agents take responsibility for the same outcome even though neither is in complete control of all the variables. When two agents take such responsibility, the resulting synergy produces powerful results.

CHART 54.1 Comparing Educational Paradigms

The Instruction Paradigm	The Learning Paradigm
Mission and Purposes	
• Provide/deliver instruction	• Produce learning
• Transfer knowledge from faculty to students	• Elicit student discovery and construction of knowledge
• Offer courses and programs	• Create powerful learning environments
• Improve the quality of instruction	• Improve the quality of learning
• Achieve access for diverse students	• Achieve success for diverse students
Criteria for Success	
• Inputs, resources	• Learning and student-success outcomes
• Quality of entering students	• Quality of exiting students
• Curriculum development, expansion	• Learning technologies development, expansion
• Quantity and quality of resources	• Quantity and quality of outcomes
• Enrollment, revenue growth	• Aggregate learning growth, efficiency
• Quality of faculty instruction	• Quality of students, learning
Teaching/Learning Structures	
• Atomistic; parts prior to whole	• Holistic; whole prior to parts
• Time held constant, learning varies	• Learning held constant, time varies
• 50-minute lecture, 3-unit course	• Learning environments
• Classes start/end at same time	• Environment ready when student is
• One teacher, one classroom	• Whatever learning experience works
• Independent disciplines, departments	• Cross discipline/department collaboration
• Covering material	• Specified learning results
• End-of-course assessment	• Pre-/during/post-assessments
• Grading within classes by instructors	• External evaluations of learning
• Private assessment	• Public assessment
• Degree equals accumulated credit hours	• Degree equals demonstrated knowledge and skills
Learning Theory	
• Knowledge exists "out there"	• Knowledge exists in each person's mind and is shaped by individual experience
• Knowledge comes in "chunks" and "bits" delivered by instructors	• Knowledge is constructed, created, and "gotten"
• Learning is cumulative and linear	• Learning is a nesting and interacting of frameworks
• Fits the storehouse of knowledge metaphor	• Fits learning how to ride a bicycle metaphor
• Learning is teacher centered and controlled	• Learning is student centered and controlled
• "Live" teacher, "live" students required	• "Active" learner required, but not "live" teacher
• The classroom and learning are competitive and individualistic	• Learning environments and learning are cooperative
• Talent and ability are rare	• Talent and ability are abundant
Productivity/Funding	
• Definition of productivity: cost per hour of instruction	• Definition of productivity: cost per unit of learning per student
• Funding for hours of instruction	• Funding for learning outcomes
Nature of Roles	
• Faculty are primary lecturers	• Faculty are primary designers of learning methods and environments
• Faculty and students act independently and in isolation	• Faculty and students work in teams with each other and other staff
• Teachers classify and sort students	• Teachers develop every student's competencies and talents
• Staff serve/support faculty and the process of instruction	• All staff are educators who produce student learning and success
• Any expert can teach	• Empowering learning is challenging and complex
• Line governance; independent actors	• Shared governance; teamwork

The idea that colleges cannot be responsible for learning flows from a disempowering notion of responsibility. If we conceive of responsibility as a fixed quantity in a zero-sum game, then students must take responsibility for their own learning, and no one else can. This model generates a concept of responsibility capable of assigning blame but not of empowering the most productive action. The concept of responsibility as a framework for action is quite different; when one takes responsibility, one sets goals and then acts to achieve them, continuously modifying one's behavior to better achieve the goals. To take responsibility for achieving an outcome is not to guarantee the outcome, nor does it entail the complete control of all relevant variables; it is to make the achievement of the outcome the criterion by which one measures one's own efforts. In this sense, it is no contradiction to say that students, faculty, and the college as an institution can all take responsibility for student learning.

In the Learning Paradigm, colleges take responsibility for learning at two distinct levels. At the organizational level, a college takes responsibility for the aggregate of student learning and success. Did, for example, the graduating class's mastery of certain skills or knowledge meet our high public standards for the award of the degree? Did the class's knowledge and skills improve over those of prior classes? The college also takes responsibility at the individual level, that is, for each individual student's learning. Did Mary Smith learn the chemistry we deem appropriate for a degree in that field? Thus, the institution takes responsibility for both its institutional outcomes and individual student outcomes.

Turning now to more specific purposes, in the Instruction Paradigm, a college aims to transfer or deliver knowledge from faculty to students; it offers courses and degree programs and seeks to maintain a high quality of instruc-

tion within them, mostly by assuring that faculty stay current in their fields. If new knowledge or clients appear, so will new course work. The very purpose of the Instruction Paradigm is to offer courses.

In the Learning Paradigm, on the other hand, a college's purpose is not to transfer knowledge but to create environments and experiences that bring students to discover and construct knowledge for themselves, to make students members of communities of learners that make discoveries and solve problems. The college aims, in fact, to create a series of ever more powerful learning environments. The Learning Paradigm does not limit institutions to a single means for empowering students to learn; within its framework, effective learning technologies are continually identified, developed, tested, implemented, and assessed against one another. The aim in the Learning Paradigm is not so much to improve the quality of instruction—although that is not irrelevant—as it is to improve continuously the quality of learning for students individually and in the aggregate.

Under the older paradigm, colleges aimed to provide access to higher education, especially for historically underrepresented groups such as African Americans and Hispanics. Too often, mere access hasn't served students well. Under the Learning Paradigm, the goal for underrepresented students (and all students) becomes not simply access but success. By "success," we mean the achievement of overall student educational objectives such as earning a degree, persisting in school, and learning the "right" things—the skills and knowledge that will help students to achieve their goals in work and life. A Learning Paradigm college, therefore, aims for ever higher graduation rates while maintaining or even increasing learning standards.

By shifting the intended institutional outcome from teaching to learning, the Learning Paradigm makes possible a continuous improvement in productivity. Whereas under the Instruction Paradigm a primary institutional purpose was to optimize faculty well-being and success—including recognition for research and scholarship—in the Learning Paradigm a primary drive is to produce learning outcomes more efficiently. The philosophy of an Instruction Paradigm college reflects the belief that it cannot increase learning outputs without more resources, but a Learning Paradigm college expects to do so continuously. A Learning Paradigm college is concerned with learning productivity, not teaching productivity.

Criteria for Success

Under the Instruction Paradigm, we judge our colleges by comparing them to one another. The criteria for quality are defined in terms of inputs and process measures. Factors such as selectivity in student admissions, number of Ph.D.'s on the faculty, and research reputation are used to rate colleges and universities. Administrators and boards may look to enrollment and revenue growth and the expansion of courses and programs. As Guskin put it, "We are so wedded to a definition of quality based on resources that we find it extremely difficult to deal with the *results* of our work, namely student learning."

The Learning Paradigm necessarily incorporates the perspectives of the assessment movement. While this movement has been under way for at least a decade, under the dominant Instruction Paradigm it has not penetrated very far into normal organizational practice. Only a few colleges across the country systematically assess student learning outcomes. Educators in California community colleges always seem to be surprised when they hear that 45 percent of first-time fall students do not return in the spring and that it takes an average of six years for a student to earn an associate's (AA) degree. The reason for this lack of outcomes knowledge is profoundly simple: under the Instruction Paradigm, student outcomes are simply irrelevant to the successful functioning and funding of a college.

Our faculty evaluation systems, for example, evaluate the performance of faculty in teaching terms, not learning terms. An instructor is typically evaluated by her peers or dean on the basis of whether her lectures are organized, whether she covers the appropriate material, whether she shows interest in and understanding of her subject matter, whether she is prepared for class, and whether she respects her students' questions and comments. All these factors evaluate the instructor's performance in teaching terms. They do not raise the issue of whether students are learning, let alone demand evidence of learning or provide for its reward.

Many institutions construe teaching almost entirely in terms of lecturing. A true story makes the point. A biology instructor was experimenting with collaborative methods of instruction in his beginning biology classes. One day his dean came for a site visit, slipping into the back of the room. The room was a hubbub of activity. Students were discussing material enthusiastically in small groups spread out across the room; the instructor would observe each group for a few minutes, sometimes making a comment, sometimes just nodding approval. After 15 minutes or so, the dean approached the instructor and said, "I came today to do your evaluation. I'll come back another time when you're teaching."

In the Instruction Paradigm, teaching is judged on its own terms; in the Learning Paradigm, the power of an environment or approach is judged in terms of its impact on learning. If learning occurs, then the environment has power. If students learn more in Environment A than in Environment B, then A is more powerful than B. To know this in the Learning Paradigm, we would assess student learning routinely and constantly.

Institutional outcomes assessment is analogous to classroom assessment, as described by K. Patricia Cross and Thomas Angelo. In our own experience of classroom assessment training workshops, teachers share moving stories about how even limited use of these techniques has prompted them to make big changes in their teaching, sometimes despite years of investment in a previous practice. Mimi Steadman, in a recent study of community college teachers using classroom assessment, found that "eighty-eight percent of faculty surveyed reported that they had made changes in their teaching behaviors as a result." This at first was startling to us. How could such small amounts of information produce such large changes in teacher behavior? Upon reflection, it became clear. The information was feedback about learning, about results—something teachers rarely collect. Given information that their students were not learning, it was obvious to these teachers that something had to be done about the methods they had been using. Likewise, we think, feedback on learning results at the institutional level should have a correspondingly large impact on an institution's behavior and on the means it uses to produce learning.

Of course, some will argue, true education simply cannot be measured. You cannot measure, for example, true appreciation of the beauty of a work of art. Certainly some learning is difficult, even impossible, to measure. But it does not follow that useful and meaningful assessment is impossible.

If we compare outcomes assessment with the input measures controlling policy in the Instruction Paradigm, we find that measures of outcome provide far more genuine information about learning than do measures of input.

Learning outcomes include whatever students do as a result of a learning experience. Any measurement of students' products from an educational experience is a measure of a learning outcome. We could count the number of pages students write, the number of books they read, their number of hours at the computer, or the number of math problems they solve.

Of course, these would be silly methods to determine institutional incentives, and we do not recommend them. Any one of them, however, would produce more useful information on learning than the present method of measuring inputs and ignoring outcomes. It would make more sense to fund a college on the number of math problems students solve, for example, than to fund it on the number of students who sit in math classes. We suspect that any system of institutional incentives based on outcomes would lead to greater learning than any system of incentives based on inputs. But we need not settle for a system biased toward the trivial. Right now, today, we can construct a good assessment regime with tools we have at hand.

The Learning Paradigm requires us to heed the advice of the Wingspread Group: "New forms of assessment should focus on establishing what college and university graduates have learned—the knowledge and skill levels they have achieved and their potential for further independent learning."

Teaching/Learning Structures

By structures, we mean those features of an organization that are stable over time and that form the framework within which activities and processes occur and through which the purposes of the organization are achieved. Structure includes the organization chart, role and reward systems, technologies and methods, facilities and equipment, decision-making customs, communication channels, feedback loops, financial arrangements, and funding streams.

Peter Senge, in *The Fifth Discipline*, a book about applying systems theory to organizational learning, observes that institutions and their leaders rarely focus their attention on systemic structures. They seldom think, he says, to alter basic structures in order to improve organizational performance, even though those structures generate the patterns of organizational action and determine which activities and results are possible. Perhaps the recent talk about restructuring, re-engineering, and reinvention in higher education reflects a change in focus and a heightened awareness of both the constraining and liberating power of organizational structures.

There is good reason to attend to structure. First, restructuring offers the greatest hope for increasing organizational efficiency and effectiveness. Structure is leverage. If you change the structure in which people work, you increase or decrease the leverage applied to their efforts. A change in structure can either increase productivity or change the nature of organizational outcomes. Second, structure is the concrete manifestation of the abstract principles of the organization's governing paradigm. Structures reflecting an old paradigm can frustrate the best ideas and innovations of new paradigm thinkers. As the governing paradigm changes, so likewise must the organization's structures.

In this section, we focus on the main structures related to the teaching and learning process; funding and faculty role structures are discussed later under separate headings.

The teaching and learning structure of the Instruction Paradigm college is atomistic. In its universe, the "atom" is the 50-minute lecture, and the "molecule" is the one-teacher, one-classroom, three-credit-hour course. From these basic units the physical architecture, the administrative structure, and the daily schedules of faculty and students are built. Dennis McGrath and Martin Spear, professors at the Community College of Philadelphia, note that "education proceeds everywhere through the vehicle of the three-credit course. Faculty members [and everyone else, we might add] have so internalized that constraint that they are long past noticing that it is a constraint, thinking it part of the natural order of things."

The resulting structure is powerful and rigid. It is, of course, perfectly suited to the Instruction Paradigm task of offering one-teacher, one-classroom courses. It is antithetical to creating almost any other kind of learning experience. A sense of this can be obtained by observing the effort, struggle, and rule-bending required to schedule even a slightly different kind of learning activity, such as a team-taught course.

In the "educational atomism" of the Instruction Paradigm, the parts of the teaching and learning process are seen as discrete entities. The parts exist prior to and independent of any whole; the whole is no more than the sum of the parts or even less. The college interacts with students only in discrete, isolated environments, cut off from one another because the parts—the classes—are prior to the whole. A "college education" is the sum of the student's experience of a series of discrete, largely unrelated, three-credit classes.

In the Instruction Paradigm, the teaching and learning process is governed by the further rule that time will be held constant while learning varies. Although addressing public elementary and secondary education, the analysis of the National Commission on Time and Learning nonetheless applies to colleges:

Time is learning's warden. Our time-bound mentality has fooled us all into believing that schools can educate all of the people all of the time in a school year of 180 six-hour days. . . . If experience, research, and common sense teach nothing else, they confirm the truism that people learn at different rates and in different ways with different subjects. But we have put the cart before the horse: our schools . . . are captives of the clock and calendar. The boundaries of student growth are defined by schedules . . . instead of standards for students and learning.

Under the rule of time, all classes start and stop at the same time and take the same number of calendar weeks. The rule of time and the priority of parts affect every instructional act of the college.

Thus it is, for example, that if students come into college classes "unprepared," it is not the job of the faculty who teach those classes to "prepare" them. Indeed, the structure of the one-semester, three-credit class makes it all but impossible to do so. The only solution, then, is to create new courses to prepare students for the existing courses; within the Instruction Paradigm, the response to educational problems is always to generate more atomized, discrete instructional units. If business students are lacking a sense of ethics, then offer and require a course in business ethics. If students have poor study skills, then offer a "master student" course to teach such skills.

Instruction Paradigm colleges atomistically organize courses and teachers into departments and programs that rarely communicate with one another. Academic departments, originally associated with coherent disciplines, are the structural home bases for accomplishing the essential work of the college: offering courses. "Departments have a life of their own," notes William D. Schaefer, professor of English and former executive vice chancellor at UCLA. They are "insular, defensive, self-governing, [and] compelled to protect their interests because the faculty positions as well as the courses

that justify funding those positions are located therein."

Those globally applicable skills that are the foundation of meaningful engagement with the world—reading, writing, calculating, reasoning—find a true place in this structure only if they have their own independent bases: the English or math or reading departments. If students cannot reason or think well, the college creates a course on reasoning and thinking. This in turn produces pressure to create a corresponding department. "If we are not careful." warns Adam Sweeting, director of the Writing Program at the Massachusetts School of Law at Andover, "the teaching of critical thinking skills will become the responsibility of one university department, a prospect that is at odds with the very idea of a university."

Efforts to extend college-level reading, writing, and reasoning "across the curriculum" have largely failed. The good intentions [have] produced few results because, under the Instruction Paradigm, the teacher's job is to "cover the material" as outlined in the disciplinary syllabus. The instructor charged with implementing writing or reading or critical thinking "across the curriculum" often must choose between doing her job or doing what will help students learn—between doing well, as it were, or doing good.

From the point of view of the Learning Paradigm, these Instruction Paradigm teaching and learning structures present immense barriers to improving student learning and success. They provide no space and support for redesigned learning environments or for experimenting with alternative learning technologies. They don't provide for, warrant, or reward assessing whether student learning has occurred or is improving.

In a Learning Paradigm college, the structure of courses and lectures becomes dispensable and negotiable. Semesters and quarters, lectures, labs, syllabi—indeed, classes them-selves—become options rather than received structures or mandatory activities. The Learning Paradigm prescribes no one "answer" to the question of how to organize learning environments and experiences. It supports any learning method and structure that works, where "works" is defined in terms of learning outcomes, not as the degree of conformity to an ideal classroom archetype. In fact, the Learning Paradigm requires a constant search for new structures and methods that work better for student learning and success and expects even these to be redesigned continually and to evolve over time.

The transition from Instruction Paradigm to Learning Paradigm will not be instantaneous. It will be a process of gradual modification and experimentation through which we alter many organizational parts in light of a new vision for the whole. Under the Instruction Paradigm, structures are assumed to be fixed and immutable; there is no ready means for achieving the leverage needed to alter them. The first structural task of the Learning Paradigm, then, is to establish such leverage.

The key structure for changing the rest of the system is an institution-wide assessment and information system—an essential structure in the Learning Paradigm and a key means for getting there. It would provide constant, useful feedback on institutional performance. It would track transfer, graduation, and other completion rates. It would track the flow of students through learning stages (such as the achievement of basic skills) and the development of in-depth knowledge in a discipline. It would measure the knowledge and skills of program completers and graduates. It would assess learning along many dimensions and in many places and stages in each student's college experience.

To be most effective, this assessment system would provide public institutional-level information. We are not talking about making public the status of individual students by name but about making the year-to-year graduation rate—or the mean score of graduating seniors on a critical thinking assessment, for example—"public" in the sense that [it is] available to everyone in the college community. Moreover, in the Learning Paradigm college, such data are routinely talked about and acted upon by a community ever dedicated to improving its own performance.

The effectiveness of the assessment system for developing alternative learning environments depends in part upon its being *external* to learning programs and structures. While in the Instruction Paradigm students are assessed and graded within a class by the same instructor responsible for teaching them, in the Learning Paradigm much of the assessment would be independent of the learning experience and its designer, somewhat as football games are independent measures of what is learned in football practice. Course grades alone fail to tell us what students know and can do; average grades assigned by instructors are not reliable measures of whether the institution is improving learning.

Ideally, an institution's assessment program would measure the "value added" over the course of students' experience at the college. Student knowledge and skills would be measured upon entrance and again upon graduation and at intermediate stages such as at the beginning and completion of major programs. Students could then be acknowledged and certified for what they have learned; the same data, aggregated, could help shift judgments of institutional quality from inputs and resources to the value added brought to student learning by the college.

The college devoted to learning first identifies the knowledge and skills it expects its graduates to possess, without regard to any particular curriculum or educational experiences. It then determines how to assess them reliably. It assesses graduating students, and the resulting information is then used to redesign and improve the processes and environments leading to such outcomes. In this manner, enhancing intellectual skills such as writing and problem solving and social skills such as effective team participation become the project of all learning programs and structured experiences. The whole would govern the parts.

Information from a sophisticated assessment system will gradually lead to the transformation of the college's learning environments and supporting structures. Such a system seeks out "best practice" benchmarks against which improvements in institutional performance can be measured in learning terms. It is the foundation for creating an institutional capacity to develop ever more effective and efficient ways of empowering learning. It becomes the basis for generating revenue or funding according to learning results rather than hours of instruction. Most important, it is the key to the college's and its staff's taking responsibility for and enjoying the progress of each student's education.

Instead of fixing the means—such as lectures and courses—the Learning Paradigm fixes the ends, the learning results, allowing the means to vary in its constant search for the most effective and efficient paths to student learning. Learning outcomes and standards thus would be identified and held to for all students—or *raised* as learning environments became more powerful—while the time students took to achieve those standards would vary. This would reward skilled and advanced students with speedy progress while enabling less prepared students the time they needed to actually master the material. By "testing out," students could also avoid wasting their time being "taught" what they already know. Students would be given "credit" for degree-relevant knowledge and skills regardless of how or where or when they learned them.

In the Learning Paradigm, then, a college degree would [not] represent time spent and credit hours dutifully accumulated but would certify that the student had demonstrably attained specified knowledge and skills. Learning Paradigm institutions would develop and publish explicit exit standards for graduates and grant degrees and certificates only to students who met them. Thus colleges would move away from educational atomism and move toward treating holistically the knowledge and skills required for a degree.

Learning Theory

The Instruction Paradigm frames learning atomistically. In it, knowledge, by definition, consists of matter dispensed or delivered by an instructor. The chief agent in the process is the teacher who delivers knowledge; students are viewed as passive vessels, ingesting knowledge for recall on tests. Hence, any expert can teach. Partly because the teacher knows which chunks of knowledge are most important, the teacher controls the learning activities. Learning is presumed to be cumulative because it amounts to ingesting more and more chunks. A degree is awarded when a student has received a specified amount of instruction.

The Learning Paradigm frames learning holistically, recognizing that the chief agent in the process is the learner. Thus, students must be active discoverers and constructors of their own knowledge. In the Learning Paradigm, knowledge consists of frameworks or wholes that are created or constructed by the learner. Knowledge is not seen as cumulative and linear, like a wall of bricks, but as a nesting and inter-acting of frameworks. Learning is revealed when those frameworks are used to understand and act. Seeing the whole of something—the forest rather than the trees, the image of the newspaper photo rather than its dots—gives meaning to its elements, and that whole becomes more than a sum of component parts. Wholes and frameworks can come in a moment—a flash of insight—often after much hard work with the pieces, as when one suddenly knows how to ride a bicycle.

In the Learning Paradigm, learning environments and activities are learner centered and learner controlled. They may even be "teacherless." While teachers will have designed the learning experiences and environments students use—often through teamwork with each other and other staff—they need not be present for or participate in every structured learning activity.

Many students come away from college with a false notion of what learning is and come to believe falsely that learning—at least for some subjects—is too difficult for them. Many students cruise through schools substituting an ersatz role-playing exercise for learning.

The first time I (Barr) studied calculus as a college freshman, I did well by conventional standards. However, while I could solve enough problems to get A's on exams, I really didn't feel that I understood the Limit Theorem, the derivative, or much else. But 15 years later, after having completed college and graduate school and having taught algebra and geometry in high school, I needed to relearn calculus so that I could tutor a friend. In only two, albeit intense, days, I relearned—or really learned for the first time, so it seemed—two semesters of calculus. During those days, I wondered how I ever thought calculus was difficult and why I didn't see the Limit Theorem and derivative for the simple, obvious things they are.

What was the difference between my first learning of calculus and the second? It certainly wasn't a higher IQ. And I don't think it was because I learned or remembered much from the first time. I think it was that I brought some very powerful intellectual frameworks to the learning the second time that I didn't have the first time. Having taught algebra and geometry, I had learned their basic structure, that is, the nature of a mathematical system. I had learned the lay of the land, the whole. Through many years of schooling and study, I had also learned a number of other frameworks that were useful for learning calculus. Thus learning calculus the second time within these "advanced" frameworks was easy compared to learning, or trying to learn, calculus without them as I did as a freshman.

So much of this is because the "learning" that goes on in Instruction Paradigm colleges frequently involves only rudimentary, stimulus-response relationships whose cues may be coded into the context of a particular course but are not rooted in the student's everyday, functioning understanding.

The National Council on Vocational Education summarizes the consequences in its 1991 report, *Solutions:* "The result is fractionation, or splitting into pieces: having to learn disconnected sub-routines, items, and sub-skills without an understanding of the larger context into which they fit and which gives them meaning." While such approaches are entirely consistent with educational atomism, they are at odds with the way we think and learn. The same report quotes Sylvia Famham-Diggory's summary of contemporary research: "Fractionated instruction maximizes forgetting, inattention, and passivity. Both children and adults acquire knowledge from active participation in holistic, complex, meaningful environments organized around long-term goals. Today's school programs could hardly have been better designed to prevent a child's natural learning system from operating."

The result is that when the contextual cues provided by the class disappear at the end of the semester, so does the learning. Howard Gardner points out that "researchers at Johns Hopkins, MIT, and other well-regarded universities have documented that students who receive honor grades in college-level physics courses are frequently unable to solve basic problems and questions encountered in a form slightly different from that on which they have been formally instructed and tested."

The Learning Paradigm embraces the goal of promoting what Gardner calls "education for understanding," "a sufficient grasp of concepts, principles, or skills so that one can bring them to bear on new problems and situations, deciding in which ways one's present competencies can suffice and in which ways one may require new skills or knowledge." This involves the mastery of functional, knowledge-based intellectual frameworks rather than the short-term retention of fractionated, contextual cues.

The learning theory of the Instruction Paradigm reflects deeply rooted societal assumptions about talent, relationships, and accomplishment: that which is valuable is scarce, life is a win-lose proposition, and success is an individual achievement. The Learning Paradigm theory of learning reverses these assumptions.

Under the Instruction Paradigm, faculty classify and sort students, in the worst cases into those who are "college material" and those who cannot "cut it," since intelligence and ability are scarce. Under the Learning Paradigm, faculty—and everybody else in the institution—are unambiguously committed to each student's success. The faculty and the institution take an R. Buckminster Fuller view of students: human beings are born geniuses and designed for success. If they fail to display their genius or fail to

succeed, it is because their design function is being thwarted. This perspective is founded not in wishful thinking but in the best evidence about the real capabilities of virtually all humans for learning. As the Wingspread Group points out, "There is growing research evidence that all students can learn to much higher standards than we now require." In the Learning Paradigm, faculty find ways to develop every student's vast talents and clear the way for every student's success.

Under the Instruction Paradigm, the classroom is competitive and individualistic, reflecting a view that life is a win-lose proposition. The requirement that the students must achieve individually and solely through their own efforts reflects the belief that success is an individual accomplishment. In the Learning Paradigm, learning environments—while challenging—are win-win environments that are cooperative, collaborative, and supportive. They are designed on the principle that accomplishment and success are the result of teamwork and group efforts, even when it appears one is working alone.

Productivity and Funding

Under the Instruction Paradigm, colleges suffer from a serious design flaw—they are structured in such a way that they cannot increase their productivity without diminishing the quality of their product. In the Instruction Paradigm, productivity is defined as cost per hour of instruction per student. In this view, the very quality of teaching and learning is threatened by any increase in the student-to-faculty ratio.

Under the Learning Paradigm, productivity is redefined as the cost per unit of learning per student. Not surprisingly, there is as yet no standard statistic that corresponds to this notion of productivity. Under this new definition, however, it *is* possible to increase outcomes without increasing costs. An abundance of research shows that alternatives to the traditional semester-length, classroom-based lecture method produce more learning. Some of these alternatives are less expensive; many produce more learning for the same cost. Under the Learning Paradigm, producing more with less becomes possible because the more that is being produced is learning and not hours of instruction. Productivity, in this sense, cannot even be measured in the Instruction Paradigm college. All that exists is a measure of exposure to instruction.

Given the Learning Paradigm's definition, increases in productivity pose no threat to the quality of education. Unlike the current definition, this new definition requires that colleges actually produce learning. Otherwise, there is no "product" to count in the productivity ratio.

But what should be the definition of "unit of learning," and how can it be measured? A single, permanent answer to that question does not and need not exist. We have argued above that learning, or at least the effects of learning, can be measured, certainly well enough to determine what students are learning and whether the institution is getting more effective and efficient at producing it.

The Instruction Paradigm wastes not only institutional resources but [also] the time and energy of students. We waste our students' time with registration lines, bookstore lines, lockstep class scheduling, and redundant courses and requirements. We do not teach them to learn efficiently and effectively. We can do a lot, as D. Bruce Johnstone, former chancellor of SUNY, suggests, to reduce the false starts and aimless "drift" of students that slow their progress toward a degree.

Now let's consider how colleges are funded. One of the absurdities of current funding formulas is that an institution could utterly fail its educational mission and yet its revenue would remain unaffected. For example, attendance at public colleges on the semester system is measured twice, once in the fall and again in the spring. Normally, at California community colleges, for example, about two-thirds of fall students return for the spring term. New students and returning stop-outs make up for the one-third of fall students who leave. Even if only half—or none at all—returned, as long as spring enrollments equal those of the fall, these institutions would suffer no loss of revenue.

There is no more powerful feedback than revenue. Nothing could facilitate a shift to the Learning Paradigm more swiftly than funding learning and learning-related institutional outcomes rather than hours of instruction. The initial response to the idea of outcomes-based funding is likely to be "That's not possible." But, of course, it is. As the new paradigm takes hold, forces and possibilities shift and the impossible becomes the rule.

Nature of Roles

With the shift to the Learning Paradigm comes a change in roles for virtually all college employees.

In the Instruction Paradigm, faculty are conceived primarily as disciplinary experts who impart knowledge by lecturing. They are the essential feature of the "instructional delivery system." The Learning Paradigm, on the other hand, conceives of faculty as primarily the designers of learning environments; they study and apply best methods for producing learning and student success.

If the Instruction Paradigm faculty member is an actor—a sage on a stage—then the Learning Paradigm faculty member is an inter-actor—a coach interacting with a team. If the model in the Instruction Paradigm is that of delivering a lecture, then the model in the Learning Paradigm is that of designing and then playing a team game. A coach not only instructs football players, for example, but also designs football practices and the game plan; he participates in the game itself by sending in plays and making other decisions. The new faculty role goes a step further, however, in that faculty not only design game plans but also create new and better "games," ones that generate more and better learning.

Roles under the Learning Paradigm, then, begin to blur. Architects of campus buildings and payroll clerks alike will contribute to and shape the environments that empower student learning. As the role structures of colleges begin to loosen up, and as accountability for results (learning) tightens up, organizational control and command structures will change. Teamwork and shared governance [will] over time replace the line governance and independent work of the Instruction Paradigm's hierarchical and competitive organization.

In the Learning Paradigm, as colleges specify learning goals and focus on learning technologies, interdisciplinary (or nondisciplinary) task groups and design teams become a major operating mode. For example, faculty may form a design team to develop a learning experience in which students networked via computers learn to write about selected texts or on a particular theme.

After developing and testing its new learning module, the design team may even be able to let students proceed through it without direct faculty contact except at designated points. Design teams might include a variety of staff: disciplinary experts, information technology experts, a graphic designer, and an assessment professional. Likewise, faculty and staff might form functional teams responsible for a body of learning outcomes for a stated number of students. Such teams could have the freedom that no faculty member has in today's atomized framework, that to organize the learning environment in ways that maximize student learning.

Meeting the Challenge

Changing paradigms is hard. A paradigm gives a system integrity and allows it to function by identifying what counts as information within the infinite ocean of data in its environment. Data that solve problems that the paradigm identifies as important are information; data that are irrelevant to those problems are simply noise, static. Any system will provide both channels for transmitting information relevant to the system and filters to reduce noise.

Those who want to change the paradigm governing an institution are—from the institution's point of view—people who are listening to the noise and ignoring the information. They appear crazy or out of touch. The quartz watch was invented by the Swiss. But the great Swiss watchmakers responded to the idea of gearless timepieces in essentially the same way that the premiere audience responded to Stravinsky's *The Rite of Spring*. They threw tomatoes. They hooted it off the stage.

The principle also operates in the other direction. From the point of view of those who have adopted a new paradigm, the institution comes to sound like a cacophony-generating machine, a complex and refined device for producing more and louder noise. From the perspective of the governing paradigm, the advocates of the insurgent paradigm seem willing to sacrifice the institution itself for pie-in-the-sky nonsense. But from the perspective of the insurgents, the defenders of the present system are perpetuating a system that no longer works.

But paradigms do change. The Church admits Galileo was right. The *Rite of Spring* has become an old warhorse. Paradigms can even change quickly. Look at your watch.

Paradigms change when the ruling paradigm loses its capacity to solve problems and generate a positive vision of the future. This we very much see today. One early sign of a paradigm shift is an attempt to use the tools and ideas of a new paradigm within the framework provided by the old or to convey information intelligible in the new paradigm through the channels of the old. This, too, is now happening.

In our experience, people will suffer the turbulence and uncertainty of change if it promises a better way to accomplish work they value. The shift to the Learning Paradigm represents such an opportunity.

The Learning Paradigm doesn't answer all the important questions, of course. What it does do is lead us to a set of new questions and a domain of possible responses. What knowledge, talents, and skills do college graduates need in order to live and work fully? What must they do to master such knowledge, talents, and skills? Are they doing those things? Do students find in our colleges a coherent body of experiences that help them to become competent, capable, and interesting people? Do they understand what they've memorized? Can they act on it? Has the experience of college made our students flexible and adaptable learners, able to thrive in a knowledge society?

How do you begin to move to the new paradigm? Ultimately, changing paradigms means doing everything differently. But we can suggest three areas where changes—even small ones—can create leverage for larger change in the future.

First, you begin by speaking. You begin to speak within the new paradigm. As we come to understand the Learning Paradigm, we must make our understanding public. Stop talking about the "quality of instruction" or the "instructional program." Instead, talk about what it takes to produce "quality learning" and refer to the college's "learning programs." Instead of speaking of "instructional delivery," speak about "learning outcomes."

The primary reason the Instruction Paradigm is so powerful is that it is invisible. Its incoherencies and deficiencies appear as inherent qualities of the world. If we come to see the Instruction Paradigm as a product of our own assumptions and not a force of nature, then we can change it. Only as you begin to experiment with the new language will you realize just how entrenched and invisible the old paradigm is. But as you and your colleagues begin to speak the new language, you will then also begin to think and act out of the new paradigm.

Second, if we begin to talk about the "learning outcomes" of existing programs, we'll experience frustration at our nearly complete ignorance of what those outcomes are—the Learning Paradigm's most important category of information is one about which we know very little now. The place to start the assessment of learning outcomes is in the conventional classroom; from there, let the practice grow to the program and institutional levels. In the Learning Paradigm, the key structure that provides the leverage to change the rest is a system for requiring the specification of learning outcomes and their assessment through processes external to instruction. The more we learn about the outcomes of existing programs, the more rapidly they will change.

Third, we should address the legally entrenched state funding mechanisms that fund institutions on the basis of hours of instruction. This powerful force severely constrains the kinds of changes that an institution can make. It virtually limits them to changes within classrooms, leaving intact the atomistic one-teacher, one-classroom structure. We need to work to have state legislatures change the funding formulas of public colleges and universities to give institutions the latitude and incentives to develop new structures for learning. Persuading legislators and governors should not be hard; indeed, the idea of funding colleges for results rather than seat time has an inherent political attractiveness. It is hard to see why legislators would resist the concept that taxpayers should pay for what they get out of higher education and get what they pay for.

Try this thought experiment. Take a team of faculty at any college—at your college—and select a group of students on some coherent principle, any group of students as long as they have something in common. Keep the ratio of faculty to students the same as it already is. Tell the faculty team, "We want you to create a program for these students so that they will improve significantly in the following knowledge and cognitive skills by the end of one year. We will assess them at the beginning and assess them at the end, and we will tell you how we are going to do so. Your task is to produce learning with these students. In doing so, you are not constrained by any of the rules or regulations you have grown accustomed to. You are free to organize the environment in any way you like. The only thing you are required to do is to produce the desired result—student learning."

We have suggested this thought experiment to many college faculty and asked them whether, if given this freedom, they could design a learning environment that would get better results than what they are doing now. So far, no one has answered that question in the negative. Why not do it?

The change that is required to address today's challenges is not vast or difficult or expensive. It is a small thing. But it is a small change that changes everything. Simply ask, "How would we do things differently if we put learning first?" Then do it.

Those who say it can't be done frequently assert that environments that actually produce learning are too expensive. But this is clearly not true. What we are doing now is too expensive by far. Today, learning is prohibitively expensive in higher education; we simply can't afford it for more and more of our students. This high cost of learning is an artifact of the Instruction Paradigm. It is simply false to say that we cannot afford to give our students the education they deserve. We can, but we will not as long as we allow the Instruction Paradigm to dominate our thinking. The problem is not insoluble. However, to paraphrase Albert Einstein, we cannot solve our problem with the same level of thinking that created it.

Buckminster Fuller used to say that you should never try to change the course of a great ship by applying force to the bow. You shouldn't even try it by applying force to the rudder. Rather, you should apply force to the trim-tab. A trim-tab is a little rudder attached to the end of the rudder. A very small force will turn it, thus moving the big rudder, and in turn, the huge ship. The shift to the Learning Paradigm is the trim-tab of the great ship of higher education. It is a shift that changes everything.

55

Beyond These Walls: Teaching Within and Outside the Expanded Classroom— Boundaries in the 21st Century

Elizabeth Grauerholz, Brett McKenzie, and Mary Romero

As we set out to write this chapter, it occurred to us that the manner in which it is co-authored is something like what we envision the classroom of the future to be—an interdisciplinary and collaborative experience, transcending physical boundaries, enhanced and executed electronically, among persons with virtually no prior connection, diverse in background and experience, who come together for a brief point in time to create a product that is greater than the sum of its parts. Our meetings for this chapter transpired entirely on the "information superhighway," a road that opened up new challenges and left us envisioning new possibilities for conducting scholarship and pedagogy in the future.

Our goal in this chapter is to shed light on how the developments within the academy and society at large that have been documented throughout this volume are likely to reshape the classroom in the 21st century as well as in our day-to-day interactions with students inside and

EDITORS' NOTE: For some innovative uses and guidelines for using technology, see Innovative Routes to Learning section, Using Technology subsection in the *Fieldguide*.

outside the classroom. These changes have, in various ways, blurred or reshaped the classroom's boundaries, either physically or metaphysically. For example, the diversification of students discussed by Calhoun (Chapter 52 in this volume) may stretch the boundaries of what traditionally has been taught and how it has been taught as well as by whom and to whom. The demand for quality teaching, described by Angelo (Chapter 9 in this volume) and by Barr and Tagg (Chapter 54 in this volume), may transport teachers and students outside the classroom walls and into other settings as they strive to make the learning experience more relevant to students' lives. Certainly, technological advances have expanded the classroom boundaries by enabling teachers and learners to access other learners instantaneously anywhere in the world. Thus, we argue that the classroom's boundaries and those separating students and teachers are becoming more unclear and diffused in response to social change. And as the boundaries of the classroom change, so too will the nature of the teacher-student relationship. These changes have the potential to enhance both teaching and learning, but they also are likely to present new dilemmas and challenges.

Social Change and the Classroom of the Future

In Steele and Marshall's (1996) analysis of the classroom in the year 2005, they make several predictions. First, "the restructuring of the teacher-learner relationship and related roles will likely eliminate the classroom as we currently know it." Second, "computers . . . and expert systems . . . will set the context." Third, "whether on or off campuses, students will increase their connectivity to a variety of information sources on campus or across the world." Fourth, textbooks will become obsolete. Fifth, "artificial distinctions between 'classroom' and daily social experience will be greatly reduced" (pp. 2-3). These predictions mirror some of those we outline in this chapter. Specifically, we suggest that the classroom of the future is likely to be more *technologically rich, supplemental, diversified and multicultural,* and *collaborative and student centered* than that in which most of us were trained and with which we are most familiar. As such, transitioning to this restructured classroom might not be readily embraced or easily accomplished.

The Technologically Rich Classroom

Considerable attention has been paid to how technology, the computer in particular, is likely to transform the classroom of the future. Certainly, computers can and have extended the temporal and spatial boundaries of the classroom and the academy. The very ideal of ubiquitous computing—with its mantra of "anyone, anytime, anyplace"—challenges the traditional ideal of the academy as an intellectual sanitarium bounded by quadrangles set in a park-like campus. Even the physical boundaries of a building or classroom are less critical than they once were as students are able to use laptop computers and wireless networks anywhere on campus, including benches under spreading elms, to attach to the campus network. Computers allow high-speed information exchanges to occur with individuals within the institution as well as with those within other institutions around the world.

One way in which computers have begun to alter the classroom structure and dynamics is through the use of electronic-based discussion groups. Discussion lists can create electronic communities that are bounded by the members of a specific class or may be open to anyone with access to the network where the exchange takes place. In the latter example, the boundaries of the classroom can be completely open. For example, a recent list associated with an American literature class attracted the attention of scholars at institutions other than the one offering the course and hosting the discussion list. In this instance, students in the class were able to discuss issues with their own instructor and also were able to consider the contributions of a different scholar. Electronic discussion group exchanges also can alter class dynamics. They may allow students who do not feel free to speak in class to contribute to a class discussion. However, the absence of face-to-face interaction that provides instructors with critical nonverbal cues during in-class discussions makes it difficult for instructors to control the tone and content of these discussions. As a result, some students can become alienated, some may become more openly hostile and derisive than they would in class, classes can become divided, and so on.

Potentially, as the classroom itself becomes a node on a network, learning possibilities within this domain could be enhanced. Unlike other technologies, the computer is not static. For example, before the computer, the action depicted in an encyclopedia cartoon of the intake, compression, firing, and exhaust strokes of an internal combustion engine had to be imagined. The same description can now be animated with the computer so that the cycle can be visualized and analyzed. The computer also can capture and display data from external sources. For example, election returns on a computer can be analyzed against predictions just as stock market fluctuations can be used to trigger an investment strategy. This aspect allows for a much richer range of demonstration in the classroom. The computer also can access data quickly without playing through all the material to reach the desired segment. This aspect allows for backtracking or jumping forward in a sequence almost instantaneously, making it less cumbersome for classroom use than more traditional technologies.

Even simpler technologies make possible new modes of teaching in a technologically rich classroom. For example, with the advent of real-time two-way communication, offered by videoteleconferencing, distance learning can now more closely approximate traditional classroom delivery. Technological advances also have ensured that the means for producing media will become decentralized in the digital era and that instructors (and students) may have the ability to create media for classroom use. If the notion of lifelong learning and the liberal ideal of higher education as a means of "learning how to learn" are taken as the direction for higher education, then the question of students creating their own material has significant merit. Literacy movements, especially those from the developing world, seem to indicate that ownership of the language is critical to increasing literacy. If our students are to become assessors of their own learning, and if they are to become more critical consumers of educational opportunities, then creating their own materials and critically reflecting on materials

created by their peers allow them more control of their learning.

Although the potential of technology for teaching is great, it poses new challenges to instructors who must continually discover ways in which to display new information, especially to their technologically savvy students. Students in the 21st century will arrive to our classrooms familiar with the technologies and expecting their use.[1] More important, their learning styles have been shaped by their experiences with technology. Even simple technological advances such as the video recorder, cable television, and the remote control may affect students' expectations within the classroom and learning styles. For example, because of the remote control, children (who are our future students) interact with television differently today from those whose experience with television anchored them to a specific channel. Channel surfing, for some, has become an integral part of the viewing experience and not an activity distinct from viewing a program. The traditional lecture, in which students are expected to sit passively and attend to one individual for nearly an hour or longer, may present a serious challenge for some of these students (and their instructors).

More generally, we need to ask, what are we actually gaining with enhanced computerization of the classroom? Its pedagogical usefulness has yet to be demonstrated. Intensive pilot projects, such as Intermedia (Beeman et al. 1988), have shown promise, but they might be examples of doing "more with more," using a highly selective population that does not transfer well to other populations. Flashy presentations alone do not ensure improved content or greater comprehension, just as the mere addition of different media might not add another dimension to comprehension. In addition, the questions of which disciplines and which levels of study are most amenable to computerization remain open. As we learn more about how learning occurs, we might change our perspectives on which are the best subjects for electronic delivery. For example, distance learning might be best suited to participants at advanced levels, where the discourse already is delimited by the discipline. This runs counter to experience with televised educational programs, which have generally concentrated on introductory subject matter.

At the institutional level, problems might arise for educators. The management and coordination of computerized classrooms will be boggling. Digital technologies require three levels of management: access to resources, hardware and software selection and maintenance (including upgrades and guarding against technological obsolescence), and the infrastructure level, which includes electrical services and sophisticated voice-data-video networks. Delivering the expected level of service requires close coordination among development offices for funding expensive campus-wide and outreach projects, physical plant offices for electrical service and data conduits, and academic offices for ensuring academic programming and faculty support. For individual educators, this probably means greater involvement in coordinating and management at the administrative level than is expected today.

The Supplemental Classroom

Technological developments have the potential to diminish the role of the classroom and, in turn, the instructor. Steele and Marshall (1996) seriously question whether the traditional classroom-lecture model can survive in an increasingly technological society:

Bringing people together to be "lectured to" runs contrary to the emerging forms of information distribution. Whether on or off campuses, students will increase their connectivity to a variety of information sources on campus or across the world. Fixed-site classrooms primarily will become locations in which face-to-face human interaction and teamwork cannot be replaced by virtual classrooms, satellite uplink, electronic classrooms, or other forms of electronic interaction. (p. 2)

Already, some faculty use e-mail and discussion lists to cover basic or definitional issues so that classroom time can be devoted to discussion and highly contentious issues. And for some, e-mail exchanges have replaced traditional office hours, whereby issues between a faculty member and a student can be resolved more quickly (although not necessarily more satisfactorily).

The classroom, as we know it, undoubtedly will continue to exist, but increasingly the classroom might assume a supplemental role. What we already know from pedagogical theory—that the majority of learning occurs outside the classroom (McKeachie 1994)—will become more widely acknowledged and realized in our teaching methods, as Angelo (this volume) predicts. Part of the push toward the supplemental classroom is likely to come from employers' demand for students who are prepared to work in the "real world" (Steele and Marshall 1996) and who are technologically knowledgeable so that they can succeed in the technological age (Raymondo 1996). The classroom may come to be seen as an arena that supplements rather than gives rise to this learning.

There already has been growing interest in out-of-classroom experiences, ranging from the satellite classroom (distance learning), in which learning occurs outside the traditional classroom walls (usually within the student's home), to situations in which learning is expected to occur off campus in other social settings. The proliferation of study abroad programs (Calhoun, this volume); Wagenaar and Subedi 1996) is a prime example of the latter,[2] as are "service learning" courses, in which students may volunteer in their communities as part of their course work (see, e.g., Corwin 1996; Ender et al. 1996; Parker-Gwin 1996). Even simple experiential exercises designed to take students out of the classroom and into other social settings (see, e.g., Boyle 1995; Chesler and Zuniga 1991) can profoundly affect students' learning and may grow in popularity as demands to make learning more relevant to students' lives intensify. Internships and exercises designed to familiarize students with the workplace (see, e.g., Lackey 1995) and to help them acquire social and communication skills necessary to succeed there (Jenkins 1995) are likely to become more common, thereby stretching the boundaries of the classroom and making it more supplemental.

The classroom space itself, as traditionally conceived, surely will remain, as will the lecture. But we might see a continued shift away from lecturing, as instructors currently are urged to do (Dunn 1994), or at least a more conscientious use of lecturing. The notion of the supplemental classroom raises new possibilities for how time spent in the classroom can be restructured. For example, rather than lecturing to passive students, students and teachers might come together in these spaces to integrate, discuss, and elaborate on ideas and understandings acquired outside of the classroom. Perhaps those courses that will continue to be conducted primarily in the classroom setting might resemble proseminars or capstone courses (Wagenaar 1993) for which classroom interaction is critical.

As the classroom becomes more supplemental, so too might the teacher's role *within* the classroom. As our knowledge of the *hows, whens,* and *whys* of lecturing and discussion become more sophisticated, teachers are encouraged to adopt the role of facilitator rather than expert or truth bearer. As Barr and Tagg (this volume) suggest, faculty become "design-ers of learning methods and environments" rather than "primary lecturers." Instructors will be responsible for keeping students on task, presenting them with challenging issues and ideas, providing vital resources for these learners, and modeling ways in which to organize ideas.

Teachers might find themselves in the actual classroom less, or at least less central to the classroom, but much more time is likely to be spent in preparation (e.g., monitoring student achievement, pondering ways in which to keep the subject alive for students, coordinating field trips, organizing guest speakers or e-mail hookups or teleconferences) and course maintenance (e.g., responding to e-mail exchanges, monitoring listserv discussions). Such a shift in responsibilities undoubtedly would increase the time demands on instructors who already are overburdened with pressures to publish, teach, and perform service. This raises several questions. In the future, will faculty have enough time to devote to teaching given the constraints and additional demands likely to face us in the future? Will it be possible to stay abreast of theories of learning and new teaching techniques and also to remain active in research and service? Will there be less time for research and, therefore, less status attached to the research role? Will there be more integration of research into the classroom and a blurring of the two roles? Or, will the conflict today experienced by devoted teachers who remain active in other ways become the norm?

Also, if instructors spend less time in face-to-face contact with students, their potential influence on students will be reduced (although their impact could be greater if time with students becomes more valuable and efficient). These changes in the teacher's role would affect students' lives as well, as students might be required to engage in more independent and active learning. This might require more support services for students, such as writing clinics or tutorial centers, to assist students in these new ways of learning. But will it be possible to have the desired impact on students? Will instructors be able to recognize when students are failing to grasp the material? This is especially critical when considering distance learning. With a live class, the instructor is sensitive to the mood of the class. It is the rare instructor who barrels forward with a class lecture when all faces remain blank. In non-face-to-face teaching, can there be the same cues? Listening to actors who contrast the stage performance with the motion picture or video performance makes one aware that the cues in live performance are different. As much as videoteleconferencing and computerization open multiple communications channels, the program remains a stylized conversation, orchestrated as much by the technology supporting the production as by the participants. The creation and adoption of innovative methods for tracking students' moods and learning, such as the "postcard" method (Metzke 1992), will be necessary but might prove to be less satisfactory than traditional methods.

A Diversified and Multicultural Classroom

Demographic changes in students' racial/ethnic background, along with the impact made by interdisciplinary scholarship and the call for an inclusive curriculum, may lead to significant changes in future classrooms. We probably will continue to see disciplinary boundaries expanding to meet the challenges of new pedagogical frameworks and an increasingly multilingual and multicultural student body. Contributions from gender studies, ethnic studies, cultural studies, and queer studies will continue to make their mark on the canon.

Future classrooms are likely to be less ethnocentric and increasingly multicultural and global.

Racial, linguistic, religious, and other cultural diversity of future classrooms can pose excellent opportunities for collaborative learning; however, they also might pose the need for new pedagogical frameworks that can address the tensions and conflicts emerging from the wide range of life experiences and values that groups such as inner-city youths, former refugees, and members of fundamentalist religious groups bring to future classrooms. One model is provided by the New London Group, an international group of American, Australian, and British scholars who propose a pedagogy for this new environment (see Cazden et al. 1996). Such changes will require that instructors adapt to a student population that is more diverse and pedagogically demanding (Calhoun, this volume). For example, older students tend to be more challenging and critical than the typical undergraduate student (Howard, Short, and Clark 1996).

As the student population continues to become more diversified, so must our teaching, both in terms of methods and materials used. As Calhoun (Chapter 52, this volume) notes, "Courses need to change not only to better educate these students but also to better take advantage of the diversity their presence brings to classrooms." For example, as we move toward an inclusive curriculum, instructors will be pressured to be more selective in adopting texts that incorporate the life experiences of their students. Also, students with diverse backgrounds are likely to have different levels of preparation that will require more time and effort on the instructor's part to teach all students. Several of the shifts discussed by Angelo (Chapter 9, this volume) (e.g., moving "from a culture of implicitly held individual hopes, preferences, and beliefs to a culture of explicit, broadly shared goals, criteria, and standards" and aspects of the learning paradigm (Barr and Tagg, this volume) will facilitate these efforts.

But the combination of curricular changes and diverse student population requires the development of new pedagogy, which may prove challenging for many teachers. For example, Mohanty (1993:51) cautions instructors about the difficulty of moving students beyond the individualistic and attitudinal parameters of discussing race in the classroom. Like many other multicultural educators, Mohanty stresses the need to move away from prejudice reduction approaches that are psychologically based to those that emphasize institutional and historical domination. More fundamentally, students (and teachers) must venture into new pedagogical domains to understand and appreciate diversity. Cohen (1995), for example, offers a model for engaging students in multicultural discussions and overcoming resistance of majority group members. (The Community Tutoring Project developed by Cohen involves college students tutoring at-risk children in the community each week.)

There also is likely to be a tremendous burden on women and faculty of color as students become increasingly diversified but the diversification of the faculty lags. Teaching courses that fulfill diversity requirements, mentoring such students, and advising such student groups might continue to fall disproportionately on the shoulders of women and minority faculty, and given their distribution in the ranks, the shoulders usually belong to professors still going through the process of tenure and promotion. To protect these faculty from the backlash of teaching to hostile students and teaching a new curriculum, it is necessary that all faculty move toward a multicultural curriculum. This goal will be difficult given that "academic segregation and selective responsibility reinforce each other when the responsibility for teaching certain substantive areas is restricted to people of color or white women while the rest of a department's faculty and curricula remain virtually unchanged" (Thompson and Tyagi 1993:87).

Thus, we might continue to find certain faculty confronting issues related to their own gender and race, especially because a significant diversification of faculty is not likely to occur in the next several decades. For example, in her study of women leaving academia, Rothblum (1988:14) identifies the role conflict created by the expectations that women faculty "emotionally work" to fulfill their duties as teachers. And like women, faculty of color frequently are confronted with contradictions in the professional role they are assigned. For example, Latina and black women faculty must counter the negative images of women of color as inferior (e.g., the perception that they are less intelligent and less competent teachers than whites) that both their students and colleagues frequently have internalized (Foster 1991; Moses 1989). The very absence of black women scholars, McCombs (1989:131) argues, gives the impression that they are unqualified.

Carter, Pearson, and Shavlik (1987-1988) identify obstacles that black women faculty face in trying to meet expectations and standards established by white males:

Their personal lives extract a loyalty to their culture that is central to acceptance by family and friends. At the same time, they must struggle with their own identity as women in a society where "thinking like a woman" is still considered a questionable activity. At times, they even experience pressure to choose between their racial identity and their womanhood. (p. 98)

If the 21st century sees greater diversification of faculty, then there are likely to be numerous pedagogical gains. Using a perspective theory to advocate for faculty diversity, Lopez (1993:113) identifies the following benefits gained by the inclusion of faculty of color representing their community ties: distinctive methodologies, reconsideration of dominant frameworks, formulations of fresh theoretical discussions, and the modification of pedagogical styles. Lopez identifies the ways in which students are empowered from exposure to scholars of color:

(1) symbolically challenging the stereotype of intellectual inferiority that burdens people of color, (2) serving as exemplars suitable for student emulation, and (3) acting as mentors to facilitate and aid the growth of students. While minority students benefit particularly, these advantages also accrue to nonminority students. (p. 109)

In general, multicultural education prepares students to move outside a monocultural environment and enables them to work together with others with greater appreciation of racial/ethnic differences. Exposure to a wider range of ideas and critical thinking provides students with the personal skills they will need to work in an increasingly diverse society.

The Collaborative and Student-Centered Classroom

The future classroom may involve more collaboration, both in terms of teaching and learning. According to Calhoun (this volume), opportunities for academics to span disciplinary boundaries will increase. As a result, the classroom in the future might become less discipline bound, where topics are approached from many perspectives rather than from the narrow approach of a specific discipline. This may occur by team teaching, but even in fairly discipline-bound contexts, student discussion

of the wide range of readings and speakers can create an interdisciplinary perspective.

Consequently, we might see an increasing demand for cross-listing and collaboration among departments.[3] An increase in interdisciplinary courses also might facilitate more "in tandem" courses (a series of courses designed to be taken sequentially) (Alexander and Sullivan 1996) and team teaching. The latter, in particular, offers teachers new pedagogical challenges and rewards and can be tremendously beneficial to students (Robinson and Schaible 1993). Students, who often are isolated from disciplinary debates, are allowed to see these debates both within the discipline and across disciplinary boundaries—debates that are the experience of education. With team teaching, the boundaries, the analytical tools, and the interpretive results can be understood in greater depth.

At the disciplinary level, there will be the question of boundaries and allegiances. Since the drift to more conservative politics in the postindustrial economies toward the end of the 20th century, the academy has witnessed attacks on its structure and organization. Many of these polemics have suggested that the disciplines are rarefied and represent members talking only to each other. At the same time, new disciplines with a narrow focus have been established (e.g., biomedical ethics). In this environment, where do the allegiances of faculty lie? Are they to the discipline that introduced them to the academy, or are they to a specific institution that supports them? Does the appointment for the ethicist move to a biology department when the philosophy department is closed? This tension in allegiance is not new to the academy, but it might be heightened as the disciplines splinter into narrower groups and as divisions among disciplines blur. Added to this conflict are allegiances to students. If the academy changes to become more student centered and if instruction for students becomes increasingly individualized, then this becomes a third dimension with which faculty must contend.

Whereas team teaching is the preserve of the instructional side of the classroom, collaborative learning involves students joining together to complete an assignment. Although collaborative learning is not without its problems (Yamane 1996), the forces discussed earlier are likely to give rise to greater emphasis on collaborative learning. Digital technologies could allow collaborative groups to engage with data and questions in class but also allow collaborative learning outside the classroom via class listservs. Furthermore, the clamor by employees that "team skills" are a requirement in the modern world, recent research on learning that demonstrates the positive effects of reciprocal teaching, and digital technologies that allow easy access to the data sets and other sources make collaborative learning exercises more attractive (Qin, Johnson, and Johnson 1995). This model of learning further stretches the boundaries of the classroom, especially boundaries dictating *who* teaches. And because students are questioning peers, an opportunity that is less daunting than challenging the experts as faculty or the experts presented in their texts, collaborative learning can enhance critical thinking as well as social and communication skills.

A collaborative class might involve a collection of people joined together for a limited time to produce a single product that is the sum of their efforts but that may seem greater than the sum of their efforts. If we imagine a class creating a World Wide Web site as the goal of the educative experience, not everyone in the class might produce the same product. Students adept at writing might present their content as text, others might present their content as images, and still others might contribute through coding the pages and developing the argument or narrative in a nonlinear fashion. Some students might discover their response to the issues from one perspective, whereas others might find it from another.

To make the example more concrete, if students were assigned to analyze voting patterns, then one group might approach the issues from the perspective of economic differences, another might consider geographic issues as paramount, and yet another group might see gender and ethnicity as the critical factors. When combined, a class project of this nature could present a view in greater depth because students could then create a web of knowledge joining the parts each has worked on to create a whole greater than the sum of the parts. The World Wide Web, with its underlying hypertext, makes this project easily do-able. Of even more interest is that this material, created by students, can become part of the course corpus for analysis, criticism, or revision by a subsequent class. Once in a digital form, the barriers to electronic publication and distribution are economically inconsequential.

This model of teaching undoubtedly would create greater time demands for the instructor. Coordinating such a class, keeping track of each student's progress (or at least the group's progress) throughout the semester or quarter, and ensuring that workloads are consistent across groups and that evaluative methods are fair pose significant problems for the instructor. On the other hand, such classes would be able to respond to individual needs and talents to a much greater degree than is common today by allowing students to focus on their own learning objectives and interests.

Issues concerning collaborative learning also relate to team teaching and the interdisciplinary debate as discussed earlier. Team teaching often is conceived of as instruction by multiple faculty members. It rarely is considered to extend to groupings that are not peers. For example, it is unusual to consider that a faculty member teaching in a computer-intensive environment would regard a student laboratory assistant as a team teacher. In similar ways, faculty relationships with teaching assistants rarely are built on a peer relationship model; rather, they usually are built on a junior/senior or apprenticeship model. As technology increasingly intrudes on the classroom, team teaching will become an enterprise among the subject matter experts, the instructional designers, and technology managers. These people will have different professional paths, have allegiances to different intellectual traditions, and will mix sentient and intellective skills (Zuboff 1988).

This raises other important questions. What will the basis of evaluation be? How will students be evaluated if learning is evaluated not on the basis of demonstrating the knowledge of concepts and facts but rather on active participation and gaining of practical knowledge or experience? Already, many instructors struggle with grading class participation and collaborative group projects; this problem is not easily resolvable. How will individuals be evaluated if much of their work is based on collaborative work? As self-assessment on the students' part becomes more common—based on some instructors' beliefs that reflection, especially self-reflection, is a critical part of education—this carries its own potential pitfalls. Are instructors' and students' assessments likely to differ? How do these discrepancies get resolved? And how will instructors be evaluated by students? Are students likely to perceive that their instructors are not working hard enough, do not care much about students, or are not knowledgeable about the material if they are not lecturing "facts" in the classroom? Might instructors' evaluations be linked to student outcomes, and if so, then how will this be achieved?

The collaborative classroom described here reflects other changes likely to take place within the future classroom. As more teachers acquire sophisticated understandings of alternative teaching methods, they might seek ways in which to transform the classroom into a more student-centered and discussion-oriented environment to engage students in the learning process (Atwater 1991; McBroom and Reed 1994; Smith 1996). The classroom in the 21st century is likely to be much more dynamic and interactive, with students better equipped to think critically (Weast 1996).

The problems that plague today's classrooms, namely student silence and passivity, could decline as we begin to challenge students to write, talk, and think (Dunn 1994). We might be forced to incorporate at least some of the ideas discussed by Long (1995) concerning pedagogy as a means to liberate students. Within this approach, students learn that their silence and passivity can be viewed in both pedagogical and political terms; as Shor and Freire (1987) maintain, student passivity and silence are in actuality "performance strikes" of students who refuse to participate in an oppressive educational system (Long 1995). At the very least, students must learn to redefine the social situation to accept their role in learning (Howard et al. 1996). We believe that new pedagogical research and theory will begin to shape teachers' approaches to students and their own teaching and that eventually the emphasis on active learning no longer will be purely theoretical but also practically applied.

The effects on teachers and students are likely to be intense. For teachers and students, teaching and learning could become more enjoyable. In the long run, we might see fewer cases of performance strikes on students' part *and* on teachers' part. Students might be challenged to think more critically. But such changes will not come without problems. In this new environment, management of the classroom experience will take priority over direct instruction. In the traditional classroom, written texts and the instructor's knowledge are central. By contrast, in the new classroom, the experience of students may be more central. Collaboration among students, student presentations to peers, student-centered discussions, and the introduction of experts via media other than written text all will become part of the educational process. This scenario challenges the presumption that the instructor is the expert, whose role is to dispense knowledge. As students "take the center" (Atwater 1991), instructors might lose some of their power and control over the classroom, thereby blurring the boundaries between teacher and student.

This blurring of roles will become more common if students' knowledge (i.e., their experiences) is increasingly validated and instructors' expertise becomes less central to the classroom experience. For example, the Anglo instructor teaching about race relations to a group of minority students may be an expert on race relations, but he or she knows virtually nothing about the experience of being a person of color. As more nontraditional students enroll in programs, the surety of the instructor having a greater range of experience than the students becomes more suspect. This range of experience might not be limited to the older and nontraditional students. As digital technology assumes a larger place within the life experiences of students, there may be some students more skilled at manipulating computers, and at accessing information contained in them, than are their instructors. In the future classroom, if students' experiences become central to learn-

ing, then the division between student and teacher may become blurred.

If the role of "teacher as expert" dissolves, then we might begin encountering new dilemmas such as the instructor's shifting power basis and possibly his or her *ability* to teach. Consider that one of the most defining features of the contemporary student-teacher relationship is its power differential (Long and Lake 1996).[4] When the teacher as expert diminishes, professors may lose significant sources of power, namely expert and informational power. Referent power also is likely to give way as students become more diversified. Older students and others familiar with abuses of social power might not be so easily awed by the college professor. One of the authors recently overheard a conversation among a group of students in which one remarked, "I've finally figured out that just because he has a Ph.D. behind his name, I don't have to like him."

What problems or dilemmas does this raise? Long and Lake (1996) caution, "Ethical teaching presumes acknowledging inequality and meritocratic elitism. It entails making and maintaining clear distinctions between roles" (p. 113). What happens when these roles become blurred? "Friendship can be an opening into unwanted importunings, unwelcome intimacies, and untoward entanglements. Fairness, or the perception of fairness, can be compromised" (p. 112). In a similar vein, their discussion of ethics in teaching alerts us to another potential problem in the classroom of the future, a classroom that makes greater use of students as experts or as researchers: "Students . . . are not a captive source of labor. . . . The authority of expertise does not sanction servitude or exploitation in the guise of education" (p. 112). As the boundaries separating students and teachers become more blurred, new questions arise. Can instructors, who no longer are regarded as the ultimate experts, effectively and legitimately evaluate students? Can instructors effectively teach if students believe that instructors' knowledge no longer is privileged or when instructors lack their students' respect? The "supplemental teacher" of the future risks what Moore (1996) suggests are "inappropriate challenges to professors' authority" (p. 202), a phenomenon already experienced by women faculty and professors of color, whose authority is more likely to be questioned by students. Finally, how well does this prepare students for the real world and future jobs that remain hierarchically structured? Certainly, other sources of power (namely reward power) will remain (unless the academy moves toward a no-grade system), but this also might pose problems. Will there be more hostility over grades if this is perceived to be the sole source of power possessed by instructors? How will instructors feel about grading students who otherwise are peers?

Is Change Inevitable?

Certainly, the changes discussed here have the *potential* to seriously alter the structure, norms, and interactions of the classroom in the 21st century in both positive and negative ways, but is such change *likely*? Most of us will recognize the potential for producing better teachers and students in the 21st century, but there is no guarantee that the changes and impacts discussed here (if they occur) will significantly improve teachers' ability to teach or students' ability to learn. *Social* change does not necessarily translate into *individual* change. As an example, witness the current underuse of computers in classrooms on college campuses despite their availability.

Yet, when viewed from a sociological perspective, the inevitability of change becomes more certain. Individual behavior *is* determined in large part by social structure (social, institutional, and subcultural norms, practices, ideals, expectations, and regulations) and social interactions. As Stryker (1980) suggests, "If the social person is shaped by interaction, it is social structure that shapes the possibilities for interaction and so, ultimately, the person" (p. 66). Thus, the social and cultural changes outlined earlier are likely to alter classroom norms and interactions and, therefore, the lives of the key social actors—teachers and students. And in turn, changes within the classroom are likely to reshape institutional structures and goals.

Although social change gives rise to new possibilities, we also must remember that social structure *constrains* individual choices and options. Despite what an individual may wish to do in the classroom, this might not be possible given university (or departmental) constraints (e.g., most of us are required to assign grades each semester or quarter, even if we are philosophically opposed to the practice). Institutions, as a rule, are slow to change, and the academy and its faculty are not exceptions. Thus, in the 21st century, we will continue to struggle with dilemmas borne from the inherent contradictions between what we *want* to do and what we *can* do in the classroom, between what students want and what instructors think students need, and between personal desires and structural limitations. There always will be students who are not interested in learning, either on that particular day or on any day, and there always will be teachers who have lost their enthusiasm for teaching. And, of course, change does not always result in more innovative or better teaching. Challenges to affirmative action programs, criticisms of "outcome-based education" programs, and decreased federal and state funding have resulted in larger class sizes and fewer faculty, making it more difficult for devoted teachers to teach well.

In the future, the various problems and challenges we confront, such as those we have discussed here, may interfere with effective teaching and learning. Furthermore, any social change produces new conflicts and dilemmas, and we undoubtedly will encounter these in our classrooms and lives as we move into the 21st century. These changes, contradictions, challenges, and possibilities will shape the classroom of the 21st century as well as our experiences and those of our students within it. And there is likely to be resistance to change from both students and teachers. For both, the changes outlined here require greater involvement and expenditure of personal resources. And as Dziech and Weiner (1990) remind us, college professors "are people who work in an environment where ideas are tested, critiqued, and retested by others before they are accepted or put into action" (p. 54). But the fundamental nature of the changes taking place—the blurring of boundaries—will make it difficult, if not impossible, for teachers and students not to change. Teachers no longer will have complete control over the classroom. As the outside world intrudes on what once was their domain, teachers will be forced to change how and what they teach.

The dilemmas and challenges discussed in this chapter may be mitigated if departments and universities restructure and reorganize priorities to meet the changing needs of faculty and students. For example, the value placed on teaching within the academy might increase. We could see a greater reconciliation of research and teaching and the elimination of the double standard that has governed academic life in the latter 20th century (Goldsmid and Wilson 1980). Teachers also might enjoy more social status in society as their work becomes more visible and as they begin to have more impact on society through service-based teaching and teaching students necessary skills to

thrive in their occupations. For the social sciences, in particular, there is likely to be an increased appreciation for what social science can tell us about society and social problems. The changes we see occurring—toward more critical thinking—are precisely those embodied within the liberal arts. We believe that these skills and values will assume greater salience in society in the 21st century.

Conclusion

Whether or not individual behavior will change significantly to profoundly restructure the classroom of the future is unclear; what seems more certain is that the opportunities, if not the motivation, to restructure the classroom will be great. Perhaps more than at any previous period in the academy's history, the pedagogical challenges, and the possibilities and means for meeting these, are tremendous. The changes explored in this volume undoubtedly will influence how we teach, how we relate to students and colleagues, and how much satisfaction we derive from these interactions. Change already is evident, and educators are beginning to glimpse new possibilities for the future, opportunities not possible a decade ago. Changes within the academy and in society at large have forced, and will continue to force, us to reexamine our methods and motives and to present us with new rewards and satisfactions.

In the 21st century, we will be confronted with new challenges that may profoundly alter our teaching ideals. As difficult as the change may be, we must recognize the exciting opportunity before us; we are in a position to reshape our own futures and those of our students in significant ways. We also may be in the position to reconfigure the institution of higher education by creating new partnerships with colleagues, students, and administrators. Teaching within and outside the boundaries of the expanded classroom of the future has the potential to expand our lives in profound ways.

Notes

1. Students today and those in the near future are growing up in a digital world. Initiatives such as Internet Day to wire public schools to the Internet, the proliferation of digital technologies within the home, and the practice students get with digital technologies (through mundane after-school jobs as cashiers at local supermarkets or more sophisticated endeavors such as working for the public access channel at the local cable television office) mean that students will be familiar with advanced technology.

2. Many study abroad programs use classrooms, but much of the learning is expected to occur outside the classroom as students interact with persons in their host countries.

3. Calhoun (this volume) warns that this move will be met with resistance, not just from academics but also from administrators, and perhaps for good reason. Consider the administrative, bookkeeping, and financial adjustments that would be required. How, for example, are the costs of such activities to be assessed among participating academic units? How is a faculty member's contribution to be evaluated for salary or promotion purposes? Will new organizational structures be required? (R. McGee, personal communication, December 20, 1996).

4. Sociologically speaking, instructors traditionally have possessed several important sources of social power (French and Raven 1959): reward power (ability to assign grades, write recommendation letters, etc.), legitimate power (authority to train students and demand academic performance), referent power (admiration from students), informational power (possessing information not easily accessible to nonacademics), and expert power (perceived to be more knowledgeable and intelligent).

References

Alexander, Susan M. and Katherine Sullivan. 1996. "Teaching 'in Tandem': Combining Sociology with Theater to Create an Interdisciplinary Classroom." *Teaching Sociology* 24:372-77.

Atwater, Lynn. 1991. "Trading Places: Teaching with Students in the Center and Professors on the Periphery of the Principles Course." *Teaching Sociology* 19:483-88.

Beeman, W. O., K. T. Anderson, G. Bader, J. Larkin, A. P. McClard, P. McQuillan, and M. Shields. 1988. "Intermedia: A Case Study of Innovation in Higher Education." Final report to the Annenberg/CPB Project, Brown University, Institute for Research on Information and Scholarship.

Boyle, Catherine E. 1995. "Seeing Gender in Everyday Life: A Field Trip to the Mall." *Teaching Sociology* 23:150-54.

Carter, Deborah, Carol Pearson, and Donna Shavlik. 1987-1988. "Double Jeopardy: Women of Color in Higher Education." *Educational Record,* Fall-Winter, pp. 98-103.

Cazden, Courtney, Bill Cope, James Cook, Norman Fairclough, Jim Gee, Mary Kalantzis, Gunther Kress, Allen Luke, Carmen Luke, Sarah Michaels, and Martin Nakata. 1996. "A Pedagogy of Multiliteracies: Designing Social Futures." *Harvard Educational Review* 66:60-92.

Chesler, Mark A. and Ximena Zuniga. 1991. "Dealing with Prejudice and Conflict in the Classroom: The Pink Triangle Exercise." *Teaching Sociology* 19:173-81.

Cohen, Lorraine. 1995. "Facilitating the Critique of Racism and Classism: An Experiential Model for Euro-American Middle-Class Students." *Teaching Sociology* 23:87-93.

Corwin, Patricia. 1996. "Using the Community as a Classroom for Large Introductory Sociology Classes." *Teaching Sociology* 24:310-15.

Dunn, Joe P. 1994. "Reflections of a Recovering Lectureholic." *National Teaching and Learning Forum* 3:1-3.

Dziech, Billie Wright and Linda Weiner. 1990. *The Lecherous Professor: Sexual Harassment on Campus.* 2nd ed. Urbana: University of Illinois Press.

Ender, Morten G., Brenda Marsteller Kowalewski, David A. Cotter, Lee Martin, and JoAnn DeFiore. 1996. *Service-Learning and Undergraduate Sociology: Syllabi and Instructional Materials.* Washington, DC: American Sociological Association, Teaching Resources Center.

Foster, M. 1991. "Constancy, Connectedness, and Constraints in the Lives of African American Teachers." *NWSA Journal* 3:233-61.

French, J. R. and B. Raven. 1959. "The Basis of Social Power." Pp. 150-67 in *Studies in Social Power,* edited by D. Cartwright. Ann Arbor: University of Michigan Press.

Goldsmid, Charles A. and Everett K. Wilson. 1980. *Passing on Sociology: The Teaching of a Discipline.* Washington, DC: American Sociological Association, Teaching Resources Center.

Howard, Jay R., Lillard B. Short, and Susan M. Clark. 1996. Students' Participation in the Mixed-Age College Classroom." *Teaching Sociology* 24:8-24.

Jenkins, Richard. 1995. "Social Skills, Social Research Skills, Sociological Skills: Teaching Reflexivity?" *Teaching Sociology* 23:16-27.

Lackey, Chad. 1995. "Preparing Students for Their Future: A Sociological Practice Approach to Teaching about Life in Complex Organizations." *Teaching Sociology* 23:269-73.

Long, David Alan. 1995. "Sociology and a Pedagogy for Liberation: Cultivating a Dialogue of Discernment in Our Classroom." *Teaching Sociology* 23:321-30.

Long, Gary L. and Elise S. Lake. 1996. "A Precondition For Ethical Teaching: Clarity about Role and Inequality." *Teaching Sociology* 24:111-16.

Lopez, Ian Haney. 1993. "Community Ties and Law School Faculty Hiring: The Case for Professors Who Don't Think White." Pp. 100-30 in *Beyond a Dream Deferred: Multicultural Education and the Politics of Excellence,* edited by Becky W. Thompson and Sangeeta Tyagi. Minneapolis: University of Minnesota Press.

McBroom, William H. and Fred W. Reed. 1994. "An Alternative to a Traditional Lecture Course." *Teaching Sociology* 22:328-32.

McCombs, Harriet G. 1989. "The Dynamics and Impact of Affirmative Action Processes on Higher Education, the Curriculum, and Black Women." *Sex Roles* 21½:127-43.

McKeachie, Wilbert J. 1994. *Teaching Tips: Strategies, Research, and Theory for College and University Teachers.* Lexington, MA: D. C. Heath.

Metzke, Linda. 1992. "The Electronic Age Creates the Postcard Professor." *The Teaching Professor,* October, p. 5.

Mohanty, Chandra Talpade. 1993. "On Race and Voice: Challenges for Liberal Education in the 1990s." Pp. 41-65 in *Beyond a Dream Deferred: Multicultural Education and the Politics of Excellence,* edited by Becky W. Thompson and Sangeeta Tyagi. Minneapolis: University of Minnesota Press.

Moore, Valerie. 1996. "Inappropriate Challenges to Professorial Authority." *Teaching Sociology* 24:202-6.

Moses, Yolanda. 1989. *Black Women in Academe*. Project on the status and education of women, Association of American Colleges.

Parker-Gwin, Rachel. 1996. "Connecting Service to Learning: How Students and Communities Matter." *Teaching Sociology* 24:97-101.

Qin, Zhining, David Johnson, and Roger Johnson. 1995. "Cooperative vs. Competitive Efforts and Problem Solving." *Review of Educational Research* 65:129-43.

Raymondo, James C. 1996. "Developing a Computer Laboratory for Undergraduate Sociology Courses." *Teaching Sociology* 24:305-9.

Robinson, Betty D. and Robert Schaible. 1993. "Women and Men Teaching: 'Men, Women, and Work'." *Teaching Sociology* 21:363-70.

Rothblum, D. Esther. 1988. "Leaving the Ivory Tower: Factors Contributing to Women's Voluntary Resignation from Academia," *Frontiers* 10 (2): 14-17.

Shor, Ira and Paolo Freire. 1987. *A Pedagogy for Liberation: Dialogues in Transforming Education*. Granby, MA: Bergin & Garvey.

Smith, David Horton. 1996. "Developing a More Interactive Classroom: A Continuing Odyssey." *Teaching Sociology* 24:64-75.

Steele, Stephen F. and Sherry Marshall. 1996. "On Raising Hopes of Raising Teaching: A Glimpse of Introduction to Sociology in 2005." *Teaching Sociology* 24:1-7.

Stryker, Sheldon. 1980. *Symbolic Interactionism: A Social Structural Version*. Redwood City, CA: Benjamin/Cummings.

Thompson, Becky W. and Sangeeta Tyagi. 1993. "The Politics of Inclusion: Reskilling the Academy." Pp. 83-99 in *Beyond a Dream Deferred: Multicultural Education and the Politics of Excellence,* edited by Becky W. Thompson and Sangeeta Tyagi. Minneapolis: University of Minnesota Press.

Wagenaar, Theodore C. 1993. "The Capstone Course." *Teaching Sociology* 21:209-14.

Wagenaar, Theodore C. and Janardan Subedi. 1996. "Internationalizing the Curriculum: Study in Nepal." *Teaching Sociology* 24:272-83.

Weast, Don. 1996. "Alternative Teaching Strategies: The Case for Critical Thinking." *Teaching Sociology* 24:189-94.

Yamane, David. 1996. "Collaboration and Its Discontents: Steps toward Overcoming Barriers to Successful Group Projects." *Teaching Sociology* 24:378-83.

Zuboff, S. 1988. *In the Age of the Smart Machine*. New York: Basic Books.

Conclusion

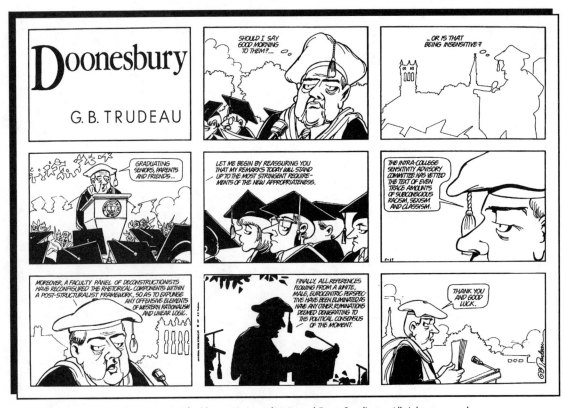

Reconstructing the Social Worlds of Higher Education: Changes, Challenges, and Dilemmas

Ronald Aminzade and Bernice A. Pescosolido

The final task that remains is to consider the shape and substance of higher education in the future. Such a vision requires that we recognize both the nature of future trends and the power of individuals within higher education to forge changes and protect the critical value in colleges and universities.

The current landscape of higher education is marked by a diversity of constituencies and purposes, a rapid pace of organizational and technological change, and enduring social dilemmas, as Trudeau's university president acknowledges. These features make it risky to generalize about shared goals and likely futures and to offer uniform guidelines about what and how to teach. Most contributors to this volume agree about certain trends such as the increasingly diverse composition of the student body, growing student demands for a relevant education, the escalating importance of technology, the loss of job security for growing numbers of part-time faculty, heightened pressures for accountability, and the growing popularity of new pedagogies involving active and cooperative learning. They disagree, however, about whether these changes bring threats or opportunities and about the resources and rules needed to grapple with them.

Teaching activities, like all human activities, are temporal in nature. One important scarce resource that shapes what goes on within our classrooms is time. The rules governing how we allocate and organize time constitute critical opportunities and obstacles for teachers in the 21st century. Here, we briefly discuss the temporal scarcities and rigidities that characterize contemporary academic life. We then identify five dilemmas routinely encountered in the classroom that are grounded in tensions between relevance and privacy, complexity and accessibility, evaluation and nurturing, passion and impartiality, and universalism and particularism. Responses to these dilemmas, we argue, must be context dependent, attentive to relations of power, authority, and trust; to our own social locations; and to larger institutional dilemmas rooted in tensions between professionalization and unionization, teaching and research, and integration and empowerment.

Time Scarcity and Temporal Rigidities

Our multiple roles as teachers, scholars, and administrators, along with our responsibilities to multiple stakeholders—students, parents, alumni, legislators, and the community—as well as to our families and friends, make it difficult for us to find time to meet our numerous obligations. As tenure demands on junior faculty escalate, and as increasing numbers of professors strive to achieve a healthier balance between work and family responsibilities, the temporal constraints of academic life become more evident. The obsession with covering all the material in a course of limited duration often leads to monologue rather than dialogue and to impatience with student participation and experiential learning. Increased demands on faculty to participate in the management of their own institutions means more time spent doing committee work, a source of frequent complaints. On the one hand, new technologies often frighten teachers, especially those of our generation, because of the demands they place on already tight schedules. Teachers must now find time to learn rapidly changing technologies, put their courses on the World Wide Web, and read and respond to the flood of electronic mail messages that fill their computer screens. On the other hand, the new technologies give us opportunities to communicate with students who might be less comfortable with face-to-face encounters, unable or unwilling to show up during our office hours, or insecure enough to prefer the anonymity afforded by cyberspace communication.

Lack of time makes professors hesitant to experiment with new pedagogies given the sunk costs invested in traditional methods and lecture notes and the scarcity of leave time or other rewards for adopting innovative teaching activities. Time scarcity prevents many teachers from adopting active and cooperative learning methods despite convincing evidence, presented in this volume and elsewhere, that the notion of a trade-off between content and pro-

cess is illusory and that such methods improve students' abilities to deal effectively with uncertainty and complexity. While convinced that the goals of our teaching should extend beyond conveying the research findings of our disciplines to encompass critical thinking, moral integrity, and citizenship, many college teachers are reluctant to adopt what they perceive to be an effective but more time-consuming pedagogy.

The temporal rigidities of academic life include the lockstep nature of career trajectories, reinforced by a tenure and promotion system with rigid socially expected durations for each rank. The system also is relatively inflexible in allowing faculty to creatively alter the balance of their commitments to research, teaching, administration, and family over the life course. For female junior faculty, tenure clocks may confront biological clocks, thus making it difficult to balance work and family aspirations. Faculty with young children, who often are up against a tenure clock, also face a "work versus family" temporal dilemma.

Institutional timetables shape student careers as well as faculty careers. The current curriculum, for example, is oriented to bureaucratic coordination and the time constraints of quarters or semesters rather than to the varied pace of student learning. The institutional sources of these temporal rigidities impeding more flexible teaching and learning suggest a need to rethink tenure, the curriculum, and the current reward system within academia. Without a reconsideration of the way in which we have structured time in higher education, we are imprisoned in an iron cage of our own making. Our ability to face the dilemmas we will encounter in efforts to bring about change will be made easier if we are freer to manipulate time as well as structures.

Exploring Dilemmas within the Classroom

Given this realization, we now turn to future challenges in the classroom, in particular, and in teaching effectively, in general. Whereas the dilemmas we face in the classroom are numerous and often pose ethical dilemmas, five dilemmas stand out as challenges to committed teachers trying to figure out how and what to teach. First, our efforts to make the material we teach personally relevant to students may conflict with a responsibility to respect student desires for personal privacy. Stimulating the sociological imagination, for example, means cultivating students' ability to make connections between their personal lives and the larger social world. But how far can we legitimately intrude on the personal worlds of our students as grist for our sociological mills, especially when these include emotionally powerful familial and sexual issues such as domestic abuse, homosexuality, and rape?

This is not unique to sociology, of course. Whenever we consider using personal journals as a pedagogical technique or ask students to relate poetry to their own experiences, we raise the specter of crossing appropriate boundaries and often boundaries for which we have little training to confront, as Lowman (1995) points out.

A second dilemma concerns the complexity and accessibility of what we teach. As social scientists trying to make sense of the world, we often use methodological tools or abstract concepts that are difficult to grasp and that readily generate boredom and inattention. The issue is complicated by our students' diverse backgrounds, skills, and levels of familiarity with course materials. Compelling stories, sometimes captured via the effective use of case studies, enable us to engage students, ground abstract problems in concrete situations, and raise compelling moral dilemmas that help students become more self-reflective about their values. But social science analysis also involves a certain distancing, made possible by tools and techniques that are less accessible than stories but that allow us to discern larger patterns, indirect connections, unintended consequences, and complex causal processes.

A third dilemma concerns the tension between evaluating and nurturing students, that is, between our roles as judge and coach. We have a responsibility to society and our institutions of higher learning to maintain standards of excellence and ensure that diplomas reflect accomplishment. But we also have a responsibility to our students to provide supportive learning environments that enable them to trust us and their own abilities. We sometimes can nurture high expectations and strong motivation in an individual student by giving a high grade, but we also have a responsibility to ensure fair standards of evaluation and provide reliable assessment. Some institutional arrangements, such as the tutorial system at Oxford and Cambridge universities, formally divide these conflicting roles, but American higher education has not institutionalized such a split.

Fourth, the tension between passion and impartiality brings yet another dilemma. Numerous contributors to this volume identify enthusiasm as a central ingredient of effective teaching. Others point out that teaching is a moral and cultural enterprise in which we impart values and worldviews as well as knowledge and valuations of different ways of knowing. How can we express our passions and value commitments while respecting the views and values of those with whom we disagree and making sure that our enthusiasm does not silence the dissident voices of those who disagree with us? Whereas some students may remain silent out of fear that their contentiousness might be punished with poor grades, others may consider it disrespectful to argue with those in positions of authority. The silent classrooms we often encounter suggest the need to be aware of our power and express our passion in a way that encourages respectful disagreement and teaches students that it is not impolite to argue with their professors.

A fifth related dilemma confronting teachers concerns the tension between universalism and particularism. Although we may strive to treat all students equally and fairly, we also typically make an effort to connect with individual students whose unique life histories and particular situations affect their willingness and ability to learn. The difficulty of coordinating activities and grading papers in very large classes, and the urge to treat all students equally, conflicts with the desire for flexibility and acknowledgment of the obstacles students from disadvantaged backgrounds face or have overcome including family responsibilities, poverty and material hardship, rapes, abortions, and drug or domestic abuse. When these make it difficult for students to meet paper deadlines, show up in class on time, or keep up with the workload, our desire to take into account their lives outside the classroom and below their necks confronts our commitment to treat all students equally.

We suggest that appropriate answers to the questions raised by these five dilemmas are necessarily context dependent. In other words, the answer to these questions is always "it depends." Thus, for example, the types of stories we use and the appropriateness of nonstory approaches depend on the composition and learning styles of students in our class, the level of the course, and whether our goal is to train future social scientists or to provide an educated

citizenry with critical thinking skills. Our response to the tension between passion and impartiality also depends on who is and is not speaking and on what positions are not being voiced. An appropriate response sometimes might involve actively soliciting the opinions of white males, although more often it is likely to require greater sensitivity to the silence of women and minority students. In short, the type of teaching that will work and serve students' needs might vary across classrooms and institutional contexts. An effective response to these dilemmas requires self-awareness about our own priorities, values, and social locations. Such an awareness enables us to convey clear expectations to our students and avoid ad hoc responses that might generate guilt and insecurity.

The answers to the questions raised by these dilemmas depend on relations of power, authority, and trust, which are mediated by the gender, age, race, class backgrounds, and sexual preferences of teachers and students. Our social locations shape our ability to gain trust and acquire greater knowledge of our students including their learning styles, expectations and aspirations, understandings of proper boundaries, lives outside the classroom, values, and assumptions about the social world. This knowledge can help us to grapple effectively with these dilemmas. As many contributors to this volume point out, access to this information requires dialogue rather than monologue and is facilitated by active, experiential, and cooperative learning techniques.

In some institutional settings, declining resources combine with growing demands on professors' time to make it difficult to deal effectively with these classroom dilemmas. Additional resources can help, for example, remedial programs for students who are inadequately prepared for college; paid leaves to enable teachers to revamp their courses to incorporate more active, experiential, and cooperative learning; and teacher training programs for graduate students that grapple with ethical as well as pedagogical issues. They can aid the creation of an academic culture that values good teaching and helps professors become more self-aware and explicit about their teaching and grading goals, their sense of proper boundaries between themselves and their students, and how their power and social location shapes individual students' willingness and ability to learn.

In addition to helping us know our audience better, active, experiential, and cooperative learning techniques enable us to move back and forth between structure and freedom. They enable us to retain our authority but to exercise it in creative ways by spreading it over time and space. They also permit us to express our passions and value commitments but to balance them with multiple voices and the alternative perspectives of classroom participants who might not share our views.

It is the mix of forms and experiences, of using the entire pedagogical tool box where appropriate and tailored to explicit learning goals (i.e., not as ends in themselves), that will result in better experiences for us and for those in our classrooms.

Institutional Dilemmas

The dilemmas we face within the classroom are related to larger institutional dilemmas that affect how, what, and who we teach. These include the tensions between professionalization and unionization, teaching and research, and integration and empowerment. These institutional dilemmas are rooted in the multiple goals, values, and constituencies; changing rules; and shifting resources in our colleges and universities.

First, as professionals, we expect a certain degree of autonomy in our workplaces, but at the same time we recognize our responsibilities as members of a profession to establish and enforce ethical guidelines and, more recently, to train future college teachers. The assault on tenure and the growth of part-time academic labor has eroded professional autonomy and stimulated the growth of faculty unions. Unions have been seen to formalize relations of production and to make us and our employers clearly accountable, protecting more vulnerable members of the teaching profession and counteracting the trend toward the proletarianization of academic labor. But, according to some, they limit our professional autonomy by creating formal rules and bureaucratic regulations that apply uniformly across varied disciplines, disciplinary cultures, and work environments and by replacing faculty governance with collective bargaining by union leaders.

Second, the relationship between teaching and research has been highly controversial, as the contributions to this volume attest. Some academics, especially those employed at elite research institutions, contend that a symbiotic relationship is possible. They point out that research can improve our teaching by enabling us to bring up-to-date findings of contemporary research into the classroom, stimulate new directions in our undergraduate teaching as research alters our understandings and interests, and provide undergraduate as well as graduate students with research opportunities. Critics have forcefully pointed out that the relationship between teaching and research more typically resembles a zero-sum game. In their view, scarce resources devoted to costly research programs that benefit corporations and governments more than students and ordinary citizens help produce high tuition and large classes, take professors out of the classroom, and make teaching a low-status activity.

The third dilemma concerns separatist demands and race-conscious policies, which can empower students victimized by racism and sexism but also create boundaries that reinforce racial and gender divisions and inhibit cross-cultural understanding and tolerance. How can we acknowledge difference and enable oppressed groups to organize to challenge racism, sexism, and classism on campus without undermining the long-term goal of creating institutions in which race, class, and gender no longer will constitute the basis for misunderstandings, inequalities, and oppression? Related questions arise concerning college admissions policies. Should the racial categories created by prior institutional policies to exclude people be recognized and used in policies of preferential treatment to overcome racial injustices?

We do not have quick and easy answers to the difficult questions raised by these dilemmas. They involve conflicting interests and values as well as differing assumptions about the likely consequences of alternative courses of action. As was the case in our response to questions raised by dilemmas within the classroom, our answers emphasize context dependency. As citizens of the larger community, we share certain responsibilities regardless of our institutional location within academia (e.g., to properly educate minority students who have been subjected to weak public education, institutionalized racism, and the failure of teachers to provide culturally appropriate education). But given very different balances across institutions between professional autonomy and administrative control, resources and rewards devoted to teaching and and those devoted to research, and emphases on graduate and on undergraduate education, as well as varying institutional commitments to multiculturalism, responses to these dilemmas are necessarily dependent on the context in which we work.

Variations in the mix of central stakeholder groups are an important feature of institutional contexts. Within the student population, there are variations in the presence of women, minorities, and students from working-class backgrounds. At the administrative level, some institutions rely heavily on career administrators and administratively appointed task forces, whereas others retain a greater commitment to a system of faculty governance. Within the faculty, the percentages of low-wage adjunct and part-time instructors vary tremendously among elite private institutions, state university campuses, and public community colleges. These differences across institutions are consequential for the allies, opportunities, and obstacles we face in confronting institutional dilemmas.

Conclusion

In many ways, colleges and universities are microcosms of the larger society, reflecting broader social goals, conflicts, and problems. Our institutions of higher learning have responded to economic crises, political trends, and consumerist culture. Historically, institutions of higher education have reflected the goals and interests of diverse constituencies—fostering national identity, educating responsible citizens, providing paths of social mobility, teaching religious values, and carrying out corporate and military research. Racial, gender, and class differences on our campuses reflect those of the wider society, just as current controversies over affirmative action, unionization, and corporatization reflect contention within the larger political arena.

At the same time that they reflect what goes on in the wider society, institutions of higher education have retained a certain relative autonomy. Institutionalized boundaries shield faculty from external pressures, ensure academic freedom (making possible the expression of unpopular ideas), and protect organizations that are not dominated by the logic of the marketplace. The issue of proper boundaries between the larger society and institutions of higher education has been a main source of contention and is likely to remain so in the 21st century.

As we shift our attention from teaching to the relationship between teaching and learning, we need to reorganize the temporalities of academic life along more flexible lines. Large-scale institutions undoubtedly will retain certain temporal rigidities in response to coordination needs, but new technologies will make it easier for students to learn at a pace determined by their own interests and abilities when and where it suits their needs. Stronger demands, especially by younger professors striving to coordinate family and work and to maintain a healthier balance between the two, might lead to expanded life course options and more flexible academic careers.

Pressures from parents, legislatures, and students to improve the quality of undergraduate teaching and increasing competition among institutions for students may reshape the reward structure to foster improved teaching and lead to a reallocation of resources to fund teacher mentoring programs and provide faculty with sufficient time to revise courses, rethink the curriculum, and learn about new technologies. Such pressures also may lead to a more coherent and integrated curriculum, based on course sequences and requirements that enable students to integrate learning experiences across disciplines. A more heterogeneous student body and growing numbers of international students may foster a more inclusive and international curriculum and expanded study abroad programs. Growing student demands for social relevance and

recognition by many faculty that we have done a poor job of making our knowledge available and accessible to the community may produce expanded opportunities for community service learning and improved university-community relations. The growth of on-line courses and off-site teachers may put pressure on professors to demonstrate the value of on-campus teaching, thereby promoting more personal student-faculty contacts and the increased use of active and collaborative learning pedagogies. Faculty unionization may reduce the number of migrant academic laborers and provide part-time teachers with better wages, benefits, and working conditions as well as protect academic freedom.

The current situation provides reasonable grounds for both optimism and despair. If the preceding optimistic outcomes occur in the 21st century, then they will not be the inevitable product of large-scale demographic, economic, or political shifts; rather, they will be the result of innumerable battles waged on campuses throughout the United States. We hope that this volume will help to prepare us for these struggles to improve the quality of the teaching and learning at our colleges and universities without decreasing the conduct of quality research through rethinking the nature of creative activity and the emphasis on quantity. Our goal in assembling this volume was to foster greater self-reflection about our teaching activities, more awareness of the dilemmas we face within the classroom, and better understanding of the distinctive character of our workplaces. We will have achieved that goal to the extent that we have provided an impetus for teachers to seek more knowledge of themselves, their students, and their institutions. We hope that the readers will close this book with a desire to learn more about their own goals, values, interests, teaching styles, and social locations; about their students' aspirations, learning styles, and life histories; and about the rules, resources, and dilemmas of their institutions.

Reference

Lowman, Joseph. 1995. *Mastering the Techniques of Teaching*. San Francisco: Jossey-Bass.

Index

Note: The **boldface** letter preceding the page number
refers to the volume, according to the following key:
H = Handbook
F = Fieldguide

Castañeda, M. B., H63
Cazden, C., H587
Ceci, S. J., H198
Celis, W., III, H324, H327
Center for Advanced Study in the
    Behavioral Sciences, Hxxxv
Center for Critical Thinking, H566
Centra, J., F302
Centra, J. A., H196, H197, H199,
    H200, H201, H202, H203;
    F293, F299, F304, F306
Cerula, K. A., H71
Chait, R., H70
Chambliss, D. F., H423, H424
Chasteen, E., H481
Chayko, M., H71
Chesler, M., H484
Chesler, M. A., H586
Chesterton, G. K., F5
Chickering, A. W., H60; F22
Chideya, F., F216, F218
Christensen, R., H99, H103
City University of New York, H65,
    H365
    ethnic diversity, H156
    minority enrollment, H155
Clark, B. R., H63
Clark, M. J., F299
Clark, O. L., H387
Clark, S. M., H587, H591
Class, planning for first day, F36-49
    coping with teaching anxiety,
        F39-40
    first period, F37-38
    sending right messages, F37
Classes, large, F144-154
    debates in, F68-69
    improving communication in,
        F147-153
    managing undergraduate seminars,
        F145-146
    office hours and, F154
    role-playing in, F69
    simulations in, F69
    smaller groups in, F69
    See also Large courses, techniques
        for better communication in
Classroom:
    as learning community, H103-104
Classroom, 21st-century, H582,
    H593-595
    changing boundaries, H582-583,
        H594
    collaborative/student-centered,
        H589-593
    diversified/multicultural, H587-589

dynamic, H591
interactive, H591
social change and, H583-593
supplemental, H585-587
technologically rich, H583-585
Classroom conflict, H66-69. See also
    Classroom interactions
Classroom interactions, F155-160
    responding to wrong answers, F156
    structuring controversy, F157-160
Classrooms, higher education trends
    in, H59, H71
    canon for teaching, H65-66
    conflicted classrooms, H66-69
    discussion, H60
    Generation X students, H64-65
    lecturing, H59-60
    less revenue, H69-70
    overly burdened students, H63-64
    reform movements, H60-62
    teaching as tradition-bound, H59
    technology, H70-71
    unprepared students, H62-63
    See also Classroom, 21st-century
Classroom time, college professors
    and, H3
Claxton, C. S., F26
Clegg, V. L., F260, F262
Clinchy, B., H445
Clinchy, B. M., H169, H171, H174,
    H176, H177, H178, H179,
    H181
Clyne, M., F226, F227
Coffman, W. E., F259
Cognition, basic principles of human,
    H92-93
    applying in classrooms, H93-94
Cohen, C., H364, H369
Cohen, H., H57, H58
Cohen, L., H64, H68, H70, H588
Cohen, P. A., H71, H200; F306
Colbeck, C., H96
Coleman, J. S., H407, H415
Coleman, R. P., H13
Collaborative classrooms, H103,
    H589-593
    team teaching, H589
Collaborative learning, H104,
    H590-591; F106. See also
    Collaborative learning
    exercises/projects; Collaborative
    learning groups (CLGs);
    Learning communities
Collaborative learning
    exercises/projects, H61, H111

Collaborative learning groups
    (CLGs), H103-104
    making successful, F142
    using in large classes, F140-141
    See also Cooperative learning
        groups
College Board, H64
College degrees:
    as "standard," H13
    numbers of, H13
    prevalence of among Americans,
        H12
Colleges and universities:
    as cultural venues, H34
    as learning communities, H110-114
    as public venues, H34
    as tourist industry, H33
    business outsourcing to, H33-34
    classification schemes, H320
    communities and, H34
    criticisms of, H9
    differentiated system of, H6-7
    funding, H578
    threat of outside bureaucratic
        control, H7
    See also specific colleges and
        universities; Colleges and
        universities, four-year
Colleges and universities, four-year:
    achievement test scores, H15-16
    as credential factories, H521
    disparities among, H16
    enrollment, H32
    private, H16
    public, H16
    See also specific colleges and
        universities; Elite institutions;
        Universities, selective
Colleges and universities, private
    sector, H50-51
    University of Phoenix, H50-51
College graduates, oversupply of, H35
College of New Jersey, H552
College Student Experiences
    Questionnaire (CSEQ), H210,
    H211
Collegiate subculture, H62
Collins, R., H13, H66, H67, H69,
    H72, H427, H521
Colombotos, J., H407, H408, H415
Columbia University, H11
Comenius, J. A., F4
Commission on National Investment
    in Higher Education, H34
Commission on the Higher Education
    of Minorities, H139

Crowfoot, J., **H484**
Cuadraz, G. H., **H497**
Cultural deficit/disadvantage theory: inadequacy of, **H138-139** institutional racism and, **H139**
Cultural diversity, higher education and, **H271-272, H276**. *See also* Anthropological imagination
Cultural literacy, **H284**
Cultural pluralism, **H246, H248, H251** competence and, **H251-252**
Cultural relativism, **H274-276** versus ethical relativism, **H275**
Cultural studies, **H65**
Culture wars, **H271; F192-193**. *See also* Cultural diversity, higher education and; Multiculturalism, educational restructuring and
Curriculum debates, **F192-193**
Curriculum preparation, **F30-35** tips, **F31-32**
Curriculum transformation: charting process of, **H462** invisible women stage, **H462-464, H469** search for missing women stage, **H463, H465** transformed curriculum stage, **H463, H468-469** women as challenge to disciplines stage, **H463, H467-468** women as subordinate group stage, **H463, H465-466** women studied on own terms stage, **H463, H466-467, H469**

D'Antonio, W. V., **H24**
d'Apollonia, S., **H71, H191**
Darrow, C. N., **H177**
Dartmouth University, **H186**
Davis, A. P., **H62**
Davis, B. G., **H197, H200, H202**
Davis, J., **F237**
Davis, J. A., **H66**
Davis, N. J., **H64, H313**
Day, R. S., **F56**
Deay, A., **H474**
Debates, **F101-102** forced, **F91** in large classes, **F68-69**
de Beauvoir, S., **F188**
Dedrick, C., **F152**
DeFiore, J., **H586**

de Lauretis, T., **H492, H494**
Delbanco, A., **H272**
Denzin, N. K., **H66**
Departments, academic: as learning community, **H104-105** collaborative, **H104** specialization within, **H105**
Derek Bok Center for Teaching and Learning, **F74**
de Sassure, F., **H161**
Descartes, R., **H220**
Dewey, J., **H98, H103, H221, H222, H224, H526**
Dews, C. L. B., **H474**
Dey, E. L., **H46, H52**
Didion, J., **F200**
Dimaggio, P. J., **H498**
Dimen-Schein, M., **H273**
Dinerstein, M., **H493, H494, H495**
Discussion approaches: breaking into smaller groups, **F90** concrete images, **F88-89** finding illustrative quotations, **F89-90** forced debate, **F91** generating questions, **F89** generating truth statements, **F90-91** goals and values testing, **F88** nonstructured scene-setting, **F93** role-playing, **F91-92** strengths, **F85-86** weaknesses, **F86** *See also* Discussions
Discussions, **H60; F84** active listening, **F97** assumptions, **F88** clarity, **F97** connections with group, **F97-98** debates, **F101-102** deemphasizing, **H61** differentiation, **F97** effective questioning, **F97** elements of effective, **F97-98** empathy, **F97** encouraging participating, **F95** evaluating, **F96** falling apart, **F94** flexibility, **F98** frequently asked questions about, **F94-96** getting started, **F94** guidelines for questioning students, **F99-100** handling discussion monopolizers, **F95-96** improving, **F85-86**

keeping conversation flowing, **F94-95** mechanisms to keep going, **F94** peripheral vision, **F97** principles, **F88** promoting in large class, **F95** self-disclosure, **F98** sense of timing, **F97** starting, **F87-93** variability, **F97** *See also* Discussion approaches
Distance education, **H46**
Distance learning, **H70, H71, H584, H585, H587**
Distar, **F184**
Ditzen, L. S., **H320, H326**
Diversity, **H249-252; F178** African American interest, **H249** Asian American interest, **H250** Chicano/Latino American interest, **H250** converging desire, **H248-249** excuses for not teaching about, **F186-187** in students' way of knowing, **F179-181** mastering discussion of, **F192-206** Native American interest, **H250** power and pedagogy and, **F182-184** taking role of "other," **F188-191** white interest, **H249** *See also* Multiculturalism; Multiculturalism, educational restructuring and; Multiculturalism debate
Donahue, P., **H155, H164**
Donnelly, P. G., **H61**
Dorn, D., **H102**
Dorn, D. S., **H59, H72**
Dorsey, R., **H464, 469**
Doyle, K. O., Jr., **H191**
Dreeben, R., **H521**
Dressel, P. E., **F262**
Dressel, P. L., **F 55**
Dressel, R. L., **F250**
Drucker, A. J., **F293**
D'Souza, D., **H9, H26, H245**
DuBois, W. E. B., **F196, F203, F207**
Dubrow, H., **F63, F71**
Duffy, D. K., **F284**
Dukes, R., **F237**
Dukes, R. L., **H481**
Duke University, **H186, H187**
Dunlap, D. M., **70**
Dunn, J. P., **H586, H591**

Federated Learning Communities, H229

Feedback:
 peer, F25
 private, F25
 student, F25
Feedback, teacher-to-student, F5-6, F7-8
 frequent, H61
 immediate, H61
Felder, R. M., H191
Feldman, K., H197, H201, H202; F293
Feldman, K. A., H67, H71, H201, H203
Felman, S., H494, H495
Feminist pedagogy, H66
Figert, A., H102, H105, H106
Finkel, D. L., H121
Finkelstein, M. J., F66, F71
Fischer, C. S., H67
Fischer, D., H340, H341, H350
Florida Gulf Coast University, H340, H352
Florida State University, H324
Fogel, A., H98
Folsom, J., H484, H485
Foner, E., H282, H288, H290, H291
Foster, M., H588
Fox, P., H69, H71
Francis, L. P., H364, H366, H369
Frank, R. H., H14
Frankel, H. H., H139, H141, H142
Frankfurter, J., H370, H380
Franklin, J., H198
Frederick, P., F24, F69, F71, F74, F75
Free inquiry, H161
Freeman, J., H102
Freidson, E., H405, H406
Freire, P., H487, H488, H489, H494, H524, H526, H527
Freire, P. A., H447, H451, H453
French, J. R., H592, H595
French-Lazovik, G., H200; F306
Friedland, W. H., F236
Friedman, M., H100
Friere, P., H591
Frisbie, D. A., F261, F265
Froh, R. C., H197, H200, H202
Froyen, L., F152
Fry, S. E., H185
Fuhrmann, B. S., F26
Fukuyama, F., H280
Fullilove, R. E., H168
Fullinwider, R. K., H379, H381
Fulwiler, T., F26

Funding, H69-70
Furman University, F25
Furniss, E. S., H161, H165
Furst, E. J., H305; F85, F251, F253, F262
Future search, H112

Gabelnick, F., H99
Gadamer, H220, H222
 theory of pedagogy, H412-413
Gagnon, P., H280, H282, H284, H288, H290, H291
Gallimore, R., H101
Gallop, J., H385, H412, H413
Gamson, W., F237
Gamson, Z., H96
Gamson, Z. F., H60; F22
Gamst, F. C., H273
Gandara, P., H139
Gardiner, L. F., H112
Gardner, H., H577
Gartner, B., H305
Garvin, D. A., H99, H103
Gates, H. L., F186
Gecas, V., H536
Gee, J., H587
Geer, B., H405
Geertz, C., H220, H223, H225, H227
Gemmill, G., F285
Gentry, R., H141
Georgetown University, H320
Geraghty, M., H63, H64, H70
German model university, H11
Giamatti, A. B., H102
Gibb, J., F148
Giddens, A., H281, H407, H415
Gilbert, P., H70
Gillespie, D., H530-531
Gillmore, G., H191
Gimenez, M. E., H64
Gingrich, N., H239-240
Gintis, H., H521, H522, H528
Giroux, H., H487, H488, H494, H508, H509, H514, H521, H522, H524, H526, H528
Gitlin, J., H401
Givhan v. Western Line Consolidated School District, H344
Glassboro State College:
 corporate connections, H318
 H. M. Rowan and, H318, H319
Glassman, J., H321, H326
Gleason, M., F21, F22
Goldberger, N., H445

Goldberger, N. R., H169, H171, H174, H176, H177, H178, H179, H181
Goldsboro Christian School, Inc., United States, H376, H381
Goldsmid, C. A., H61, H104, H313, H481, H594
Goldstone, J. A., H66
Goodenough, D., H444
Goodenough, W. H., H274
Goodman, N., H498
Goody, J., H274, H277
Gordon, E., H142
Gose, B., H63
Government connections, higher education and, H318, H320-321
Gow, L., H60
Gracey, H. L., H521
Grade inflation, H63. *See also* Grade inflation myths
Grade inflation myths, H185-186, H192-193
 as increasing problem, H186-189
 business-centered university/college policies and, H191-192
 "C" grade as "average," H189-190
 changes in classrooms and, H188-189
 changing composition of students and, H188
 good grades—good teaching evaluations, H190-192
 improving student credentials and, H188
 media reports and, H187
 rise in professional schools and, H189
 student activism and, H190-191
 withdrawal inflation and, H189
Grades, F247-248, F290-291
 grade-averaging sheet, F247-248
 grade monitoring sheet, F247-248
Graduate associate instructors (GAIs), H507-515
 facing classroom challenges, H512-515
 marginality of, H508-509
 mastering course preparation, H510-512
 thoughts about teaching, H507-510
Graduate education, growth in, H552-555
Graduate education, structural realities of, H496-497, H500-501

Historians:
 as forecasters, H289
 new cultural, H287
Historical context, H283-284
 forms, H286-287
 importance of, H286-288
 levels, H286
 See also Historical imagination
Historical imagination, H284-286,
 H290
 case studies and, H285
 first-person sources and, H285
 visual materials and, H285
Historical literacy, H284
Historical understanding, uses of,
 H288-290
History, H280
 importance of, H283-284
 instructional uses, H287
 revising, H280-281, H282-283
 rewriting, H281
History teaching:
 changes in, H281-282
 revising history and, H282-283
 See also Historical context;
 Historical imagination
Hobsbawm, E. J., H280, H282,
 H288, H289, H291
Hochschild, J., H473
Hodges, L., H414
Hodson, R., H33
Hoffman, B., H364
Hollings, E., H321, H326
Hollingsworth, J. R., H407
Honan, W., H321, H326
Honan, W. H., H69
Honneth, A., H302
Honnold, D., H522
hooks, b., H409, H411, H413,
 H491, H492, H493, H494,
 H495, H507, H508; F196,
 F206, F207
Hoover, G., F25
Hopkins, K. D., F263
Horowitz, H. L., H60
Horowitz, I. L., H62, H66
Horton, M., H100
Hossler, D., H64
Hotaling, G. T., H65
House, J., F228
Howard, A., H138
Howard, J., F205, F207
Howard, J. R., H587, H591
Howard University, H376
Howe, R., H402
Howery, C. B., H60

Huber, J., H66
Hubert M., Jr., Hxxix
Hughes, E. C., H405; F236
Hughes, H. S., H280
Hull, R., F5
Human Relations Area Files (HRAF),
 H276
Humor, integrating into classroom:
 ground rules, F121-122
 techniques, F122-123
Hunt, L., H280, H281, H282, H285,
 H288, H291
Hutchings, P., H62, H201, H202

Illinois State University, H96
 teaching-learning center, H97-98
Indiana University, H186, H187,
 H188, H189, H190, H191,
 H507, H510, H512, H515
 Office of Diversity Programs and
 Instructional Support, H155
Indiana University-Purdue University
 at Indianapolis:
 minority enrollment, H155
Institute for the Study of Social
 Change, H474
Institutional overload, H39
Instructional awareness:
 checklist, F53
Instruction paradigm, H565, H566,
 H567, H574, H580, H581
 as theory-in-use, H566
 criteria for success, H568,
 H570-571
 criticisms of, H565-566
 learning theory, H568, H575,
 H576, H577
 mission and purpose, H567,
 H568, H569, H570
 nature of roles, H568, H578
 productivity/funding, H568, H577
 teaching/learning structures, H568,
 H572-573
Intellectual arrogance, H129, H132
Intellectual virtues, H128-129,
 H130-131, H136
 analyzed experiences and, H135
 defense mechanisms and, H133
 interdependence of, H132-133
 intellectual confidence in reason,
 H128, H131
 intellectual courage, H131, H132
 intellectual empathy, H128, H131,
 H132, H133, H174-175

intellectual good faith, H131,
 H132
intellectual humility, H130-131,
 H132, 133
intellectual perseverance, H128,
 H131, H132
intellectual sense of justice, H128,
 H132-133
meta-experiences and, H134
teaching for, H134-136
See also Critical thinkers; Critical
 thinking
Intercultural discourse, F193
Intercultural education, F193
International students, facilitating
 classroom communication with,
 F224-225
International teachers, cross-cultural
 stumbling blocks for, F226-227
 differences in organization of
 salient information, F227
 differences in signaling
 organization of material, F227
 directness and social skills, F228
 stage presence/public speaking
 experience, F227-228
Internet classes, preparing to teach,
 F118-119
 planning/preparation, F119
 presentation/feedback, F119
 See also Technology
Irish, S., H64
Isaacs, W., H100
Ishiguro, K., H161

Jackson, P., H452
Jackson, P. N., H521
Jacob, M., H280, H281, H282,
 H288, H291
Jacobs, G. M., H285
Jacobs, W. R., H508, H512, H515
Jacobson, L., H459
James, W., H55, H107; F21
James Madison University, H163
Janowitz, M., H497
Jencks, C., H62, H63
Jenkins, K., H280
Jenkins, R., H586
Jennings, B., H288, H291, H405,
 H406, H414
Jensen, A. R., H138
Joas, H., H302
Johns Hopkins University, H11, H12,
 H577
Johnson, D., H114, H590

Johnson, D. W., F125, F275
Johnson, L. B., H362, H363
Johnson, R., H114, H590; F275
Johnson, R. T., F125
Johnson, S., F4
Johnston, K., F179
Johnstone, D. B., H578
Jones, A. E., F270
Jones, J., H102
Jones, J. W., F284
Jourard, S., F151
Joyce, B., H103
Jung, C., H436

Kalantzis, M., H587
Kallen, H., H 246, H251
Kampf, L., H485
Karabel, J., H15, H27, H155, H156, H157, H251, H253
Karcher, B. C., F188
Karen, D., H251, H253
Kasper, G., F228
Katz, J., H201, H211, H484
Katz, M., H358
Katz, M. B., H283, H288, H289
Katz, S. N., H61
Keeley, S. M., F21, F26, F130, F131
Keen, S., H385-386
Kegan, R., H181
Keig, L., H201
Keirsey, D., H438
Kekes, J., H365
Keller, E. F., F196, F200, F207
Keller Plan, F152
Kellner, H., H281
Kelly, D., H340, H350
Kember, D., H60
Kennedy, J. F., H362, H363
Kent State, part-time faculty unionization at, H333
Kerlin, S. P., H70
Kerr, S., H539
Kett, J. F., H62
Key, S., H63
Keyishian v. Board of Regents, H341, H350
Kierkegaard, S., H435
Kimball, R., H9, H26
King, P. M., H171
Kirchner, C., H407, H408, H415
Kirschner, S., H462, H469
Kitcher, P., H171
Kitchner, K. S., H171
Klein, E. B., H177
Kleinfeld, J., H144

Kline, M., H170
Klitgaard, R., H371, H372, H373, H380, H381
Kluckhohn, C., H274
Knapp, M. L., F153
Knefelkamp, L., F202
Knefelkamp, L. L., H178, H179, H181
Knowledge workers, H94
Knowlton, S., H65
Kohn, A., H521
Kolb, D., H444
Kominsky, R., H14
Koos, L., H48, H49, H52
Korn, W. S., H46, H52
Kottak, C. P., H276
Kotthoff, H., F226, F227, F228
Kowalewski, B. M., H586
Kramer, L., H282, H283, H287, H288, H290, H291
Krashen, S. D., H142
Krathwohl, D. R., H305; F85, F251, F253, F262
Kress, G., H587
Kretschmer, E., H438
Kristol, I., H245
Kroeber, A., H274
Kuber, K., F237
Kuh, G. D., H60, H67
Kuhn, E. D., F228
Kulik, J. A., F293
Kulis, S., H497
Kupperman, J. J., H366, H369
Kurfiss, J., H181
Kurland, J. F., H341, H350

Lackey, C., H586
Lafayette College, H162-163
Lake, E. S., H592
Lakoff, G., H178
Lambert, L. M., H197, H200, H202
Landes, D. S., H280
Landrum, M. S., F43
Lane, A. J., H412
Langer, E. J., H101
Laosa, L. M., H138
Large courses, techniques for better communication in:
    create supportive climate, F148-149
    "get personal," F151-152
    get students involved, F152-153
    let receivers become senders, F150-151
    make space small, F148

See also Classes, large
Larkin, J., H584
Larson, D. R., F112
Larson, M. S., H406
Lauderdale, P., H70
Laumann, E. O., H413
Law, C. L. B., H474
Lawrence, G., H436, H440, H441, H442
Layzell, D. T., H48, H52
Lazar, A. M., F275
Leacock, S. B., H256, H262
Learners, H435
    encountering new information, H92
    ways of organizing knowledge, H92
Learning, H98, H494
    accommodation and, H458
    approaches, H46-47
    as communal activity, H98
    assimilation and, H458
    double-loop, H101
    levels of, F254
    teacher expectation and, H459
    transformative events, H447
    trust and, H447-454
    vaccination model of, H112
    versus teaching, H43
    See also Active learning; Learning Paradigm
Learning communities, H61
    benefits of, H111
    colleges and universities as, H110-114
    collaboration in, H110-111
    communal principles of, H100-102
    communication in, H100
    competency-based, H114
    double-loop learning in, H101
    freedom/structure dialectic in, H102
    fundamental features, H99
    idea of, H97-100
    mindful engagement in, H101
    mutuality in, H100-101
    power of dialogue in, H100
    zone of proximal development (ZPD) in, H101-102
Learning communities, creating, H95, H106-107
    academic settings for, H102-105
    improving instructional productivity, H111-114
    improving learning quality, H111-114

in action research partnerships,
H103
in classrooms, H102, H103-104
in departments, H102
teaching as lonely work, H95-97
university-community partnerships,
H105-106
See also Learning communities
Learning disabilities, students with:
characteristics of , F231-232
instructional interventions for,
F235-238
suggestions for, F234
suggestions for teachers of,
F233-234
Learning disability, description of,
F231
Learning disability issues, F230-238
See also Learning disabilities,
students with:
Learning groups:
how to use in classroom, F133-138
See also Collaborative learning
groups (CLGs); Cooperative
learning groups
Learning (higher), principles for
improving, F4-9
Learning paradigm, H565, H566,
H567, H580-581
as espoused theory, H566-567
criteria for success, H568,
H570-571
implications, H566
learning outcomes and, H580
learning theory, H568, H575-577
mission and purposes, H568,
H569-570
nature of roles, H568, H578-579
productivity/funding, H568,
H577-578
quality learning and, H580
teaching/learning structures, H568,
H573-575
Learning styles, H444-445
field-dependent learners, H444
field-independent learners, H444
Gregorc Adult Transactional
Ability Inventory, H444
Inventory of Learning Styles, H444
male versus female, H444-445
multimodal Learning Style
Inventory, H444
new technology and, H584
See also Myers-Briggs Type
Indicator (MBTI); Psychological
types, Jungian;

Teaching-learning process;
Teaching process
Leatherman, C., H70, H412
Lectures, F53
change-up in, F72-76
controversial topics and, F74-75
criticisms, F62-63
emotional media, F69-70
energy shifts, F66-67
enhanced, F60-61
exquisite oral, F64-65
feedback/interaction, F58-59
generating ideas and, F74
guided, F60
importance of variety, F64
improving, F54-59
intellectually exciting, F82-83
justifications of, F63-64
lively, F62-70
participatory, F65-66
pause procedure, F60
preparation/organization, F56-57
presentation/clarity, F57
problem solving, F, F73-74
responsive, F60-61
short writing exercises, F60
stimulation/interest, F57-58
strengths, F54-55
student-generated questions and,
F72-73
student self-evaluation and, F75
textual exegesis, F67-68
varying media in, F75-76
weaknesses, F55-56
See also Lecturing; Speaking skills
Lecture support media:
relate to learning objectives, F109
main ideas in simple format,
F109-110
match to instructional level, F110
overhead visuals, F112-115
support main ideas, F110
Lecturing, H8, H59-60, H103
deemphasizing, H61
future of, H586
learning paradigm and, H566
suggestions for bad, F82-83
suggestions for good, F83
Lehmann, I. J., F254, F265
Leik, R. K., H70
Lemert, C., H66
Lensink, J., H493, H494, H495
Lerner, G., H462, H467, H469,
H470
Lesko, P. D., H333
Leslie, L. L., H21, H29, H64

Levi, G., H286, H287
Levine, A., H47, H52, H59, H64;
F205
Levine, D., H63, H66
Levinson, D. J., H177
Levinson, M. H., H177
Levinson, S., F226, F228
Levy, F., H35
Lewin, K., H103, H438
Lewis, L. S., H20, H21, H22
Lewis, S., H159, H162, H163
Liberal arts colleges, H320
decline in, H17
number of, H17
Liberal education:
bored college students and, H84-85
value of, H158
Library:
as college cornerstone, H164
Lieberson, S., H66
Light, R., F180
Lilly Teaching Fellows Program, H201
Limerick, P., F193, F206
Lincoln, A. J., H65
Lincoln, Y. S., H66
Lipset, S. M., H496
Liston, D. P., H487, H494
Litt, E., H62, H63
Little, J. K., H60
Lively, K., H332
Lochhead, J., F129
Loewen, J. W., H282, H290
Lomperis, A. M. T., H330, H336
Long, D. A., H591
Long, G. L., H592
Lopez, I. H., H589
Lorde, A., H484
Lortie, D. C., H96
Lowi, T., H407, H415
Lowman, J., H191-192, H194,
H409, H410, H510, H537,
H603; F22, F226, F227, F284
Lucas, C. J., H10
Luckmann, T., H313
Ludewig, L. M., H68
Luke, A., H587
Luke, C., H587
Lund, J. P., H64
Lunneborg, C. E., H138, H142
Lunneborg, P. W., H138, H142

MacCorquodale, P., H493, H494,
H495
MacGregor, J., H99; F75
MacIntyre, A., H241, H242, H243

Multiculturalism, H67, H271
  See also Diversity;
    Multiculturalism, educational
    restructuring and;
    Multiculturalism debate
Multiculturalism, educational
  restructuring and, H220, H231
  courses addressing power/privilege,
    H473-475
  democratic pluralism, H224,
    H226, H227-229
  frameworks, H220-222
  hierarchism and, H221, H224
  interpreting diversity, H222-226
  in 21st century, H587-589
  objections to, H229-231
  organizational philosophy,
    H226-227
  perennialism/universalism and,
    H221, H223-224
  pluralism and, H221
  relativism and, H221, H223
Multiculturalism debate, H245-248
Murchison, W., H35, H40
Murnane, R. J., H35
Murray, H. G., F22, F23
Murrell, P. H., F26
Mwachofi, N., H70
Myers, I., H436, H442
Myers-Briggs Type Indicator (MBTI),
  H436, H441, H444; F106
  bipolar scales, H436
  for identifying student preferred
    learning styles, H438-440
  temperaments, H438
  See also Psychological types,
    Jungian

Nakata, M., H587
Nakata, Y., H63, H64
Naroll, R., H99
Nash, G., H282, H290
National Association of Scholars,
  H245, H480
National Association of State
  Universities and Land Grant
  Colleges, H352
National Association of Student
  Personnel Administrators, F24
National Center for Educational
  Statistics, H13, H15, H16, H23,
  H27, H46, H52
National Center for Teaching,
  Learning, and Assessment, H114

National Center on Educational
  Statistics, H187
National Commission on Time and
  Learning, H572
National Council on Vocational
  Education, H576
National Education Association
  (NEA), H333, H334
  report, H160
National Joint Committee on
  Learning Disabilities, F235
National Research Council, H484
National Survey of Postsecondary
  Faculty, H23
Navarrette, R., Jr., F202
Neitz, M. J., H514
Nelson, C., H240, H508
Nelson, C. E., H168, H169, H175,
  H178, H179, H181, H282,
  H290
Nettles, M. T., H138
Neustadt, R. E., H288, H291
New London Group, H587
Newman, J. H. C., H158
Newmann, K. M., H508
New Mexico State, H333
Nicklin, J. L., H70, H319, H325
Nidiffer, J., H47, H52
Nietzsche, F., H222, H242
Nixon administration, H363
Nora, A., H63, H67
Norbeck, E., H273
Nordvall, R. C., H70, H72
Norman, D. A., F6
Northwestern State University, F118
Novick, P., H178
Nunn, C. E., H60
Nyden, P., H102, H105, H106

Oakley, F., H10, H15, H16, H17,
  H25, H28, H30, H551
Obear, K., F204, F207
Oberdorfer, D., H157
Oberlin College, H10
O'Brien, G. D., H548, H560
O'Connor, K., H288, H291
O'Connor, S. D., H345
Office hours, large classes and, F154
Office of Diversity Programs and
  Instructional Support, H155
Office of Student Research, H249,
  H253
Ohmann, D., H485
One-minute paper, H61; F5, F73
Open-space technology, H112

O'Rand, A. M., H539
Oren, D. A., H362, H368
Oreovicz, F. S., F125
Ory, J. C., H195, H196, H197,
  H200, H202
Osborne, M. D., H181
Ottinger, C. A., H16, H27
Outcome-based education, criticisms
  of, H593
Overall, J. U., F293, F294
Overbook Press, H163
Owen, D., H372, H380

Pace, C. R., H60, H210
Pacht, A. R., F24
Palladino, J. J., F26
Palmer, J., F294
Paludi, M. A., H497
Panitz, T., F43, F285
Paper services, H159
Park, R., H101, H105
Parker, C. A., H181
Parker, R., F285
Parker, W. C., H488, H494
Parker-Gwin, R., H586
Pascarella, E., H138
Pascarella, E. T., H63, H67, H112
Passell, P., H63
Patrons, higher education:
  changing attitudes/demands,
    H42-44
Paul, R., H175, H181, H566
Paul, R. W., H71
Paulsen, M. B., H201, H203
Paz, O., H221
Peacock, J., H277
Pearson, C., H588
Pease, B., H481, H484
Pedagogical knowledge:
  as taboo, H181
Pedersen, D., H63
Pennsylvania State University:
  Instructional Development
    Program, F147
  instruction expenditures, H323
  research expenditures, H323
Performance-based assessment,
  H214-215
Perkins, D. N., F129
Perry, W., H444
Perry, W. G., Jr., H169, H173, H174,
  H177, H178, H181
Perry v. Sinderman, H343, H350

Traub, J., H155, H164
Toth, S., F202
Treisman, P. U., H168
Treisman, U., H168
Trust-building, teachers and, H447
  admit errors, H450
  balance credibility and authenticity, H453-454
  don't deny credibility, H448-449
  don't play favorites, H451-452
  express organizing vision explicitly, H449
  make words and actions congruent, H449-450
  realize role-modeling power, H452-453
  reveal non-teaching personality, H450
  take students seriously, H451
  teacher authenticity, H447-448
  teacher credibility, H447
Tschirhart, M., H70
Tuilier, A., H156
Tuition, rising, H37-39, H44
  private schools, H38
  public schools, H38
  technology costs, H37-38
  time allocation of faculty and, H37
  See also specific colleges and universities
Turner, J. H., F237
Turner, R., H499
Turner, S. E., H551
Twain, M., F6, F25
Twitchell, J. B., H188
Tyagi, D., H588
Tyler, J., H35

U.S. Bureau of the Census, H12, H13, H26-27, H32, H33
U.S. Department of Education Office of Educational Research and Improvement:
  PETS project, H209
Universities, selective, H370
  subjective admissions policies, H372
  See also specific selective universities; Elite universities
University and Small Business Patent Procedures Act of 1980, H320, H321, H325
University-community partnerships, H105-106
University of Alabama, F23

University of Arizona:
  minority enrollment, H155
University of California:
  as military subcontractor, H243
University of California, Berkeley, H62, H241, H245, H246, H247, H248-249, H250, H251, H252
  diversity controversy, H247
  fraternities, H246
  Institute for the Study of Social Change, F194
  minority enrollment, H155, H247
University of California, Los Angeles, H573
  corporate connections, H318
  Higher Education Research Institute, H4, H46, H49, H139, H341
  minority enrollment, H155, H157
University of Chicago, H12, H62
  Dewey's laboratory school, H99-100
  Human Dynamics Laboratory, H103
University of Colorado, F193
University of Colorado (Boulder):
  instruction expenditures, H323
  research expenditures, H323
University of Florida:
  instruction expenditures, H323
  research expenditures, H323
University of Georgia:
  board of regents, H354
  instruction expenditures, H323
  research expenditures, H323
University of Illinois-Chicago Circle:
  minority enrollment, H156
University of Maryland:
  instruction expenditures, H323
  research expenditures, H323
University of Maryland at College Park:
  longitudinal study, H211
University of Michigan, H69, H480
  fraternities, H246
  instruction expenditures, H323
  research expenditures, H323
University of Minnesota, H324, H340
  board of regents, H354
  Humphrey Institute for Public Policy, H319
  instruction expenditures, H323
  research expenditures, H323
  tenure changes, H163

University of Missouri-Columbia, H46
University of Nevada at Las Vegas:
  corporate connections, H319
University of New Mexico:
  minority enrollment, H155
University of North Carolina, H15, H16
  Chapel Hill campus, H303, H538
  instruction expenditures, H323
  research campuses, H24
  research expenditures, H323
University of Northern Iowa (UNI), H522-523
  Center for the Enhancement of Teaching, H523
University of Oklahoma, F209
University of Pennsylvania, H320
University of South Carolina:
  minority enrollment, H155
University of Southern California, H340
University of South Florida, New College of, H552
University of Texas at Austin:
  minority enrollment, H155
University of Wisconsin:
  instruction expenditures, H323
  Madison campus, H62, H69
  Milwaukee campus, H324, H412
  research expenditures, H323
Uranowitz, S., H91

Vanden Brook, T., H64, H324, H327
Vasquez, J. A., H143
Veatch, R., H407, H411
Veblen, T., H69, H256
Vesper, N., H60
Veysey, L. R., H12, H26
Victoria, H481
Vygotsky, L., H98, H101, H101

Wagenaar, T., F188, F191
Wagenaar, T. C., H585, H586; F237
Wagenheim, G., F284, F285
Waggoner, M. D., H201
Walker, E. L., F54
Waller, W., H95
Walzer, M., H370, H380
Wankat, P., F125
Warren, E., H341
Washington University, H310
Wasserstrom, R., H366, H369
Wasserstrom, R. A., H379, H381

Fieldguide for Teaching in a New Century

BERNICE A. PESCOSOLIDO
Indiana University

RONALD AMINZADE
University of Minnesota

PINE FORGE PRESS
Thousand Oaks, California
London • New Delhi

Contents

Section II: The Basic Topography   51

Section VI: Assessing the Journey: Assignments, Grading, and Course Closure   239

Preface

One of our challenges in trying to bring a comprehensive set of materials to college and university teachers was how to sort out the plethora of issues, perspectives, and tools that mark the borders of higher education. After struggling with a range of formats and types of materials, we decided on the present division of labor. The *Handbook* targets issues and perspectives along the landscape of higher education, and the *Fieldguide* provides practical tools and "pointers" to navigate the terrain successfully. We have tried to cross-reference the two volumes to provide a link between theory and practice.

We have organized the hundreds of pieces along the journey from our preconceptions of the teaching enterprise, to our initial impressions of classroom and students, to the rhythm of the semester or quarter, to an evaluation of the trip and preparations for the next voyage. We also have set up the *Fieldguide* to be in a user-friendly computer format so that the overall journey can be surveyed and special points of interest picked up. Because many of the materials may be useful in classrooms or for teaching workshops, we decided on a diskette format so that pieces can be reproduced.

All of us searched our own files from classes, from our teaching dossiers and portfolios, and from meetings and workshops we had attended. We asked our colleagues, called teaching and learning centers across the country, and scoured the literature including general and disciplinary-based teaching journals, newsletters, and books on higher education, very broadly defined. We ended up with thousands of pages of interesting and useful material. Even with the computer format, we were limited to what could be included. In the end, we decided to use the *Fieldguide* as part resource to hands-on materials and part "pointer" to resources. To that end, we often use a page from a wonderful book or a list from an article with a brief introduction. In so doing, we hope not to have done major injustice to the works. The purpose of including these excerpts is twofold. First, we want to introduce college and university teachers to the wide and rich range of sources available, even if providing only a glimpse of each. Second, we hope that this diversity leads teachers to consult the full book (*Handbook*), the ongoing periodicals, the presses that have book series on teaching and learning, and the like. Too often, these are compartmentalized by discipline, and this project, in total, was designed to escape that insulation.

We have so many people to thank in getting this done—our editorial and advisory boards, colleagues, directors of teaching centers, librarians, journal and newsletter editors, authors, and college teachers. In particular, we thank Joan Middendorf, director of the Teaching Resources Center, College of Arts and Sciences, Indiana University; and Carla Howery, director of the Teaching Service Program of the American Sociological Association. We also thank those who produced these materials, both authors and journal/newsletter editors, for granting permission to use them in "pieces." Special thanks go to Ed Kain, who provided us with a thorough and insightful review of an early draft. We acknowledge Indiana University (including the participants of the Faculty Colloquium for Excellence in Teaching) for its support of this project and its attention to issues of teaching and learning. Mary Hannah, our secretarial whiz, labored over every phase of getting these materials in shape for Pine Forge Press. She became expert in contacting and getting permissions, scanning in materials, cleaning them up, proofing, and (not least) nudging us to get things done. This book could not have happened without her. Finally, we thank Steve Rutter for his long-standing support for this unusual project (and unusually long process) and Jean Skeels, Windy Just, and Sherith Pankratz at Pine Forge for their assistance all along the way.

How to Use This Fieldguide

The *Fieldguide* is designed along a Microsoft Windows Explorer format to facilitate searches on the diskette by topic. It also can be printed out, in total, to create a full, integrated document. This flexible format permits the *Fieldguide* to serve a number of purposes.

Part of our own thinking emerged from the sequence of courses that are taught in the Preparing Future Faculty Program in Sociology at Indiana University. Our first course, the "nuts and bolts," discipline-oriented course, is designed for first-time teachers and focuses on basic issues and tools. The second course gets beyond introductions to syllabi construction, assessment, and basic learning theories and introduces teachers to the wider debates and the critiques of what we do, how we do it, and why. It places issues of teaching and learning in larger context. It serves, in essence, to introduce individuals to issues intimately tied to but beyond their own classrooms, disciplines, and even higher education itself. Four possibilities follow:

1. Using the *Handbook* as a follow-up to the *Fieldguide* by considering the work that college teachers do once they have classroom experience and have the time after new "preps" to reflect on teaching and learning in larger perspective

2. For first-time teachers, using the *Handbook* initially to anchor individuals' decisions in their own agreement or disagreement with the diversity of perspectives presented, followed by the *Fieldguide* to prepare materials

3. Using the *Fieldguide* as an accompanying volume to the *Handbook*, facilitating the interchange between thinking and doing, and between theory and practice, in college teaching (to that end, it can be used in integrated course work)

4. Taking parts of the *Handbook* and *Fieldguide* that address similar issues and using these segments/parts in seminars, "brownbags," and workshops.

An explicit purpose of the *Fieldguide* is to provide materials that can be used to enhance college teaching. To that end, they can be reproduced under limited conditions. We have, of course, acquired permissions for every piece in the *Fieldguide*, and all copyright policies apply, including the fair use of materials for educational purposes.

Acknowledgment

Grateful acknowledgment is made to all of the contributors to this volume and for special permission to use their materials. All rights are reserved.